ROBERT GRAVES

ROBERT GRAVES

AND THE WHITE GODDESS
1940–85

RICHARD PERCEVAL GRAVES

WEIDENFELD AND NICOLSON · LONDON

FOR
MY FORMER TUTOR
KEITH THOMAS

First published in Great Britain in 1995 by
Weidenfeld and Nicolson

The Orion Publishing Group Ltd
Orion House, 5 Upper Saint Martin's Lane, London WC2H 9EA

Copyright © 1995 Richard Perceval Graves

A CIP catalogue record for this book is available
from the British Library

ISBN 0 297 81534 2

Typeset by Deltatype Ltd, Ellesmere Port, Cheshire
Printed in Great Britain by The Bath Press, Bath, Avon

CONTENTS

BOOK NINE DEATH'S NARROW SEA 1975–85

ILLUSTRATIONS

1   A 1938 portrait of Beryl (*née* Pritchard), who was then married to Alan Hodge, but would set up home with Robert Graves in October 1939 (Beryl Graves).

2   Robert Graves in the mid 1940s, when he and Beryl were living at Galmpton in Devon (Beryl Graves).

3   Robert and Beryl Graves with their children Lucia, William and Juan in 1949 at Kneesworth Hall where they were visiting their friends Dorothy and Montagu Simmons (Beryl Graves).

4   Robert Graves's mother Amy at Harlech in 1949, with his brother John and nephew Richard.

5   An early portrait of the artist Judith Bledsoe, who became Robert Graves's Muse in November 1950 (Judith Bledsoe).

6   The only surviving letter from Robert Graves to Judith Bledsoe, written in December 1951 (Judith Bledsoe).

7   Robert Graves in 1951 with his friend Tom Matthews of *Time* magazine (Beryl Graves).

8   The composer Peggy Glanville-Hicks in Deyá in 1955 with Robert Graves, whose *Homer's Daughter* she was using as the basis for her opera *Nausicaa*, and with her collaborator, Robert's close friend Alastair Reid (Beryl Graves).

9   In Deyá in 1959 with Martin Amis, Hilly Amis, Tomas Graves and Kingsley Amis (Beryl Graves).

10   Margot Callas in June 1960, when she became Robert Graves's Muse. This is a still taken from a film by Mati Klarwein in which she and Robert both took part (Mati Klarwein).

11   Robert Graves and his daughter Lucia on a beach in Greece in 1961 with Eleni, the Greek sculptress who became Robert's 'spiritual sister' (Beryl Graves).

12   With his daughter Lucia in 1962 (Douglas Glass).

13   With his daughter Jenny Nicholson, with whom he had been collaborating on the musical *Solomon and Sheba*, in 1963 (Beryl Graves).

14   *The Indigo* in Palma in 1963. On Robert Graves's left (and wearing his hat) sits 'Cindy' Lee, later known as Aemilia Laraçuen, who became Robert's Muse in July 1963. On his right is his friend Ralph Jacobs.

Across the table sit Beryl and Lucia with their friend Helen Morningstar, while Ramon Farran, Lucia's husband, sits at his drums in the background (Beryl Graves).

15   Robert Graves in 1964 with his niece Sally Chilver, who had often helped him with his researches. The title *The Mob* was given to the snap by Aemilia Laraçuen.

16   A play rehearsal in the summer of 1965 in the theatre below Canelluñ: Ralph Jacobs, Esteban Frances and Robert Graves, with Tomas Graves on guitar (Beryl Graves).

17   Robert Graves in Deyá on 27 July 1968, walking with his god-daughter Helena Simon on his way to be made an adoptive son of the village (Helena Simon).

18   Robert Graves's sister Clarissa Graves in 1968.

19   Robert Graves in 1969 with Juli Simon, who had become his Muse in October 1966 (Helena Simon).

20   Giving a poetry-reading (Beryl Graves).

21   With the Sufi philosopher Idries Shah in 1970 (Beryl Graves).

22   With his friend Ava Gardner (Beryl Graves).

23   With his daughter Catherine Dalton in 1978, when his memory was already severely impaired (Beryl Graves).

24   Robert Graves leaning on one of the olive trees on his land below Canelluñ (Beryl Graves).

Unless otherwise acknowledged the pictures reproduced here belong to the author.

ACKNOWLEDGEMENTS

The author would like to thank the Trustees of the Robert Graves Copyright Trust for permission to quote from published and unpublished writings by Robert Graves. However, he is required to point out that the fact that this permission has been granted by the Trustees in no way implies that they agree with the text.

The author would also like to thank Sir Kingsley Amis, for extracts from one of his letters to RG and from his writings about RG. In addition, an extract from a letter by W. H. Auden to RG appears by kind permission of the Estate of W. H. Auden; extracts from letters from Ingrid Bergman to Robert Graves, appear by kind permission of her daughter Isabella Rossellini on behalf of herself and her co-executors Ms Pia Lindstrom, Ms Ingrid Rossellini and Mr Roberto Rossellini; an extract from a letter by Judith Bledsoe to Robert Graves, by kind permission of Judith Bledsoe; extracts from letters by Bridget Boland by kind permission of her executors; an extract from a letter by Agatha Christie to RG by kind permission of Hughes Massie Limited; extracts from letters by Alexander Clifford, by kind permission of Elizabeth Davies; extracts from his letters to RG by kind permission of Alexander H. Cohen; extracts from letters by Rosaleen Cooper by kind permission of her sons Paul and Roger Cooper; an extract from one of her letters to RG by kind permission of Ruth Fainlight; an extract from a letter by Lord Falkland by kind permission of the present Lord Falkland; an extract from one of her letters to RG by kind permission of Christina Foyle; an extract from one of her own letters to RG by kind permission of Martha Gellhorn; an extract from one of her letters to RG by kind permission of Cecily Gittes; extracts from the letters of Peggy Glanville-Hicks by kind permission of James Murdoch and Shane Simpson; extracts from letters by Dick Graves to his half-brother RG, by kind permission of Dick's grandson, Simon Gough; extracts from letters by David Graves, Sam Graves and Nancy Nicholson, by kind permission of Sam Graves; extracts from their letters to RG by kind permission of Sir Alec and Lady Guinness; extracts from letters by Alan Hodge to RG and BG, by kind permission of Jane Aiken Hodge; an extract from a letter to RG by kind permission of Ted Hughes; extracts from letters by Selwyn Jepson to RG by kind permission of his grandson Timothy Landfield; extracts from letters by Vincent Korda to Robert Graves appear by permission of Michael V. Korda on behalf of the executors of Vincent Korda; extracts from a letter by Betty Sicre to RG and BG by kind permission of Betty Lussier; extracts from letters by Tom Matthews to RG and BG, and from TM's *Under the Influence*, by kind permission of his literary executor the Rev. Tim Anderson; extracts from letters by Dorothy Simmons to RG and BG by kind permission of her daughter Marcia Jones; an extract from one of her letters to RG by kind permission of Dame Maggie Smith; a telegram from Sam Spiegel to RG by kind permission of the Estate of Sam Spiegel; extracts from her letters to RG by kind permission of his daughter Catherine Nicholson; an extract from one of her letters to RG by kind permission of Edna O'Brien; an extract from one of her letters to RG and BG by kind permission of Marnie Pomeroy; an extract from a letter by Jacquetta Hawkes to RG by kind permission of Mrs J. B. Priestley; extracts from *Robert Graves: His Life and Works* by Martin Seymour-Smith, by kind permission of the author; an extract from a letter by Peter Quennell to RG by kind permission of his widow Lady Quennell; extracts from letters to RG and for his poem 'To Robert Graves in Deya' by kind permission of James's daughter Stella Irwin; extracts from his letters to RG by kind permission of Mr Jerome Robbins via Fitelson, Lasky, Aslan & Couture of 551 Fifth Avenue, New York City; extracts from his address on Jenny Nicholson Crosse by kind permission of Nigel Ryan; extracts from his letters to RG by kind permission of Alan Sillitoe; extracts from letters by George and Joanna Simon to RG and BG by kind permission of Joanna Simon; an extract from one of her letters to RG and BG by kind permission of Juli Simon; extracts from his own writings appear by kind permission of David Sutton; extracts from letters written by Bill Watt and Michael Hornimann while employed by A. P. Watt by kind permission of A. P. Watt Ltd; extracts from letters by Frances Weismiller and her son Peter Weismiller to RG by kind permission of Peter Weismiller; and an extract from a letter to RG by Charles Williams by kind permission of David Higham Associates.

The author would also like to thank those institutions who do not control copyright, but own the physical property rights over a number of documents quoted. These include materials from the Nancy Nicholson, Karl Gay and Richard Hughes collections in the Lilly Library, Indiana University, Bloomington, Indiana; while extracts from a number of letters from Robert Graves to Selwyn Jepson are provided, courtesy of the University of Victoria, McPherson Library, University Archives and Special Collections (Victoria B. C., Canada) who hold the originals of those Graves letters to Selwyn Jepson.

In addition, the author acknowledges the use of small amounts of published material by Kenneth Allsop; Omar Ali-Shah (from *The Fitz-Omar Cult*); Deborah Baker (from *In extremis: the Life of Laura Riding*); Edmund Blunden; Jonathan Cape; Catherine Dalton (from *Without Hardware*); Robert Harling; Richard Hughes (from *The Wooden Shepherdess*); Betty Lussier (from *Amid My Alien Corn*); Harold Macmillan; Spike Milligan and Pauline Scudamore (from *Dear Robert, Dear Spike*); Idries Shah (from

Between Moon and Moon); Sir Stephen Spender; Gertrude Stein; Philip Toynbee; the Vice-President of 'Creative Age'; H. D. Vursell; Gamel Woolsey (from 'Immutable' in *Middle Earth*) and Sir Peregrine Worsthorne.

The author gratefully acknowledges Alastair Reid's permission for the use both of extracts from his letters to RG and from an important unpublished article entitled 'Remembering Robert'; and he also thanks Mr Reid for a number of factual corrections to that small part of the text which he has seen.

In addition, the author asserts that he has used his best endeavours to trace copyright owners, and will happily acknowledge any he has been unable to reach, or who have not yet replied to his letters, in future editions of this work.

GRAVES

Partial family tree
accurate as of
3 November 1977

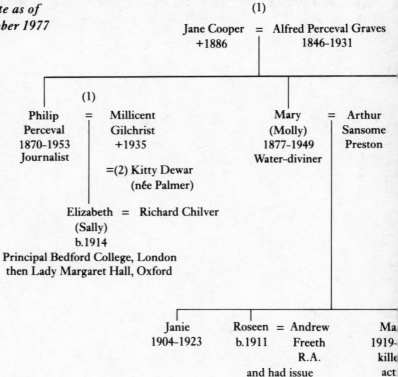

(1)

Jane Cooper = Alfred Perceval Graves
+1886   1846–1931

(1)

Philip   =   Millicent   Mary   =   Arthur
Perceval   Gilchrist   (Molly)   Sansome
1870–1953   +1935   1877–1949   Preston
Journalist   Water-diviner

                 =(2) Kitty Dewar
                     (née Palmer)

      Elizabeth = Richard Chilver
      (Sally)
      b.1914
Principal Bedford College, London
   then Lady Margaret Hall, Oxford

            Janie   Roseen = Andrew   Ma
            1904–1923   b.1911   Freeth   1919–
                                    R.A.   kille
                             and had issue   act

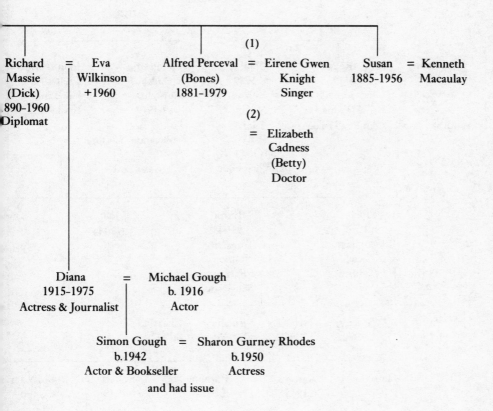

(2)

= Amalie von Ranke
1857-1951

Richard   =   Eva   Alfred Perceval = Eirene Gwen   Susan = Kenneth
Massie   Wilkinson   (Bones)   Knight   1885-1956 Macaulay
(Dick)   +1960   1881-1979   Singer
890-1960
Diplomat

(1)

(2)

= Elizabeth
Cadness
(Betty)
Doctor

Diana   =   Michael Gough
1915-1975   b. 1916
Actress & Journalist   Actor

Simon Gough = Sharon Gurney Rhodes
b.1942   b.1950
Actor & Bookseller   Actress
and had issue

GRAVES

*Partial family tree
accurate as of
3 November 1977*

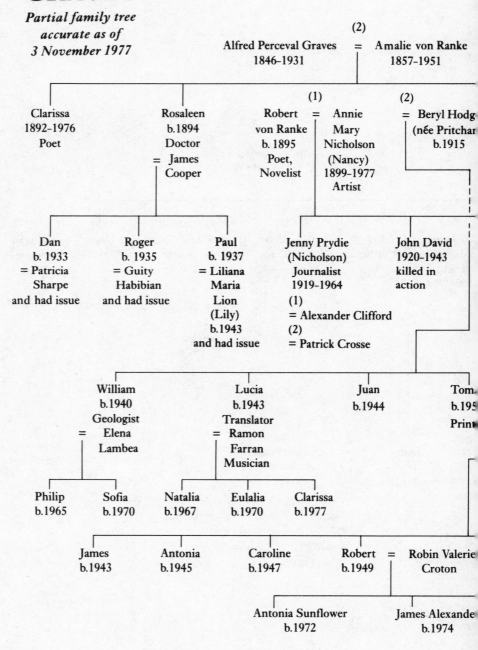

(2)

Alfred Perceval Graves = Amalie von Ranke
1846–1931   1857–1951

Clarissa
1892–1976
Poet

Rosaleen
b.1894
Doctor
= James
Cooper

(1)
Robert = Annie
von Ranke   Mary
b. 1895   Nicholson
Poet,   (Nancy)
Novelist   1899–1977
Artist

(2)
= Beryl Hodg
(née Pritchar
b.1915

Dan
b. 1933
= Patricia
Sharpe
and had issue

Roger
b. 1935
= Guity
Habibian
and had issue

Paul
b. 1937
= Liliana
Maria
Lion
(Lily)
b.1943
and had issue

Jenny Prydie
(Nicholson)
Journalist
1919–1964
(1)
= Alexander Clifford
(2)
= Patrick Crosse

John David
1920–1943
killed in
action

William
b.1940
Geologist
= Elena
Lambea

Lucia
b.1943
Translator
= Ramon
Farran
Musician

Juan
b.1944

Tom.
b.195
Print

Philip
b.1965

Sofia
b.1970

Natalia
b.1967

Eulalia
b.1970

Clarissa
b.1977

James
b.1943

Antonia
b.1945

Caroline
b.1947

Robert = Robin Valerie
b.1949   Croton

Antonia Sunflower
b.1972

James Alexande
b.1974

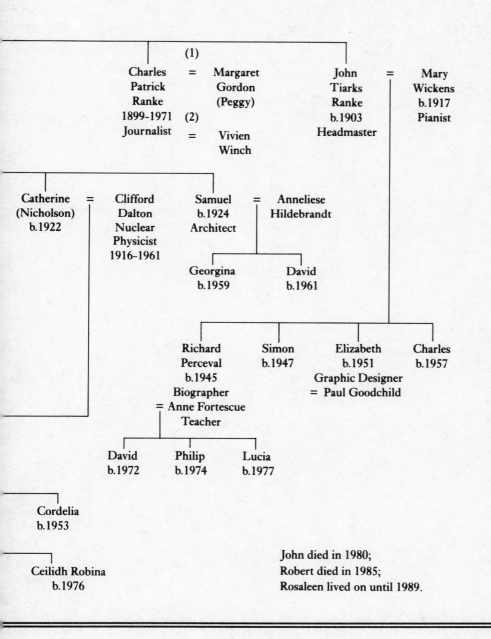

(1)

Charles
Patrick
Ranke
1899–1971
Journalist

=

Margaret
Gordon
(Peggy)

(2)

=

Vivien
Winch

John
Tiarks
Ranke
b.1903
Headmaster

=

Mary
Wickens
b.1917
Pianist

Catherine
(Nicholson)
b.1922

=

Clifford
Dalton
Nuclear
Physicist
1916–1961

Samuel
b.1924
Architect

=

Anneliese
Hildebrandt

Georgina
b.1959

David
b.1961

Richard
Perceval
b.1945
Biographer
= Anne Fortescue
Teacher

Simon
b.1947

Elizabeth
b.1951
Graphic Designer
= Paul Goodchild

Charles
b.1957

David
b.1972

Philip
b.1974

Lucia
b.1977

Cordelia
b.1953

Ceilidh Robina
b.1976

John died in 1980;
Robert died in 1985;
Rosaleen lived on until 1989.

INTRODUCTION

Although I don't propose raking up the past, if it *is* raked up,
I want the whole story told.

> Robert Graves, 16 February 1968

When Robert Graves wrote these words, he was referring to the story of
his relationship with Aemilia Laraçuen Lee, usually known as 'Cindy', the
muse with whom, after Laura Riding, he had the most tempestuous
relationship of his life. Graves knew the dangers of a story only partly told.
What he hoped for was a biographer who would search out the whole
truth, told sympathetically (or with what John Cowper Powys once
described as 'the clairvoyance of love').

Searching for the truth about the life of my late uncle Robert Graves,
and then setting down my findings as accurately and as readably as
possible, has been my principal task since I began my researches back in
1982. For this volume – designed to be read alone, though it also takes its
place as the final part of the trilogy which begins with *Robert Graves: The
Assault Heroic 1895–1926*, and goes on with *Robert Graves: The Years with
Laura 1926–40* – that task has been particularly difficult.

There are two principal reasons:

First, the vast quantity of raw material. Once again, there was much to
be found among the family papers which I inherited from my father John
Graves, Robert's youngest brother; although they are generally less
interesting after 1951, when my grandmother Amy Graves died of cancer,
and ceased to act as a clearing house of family information. More
important on this occasion have been the archives at Canelluñ which
contain, among other things, most significant letters received by Robert
Graves since 1940. I have also used vital sets of unpublished letters from
the Berg Collection in the New York Public Library; from the Lilly
Library in Bloomington, Indiana; from the University of Victoria in
British Columbia; and from the burgeoning Graves collection being
amassed by the Robert Graves Trust at St John's College, Oxford.

Second, the fact that this volume extends so nearly to the present day:
which means that here and there I have felt it necessary to suppress
certain facts on the ground that it would be cruel to reveal them during the

lifetime of certain persons still living: some of whom are still only in their forties or fifties.

Incidentally, it has been strange to find myself becoming a character, even though a very minor one, in my own story; and to replay in my mind scenes which I did not fully understand at the time (because when, for example, I first visited Canelluñ I knew so little about what was going on in Robert's private life), but which now become perfectly intelligible. To distance my current perceptions from those of, say, 1961 or 1967, I have written about myself in the third person throughout.

When this volume opens, in February 1940, Robert Graves has ended his remarkable fourteen-year association with the American poet Laura Riding, and is living in a converted chapel in an Essex village with his new companion Beryl Hodge, who is expecting their first child.

Robert would remain with Beryl until his death in 1985. They spent most of the Second World War together at Galmpton in South Devon. Then they went out to Majorca, where everything at Canelluñ had remained untouched since Robert and Laura had fled from the island in the summer of 1936.

With Karl Goldschmidt's editorial eye replacing that of Laura Riding until the mid-1960s, Robert remained a prolific professional author of all kinds of work, from historical novels such as *Wife to Mr. Milton* and *The Golden Fleece*; to essays and short stories and a rewriting of the Greek myths; and to *The Nazarene Gospel Restored*, a brave attempt (with Joshua Podro) to discover the truth behind the authorized version of the life of Jesus.

Poetry, however, remained Robert Graves's principal calling; and apart from the poems, his main achievement during these years was the writing of *The White Goddess*, that 'historical grammar of poetic myth' which is also the classic work on what it is to be a romantic or 'muse-inspired' poet.

But the muse is always 'the other woman'; and Graves's devotion to the muse led him and his close family into the most extraordinarily difficult situations. In this volume, the story of his stormy relationships with four muses: Judith Bledsoe, Margot Callas, Aemilia Laraçuen Lee and Juli Simon, is told in detail for the first time. They were relationships which inspired him to write some of the finest love poems of the twentieth century.

Once again, I am very much in the debt of all those who have helped me. In particular I thank my Aunt Beryl, who welcomed me to Deyá (now more properly Deia) in February and December 1993 and in September

1994. On each occasion I stayed with her at Canelluñ (now more properly Ca N'Alluny) and spent many hours combing through the family archives. Beryl herself has continued to be unfailingly helpful and encouraging, and has spent many hours answering my questions and resolving my difficulties.

Others who have supplied me with first-hand information include Karl Gay (who as Goldschmidt was Robert and Laura's secretary from 1934, and continued working for Robert alone from 1947 until 1965); Karl's wife Rene, who made many valuable observations; and Alan Sillitoe and Ruth Fainlight. Of the muses, I have interviewed both Judith Bledsoe and Juli Simon. 'Cindy' has disappeared so completely that she is probably dead; while Margot appears to have decided to remain silent. Among members of my family, I have had useful conversations with my mother Mary Graves (Robert's sister-in-law), my brothers Simon and Charles, and my sister Elizabeth; and with many of my cousins, especially Catherine Nicholson, one of the surviving children of Robert's first marriage; Sally Chilver, the daughter of Robert's half-brother Philip; and Beryl's children William, Lucia, Juan and Tomas. William's wife Elena has also been extremely helpful with her shrewd observations.

Others who have kindly given me both advice and information include Brian Bliss, Susie Bradbury, Charles Corbett (a friend of Cindy's first husband Owen Lee), Jane Craddock, the late Patrick Crosse (Jenny Nicholson's second husband), Mrs Maureen Pilling (a friend of Jenny's), Stella Irwin (James Reeves's daughter), John de St Jorre (who once had an affair with 'Cindy'), Robert Kee, Helen Morningstar (one of Robert's circle especially during the 1950s and 1960s), Paul O'Prey (editor of Robert's letters), Helena Simon (Robert's god-daughter), Joanna Simon (Robert's friend from the 1940s onward), Martin Seymour-Smith (Robert's first biographer), Martin Tallents (a close friend of Robert's from the late 1960s onward), Suzy Townsend (one of the team who looked after Robert with such devotion during his declining years), Sir Peter Ustinov and Mr Tim Whalen (who acted as a clearing house for information from the United States of America). And once again, I thank Eric Norris, master bookseller, for his work in hunting down many of the books which I needed to consult.

I also thank Philip Hunter, research assistant and archivist to the St John's College Robert Graves Trust, for his valuable help.

I also thank Ion Trewin of Weidenfeld for his encouragement, and for his continuing faith in the value of my work; and finally I thank both the Arthur Welton Foundation and the Authors' Foundation for giving me grants without which this volume could never have been completed.

BOOK ONE

THE SHADOW OF THE PAST

1940–43

CHAPTER 1

A Letter from Laura Riding[1]

Great Bardfield, in the heart of the Essex countryside, during the early hours of a February morning in 1940. A very cold, white world with snow heavy on the branches, and more falling. At one end of the village, a large house known as The Place, set in its own snow-covered grounds; and beside those grounds, a barn-like building, which was once a chapel. Inside, out of the snow, it seems colder than ever; but a wooden staircase leads up to a kind of flat: one large room, with a desk and a typewriter and some chairs and a makeshift kitchen in one corner; and a small bedroom leading off.[2]

In the bedroom, a dark-haired woman of twenty-four with large cat-like eyes lies in bed beside her forty-five-year-old lover. She is four months' pregnant, and sleepily she turns towards this large handsome man with his broken nose and his shock of greying hair, and murmurs something in his ear. Her words please him; and he will later write of this moment:

> She tells her love while half-asleep,
>   In the dark hours,
>   With half-words whispered low:
> As Earth stirs in her winter sleep
> And puts out grass and flowers
>   Despite the snow,
>   Despite the falling snow.[3]

Robert Graves and Beryl Hodge have found an unexpected happiness in what Robert describes simply as a real 'home, with a cat and all'.[4] No longer a chapel, it remains for them a sanctuary, from which, for the time being, neither of them wish to venture very far.

For it is only a short while since they were both caught up in a series of events so nightmarish that Robert was brought to the very edge of madness. The experience was far worse than anything he had yet endured, though he is no stranger to mental suffering.

Extreme bullying when Robert Graves was a schoolboy at Charterhouse had been followed by the horrors of trench warfare on the Western Front. First he had endured the Battle of Loos in 1915; and then during the Battle of the Somme in 1917 he had been wounded so badly by a piece of shell, which had travelled right through his back and chest, that at one point he had been left for dead. Jolted in and out of screaming consciousness first in an ambulance and then on a hospital train, he had somehow survived to read his own obituary in *The Times*. Later, in the mid-1920s, Graves had suffered from the cumulative effects of shell-shock, a failing marriage to the artist Nancy Nicholson, and a fading career; and had begun to feel that his personality was on the verge of disintegration.

Then had come the appearance on the scene of Laura Riding, the young American poet of forceful intellect and magnetic sexuality who had rescued him from his earlier difficulties, and upon whom he had rapidly come to depend not only as lover, companion, critic and mentor; but also, in his view, as a unique source of ultimate wisdom.

When, in 1929, Laura had finally torn him away from his wife, from his four children (Jenny Nicholson, David Graves, Catherine Nicholson and Sam Graves), from his wider family and from most of his friends, Robert had described her to his sister Rosaleen as being 'seamless, like the garment of Christ'; and five years later he had told the poet James Reeves, one of the new circle of friends that had grown up around Robert and Laura in their new home on the island of Majorca, that it was quite useless to argue that Laura should be other than she was. 'She is a great natural fact,' he wrote, 'like fire or trees or snow ... By natural I don't mean human or inhuman or non-human but just naturally acceptable to anyone with a good mind and heart.'[5]

Assimilating himself into the world of this 'great natural fact' had not been easy. Riding had become sexually disenchanted with someone whom she could so easily control; and although she wished to continue living with Graves (who, under her tutelage, became famous as the author of *Good-bye to All That* and the *Claudius* novels), she had soon been doing so in the light of her philosophy (elaborated after a failed suicide attempt in which her pelvis had been broken in three) that 'bodies have had their day'.

This had set up a powerful conflict in Graves's mind between his devotion to Riding and his steadily increasing resentment of her manipulative treatment. Later he would reflect that:

Chastity in man is obviously unhealthy … I know I was in a very bad state during those years with Laura and certainly don't think that my spiritual or poetic prowess were any the better for the regime though I did learn to think.[6]

But at the time he could not consciously think ill of his muse. Where the conflict had surfaced in his dreams, it had produced terrifying visions of blazing buildings and burning railway coaches; and those visions had been prophetic about the horrific end of their relationship.

The last period of their life together had begun with the outbreak of the Spanish Civil War in 1936, which had driven them from their island home and sent them wandering through Europe like some peripatetic mediaeval court: Queen Laura presiding, her devoted Chancellor Robert seeing to her slightest wish, and a small group of loyal courtiers always in attendance. Finally, in April 1939, Robert and Laura had set out for the United States of America, drawn there partly by their long-standing friendship with Tom Matthews of *Time* magazine; but principally by Laura's interest in Schuyler Jackson, an ex-Princeton friend of Tom's who, much to her joy, had publicly described her *Collected Poems* as the 'book of books of the mid-twentieth century'.

Having decided that the handsome Schuyler must be hers, Laura had behaved with calculated ferocity. Schuyler Jackson's wife Kit, the good-natured mother of their four young children, was a serious obstacle; but within six weeks, through sheer force of will, Riding had reduced her to a demented and violent creature prepared to 'confess' to witchcraft before being removed to an insane asylum. By then, the atmosphere of horror had become so pervasive that many of those present would come to believe that they had been in the presence of great spiritual evil.

On Kit's departure, Laura Riding had taken over the running of the Pennsylvania farmhouse in the hamlet of Brownsburg, just south of New Hope, Pennsylvania, which she and Robert and a few other members of her inner circle had been sharing with the Jacksons. Soon afterwards, she had disappeared into a bedroom with Schuyler for two days, emerging to announce (for the benefit of anyone who was uncertain about her present views on the subject) that 'Schuyler and I do'.

Robert, who had already endured the dreadful strain of living at close quarters with someone who was going mad, and the further strain of watching himself being gradually displaced in Laura's affections by Schuyler Jackson, had then had to face the fact that his special relationship with Laura had come to an end. Encouraged to set out for England at the beginning of August (there was some idea in Laura's mind, not wholly fanciful, that after eleven years she might still be able to return him to his wife), Robert had seemed to Tom Matthews, who saw him off from the dockside in New York, to be 'desperate and wretched, near the end of his tether'.

It was only Beryl Hodge who had saved him from a complete breakdown. The daughter of a distinguished London solicitor, she had first met Robert in July 1937 as Beryl Pritchard, a twenty-one-year-old Oxford undergraduate, and the girlfriend of his friend Alan Hodge. Early in 1938, Beryl and Alan had married (partly at Laura's instigation, for she was aware of the attraction which had sprung up immediately between Robert and Beryl); both had been present during those terrible events in Pennsylvania; and afterwards it was in Beryl's company that Robert had found periods of the 'lovely calmness' which had preserved him.

Even the horrors of Brownsburg had been overshadowed by the outbreak of the Second World War in September 1939. Beryl had remained in America (where Laura monitored the progress of her increasingly intimate correspondence with Robert); but Alan, who had crossed the Atlantic on the same boat as Robert, had been in Warsaw when Hitler's armies invaded Poland, and had only just managed to escape the German bombers before returning to England via Estonia, Finland, Sweden and Norway.[7]

Robert, hoping to see active service once again, had gone before a medical board for the Officers' Emergency Reserve. However, as he had explained to his friend Basil Liddell-Hart (the military expert), he had only been 'passed Grade 2 which means that I can only be accepted for non-combatant and very dull corps'. At that stage, encouraged by letters from Laura Riding which suggested that a *rapprochement* was possible, Robert had decided on a return to America; until a further letter from Riding had made it clear that she would not tolerate any kind of relationship with him which involved Beryl, too, playing an important part in his life.

This had plunged Robert into a renewed state of acute misery. Since returning to England he had been living at The Place, Great Bardfield, with his artist friends John and Lucie Aldridge; and Lucie, encountering in her garden Brian Bliss (a young writer in his twenties who had become one of the Graves/Riding circle as recently as 1937, and was using the Aldridges' converted chapel for weekends and holidays) would tell him nervously: 'Robert's showing the whites of his eyes again.'[8]

Fortunately, in October 1939, Beryl had made a decisive intervention. Crossing the Atlantic, she had been met by Robert in Liverpool; and then, as Robert recounts in his poem 'The Oath', part of which runs:

The doubt and the passion
Falling away from them
    In that instant both
Take timely courage
From the sky's clearness
To confirm an oath ...

She knows, as he knows
Of a faithful-always
    And an always-dear
By early emblems
Prognosticated,
    Fulfilled here.[9]

A few weeks later, after Alan had stepped graciously aside, Beryl had joined Robert in the chapel at Great Bardfield which Brian Bliss had been 'only too pleased' to relinquish in their favour.[10]

For some months a *rapprochment* with Laura had once again seemed possible. 'Very dear very good Beryl,' Robert had written one November morning when Beryl was away from Great Bardfield for a few days,

I was so happy this morning with your letter: and about Laura's acceptance. Things will really untangle themselves now at last I feel. Tabby was on my bed between 7.30 and 8.30 playing with my toes through an untuck of the blankets. I had a splitting morning headache which always seems to occur in your absence but went for a *run* around the fields where we went for that depressed walk (and left most of it behind) ...[11]

In what they assumed were changed circumstances, Robert and Beryl had proposed to return to Pennsylvania in the spring of 1940; but Schuyler had other ideas. Revealing himself as the dominant partner in his relationship with Laura, he had compelled her to write a letter in January 1940 saying that she and Robert could no longer work together, and had enclosed a violent letter of his own which, as Robert had told his former secretary and current research assistant Karl Goldschmidt,

is aimed at breaking all connexion between me and Laura and speaks of Beryl and me in a way for which I really could get him prosecuted for sending indecent matter by the mails (this is *not* exaggerated).

'Don't let all this sadden you,' he had added. 'Be happy in what good Laura bequeathed to us before she left us.'[12]

Much though he loved Beryl, the loss of the woman who had been his guiding light for so many years had left Robert feeling in a kind of limbo; and when (on a later, less snowy morning in February 1940 than the one with which we began) the postman arrived with a letter from Basil Liddell-Hart, Robert read it and replied:

> Everything has been frozen here and I have (as it were) been waiting for a bright sky to answer your [earlier] letter by: which was a very warm one and deserved an unfrozen answer. Today there is a faint dripping of snow off the trees and your letter has come as a reminder ... What can I say about Laura? She reached (for me) a point of shall we say poetic (i.e. hyper-moral) excellence that nobody has ever attained before; and then – what shall I say? Her oldest friends consider it an inexplicable abandonment of the principles that she once guarded with the fiercest intensity.

'The explanation', he concluded, 'is that she has made the centre of the universe no longer herself but Schuyler Jackson and herself, and thus admitted into her scope so many foreign elements that it is difficult to regard her as the same person.'[13]

Not long afterwards, Robert received his final letter of dismissal. Writing on 17 February, Laura addressed him with sudden formality as 'Robert Graves', and told him that she was terminating their correspondence. As he read on, it became clear that under Schuyler's influence she had rewritten the entire fourteen years of her association with Robert; and she concluded her letter with some extraordinarily bitter words for the man who had been so devoted to her for so long. By joining him in England in 1926, she declared, she had made a serious error of judgment; and with her current understanding of the true nature of their time together, it was now impossible for her to feel the slightest gratitude for a single thing that he had done.

However, Robert remained faithful for many years to the memory of the Laura who had once meant so much to him. When he received her letter, he was still hard at work for Methuen on a long discursive novel about the American War of Independence, based upon the *Journal* and *Memoir* of a Sergeant Roger Lamb of the Royal Welch Fusiliers; but he was also about to begin a collaboration with Alan Hodge on *The Long Weekend*, a social history of England between the wars. Towards the end of May 1940, when Robert came to write about Laura ('to leave her out', he told Alan, 'would have been dishonest')[14] he began with the words:

It was in 1927 that Laura Riding, a young American who had recently come to Europe, first published her poems and critical work in England. Wiping her slate clean of literary and domestic affiliations with America, she became for the next twelve years the best of 'good Europeans'; the Americans only knew her as 'the highest apple on the British intellectual tree'. In England she was assailed as a 'leg-puller', 'crossword puzzle setter', 'Futurist', 'tiresome intellectualist', and so on: none of her books sold more than a few dozen copies, nor did she ever (as Gertrude Stein did after the Wall Street Crash, in her chatty *Autobiography of Alice B. Toklas* and during her American lecture tour) consent to give the larger public what it really wanted. She was the one poet of the time who spun, like Arachne, from her own vitals without any discoverable literary or philosophical derivations: and the only one who achieved an unshakeable synthesis. Unshakeable, that is, if the premiss of her unique personal authority were granted, and another more startling one – that historic Time had effectively come to an end.

And he concluded:

Laura Riding was remarkable as being in the period but not of the period, and the only woman who spoke with authority in the name of Woman (as so many men in the name of Man) without either deference to the male tradition or feministic equalitarianism: a perfect original. At the very end of the period she returned to the United States, surprisingly rediscovered her American self, and wiped the slate clean once again.[15]

This generous tribute reads very well; and it shows how Graves had coped with Riding's defection by attributing it to some fundamental change in her nature. This enabled him not only to ignore his own crucial role in the collapse of their relationship; but also to avoid a more detailed and complex analysis of Laura herself. It was therefore an unaltered image of Riding as she had been, especially in the earlier years of their relationship, which rapidly sank into Graves's subconscious mind; from where within a few years it would re-emerge as one of the principal constituents of his most influential work.

CHAPTER 2

The Vale House

As soon as Robert Graves realized that there was no future for him and Beryl and their unborn child in Pennsylvania, he began thinking about setting up a more permanent home in England. London, which in other circumstances would have been the most obvious choice, was out of the question because of wartime dangers. The Oxford area, where Robert had lived before, would have meant being too close to Nancy Nicholson, who lived on Boars' Hill (where she ran a small printing press, though she was chiefly dependent upon substantial quarterly payments from Robert), and who had already made it clear that she was bitterly opposed to his new liaison. Harlech in North Wales, whose 'rocky acres' had always been Robert's spiritual home, was also out of the question. Local society there was dominated by his eighty-two-year-old mother Amy, a deeply religious woman who was still hoping and praying that he would return to his wife and family.[16]

So Robert thought instead of South Devon, where Basil Liddell-Hart had set up home with Kathleen Norris; and where Robert's forty-six-year-old sister Rosaleen, her marriage to Jim Cooper in ruins,[17] practised as a doctor and lived alone with her three young sons Dan, Roger and Paul in Bishopsteignton, a little village set in rich red-earth countryside on the estuary of the River Teign, only a mile or two inland from Teignmouth, with its dramatic cliffs of red rock. Like Rosaleen, Robert wanted to live near the sea; and by mid-March he and Beryl had found exactly what they were looking for.

This was The Vale House, in the village of Galmpton, some twelve miles southward along the coast road from Teignmouth. Robert described it in a letter to his eldest son, twenty-year-old David Graves, as 'an early 18th century house, very agreeable in shape and windows and so on', and he hoped that it would be a real home not only for himself and Beryl, but for the children of his first family. 'I realise,' he told David, how much Laura came between you all and me. I will never try to go back to life with Nancy, because that wore out too long ago: you must forgive me for this, but realise its impossibility. I hope to see a lot of you all now.[18]

However, there was still 'a good deal of work to be done' before it was habitable, and by 2 April, as Robert reported to Karl, the pressure on him was almost inconceivable.

First there is this move to Devonshire in prospect about a fortnight off ... I have to wrestle with lawyers, agents and contractors there, and also buy a houseful of furniture, to put into it; Beryl isn't able to do as much work as she would like to do, because she hasn't been at all well and still looks forward to 'never feeling better in her life' as other women promise her ...

As for *Lamb*: since I can't compress his story without making it read dry I have to follow it out at leisurely length feeling anything but leisurely myself and in the last eleven days I have written six and a half chapters.[19]

He added that 'with a little doctoring at the join', it would break into two volumes of around 90,000 words each: *Sergeant Lamb of the Ninth*, and *Sergeant Lamb of the Twenty-Third*. In the meantime, money was very short,[20] and he asked Karl if he could 'wait to be paid for the rest of the typing until my affairs are more in order'.

In mid-April 1940, when Robert and Beryl were almost ready to move to Galmpton, Robert asked Molly Waters, a close friend of Brian Bliss, whether she would help him to prepare The Vale House to receive Beryl. When Molly agreed, she and Robert travelled down to Galmpton together by train and bicycle. The preparations were hard work, though Molly recalls lighter moments, such as the time when Robert asked her:

Molly, would you mind lifting the dining-room table while I switch round the carpet – or would you rather I lifted the table and you did the carpet? And, on discovering that a mattress was too long for a newly-bought second-hand bedstead: 'Molly, would you mind just shortening this mattress?'[21]

Basil Liddell-Hart drove over from Dartington in his ancient Rolls-Royce several times to see how things were going;[22] and before long Robert and Molly were joined in their efforts by Robert's eighteen-year-old daughter Catherine,[23] who had been working at the Zoology labs in Oxford in preparation for studying medicine.[24] Finally all was ready and Beryl herself arrived at her new home.

The Vale House was separated from the road only by a low dry-stone wall with a gate, and a small front lawn; but it was a surprisingly spacious building. On entering the house, there was a large room to the left of the front hall which was used for most purposes, since it had a fireplace and in winter, apart from the kitchen, it was the only really warm room in the house. It also contained a small desk for Robert's typewriter, an easy chair or two, and a large table which was usually covered with work.[25] To the right was another large room in which, as one wartime visitor discovered:

> there was a radio, and little else – though it could serve as a dining room if there were many guests. The radio was switched on for the news, Churchill's speeches – and for 'ITMA' ('It's That Man Again'), the comedian Tommy Handley's show ...[26]

A passage led from the front hall behind this room to a typical stone-floored farm kitchen, with a substantial range: it was here that Robert and Beryl usually ate their meals. Through the kitchen there was a wash-place with a boiler;[27] and at the back of the house, looking out over a garden in which Robert immediately began growing vegetables, there was a dairy with long slated tables which made an excellent larder and storeroom.[28]

The only drawback to living in Galmpton was that at first the villagers were suspicious of them – apparently the local police constable had learned that Robert's middle name was von Ranke, and believed that he might have German sympathies. But in every other respect it was 'a lovely place to live', with many advantages. For one thing, the surrounding countryside was lush and beautiful, and there were no fewer than five separate walks to be enjoyed from the front gate, including one which led over the hills to Dartmouth from where the Pilgrim Fathers had set sail for the New World.[29]

For another, despite the increasingly severe food rationing, it was always possible to obtain rich Devonshire cream, which Robert and Beryl code-named 'O Be Joyful', from the farm up the road where they bought their milk; and the little fishing port of Brixham, at the southern end of Tor Bay, was within an hour's walk. Brixham was home at that time to the Belgian fishing fleet; on the quayside there was usually a plentiful supply of fresh crabs and lobsters; and the local inhabitants included a number of colourful characters with whom they became friends.[30]

Among the first of these was Douglas Glass, a wild-looking New Zealander who ran a photographic business from a little shop in Brixham harbour where he lived with his wife and son. He was soon visiting Robert and Beryl at The Vale House, where he further aroused the suspicions of the villagers not just by wandering about Galmpton with a camera, but by pausing to take a photograph of a dandelion in a stone wall. This, to them, insane act could only be explained by the fact that he was a spy. The camera, it was concluded, was not a camera at all, but some kind of radio transmitter with which, as von Ranke's friend, he was reporting back to their German masters.[31]

Other visitors came from further afield. Towards the end of May 1940, just as Robert was completing his Sergeant Lamb novels, his twenty-one-year-old daughter Jenny Nicholson 'rushed down to call, by midnight train, for a very short weekend'.[32] A former showgirl (she had been one of Cochran's 'Young Ladies'), Jenny was now both a professional actress who had successfully completed two seasons with the Liverpool Repertory Company, and a writer, several of whose sketches had recently been performed upon the London stage.[33] 'She has a good mind', Robert wrote to Nancy, 'and once she can learn to concentrate will do very good work as a dramatist.' In recent years his relationship with Jenny had been troubled; but now he found that he 'liked her very much'.[34]

In the outside world, the danger from Nazi Germany was intensifying. Robert's forty-year-old brother Charles, a highly-paid Fleet Street journalist and Robert's hated rival, was also too old for active service, but had been in Paris as late as mid-April 1940 as a war correspondent;[35] since then the British Expeditionary Force had been withdrawn over the Dunkirk beaches with the loss of many of its men and most of its equipment. Robert's nephew Martin Preston, the son of his half-sister Molly, was among those who had been declared missing.[36] 'The only safety', Robert wrote to Nancy Nicholson, 'is in personal integrity.'[37] And then in June France fell, and the invasion of England seemed imminent.

CHAPTER 3

The Birth of William

Twenty-year-old David Graves had spent the previous three years reading English at Jesus College, Cambridge. A quiet, serious-minded man with a great love of literature, he not only wrote poetry but also painted exquisite watercolours in a non-representational style somewhat akin to that of Miro, and looked as though he might prosper equally well as writer or painter.[38] When he secured only a Third in his Finals in June 1940, his uncle John Graves (who had been working with the Oxford Education Authority for some months, and at the age of thirty-seven was about to accept a teaching post at Malvern College) told Amy that he was neither surprised nor depressed: this was simply 'the penalty for having read *too* widely', and there could be no doubt of his success later on[39] – a sentiment echoed soon afterwards in a letter from David's tutor, who declared that he was 'much better than a third'.[40]

In the meantime, with the war situation looking so desperate that Basil Liddell-Hart was said by Robert's niece and confidante Sally Chilver to be 'feeling defeatist' (she herself, working as a secretary in the offices of the War Cabinet, still believed that 'we might win the war if we got rid of a lot of dead-heads'[41]) David Graves was about to become a soldier. On his father's advice, he had applied for a commission in the Royal Welch Fusiliers. 'It would *greatly please me* if you did go into the Regiment', Robert had written to him earlier in the year,

> because it is and always was a corps d'élite and thus has always had the pick of the market in recruits and officers. As I think I told you, one feels much *safer* in a really good regiment; does not have to worry about being let down by one's own men or brother-officers.[42]

First, however, David and his sister Catherine went up to Erinfa for a holiday with their grandmother.

After Amy had met them by car at Barmouth station, they were stopped twice at checkpoints along the caost road, which had been narrowed in places with stone pillars or tree trunks;[43] and before long Amy would be reporting that she had been asked by the Harlech Local Defence Volunteers (or LDV, later the Home Guard) whether she would interpret if they captured any German parachutists who could not speak English. 'I agreed, of course', said this formidable old lady.[44]

Catherine left for Galmpton on 8 July, summoned there by a reply-paid wire from her father; and David also left Erinfa, intending to visit friends and then to spend a few days with his mother before joining up.[45]

Arriving in Devon, Catherine found that her father had very little time to look after Beryl, since in addition to his normal work he had now joined the Galmpton LDV which, as his contribution to the war effort, he was enjoying 'bringing … up to scratch'.[46] In particular, as he explained in a letter to David, he had found that there was 'no co-ordination' between the LDV and the Special Constables,

> so I introduced them to each other apparently for the first time: the idea being that the L.D.V. who very few of them know how to handle a rifle but have them, should not shoot the S.C.s [Special Constables] who almost all of them can handle a rifle but are not allowed them – on occasions when both are called simultaneously to deal with parachutist scares and not warned of each other's presence.[47]

Beryl herself was not only heavily pregnant but in poor health (probably suffering from mild anaemia), and was very grateful for Catherine's assistance; while Catherine was relieved that, after all his years with Laura Riding, her father had finally allied himself with someone really good; and the two women, who were separated in age by only seven years and nineteen days, began to become friends. When, on Sunday 21 July (just three days after David had joined up[48]), it became clear that Beryl's child was about to be born, Catherine accompanied her to Paignton hospital, and then walked anxiously around the town with her father. All went well, and before long Beryl had given birth to a son whom she and Robert named William.

Since in those days illegitimacy was a social disaster, Robert had already consulted a Somerset House Registrar named Earp, who had told him that the first paperwork on any child's name was crucial: so instead of being registered under his mother's name of Hodge (the normal procedure) William was registered as a Graves; and on his first ration book he also appeared as William Graves.[49] A much more fundamental problem was that Robert Graves was now trying to support two families.

When his next quarterly payment to Nancy was due, he cut the amount he was paying from £150 to just £100, telling his wife: 'I hope this is all right. As David is now off our hands and as by having to live in England my taxes are up 25% and the book market is very bad, it has been difficult enough to raise this.'[50] Nancy replied that his letter was:

> a complete blow. I had taken it for granted that you were going to send the usual amount and David knocking off a year at Cambridge & being self-supporting now would make it possible for Catherine to get to Oxford & Sam to have his essential cures.

She then reminded Robert that she had written to him when Catherine had been offered a vacancy at Lady Margaret Hall, Oxford; and that Robert had then written and congratulated her. 'I've taken it for granted', Nancy concluded angrily, 'you meant to see your first family through in spite of starting a second.'[51]

'I don't see what I can do about it', Robert replied by return of post, 'and honestly, I haven't the least sympathy with giving the children that sort of education in these times.' He would be happy to take over Sam's schooling, since he was 'a natural genius with both eye and pen' (as was Jenny 'in the matter of dramatic vision'). But Catherine, in Robert's opinion, had no real desire to go to L.M.H.; and it would better for her 'to break the Oxford thing ... and let her start adult life now'.[52]

Nancy's reply must have been blistering, for Robert's next action was to send both Catherine and Nancy deeply apologetic letters. To Catherine he wrote explaining quite simply that her first year at Oxford would cost him close to £310, which, with income tax where it was, meant that he would 'have to earn £600 *for you alone* for the next four years ... In peacetime my average income is £900. This war has greatly reduced it. In other words there isn't the money to go round.' The presence of Beryl and William, he assured her, did nothing to complicate things, as 'Beryl pays for her expenses & Wm. costs nothing extra as there is no nurse'; but he realized that she might be disappointed, and he ended: 'Dearest Catherine, please forgive me for being a fool.'[53] In his letter to Nancy he added that he had been working eighteen hours a day since the previous September;[54] and just over a week later he sent her £20, the product, he told her, of selling some of his old books.[55]

CHAPTER 4

Work in Hand

Three weeks after William's birth Karl Goldschmidt, who was visiting the Graveses for a day, noticed that Beryl still looked 'miserably pale'; though she was able to accompany him and Robert on a walk down to the sea. Finding a small beach to sit on, though it was fortified with barbed wire against enemy invasion, they gazed out at the ocean and listened to the waves beating on the shore, and discussed such things as Karl's current status and Robert's work in hand.[56]

Earlier in the year, thanks to his German origins, Karl had been interned as an enemy alien. Since he was also Jewish (in 1936 he had narrowly escaped being removed from Majorca to Germany, where he would have been thrown immediately into a concentration camp) this was a shocking injustice. However common sense had eventually prevailed, and Karl had been allowed to leave his internment camp and join the Army Pioneer Corps. He was now stationed temporarily at Ilfracombe in North Devon; but did not expect to remain there for long, and indeed it would be four years before he saw Robert and Beryl again.

As for Robert's work in hand: within a week of Karl's visit, Robert entrusted the completed manuscript of *The Long Weekend* to a friend, who conveyed it by hand to Faber and Faber's London offices.[57] A few editorial amendments were made: T. S. Eliot, for example, 'objected to having his earlier poems described as "rather pornographic" '; and, as Robert explained to his collaborator Alan Hodge, 'Faber changed it himself, giving me no time to approve: he just omitted it.'[58] Publication had already been decided for November; and in the meantime, in September, Faber would publish a volume of Robert's selected poems under the title *No More Ghosts*.

September 1940 would also see the publication of *Sergeant Lamb of the Ninth*; whose sequel, now renamed *Proceed, Sergeant Lamb*, was scheduled for February 1941. Graves seemed pleased with 'the only books in existence to give an account of the whole war [of Independence] while also contriving to be readable'; and he thought there was a good chance that they would 'find their way into all school libraries especially in the U.S.A.'.[59]

He had certainly done his research well, and his re-creation of late eighteenth-century American life and manners and landscape is vivid and wholly believable: but although there are some excellent set pieces, the story is not merely 'discursive', as he had intended, but rambling to the point of tedium; while Sergeant Lamb himself, the main character and narrator, is extraordinarily shadowy. Just occasionally, the narrative is illuminated by flashes of pure horror (such as accompany the appearances and disappearances of the sinister John Martin, who may or may not be the Devil), which remind us that Graves was writing this novel within a year of his appalling experiences in Pennsylvania; but for much of the time he appears to be emotionally disengaged – like Sergeant Lamb, when he says: 'My mind is like a lake over which a storm has raged. It reflects only the blue sky and forgets the thunder and lightning.'[60]

With *The Long Weekend*, the *Sergeant Lamb* novels and his *Selected Poems* more or less ready for the press, Graves was already searching for new projects, and for a while he thought of producing a work based on a set of ideas deriving from his final years with Laura Riding. It was in London in March 1938 that Riding had presided over a meeting of twenty-six of her closest associates, 'to decide [in the face of widespread intellectual despair about the drift towards war] on moral action to be taken by inside people for outside disorders'. Out of this meeting had grown the twenty-six articles of a *Covenant of Literal Morality*, more conveniently known as the *First Protocol*, in which the 'inside people' (that select body of those who agreed with Laura and were therefore 'innately appointed to fulfil the most serious responsibilities of existence') declared their solidarity and their general purposes. Subsequently, during Robert and Laura's final months together, there had been much talk about a *Second Protocol*, described by Tom Matthews as 'in effect a program for inside action ... [in which] by declaring ourselves with effective intensity, [we would attempt] to save the world from war'.[61]

When Riding broke with Graves, she also announced that she had rejected the *First Protocol* as an 'infected document'; but Graves had continued to believe that it 'should be reaffirmed and carried on';[62] and in the summer of 1940 he began planning a Utopian novel (its social and political organization founded chiefly upon Riding's discarded ideas), which would in time inspire a 'practical organisation of decent people'.[63]

Among the 'decent people' who descended upon The Vale House during the remainder of that summer were sixteen-year-old Sam Graves, nervous, warm-hearted, a little disorganized and rather deaf, whom Robert asked to regard The Vale House as another home;[64] Lucie Aldridge;[65] and Jenny Nicholson.

Arriving in Bristol in September 1940 after being bombed out of London, Jenny had rapidly secured the promise of work in the local BBC studios, before moving on to nearby Bath. There she had tracked down Diccon Hughes, the author of *A High Wind in Jamaica* and a long-standing family friend who was now working for the Admiralty, and had borrowed money from him so that she could travel down to Galmpton.[66]

Robert was enormously impressed by her initiative. His respect was increased when he discovered that she had brought with her a typewriter (Jenny diplomatically failed to mention that it was a gift from his brother Charles),[67] upon which she proceeded to hammer out a short piece for broadcasting; and when Robert next wrote to David, chiefly to tell him of his ideas for the Utopian novel, he described her as 'marvellous'.[68]

'Jenny *is* marvellous,' replied David, 'never at a loss for a job.' He himself was still doing basic training in Lincolnshire, from where he had already sent his father some notes describing its 'pitiable silliness', in case they were worth showing to Liddell-Hart.[69] And now he told his father: 'This life is exactly as you imagined: healthy, stupid, monotonous … cleaning one's kit takes up most of life.' He was equally critical of Robert's ideas for a novel, asking him, for example, whether the Queensberry rules would be:

accepted by woman garotters? Would your rules for safe government be accepted by careerists, reactionaries, the prejudiced & selfish, the ignorant & mutinous? There is no will for such a scheme, surely … Besides, it's no use whitewashing the outside. The present social system, with its business & working-class rivalries, its petty national outlook, its utter vulgarity, could never cooperate. The book might be an amusing tour-de-force, but never a practical scheme, I think.

David added gloomily that: 'Any practical organisation of decent people' along the lines which his father had suggested, 'would be suppressed at once by the government … I think it is time this Western industrial civilisation was ended.'[70]

Robert took these strictures seriously enough to lay his Utopian novel to one side for almost seven years. Instead, he began working (once again with Alan Hodge, though Alan could only undertake a limited share of the work as he now had a full-time job with the Ministry of Information) upon a 'new book about English prose ... for the general reader, and also for intelligent colleges and VI-forms'.[71]

In the meantime, despite Robert's work in reorganizing the local LDV, he continued to be regarded with deep suspicion by the village policeman who, as Robert complained to a friend in October 1940, evidently took him for a fifth columnist.[72] Douglas Glass's eccentric photography had been bad enough; but since then Robert and Beryl had been visited by friends who were learning Spanish, and had played a gramophone record with Spanish voices: so it was reliably reported that foreigners had been heard talking behind a wall ... To make matters worse, some of Beryl's friends visited Galmpton with a dachsund. German dogs were considered highly unpatriotic. One of the villagers greeted the dachsund with a Heil Hitler as he passed it on the street; then another villager wrote HEIL HITLER on a marrow in their garden – and the words had grown with the vegetable.

The Graves household began to seem a little more normal when, early in October, they took in the Sullivans, a 'bedraggled family bombed out of Highgate'. Robert explained to Alan Hodge that when the Sullivans knocked on the door of The Vale House, having had nothing to eat for twenty-four hours, 'It was raining so I brought them in to lunch and once they were in, we couldn't send them off again and so here they are.' Fortunately, it seemed that they were 'a great acquisition'. Mrs Sullivan was a farmer's daughter who had been a lady's maid, and was an excellent cook; her fourteen-year-old daughter Lily could type and also knew how to look after babies; and Robert added humorously that, since Mrs Sullivan's three-year-old son Johnny was a great-nephew and spitting image of the famous boxer John L. Sullivan, and like him had 'huge hands and a terrific punch', he and Beryl and William were 'now properly looked after, and defended'.[74]

Then, the following month, Robert and Beryl were given the seal of approval by the upper rank of Galmpton society when they were called upon by 'a large, impressive Mrs Mallow or Mellon or something "from Greenway House" ... with an archaeological little husband'. They were in fact Mr and Mrs Mallowan; and after twenty minutes Robert and Beryl suddenly realized (as Robert reported to Alan Hodge) that Mrs Mallowan 'was p. 57 (or whatever) of [*The Long Weekend*] – Agatha Christie herself'. When Robert, with typical directness, asked her 'why if she never noticed anything (as she confessed) she had become a writer', she impressed him by answering equally directly that 'she had been an only child and told herself stories, all plot & no characterisation'.[75]

CHAPTER 5

Lament for Pasiphae

From time to time, the most extraordinary news reached Robert Graves about Laura Riding and her current circle of friends, which now included Kit Jackson. After receiving electric shock treatment in the mental hospital to which she had been committed after her second breakdown, Kit appeared to one of her visitors, Tom Matthews, to have forgotten or distorted:

> all memory of what had happened to her in her last weeks at the farm. More than that, her feelings about Laura, far from being resentful or hurt, were affectionate and admiring, not to say worshipful. She revered Laura with the same fervor as Robert's in the days of his humble discipleship. She either could not remember or angrily brushed aside all evidence that Laura's presence had contributed to her collapse.[76]

Kit spoke of Schuyler Jackson 'with a disdain almost impersonal; but of Laura herself as of someone unique, extraordinary, more than human'. And early in 1940, when she was well enough to leave hospital, she voluntarily returned to the farm, where for some months she and her children lived at close quarters with the woman who had stolen her husband and sent her temporarily insane.[77]

Since Kit was now clearly harmless, Laura dealt with her kindly; but Robert was still treated with implacable hostility. In June, for example, Laura told Ward Holgate, a former member of the Graves/Riding inner circle, 'that communication between him and her should cease as he had written saying how good in mind and body Robert was now'; though if Ward came to America, 'then negotiations could reopen'.[78]

Riding's hostility was fuelled by the cruel jealousy of a woman who has rejected her lover, but wants no one else to enjoy him; and since she knew Robert extremely well, her analysis, though not wholly accurate, had some force. In particular, she believed that Robert had tried to make his relationship with Beryl into an imitation of his former relationship with herself, so that Beryl had become a kind of 'pseudo-Laura'. This was also the opinion, at first, of the sculptor Dorothy Simmons, who remained firmly attached to Laura, and who explained in a letter to Robert and Beryl that while she fully accepted that their being together represented their effort 'to be really honest', she thoroughly disliked their concomitant 'attempt to make a different set of facts and persons, carry a make-believe of what had been before'.[79]

Robert recognized that there was an element of truth in this when he wrote his poem 'To Sleep', which includes the telling lines:

> The mind's eye sees as the heart mirrors;
> Loving in part, I did not see you whole ...
> And the words I chose for your voice to speak
> Echoed my own voice with its dry creak.[80]

However, there was no doubt that Beryl had become a source of genuine inspiration; and the poems that he wrote for her reveal a gentler Muse than Laura. Loving and charming, they are the poems of a sensitive child abandoned in a dark forest, who has found a friend to alleviate his suffering and share his wanderings. In 'Mid-Winter Waking', for example, Graves writes movingly:

> Be witness that on waking, this midwinter,
> I found her hand in mine laid closely
> Who shall watch out the spring with me.
> We stared in silence all around us
> But found no winter anywhere to see.[81]

And in another poem, 'Despite and Still', he makes this touching promise of domestic fidelity:

> We have been such as draw
> The losing straw –
> You of your gentleness
> I of my rashness,
>
> Both of despair –
> Yet still might share
> This happy will:

> To love despite and still.
> Never let us deny
> The thing's necessity,
> But, O, refuse
> To choose
> Where chance may seem to give
> Loves in alternative.[82]

Sadly, these lines, with their mention of 'The thing's necessity', also show that Graves retained ambivalent feelings about the wholesomeness of sexual pleasure; and in his poem 'The Thieves' he would conclude that sexual intercourse was essentially dishonourable, for:

> Theft is theft and raid is raid
> Though reciprocally made.
> Lovers, the conclusion is
> Doubled sighs and jealousies
> In a single heart that grieves
> For lost honour among thieves.[83]

And when, at the beginning of 'Mid-Winter Waking', Graves writes memorably:

> Stirring suddenly from long hibernation
> I knew myself once more a poet
> Guarded by timeless principalities
> Against the worm of death, this hill-side haunting;
> And presently dared open both my eyes ...[84]

what does he see when he opens his eyes, but love and friendship and domestic happiness? Unfortunately, for Robert Graves, having experienced the violent joys and equally violent horrors of his years with Laura Riding, domestic happiness could never be enough.

In the meantime, Robert continued to be intrigued by Laura's progress. In November 1940 (not long after publication of *The Long Weekend*, which he told his brother John seemed 'to be selling well, though boycotted by the daily and Sunday book reviewers'[85]), he wrote enquiring about Laura and Schuyler to Bill Chapman, one of their neighbours in Pennsylvania. Chapman replied that 'Laura seemed gentler than ever before, quite composed, and seemed to be trying, quite embarrassedly, to be friendly and interested in people'; but she and Schuyler had now left Kit and her children at the farm, and decamped to New York.[86] There, as Robert learned later from Tom Matthews, they were living 'in a walk-up flat on the West Side', where 'a card beside their door-bell announced falsely that "Mr and Mrs Jackson" lived there', while they waited for Kit to bring divorce proceedings, to clear the way for their own marriage.[87]

By this time Robert was immersed in his collaboration with Alan Hodge on their 'new book about English prose'. His domestic burden had become much more difficult, since Beryl's health continued to be poor and Mrs Sullivan, unable to bear being parted from her husband, had decamped to London with her two children.[88] However, Alan came down to Devon for Christmas;[89] and by New Year Year's Day 1941 the two men had prepared a synopsis and specimen pages of what would become (the title was Jenny's idea[90]) *The Reader Over Your Shoulder*. Faber, who were pleased with the success of *The Long Weekend*, liked this new project so much that when Robert's brother Charles appeared in Galmpton in the second week of January, he learned that a contract had been signed almost immediately.

For once, the brothers were in harmony. The reason was that Charles had recently been commissioned to write a book about the RAF in order to stimulate recruiting. It was to be 'a novel, with documentary features'; and, as Robert explained to another member of the family, Charles had written 'to ask my advice. An Air Force neighbour, their new friend 'Crab' Searle, a most intelligent man to whom I mentioned this, then got himself appointed as liaison officer between the Air Force & Charles to keep him on the rails', and Charles had come down to Galmpton 'to be primed'.[91] Robert had enjoyed his role in the business; and Charles's book, written and published within three months as *The Thin Blue Line*, was a useful contribution to the war effort.[92]

On 12 January, while Charles was still in Galmpton,[93] Robert wrote to their brother John telling him that *The Long Weekend* was due for a new edition soon and asking whether, as 'a great favour,' he would check:

> our educational references, and whenever an error in fact, as opposed to what you think merely a wilful opinion, occurs would you please suggest the appropriate revision, in such a manner as to spare printing fees by using just the same number of words as were there.

Robert also mentioned that when the text of *The Reader Over Your Shoulder* was 'in an advanced stage', he would be *'very glad* of your scholastic advice if you would give it, especially as to any omissions or obscurities'. In the meantime, he explained that it was certainly not, as John might have supposed:

> intended to conform with the principles embodied in *The Teaching of English* [a 1921 best-seller] ... which was very bad I thought on the subject which interested me most at the time – the teaching of poetry. Recently I have looked at Q and Fowler as writers of English and they both take a Charity Third instead of a First.

'So I imagine,' he concluded, 'that this book will not conform, but rather demand conformation with.'[94]

Besides these projects, Robert was also helping Liddell-Hart with the proofs of his latest book *The Current of War*, and putting together *Work in Hand*, intended to be a slim volume of poems by himself, and by his friends Alan Hodge, Norman Cameron, James Reeves and Harry Kemp. He was also busy in his vegetable garden;[95] and spending some time with Sam. Now seventeen years old, Sam had abandoned his formal education at Christmas. After being employed by a builder for a while, and finding it 'too slow', he was now very happily 'working for the Admiralty in their local shipyard', and playing football for Paignton.[96]

The only other family news of importance was that Amy had suffered from a severe attack of bronchitis.[97] It was a great relief to Robert when, on 6 February, having half-expected that he would have 'to dash up' to Erinfa to see his mother,[98] he heard that she was better;[99] and then within a week he had also received an extraordinary letter from Laura Riding.

In her letter, which was sent jointly to both Robert and Beryl, Laura Riding most unexpectedly apologized for her behaviour towards them. They were so astonished that they immediately sent a copy of the letter to John and Lucie Aldridge and asked for their reaction.

John, who had once been a great favourite of Laura's, was circumspect in his reply. All he would say about what he described as 'Laura's Peace Offensive' was that: 'there is always a problem when people apologise but in this case Lucie's diagnosis is not unfair.'[100] By contrast Lucie's accompanying letter (addressed to Beryl), was direct and forceful. 'It was good of you,' she wrote,

> to send Laura's letter on. It appals us ... British propaganda in America may be the reason, or some wish to identify herself with us now that Britain is such a wow in America. Of course she and Schuyler

may want money I presume. Robert's books may be selling in America but Robert has always been a lucky star for Laura in other ways which she has now had time to miss.

She concluded that she had 'a complete and utter mistrust of Laura which it would take a great deal to ever remove', and she guessed that Robert and Beryl would 'probably' not send Laura a reply.[101]

Towards the end of February, however, Robert told her that after much thought he had decided to accept Laura's apology. Lucie immediately congratulated him on having done the 'better thing'; but she added that she herself was still unable to:

feel the same way about her as you. I think you regard her as a changed person, whereas I think she is the same person I knew nine years ago in Deyá whose behaviour then had all the potentialitites of what became apparent during her movement from you to Schuyler ... I could never quite reconcile myself to her way of power nor her lack of what I consider the first human grace: if I say 'decent humility' I hope you will understand what I mean. I mean seeing oneself in accurate relationship with the rest of the Universe.

She added that, 'Since Laura has been in love with Schuyler she has changed her technique to suit her life with him but I think her character is the same';[102] and had Robert then known of a recent letter which Laura had sent to Kit, he might well have agreed with her.

Divorce proceedings were in progress between Kit and Schuyler, and as Tom Matthews later recorded, Laura had written:

one of her massive manifestoes to Kit. Griselda, although she was then only fourteen, had power of attorney for her mother; she intercepted the letter and read it. She had not lost her fear of Laura – she never altogether lost it – and she felt Laura's power in this letter which she thought, as it was written in the knowledge that Kit was already ill, was 'beyond anything one could describe'.[103]

Robert did not break off all contact with the Aldridges after Lucie's two anti-Laura letters, as he would have done a year previously. Indeed, a few months later (when John had been called up and was serving as a private in the army, which he found 'like one of those awful dreams of being back at school'[104]), Robert went over to stay with Lucie at Great Bardfield for about a week.[105] But he persisted in believing that Laura Riding, in her pre-Schuyler Jackson days, had embodied some kind of divine inspiration; and the poem he wrote at this time which has the greatest emotional force is undoubtedly his 'Lament for Pasiphae', which might just as well have been entitled 'Lament for Laura'. It concludes:

> Faithless she was not; she was very woman,
> Smiling with dire impartiality,
> Sovereign, with heart unmatched, adored of men,
> Until Spring's cuckoo with bedraggled plumes
> Tempted her pity and her truth betrayed.
> Then she who shone for all resigned her being,
> And this must be a night without a moon.
> Dying sun, shine warm a little longer![106]

CHAPTER 6

Nancy's Children

Proceed, Sergeant Lamb was published towards the end of February 1941 to excellent reviews, in some of which Graves was compared to William Cobbett, or even to Daniel Defoe.[107] In his 'Foreword', he had recorded with some satisfaction that Lamb's story had come close to him in several ways: for example, his paternal grandfather Charles and his great-grand-father John Crosbie Graves had been Dubliners of Lamb's day; and during the American War of Independence John Crosbie's cousins had successively commanded the British fleet in American waters. Robert's 'chief link', however, was that 'I had the honour of serving, like [Lamb], in the Royal Welch Fusiliers during a long and bloody war; and found their character as a regiment, and their St. David's Day customs, happily unaltered since his day.'[108] And the family link with the regiment was continued when his son David, who had recently completed his officer's training, was commissioned as a second-lieutenant into the Royal Welch Fusiliers.[109]

Before joining the RWF at Wrexham, David was given a short leave, and on 7 March 1941 he celebrated his twenty-first birthday with his grandmother at Erinfa. Amy found him looking 'very well and happy in his brand new battledress', and passed on a birthday telegram from his father. The next day, David went on to visit 'Nancy in Somerset & Robert in S. Devon'.[110] (By this time his sister Catherine, incensed by the blitz of Coventry, had also joined up and was training to be a radar operator with the Women's Auxiliary Air Force.[111])

During his brief visit to The Vale House, David made a great impression. Afterwards, Robert told Nancy that he had found their eldest son 'very much improved by the Army', and that he had introduced him to 'the Colonel of the "Irregular Troops" here, who are the people who do raids on the French coast ... etc – a sort of *corps d'élite*'. The colonel had promised to ask for David to be sent there once his training was complete, and Robert explained that it was paradoxically safer being a commando than being in an ordinary battalion.[112]

By this time, Robert Graves was heavily engaged on the *Work in Hand* collection. Liaising between his three co-contributors (who wrote frequently, commenting at length on each other's poems), he began to 'feel like a correspondence club secretary or something'.[113] He and Alan Hodge also continued their work on *The Reader Over Your Shoulder*, with Robert concentrating for the time being upon an introductory chapter, while both men collected 'epitomes', or 'epittymes'. This was their name for prose extracts, preferably from the works of eminent writers, which were so sloppily written that they could be usefully analyzed as examples of bad practice, before being thoroughly revised.

There were occasional distractions: especially as Robert fell easily into conversation with strangers. One day, for example, he was waiting to buy carbon paper in a shop in Paignton, a small town a few miles north of Galmpton, when he heard:

the shop man ... being rude to a nice girl of eighteen or nineteen who wanted to rent a typewriter. 'There's not a typewriter to be had in the whole of Devon,' he told her. So I said 'You're a liar!' and asked the girl what she wanted one for. She said: 'To type out a list of all the El Grecos' in existence'. This seemed to be a hopefully paradoxical sign; so I at once offered to lend her our spare typewriter, and we made friends.[114]

The girl was Marion McFadyen. Robert soon learned that she was half-Jewish, that she had escaped from Nazi Germany and married a Scot, that she was now living in Paignton with her father (described by Beryl as 'a nice old fellow'); and that the list of El Grecos was for the great collector Tomàs Harris.[115] By chance, Marion lived opposite a man named Joshua Podro, 'whose press-cutting business had been evacuated to Paignton, and who went to play bridge with her father'.[116] Podro had fought in France in the First World War,[117] and was also a considerable scholar. When he and Graves were introduced they had enough in common to strike up a lasting friendship.[118]

In May there was a pleasant visit from Norman Cameron;[119] and then at the beginning of June, Robert travelled to London where he stayed briefly with Alan Hodge. The chief purpose of his journey was to appear as one of the panel on the popular wireless show 'Any Questions',[120] on which he held his own quite comfortably and enjoyed making the point that intelligence is more than just reasoning power.[121]

Shortly after his return, however, Robert was involved in a most unpleasant quarrel with Sam,[122] who had now been staying at The Vale House for over five months. At first Robert had welcomed the opportunity of giving him a helping hand, had introduced him to his local friends, had flattered him by describing him as a genius, and had taken him partially into his confidence on the reasons for his break-up with Laura Riding. However, father and son were so different that in due course Robert began to find Sam's presence a considerable strain. The burden was not eased by Robert's awareness that many of Sam's difficulties almost certainly stemmed directly or indirectly from his own behaviour in having abandoned him back in 1929, when Sam was only five years old.

At length it was agreed that Sam should return to live with his mother who was now at Forest Hill near Oxford,[123] and think once again about trying for his School Certificate – though as the syllabuses changed each year, 'it would mean a lot of new books to be got up'.[124] However, shortly before Sam left The Vale House, he discovered that 'Crab' Searle had an old motor-bike which he no longer wanted. He asked whether his father would buy it for him, explaining that it would not only be useful for himself but also for his mother. When Robert, who was 'feeling terribly poor',[125] refused to help, Sam asked Crab if he would consider giving him the bike for nothing.

Before Crab had decided what to do, Sam left Galmpton to join Nancy and Catherine, who were holidaying on the other side of the county. And a few days later, when the motor-bike unexpectedly turned up on his doorstep, Sam quite wrongly assumed that it was a present from Crab.

In fact it was Robert who had paid for the bike and sent it on, partly against his better judgment, since he was feeling annoyed with Sam for not having thanked him properly after such a long visit. Now, at least, he could expect some expression of gratitude from his middle son ... Robert was therefore astonished when, a few days later, he received a letter not from Sam but from Catherine, telling him that, at Sam's request, she had sent the motor-bike back to a nearby repair shop, and asking him, again at Sam's request, to supervise the necessary work and have it sent on by rail to Oxford as soon as it was in good order. From Sam himself there was 'not even a message of love'.

Robert immediately wrote to Sam, explaining that the bike was a present for which he had paid Crab £5-10s-od, and asking whether Catherine had relayed his 'instructions' correctly, as he could not quite believe that Sam had meant to cause him so much further trouble and expense. This, of course, was the cue for Sam to make profuse apologies.

In his reply, he certainly agreed to pay for the repairs if Robert sent on the bill, and even to repay the £5-10s-od if his father could not really afford it; but there was no hint of either thanks or apology: far from it. Catherine had got nothing wrong; the trouble he had caused Robert was 'unavoidable', and he asked Robert to send him some money to repay him for having purchased, out of his own pocket-money, some food for Crab Searle, and some medicine for Beryl. He pointed out that he had given his father two reminders on the subject …

Robert spent half an hour making furious annotations all over this letter, in the least angry of which he declared that his son was 'like the man in the Parable who was forgiven his debt of a hundred talents & took a bloke by the throat who owed him a hundred pence'. Then, realizing that he could not write directly to Sam when he was in this mood, he wrote a slightly less fierce letter to Nancy, putting his point of view and complaining that Sam had 'refused to understand the situation'.

However, Nancy was herself near breaking point on the subject of her errant husband. She had been devastated by Robert's having set up home with Beryl; she had been amazed by his evidently expecting her to be pleased by William's birth (after which she had politely declined Robert's request that she should visit The Vale House in order to admire his new-born son). More recently, though she was too proud to show it, she had been upset by the way in which Robert had so easily recaptured the affections of all four children; and now, just when he had succeeded in building up Sam's confidence, he appeared to be about to undo all the good he had done with a silly quarrel which inevitably reminded Nancy of the equally silly quarrels he had carried on with her and her lover Geoffrey Phibbs back in 1929.

Nancy showed Robert's letter to Sam, and then something in her gave way, and out poured all the dammed-up resentments of the past twelve years. For the first time, she told Sam in detail her side of the story. He listened, and could hardly believe. He mulled it over for almost a week; and then sat down in private and secretly wrote his father a fifteen-page letter. 'Look here, Father,' he began,

I am no longer in the darkness as regards to your history since you married Mother … I have been told more of my childhood; of that scene on the barge at Hammersmith, when you came down from your house in St. Peter's Square, when you demanded that J.D.C. & I should either come with you to Spain or you would never see us again; of that sub-scene in which Catherine, realising the gravity of the situation, asked you whether you could choose Laura or her, & you had the courage to put a stranger before your own child …

On and on he went, page after page, down to the comparatively recent occasion when Robert had asked him 'to look on [his] house as a home'. Sam now declared roundly that he:

> could not. I shall always, so long as I live with Mother, regard her home as my real home. For it was Mother who brought me up, having undergone terrible sufferings and trials ... do you not wonder that David is paying for Mother's new artificial hair, the cause of which may have been you and your thoughtless actions?

However, there was a large measure of understanding for both his parents. 'Mother has her faults,' Sam wrote,

> & she said so ... I can readily forgive her for them, as she was terribly honest & had, despite everything, a mother's real affection for her children ... But she told me one. It was her fault, she said, that she allowed Laura to get the better of you. But, as a rule, Scotch maids never flirt, & she said so. So she never suspected ... that Laura had any designs on you ... she regarded you as one who could look after himself and the family ... [but] it was not so ...
>
> However I will not blame you wholly for this, as, even at my young age, I fully understand your feelings then.
>
> But what a pity that you spent such a fortune on your dream island under Laura's guidance, while, if you had a telescope that had no respect for distance & the contours of the earth, you would have seen, through the thick smog of Hammersmith, and trudging through the alleys, cobbled & dirty, a girl of 13 with her satchel on her way to a day school. Jenny. Another figure, her younger brother, & another, C.N.

Sam finished with words of desperate sadness. He knew, he said, that this letter might end his new friendship with his father. He might have to 'cease to be your son ... I may not see Galmpton again. When people ask me if the great poet Graves is my father, I will say that he isn't ...'

What Robert felt when he read this letter can only be imagined. But afterwards he wrote very kindly to Sam, and there was no more mention of the motor-bike, and not a word about his long letter. 'I see you are not inclined to touch upon the subject I brought in', Sam wrote in reply. 'Very well, let the whole thing blow over, and let me hope for the best. With much love, Sam.' That was the end of the matter; and Robert was soon writing proudly about his children by Nancy and their contribution to the war effort.

Jenny had recently followed Catherine into the WAAF. When she had completed her basic training, Jenny joined a WAAF recruiting unit in London;[126] and on the last Sunday in June she spent a day in Oxford with her mother, Sam, and David and Catherine who were both briefly on leave. Nancy, though 'nervous at times through lack of cigarettes', seemed 'quite well and happy';[127] and, as Jenny reported to Robert, she herself found her 'handsome brother' David 'enchanting'. They had 'a long service talk';[128] and he was able to tell her that Robert had kindly sent him the £10 he needed to take his degree.[129] Her own news was that she had already been recommended for a commission;[130] and not long afterwards Sam, after asking his father's advice, and telling him that it was his ambition to join the Royal Welch Fusiliers,[131] became a member of the Forest Hill Home Guard,[132] and was put in charge of the village mortar.[133]

CHAPTER 7

Wife to Mr. Milton

The domestic pressures on Robert Graves, already eased to some extent by Sam's departure from Galmpton, were further reduced for five or six weeks[134] when in August 1941 he and Beryl and William were joined at The Vale House by a housekeeper. This, curiously enough, was 'Jenny's first nurse, Margaret Russell',[135] the woman who had been sacked by Nancy back in February 1921, at a time when she had been 'almost the mistress of the house, having charge of the money, & giving R & N pocket-money weekly out of their own money'.[136] Margaret had remained devoted both to Jenny and to Robert; and when her former employer somehow resumed contact with her, she wrote to him most warmly as 'Dearest Captain',[137] and was pleased at once again becoming a member of his household.

Shadows from the past continued to fall across Graves's path. In mid-September, for example, came a long letter from Tom Matthews with fresh news about Laura Riding and Schuyler Jackson. 'As you must have heard,' wrote Tom,

> Kit's divorce from Schuyler went through with no hitches and he and Laura were married sometime last June I think. We were all glad that Kit stuck to her guns about divorcing him. The proceedings took place very quietly at Doylestown PA. Kit's witnesses (the hearing was in the master's chambers) were her brother Jimmy, Haven Page (an even older friend of Schuyler's than I) and myself. It was not fun but it could have been worse ... Now we hear that L and S have bought a place in [Wabasso] Florida (how or with what I don't know), plan to spend the winters there and the summers on the farm.

Tom added that he and Julie had not seen Laura 'since a year ago last Christmas'; but that he had 'r[u]n into Schuyler about six months ago in the lobby of the *Time* building and we just said Hello. The awful thing about it was that it wasn't more awful. He might have been almost anybody.'[138]

While Graves absorbed the news of Laura's marriage to Schuyler, he completed the *Work in Hand* collection, which now consisted solely of poems by himself, Norman Cameron and Alan Hodge, the Hogarth Press having determined to exclude poems by Harry Kemp and James Reeves. There was also work to be done on *The Reader Over Your Shoulder*; and in late October he gave a wireless talk on 'War Poetry' of which a version appeared in the *Listener* entitled 'Why has this War produced no War Poets?'[139] This talk and the subsequent article brought Graves two new correspondents, both of them poets aged twenty-six: Keidrych Rhys, co-editor with Dylan Thomas of the magazine *Wales*, who had 'got himself into muddy waters' in the *Listener* correspondence following the publication of Graves's article, and was advised by him 'not to get involved in literary politics'; and Alun Lewis, a second-lieutenant in the South Wales Borderers.

Alun Lewis wrote in the first instance complaining that his poem 'The Soldier' had been quoted in Graves's talk 'to express a point of view I don't endorse: to wit, the isolation or *difference* of the poet'. However, he did not blame Graves for this, but Stephen Spender, who had lifted out of context a number of lines from a longer poem. The complete version, he added, was to be published shortly by Allen and Unwin in a selection of his poems (to be entitled *Raider's Dawn*).[140] Robert replied on 6 November that he was sorry about his mistake, but that it had been a natural one to make in the circumstances which Lewis had outlined; he also suggested that they should exchange their forthcoming volumes of poetry, and asked him to call in 'if you are ever down this way'.[141]

Robert's next visitor was another second-lieutenant: his son David who had been given embarkation leave after being informed that the First Battalion of the RWF, to whom he had recently been posted, might be going abroad very soon. Having purchased 'tropical kit and a good number of books to last me for the voyage',[142] he had spent four days with Nancy and Sam, and then (*en route* for Galmpton) had gone to see Jenny in London[143] where, having won her commission, she was now working for the WAAF as a public relations officer.[144]

Jenny's principal function at that time was acting as liaison officer between the WAAF and the BBC, a role which she fulfilled with enormous success. 'It was more than exhilarating', wrote one of her colleagues, 'sitting next to one of the most enchanting women I have ever met.' Jenny seemed 'irresistible with her blonde hair (slightly longer than the approved length) shining eyes and vivacious mouth'; she had tremendous energy and enthusiasm; and when (for instance), the recruiting for WAAF Cooks became an urgent issue, Jenny found a girl in a RAF Cookhouse ... with a splendid voice and got her on the "Forces Broadcast" – the Singing Cook – and so gave a glamorous twist to that mundane operation'.[145]

At The Vale House, Robert listened to David's news about Jenny, before giving him some careful advice about what he should take abroad with him – suggesting in particular morphia, and gold tokens. Then, on Sunday afternoon,[146] father and son bade each other 'a fond and sad farewell'.[147]

The following morning there was a further letter from Alun Lewis, who declared that he was 'surprised, excited and honoured' by Graves's letter. He would 'dearly like' to call on him if an opportunity arose, and would 'count it a privilege' to send Graves his poems. However, he wanted him to:

> know beforehand the course from which my writing comes. *Humility* ... the source of all my long struggles, for it brings me into conflict with self-pity and pity for the world, with authority and presumption on the part of those who are not humble, with intolerance and cruelty, and with submission.[148]

Graves replied that humility was 'a characteristic of poets, as they learn the impossibility of poetry by experience'. But he added a warning. 'I think it is important', he wrote,

> to make the humility something that one puts between oneself and one's impossibly high standards, not between oneself and others. After all, nobody can possibly succeed in being Alun Lewis so well as yourself, and gradually you in that favourable position of being in his position can find out far better than anyone else what being him entails.

He added that he did not like 'synthetic work, from Virgil on through the centuries – including Milton ...'[149]

This dislike of Milton was deep-rooted, and was about to be incorporated by Graves into an historical novel far more powerful than his recent volumes on Sergeant Lamb.

Work on *The Reader Over Your Shoulder* was now well advanced, but Faber, the prospective publisher, had lost their nerve and backed out; and so Robert, needing a new source of income, had been thinking hard about a subject for another popular historical novel. He had almost settled on the story of Jason and the Argonauts when, as he told Alan Hodge,

> I had a sudden inspiration that I know all about Milton and his wife whom he was living with when he wrote about divorce. Historically I know very little and will have to get all the relevant books together – tell me, didn't you read up Mrs. Milton for Laura?[150] … hair was [Milton's] obsession and bound up tightly with his Samson complex.[151]

Graves immediately began researching for this novel, in which he tells the story, from her point of view, of Marie Powell, the daughter of a Royalist squire who in 1642 at the age of sixteen married the thirty-four-year-old Puritan poet John Milton. Published as *Wife to Mr. Milton*, it made such an impression that it remains in print after more than fifty years.

This is not surprising for it has an emotional charge second only, in Graves's fiction, to that which had powered the *Claudius* novels. His 'sudden' lightning flash of inspiration had welded not only a number of immediate preoccupations, but also long-standing guilt, hatred and prejudice: much of it deeply buried. And although *Wife to Mr. Milton* is largely sympathetic to Marie Powell, it displays towards John Milton the kind of virulent hatred which indicates some deeply personal motive.

The unsympathetic side of Milton's nature had already been well documented. In 1900 Sir Walter Raleigh (subsequently Graves's friend and mentor) had published a volume on Milton in which he lamented that, after describing in *Comus* 'one whole realm of pagan loveliness', Milton had 'turned his face the other way, and never looked back'. His guiding star had become 'that severe and self-centred ideal of life and character which is called Puritanism'; he had elected to 'reject common ambitions, to refuse common enticements, to rule passions, desires and fears'; and to think of himself as 'a "cause," an agent of mighty purposes'.[152]

Graves (who had once described Poetry as 'a modified descendant of primitive Magic'[153]) shared Raleigh's admiration for *Comus*; but where Sir Walter could admire the spiritual grandeur of *Paradise Lost*, 'spanned on frail arches over the abyss of the impossible, the unnatural, and the grotesque',[154] Robert regarded everything but Milton's earliest work as a betrayal of his true poetic gifts. For poetry, in Graves's view, was principally about the relationship between the poet and his Muse; and the 'classical' poetry of a Virgil or a Milton was not true poetry at all, but an artificial construction chiefly concerned with impressing its hearers and enhancing the reputation of its author.

Milton admits in Graves's novel that in his youth he 'conceived strange amatory fancies for persons of my own sex';[155] and he is portrayed as 'small-minded, vengeful, self-righteous',[156] proud, vain and ruthlessly ambitious. He decides to marry partly because Marie Powell, as he notes, is 'remarkable for the glory of her hair',[157] so 'copious' that in his eyes it 'bespeaks perfect femininity';[158] and partly because he believes that only 'the chastity of the married', which is 'neither to commit adultery nor to be greedy of the sensual pleasures by Nature permitted to a married man' will enable him to become a great epic poet.[159]

Marie Powell, who marries John Milton in 1642 only because her family owes his family a large sum of money, is shown as being treated abominably. Milton's arrogance causes so many misunderstandings that the marriage remains unconsummated, she is sent back to her parents, and Milton proceeds to write a number of tracts advocating 'that such contrariety of mind between husband and wife as will blight the peace of marriage is a just and sufficient cause not only for their separation, but for their divorce'.[160]

Within three years, learning that Milton is planning bigamously to acquire a second wife, Marie effects a return, cunningly appealing to her husband by throwing herself upon her knees in such a way that 'my hood tumbled off and showed him my hair'.[161] Their marriage is finally consummated, though Milton is too selfish to notice that his love-making gives his wife no pleasure, and she bears him three children before dying in childbirth in 1651.

Tom Matthews was in no doubt about the motive which lay behind Graves's savage assault upon his fellow-poet. 'I believe', he wrote, 'that he visited on Milton the bitter detestation he felt for Schuyler [Jackson]: that the Milton he was writing about *was* Schuyler.'[162]

Graves certainly hated Schuyler Jackson. Earlier in 1941 he had described him to Alan Hodge, deliberately misquoting a Riding poem, as 'madder than before,/ With nothing but a nasty grangrened spot/ Where once had been his heart ...'[163] His portrait of John Milton clearly has Schuyler Jackson's selfishness and arrogance; and in retelling the story of how Milton refused to pay his mother-in-law a sum of money to which she felt entitled,[164] Graves also attributes to Milton the 'cynical dishonesty in business affairs' which he thought of as the most shocking feature in Schuyler's character. But there is something more. Graves's hatred of his Milton/Jackson figure is so extreme that, as Eddie Marsh would comment,

I don't think it's an exaggeration to say that you never show him doing a kindly action or saying a civil thing. Is this really credible, that a man who shows such nobility and greatness of mind in his poetry could have been so completely lacking in those qualities in his daily life?[166]

In expressing such hatred, Graves was also holding up a mirror to the dark side of his own soul.

In his novel, *The Wooden Shepherdess*, Graves's friend Richard Hughes would write that:

No man can see his own soul clearly and live: he must hood his eyes which look inwards as if against a dazzling by light when the light is too much – though this is a dazzling by darkness, his soul is too dark to bear looking at.[167]

So when we look over Graves's shoulder, as it were, into that sinister reflection, the picture is often shadowy and indistinct. Yet we can see clear hints in the foreground of the connection between Milton's story and his own.

For example, Graves's conviction that Milton had an obsession about hair was derived partly from the passage in 'Lycidas' in which Milton had asked:

> ... What boots it with incessant care
> To tend the homely slighted Shepherd's trade,
> And strictly meditate the thankles Muse,
> Were it not better don as others use,
> To sport with *Amaryllis* in the shade,
> Or with the tangles of *Neaera*'s hair?

But alongside Neaera we may also imagine two likenesses of Nancy Nicholson: one very recent, and one dating back to 1926. In each of them she is ill, her hair is falling out, she holds a wig in her hand, and she stares accusingly at her husband and tormentor. By her side is a single image of Laura Riding, whose hair had once been cropped close, but who here, in 1928, in the process of stealing Robert away from his wife, has grown her hair long, so that it falls luxuriantly across the breasts between which she flaunts a silver locket containing Nancy's picture.

Further back in the reflection, their images clouded with guilt, stand Nancy's children; with Beryl not far away.

How roundly Graves attacks Milton for the treatment of his wife; yet where Milton rejected Marie for three years, and was then reconciled,

Graves has already rejected Nancy for twelve years, and will continue to reject her for the rest of his life. How forcefully Graves attacks Milton first for his dishonourable wish to divorce Marie; and then for his still more dishonourable plan, once he has realized that a divorce is out of the question, of marrying bigamously. Yet where Milton ultimately remained faithful to his wife, Graves had deserted Nancy and their four children for Laura Riding, and was now living as though married to Beryl Hodge.

John Milton is also implicitly ridiculed for his relationship with a woman eighteen years younger than himself; yet Beryl was almost twenty years younger than Robert Graves. Milton is attacked for his puritanical notion of 'chastity' within marriage; yet for much of his relationship with Laura Riding, Robert had embraced the far more puritanical ideal of total sexual abstinence. Milton is attacked for his early homosexual leanings; yet Robert too had passed through what he would describe as a 'pseudo-homosexual' phase in his early manhood. Milton is attacked for spending part of his youth dependent upon his father's generosity; and yet on more than one occasion it was only Alfred Perceval Graves who had saved Robert from financial ruin.

In this mirror held up to the dark side of Robert Graves's soul, the figure of his father is almost completely obscured; as is that of his once beloved school-fellow Peter Johnstone.

In the background of all these figures swathed in guilt there is a great darkness; and the strongest element in that darkness is arrogance, closely intertwined with the desire for fame. How fiercely Graves attacks Milton for his arrogant belief in the excellence of his own poetic powers, and for his determination to write some great work that would live for ever. Yet Graves had long ago declared that: 'with the poet there is always the tinge of arrogance in the thought that his own poetry has a lasting quality which most of his contemporaries cannot claim';[168] and in his recent correspondence with Alun Lewis, he had specifically cautioned him against too much humility.

Graves believed not only that a measure of arrogance was an essential ingredient in the personality of any writer or artist;[169] but also that at any one time there were only a few people in the world ('proper chaps' he had called them in *Good-bye to All That*) whose lives were of any real importance. Riding, with her own conspicuous failure either to earn money or to achieve the recognition she felt she deserved, had subsequently taught him that he should despise both fame and commercial success; yet, although he could never acknowledge it, even to himself, Graves retained for both these things a powerful longing which fuelled his creativity, even if at times it unbalanced his critical thought.

Once Graves had signed a contract for *Wife to Mr. Milton* with Cassell, he intensified his researches, although he was deeply committed to his point-of-view and wrote to James Reeves on the subject: 'Nothing can make me like, admire, or even pity John Milton. That was my earliest judgment and the more I read the sounder it seems.'[170]

CHAPTER 8

Family and Friends

Alan Hodge visited Robert and Beryl for Christmas 1941. After sharing in the seasonal festivities, he stayed on to help Robert with *The Reader Over Your Shoulder*, which the friends had now decided should be divided into two volumes. The first, which was chiefly concerned with 'the principles of clear statement', was completed on 28 December. One typescript copy was sent immediately to the London agent A. P. Watt; and at the same time Robert wrote to his brother John, asking whether he would be prepared to comment on the text, and explaining that:

> The second volume consists of detailed analyses of 66 short passages from prominent writers, with an average of 30 errors pointed out in every twenty lines of text. This is [also] done now, but not yet typed or cross-copied. It will be a bit difficult to get the second volume published: it is dynamite under so many chairs – though not a malicious or snorty book.[171]

Robert also had some news to retail about his younger daughter.

Not long after joining the WAAF, nineteen-year-old Catherine had met and fallen in love with Clifford Dalton, a brilliant twenty-five year-old engineer from New Zealand. After studying at both Canterbury and Auckland University, Clifford had been elected to a Rhodes Scholarship at Oxford; the outbreak of the Second World War had interrupted his studies, and when Catherine met him, he was serving in the RAF as a research officer.[172] Catherine had already introduced Clifford to her father, who thought him 'a very very good chap'; but, as Robert explained to John, there were difficulties with Nancy. She and Clifford had 'got on badly as I feared they might – I don't know what will happen ... Clifford is too clear-minded on the subject of Nancy's oldest obsession – male and female equalitarianism.'[173]

However, much to Robert's relief, as he came to like Clifford 'more and more'[174] and considered that he had 'one of the keenest minds I know',[175] Nancy had soon announced that she would not actually oppose a wedding.[176] So Catherine and Clifford were married on Saturday 31 January 1942 in a Registry Office at Aldershot; and after a forty-eight-hour honeymoon they each returned to their respective units.[177]

In the meantime, David's embarkation had been delayed for several months;[178] and there was excellent news of Sam, who had passed his School Certificate with three credits and two 'very goods',[179] and would soon be travelling down to London. There he would combine speech-training in Kensington with preparation for an army career in an officer's training corps at a Harrow day school.[180] However, Robert privately told Nancy that he thought it unlikely that Sam would pass his medical; and he added that he did not 'feel sorry because the Army will be doing real fighting this year and it's bad enough to have David engaged for that'.[181]

There was less good news from Erinfa. Robert had been corresponding regularly with his mother since the spring of 1941, and on 15 December that year, much to her delight, he had sent her 'a poetic telegram' to mark her 84th birthday.[182] But Amy was extremely ill over Christmas with gastric flu; she remained in bed for the first half of January 1942;[183] and in February there was a letter from John explaining that their mother was 'very exhausted & must not write except by dictation if she is to pull through the next few weeks'. He also asked whether Robert had any money to spare, since the doctor:

> now says she must have the nurse till the middle or end of March. This costs nearly £4 a week, apart from food etc. Susan [Macaulay, *née* Graves, their ailing but sharply intelligent half-sister] paid for the first fortnight, & I paid for the Consultant's fee & for another fortnight.

'As mother's finances are not too good,' John concluded, 'any spontaneous help you could give would probably make her enforced rest less anxious.'[184]

Robert replied that unfortunately his own financial affairs were 'in a precarious position', and that:

> When I am assessed by income tax, [I] expect to find I am insolvent. I am working hard to get some money back into the till with this Milton novel. If I sent Mother money, I should only be robbing someone else: of course, if there *is* none to be had I can, and will, forthcome.

He added that for the sake of his novel he had 'had to buy £50 worth of books, no library being adequate to my purposes, to sell back when finished'.[185]

A fortnight later, Robert heard from Susan that both she and the doctor thought Amy was approaching the end of her life; and he remarked in a letter to Nancy that his mother was 'a *good woman* despite her religion, and I will miss her very much indeed when she dies'.[186] However, much to everyone's surprise, Amy once again defied medical opinion and within three months had staged a complete recovery.[187]

In the meantime, Robert worked furiously on *Wife to Mr. Milton*. By 5 February he had already 'done 3 chapters now & see my road clear';[188] and for a while there were very few distractions, although mid-February saw the arrival of Alun Lewis's first book of poems, *Raider's Dawn*,[189] which led to some further correspondence between the two poets;[190] and at the beginning of April there was a welcome visit to Galmpton by David Graves, on his second and final 'embarkation leave'. When, just a few days later, he and his battalion were about to set sail, David announced that it was about time: having been inspected by 'General Montgomery ... Winston Churchill and the King ... only God Almighty' was left to see them off.[191]

Other family visitors included Rosaleen, who would drive over about once a fortnight with her three young sons: the difficult nine-year-old Dan, the sensible seven-year-old Roger and the sensitive five-year-old Paul; Catherine, who would often hitch-hike over to Galmpton; and Jenny, who telephoned one evening in great excitement with the news that *Lilliput* had commissioned her to write an article on Lord Louis Mountbatten.[192] As a result of his part-time work for the local 'Air Raid Precautions' (ARP), which had a post in the village school just opposite The Vale House, Robert had also made two important additions to his list of local friends and callers.

It happened like this: one evening Graves had been working hard on *Wife to Mr. Milton* and was close to the end of a chapter when it was time for him to report for duty. On doing so, he found that the elderly gentleman whom he was due to relieve was in the middle of a chess game, and told Graves, after introducing himself as Lord Falkland, that he was quite happy to remain on duty while Robert returned to The Vale House to complete his chapter.[193]

Lord Falkland (the thirteenth viscount of that name, and the premier earl of Scotland) now lived quietly in Brixham, but he had led an extraordinary life. An ex-governor of Wandsworth prison, he had also travelled extensively; and Robert began inviting him over to The Vale House, where he would sit by the fire and enthral his host with tales of his adventures in remote parts of the world. His *pièce de résistance* as a story-teller was his description of the occasion on which he had been served 'lady' by a cannibal chief – apparently it had tasted good. He and Robert had soon become firm friends.[194] By a strange coincidence, which lent a little piquancy to their friendship, Falkland was also the direct descendant of a minor character in *Wife to Mr. Milton*: the second Viscount Falkland, who had died fighting for King Charles I.[195]

Falkland also introduced Robert and Beryl to Irene, usually known as Rene, a very striking young woman in her twenties with long, honey-coloured hair,[196] whose husband was a friend of Falkland's son. She had been married for less than two years and had a daughter a few months younger than William; but she was living with her parents in Brixham because her husband was away in the services. In his absence, Falkland kept a friendly eye on her. The custom developed that on Friday evenings he and Rene would call on Robert and Beryl at The Vale House, where Rene, using ingredients she had brought with her from Brixham, would cook a splendid fish supper for them all: in those penurious days, probably their best meal of the week.[197]

By the end of April a first draft of *Wife to Mr. Milton* had been completed;[198] on reading it over, Graves recognized its power, and began to believe that 'after Claudius' it would become 'the most popular of my novels'. Towards the end of May Robert was able to tell his brother John (now living at Harrow, since Malvern College and Harrow School had merged for the duration of the war) the excellent news 'that Cape will do *The Reader Over Your Shoulder* book with a 20% cut in length – that is Okeh by me – you see how pedantically I spell O.K. in its original Cherokee form, and I will have pleasure in incorporating your points ...'[199]

Now that *The Reader Over Your Shoulder* had been accepted, there was the time-consuming and occasionally difficult task of obtaining permission to reproduce the passages which were to be used as examples of bad writing. Alan Hodge undertook the routine work; but when 'any delicate problem' cropped up, it was left to Robert to deal with the matter,[200] and this led to some awkward correspondences.[201]

In the meantime, both Robert Graves and Nancy Nicholson had been worrying about their son David. At length Robert received a reassuring letter, written when he had been at sea for a month. Apparently he had found himself 'sharing a cabin with a well-known actor called Jack Hawkins ... a pleasant and amusing person [who] does not get on one's nerves [and who had] acted opposite Jenny at the Liverpool Rep once'. David had also been lecturing about the battles of the last war, with the help of *The War the Infantry Knew* by Robert's old comrade-in-arms Dr Dunn; and 'for the first time in my life' he had begun 'to drink a little whisky & gin, as I find they settle my stomach'.[202] Not long afterwards, Nancy received a cable: David had reached India and announced that he was 'extraordinarily well'.

On 14 July Robert posted a long letter to his eldest son,[203] to whom he also sent £15,[204] but fears about David's safety persisted throughout the family; and ten days later, on Robert's forty-seventh birthday, he received a letter from Sam telling him that Catherine had recently dreamed of David's death.[205] This news, coming on top of other difficulties such as a fresh and ungrateful set of evacuees,[206] made Robert feel extremely gloomy, and he wrote a depressed set of verses which begin:

> July the twenty-fourth, a day
> Heavy with clouds that would not spill
> On the disconsolate earth.[207]

Shared family worries had drawn Robert and Nancy a little closer in recent months. Together they agonized not only about David's chances of surviving the war, but also about Jenny's living beyond her means [208] (though later in the year she was promoted to the rank of Flight-Lieutenant and began receiving a handsome £6 a week[209]); and about Sam's continuing deafness, which meant that although he had been longing to get into uniform, he was classified Grade IV and thus effectively debarred even from the Pioneers.

Catherine's news was more cheerful: at the age of twenty she was pregnant with her first child. Robert immediately invited her and Clifford down for the weekend of 14 August, and offered to put her up for a few weeks when she received her discharge from the WAAF.[210]

It was shortly after Catherine's visit that Robert received a letter from Alan Hodge saying that he wanted:

> to raise a dire spectre and that is divorce. I've mentioned this before and never done anything about it but now I think I should like to pay a visit to a lawyer and if possible start the horrid business going. I am so sorry ...[211]

This would be the start of a further set of severe difficulties between Robert and his estranged wife.

CHAPTER 9

A Divorce in the Family

In late August 1942, with *Wife to Mr. Milton* revised and work on *The Reader Over Your Shoulder* virtually complete, Robert Graves began researching for his novel about Jason and the Argonauts, which he would call *The Golden Fleece*. He also decided to allow himself a brief holiday, and arranged to take Beryl and William to stay with the Aldridges for a week.[212] But first there was a party in Brixham given by Desmond Flower of Cassells; and Robert and Beryl soon found themselves talking animatedly to a highly intelligent couple named George Simon and Joanna Shuckburgh, whom they had never met formally, but who by a coincidence had been observing them earlier that very day.

George and Joanna had been walking along the beach at Paignton with Elizabeth, George's daughter by his wife Charlotte, from whom he was in the process of arranging an amicable divorce. Suddenly they had been struck by the sight of an 'amazing-looking' couple, who were introducing their infant son to the sea. The man looked 'spectacular', the woman 'very beautiful'; and now here they were at Desmond Flower's party (to which George and Joanna had been taken by Charlotte and her new partner Desmond MacCarthy, a nephew of his more famous namesake), and the man turned out to be Robert Graves, whose work they had both read and admired, while the woman was his partner Beryl ...[213]

George himself was a forty-year-old Jewish radiologist at St Bartholomew's in London, a brilliant and delightful man with an engaging smile and a great love of literature who enjoyed nothing more than a good conversation. He also had a brother who was a famous printer, and he was related to the Rothensteins, one of whom, Michael Rothenstein, Robert had met in Great Bardfield. As for twenty-six-year-old Joanna, whom George intended to marry as soon as he was divorced from Charlotte: she was a handsome woman with an enquiring mind who had studied German at Munich University before the war. Joanna said little about her work: when pressed she mentioned something about 'passport control'; but in fact she was working for British Intelligence. In any case, the rapport was immediate. Within a few minutes Robert, Beryl, George and Joanna had fallen easily into a friendship which would last for the rest of their lives.[214]

Shortly after this meeting, Robert, Beryl and William went to stay with the Aldridges at Great Bardfield.[215] Falkland kept them in touch with the local news, writing to them, for example, on 28 August, while they were still away, about Daisy Kitto 'a well-known and much-respected prostitute' having been 'murdered in Brixham by a Canadian soldier. It is thought that he will be found not guilty', Falkland explained,

> as he is pleading incompatibility of temper. A most formidable rival Shanghai Lil succeeds to her practice without having to pay a penny for the goodwill. We have had many alerts and a few bombs since you left but have suffered only slight damage.

He added that he missed 'you all three very much and hope you will not stay away longer than you at first intended'.[216]

When they returned (to find a letter from Tom Matthews, announcing that he was being sent to take charge of the London branch of *Time* magazine for three months and hoped to see something of them[217]), Robert was soon busy with *The Golden Fleece*; while Beryl wrote to Alan Hodge enclosing Tom's letter, and enquiring about progress on their divorce. 'Dear Beryl,' Alan replied on 6 September,

> I am returning Tom's letter. It is good news that he is coming over.
>
>   This is a collusive letter by the way and legally should not be written for I saw Mr. Winterbottom on Wednesday and opened a docket labelled Hodge v. Hodge + Graves. It all looks pretty plain sailing – I'm not disclosing having stayed with you since that would amount to admitting acquiescence.

It would, however, be on the record that he had 'visited you several times to see if there was Any Hope of Reunion'.[218]

When Beryl asked whether it was necessary for Robert to be brought into the case, Alan consulted his solicitors and wrote again on 1 October:

> It can't be done on grounds of desertion, it seems if you just leave somebody in order to go back to Mother or some such, that is desertion, but if you leave somebody for Another Man, that is adultery. I'm sorry about this too but that's what Mr. W. tells me.

Alan added that Tom Matthews 'came in the other day. He's pretty busy at the moment. Norman [Cameron] is giving him lunch tomorrow and I next week.'[219] In between those two lunch dates, Tom travelled down to Galmpton for the weekend.

He found a household even busier than usual, for two of Robert and Beryl's Great Bardfield friends, Dr Maurice Newfield[220] and his wife Sigrid, had been staying in rooms nearby for almost a week. Of Beryl herself there was no sign for the first twenty-four hours of Tom's visit: she

> kept to her room; she was not well, Robert said, but nothing serious. Besides his writing, an unbreakable daily habit, he did the cooking and all the household chores, as well as minding William, their obstre-perously lively child. When he had a spare fifteen minutes Robert would seize a pair of scissors and a pile of magazines and cut out coloured pictures from their illustrations and advertisements, to paste into a scrap-book for William's amusement.[221]

Tom was shocked to see that Robert appeared to enjoy acting as William's 'devoted slave', weakly placating him with blackberries after justifiably reproving him for pulling his ears at the end of a tea-time expedition to visit 'Agatha Christie'; and he also noted a considerable change in Beryl. Before she left her room and came downstairs, he:

> had heard her voice, querulous and weakly strident, calling to Robert, unbraiding, complaining, impatient. And I had heard his responses, or the tone of them: seriously conciliatory, humble, apologetic. Exactly the tone he had used to Laura.

When he saw them together, this resemblance was hardly noticeable; and yet it seemed to him:

> that Beryl was making a conscious effort to be or do something that was not natural to her – to rule the roost – and that Robert played his part in the game much more easily than she did. I was not alone in this opinion: other friends of Robert's[222] told me that when he and Beryl first set up house together her treatment of Robert had been strikingly and unexpectedly reminiscent of Laura's.

By the time he saw them, however, 'this phatasmagoria had begun to fade'. Beryl was moving from her role as Muse to a new role, not necessarily more natural to her, as 'housekeeper, wife and mother': which left Robert in an emotional and creative dilemma similar to the one he had faced in the mid-1920s, when he had first come to believe that domesticity was death to poetic inspiration.[223]

Robert was not yet consciously seeking an alternative Muse – or at least, not one made of flesh and blood. But in his spiritual life he was reaching out for some new revelation, and he began feeling things with the heightened intensity of the period in 1926 when he had been falling in love with Laura Riding. This was deeply associated with his researches for *The Golden Fleece*, for as he read more and more about the religious beliefs of the early ancient world, he spent more and more of his time in a world at a slight tangent to normal reality.

Robert had recently told James Reeves, another recent visitor, how he and William had accompanied the Newfields on an outing to Pomeroy Castle, a few miles inland from Galmpton. With a shock of horrified recognition, Robert had immediately 'identified' Pomeroy 'as my nightmare castle of many years standing'; and he referred James to 'The Castle',[224] a poem written during the time when he had been inconveniently in love with both Nancy and Laura, and had declared that there was:

>   ... No escape,
> No such thing; to dream of new dimensions,
> Cheating checkmate by painting the king's cheek
> So that he slides like a queen.
> Or to cry nightmare, nightmare,
> Like a corpse in the cholera-pit
> Under a load of corpses.
> Or to run the head against these blind walls,
> Enter the dungeon, torment the eyes
> With apparitions chained two and two.
> And go frantic with fear ...[225]

But whatever his subconscious aversion to being 'chained two and two', Robert had consciously decided that he wished to regularize his position with Beryl; and, not long after spending a few days in London with Norman Cameron,[226] he wrote on the subject first to his mother and then to his wife.

Amy, on learning that Robert hoped to divorce Nancy and marry Beryl (partly, he told her, for William's sake), replied with a letter in which she took great care never to mention Beryl's name.[227] 'That I cannot interfere with your life at forty-seven years of age I know,' she told him, but I must tell you how sad I am about what has happened since you came back from America. I had continued to hope that you & Nancy would go back to each other as your 4 fine & clever children definitely belong to you both & over their heads you might have forgiven each other & made a fresh start. Now all that is impossible & Nancy must go lonely through life, though she has worked herself to the bone for the children & is much wiser than she was in the early years. Nevertheless I am sorry for you & very sorry for little William, who seems to be a very promising child.[227]

She concluded that she still loved Robert, '& can continue to call myself Your affectionate Mother Amy Graves'.

The day after receiving this maternal broadside, Robert wrote to Nancy telling her that Alan Hodge (who was still working for the Ministry of Information) was 'beginning divorce proceedings against Beryl, his wife, for adultery and I would be very grateful to you if you would use the same solicitors as he, and the same evidence, for a divorce against me'. He knew that Nancy hated the idea of divorce, but it would be 'far less awkward' for everyone if he and Beryl were married. He assured Nancy that she would not have to appear in court and that he would pay all her costs; and he added that this was 'a collusive letter, so please destroy it'.[228]

Nancy did not destroy the letter; nor did she answer it for nearly three weeks, reserving her judgment about a possible divorce, and finally writing only to tell Robert that she was 'finding out about things & will let you know'.[229]

In the meantime Robert had written another letter to Amy telling her that he intended to marry Beryl, and that he hoped that she could then be pleased with William 'who is such a decided Graves, Rosaleen said a Ranke'.[233] He was also drafting pages of *The Golden Fleece*; but the divorce question had unsettled him, and he became so dissatisfied with what he had written that by the time he received Nancy's letter on 5 November he had scrapped an entire opening chapter and started again.[231]

Two weeks later, Nancy was advised by a Brixham firm of solicitors that they had served Robert with a Petition in the case of Hodge v. Hodge & Graves;[232] she also received a further letter from Robert begging her to proceed against him herself.[233] At this point, Nancy wrote to a London firm of solicitors telling them that she wished to divorce Robert, provided that she did not have to appear in court herself; she also explained that she would be proceeding under her proper name of (Miss) A. M. P. Nicholson.[234]

When the solicitors wrote back to tell her that the proceedings would 'have to be in your married name and it will be necessary for you to appear in Court personally',[235] she immediately forwarded their letter to Galmpton, with a covering postcard to 'Dear Robert' which ran:

> Enclosed. I put it all so plainly I suppose he couldn't see it. I wondered if you would like to type a letter that I could sign if you think a different technique might be effective.
> One can't change a name one hasn't got by deed poll to one that one has got. And the whole business of legality of a woman keeping her own name was thrashed out publicly years ago – about 7 I think – even a long article by Helena Normanton in Good Housekeeping about it.

'Don't see', she concluded, 'why one should have to do lawyers' jobs for them & keep them up to date with their law.'[236]

Nancy's feminist principles had been outraged; and as her correspondence with Robert continued, she became increasingly angry. 'I can't do this obviously', ran her note of 23 November. 'And what the dickens has A.H. got to do with my affairs. Believe *you* can get a divorce on grounds of long separation these days.'[237] To which Robert replied patiently that he could not divorce her while he was living with another woman. And although he agreed with her about the use of her name, he reminded her that when Geoffrey Phibbs's wife Nora had attempted to divorce him on the grounds of his adultery with Nancy, she had allowed 'Annie Mary Graves' to 'stooge' for her; and he arged that 'it would in a real sense be truer to get Annie Graves to undo a legal knot that she tied herself and then disappear for ever, than to involve Nancy Nicholson in the matter'. He added that once they were divorced, he could see her again, which would be easier for the children, and especially for Sam.[238]

This drew an explosion of anger from Nancy. 'The only reason I am thinking of going on with the divorce', she told him, 'is the aversion one had to damaging a child's future status. Just that. I consider I owe you less than no consideration.' And then, referring back to the time when Robert had frustrated her hope of marrying Geoffrey Phibbs, she wrote:

> Justice is outraged considering how you refused to let me get my divorce until it was too late, and when it would have made all the difference to my life ... [and] if the divorce business does come off there is going to be none of that easy friendship business as far as I am concerned – sorry to be so rude.

She added that it was 'a preposterous suggestion' that she should sign anything except in her own name; that the use of 'Graves' instead of 'Nicholson' in the Phibbs case had been 'sharp practice' by the lawyer concerned, and that in any case 'Laura ought to have been co-respondent. But she was in Spain.'[239]

Robert replied as placatingly as possible that he did not understand some of her remarks; but he did not wish to rake up the past, and could 'only conclude that there was at some time or other a deep misunderstanding between us and apologise if the fault was mine'.

However, the case was hopeless. No solicitor could be found who would accept Nancy's reading of the law. So Alan's divorce from Beryl went ahead; but Robert and Nancy remained married. 'This divorce business is indeed silly', Robert would tell Alan early in 1943:

how much better the Mahommedan formula: 'I divorce you, I divorce you, I divorce you,' spoken in front of witnesses, and the woman goes back to the father's home with her dowry and a decent sum for wear and tear ...[240]

Robert himself, freed for a while from these recriminations about his past life, was able to focus more sharply upon the mythology of the ancient world. In doing so (with growing excitement), he would come to discern the outlines of an ancient religion whose tenets, imaginatively rediscovered, would provide him both with a coherent poetic philosophy and with a solution to his complex emotional difficulties.

BOOK TWO

THE WHITE GODDESS
1943–46

CHAPTER 1

The Golden Fleece[1]

The legend of Jason's Argonauts and their voyage to recover the Golden Fleece from King Aeetes of Colchis had a long and distinguished history; and Robert Graves believed that, like the ancient legend of the Fall of Troy, dismissed as pure fiction until Schliemann's excavations at Hisarlik in the 1870s and 1880s, it had a basis in solid historical fact. As he pointed out:

> The Greeks, on the whole a level-headed people, regarded the voyage as an historical event that took place about two generations before the fall of Troy ... The voyage was a good deal nearer in time for Homer and Hesiod than Columbus's discovery of America is for us; and though in the fifth century B.C. Thucydides found the story too intractable for inclusion in the First Book of his history, no Greek, so far as I know, ever ventured to deny that *Argo* was a real ship which sailed from Thessalian Iolcos to Aea on the Colchian river Phasis – and back again.[2]

Graves's task was therefore to study all the surviving accounts of the voyage, such as the Argonautic epic written in the third century BC by Apollonius Rhodius, who had access to the famous Royal Library at Alexandria; and then, using a combination of shrewd detective work, imaginative reconstruction, and what he called analeptic thought (that is, the kind of associative thought by which Graves believed that he could find solutions to historical, religious, moral and poetic problems that could not be solved by reason alone) to present the most truthful narrative possible of what had actually occurred.

Although *The Golden Fleece* could do with being shorn of thirty or forty pages of excessive background detail (the number of minor characters, fleetingly mentioned, makes some chapters rival the more genealogically minded books of the Old Testament), the central story of the voyage of the *Argo* and the recapture of the Golden Fleece is excellently told. The larger-than-life portrait of Hercules (who is easy to please, but quick to take offence, and has been given several other Gravesian characteristics) is outstanding among a gallery of vividly drawn characters including Jason himself (a generally uninspiring and even wrong-headed leader, whose chief gift is that all woman fall in love with him), and Medea, the yellow-haired and dangerously fanatical priestess of Artemis. The narrative itself is full of magical, erotic and dramatic incident, as when Graves introduces us to the great mysteries of Samothrace; or when he depicts the 'merry repopulation' of the island of Lemnos (whose women, having killed all their men-folk, fall greedily upon the Argonauts by whom they conceive vast numbers of children); or when he describes the recapture of the Fleece and the killing of King Aeetes.

However, the orginal seizure of the Fleece is perceived as 'an episode in a religious conflict between the supporters of the matriarchal Moon Goddess of the "Pelasgians" and those of the patriarchal Thunder God of the Greeks';[3] and it soon becomes clear that Graves's main interest does not lie in telling of the excitements and dangers of the voyage. Instead, he is preoccupied with the religious background against which that voyage takes place.

When writing his 'Biblical romance called *My Head, My Head!*' in 1924, Robert Graves had outlined his belief, shared by numerous anthropologists of the day, that society had once been matriarchal; and he had added that in his private view 'the beginning of our present misery' dated from the time when 'the mother lost her rule'.[4] It was when he realized that the change from matriarchy to patriarchy was to be the central theme of *The Golden Fleece* that Graves had scrapped his unsatisfactory first chapter;[5] and when he began his novel a second time, he showed how close this theme was to his heart by drafting a prologue set in Majorca, the island which had been his home for seven years, and which he hoped would be his home again.

But this is Majorca in 1300 BC, one of the Islands of the Hesperides; and Graves imagines it being ruled by a Chief Priestess whose loyalty is to the Triple Goddess, and one of whose daughters is 'the Nymph of the sacred orange-grove at Deia'.[6] To this Nymph comes Little Ancaeus, 'Last survivor (it is said) of all the Argonauts who sailed to Colchis in search of the Golden Fleece'.[7]

In the exchanges which take place between the Orange Nymph and Ancaeus (before she orders her followers to hunt him to his death), we are given a few glimpses of a world which, though violent in many respects, has not yet been corrupted by patriarchy. The Orange Nymph herself is:

tall and beautiful. She wore a flounced bell-shaped skirt in the Cretan fashion, of linen dyed the colour of orange with heather dye, and no upper garment, except a short-sleeved green waistcoat that did not fasten in front but showed the glory of her full breasts. Her badges of office were a belt of countless small pieces of gold linked together in the form of a serpent with jewelled eyes, a necklace of dried green oranges, and a high caul-cap embroidered in pearls and surmounted by the golden disc of the Full Moon.[8]

Here, we learn, the old religion is practised. 'Maiden, Nymph and Mother are the eternal royal Trinity of the island, and the Goddess, who is worshipped there in each of these aspects, as New Moon, Full Moon, and Old Moon, is the sovereign deity.'[9]

Following this religion means that the Orange Nymph, as she tells Ancaeus, was 'initiated into nymph-hood' by 'companying' with nine men 'in the open furrow of the field after the sowing'; but when she subsequently bore a child, 'it was not a girl, to be preserved, but a boy; and in due course he went, torn in pieces, to the furrow from which he had sprung. The Goddess gave and the Goddess took away again.'[10]

When Ancaeus explains that the mainland to the north of Crete, once known as Pelasgia, has been invaded by 'the Greeks, a barbarous pastoral people from the north', who 'worship the Father God as their sovereign Deity and secretly despise the Triple Goddess', the Orange Nymph wonders:

> whether she had misheard his words. She asked: 'Who may the *Father God* be? How can any tribe worship a *Father*? What are fathers but the occasional instruments that a woman uses for her pleasure and for the sake of becoming a mother? ... Fathers, indeed! I suppose that these Greek fathers suckle the children and sow the barley and caprify the fig trees and make the laws, and in short, undertake all the other responsible tasks proper to women? ... Is it not the woman who rules in the cave, and if any of her lovers displeases her by his surly or lazy behaviour, gives him the three times repeated warning to take up all his gear and begone to his fraternity lodge?'[11]

When Ancaeus explains that Greek men are masters of their women and their houses, the Orange Nymph calls them 'the most impious and disgusting people in the world'; and she is still more shocked when Ancaeus tells her that they reckon descent through the father. 'No, no,' she cries,

that is manifestly absurd. Though it is plain and indisputable, for
example, that little Kore is my daughter, forasmuch as the midwife
drew her out of my body, how can it be known certainly who was her
father? For the impregnation does not necessarily come from the first
man whom I enjoy at our sacred orgies. It may come from the first or it
may come from the ninth.

'That uncertainty the Greeks attempt to dispel,' said Ancaeus, 'by
each man choosing what he calls a wife – a woman who is forbidden to
company with any but himself ...'[12]

But to the Nymph this is a wholly unnatural state of affairs, as no woman
'can be so ruled and watched and guarded as to be prevented from
enjoying any man whom they please.'

However, the tide of history is running strongly against the Nymph and
her view of things, and inevitably, social and moral changes in the new
'Greece' have been accompanied by theological changes. As to how these
have come about: Graves imagines a series of meetings between
adherents of different religious cults to decide upon the changing
relationships between the gods and goddesses whom they worship. (Not
altogether implausible, when one recalls that the bishops of the Christian
church would later hold councils at which they adjudicated on such
matters as the precise nature of the relationship between Father, Son and
Holy Ghost.)

As successive waves of Greeks overcome the original Pelasgians, so the
Triple Goddess finds that her supremacy is challenged. At first she is
allowed to be the mother of the Greek sky god Dios (later Zeus); but
eventually Zeus becomes head of an Olympian family of gods and
goddesses; and the Triple Goddess, though represented as Hera (wife of
Zeus) in her capacity as Mother; as Aphrodite, in her capacity as Nymph;
and as Artemis, in her character of Maiden huntress, is everywhere
'under male tutelage'.[13]

These theological changes are not, however, to be regarded merely as
intellectual games played chiefly for political ends. Robert Graves had
been deeply religious all his life. He had long recognized what has always
been understood by the great Christian mystics, and is now also
recognized by the great physicists, that the universe is a much stranger
place than it seems; and that the obvious material world, known directly
through the five senses, is only a small part of a reality perhaps more
spiritual than material, and certainly so complex that it can never be fully
understood.

Within this complex reality there appear to be numerous forces both creative and destructive; and when, in an attempt to place themselves in a proper relationship with the universe, men assign to those forces the names of gods and goddesses (or even a single three-personed God who encourages His followers to renounce the devil and all his works), then the names may be only names; but, just as a rose by any other name would smell as sweet, the forces are real forces, and just as real for a believer in Mithras or Pallas Athene as they are for a believer in the Christian God.

'By their fruits ye shall know them'[14] runs the Christian injunction familiar to Graves since childhood. His primary consideration, therefore, as he examined the various religious cults of the ancient world, was the actual effect of a particular belief upon its adherents; and as he tells the story of *The Golden Fleece* it becomes clear that he himself favours the cult of the Triple Goddess, sometimes known as the White Goddess, who says of herself:

I am the Triple Mother of Life, the mistress of all elements, the original Being, the Sovereign of Light and Darkness, the Queen of the Dead, to whom no God is not subject. I rule the starry skies, the boisterous green seas, the many-coloured earth with all its peoples, the dark subterrene caves. I have names innumerable. In Phrygia I am Cybele; in Phoenicia, Ashtaroth; in Egypt, Isis; in Cyprus, the Cyprian Queen; in Sicily, Proserpina; in Crete, Rhea; in Athens, Pallas and Athena; among the pious Hypoboreans, Samothea; Anu among their dusky serfs. Others name me Diana, Agdistis, Marianaë, Dindymene, Hera, Juno, Musa, Hecate.[15]

It is she, outraged by the rededication of her shrine at Pelion to Zeus, who encourages Phrixus to steal from it the great ram's fleece (fringed with locks of gold wire, and therefore known as the Golden Fleece) which has been placed there to aid Zeus with his rain-making. And later, when Phrixus, having taken the fleece to Colchis, has died and been left unburied, it is the White Goddess who promises to help Jason to recapture the Fleece – provided he ensures that Phrixus is properly interred.

For although Graves has found plausible explanations for the most bizarre aspects of the story of Jason and the Argonauts, such as the Harpies which tormented the blind King Phineus, the clashing rocks of the Symplegades, and the fire-snorting bulls of King Aeetes, he happily allows the White Goddess herself to speak, either in dreams or, more normally, through the mouthpiece of one of her priestesses. This came easily to a man who was of the opinion that Laura Riding, in her pre-

Schuyler Jackson days, had been a manifestation of the divine power; and who had described her in 1932 as an incarnation of the Goddess Isis.[16]

Graves firmly believed, as he wrote *The Golden Fleece*, that the White Goddess was not only a convenient description for a particular creative force, but also, provided that she had worshippers, a living reality. For Graves also believed that, just as a scientist's expectations are said to determine to some extent the outcome of his experiments, so our conscious beliefs can act upon the substance of the universe and shape it. Therefore he makes the White Goddess herself explain that 'the power of a Goddess is circumscribed by the condition of her worshippers ...'[17]

This rediscovery, as he saw it, of an ancient religion was utterly intoxicating. Early in December 1942, Graves wrote to friends in Sweden, telling them that his novel was progressing with enormous speed;[18] and despite a traditionally merry Christmas (with Cliff and the heavily pregnant Catherine welcome guests at The Vale House),[19] his pace of work hardly slackened as he entered the New Year.

For several months, the outside world made little impact, although in January there was an awkward correspondence with Norman Cameron about the use of Ca'n Torrent in faraway Deyá. Cameron had long ago given the house to Laura Riding, who in turn had passed it on to Robert Graves. More recently Graves, realizing that Cameron had been heavily out-of-pocket in the matter, had offered his old friend the use of the house once the war was over; but had then been offended when Norman had talked of transferring that offer to a woman friend of his. However, Norman resolved the situation in a touching letter which began 'Dearest Robert – really dearest Robert – rather than become estranged from whom I would sacrifice any wealth ... before God and man and in all equity C'an Torrent belongs to you 100%.'[20]

In February came the disappointing news that, because of a paper shortage, Graves's earlier historical novel *Count Belisarius* could not be reprinted as had been planned.[21] However, that month also saw the English publication of *Wife to Mr. Milton*. The reviews were extremely mixed, and several private correspondents complained about Graves's treatment of Milton. (It was a treatment which had already led Random House, the New York publishers of Graves's work since *Antigua, Penny, Puce* in 1937, to turn down *Wife to Mr. Milton*; when it appeared in America in 1944 it would do so under the relatively unknown imprint of the Creative Age Press.[22])

Eddie Marsh, in particular, declared that although he realized that there was 'a horrible side' to Milton's character, he himself would 'continue to believe in my heart of hearts that the man who wrote "L'Allegro" and "Il Penseroso" can't have been the *unredeemed* monster you have depicted'.[23] However, Graves defended himself ably enough in the *Listener*[24] and other places; and the controversy did nothing to harm sales: the Cassell edition of 10,000 sold out so rapidly that a new impression of 3,000 was needed within a fortnight.[25]

But beyond his writing of *The Golden Fleece*, there was little that touched Graves apart from worries about the war, which had gradually caught up more and more of his family. Although Sam still had no occupation, Nancy had been in uniform as an ambulance driver since the previous September;[26] and as for David ... On 17 February 1943 Catherine (with a month to go before her baby was due) sent him a long letter telling him that Jenny had finished *Kiss the Girls Goodbye*, her amusing account of life in the WAAF; that their father was 'getting on well with *The Golden Fleece*'; that she was 'cutting Robert's *Lawrence* book by 1 in 5 for an abridged edition'; and that the Milton book was receiving a lot of attention. Tragically, she might as well have saved her ink. Two months later the letter was returned to her on the ground that the 'addressee' had been 'reported missing'.[27]

CHAPTER 2

'Missing, Believed Killed'

Despite his terrible experiences in the Great War, Robert Graves believed that his country had been right to declare war upon Nazi Germany; and early in March 1943 he wrote a letter to *The Times* in which, looking back to the events of 1940, he drew 'the parallel of Horatius holding the bridge alone, after losing some allies, and Great Britain standing alone against tyranny after the fall of France'.[28]

When that letter was published, Robert's eldest son David was far away in the east with 'B' Company of the First Battalion of the Royal Welch Fusiliers. After arriving in Bombay the previous summer, the battalion had moved some 150 miles inland to Ahmadnagar, where it was learned that it was to be deployed not against the Germans in Egypt, as had been thought, but against the Japanese in Burma.

Training in jungle warfare had followed. In December 1942 the battalion had been moved to a tented camp near Chittagong in eastern Bengal. There it had engaged in further arduous training whose purpose, a well-kept secret,

> was an attack from the sea on the enemy-held port of Akyab [on the Arakan coast] ... 250 miles to the south, and a possible jumping-off place for a Japanese invasion of India ... Indian troops were already advancing down the Arakan coast towards Akyab, and by the beginning of January were within fifteen miles of their objective.[29]

But their advance had been halted at Donbaik, where the Japanese were 'well dug-in and extremely difficult to locate'.

On 8 February, David's battalion had begun moving from Chittagong to Teknaf, 'near the southernmost prong of Bengal and separated from Burma by only a narrow strip of water'.[30] An immediate assault on Akyab was expected, but since that was cancelled (as was a later plan for a landing by sea, in an attempt to take the Japanese positions at Donbaik from the rear), the battalion was still at Teknaf on St David's Day.

David Graves marked the day with a light-hearted 'Ode on the difficulties of celebrating St David's Day in a foreign clime in a proper and fitting manner', which began:

> What is there in this land accursed
> With which to honour March the first?
> The goats round here are far from royal,
> Pot-bellied small and unhygienic.
> Not wishing to appear disloyal
> Our uniforms are far from scenic ...
> Our leeks will just be lengths of marrow
> Cut down to shape and long and narrow ...[31]

The following afternoon, orders were received for a march to the Donbaik front. There, in the early morning of 18 March 1943, the battalion went into action for the first time for more than two and a half years.[32]

With an element of surprise, they might have had a chance. But their attack was preceded by a light artillery bombardment which 'made no impression on the strong Japanese positions [which lay astride a sunken stream, or chaung] beyond warning them of the assault which was to follow'. At twenty minutes to six the three forward companies ('A', 'C' and 'D') launched concentric attacks on their objectives. 'A' Company reached the strong points it was due to attack, but was repulsed with heavy casualties; 'D' Company also reached their objective, but was then pinned down under heavy grenade and rifle fire; while 'C' Company, which attacked down the chaung, fared no better. Held up by light-machine-gun fire from concealed posts, as well as by mortar and grenade fire, it was forced to withdraw to its original starting point with severe losses.

Speaking in Welsh over loudspeakers, Colonel Williams ordered the survivors of 'D' Company to hold their ground while 'B' Company, not yet formally engaged, though its second-in-command had already been wounded,

> put in an attack along the north bank of the chaung, in order to eliminate the posts in the chaung itself which had held up 'C' company, and to link up with 'D' ... [This] attack was carried out by No. 11 Platoon ... but after an advance of about forty yards it was held up by enemy fire and the platoon could only cling to the ground it had gained.

It was at this point, seeing that the advance was held up on every side, that Lieutenant David Graves of 'B' Company made an heroic intervention.

In the absence of his company commander, who was out on the north bank of the chaung, Graves ordered a sergeant and a Bren gunner to accompany him. Then, displaying what Colonel Williams would describe as 'most conspicuous gallantry', he:

> advanced on the first enemy post. With the Bren gunner giving covering fire Lt. GRAVES bombed his way into the position. During this period the Sgt. and the Bren gunner were wounded and put out of action. Quite undeterred, Lt. GRAVES coolly returned for a further supply of grenades, and going out again over completely open ground swept by enemy fire, proceeded to carry out a lone attack on the next post from which the enemy had been throwing large numbers of grenades.
>
> This post Lt. GRAVES took with a fearless charge, and was seen to be continuing his advance when he was shot.[33]

Graves was last seen falling into a trench after being hit, but no one could reach him to see whether or not he was dead; so on the following day, after the battalion had withdrawn (with the terrible loss of thirteen officers and 162 other ranks killed, wounded or missing),[34] he was posted 'Missing, believed killed'.

The news reached The Vale House on 3 April,[35] just twelve days after Catherine Nicholson had given birth to a boy whom she had named David James.[36] (Robert had invited Catherine to Galmpton for her 'lying-in' and she and her baby son stayed with him and Beryl until the end of May.[37]) Rejoicing over his first grandson (and over the approaching birth of his second child by Beryl, who was six months pregnant) was immediately displaced in Robert's mind by a terrible anxiety.

Robert had been halfway through a letter to his sister Clarissa, still out in Palestine, where she was now housekeeping for their civil servant half-brother Dick, when the telegram arrived. Having begun his letter by telling her cheerfully that the news of David was good, he ended it despairingly with the words: 'We can only wait.'[38] The following day he wrote to Nancy:

> I couldn't trust my voice over the phone to you, so sent a telegram and later phoned Jenny.
>
> I will send you at once any additional details that come in the letter that 'follows shortly' ... Jenny is a wonderful person. After talking twice

to her I feel that I can break the news to Catherine today. She leaves hospital tomorrow. The baby has been gaining weight phenomenally.[39]

And a few days later Robert told Alan Hodge that:

The war has just given me a body-blow; the usual horrible telegram has arrived saying that David is missing ... Of course 'missing' may mean a whole lot of things, just as 'died of wounds' in my case meant 'unconscious'; but it's no place to be missing at the best of times,

he concluded, 'and the Japs aren't too good to prisoners.'[40]

The news spread rapidly round the family. Charles heard that Robert was 'taking it badly';[41] while Nancy, according to Sam, was 'so full of home-made philosophy that she has taken the news very well indeed'.[42] Sam himself was haunted by an image of the brother he felt he had known too little: 'I can see his face remarkably vividly,' he wrote to Robert,

as he runs across that terrible open ground; I know he was sensitive of things hitting him in the front, & would bend his arms in that peculiar way of his, & his face looking as though a fragile tumbler was on its way there, his eyes clenched almost shut so that he could hardly see his way ...[43]

But nothing certain was known. 'We can only hope and pray,' wrote Amy from north Wales; while Clarissa comforted herself with the thought that David was 'only missing from the human point of view'.[44]

There were numerous other letters of commiseration: notably from Maisie Somerville, an old friend who wrote that her own adopted son was missing;[45] from Robert's half-brother Perceval, who described David as 'a grand companion with a kind of quiet charm which I find it impossible to describe';[46] and from his half-brother Philip's wife Kitty, who reminded Robert that he had once brought David to see her and Philip in their London house, and wrote: 'I knew that you were very fond and proud of him.'[47] Robert himself found his hopes and fears fluctuating from week to week.[48]

Perhaps it was just as well that April and May were fiendishly busy. Two-year-old William had measles;[49] and there was a houseful of guests over Easter (including Alan Hodge,[50] whose divorce decree nisi from Beryl went through on 10 May[51]). Afterwards, Beryl was so exhausted that she had to take to her bed for a while;[52] and then, since she realized that even when her divorce from Alan was made absolute, Nancy's opposition would mean that it was still impossible for her to marry Robert, she was involved in the legal process of changing her surname from Hodge to Graves by deed poll.[53] May also saw the successful publication of *The Reader Over Your Shoulder*, and all this time Robert was working furiously hard on *The Golden Fleece*, a first draft of which had been completed by the beginning of June.[54]

By this time, David's heroic action had been widely reported in the press, and Robert was feeling more hopeful about his survival. 'I expect you read about David?' he asked his brother John:

> A good show, & I am glad it was with our 1st Battalion, which has been twice knocked out this war and is the only organisation of any sort (school, college, society etc) that I am childishly proud of having belonged to myself. I think David has a good chance of being alive; the Japs respect courage, and little else.[55]

Later that month, however, came the news that some of the men in 'B' Company had reported David's death; although Basil Liddell-Hart advised Robert that this was not conclusive, as they would have had to report his death 'to excuse [themselves from] not suicidally rescuing him'.[56]

Then a few weeks later, on 21 July (coincidentally William's third birthday), Beryl gave birth to a daughter whom she and Robert named Lucia. The contrast between this happy occasion, and the horror of a war in which he had probably lost his eldest son, inspired Robert to write his poem 'To Lucia at Birth', which begins memorably:

> Though the moon beaming matronly and bland
> Greets you, among the crowd of the new-born,
> With 'welcome to the world' yet understand
> That still her pale, lascivious unicorn
> And bloody lion are loose on either hand:
> With din of bones and tantarará of horn
> Their fanciful cortège parades the land –
> Pest on the high road, wild-fire in the corn.[57]

The following month, Robert received a letter from Colonel Williams, who wrote:

> I was very grieved to lose David who was an outstanding platoon commander and a most inspiring leader. He attempted to restore a

situation which was looking bad by one of the bravest actions I have ever seen. I shall never forget the sight of David sallying out with an armful of grenades as if he were demonstrating on the assault course ...[58]

However, he had to break the news that, although David had been recommended for a DSO, there would be no medal of any kind. The action in which David had been engaged had ended in failure and therefore, as Colonel Williams explained, 'the regulations on awards precluded our securing for him the recognition his bravery merited'.[59]

Nor could there by any certain knowledge about David's fate until the end of the war. However, the conviction steadily grew upon Robert that Catherine's dream of the previous summer had been prophetic, and that David was almost certainly dead.[60]

CHAPTER 3

Matriarchal Days

While Robert Graves and Alan Hodge had been collecting copyright permissions for *The Reader Over Your Shoulder* back in the summer of 1942, they had considered collaborating on another book, this time about poetry, and Robert had written a thoughtful letter in which he had emphasized the difference between 'real' and 'artificial' poetry. In particular, he had talked of:

> The aura, or halo, or whatever, that clings to the name 'poet' in spite of the lamentable history of poetic behaviour. How this shows the dim popular awareness of the supernatural power in poetry: a poem being the magic circle in which poets by their strange dealings with living things enclose a living power. The existence of charlatan poets who try to reproduce a genuine poetic phenomenon by literary means (gorblimey vocabulary, metrical tricks, etc.) is an indirect indication that the real thing exists.[61]

Since there was not enough time to work on this book alongside his story of the Argonauts, Robert had agreed with Alan to put it 'on to simmer very, very slowly'. Indeed it was almost a year later (early in July 1943, when Graves was trying to concentrate on drawing '4 large and highly complicated maps of the Argo voyage',[62] and when his head was still full of the ancient Greek mythology upon which he had drawn for *The Golden Fleece*) that he found himself becoming obsessed by an altogether new perspective on the history of poetry.

Explaining this to Hodge on 13 July, Robert told him that he had recently become worried:

> by thinking about poetry and finding that all the poems that one thinks of as most poetic in the romantic style are all intricately concerned with primitive moon-worship. This sounds crazy, and I fear for my sanity,

but it *is* so. The old English ballads ... are all composed with a sort of neurosis compulsion for arranging things in 3s ... which is the chief characteristic of the Moon Goddess – Triple Goddess – ritual ... Of course, Apollo originally pinched Parnassus and Pegasus from the Moon Goddess. And the Muse, whom poets habitually address, was the Moon originally in her Mouse aspect ...

'This may lead me nowhere,' he concluded, 'and I am anxious not to get dogmatic or psychological. But I find myself making the Bards into Moon-men and the minstrels into Sun-men. Help!'[63]

This was the first time that Graves had directly associated the White Goddess of Pelion or Triple Goddess with the Muse or source of poetic inspiration, though his belief in such a magical source was of long duration.

As far back as 1919, in his poem 'Unicorn and the White Doe', Graves had written a striking parable about the poetic life in which the poet is seen as a Unicorn, and his Muse as the White Doe:

> 'Seek me not here
> Lodged among mortal deer,'
> Says the White Doe;
> 'Keeping one place,
> Held by the ties of Space,'
> Says the White Doe ...[64]

This source of inspiration had appeared to be 'unattainable' once Robert was married, and his poetic relations with Nancy Nicholson had become complicated by domesticity.

Five years later in 1924, about the time that Graves had first outlined his belief that society had once been matriarchal, he had written his magical lines 'On the Poet's Birth', in which he had suggested that a poet's true origins are in a mythical realm far removed from the everyday world. 'Acknowledge only me; be this enough' the poet's mother tells him when there is some dispute over his parentage:

> For such as worship after shall be told
> A white dove sired you or a rain of gold.[65]

Then, in 1926, Robert had begun his long association with Laura Riding; and by the end of 1928, Riding had revealed to Graves that she was more than human. She could be thought of, if he liked, as a goddess: she was certainly a figure of destiny or, as she herself preferred to say, she embodied finality. Soon he had begun describing her as 'seamless, like the garment of Christ'; then as an incarnation of the Goddess Isis;[66] and now she was becoming associated in his mind with the White Goddess of Pelion. Elsewhere, in the background of his thought, unseen, but with her own spiritual and psychological legacy, loomed the powerful influence of his mother Amalie von Ranke Graves.

The new revelation towards which Robert Graves was making his way, in a state of enormous spiritual and intellectual excitement, would provide him with the moral and religious and poetic synthesis for which he had been groping for much of his adult life.

In the meantime (as George Simon and Joanna Shuckburgh learned from Robert's letters) he was obsessed by everything connected with the moon. After Lucia's birth, George had written to Beryl urging her 'to get Robert to compose a moon poem' for her baby daughter; and soon received a cheerful reply telling him that Robert had done so (in those lines beginning 'Though the moon beaming matronly and bland') without having to be asked.[67]

Beryl had brought Lucia home from the hospital towards the end of July, but had then had to spend most of the next fortnight in bed, which meant a busy time for Robert. In mid-August he told James Reeves that he had at last sent off the maps of the *Argo* voyage; but that they currently had eight people in the house, including:

> the Sullivan family of 3, our ex-evacuees, who are no trouble and much help, and Beryl's twin Hardinge, who has been up 8 times in an aeroplane but never come down in one i.e. he's an R.A.M.C. paratroop learning his job, and on embarkation leave ...[68]

In addition, he would soon be reading the proofs of Basil Liddell-Hart's *Thoughts on War*.[69]

The good news was that he was no longer under such acute financial pressure. *The Reader Over Your Shoulder* had nearly sold out, and although there was no paper for a full reprint, the Reader's Union were to launch an edition of 5,000 copies in the New Year; Macmillan were to publish it in the USA; and Cape were committed to a concise version aimed at primary schools. At the same time, as Robert told his brother John, he had been relieved to hear that *Wife to Mr. Milton* had 'sold out the first two editions of 12,000 & will find paper for a reprint; so I am solvent again!'[70]

Robert Graves therefore felt free to devote most of his time to collecting material for his proposed book on poetry.

Earlier in the year, Graves had been visited at The Vale House by a precociously intelligent fourteen-year-old admirer named Martin Seymour-Smith, son of the bibliographer and librarian Frank Seymour-Smith used by Graves to obtain rare books.[71] Martin had impressed Robert with his admiration for the poetry of Norman Cameron;[72] and now Robert wrote to him explaining that his new book would be:

> for people of good sense who have shelved the consideration of poetry because it is too muddled a study, and for anyone else who is interested. It's going to be exciting to write because of the discoveries I have already made, in the course of *Golden Fleece* researches, about Apollo and the Muse and the tenancy of Mount Parnassus. This sounds nonsense, but isn't it queer that English poets have always owed loyalty to the Muse rather than Jehovah?

He added that the Muse was 'the mouse-aspect of the Moon, and it all starts with that, i.e. with Big Medicine under the Moon on Mount Parnassus in matriarchal days'.[73]

In late August Graves began a useful correspondence on the subject of this proposed book with a young Welsh poet whose verses appeared under her maiden name of Lynette Roberts. After one of his letters to her husband Keidrych Rhys (still editing the magazine *Wales*), Lynette generously 'offered to look up things for him in the British Museum and to send him essential source books'.[74] In his reply, Graves wrote that he was 'very grateful' for her offer. In the meantime, he had decided that the English poetic tradition, in its highest sense, was 'predominantly Celtic'; and he was beginning to investigate the links between Gaelic and Brythonic influences and Greek poetry. It was already plain to him 'that at a certain socio-economic stage' in Western and southern European nations, 'you get a Llew-Lugh-Apollo god who patronises poetry of a *bardic* sort ...' What he was chiefly interested in, he declared, was 'the previous stage – marked in England by the three Brigids. In Wales ...?'[74]

By this time it was becoming clear that Graves was thinking along highly idiosyncratic lines, and Alan Hodge began to have doubts about whether he would be able to make any significant contribution, at least to the early chapters. 'I am most interested in your epitome of early poetic history,' he wrote to Robert on 22 September,

> but I cannot much help you to write it out – at least, the historically early part of it, because I know so little of Latin and Greek literature and religion. I should regard your epitome as a kind of myth (in the sense

that Jason's story is a myth), needing telling and interpreting as only you can do it.

'I think it is a good myth', he added wisely; 'that is, it has truth, and it is not necessary to ask whether it is entirely factually true.'[76]

Within six weeks of receiving this letter, Robert Graves found himself moving in yet another direction, and he began to research on a new historical novel about the life of Christ[77] to which he gave the provisional title *The Angry Shepherd*. Clearly, he needed to produce popular works at regular intervals to subsidize his old family as well as supporting his new one; but, as his first biographer Martin Seymour-Smith has wisely pointed out, there was a far more important reason for his choice of subject.

Having begun to understand the religion of the ancient world, and having discovered, at least to his own satisfaction, how the once all-powerful Triple Goddess had been supplanted by Zeus and his followers, Graves now needed to come to terms with the Triple God who had in turn supplanted the Olympians.[78] Until he could do this, it would be impossible for him to write the book on poetry in which he intended to take his theme of Goddess-worship and Muse-inspiration from ancient times, right through the Christian-dominated era, and up to the present day.

CHAPTER 4

The Angry Shepherd

One day at the beginning of November 1943, Robert Graves had been leafing through a copy of the New Testament when he was struck by a passage in the thirteenth chapter of the Acts of the Apostles,

> in which Sergius Paulus the Roman Procurator of Cyprus is recorded to have been 'amazed' by Paul and Barnabus when they told him about Jesus ... I knew that it took a great deal to amaze one of Claudius's hard-headed Governor-Generals, whose guiding juridical principle was *title*: for example, they would have classed the followers of a man who had falsely claimed to be King of the Jews with the abettors of one found in possession of stolen Government property.

Since Paulus was also 'unlikely to have been in the least interested in religious or ethical theory', and there was 'no suggestion in the Acts that he was baptised into the Christian faith', what could have so amazed him? Graves's mind ran on to:

> ponder on Pilate's extraordinary favour in granting Jesus a private interview, usually reserved for Roman citizens, and on the unconventional *titulus* ['JESUS OF NAZARETH THE KING OF THE JEWS'] which was fixed to the Cross at his orders. The logical development of these inter-related problems, in the light of certain passages in the *Gospel to the Egyptians* and the *Proto-evangelism*, was so startling that I did not know what to make of it.[79]

However a few days later, Robert Graves's friend Sir Ronald Storrs, the Classical scholar and Orientalist, came down to Galmpton for a brief visit,[80] and Graves decided to confide in him.

Robert had a high regard for his guest, a large, broad-shouldered, good-humoured man with whom he would sing folksongs over the washing-up.[81] Sir Ronald was also a close friend of his half-brother Philip, and a man whom Robert had come to know chiefly because of their shared interest in T. E. Lawrence, in whose *Seven Pillars of Wisdom* adventures he had played an important part. Like Pontius Pilate, Storrs had once been the Military Governor of Jerusalem; and he listened carefully to Robert's astonishing theory: which was that Jesus really had been a legitimate claimant to the throne of Israel. Storrs was intrigued; and Graves records that, 'It was his generous encouragement – though he did not commit himself to accepting my hypothesis – that started me working on the book.'[82]

Graves immediately put all his other work to one side, and began a massive course of background reading, which not only confirmed him in his point of view, but led to all kinds of new discoveries. On 24 November, after several weeks of research, he told James Reeves that his proposed novel would be:

> all about Jesus Christ and his royal parentage. Quite new, and confirmed by all the authorities, new and old. I wish it was off my desk: it is too big, and I don't like the way it grows in all directions. Not esoteric; I am still non-Christian, but also completely convinced of the truth (historic) of the Gospels when read in terms of the religious politics of the day … it makes a very queer story from the journalist's point of view.

'It is also very queer,' he concluded, 'that nobody has hit on the story before; not even those who know about rules of divine inheritance – how this is conveyed in different tribes. I don't know when I'll finish.'[83]

In the meantime, everything was grist to his mill. Early in December, for example, Lynette Roberts sent him a copy of the Reverend Edward Davies's *Celtic Researches*, which she hoped would help him with his book on poetry. Graves replied by telling her that she had helped him more than she knew. Although the Edward Davies book was 'crazy in parts', it contained:

> the key (the relations of bardic letters to months and seasons, which he himself doesn't realise; but he gives all the elements in the equation, so it's easily worked out) to Celtic religion: a key which unlocks a succession of doors in Roman and Greek religion and (because the Jewish religion was a Semite one grafted on a Celtic stock) also unlocks the most obstinate door of all – the story of the Nativity and Crucifixion.

He added that he could 'now make out a good historical case for the more improbable gospel elements', and that his thesis was confirmed 'by a study of early Christian literature ... and Egyptian and Talmudic tradition, and of Josephus, etc.'[84]

Graves was one again writing an historical novel using 'the analeptic method', which he defined as 'the intuitive recovery of forgotten events by a deliberate suspension of time'. For this to work, he would declare in his 'Historical Commentary' to his novel,

> one must train oneself to think wholly in contemporary terms. This is most easily done by impersonating the supposed author of the story, who has much the same function as the carefully costumed figure placed in the foreground of an architectural drawing to correct misapprehensions about its size, date and geographical position.[85]

In writing *The Angry Shepherd*, 'Graves chose to be the mouthpiece of old Agabus the Decapolitan, who wrote in the year A.D.93'; and the story told by Graves/Agabus, though initially weighed down, like *The Golden Fleece*, by too much detailed learning, develops into an enthralling reinterpretation of both the Jewish and the Christian tradition.

Graves's theory is that Jehovah, the God of the Old Testament, 'was once regarded as a devoted son of the Great Goddess';[86] that in ancient Israel descent was matrilinear, and every chieftan or king had ruled 'by woman-right: namely by marriage with the hereditary owner of the soil';[87] that later, Jehovah had formed a Trinity with two of the Goddess's three persons, Anatha of the Lions and Ashima of the Doves, while 'the remaining person, a sort of Hecate named Sheol' retired 'to rule the infernal regions';[88] that still later, Jehovah divorced 'his two partner-Goddesses', who are named in chapter twenty-three of the Book of Ezekiel as Aholah and Aholibah; and that since then, although remnants of Goddess-worship had survived here and there, the Jews had been sadly obsessed with 'celestial patriarchy'.[89]

Jesus himself is introduced to us as the offspring of a secret marriage between Herod the Great's son Herod Antipater, the rightful heir to the throne of Israel under Roman law, and Miriam, later known to the Christians as Mary, a temple virgin who is both the matrilineal heiress of Michal, wife of King David, and a 'goddess': that is to say 'one of a line of priestesses in whom a divinity is held to be incarnate'.[90] Herod Antipater has married Miriam, we are told, because his title to the throne of Israel by Jewish law 'can be traditionally perfected only by marriage to the heiress of the still extant Michal line'.[91] However, Antipater himself falls prey to the scheming of his increasingly insane father, who secures permission from the Empress Livia (making a brief but delightfully sinister return to the pages of Graves's fiction) to have him executed on a trumped-up charge of treason.

As Jesus grows up in obscurity with Miriam and her husband Joseph, he learns that he is the rightful heir to the throne of Israel, and he becomes determined to enter into his inheritance. However, as a true follower of Jehovah, he dedicates himself utterly to oppose the feminine principle. When, therefore, a bride (Mary of Cleopas) is found for him, he refuses to consummate their marriage. By 'defeating' the seductive power of women in this way, he believes that he has also defeated death; and that it will soon be possible for him to inaugurate the tumultuous 'last days', so long prophesied in the scriptures. He will then set up 'the Kingdom of Heaven' on earth, and reign over his followers for a thousand years ...

But in rejecting the female principle, Jesus has made a profound error; and indeed on his crucifixion he is ironically fated to die a ritual death presided over by the White Goddess herself in her triple aspect as Mother (Miriam/Mary), Lover (Mary of Cleopas) and as Layer-out (Mary Magdalene, vividly represented as a follower of the old religion).[92] In this brilliantly sustained *tour-de-force*, in the course of which he 'solves' riddle after riddle and difficulty after difficulty to provide us with a 'rational' interpretation of the New Testament, Graves has therefore rescued the figure of Jesus for the religious tradition in which he had come to believe as he examined the origins of poetry.

Alan Hodge came down to Galmpton for Christmas 1943 and found Robert still busily researching for *The Angry Shepherd*, turning for help on 'the Hebrew-Aramaic side of the story' to his near-neighbour Joshua Podro,[93] and for advice on any medical matters to George Simon,[94] now divorced from his first wife and shortly to marry Joanna Shuckburgh.[95] Robert's total immersion in his esoteric researches, at that time he was chiefly interested in Greek and Babylonian mythology,[96] was becoming a little unnerving; but when Alan returned to London he wrote to Beryl reassuring her that: 'Robert's world of moth-myth is a very real one. Now I am back in the Ministry I see this perhaps more clearly than you do who live in it.'[97] In any case, Robert's feet were kept on the ground to some extent by his constant involvement with household duties, since Beryl's health continued to be poor, and there were now two children to be looked after.

There was also the usual flood of letters to be dealt with, including an interesting correspondence with the poet Alun Lewis, whose battalion had sailed for India back in 1942. Since then Lewis had undergone 'an "alarmingly prolific" phase of writing poetry';[98] and when in 1943 he considered that he had enough for a second volume, he had written to Graves asking him 'to read the manuscript and decide for him how much should be included and whether any rewriting was needed'.[99] Graves had soon returned the poems with a 'long list of comments and criticisms'; and Lewis wrote again on 23 January 1944 saying that he was 'very very indebted to you ... For both your purgative criticism and your general fiat I am more grateful than I can say.'[100]

By mid-February 1944, Graves had begun the actual writing of *The Angry Shepherd*. Then, towards the end of March, only a few days after Lewis's letter had reached him, he opened his morning newspaper to read 'the heavy black headlines' which told him that 'Alun Lewis the Poet is dead'.[101] The news was given a bitter twist by the fact that he had died in Arakan, not far from where Robert's son David had gone missing; and Robert began thinking grimly about the relationship between a poet and the general public. 'Search the back files', he wrote some months later,

> and you will find no preparatory announcement: Alun Lewis writes great poetry. An ancient Triad runs: three sacred things: Poets, Groves, Kings – for in ancient Wales or Ireland a poet was not merely a professional verse-writer: he was acknowledged to exercise extra-ordinary spiritual powers. His person was sacrosanct, like that of the King, with whose well-being and well-doing the prosperity of the Kingdom was magically bound up ...

'When he died', Graves declared, 'the people felt a sudden loss of power and sorrow stole over them all, even over those who were incapable of understanding the meaning of his simplest poems ...'[102]

Alun Lewis's death had turned Robert's thoughts back towards his book on poetry, at a time when in any case he had temporarily laid *The Angry Shepherd* to one side. Publication of *The Golden Fleece* had been held up for some months[103] because the maps of the voyage of the *Argo* were judged to be unsatisfactory;[104] and in late March or early April 1944 Robert turned his attention to redrawing them.[105]

A frantically busy Easter intervened on the weekend of 8–9 April, with visits to Galmpton by James and Mary Reeves and their infant daughter Stella; by Catherine Nicholson and her baby son David James; and by Alan Hodge, who had been told that it would be 'rather like a Russian farce about Moscow housing conditions'.[106]

When Graves was once again making serious headway with his maps, he could not get out of his head some lines from Alun Lewis's last letter, in which Lewis had written of his dedication, as a poet, to 'the *single* poetic theme of Life and Death'.[107] And then Graves was seized by 'a sudden overwhelming obsession', which took the form, as he later recalled,

> of an unsolicited enlightenment on a subject which had meant little enough to me. I stopped marking across my big Admiralty chart of the Black Sea the course taken (the mythographers said) by the *Argo* from the Bosphorus to Baku and back. Instead, I began speculating on a mysterious 'Battle of the Trees', fought in pre-historic Britain, and my mind ran at such a furious rate all night, as well as all the next day, that it was difficult for my pen to keep pace with it.[108]

The result was that within only two months[109] (by 12 June 1944[110]) Graves had drafted and revised a seventy-thousand-word book which he called *The Roebuck in the Thicket*.

CHAPTER 5

The Roebuck in the Thicket

Having written at some length in *The Golden Fleece* about the cult of the White Goddess of Pelion, Robert Graves 'now had thrust upon me ancient secrets of her cult in Wales, Ireland and elsewhere'.[111] His starting point was the thirteenth-century *Red Book of Hergest*, a volume which contains the traditional romances of the Welsh minstrels (known as the *Mabinogion*), a jumble of fifty-eight poems called *The Book of Taliesin* (some of which may actually have been written by a famous sixth-century Welsh bard of that name), and the incidental verses of a *Romance of Taliesin*.

That *Romance* contains a long poem (237 lines) on the subject of 'Cad Goddeu', or 'The Battle of the Trees'. In its surviving form it makes very little sense, but Graves decided that this was because the lines had been deliberately 'pied', and that 'less than half of them belong to the poem which gives its name to the whole medley'. He then ingeniously extracted from this apparent nonsense a poem of 100 lines, part of which runs:

> From my seat at Fefynedd,
>   A city that is strong,
> I watched the trees and green things
>   Hastening along.
>
> Retreating from happiness
>   They would fain be set
> In forms of the chief letters
>   Of the alphabet.
>
> Wayfarers wondered,
>   Warriors were dismayed
> At renewal of conflicts
>   Such as Gwydion made …

> The alders in the front line
> Began the affray.
> Willow and rowan-tree
> Were tardy in array ...

This rediscovered poem now had to be interpreted, and Graves learned from another source, the *Myvyrian Archaiology*, that the Battle of the Trees:

> was on account of a white roebuck, and a whelp; and they came from Annwm [The Celtic Underworld] and Amatheon ap Don brought them. And therefore Amatheon ap Don, and Arawn, King of Annwm, fought. And there was a man in that battle, who unless his name were known could not be overdone ... And Gwydion ap Don guessed the name of the man [which was Bran].[112]

The subject of this myth is apparently 'a battle for religious mastery' between the King of Annwm and the armies of Don, 'a confederacy of tribes in which the kingship went by matrilineal succession', their ancestors having been driven from Greece in the days before the voyage of the Argonauts.[113] The theft of the Dog and Roebuck from the Underworld supports the link with Greece, Graves tells us, since there are:

> several analogous Greek legends of Bronze Age origin. For example, that of Hercules ... who was ordered by his task-master King Eurystheus of Mycaenae to steal the dog Cerberus from the King of the Underworld, and the brass-shod white roebuck from the Grove of the Goddess Artemis at Ceryneia in Arcadia.[114]

As Graves's argument unfolds, it is backed not only by an astonishing wealth of obscure knowledge, but also by a certain amount of inspired guesswork whose conclusions time and time again were borne out by subsequent research.

Before long, he is postulating a close link, stemming from a mass exodus of population following upon the overthrow of the Goddess-worshipping Pelasgians in ancient Greece, between ancient British, Celtic and Hebrew religion; he is discovering ancient secrets of the Goddess-cults, such as names concealed in tree-alphabets; and he is introducing his readers to the White Goddess as famously celebrated in

Apuleius's *Golden Ass*, where she is invoked by the miserable Lucius, and replies, under her 'true name' of Queen Isis:

> Behold, Lucius, I am come; thy weeping and prayer hath moved me to succour thee. I am she that is the natural mother of all things, mistress and governess of all the elements, the initial progeny of worlds, chief of the powers divine, queen of all that are in Hell, the principal of them that dwell in Heaven ... At my will the planets of the sky, the wholesome winds of the seas, and the lamentable silences of hell be disposed ...

'Behold,' she concludes, 'I am present to favour and aid thee; leave off thy weeping and lamentation, put away all thy sorrow, for behold the healthful day which is ordained by my providence.'[115]

Understandably alarmed by the speed with which his mind was racing, Graves occasionally sent extracts from his recent work to be examined by close friends: in mid-May, for example (shortly after he had been asked to write a foreword to Alun Lewis's poems by Alun's widow Gweno),[116] he also received a letter from Alan Hodge, telling him that Alan had been 'glad to read your piece on Taliesin'.[117] And by then, Graves had also sent to Keidrych Rhys not only a first draft of the entire work, but also a revised chapter entitled 'Dog, Lapwing and Roebuck', which contains his interpretation of 'The Battle of the Trees'.[118]

Rhys liked the revised chapter well enough to decide to print it in a forthcoming issue of his magazine *Wales*; and when Graves posted *The Roebuck in the Thicket* to his agent Watt on 12 June (after which he returned to work on *The Angry Shepherd*), he was hopeful that Jonathan Cape could be persuaded to publish.[119] However, when Cape wrote on 16 June, he was not at all encouraging. He explained that Keidrych Rhys had sent him a proof of the 'Dog, Lapwing and Roebuck' chapter, and 'I have to say', he wrote, 'that it was beyond me and failed to stir any spark of interest.' He added that:

> A Publisher frequently publishes many books which are too good for him; i.e. they transcend his individual taste and scholarship, but at least he has some inkling of what the author is aiming at and can see that there is some reasonable ground for publication.

'Here,' he concluded, 'it seems to me that the interest is so obscure and so limited ... [that] you need for this book a publisher who is humble enough to take it ex cathedra ...'[120]

Graves subsequently wrote to Charles Williams of the Oxford University Press, who replied on 23 June that he would 'do my utmost, if it is needed, for your book here … And of course I look forward very much to reading it myself';[121] but once he had done so he was as sceptical as Cape, though he rejected *The Roebuck in the Thicket* 'politely, saying that he would not venture to persuade his colleagues of its merit, though convinced himself'.[122] Much later in the year another publisher, Richard Church of J. M. Dent, also rejected the book, though he subsequently apologized for having had:

> no opportunity to read it carefully because a quick decision was wanted; but that quick decision was inevitable because the paper shortage with Dent is particularly acute owing to the huge appetite of Everyman's Library.[123]

The result of this paper shortage, he explained, was that their policy was only to print the work of authors already on their list.

Despite these disappointments, Graves continued to look for a publisher for *The Roebuck in the Thicket*. However, it was just as well that no one took an immediate interest, for he continued to gather fresh material (for example, from the poet Valentin Iremonger, who wrote to him in July about the Ogham letter QUERT, and the ancient Irish division of trees into three classes[124]), and the end result would be a far more important contribution to the understanding of a certain type of poetry.

In the meantime, Graves continued to work hard on *The Angry Shepherd*, for which from mid-August 1944 he was fortunate enough to have the assistance of his former secretary Karl Goldschmidt, who was now officially Kenneth Gay, since all Germans serving in the Navy had had to change their names to English ones, for fear of being taken prisoner. However, he was still known to all his friends as Karl;[125] and Robert explained to James Reeves that despite having been 'invalided out of the Navy (nerves)', Karl was 'as efficient and sweet as ever'.[126]

CHAPTER 6

The Winter Solstice

When, in August 1944, Karl Gay left the Navy and visited Galmpton after a four-year absence, his arrival was too grand an opportunity for the hard-pressed Robert Graves to miss. Karl found himself being invited to move into a spare bedroom in The Vale House, and to resume his secretarial duties. He accepted the invitation, though it meant leaving his wife Marie in Sussex with her parents, as he could see that although Robert was evidently happy (and 'head-over-heels' with excitement about his work on *The Roebuck in the Thicket*), he was also dreadfully overworked.

Once again there was no help in the house; there was Lucia to be looked after as well as William; while Beryl looked terribly anaemic, was often in bed, and was already five months' pregnant with a third child. The result was that Robert had to work from the time when he climbed out of bed in the morning until late at night;[127] and in one of her letters that year, his daughter Catherine wrote him a sympathetic letter beginning, 'Dear Robert, housekeeper, baby-minder, stove-stoker, pen man, wood gatherer and telephone answerer ...'[128]

There were other interruptions: in August, for example, Alan Hodge arrived in a cheerful mood for a few days' holiday;[129] while in September Douglas Glass came to photograph Robert, whom he considered 'a first-rate subject'.[130] There was also the shock of realizing, as Robert wrote to his mother at the beginning of October, that he was up to his neck in a quagmire of back-income-tax claims. He told her that he owed more than £1,300,[131] and that when the war was over he would have to go abroad again, as the level of taxation made it 'impossible for him to go on living here'.[132] 'Shall you have to go bankrupt, poor Darling?' Amy replied. She explained that she had no money to spare (though later she sent him ten shillings and six pence[133]), but she added that she had begun knitting him another pair of socks.[134]

Karl noticed that during these difficult days, Robert's thoughts often turned to Deyá; and when Beryl was ill again (she had to spend a complete week in bed during November[135]), Robert painted a rosy picture of life as it would be when they could leave England's grey skies and move from The Vale House into sunny Canelluñ.[136]

Meanwhile there was exciting news from Jenny. Since the Allied invasion of France in June 1944, she had succeeded in attaching herself to the official war-films unit as a 'military adviser',[137] while acting 'on the side' as a front-line war correspondent. Robert was extremely proud of her subsequent exploits, reporting to Amy that she was wearing, as a kind of talisman, 'the famous ring that I had when I was officially killed & that I gave to David, who passed it on to Jenny'. It had been on Jenny's finger when she took part in the liberation of Paris on 25 August and the liberation of Brussels on 3 September, and had 'guarded her through some nasty places including a town still occupied by some Germans'[138] where, in pursuit of a good story, she had bravely gone into one hotel thought to be in German hands, disguised 'as a flower-girl'.[139]

Jenny survived these dangers, but suffered a serious loss. She had been engaged to Anthony Cotterell, a doctor who was also the author of a popular novel called *An Apple for the Sergeant*. But in September he jumped with the parachutists at Arnhem and for him, as for so many others, it was 'a bridge too far': he was severely wounded, and died not long after being captured by the Germans.[140]

After a brief spell in England, Jenny returned to the front line, first in Holland and then in France. There, as she told her father, she found herself:

> an accepted member of the exclusive clique of war correspondents comprising Alan Moorehead, Alexander Clifford *Daily Mail*, Christopher Buckley *Times* David Woodward *Manchester Guardian* and whatever general they happen to favour. Two nights ago I dined with them and Monty's Chief of Staff. We were all sunbathing the following day by a river in the shadow of a chateau two Panther tanks and a Sherman.[141]

More important, it was in Alexander Clifford's arms that she found renewed hope for the future. By Christmas they were secretly engaged to be married – 'Secretly,' explained Robert to another member of the family, 'because of the apparent indecency of making her choice so soon after Anthony's death; but of course I quite understand.'[142]

Robert was equally delighted by news of another engagement: his youngest brother, who at the age of forty-one was about to throw up his teaching career and take a job as Assistant Editor of the *Times Educational Supplement*, announced that he was engaged to be married to twenty-seven-year-old Mary Wickens, a graduate of the Royal College of Music who had been teaching at Harrow since September, and had been described by Nancy in a letter to Amy as 'sensible, agreeable & incredibly pretty'.[143] 'I hope you'll get married soon', Robert wrote to John on 12 December 1944.

> I am not competent to give you any advice except that life is hell with small children in the house, but far worse without. Beryl & I are expecting our third child in a few days' time: my seventh. I must say that the older family have all turned out, or are turning out, very well and I am deeply attached to them all. Jenny has been the most difficult by far, but is also the one to whom I feel the closest.

He added that he still had 'pangs of gratitude for your advice in the *Reader Over Your Shoulder*', and he passed on some excellent news about his financial position, which had improved dramatically. 'I am very glad to say', he wrote,

> that I'm getting out of my back income-tax quagmire ... Mrs. Milton [despite extremely hostile reviews] has had a sudden spectacular success in America & someone even hopes to stage it on Broadway. It sold 15,000 copies at 3 dollars 50 before publication. Here my *Golden Fleece* sold out (9,000 copies) in ten days ...[144]

His only disappointment was that, although *The Golden Fleece* had received 'the best reviews of any book I've ever published',[145] the paper shortage ruled out an immediate reprint: so that good reviews continued to come in, when there were no copies left for sale ...

However, with Karl to help him, Robert's rate of production had substantially increased, and he told John that future numbers of *Lilliput* (a magazine to which Jenny occasionally contributed) would contain pieces on 'the authentic story of Thomas Atkins of the 23rd Royal Welch Fusiliers'; and on 'the historical (not cranky) solution of the Number of the Beast which has been a standing problem since the 2nd century A.D. How we get about in Devon!'[146]

Early in the morning of 22 December, Beryl went into hospital for the birth of her third child, a boy, whom she and Robert named Juan: 'pronounced with a J', Robert would explain, 'because this is England,

and when we go to Deyá (if we do) it will be pronounced with a J also because that is the Majorcan (as opposed to the Spanish) way'.[147] Leaving William and Lucia with George Simon's first wife Charlotte,[148] Robert spent the morning at Beryl's bedside; and then, when he went home, sent her a letter which began: 'Dearest darling, Congratulations on the boy. He really is all right …'[149]

During the next few days, Robert and Beryl wrote each other a number of touching love letters in which they swept aside the difficulties of the past twelve months. 'This is about all', Robert closed one letter,

> except that there is so much that you and I say to ourselves about each other in a secret way which can't be and shouldn't be expressed and that comes up a lot on occasions like this and makes them very happy. I am very very happy tonight and I can feel you are too. Your Robert.[159]

'Darling', Beryl replied when she had received no fewer than three letters from Robert in a single day,

> Yes I was very happy last night but that is nothing unusual … I *love* Juan. He seems very well though I don't know how he is doing … Most of the time I am just lying and thinking about you. Goodness, how I do love you and it's so wonderful to think it has all really happened.

'Juan reminds me', she added, 'of the winter at the Chevrie' – that time in January and February 1939 when they had first been attracted to each other.[151] 'My only fear', Beryl continued, 'is of tiredness and crossness which I know is the only thing that comes between us. Actually, I am sure that being so much in love takes up a lot of energy. It's wonderful how the sun has shone since Juan was born …'[152]

Meanwhile, Robert had been struck by the coincidence that Juan had been born on the winter solstice, the day when, as he had written in *The Roebuck in the Thicket*, the Sun-god is born,[153] the day which had once been celebrated as the true beginning of the sacred year. The result was one of his most memorable poems, 'To Juan at the Winter Solstice', which begins:

> There is one story and one story only
> That will prove worth your telling,
> Whether as learned bard or gifted child;
> To it all lines or lesser gauds belong
> That startle with their shining
> Such common stories as they stray into.

Is it of trees you tell, their months and virtues,
Or strange beasts that beset you,
Of birds that croak at you the Triple will?
Or of the Zodiac and how slow it turns
Below the Boreal Crown,
Prison of all true kings that ever reigned?

Water to water, ark again to ark,
From woman back to woman:
So each new victim treads unfalteringly
The never altered circuit of his fate,
Bringing twelve peers as witness
Both to his starry rise and starry fall.

Or is it of the Virgin's silver beauty,
All fish below the thighs?
She in her left hand bears a leafy quince;
When with her right she crooks a finger, smiling,
How may the King hold back?
Royally then he barters life for love.[154]

Robert was so pleased with this poem that he had it printed before presenting it to Beryl when he was visiting her in hospital on the Friday after Christmas. She waited until his visit was over before reading it, and then she wrote to tell him: 'it quite took my breath away and I hardly dare look again. O darling Robert it was lovely seeing you this afternoon ...'[155]

Robert was delighted. 'Darling: Happy New Year!' he wrote back on Sunday evening, New Year's Eve:

I read your letter as I wheeled my bicycle up the hill: it was lovely and I was so reassured about the poem – I never feel right about a poem unless you pass it and this one I'd been rather insolently quick in printing.[156]

He had more good news: only a few evenings previously, he and Karl had successfully resolved some remaining problems connected with 'the Jesus tangle',[157] after which Robert had been able to complete his first draft of *The Angry Shepherd*.[158] 'I think the year made up for its general awfulness very well right at the end', he commented. 'I mean, I never expected I'd feel so happy as I do now thinking of you and me and the children and so many good friends.'

Rene had been particularly helpful. On the verge of a permanent separation from her husband,[159] she was spending more and more time at The Vale House, which was 'festive with holly and Christmas cards', and where she shared in the Christmas goose, before returning to welcome in the New Year.[160] Karl also stayed up 'to be first foot over the threshold for 1945'; and while he waited for the old year to end, Robert wrote to Beryl asking her to be 'strong-minded enough' on her return from hospital 'not to worry about details of food and clothing and housework and what-not'. He ended 'ever always very truly meaning it, Yours and yours only Robert'.[161]

CHAPTER 7

Jenny's Wedding

In January 1945, with Beryl and Juan back from hospital, Robert Graves was busier than ever. 'I am nurse to William & Lucia, & mother's help for Juan', he wrote to his brother John towards the end of the month, explaining why he had taken so long to answer a letter; 'as you know nurses are as extinct as the pterodactyl.'[162] Karl (whose wife Marie had joined him in Galmpton for a few days after Christmas)[163] looked on sadly at all these interruptions to Robert's work, and would later declare ruefully that at least he had been able to help with the washing-up; while Rene, who continued to be a frequent visitor, recalled that Robert's best poems were often written at the stove or the sink, even if his sudden preoccupation meant that the porridge was burnt again.[164]

When domestic duties allowed, work continued on revising and tightening up *The Angry Shepherd*; and Robert enjoyed teasing believers like John by declaring that, having finally discovered 'a perfectly consistent explanation' for some of Jesus's more perplexing actions, he would 'now have to convert our atheistic bishops to their true faith!'[165]

In the meantime Robert learned that his agent had sent the typescript of *The Roebuck in the Thicket* to Faber & Faber; and he wrote a personal letter on the subject to T. S. Eliot, one of the directors, saying that he supposed the book would:

> go through your hands. This is gratifying, because you are one of the few people who will be able to check the Classical and Biblical references: I don't know how expert you are in Celtic archaeology, but I can guarantee that I have used only the soundest sources.[166]

The point of his letter, he explained, was that the typescript was now out of date, since he had added two more chapters. One of these, 'essential to the completeness of the book', accounted for 'the heresy in the Taliesin conundrum with which the book begins'; while the other was 'an embellishment ... on the logical connexion of nuns with fish'.

Eliot replied encouragingly on 19 January that he was 'extremely interested in the book and was sure that it ought to be published':[167] and so Graves sent him the new material, with a few additions, and told him that once *The Angry Shepherd* was completely finished, he would return to *The Roebuck in the Thicket*, and 'get the argument still neater'.[168]

In the meantime Jenny's wedding day was rapidly approaching. First came her twenty-sixth birthday, celebrated in Brussels, where her fellow journalists arranged a party at which, as Robert reported to Amy, 'besides Press people nobody was to be invited of less standing than Ambassadors (several of these) divisional Army Commanders and Air Commodores ... Jenny really is a Star, isn't she?'[169] Then on Friday 16 February (thirteen days after John's wedding to Mary), news of Jenny's engagement appeared in *The Times*;[170] and she was married to Alexander Clifford the following Thursday, in the Savoy Chapel.[171]

There was a pre-wedding lunch in the Savoy River Room,[172] where Robert and Alex met for the first time. Nancy had already pronounced Alex 'just right',[173] and Robert thought him 'reliable, intelligent, warm-hearted, firm and capable'.[174] Sam was also there; as was Catherine (who only five weeks earlier had given birth to her second child, a daughter named Antonia).[175] Charles was also there, accompanied by Philip (still working for *The Times*, but suffering from heart trouble[176] and looking years older). John was also present; and Catherine was 'staggered' to find him 'changed so much for the better' by his recent marriage. 'He is quite human', she reported to Rosaleen, 'and getting more so every minute.'[177]

Amy was not well enough to travel; and when she saw the wedding photographs she thought that Robert, whom she had not seen in person for five and a half years, looked 'sad in repose'.[178] This was not surprising: as he had confided to Jenny at the time, he had only just received a 'gunny-bale' of David's personal belongings.[179]

After lunch, the wedding party proceeded to the chapel, described by Catherine as:

> decorated by the most lovely arrangement of spring flowers in two huge stone vases that I have ever seen. Jenny's bouquet was the same ... [she] wore a white dress. She had some beautiful brocade given her and she made it up with ballet dancer's net with white sequins sewn in the same design as the brocade. And a net vail trailing from her head fastened by a small bunch of orange blossom.

Catherine added that it was 'wonderful' to see Jenny 'really happy again', and that Alex had 'that humbleness of manner which makes great people'.[180]

Robert then marched cheerfully enough down the aisle with his eldest daughter on his arm before giving her away 'with dignity', and standing up 'as straight as if he were in uniform … We were all proud of him', wrote Catherine. 'He stands out so from other people in any crowd by his sheer charm.' Nancy she described as '*very* smart – with a black suit, white blouse, yellow silk scarf and a black and grey panelled coat. And black felt hat. She did look young. And happy.'[181]

Afterwards, Nancy presided elegantly over a simple reception with 'just tea and sandwiches, and of course the cake – a beauty'.[182] In the evening there was a further and much larger reception at the Savoy, this time without Nancy. Robert was there, his arm round Alan Hodge; Charles and John had returned, this time with their wives; and the evening was enlivened by a number of Jenny's actress friends, one of whom, Judy Campbell, was then so well-known that her entrance created quite a stir.[183]

A few days later, Robert sent Jenny and Alex a set of verses entitled 'At The Savoy Chapel'[184] in which, after gently teasing relatives who meet 'Only at weddings and funerals', and describing how:

> Each eyes the other with a furtive pity:
> 'Heavens, how she has aged – and he,
> Grey hair and sunken cheeks, what a changed man!'

Robert went on to give a very simple 'loving blessing' for 'you, loving ones, who kneel at the altar'.

After the wedding Robert had returned to Galmpton, from where he sent on David's 'gunny-bale' to Nancy,[185] having learned from Jenny that she intended to keep 'everything of his religiously until two years after the Japanese war'.[186] As for Jenny and Alex: after a brief honeymoon they spent a week in Harlech, where they visited Amy every day. Then they returned to London, where a little later in the year Alex would be overwhelmed by a multiplicity of late wedding presents from Robert, including a 'patchwork quilt which delights my mother who is an expert, the Wedgwood Plate, the Aldridge picture and a number of charming and valuable odds and ends which Jenny keeps producing from cupboards and trunks'.[187]

When, on 7 May 1945 the war in Europe ended with the unconditional surrender of Germany to the Allies, Alex persuaded the *Daily Mail* that there was 'no future in Germany – the country is too hopelessly ruined to provide any news of its own',[188] and after a few months in Paris, he and Jenny were both transferred to Rome. He was set in overall charge of news-gathering from the entire Mediterranean area, while Jenny became the paper's Rome correspondent.[189] It would be an extremely happy arrangement for them both.

CHAPTER 8

Clarissa at Galmpton

In mid-March 1945, as Robert Graves settled back into work on *The Angry Shepherd*, he was delighted to hear from T. S. Eliot that publication of *The Roebuck in the Thicket* was 'agreed in principle'; and he replied saying that he intended to have a revised version in Eliot's hands 'by September at latest'. He was then hoping to complete *The Angry Shepherd* within a few weeks',[190] but in practice it was not until 6 June that he managed to complete the typescript and post it to Cassell.[191]

In the meantime, Robert had received a long letter on the subject from Clarissa, who had returned to England in January and was living with their mother at Erinfa.[192] After telling her brother that *The Angry Shepherd* would 'have scholars after you like a pack of hounds', she wondered 'whether the intensive study of Christ has done something to you personally which you did not expect. It got Saul ... Christianity is like radium. You cannot play with it with impunity.'[193] As for Robert's poem 'To Juan at the Winter Solstice', which he had sent her, she commented that Juan was a 'poor little boy', who had 'much to forgive you for. And why because, like Ariosto, you suffer the endless "muliebrita" (we have no word for it in English) must you put it upon the child? Anyway', she concluded, 'it is a great poem, and you cannot pick and choose but must accept the poetic fluid when it comes your way, whatever the source.'

Knowing that his sister was a real poet (though she had only published one slim volume in 1927[194]), Robert very much respected her critical opinion. She was possibly the only member of the family who never flinched from telling him when she thought his work was below his usual standard; and so when she announced that she was shortly coming south to stay with Rosaleen, and was looking forward to seeing him,[195] he at once invited her to visit him.

Clarissa, who was driven over for the day by Rosaleen,[196] found Robert 'haggard but happy, with his long, grey curling hair & his elbow through the sleeve of his jersey'; and she reported to John that their brother's nose was firmly 'to the domestic grindstone'. It was, she wrote, 'amazing that he manages to write at all, let alone great books'. While she was with Robert, she talked to him about Amy, making it clear that their mother was very anxious about *The Angry Shepherd*, and yet wanted to see him again more than anything in the world. Only six months previously, Robert had not even bothered to tell his mother of Juan's birth, explaining to Amy, when she reproached him, that 'I didn't think it would be as welcome to you as it is to me.'[197] But Clarissa's intervention made him think again, and he immediately wrote to Amy a loving letter which drew this reply:

> Many thanks for your last letter, about your latest book, which you have sent off. I had been sad and uncomfortable about it, but will now hope for the best. You were a sincere follower till you were 16, so you know exactly how I would feel.

Amy added that she was 'sorry to hear you definitely think of going back to Deyá ... you have such a high opinion of William's endowments that it is worthwhile to send him to a good English school and University'; but she was also 'glad of your promise to come and see me before starting for Deyá at any rate ...'[198]

Clarissa's visit had been such a success that she was invited back to stay at The Vale House for a few days the following week. She told John in advance that she intended to 'darn & wash up those few days, then melt away';[199] and Robert found her 'charming: quiet, helpful and unself-assertive'. He was able to tell her that his 'Jesus book', which he had now somewhat obscurely renamed *The Power of the Dog*,[200] was being printed; and that he was working again on *The Roebuck in the Thicket*.[201] He also passed on the family news that Sam, who had been studying forestry in Edinburgh, now wanted to move to Cambridge to study architecture instead, and (now that Robert was solvent again) he was intending to finance Sam's going there.[202]

Clarissa for her part had more time to assess Robert's domestic situation. Afterwards she wrote to him sympathizing with his wish to return to Deyá[203] (apparently the Foreign Office had recently reported that his property there was 'in as good a state as when I left it'[204]); and she asked him to give her love to Beryl, saying how much she liked Beryl's 'deep voice & sensible attitude: and she is a pleasure to look at, with the beautiful contrast between her hair and skin'.[205]

Clarissa had also been persuaded that another effort should be made to encourage Nancy to divorce Robert, for the sake of the children of his second family; and on the day after her return to Harlech, she had a long talk on the subject with Amy. 'I painted her a graphic picture', she reported to Robert,

> of your present life and its hardships, which, though they may be and obviously are conducive to creative work on your part, are a great strain on Beryl, as one notices from her slight stoop, & the fact that occasionally she gets a bit on edge in spite of her deep, deliberate nature, with its 'cello ring, which resists being flustered.

Clarissa added that she herself was:

> all out to help you if I possibly can, in any way that you may choose: so is Mother, that wonderful woman, who longs to welcome your three little ones into the family, and Beryl too. She realises that your present union is in fact a real marriage at last, in a sense that neither of the others could be, because they did not bring you peace of mind.[206]

She added that 'Mother definitely wants to help you with your darning'; and for a number of months there was a regular traffic in mended and unmended clothing between Erinfa and The Vale House.[207]

In the meantime, Amy wrote to Nancy about divorcing Robert, telling her that 'no expenses should fall on her', though she realized 'what a sacrifice' it would be for her;[208] but Nancy replied:

> My dear Grandmother,
> ... as it can make no difference (for some time anyhow) to Robert's other children, I am postponing any idea of getting a divorce anyhow until Sam, the last of our children, is through Cambridge and well on his feet. I think you do not quite realise what a front page scandal it might be and just what a grim ordeal for me.[209]

So Amy had to tell Robert that she could not, after all, help him 'to legalize your irregular union, which I have been so sad about'.[210]

In return he sent her some more mending, and what she described as 'a very affectionate letter' announcing that he had once again altered the title of his new book. It was now to be called simply *King Jesus*; it was likely to be published in the New Year; and 'No one who has read it has felt that it is anyway derogatory to the dignity of Jesus.'[211]

CHAPTER 9

The White Goddess

Robert Graves's principal work from June 1945 to January 1946 was a comprehensive rewriting of *The Roebuck in the Thicket*.[212] This involved him in further prodigious quantities of research, which he had to do himself since at one stage he had been hoping to return to Majorca before the end of the year, and he had therefore found a job for his secretary Karl Gay with Joshua Prodro's press cutting agency in Paignton.

His research involved a good deal of correspondence with Lynette Roberts and Keidrych Rhys. In mid-July 1945, for example, Robert wrote to Lynette to ask for the loan of some relevant books, and to tell her that the rewriting was being done 'in a more scholarly way'.[213] Later that month, announcing that he had now disentangled two of the poems muddled up in the 'Cad Goddeu', he promised to rededicate 'The Battle of the Trees' to Lynette and Keidrych's daughter Angharad,[214] who became Robert's godchild in the autumn. Rather surprising, perhaps, for an unbeliever to be a godfather; but then, as he explained to Angharad's parents, 'infant baptism is a heathen rite practised by the ancient Welsh and Irish, adult baptism only was practised by the early Christians; so old Druid Robert is just the chap for the job.'[215]

Robert also corresponded regularly with Clarissa about his poetry and hers; and (partly to help her brother with *The Roebuck in the Thicket*, but also in the hope that he might one day write an historical novel about ancient Ireland) she persuaded Amy to send him 'the 2 volumes of Joyce's *Social History of Ancient Ireland*'.[216]

By now, Robert was once again in regular contact with his mother, 'My dear Robert,' she had written on 9 September, 'Your long letter gave me very great pleasure, making me feel I have not lost you';[217] and before long, he was planning a visit to Enrinfa.[218]

First Robert and Beryl went up to London, where they and their three children stayed with George and Joanna Simon, who were now living in a substantial terraced house at 12 Drayton Gardens.[219] Then, on 28 October, after several days of seeing friends[220] and doing business, Robert caught the night train for north Wales.

Arriving at Erinfa early on Monday morning, Robert found his mother in a highly nervous state. A few days earlier she had been worrying that it would be 'difficult for me to know what to say' to the son she had not seen for over six years;[221] but although Robert's visit was short (he explained that he had to leave the following evening so as to be in time for an engagement in London on Wednesday morning), it was also very successful.[222]

On Tuesday Robert, Amy and Clarissa lunched with Susan, where they enjoyed 'a very nice & very friendly time';[223] and then after lunch they were driven up into the hills to Cwm Mawr, a remote farmhouse near the sinister Cwm Bychan Lake. Leaving Amy in the car (where she was busily 'trying to finish Robert's mending of his silk pyjamas, which have already lasted for 6 years, & may last several more'), Robert and Clarissa went on a brief tour of inspection,[224] as Rosaleen was thinking of buying Cwm Mawr as a holiday home and Robert had offered to help her with the purchase.[225]

Tea followed at Dolreiddiog; and then after 'a little meal at Erinfa' Robert and Amy were driven to Barmouth station where, as Amy recorded, they were 'in good time for the 7.15 train that would bring him to Euston in the early hours of [Wednesday] morning'.[226] But after leaving Robert at the station, Amy immediately began to feel miserable. She did not think her son looked well. She doubted whether he was eating enough. She wished he had accepted the offer of her rug ... Back in Erinfa, she spent a tortured night before writing:

Dearest Robert,
Your short visit was well worth while as we got to know each other afresh & I love you very much. But yet there is an ache in it – may God draw you still closer to himself. I felt miserable to leave you when I did, before even the train was alight ... I felt quite reluctant that night to get into my comfortable bed, while you were travelling, cold, in the train. If you only had taken my rug! Try & take care of your health my darling Robert ...[227]

When he reassured her that he had been quite all right, Amy wrote again, thanking him for 'a very loving letter which I thoroughly appreciated. I am so glad', she continued, 'you did not regret all the difficulties personal &

financial, in getting to me for only one night. I hope you were none the worse for those two long night journeys ...'[228]

Amy was full of anxieties: partly about her immediate family, and partly about those German relatives who had survived the war, one of whom, for example, was a prisoner of the Russians, while two were said to be subsisting chiefly on potatoes.[229] And then, in mid-October, there was bad news from the War Office. There was now little doubt, they announced, that David had lost his life. He had been 'shot, sustaining what appeared to be a penetrating wound between the eyes', and was seen to 'fall into a forward enemy trench', after which there had been 'no sign of movement'.[230]

Towards the end of November (when Clarissa was just beginning a second brief stay at The Vale House), the pressure became too much and Amy had to take to her bed after massive nose-bleeding. Clarissa rushed home; the doctor said that in view of Amy's high blood pressure, the nosebleeds had been fortunate and had probably prevented a stroke; and Amy was soon making another of her famous recoveries.[231]

By then, Robert had entirely given up hope of David's survival. 'Dear David', he had written about him to Sam at the end of October, 'all my memories of him are good ones: he never gave me the least unkindness or trouble or anxiety; and I still have continual pangs about him.'[232] And in mid-December, the seal was set on David's death by a formal message from Buckingham Palace:

> The Queen and I offer you our heartfelt sympathy in your great sorrow.
>   We pray that your country's gratitude for a life so nobly given in its service may bring you some measure of consolation.
>   George R.I.[233]

Fortunately for Amy's peace of mind, it was not long before the loss of one grandchild was to some extent balanced by the birth of another: John's wife Mary gave birth on 21 December 1945 to a son whom they named Richard Perceval. He was a sickly child, who seemed unable to keep anything down, and spent the first few months of his life in and out of hospital; but Amy welcomed him with joy as the first of her grandchildren born in wedlock to bear the Graves surname since the birth of Sam in 1924.

In the meantime *The Golden Fleece* had been published by Creative Age Press in America where, although it was poorly reviewed and disappointingly produced,[234] it sold in large numbers. Graves himself, despite the usual domestic pressures which meant that at one point in November he had even thought of paying Clarissa a small salary to live at The Vale House as his housekeeper,[235] had been not merely revising but also considerably extending *The Roebuck in the Thicket*. It was fortunate for him that Karl, despite his full-time job, found time to type the various drafts which streamed from his pen: at least five before it was judged to be reasonably complete. 'Dearest Karl', he had written on 8 November after receiving a clean typescript,

> Thanks very much for the letter and the beautiful typing. I can't do much with it at present in the way of further disfiguration although when I was up in Wales I found a set of learned books on the subject of Taliesin and the bards generally in my father's library and will read them through to get more gen on the subject …

He added that he had also been sent 'a book on tree-cults in Palestine' by his niece Sally Chilver, a constant source of help, 'which may before long provide you with work'.[236]

In his new chapters for *The Roebuck in the Thicket*, the White Goddess of Pelion was firmly identified with the Triple Muse, whom Graves began to regard as the only source of inspiration for true poetry. He had already told the story (from the *Romance of Taliesin*) of Caridwen, whom he regarded as one of the aspects of the Triple Muse. For it was Caridwen who had:

> boiled up a cauldron of inspiration and knowledge, which had to be kept on the simmer for a year and a day. Season by season, she added to the brew magical herbs gathered in their correct planetary hours. While she gathered the herbs she put little Gwion … to stir the cauldron. Towards the end of the year three burning drops flew out and fell on little Gwion's finger. He thrust it into his mouth and at once understood the nature and meaning of all things past, present and future, and thus saw the need of guarding against the wiles of Caridwen who was determined on killing him as soon as his work was completed.[237]

As he ran away, he used his new powers to change his appearance; but when in his final metamorphosis he became a grain of wheat, she became a black hen and swallowed him. The result was that 'when she returned to her own shape she found herself pregnant of Gwion and nine months later bore him as a child'. She then placed him in a leather bag and threw him into the sea, from which he was rescued by Prince Elphin, who renamed him 'Taliesin' – the name by which he was known when he became a famous poet.

Now, referring to the 'Romance of Pwyll, Prince of Dyfed', one of the tales of the *Mabinogion*, Graves tells of Rhiannon, who once took the form of a white mare, and who is clearly a Muse-goddess, 'for the Sirens that appear in the *Triads*, and also in the *Romance of Branwen*, singing with wonderful sweetness are called 'The Birds of Rhiannon'.[238] To this discovery, Graves adds a history of the Greek Muses, pointing out that:

> The Triple Muse, or the Three Muses, or the NineFold Muse, or Caridwen, or whatever else one may care to call her, is originally the Great Goddess in her poetic or incantatory character. She has a son who is also her lover and victim, the Star-son, or Demon of the Waxing Year. He alternates in her favour with his tanist Typhon, the Serpent of Wisdom, the Demon of the Waning Year, his darker self.[239]

The true Muse-obsessed poet is therefore the man who is first the son, then the lover, and finally the victim of his Muse (so that one of the truest Muse poems is Keats's 'La Belle Dame Sans Merci'). But with the victory of Apollo over the Triple Goddess, 'poetry becomes academic and decays';[240] and the Apollonian is a mere versifier whose work is of no lasting value.

There was a pause in work on *The Roebuck in the Thicket* towards the end of November 1945, when Graves had to deal with the galley proofs of *King Jesus*;[241] but by New Year's Day 1946, Robert could tell Karl that he had 'once more ... come to the end of [*The Roebuck in the Thicket*], and this time, if you can type the amendments and insertions, it will be ready to send off ... What a plum-pudding it is!' he added,

> Too much of it, and yet, why not? The whole point is the method of thought, not the results, and as many examples of the method as I can give, the better. It warms up towards the end, and I don't think that there's a dull chapter.

He added that he and Beryl were hoping 'not to spend another winter in England for a long time'.[242] Canelluñ was their aim; and Jenny, whose work was about to take her on a journey to Portugal and Spain, had promised to call in at Deyá with 'a long letter of questions and news of us all'.[243]

Despite having sent Karl these 'final' amendments, Robert's mind went on racing down unfamiliar paths ('I am still making more and more illuminating inserts into the *Roebuck*', he wrote to James Reeves on 8 January, 'e.g. why pigs can see the wind ...'[244]); but at last, on 28 January, he was ready to send what he hoped was the completed work to T. S. Eliot. And since his set of ideas about the relationship between the poet and his Muse had gradually developed into the core of the book, Graves had decided to change its title from *The Roebuck in the Thicket* to *The White Goddess*.

Having changed his title, Graves would feel inspired to write what, in this revised version, remains one of his most memorable poems:

IN DEDICATION

> All saints revile her, and all sober men
> Ruled by the God Apollo's golden mean –
> In scorn of which I sailed to find her
> In distant regions likeliest to hold her
> Whom I desired above all things to know,
> Sister of the mirage and echo.
>
> It was a virtue not to stay,
> To go my headstrong and heroic way
> Seeking her out at the volcano's head,
> Among pack ice, or where the track had faded
> Beyond the cavern of the seven sleepers:
> Whose broad high brow was white as any leper's,
> Whose eyes were blue, with rowan-berry lips,
> With hair curled honey-coloured to white hips.
>
> Green sap of Spring in the young wood a-stir
> Will celebrate the Mountain Mother,
> And every song-bird shout awhile for her;
> But I am gifted, even in November
> Rawest of seasons, with so huge a sense
> Of her nakedly worn magnificence
> I forget cruelty and past betrayal,
> Careless of where the next bright bolt may fall.[245]

As Robert Graves laid down his pen, and carefully blotted the sheet of paper on which this poem had been written, Irene of the honey-coloured hair strolled into the room where he was working. She noticed that he seemed miserable and wretched. 'Look at this: I've just finished a poem about the White Goddess', he told her. 'All the women I've loved had dark hair. But somehow you got in the way.'[246]

BOOK THREE

WATCH THE NORTH WIND
1946–50

CHAPTER 1

A Flight from Croydon

After six years of war, peace had come as a severe shock to many of the survivors, including Alan Hodge, who had written to Beryl Graves on Whit Monday 1945, only a fortnight after the unconditional surrender of Germany, that he did not like peace at all.

> It is frightening as you say. I should like to go to sleep for a few months and wake up at La Chevrie or Canelluñ with a book to write. Now I find myself short-tempered, and really angry if I am expected to think of something more than a day ahead. There is no Horatian choice of Carpe Diem: the days are already cepti; mortgaged it seems to me, for years ahead.[1]

By October, about a month after the official surrender of Japan, Alan had found his way from the Ministry of Information into journalism;[2] and the surviving children from Robert's first family were also secure: Jenny was living with Alex in Rome; Catherine was looking after her children while her husband lectured at Oxford; and Sam, who had found at last an occupation which truly suited him, had gone up to Jesus College, Cambridge to study architecture.

At the end of the Great War in 1918, sorrow about the loss of life had been mingled with hope for the future. This time it was very different. 'I am frightened of these split Atom bombs', Amy told Robert in August 1945. 'What a future threatens our children!'[3] Her stepson Philip Graves, the wise elder statesman of the family (having decided at the age of seventy to retire from *The Times* and to move to Ireland where he and Kitty would run a small hotel), wrote in March 1946 that he was 'more and more pessimistic about our civilisation lasting & will be glad to get to Ireland which may be a refuge, as in the dark ages'.[4]

Robert shared his half-brother's pessimism. While working on *The White Goddess*, he had become increasingly convinced that in turning, as it were, from the worship of the Triple Goddess to that of Zeus, in replacing feminine with masculine control, society had made a disastrous mistake. To worship the Goddess was to keep in natural balance with one's surroundings. To worship a male God, on the other hand, was to unleash a terrible destructive power upon the world, in the form of the 'restless and arbitrary male will'.[5] Before publication of *The White Goddess*, Graves would add several paragraphs in which he described how the western world had 'come to be governed by the unholy triumvirate of Pluto god of wealth, Apollo god of science and Mercury god of thieves'.[6]

Eventually, he believed, there would be a return 'to some practical form of Goddess worship,' But he warned that:

> the longer the change is delayed, and therefore the more exhausted by man's irreligious improvidence the natural resources of the soil and sea become, the less placid and merciful will be the five-fold mask that the Goddess ultimately assumes, and the narrower the scope of action that she grants to any god whom she chooses to take as her consort in godhead.[7]

In the meantime, practical politics was not a poet's concern (Milton had made that mistake); and Graves wished above all to escape from dreary, conformist postwar England, perhaps even more stifling than the England from which he had escaped in 1929, to a place where he and a few close associates could live life as it should be lived, in harmony with the natural world.

Graves's continuing sense of despair when confronting the mass of his fellow human beings was forcefully expressed in the 'Foreword' which he wrote for his *Poems 1938–1945*, a slim volume of forty pages published by Cassell in a green cover towards the end of January 1946, and including such gems as 'To Lucia at Birth' and 'To Juan at the Winter Solstice'. 'Since poems should be self-explanatory', declared Graves,

> I refrain from more foreword than this: that I write poems for poets, and satires or grotesques for wits. For people in general I write prose, and am content that they should be unaware that I do anything else.

'To write poems for other than poets', he added scathingly, 'is wasteful'; and then, in case anyone had missed the point, he observed that:

> The moral of the Scilly Islanders who earned a precarious livelihood by taking in one another's washing is that they never upset their

carefully-balanced island economy by trying to horn into the laundry trade of the mainland; and that nowhere in the Western Hemisphere was washing so well done.[8]

Graves had written as if defying in advance the opinions of any critics who happened not to be poets; and to begin with the only good opinions came from those who had been sent copies as gifts.

By the end of March, however, there were some encouraging signs. The first edition of 3,000 copies had sold out, and Cassell were printing 5,000 more. (Graves, still inclined to be pessimistic, declared that these sales were 'solely on the strength of my novels, I expect'.) The reviews had been favourable, but there were very few of them: one by Norman Cameron, two others by uninfluential critics, and, as Graves told James Reeves, a fourth 'long polite one in the T.L.S. which I threw away; otherwise nothing. I belong to no racket so *Observer, Statesman* & *S. Times* etc. will give me a miss probably'.[9]

James replied sympathetically: 'I think the public hasn't caught up with you yet.' He believed that they had 'said goodbye to Georgian Robert about the time you did yourself, and haven't rediscovered Robert of the 1930s. Give 'em time. I prophesy recognition about 1950 ...'[10] But the sales figures continued to climb, and more friendly reviews came in, and within a few weeks Robert was telling Lynette Roberts that:

I have been rather amused ... Everyone has suddenly decided to 'recognize' me as one recognizes a new Government of some troublesome country. This is the first really cordial batch [of reviews] I've had since – 1916! I suppose I'm getting old and am no longer considered a rival to the younger generation.

'Anyhow', he added, 'what the hell! Letters from friends like you who are also poets is another matter: especially if you can tell me how to improve anything there.'[11]

In July 1943, knowing that David wrote poetry,[12] Robert suggested to Sam that in due course they should gather up and publish as much of his work as could be found. Nancy had been 'quietly pleased' by this idea;[13] but it had been shelved for the time being. Then, in December 1945, Robert had suggested to Nancy that he should wind up David's financial affairs – and perhaps there should be a formal obituary?

Nancy had no objection to their son's financial affairs being wound up, but on 2 January 1946 she wrote firmly:

Please don't do anything about an obituary for David. The one thing
David loathed was publicity. And the only non-private thing he did has
had the publicity. I think it would be extremely bad taste. And the
outstanding thing about David was his sensitiveness and taste.[14]

Robert completely ignored this directive, for on 6 February Amy reported
to John that she had opened her *Times* and read:

the full account of David's heroic deeds and his presumed death. I
suppose Robert put it in. I have written to him about it ... I had for a
long time been looking for some notice, so it gave me a painful
satisfaction to see it at last.[15]

Robert had also remained interested in publishing his son's poems; but it
seemed that David had taken with him anything of value when he was
posted abroad, and so when Sam visited Galmpton for a brief visit at the
end of March 1946, Robert asked him to persuade Nancy finally to open
David's 'gunny-bale' to see what could be found.

On the evening of 3 April, it was done. David's officer's uniforms were
there; the white feather plume or 'flash' of the Royal Welch Fusiliers; a
few books, including Malory's *Morte d'Arthur*, some poetry anthologies,
and Sam's inscribed copy of Robert's *No More Ghosts*; but sadly, as Sam
reported to his father, there seemed to be 'a good deal missing'[16] –
including 'an appreciable quantity of David's work'.[17] So the idea of an
anthology was abandoned. However, a handful of David's poems still
survived, among them:

IN CONCLUSION[18]

It will be small loss, never to return.
The summer-house will be cobwebbed,
the plaster flaked;
The nets over the unpruned fruit-bushes
holed and torn,
And wild grasses dropping seeds on the sundials;
And the Penny-farthing and the saddlery
grown dusty in the stables,
And mildewed the embroidered dressing-up
clothes in the chest.
The artificial lake will be stagnant and undrained,
The hedges unclipped, the boarding rotten;

The lawn rough-floored under the cedar trees;
And in the pigeon-cot stairs will be broken,
the swing hanging broken.
The engine in the boiler-house will have ceased its beating;
The known voices will no longer be heard about the house.
There will be weeds and crumbling and desolation only.
    We should be sorry we returned.

Robert was so moved by these lines that he polished them up a little (they are given here in their original form) and sent them to the *Cambridge Review*, in which they were published on 25 May 1946.

The end of the war had brought with it a few quite unexpected responsibilities. When Robert had visited his mother in the autumn of 1945, he had found her understandably anxious about the fate of her various German relatives; and then in January 1946 he received a letter begging for help from Hubert Ranke, the eldest son of his uncle Harry, Amy's brother, whom he had last met at Laufzorn on one of his memorable childhood holidays in 1906 or 1907.

Hubert explained that after the 1914–18 war he had gone into civil aviation; he had then been imprisoned for his liberal views by the Nazis, but had escaped in 1934 to France; two years later he had gone south with Malraux, and fought for the Republicans during the Spanish Civil War, as a result of which, after surviving several apocalyptic battles, he had suffered a serious nervous breakdown. In 1938 he had returned to France, where he had stayed in the Haute Savoie not far from Gertrude Stein; he had then joined the French Army, had subsequently fought in the Resistance, and was now living in Paris with his second wife and their baby in a highly impoverished state, desperately wanting funds to enable him to return to Germany to see his family.[19]

Robert decided to help his cousin with the very substantial gift of £50;[20] but strict exchange controls were in force, and he was not at all sure how to transfer the money to Paris. In the meantime, Hubert's letter had stirred his conscience in another direction, by reminding him of Gertrude Stein, who had originally encouraged him and Laura Riding to try living in Majorca; and soon he had posted the first letter he had written to her since she and Laura had quarrelled in the summer of 1930.[21] He was delighted when Stein replied, and wrote a further letter telling her:

I don't know why it is, but you have always been very close to my heart since we stayed at Belley in 1929 and I was very sorry when Laura broke with you in a fit of spleen: I think because you always mentioned the weather, and that seemed unworthy. But of course the weather is very important in the short run, and the long run consists of short runs.

He then asked whether it would be possible for her to pay 2,400 francs to Hubert, if he could 'arrange for Pavois Frère, who are publishing my *Marie Powell, Wife to Mr. Milton*, to pay the advance to you. But say nothing to him until I know that it can be arranged.'[22]

Graves's plan proved unworkable; and later that year Gertrude Stein died at the age of seventy-two. But first they exchanged two more letters in which they set down their views on Laura Riding. Robert sent the first: 'Laura – it's a strange but familiar story', he told Stein. 'She was possessed for a great many years by a very cruel and beautiful Muse with which she identified herself; and then she found the position intolerable, and the spirit left her and she become common clay.' He added that 'these last years ... with Beryl have been the happiest of my life and I have done my best work in them.'[23]

To which Stein replied that she was 'very much interested in the Laura story', for:

of course it was terribly important for you to have lived her [sic]; for your Jesus book, after all, she was Jew every single bit of her, but and that was really the basis of our break, she was the materialistic Jew camouflaging her materialism by intellectualism, a very very common thing in the race ... really the intellectualism is the reactionary violence of their materialism ...[24]

Graves disliked this interpretation, and wrote:

About Laura. It was not quite so simple as you make out. She was a Jew, yes, but not Jehovah-Jew; she was a sort of embodiment of the Queen of Heaven – Jehovah's former wife and mother – alias Lilith, Kadesh, Alukah, Michal, Aholibamah, Ashtaroth, Ashima, Anatha, etc. ... who has been the *cherchez la femme* torment of the Jewish soul since he first divorced her during the Exile ...

He added that he did not 'regret a moment of the life I spent with Laura. I was learning all the time and she was a wonderful poet at her best and as good to me as I deserved, I suppose ...'[25]

The payment to Hubert Ranke was finally arranged with Jenny's help;[26] after which Amy told Robert she was 'very proud that you are so generous to one of your German relatives'.[27] Robert also paid for Clarissa's air fare to Jerusalem:[28] an excellent idea, because Amy enjoyed her independence, and found Clarissa's efforts to look after her 'very kind, but trying'.[29]

In March 1946, Jenny visited Majorca in order to find out what had happened to her father's home and possessions. These had been left in the hands of Gelat, the likeable rogue who had been so much admired by Laura Riding and Robert Graves in the thirties; and soon after arriving in Palma Jenny ran into Gelat's son Juan, who:

> drove her out to Deyá at once in their ancient charcoal-burning bus, and Gelat, who was delighted to see her, walked with her to Canelluñ, where he unlocked the front door with a flourish. There on the hall table where he had flung it ten years before was Robert's straw hat, carefully dusted, proofs of *I, Claudius* were spread out neatly along the top of the book-case ... The curtains had been washed and starched, the typewriter oiled, clothes and hand-linen aired. As the weather was still cold, Jenny found a log-fire burning in the sitting-room grate.[30]

Before long she had reported to her father that she had received a warm welcome;[31] that 'there was no political trouble in the neighbourhood', and that 'everything was in wonderfully good order':[32] just as he had left it, so far as she could tell, down to 'a half-written letter beginning "Dearest Jenny" on your writing-desk.'[33]

So there seemed nothing to prevent Robert's return, apart from a good deal of paperwork, and the necessity of finding some convenient method of transporting himself, Beryl, three very small children and a houseful of books and other belongings across three countries and two substantial stretches of water at a time when the frontier between France and Spain was closed, and there were no regular civilian passenger flights or sea voyages. There was also a moral dilemma to be faced.

Since the end of the Spanish Civil War, Spain had been governed by the Fascist dictatorship of General Francisco Franco; and although Franco had remained neutral during the Second World War, he had such strong ideological links with the Axis Powers that their defeat seemed to presage his own fall from power. Graves himself had felt so sure of this that in July 1945, when writing about his hopes of returning to Majorca, he had assumed that although he must 'wait patiently for Franco to fade out',[34] he would not have to wait long.

When, to his surprise, Franco remained safely in power, Graves had to ask himself whether he was prepared to live under a dictatorship. After much thought, he came to the conclusion that it was the people who mattered, not the government; and he wrote in this vein to Ricardo Sicré, a Spaniard to whom he had introduced himself when he overheard him talking Catalan in a public house in Great Bardfield during the early months of the war.[35]

Robert had sympathized with Ricardo, a would-be writer and a refugee from Fascist Spain where he had been a captain in the Republican Army during the Civil War,[36] found him some gardening work, encouraged his writing, and became his friend. Later, the fall of France and the invasion scare had meant that foreigners were compelled to move further inland; and Ricardo had eventually decided that he was tired of England, and would like to try his luck in America. Robert gave him a letter of introduction to Tom Matthews; and the next part of his story reads like pure fiction.[37]

Travelling to New York by sea in 1941, at a time when the German U-boat fleet was sinking some 300,000 tons of shipping each month, Ricardo Sicré overcame an embarrassing lack of papers by diving fully clothed from his boat while it was travelling up the Hudson River, and swimming to the shore. 'The conditions of my landing', he told Robert,

> were so exciting and sudden that I put my foot on soil with my clothes on ... and all the hours of work and dreams that I put on the manuscript that you indicated me to write, I'm afraid are lying today in the fondo del mar. Well, it was good enough for me to arrive safely.[38]

Before long Ricardo was making a living giving Spanish lessons, some of them to Tom Matthews and his colleagues, and writing occasional articles while he worked hard 'on the legalisation of my status'.[39] Later he moved to Washington where he was employed by the American Government, who wanted someone from another country to spy for them against the Japanese;[40] he then worked for the O.S.S. (the Office of Strategic Services) in Algiers; and towards the end of the war he landed in France with the invasion forces, and fought alongside the 'maquis' in the French Resistance.[41]

Now that the war was over, Ricardo and his wife Betty (who in 1942, at the age of twenty-one, had been delivering new aircraft from British factories to operational bases, 'and nursing the old, beat-up planes back to the factories for overhaul'[42]) had together set up an import-export business and were 'trying to stir up trade between the US and France and North Africa'. It was Betty who wrote to Robert and Beryl making it clear that she and Ricardo believed that they were 'wise not to wait any longer. After all, as you say, it is the people and not the government. And the change should not be too long in coming, anyway.'[43]

Shortly before Betty's letter arrived, Robert had heard from 'Crab' Searle, who explained that he was now a Wing-Commander. He had been in charge of all the training schemes before the 1944 Normandy invasion;[44] and now that the war was over, he was running an aviation company.

This gave Robert the idea of chartering a small aircraft, and he wrote to ask how much it would cost to fly him and his family all the way to Palma. Crab replied on 1 April that he could 'get a charter aircraft to take you to Majorca by way of Paris and Marseilles. For this journey and your crew a twin-engined Rapide would have to be used and it's rather costly: £305.'[45] Robert sent him the necessary cheque by return of post; and asked whether Crab himself could fly them out to Majorca on 15 May?[46]

'No', Crab replied, 'I fear I can't fly you there although it was my original intention to do so.' He was leaving on a long-haul flight to South America towards the end of April, so he had 'fixed for another man called Bebb to take you. He flew Franco into Spain so he stands well with the present regime which is also useful.'[47]

Once the decision to leave England had been taken, Robert and Beryl found themselves 'dreadfully busy settling up ... and planning'.[48] One unforeseen task was helping to organize a sensible division of some family silver which had been buried away in a bank vault for years:[49] Robert's share included two fine Tiarks silver candlesticks, a delightful silver coffee pot, and some Cheyne teaspoons.[50] Another unexpected chore was dealing with a letter from T. S. Eliot, who had asked Robert to sign a plea for clemency on behalf of Ezra Pound, who was 'awaiting trial for treason because of pro-Fascist wartime broadcasts he had made to American troops from Rome'.

Unfortunately, the plea 'made no reference to his guilt or innocence but simply affirmed the importance of Pound's contribution to twentieth-century literature';[51] and Graves had to reply that:

since 1911 when I first read Pound in Harriet Monro's *Poetry* magazine; and since 1922 when I met him for the first and last time at All Souls in T. E. Lawrence's rooms, I could never regard him as a poet and have consistently denied him the title ... If there were a single line or stanza of Pound's that recurred to my mind as true and beautiful, or merely as true, I should join in your plea – but to do so just because he is a 'name' would be unprincipled.

'Forgive me', he concluded. 'May I myself be judged with equal severity in the Last Day.'[52]

Then came a curious letter from George Simon. After suffering a second miscarriage, Joanna had begun to feel that medical science had failed her; and so in desperation George asked Robert for 'magical instructions' to avoid a third such disaster. Robert took this very seriously. Earlier in the year, hearing that John's son Richard was very ill, he had written to John to tell him:

> My astrological theory is that a child born on the day before the winter solstice who makes a poor start will make a marked recovery at the spring solstice and be in perfect trim by midsummer.[53]

And now he advised the Simons to:

> Clear out all rubbish from the house (backs of drawers, under stairs etc., between May 14 and June 14) and burn it, unless classifiable as salvage, in the backyard. A bunch of primroses would please the Goddess and, when nobody is snooping, a handful of pearl barley laid on a raised stone. The birds will eat it; but they belong to her.

He also advised the use of the following charm, 'chockful of astrological magic':

SUFFICIUNT TECUM CARYATIS DOMINA QUINA

Graves explained this as meaning:

> 'the five feasts are enough for us, Artemis of the Nut-tree, when you are about' (i.e. the working week, excluding the Sabbath and Sunday both of which Jehovah appropriated to himself). The formula S.T.C.D.Q. can also be represented with willow, holly, nut, oak, apple. The five-petalled primrose is an even neater sign, as John Donne recognized.
>
> > Live primrose, then, and thrive
> > In your mysterious five.

'I think', he concluded, 'Wizard Graves has said enough for the present.'[54]

Besides dealing with these letters, there were residential visas to be applied for, papers to be sorted, and unwanted furniture to be disposed of.[55] There were also numerous goodbyes to be said; and in the midst of all this activity, Karl Gay paid a momentous visit.

It was already understood that in due course Karl should follow Robert and Beryl out to Majorca; but now, while he was helping Robert at the sink, he announced that he would not be bringing with him his wife Marie. He and Rene had fallen in love, he explained; and they hoped to be lifelong companions. This news came as a shock to Robert.

Karl had already observed that despite Robert's happiness with Beryl, he was occasionally attracted to some potential Muse over whom he would sigh for a few weeks: Dido Mulroy, a 'rather busty play-doctor', had been such a one; and recently (like Alan Hodge) he had begun to take a special interest in Rene: hence her 'getting in the way' when he wrote his White Goddess poem. So now he flared up for a few moments 'trying to get on his high horse' as Karl recalls. But then he subsided just as quickly, accepted the situation, and wished them both well.[56]

The Graveses had decided that before flying south, they would spend a few days in London, where Robert had to collect the necessary visas,[57] and tie up a few more personal and professional loose ends. So by 8 or 9 May they and their three children were installed in Brown's Hotel in Dover Street.[58]

This prestigious establishment was rather too grand an hotel for the relaxed family life to which Robert and Beryl had become accustomed, and which was unconventional enough to mean that on one of Beryl's walks with the children, a road-sweeper politely enquired whether they were 'part of a circus'. And since they had been unable to find a nanny, Robert was needed to help with the children. This meant that at meal times, when Beryl ate in her room with one-year-old Juan, Robert was expected to take charge of five-year-old William and three-year-old Lucia in the restaurant. Egg was trodden into the carpet, soup plates were held up to the face, and eventually, with Robert declaring how ashamed he was of the way his children behaved, screens had to be set up round the table to protect the sensibilities of the other guests.[59]

However, Brown's Hotel was a splendid base for the 'hectic meetings with friends and relatives'[60] which occupied most of the next ten days. Karl was a frequent visitor; Mary Reeves put in an appearance;[61] Catherine and Sam turned up;[62] and John Graves came along to say goodbye and tell of Clarissa's recent departure for Palestine.[63] Robert also met for the first time Lynette Roberts,[64] who had given him so much help with source material for *The White Goddess*, the typescript of which he was taking with him to Deyá, having told Eliot that he needed it 'for some last-minute emendations'.[65]

After a final leave-taking party,[66] Robert and Beryl and their three children departed on schedule from Croydon airport at three o'clock on the afternoon of 15 May. Beryl's mother was there, as was Karl. Curiously enough, the sky was so overcast that it was almost pitch dark; but they watched as the little plane lumbered down the runway, so heavily laden that it could only just take off; but take off it did, with Bebb at the controls; and then banked toward the southeast and disappeared into the darkness.[67]

Within the areoplane, there was much hope and much excitement, mingled with some anxiety. For years, Robert had been telling Beryl that Deyá was an earthly paradise.[68] More recently, he had begun to think of the drawbacks. It would certainly, he had confided to Lynette Roberts, be 'a bit lonely for Beryl and the children for a time, until they get to speak Spanish'. And, despite Jenny's enthusiastic report, much might have changed in village life after ten years. But the choice had been made. Before long they had left behind the white cliffs of the Kentish shore, and were flying across the Channel towards a remote Mediterranean island and an entirely new way of life.

CHAPTER 2

Return to Canelluñ

In the early evening of 15 May 1946, the twin-engined Rapide carrying Robert and Beryl Graves and their three children landed at Rennes in northwestern France. The weather was poor, and William and Lucia had been airsick;[69] but at Rennes they were all given a warm welcome by Gelat's sister, their old friend from prewar days, Anita Vives. She had prepared a 'grand reunion meal'[70] with a delicious roast chicken, and the pungent smell of garlic, something quite forgotten after years of wartime austerity.[71]

After staying for a night at Rennes they flew on to Toulouse, which, as Beryl reported to James Reeves, was:

> hopeless, no petrol ready for us, nobody knew or cared but liked to look at the plane and talk about the war. Eventually we had to fly to the nearby civilian airfield where they actually did put in the petrol but with about 6 chaps hanging round smoking cigarettes right over the petrol [which] frightened us out of our wits.[72]

From Toulouse they took off again, bound for Barcelona.

There they 'nearly landed on a flock of sheep and then ran through a wire'; and although they were 'received with much politeness and everyone looked very smart and efficient',[73] they were considerably delayed. As Robert takes up the story:

> they had only recently opened the civil aviation port, and we were the first air-taxi to make the hop to Majorca which is a military zone. It needed 24 hours and the British Embassy at Madrid to straighten things out. It all turned out lucky in the end because the bad weather improved and we had a non-air-sick flight over the Foradada and Valldemossa and could see our house in the distance. The island looks

wonderful from the air, the terraces and compact villages and everything was still very green because of late rains.[74]

Less than an hour after setting out from Barcelona, they had crossed a hundred miles of Mediterranean, and flown over the mountains of northwest Majorca, and across the large central plain, and down to Palma. There, on 18 May 1946, Robert and his family 'had the distinction of being the first civilian passengers to alight' since before the war.[75]

Gelat and his son Juan were waiting for them with two cars and 'much emotion'; and drove them to Deyá, along a route so well known to Robert, so completely new to Beryl and their children. The heat was intense, the light almost blinding in its clarity; the landscape was flat, with white, flat-roofed houses and palm trees and orchards of oranges and olives and dozens of ancient windmills. There followed the climb from the plain up into the mountains of the northwest; they drove through ancient Valldemossa, famous for its connection with Chopin and his mistress George Sand; and then they travelled northward along the coast road, between olive groves and clumps of pine, with the sea hundreds of feet down below to the left, and the mountains hundreds of feet up above to the right.

At last they swept round a turn in the road, and found themselves in a broad semicircular valley. On the west, it ran all the way down to the sea. On the east, it settled itself against a tall mountain range. Some distance below the head of the valley, at the point where the road wound through a cluster of houses, a long ridge of ground extended itself for a quarter of a mile towards the sea, climbing up to the village church, and beyond the church to an ancient graveyard.

This was Deyá. As they approached, they passed by Casa Salerosa, the house where Robert had first lived with Laura Riding in 1929. Then they came to the edge of the village, and a public open-air washing place, where a handful of villagers were doing their laundry. Through the village they drove; and then about a mile beyond it, after two more bends in the road, they came to an iron gateway; and through the gateway, they drove up a narrow drive which led to an attractive two-storey house with shuttered windows and walls of hand-hewn limestone.

They had reached Canelluñ, the 'house further-on', which had been Robert and Laura's home from 1932 to 1936. Built on three sides of a small east-facing courtyard, it was entered through the kitchen which lay to the south of the courtyard, and which looked out across a large square terrace towards the village and the distant mountains. Beyond the kitchen was the living room, with a stone fireplace, a few easy chairs, and a dining table. Through the living room, to the west of the courtyard, was a large hallway, from which double doors opened into a small terrace with spectacular views of the sea. Beyond the hallway, was the room which had been used by Robert and Laura for their private press, which Robert would now sell to a priest for 500 pesetas, so that Beryl could use the room as her study;[76] and leading out of that, to the north of the courtyard, was Robert's study, a cool, quiet, book-lined room with the large desk at which he had written *I, Claudius* and *Claudius the God*.

On returning to his old home, Graves was so pleased by Gelat's welcome that he shut his mind to the fact that a few items had disappeared both from Canelluñ and from the neighbouring cottage, C'an Torrent, which was also his.[77] What was chiefly remarkable in his eyes was that:

> everything was ten years older, but just the same; for example, all my shirts and trousers and socks wearable; and five jars of green tomato chutney eatable, and cigarette tobacco in my tobacco jar smokeable. And the *Encyclopaedia Britannica* and *Times Atlas* ten more years out of date ...[78]

As he told Tom Matthews, his 'hat was hanging on the same peg, his stick was leaning in the corner, all his books and papers were in order. On the table in the hall a shallow bowl still held the varicolored pebbles he had put there'. It appeared to Tom that Robert was 'touched by this evidence of [Gelat's] trustworthiness and at the same time delighted by the vindication of his own judgment – like a gambler who thinks he has won his bet not because he is lucky but because he knows the winning system'.[79]

The Cala, that semicircle of sandy beach set far below Deyá in an amphitheatre of rock, was also almost exactly the same: the only difference being, as Robert reported to James Reeves, that there was 'more sand now, at both ends of the beach. Wm. can manage the climb without effort, Lucia with a little coaxing. She had her 3rd birthday on July 21 so that isn't bad, is it?'[80]

What was most obviously different was that the children Robert remembered had grown up. For example Francisca, the little girl about whom Laura had written her poem 'Laura and Francisca', was 'now a deep-bosomed strapping girl of, I suppose, 19, and Miguel the loutish Fonda boy is a Guardia Civil ...[81] Another difference was that although saints' days were still celebrated, so that a month after they arrived there was a feast in honour of San Juan, the patron saint of Deyá, with '*arroz paella*, roast kid, *ensaimadas* etc.',[82] there had been a general demise of 'those beautiful pagan or semi-pagan village fiestas' which had been at the heart of village life in the prewar years.[83]

Equally unexpected, there were 'severe food shortages'.[84] One and a half pounds of sugar, for example, had to last the entire family for six weeks; and they found themselves having to resort to the black market for essential supplies. And although Gelat promised that while there was 'any food left on the island we shall eat it', Graves's relationship with him was very different from what it had been in the 1930s. Within a few weeks of his return, Graves had noted that: 'he and I are so mutually (or is it reciprocally?) grateful to each other for past services that it is almost uncomfortable'.[85] And 'uncomfortable' was the operative word. Their past friendship had depended substantially upon the powerful attraction that had existed between Gelat and Laura Riding, an attraction which fortunately never developed between Gelat and Beryl.

And where Deyá had once been a hive of expatriates, there were now 'no foreigners at all in the village except [Jessie Broadwood],[86] an old lame English spinster who paints flowers all day in a Bloomsbury attic she has made for herself at the Fonda ...'[87] The villagers were delighted to see Graves, mistakenly seeing his arrival as a hopeful sign that the tourist trade would soon be in full swing. But until Beryl had improved her Spanish, she and the children were extremely isolated.

In the circumstances, news from England became very important, and both Robert and Beryl kept up numerous correspondences with their friends. Robert also arranged to have the airmail *Times* sent out to Canelluñ; and he enjoyed telling Alan Hodge, who had written Beryl a sympathetic letter about her probable loneliness, and 'all the minor disadvantages of living abroad which one forgets in England',[88] that their 'Philips radio set ... gets England rather more clearly than we got it down in Devon', so he and Beryl were '*au courant* with all your latest climatic and dietetic disasters'.[89]

At first, Laura's presence hung over Canelluñ which, as Robert wrote to Tom Matthews, needed converting from 'a childless and carefully-arranged museum place into a free-and-easy family one'.[90] Beryl gradually made the house her own, though some of her schemes, such as whitewashing the patio, thoroughly annoyed Gelat;[91] and by the end of June she was telling Alan Hodge:

> I like living here very much. It was very strange at first, but chiefly because of the evidences of Laura in the house, the strange designs she drew on the walls, the clutter of furniture in her rooms, empty and half-empty bottles of medicine and all the other things ...[92]

As for Robert, 'Fulfilling Laura's behests', one of his first tasks was to destroy 'all her loose writings – several half-finished or 1/4 finished books and bundles of scrawled notes. She left a lot of unhappiness behind', he told Alan Hodge; 'but we are clearing it off gradually: unhappiness breeds clutter.'[93] To Karl Gay, he explained with some relish that he had also sold several sackfuls of Laura's poetry and prose to a Palma wastepaper merchant: 'a pity, but they will make good cardboard and wrapping paper'.[94]

The move back to Canelllñ had unsettled Robert enough to make it impossible for him to write poems for several months; but he very soon began making more amendments to his typescript of *The White Goddess*; and when that was done, and it had been posted to Karl for retyping, he set himself 'to revise and see what was worth keeping of my early essays'. Then in mid-July, 'because Beryl teases me that I can't write modern fiction', he wrote 'a 10,000 word story for *Cosmopolitan* which offered me a large fee; the result is a bit prostitutish, but as the proceeds will be spent in the black market she thinks this is excusable'. Sadly there were no proceeds, as *Cosmopolitan* rejected the story; and Robert settled down to wait for the September publication, in England and the USA, of his *King Jesus*, and to wonder 'what books I will be able to afford to write, and whether we can give ourselves a bit more liberty by getting a car ...'[95]

CHAPTER 3

Family, Friends and the Queen of Heaven

In July 1946, shortly after receiving a cutting from the *New Statesman* with the only seriously hostile review to his *Poems: 1928–1945*, Robert Graves also had a letter from Amy to remind him that it would soon be the centenary of his father's birth. Special programmes celebrating Alfred Perceval Graves's life and work would be broadcast from Belfast and Dublin on 22 July; Amy herself would be placing flowers on his grave; and Robert's half-sister Susan and a group of their friends would be coming to supper at Erinfa to hear a wireless recital of APG's poems and songs.[96]

Robert ignored his father's centenary, although there were many ways in which, as he advanced into middle age, his life was beginning to echo that of the witty Anglo–Irish poet whose paternal love he had long ago rejected. They both hadsecond families, for example, and large numbers of children. Erinfa and Canelluñ, their respective homes, had both been built to their own specifications in remote areas on hillsides with the sea down below and the mountains at their back; and bothwere situated a little to the north of villages over which their owners had gradually come to exercise a great deal of unofficial influence. More than this: both Alfred and Robert had a consuming interest in poetry and mythology; both had a gift for bringing out the best in their friends; and above all, both were deeply religious, and both wanted to lead virtuous lives, even though one acted according to the edicts of the Christian God, the other according to the dictates, as he understood them, of the Queen of Heaven.

In the event, as Robert heard soon afterwards, APG's centenary was very nearly marred by a considerable family tragedy. In Jerusalem his half-brother Dick Graves, then Director of the Labour Department in Palestine,[97] had arranged to meet Clarissa at the King David Hotel for a celebratory lunch party. They were both on the way there when by chance they met in the street about half a block away, and stopped to talk. A few minutes later, while they were still engrossed in conversation, a wing of the hotel was blown up by Jewish terrorists.[98]

During August advance copies of the Creative Age Press edition of *King Jesus* became available in the USA, and Tom Matthews wrote from New York to tell Robert frankly of his serious reservations, comparing it as a work of doubtful scholarship with George Moore's 1916 best-selling novel about the life of Christ, *The Brook Kerith*.[99] Robert replied equably that:

> your criticism interests me very much, especially as I know that it comes straight from your heart, and gives me a foretaste of the bludgeoning that the book will get from a large part of the solid core of educated Americans, especially in the Middle West ... it is, however, an oversimplification of the case: I mean, the comparison with George Moore.

Moore, said Graves, 'had no historical conscience and imposed a theme on the story rather than letting the story emerge logically from the historical data'. He added that *King Jesus* was 'literally the first book to reconcile all the known historical data', and that at least one Catholic priest had admitted that he had explained the story 'better than the Church herself'.[100]

Tom Matthews's letter was accompanied by one from his wife Julie, who announced sternly that she had decided not to read *King Jesus*, as she had become a Christian and did not want her new-found faith to be put at risk. Robert replied wittily that in the circumstances she was probably 'wise not to read the book', as the 'Christian life' revealed in his book would involve her 'in Judaizing yourself completely, and in embracing a sort of Stalinite communism laced with Seventh Day Adventism – and how awkward for your family that would be'. He added that Beryl (whose health continued to be poor) 'often wishes she were religious, in her low moments: this is a dreadful epoch, and religion seems to be the only thing to keep one going in bad weather of all sorts'. He personally had never had that wish, since:

> poetry has always supplied my religious needs. This may seem a stupid statement but I am realizing, have been realizing for the last three years, that real poetry, there is very little of it like the trace of gold when they wash gravel, is an epitome of the ancestral religion of Europe.

However, he quite understood that anyone who wanted 'to be in touch with as many people of religious life as possible, as you do', would find that 'Catholicism (or Anglo-Catholicism)' was:

the only solution of the problem; and I should obviously become a Catholic, if I thought that it added up historically and was compatible with my poetic principles. It is just too bad.

At any rate I agree with you that these are times in which one is returned to first principles and in which 'the good life' as it is sometimes called, which you define as 'the Christian life' is the only thing of real interest, apart from family happenings.

'So don't think', he assured her, 'I am anything but sincere in my pleasure that you have become a 'believer'.[101]

Early in October 1946, Jenny and Alex came to stay in Ca'n Torrent for a week. Jenny saw a great deal of her half-brother William, who at the age of six was already swimming, rowing and riding a bicycle, had picked up a good smattering of Spanish and of Mallorquin,[102] and had recently begun attending the village boys' school; but she became particularly attached to three-year-old Lucia, who had already begun some elementary education with the village nuns.[103] 'We love the children,' Jenny would write in her 'bread-and-oil' letter,

> though we don't hold out any very correct or proper future for Lucia. Send her to [stay with us] when she gets out of hand and home – as we are sure she will – and we will at least guarantee to show her the best of the bad things in life.[104]

Jenny and Alex left Deyá in weather so wild that on the road to Valldemossa their driver 'had to keep getting out … and removing great pieces of plane and olive tree before we could pass on'; there were floods down on the plain; and a terrible storm on the sea-crossing to Barcelona. However, Jenny's enthusiasm for her father's island home was undiminished. 'Now we have seen Majorca in flower, fruit and flood', she wrote, 'and all of them become her.'

No other visitors had made their way out to Majorca that spring or summer, though there was news on the family grapevine of Robert's old friend Diccon Hughes who, according to Amy, had suddenly reappeared in the Harlech area 'with his wife & five children & a big black beard' and was holidaying at Môr Edrin, on the river estuary opposite Portmeirion.[105] Not long afterwards, Robert Graves re-established contact with Peter Quennell, Diccon's former protégé, and one of the numerous folk with whom Robert had quarrelled during his years with Laura Riding. Now editor of the *Cornhill* magazine, Quennell replied to a conciliatory letter from Graves that: 'It was delightful to hear from you and to know that our ancient difference has now been forgotten and forgiven'; and he hoped that Robert might be able to 'extract an article of 2–4,000 words' for the *Cornhill* 'from your romantic muse book'.[106]

There was also news of John Aldridge, who had been away in the armed forces for much of the war and was finding it difficult to settle back into life at Great Bardfield; and of Len Lye (the pioneer in the art of making animated films who had been a member of the Graves/Riding circle from the late 1920s). When Len's wife Jane had followed him out to New York, she had arrived 'about all-in with fatigue to find Len had got a glamour-girl who he has told Jane he prefers to her'.[107] Robert later had 'a most distressing letter' on the subject from Jane. It seemed to him that Len had been 'very clumsy and cowardly'; but by and large, as he explained when he retailed the news to Tom Matthews, he reserved his judgment. 'Who am I', he asked, 'to cast stones?'[108]

As for Norman Cameron: after spending the war in military intelligence (at one time attached to the Eight Army in Africa, for whom he prepared propaganda leaflets to be dropped behind enemy lines), he was now working for the Occupation Forces in Austria;[109] while James Reeves wrote to tell Robert that although their joint efforts to prepare a school poetry book for Cassells had come to nothing, he had given Heinemann 'a rough scheme for a more or less modest one-volume anthology for fifteen-year-olds' which had suddenly been accepted.[110]

Relations with Alan Hodge were more complicated, chiefly because Hodge could not resist playing a game which involved Robert, Beryl, Karl, Rene and himself. Back in June, Alan had indicated in a letter to Beryl that he knew all about the romance between Karl and Rene: he had 'seen Karl since you left', he wrote, 'and Robert's letter to him and heard of yours to Irene.' Since both Karl and Rene were still married to other people, while Alan himself was single; and since there was also an attraction between Robert and Rene, it was a situation ripe with both comic and tragic potential. Fortunately Alan contented himself with teasing the various players concerned. After telling Beryl that he and Rene had been 'striking up quite a correspondence', he had added, as an apparently casual afterthought: 'I have, by the way, offered to convey Irene to Majorca if Karl can't (and if you want her) sometime in the autumn or winter ...'[111]

'No, please', Beryl replied at the end of June, 'for heaven's sake do not bring Rene out if Karl is delayed. It is entirely Karl's show as far as we are concerned';[112] but in August Alan was still teasing her with the possibility. 'Whether to bring [Irene] to Majorca in the winter', he wrote, is a thing I must talk about to Karl – for it looks as if many months may go by before he gets his nationality, and I think your first reaction against having Rene by herself was a wise one. She ... would get bored in Hesperidean peace ...[113]

Much later in the year, when Alan wrote to tell Robert that he was thinking about visiting Deyá in February or March 1947, he mentioned that Rene was 'coming to stay here for a couple of days on her way to Brussels to stay with her ... husband', and added gleefully in a note at the side of the page, that: 'When I rang up Karl to tell him and ask him along he sounded highly cross and suspicious.'[114]

Then came a letter from George and Joanna Simon, with news that Robert's magical charms appeared to have worked to the extent that Joanna had once again become pregnant, and so far there had been no miscarriage. However, George had recently failed to be elected to a coveted post, so they had become alarmed that they might have unwittingly offended the gods; and they wanted further advice, to give them both better luck and to safeguard Joanna's pregnancy. 'Our first reaction', Beryl replied,

is that you are too good for this world but that is small comfort. Speaking rather more practically, Robert suggests that you should cultivate the Queen of Heaven. She is at least a dispeller of gloom and it is due to their rejection of her that the Jews for instance have become such a gloomy and ill-fated race. So get yourselves for Christmas a statue of the Virgin Mary who is Queen. And burn incense to her. This is the beginning and you will probably get inspiration of other things to do ... Another important thing is music. Avoid symphony concerts chamber music and all ... music which belongs to Apollo and concentrate on music written before the Civil War that is before Merry England came to a finish at the Battle of Naseby.[115]

After Beryl had finished writing, she showed her letter to Robert, who added some details in the margin about the Virgin Mary, who had 'taken over all the characteristics of the Queen except her decolletage and sexual caprice'; and had been 'very merry indeed' in mediaeval England as Our Lady of Walsingham.

Robert also suggested pleasing the Queen of Heaven by fastening scarlet thread horizontally to their bedroom door. Other ideas were that George should propitiate Venus by wearing 'a thumb-ring, if permitted by professional etiquette a silver one'; and that Joanna should propitiate the birth-goddess Artemis by bowing nine times to the next silver fir that she saw, and by uttering 'a silent wish'.

Finally, he added that *King Jesus* was 'out in America', and that the early American reviews had been 'extremely good'.[116] Some of the later ones were less so. Eileen Garrett, the owner of the Creative Age Press and a well-known psychic,[117] had lunched with Tom Matthews in an effort to secure as much review space as possible in *Time* magazine. Afterwards she reported that she was satisfied with the results, as although Matthews personally disliked the book, 'in this particular instance quantity was as good as quality'. But it had not been an easy interview. Garrett was fascinated by *The White Goddess*, of which she had recently read a typescript; and when she told Matthews how much she would like to sit at Graves's feet and discuss it with him, he had 'flushed rather red' and told her 'what dire consequences would result if I ever "tried that on"'.

In mid-October, Graves wrote to his mother to tell her that *King Jesus* had caused 'much controversy' in the USA; and he advised her not to read his novel on its English publication in case it unsettled her mind. He added that he was now busily engaged on a translation for Penguin Classics of Apuleius's novel *The Golden Ass*. This, as Amy explained when retailing the news to other members of the family, was 'a pagan religious work', which Robert was finding 'most interesting'.[118]

CHAPTER 4

The Golden Ass

Lucius Apuleius, whose novel Graves had chosen to translate, was born early in the second century AD in the Roman province of Numidia in North Africa. His father, a provincial magistrate, died leaving him to share with his brother a fortune of some two million sesterces. Educated first at Carthage and then at Athens, where he studied Platonic philosophy, Apuleius went to Rome, and made a success at the Bar.

When, however, he married an elderly widow whose son soon afterwards died, the rest of the widow's family charged him with having poisoned the son, and gained the mother's affections by magic. Apuleius spoke successfully in his own defence; and later he wrote *The Transformations of Lucius Apuleius of Madaura*, a title soon shortened to *The Golden Ass*, in part a satirical account of the manners and morals of his day.

Graves had been attracted to Apuleius's work since discovering that he had been initiated into the mysteries of Isis, considered by Graves to be one of the 'true' names of the Queen of Heaven. In writing *The White Goddess*, he had included a passage from a 1566 translation of *The Golden Ass* in which Lucius, who has been transformed into an ass and involved in all kinds of dangerous and often bawdy adventures, begs Isis for her help and protection;[119] for Graves recognized that *The Golden Ass* was 'above all, a religious novel'.[120]

'The main religious principles that Apuleius was inculcating', Graves explains in his introduction, 'were wholly opposed to those of the Christianity of his day.' The first of these was:

> that men are far from equal in the sight of Heaven, its favour being reserved for the well-born and well-educated, in so far as they are conscious of the moral responsibilities of their station: that only such can be initiated into the divine mysteries ...[121]

The second was that ill-luck is catching; and the third, that one should avoid meddling with the supernatural. To be precise:

> A nobleman should not play with black magic: he should satisfy his spiritual needs by being initiated into a respectable mystery cult along with men of his own station; even then he should not thrust himself on the gods but patiently await their summons.[122]

Two of these precepts were particularly attractive to Graves: the first fitted in with his own views about there being only a chosen few who were of any importance; while the third enjoined the kind of spirtual decency which, as an English officer and a gentleman, he had been brought up to admire. As for the second: while not so enticing for a man who had suffered from his own share of bad luck, it did at least suggest that no guilt could be attached to anyone for leaving unlucky people to their fate.

Early in December, when his translation of *The Golden Ass* had to be laid aside, it was to work on a related subject. As Graves told Derek Savage, a poet who, on his recommendation, had recently been given a £200 Atlantic Award in literature,[123] he was:

> having an enjoyable time now on proofs of my *White Goddess*, a sort of historical grammar to the language of poetic myth; a dreadful book to write because the subject had never been attempted – and my problem was like Jehovah's on the Sixth Day of Creation, how to forge a pair of tongs with which to hold the red-hot metal when one is forging a pair of tongs.

'In the end', Graves declared, 'He created 'em ... together with the Rainbow and other necessary odds and ends.'[124]

Christmas brought amusing letters from Alan Hodge, who told them that Rene was 'gorging on the Belgian Black Market';[125] and from 'Agatha Christie', enclosing her 'latest bit of blood', and telling Robert that his former house appeared to be 'full of curates. Perhaps there is only one, but he always seems to be coming out whenever I pass and makes me feel guilty for persistent non-attendance at church.'[126]

Christmas also brought some unexpected guests: John and Frances Knittel, the parents of an executive at the Creative Age Press who was a Graves enthusiast. Frances turned out to have no sense of humour;[127] but she doted on the children, and some months later wrote to ask:

Is William still drawing, Lucia still kissing the cross and learning to sew, and has Juan stopped falling on his head and making bumps? They still feel so close to me, that darling little family.

'I hope', she added, 'Beryl has regained some strength.'[128]
Early in the New Year, Beryl, who had once again been feeling extremely listless, underwent a small internal operation;[129] but sadly it was not enough, and her ill-health continued.

Meanwhile Robert went on with his *White Goddess* proofs; but once again he was doing almost as much new writing as correcting. On 19 January 1947, he wrote to Eliot to tell him that he had:

> yielded to a poetic compulsion in *The White Goddess* to answer Sir Thos. Browne's 'puzzling questions not beyond all conjecture' about Achilles' assumed name among the women and what songs the Sirens sang ... the answer to the first is Drosoessa ... [and] to the second, a Hellenization of the corresponding early Irish addresses to heroes from priestesses of Avalon islands, makes it quite a nice poem.

'Well,' he concluded, 'I'll try to stop improving the book, but my mind gives me little peace.'[130]
Graves was well aware that time spent either on *The White Goddess* or on *The Golden Ass* was unlikely to bring him much financial reward; and, as he told Karl in mid-February, he reckoned that 'Expenses in ordinary living (but with two maids to feed) work out at about £1000 a year for us ... So I'm hoping in the Lord Jesus.'[131] The sales of *King Jesus* in England were certainly good, and in the USA, where they had begun to flag, Robert Knittel placed an article by Graves on the 'History and Logic of King Jesus' with the *New York Herald Tribune*[132]. With an uncomplimentary but thought-provoking preface by Tom Matthews, it was 'given a big spread' on 4 February; and by then Graves's novel had also 'been sold to Sweden, Holland, Hungary, Czechoslovakia, Denmark and I forget where else'.[133]

Every evening, Robert and Beryl listened on their radio to the news from London, which was now in the grip of one of the most severe winters of the century; and on 11 February 1947 Robert wrote to Amy:

Dearest Mother:
   In this time of warm southerly breezes, new potatoes, almond blossom, roses, green peas and so on ... we have been thinking very

sadly of you in England. Our 9 o'clock news (which we get at 10 because Spain keeps summer-time all winter) has been terribly gloomy with its tales of electricity cuts & coal shortages. I hope at least you can get wood to burn.[134]

There had also been much news about the continuing troubles in Palestine. Robert had been amused to hear of a certain Judge Wyndham who, having been captured and then released by Zionist terrorists, had expressed himself very much impressed by his treatment – 'talk of art and politics, in English & German, & a cup of coffee, a morning paper, and Robert Graves's *King Jesus* to read!' But Robert was also deeply concerned about the safety of his eldest sister. 'Can you tell me about Claree?' he asked Amy. 'Is she "standing put" as a Palestine citizen, or is she on her way home?'

As he wrote, there was a cheerful letter in the post from Clarissa, enclosing an account by their mother of a nativity play in Harlech church, 'where all the performers seemed to be wearing her [cast-off] clothes, from the Blessed Virgin Mary downwards'; telling him that he was 'seldom out of my thoughts'; and completely ignoring the danger she was in.[135]

But that danger was very considerable and, as Robert had suspected, Clarissa was already racing her letter back to England. Despite having become a Palestinian citizen, she had been included among the British women and children who, on 2 February, 'were suddenly given 48 hours notice to leave Palestine, possibly for good, & were told that they could take two suitcases only, and £20 for the journey'.[136]

Dick also returned to England, for an operation and some leave; but in the third week of March, Robert learned from Molly, now so hopelessly crippled with arthritis that she had to dictate her letter, that 'Graves Superieur' (as he had been nicknamed long ago) would shortly be returning to Palestine in a much more dangerous role. 'Dick', she told him,

has been asked to be mayor of Jerusalem [and Chairman of the Municipal Commission] and has accepted the honour. I personally call it a great risk. I hope he will be safe, because you know, I love him very much. I think I always loved Dick and you best of all my brothers.[137]

Dick, as might have been expected, filled his new position with great courage, travelling about Jerusalem with an armed bodyguard in a car whose windscreen was shattered at least once by a would-be assassin's bullet.

Other family news was that on 14 March Catherine had given birth to Caroline, her third child and second daughter;[138] that Charles was now so wealthy that, as Rosaleen reported, he was now employing '5 resident maids for him and Peggy', not to mention 'a char and a secretary';[139] that John was writing a history of the Royal Welch Fusiliers;[140] that Jenny had been touring America for the *Daily Mail*;[141] and that she and Alex had bought a mediaeval castle, known as the Castelletto, overlooking the Port of Porto Fino in the Gulf of Genoa.[142]

As for Robert himself: by the start of April he had at last completed work on *The White Goddess* galley proofs. He forwarded them to Eliot with a handsome apology for having added some 15,000 words to the text, including a final chapter,[143] 'War in Heaven', in which he had dealt 'more particularly' with 'the Sacred King as the Moon-goddess's divine victim; holding that every Muse-poet must, in a sense, die for the Goddess whom he adores, just as the King died'.[144] He had also written this memorable definition of 'the main theme of poetry' which was 'properly', he declared,

> the relations of man and woman, rather than those of man and man, as the Apollonian Classicists would have it. The true poet who goes to the tavern and pays the appropriate silver tribute to Blodeuwedd goes to his death. As in the story of Llew Llaw: 'All their discourse that night was concerning the affection and love that they felt one for the other and which in no longer space than one evening had arisen.' This paradise lasts only from May Day to St. John's Eve. Then the plot is hatched and the poisoned dart flies; and the poet knows that it must be so. For him there is no other woman but Cerridwen and he desires one thing above all else in the world: her love. As Blodeuwedd, she will gladly give him her love, but only at one price: his life. She will exact payment punctually and bloodily. Other women, other goddesses, are kinder-seeming. They sell their love at a reasonable rate – sometimes a man may even have it for the asking. But not Cerridwen: for with her love goes wisdom. And however bitterly and grossly the poet may rail against her in the hour of his humiliation – Catullus is the most familiar instance – he has been party to his own betrayal and has no just cause for complaint.
>
> Cerridwen abides. Poetry began in the matriarchal age, and derives its magic from the moon, not from the sun. No poet can hope to understand the nature of poetry unless he has had a vision of the Naked King crucified to the lopped oak, and watched the dancers, red-eyed from the acrid smoke of their sacrificial fires, stamping out

the measure of the dance, their bodies bent uncouthly forward, with a monotonous chant of: 'Kill! kill! kill!' and 'Blood! blood! blood!'[145]

Having posted this powerful new material to Eliot, Graves returned to his much-delayed translation of *The Golden Ass*. At the same time, he was dealing with some important financial business.

In 1940, when Laura Riding had agreed to transfer to Robert Graves the ownership of their Majorcan property (nominally held by Gelat, though it had been paid for by Robert, and Laura's name was on the title deeds), she had forgotten that Gelat had been left with power of attorney; so nothing effective could be done until after the war. Graves had recently approached Gelat on the subject, and Gelat had therefore written to Laura, who obliged him with:

a document instructing him to 'sell' Graves [Canelluñ and Ca'n Torrent], though stating that no money was to change hands. This was, however, not legally acceptable and although Graves's ownership of the houses was finally established, the land (a considerable amount) remained in Gelat's name.[146]

Although this was a hopelessly unsatisfactory situation, Robert trusted Gelat too completely to admit that there was any threat to his interests; and his chief feeling was one of profound relief that he had 'at last got the houses under my own name. I had a half-fear', he told Alan Hodge, 'that Laura would refuse to play ball at the last moment, but since Gelat did the letter-writing she was not tempted.'[147]

Robert's letter crossed with one from Alan to Beryl which contained dramatic news about their friend Norman Cameron. Back from Vienna on a fortnight's leave, he had found himself an advertising job; and then, having secured his future, he had borrowed money from Alan to buy a wedding ring, and sent a telegram proposing marriage to a twenty-eight-year-old Austrian journalist named Gretl. Then, in Alan's words, after:

several cat-on-hot-brick days an answer came saying 'Wahr Scheinlich Ya'. N[orman] was much perturbed by the Wahr Scheinlich and set off for Vienna loaded down with soapflakes stockings needles shampoo toothpaste facecream tennis balls and wedding and engagement rings.[148]

Norman had confided that he was 'not madly in love' with Gretl, but simply wanted 'to marry a nice girl'; and the result was a happy marriage which lasted for the rest of Norman's life.

In the meantime Graves continued with his translation of *The Golden Ass*. He had now reached the final chapters, in the course of which the ass is transformed back into a human being again, after being told by Queen Isis:

> Only remember, and keep these words of mine locked tight in your heart, that from now onwards until the very last day of your life you are dedicated to my service ... Under my protection you will be happy and famous, and when at the destined end of your life you descend to the land of ghosts, there too in the subterrene region you shall have frequent occasion to adore me.[149]

Later Lucius is advised to enrol himself in a religious order dedicated to Isis, 'voluntarily undertaking the duties to which your oath binds you; for her service is perfect freedom'.

Graves, who was in the process of committing himself to lifelong service to the White Goddess, enjoyed the irony that he had recited the words 'whose service is perfect freedom' at Morning Prayer throughout his childhood – the adherents of the usurping male deity having clearly stolen this concept long ago from the followers of the Goddess. He was also very much interested in deepening his understanding of what he now took to be the truth. So he was intrigued by the fragmentary account given in *The Golden Ass* by Apuleius, who wrote from first-hand experience, of how Lucius was initiated into 'the mysteries of the holy night'.[150]

'I will record as much as I may lawfully record for the uninitiated,' Lucius tells us,

> but only on condition that you believe it. *I approached the very gates of death and set one foot on Proserpine's threshold, yet was permitted to return, rapt through all the elements. At midnight I saw the sun shining as if it were noon; I entered the presence of the gods of the under-world and the gods of the upper-world, stood near and worshipped them.*

'Well', Lucius concludes, 'now you have heard what happened, but I fear you are still none the wiser.'

Graves, however, wished to be wiser and to be initiated into the mysteries of the ancient cult which he had chosen, in his own personal life as a poet, to revive. And curiously, it was not long after completing *The Golden Ass* that he underwent a strange kind of mystical experience: one which almost cost him his life.

CHAPTER 5

Silver Island

By June 1947, when he was casting around for a new subject, Robert Graves began thinking again about his ideas for a Utopian novel, ideas which he had laid to one side on his son David's advice almost seven years before.[151] But this time, instead of making his Utopia a 'decent organisation of practical people' along the lines of Laura Riding's 'Protocols', he would learn from David's words about western civilization being finished in its present form, and write about a society living according to the primitive religion of the White Goddess.

In the meantime Karl Gay and Rene had finally arrived in Deyá, where they were soon installed at C'an Torrent, and Karl began typing out a fair version of *The Golden Ass*. Karl found it strange to be looking out on a local world which had changed so dramatically since Laura Riding's will had been law. He was reminded vividly of those days when, a few weeks after their arrival, Robert called him and Rene to a rubbish pit near C'an Torrent. It was filled with a pile of Laura's manuscripts which had escaped his earlier clearing-out; and as Robert set fire to them, he called on Karl and Rene to witness that he was obeying Laura's demands. After he had finished, he found still more of her manuscripts; and a day or two later, he used them to light a fire in Canelluñ.[152]

In many ways Karl regretted Laura's absence. He regretted, for example, that she was no longer there to dress Robert in fine, elegant clothes, as she had done in the 1930s. He regretted that Canelluñ was no longer a place of such artistic perfection, but a family home with children running wild. He regretted, above all, that the special relationship which had once existed with Gelat was gradually breaking down.[153]

This had consequences. For example, at about three o'clock each afternoon, Robert would get out the pram and take Lucia and Juan for a walk. Usually he took them to C'an Medo, a small property which Robert and Laura had bought in the 1930s, and which had a valuable water supply, and a delightful garden with plum-trees and other fruit. But as relations with Gelat deteriorated, the visits to C'an Medo ceased; and ownership of the property, which had remained in Gelat's name, gradually fell completely into Gelat's hands.[154]

It was on one of Graves's walks into the village that he met Dr Otto Kubler, an Austrian historian who persuaded him to lay his 'Utopia' idea to one side. Instead, the two of them would collaborate on an historical novel based upon the sixteenth-century exploits of Ysabel de Barreto.

This Ysabel was the wife of the Spanish explorer General Alavaro de Mendana de Neira, who took her with him when, in 1595, he sailed from Peru into the South Pacific to colonize the Solomon Islands. It was a disastrous expedition, but for that very reason it involved many moments of high drama. An excellent original report had survived which could be adapted to form not only the bare bones of the narrative, but a good deal of the flesh;[155] and Graves was also attracted to the story because on her husband's death, Dona Ysabel had assumed command of the expedition. This presented Graves with the chance of portraying a powerful woman in a position of authority. His provisional title was *The She-Admiral*; and his initial intention that Ysabel should represent one aspect of the White Goddess ('Whose eyes were blue', and so on) is clearly signalled when he introduces this lady of rank and beauty and describes her 'blue eyes' which 'danced like stars under her crown of wheat-coloured hair'.[156]

In July 1947, after living continuously in Deyá for more than a year, Robert and Beryl accepted an invitation from Ricardo and Betty Sicré, and joined them for a holiday at Ariège in the French Pyrénées.[157] It was while they were staying there, in 'a large rambling dirty charming house' where Ricardo's parents and sisters lived, that they received a letter from George and Joanna Simon with the news that, on 27 June 1947, Joanna had safely given birth to 'a fine baby girl' whom they named Helena.[158]

Robert was not at all surprised when he learned that Helena's birth was attributed entirely 'to you and your various devices'.[159] He had already told George and Joanna that in order 'to avert Nemesis', they should treat their first-born with what he described as 'salutary neglect';[160] and now he added that they should dress her 'very plainly', on the grounds that she would be 'very beautiful and a danger to men, with a nativity so close to midsummer'.[161]

Robert was halfway through this letter when he put it to one side and went out for a walk with Juan, whom he carried down to a little stream some distance from the house. And then Robert was stung on the heel by an adder. Almost at once, his leg began to go numb, and his head to ache.

Somehow, he managed to get back home with Juan.[162] And then, in one corner of his vision, there appeared the silver pattern of an irregular oval shape fringed on one side by a narrow indented border.

This pattern gradually grew larger and larger 'until it enclosed the whole field of vision and then began turning round'. At first it seemed to be a revolving island; and then, before he lost consciousness, he was aware that he was looking at a glass castle.[163]

The local doctor was called; but although Robert regained consciousness, and was able to explain what had happened, the doctor could see no sign of a bite and assumed that Robert was suffering from a violent stomach upset which had made him feverish. It was only when he was called back again in the evening that he saw the fang marks. This time, looking highly alarmed, he injected Robert with a powerful antidote. For a while this appeared to make Robert very much worse; but at length he began to recover, though he had a swollen leg for weeks;[164] and soon he had resumed his letter to George and Joanna, telling them, 'I still can't walk for pins and needles, but feel all right otherwise.'[165]

What chiefly interested Robert about this extremely dangerous experience (it was George Simon's professional opinion that 'only your strong constitution pulled you through'[166]) was its 'unusual and mythologically interesting' nature. 'Really', he explained, 'it was very strange, because in my *White Goddess* there is a whole chapter devoted to this. The God of the Year used to end this way before being conducted to the Silver Island of the dead.' He supposed that the pattern he had seen 'must have a connection with Silver Island'; and its turning round perhaps explained 'why the Islands of the Dead were said to revolve'.[167]

Mythologically interesting though it may have been, Robert's accident had blighted their holiday. Seven-year-old William was enjoying himself well enough, fishing for 'lots of tiddlers which are fried for the children's tea'; while four-year-old Lucia happily spent her time 'in personal adornment and sewing'; but their father found himself unable to 'settle here to any work. No privacy,' he complained to George and Joanna, 'no ink, no thoughts and a heat-wave, the worse for this valley being very green and damp.'[168]

Another difficulty was that Beryl, who had been in a generally anxious state even before his adder sting,[169] was 'having too much work to do, for a real holiday, because I can only hop at present and Juan needs a strong man to cope with him'. To make matters worse, there was 'a deaf aunt' who acted as a help in the house 'and is very much shouted at, and retaliates by hiding everything we need in off corners and watching us search for them with poker-faced glee'.[170] So, although it was not an easy journey back,[171] Robert and Beryl were relieved when the time came to return to Deyá. There, however, fresh troubles awaited them.

CHAPTER 6

Watch the North Wind Rise

William was bicycling in the village with one of Gelat's grandsons one sunny morning in the first week of August 1947, when they went much too fast round a dangerous corner. A taxi was coming the other way. William was knocked down, and dragged along the road. One foot was badly injured, and he was rushed into Mare Nostrum, the insurance hospital in Palma.[172] Robert and Beryl followed him, and for a few nights they took turns sleeping on a chair by his bedside.[173]

It was soon clear that William, who endured his sufferings very bravely,[174] had a good chance of being able to walk again on his damaged foot. But even when he had been discharged from his hospital bed he would need to have out-patient treatment every day for some weeks; and as soon as he had recovered from the immediate after-effects of the accident, he would need a series of skin-grafting operations.

After the first few chaotic days and nights, Robert was alone in Palma one Wednesday evening. He wrote to Beryl suggesting that since the present system was 'killing' them, they should accept an offer from their friend Cecily Gittes. Cecily, a pianist who lived with her artist husband and their four sons,[175] had promised William a bedroom in her Palma home. This would mean, as Robert pointed out, that he and Beryl could:

> sleep both of us every night in Deyá and one of us mostly me because I can work in the train go in every day ... All that would be needed would be William's bed brought in by camion sheets and a contribution to household expenses.

The future was more problematic. They had been wondering whether to fly William back to England for the skin-grafting, and Robert had already written to make enquiries; but a 'German surgeon woman' had now told Robert that the local specialist was 'perfectly capable of grafting and on a child of his age in good health it always takes'. However, it might not be so neat a job; and English nursing would probably be better.

'I wish I could make up my mind', wrote Robert gloomily. 'The two bright spots in this nightmare,' he continued,

> are that we love each other and that William will eventually be all right. I daresay your worries have been a sort of intimation of all our present troubles and will now dissolve. Sleep well, eat well, take it as easy as you possibly can. Kiss the children for me and see me on Friday. All my love, Robert.[176]

Beryl agreed that William should move into the Gittes household; and a few days later the decision about what to do next was settled for them by a letter from a London surgeon dated 12 August. In it, Robert was 'strongly advised' that William should be 'transferred immediately to Barcelona under the care of Dr. P. Gaburro', who had recently returned there after working with orthopaedic and plastic surgeons in England, and who was said on the best authority to be '100% good'.[177]

In the midst of preparations to transfer William to Barcelona (it had been decided that Robert should accompany him, leaving Beryl in charge of the other children at Canellun) there was another brief period of intense anxiety. Sam, still pursuing his architectural studies at Cambridge, had come to Deyá on holiday. One day he went out for a walk, and simply failed to return.

Sam had decided to walk up into the mountains, but had not set out until four o'clock in the afternoon; and had then become hopelessly lost. The following morning, when he made his way home down to a house, it was one where there had recently been an unsolved murder, and the inhabitants were terrified.[178]

Fortunately, a passing motorcyclist rescued Sam and his new acquaintances from each other; and towards the end of August Robert and William set off by sea for Barcelona, where William was soon installed in the Clinica Adriano. It was a handsome, well-run establishment. 'You'd love this place', Robert told Beryl on Thursday 4 September. 'The nurses are all so sweet and everything runs so smoothly.' He added that he had:

> entirely lost my distaste for Barcelona and have a lot of friends at the ... tavern round the corner where I have my morning coffee and my before-dinner beer ... I have realised how necessary it was that I should have brought William here and kept him in a happy and busy

condition, not because I like being away from you any better than I thought I would.[179]

Gaburro, whom Robert had found 'wonderfully good and humane'[180] had examined William that morning and had decided to do the graft the following Wednesday, 10 September, taking some skin from the top of the thigh, and then placing the foot in plaster for a few days.

Payment might have been a severe problem: the operation and charges for nursing care at the clinic would swallow up at least £500;[181] and Robert's finances were at another low ebb. However, he had managed to borrow a substantial sum of money from Ricardo Sicré;[182] and once William was happily settled into the clinic, Robert began spending a good part of each day working on a novel: not *The She-Admiral*, for which he and Kubler were still busy researching;[183] but his 'Utopia' novel.

The circumstances for doing so were both practically and emotionally favourable. Practically, because the 'Utopia' novel by its very nature required no reference books, and because for the time being, apart from sitting in the clinic at William's bedside, Robert had no domestic responsibilities of any kind; and emotionally, because Graves was so far removed from the world in which he normally lived. His friend Richard Hughes once declared that an author writes best not about what is under his nose, but about what is under his skin; and in the course of this novel Graves analyzed with appropriately clinical precision the exact nature of his own emotional needs.

Watch the North Wind Rise (as the novel would be called in its American edition; the English bore the more prosaic title *Seven Days in New Crete*) tells how the English poet Edward Venn-Thomas, a Gravesian clone, is transported from his own time to a date in the remote future. His hosts, experts in primitive magic, have summoned him to their 'New Cretan Epoch' so that they can learn from him about the 'Late-Christian epoch' to which he belonged but which ended when it was realized that mankind must either perish, or replace the masculine principle with the feminine. So, although New Crete is divided into kingdoms, the 'real gold crowns' of the kings are 'entrusted to them by their queens'.[184] The 'governing principle'[185] is a custom based 'not on a code of laws, but for the most part on the inspired utterances of poets; that is to say, it's dictated by the Muse, who is the Goddess';[186] and the system as a whole is maintained by women, who 'act directly on behalf of the Goddess', and are 'naturally' treated by men as the superior sex.[187]

This is a society living in harmony with the natural world; and each individual is allocated to one of the 'five Estates' not by birth, but by capacity.[188] Money has been abolished; different villages have different social customs, so that one may live in a monogamous, polygamous, or polyandrous society and yet be perfectly virtuous; there are even 'bagnios', brothels which it is no disgrace to visit, and 'where one goes when one isn't in love with anyone in particular but feels unhappily lecherous';[189] while war has become ritualized into a kind of moderately violent rugger, so that the only deaths, apart from those by natural causes, occur as part of the ritual of goddess-worship.

It is a sane society, and yet something important is missing. The New Cretans lack 'the quality that we prize as character: the look of indomitability which comes from dire experiences nobly faced and overcome'; they have no sense of humour; and the atmosphere, 'if it could be acclimatized in an evil epoch like ours', says Venn-Thomas, 'would be described as goody-goody, a word that conveys a reproach of complacency and indifference to the sufferings of the world'.[190]

However the Goddess, just like the Tennysonian God of Graves's youth, fulfils herself 'in many ways,/Lest one good custom should corrupt the world'; and Venn-Thomas discovers that he has been deliberately introduced into this apparently idyllic society to be 'a seed of trouble, to endow you with a harvest of trouble, since true love and wisdom spring only from calamity'.[191] So Graves's 'Utopia' novel ultimately turns out to be a ferocious attack upon all so-called Utopian visions of society.

Along the way there is a great deal of searching self-analysis. Soon after his arrival in New Crete, Venn-Thomas begins to fall in love with Sapphire, a seventeen-year-old nymph who tells him that he is:

> the sort of man to hold nothing back when you fall in love; and that's right. But you're content to go on seeing what you first saw. Has it ever happened that the woman who was pleased by the first image of herself in your eyes grew dissatisfied when she found that it didn't change as she changed?

She adds that since Venn-Thomas has never been out of love 'for more than a miserable few days', he will always, when necessary, 'look around for a fresh focus of your love'. To which he agrees, explaining that he 'can't love a woman unless I can convince myself, in spite of all my previous failures, that I'll love her for the rest of my life. So I try to see her always as I saw her first. A deception, perhaps, but that's my way.'[193]

When Sapphire asks whether it was unkind of the New Cretans to have fetched him here without his wife, Antonia, Venn-Thomas answers somewhat inconsequentially that he 'can really love only one woman at a time'. 'But her time and my time aren't the same', Sapphire replies. 'You can still love her faithfully all your life, and love me as long as you please.'[194] Venn-Thomas is forced to the conclusion that 'the theory of marriage doesn't correspond in the least with the facts'; that it is possible for a man to love different women at the same time and yet 'in entirely different ways';[195] and he learns from Sapphire that the consummation of love can be separated from the reproductive process; and that those in the New Cretan 'magician' class are not physically promiscuous. They 'avoid congress' unless they want children; and at all other times:

> consummation is achieved by a marriage of mind and body, while the reproductive organs are quiescent but our inner eyes are flooded with waves of light. In cases of complete sympathy we lie side by side ... and our spirits float upward and drift in a weaving motion around the room.[196]

When they *do* want children, they mentally 'remove, and our bodies remain locked in torment far below us'.

The plot had reached approximately this point on Tuesday 9 September when Robert Graves was visited by Alan Hodge, who found him 'at ease and working well on *Utopia*'.[197] Alan had been spending a week in Deyá, giving Beryl moral support while Robert was away;[198] and after calling in at Barcelona on his way back to England, he reported to Beryl that he liked the look of the clinic; that William had put on weight and looked happy; that the nurses had been exercising his legs 'most impressively'; that the doctor had 'found all sorts of pebbles in the wound and it's all the better for having them out'; and that the skin-grafting operation was planned for the following day.[199]

In the meantime, he added his voice to Robert's in urging Beryl to come over to Barcelona, share William's room in the clinic, and have the minor operation she had needed for so long. 'I really think that would be sensible', Alan told her. 'No wonder you were shattered by last winter when you were losing so much blood – and you anaemic anyway. I do think you ought to fall in with R's suggestion.'

The skin-grafting operation was a success, and by the following Tuesday, 16 September, Robert was telling Beryl that William was:

> very well again though with not much of an appetite yet, a bit of ether being still in his blood ... Gaburro says William can go for a car ride on Sunday if he likes ... Now I must do some more *Utopia*. Sapphire

hasn't been active in the recent chapter, which is about schools and so on ...

'I miss you and love you', he added, 'but I am all right. I sleep well and only wish I could take more exercise especially in going to the sea though I do like my hot baths here.'[200]

As he began the sixth chapter of *Watch the North Wind Rise*, Graves continued with his ruthless self-examination. (Later, he would be mildly embarrassed by the precision with which he had taken a scalpel to his personal predilections, and dismiss one of his most interesting novels by saying: 'Don't like it, really, it smells too much of the Barcelona clinic where I wrote it'.[201])

First he inspected his relationship with Laura Riding, who appears here thinly disguised as 'Erica Turner', a 'half-American' (and one of the manifestations of the Mother Goddess) with whom Venn-Thomas has once had a passionate love affair, but who 'had not only treated me foully but managed at the same time to put me in the wrong and make me feel a thorough heel, before suddenly breaking with me and going off with a man I detested and despised'. In a veiled reference to Laura's having immorally kept some royalties of Robert's which had been sent to her in error soon after their break-up, Venn-Thomas adds that she withdrew 'all the money from our joint account ... and left me flat'.[202]

Next, Graves/Venn-Thomas compared his feelings for Laura/Erica with his feelings for Beryl/Antonia. 'To be precise', says Venn-Thomas,

> had I ever loved Antonia, who was a one-man woman, as much as I had loved Erica, a queen-bee if ever there was one? Not as intensely perhaps, not as insanely certainly, and how else can one measure love, except by its intensity and insanity? But then I had never hated Antonia even for a moment, as I had hated Erica quite half the time we were together.

So Antonia has his heart; but Venn-Thomas nervously recalls 'the old days' when Erica could 'switch ... on and off at pleasure ... an almost phosphorescent aura of sexuality that etherealised her not at all faultless features'. When it was 'in full swing', Venn-Thomas had been 'at her mercy'; but now he:

> greatly hoped that she had lost the knack ... There was a peace in my love for Antonia, peace and confidence, which I wanted never to be

disturbed. Antonia was good, in the simplest sense of the word, and with a quiet constructive humour;

'Erica', on the other hand, 'was evil, with a beautifully destructive wit that matched the intense dislike I felt for my age.'[203]

Towards the end of September 1947, Robert and Beryl changed places at Barcelona. Beryl joined William in the clinic where, much to Robert's relief, she had agreed to have her operation; while Robert, 'after a frightful crossing' to Palma, was soon back at Canelluñ,[204] where he looked after Lucia and Juan, and continued working on *Watch the North Wind Rise*.

It was not long before Beryl and William had rejoined him. Both mother and son made an excellent recovery;[20] and by mid-October William was able to go for short walks in the garden, now producing such vast quantities of walnuts and figs that the children were said to be 'chiefly living' on them. By this time, too, Robert's latest financial crisis had been 'relieved', as Amy retailed, 'by the enthusiastic reception by the Penguin book people to his translation of *The Golden Ass*';[206] the contract was 'far better' than he had expected and, as he told Ricardo, he was hoping for 'a big sale' in the USA, 'for all the wrong reasons; it certainly is full of obscenity as well as religion'.[207]

In the meantime, there was exciting news from London about Alan Hodge. He had stayed on in Norman Cameron's flat after Norman's marriage to Gretl; but had inevitably begun to feel something of an outsider. Now, however, there had been a dramatic improvement in his life.

It happened like this. Bill Chapman of *Time* magazine had received a telephone call from Alan, announcing rather gloomily that he was back in London; and so Bill, as he later recalled, invited Alan to look in on him, mentioning that he had:

a whole bottle of Irish whiskey. Alan came up and we drank it, naturally. The following day Jane Aiken [one of Bill's colleagues, and the daughter of Conrad Aiken the American poet] said: 'Can you have dinner with me and my step-mother tonight. She has a friend arrived in town and she would like you to meet him. His name is Alan Hodge.' I put my hand to my aching head and said: 'I know him very well.'[208]

So that evening Alan met Jane for the first time 'in the York Minster pub in Lower Dean Street. After which', according to Bill, they all 'wound up in a joint called the Gargoyle, where Hodge and Jane seemed to have taken a deep look into each other's eyes and have never been the same since'. They were very soon engaged to be married, and it was announced that the wedding ceremony would take place on 3 January 1948.[209]

Robert Graves himself was 'very busy' during December. *Watch the North Wind Rise* had been laid aside while he worked 'on revised proofs of *The White Goddess*. It is a pity', he told Joshua Podro, 'that there's no room for a lot of new mythological discoveries I have made'.[210] He had also drawn up an outline for his proposed novel about Ysabel de Barreto; and by the beginning of January 1948 he and his collaborator Dr Kubler had signed a contract for *The She-Admiral* with Doubleday.[211]

When news of this contract reached Creative Age, they were extremely upset. Having agreed to publish *The White Goddess*, they felt they had a right to Graves's more commercial works; and they wrote telling him that 'rightly or wrongly ... we are your American publishers ... we surely feel that we have first claim to you'. Graves, who had been lured away from Creative Age by the prospect of a substantial advance, wrote to them to explain his precarious financial position, and to remind them that he had promised them his 'Utopia' novel, of which Watt would shortly be forwarding an outline and some sample material.[212]

Not long after returning the final portion of the corrected proofs of *The White Goddess* to T. S. Eliot, Robert Graves congratulated him on having been named in the 1948 New Years Honours List as a member of the Order of Merit: a substantial honour, which Graves came to believe was Eliot's divine reward for having accepted *The White Goddess* for publication.

Neither Jonathan Cape nor Desmond Flower of Cassell appear to have suffered from any divine retribution for having rejected the work, but unpleasant things had certainly happened to others, and Graves would later take a keen delight in recounting how he had:

offered *The White Goddess* in turn to the only publishers I knew who claimed to be personally concerned with poetry and mythology.

The first [Charles Williams of the Oxford University Press] regretted he could not recommend this unusual book to his partners, because of the expense. He died of heart failure within the month.

The second [an un-named American publisher] wrote very discourteously, to the effect that he could not make either head or tail of the book, and could not believe it would interest anyone. He died too, soon afterwards [having] dressed himself up in a woman's panties and bra one afternoon, and hanged himself from a tree in his garden. ['I saw the White Goddess's terrible hand in that' wrote Graves in another version of the story, 'but never found what sort of tree it was. Yew? Elder?']213

But the third, who was T. S. Eliot, wrote that it must be published at all costs.

'So he did publish it', Graves concluded, 'and not only got his money back, but pretty soon was rewarded with the Order of Merit, the Nobel Prize for Literature, and a smash hit on Broadway.'214

Publication of *The White Goddess*, in May 1948 in England and a few months later in the USA, brought mixed reviews.215 The reaction of the BBC producer Rayner Heppenstall was typical. After reading a set of page proofs in March, he had told Graves frankly that *The White Goddess* was 'not an easy book in its present form. I have alternated between thinking it the definitive poet's Bible and thinking it preposterous';216 and many other reviewers were equally baffled.

In England there was a handful of excellent notices, including one in the *Sunday Times* by James Laver;217 while in the USA, the vice-president of Creative Age declared himself 'much amused' to see:

the diffidence and fright with which the reviewers approached the book. They were obviously (even as I) scared out of their pants at the thought of saying something stupid so they circled round Hecate making tentative and, they hoped, acceptable salaams.

'The book', he added, 'has terrific admirers and also detractors ... Katherine Anne Porter and Thomas Sugrue ... think it a very great work', while 'Prescott of the [*New York*] *Times* loathed it.'218

Laura Riding, fully aware of her own crucial role in the development of Graves's thinking on the subject of *The White Goddess*, was utterly furious. As her biographer writes:

The wickedness of this book, she claimed, lay not only in the large-scale appropriation of her thought ... The centre of his travesty had been in the assassination of her self and the human truth of her being, and the distortion of the human wisdoms and cosmic realities that belonged to herself alone.219

'Where once she had reigned', Riding concluded, 'now a whorish abomination had sprung to life, a Frankenstein pieced together from the shards of her life and thought.' However she made no direct approach to Graves on the subject, and although he had recently heard of her, it was in quite another context.

Margaret Russell, a former employee who had remained a friend, had written to tell him that Dorothy and Montagu Simmons and their two children had sailed to America to join Laura Riding and Schuyler Jackson on their farm at Wabasso. 'They have a bungalow near the Jacksons', Margaret had reported,

> and are now in the throes of grapefruit picking and packing for export ... I feel they have done the wrong move, but I am such a stick-in-the-mud I may be wrong. Time will tell. Montagu threw up his job at the Home Office and had just been earning £1,700 a year and would have had a pension of £1,000 a year which is security these days.[220]

Margaret's instinct proved to be correct. Having 'come as friends', Dorothy and Montagu were 'treated like slaves';[221] and within a few months, as Robert learned, 'A frightful bust-up ensued ... [Dorothy]'s now had to ask Papa to send her the return fare for herself and the children, while Montagu washes dishes somewhere in the hopes of rejoining her.'[222]

All this time, Robert had been hard at work on *Watch the North Wind Rise*; he was also, as he told James Reeves in mid-May 1948, 'working on a mythical ballet with [the Catalan artist] Joan Junyer by correspondence'; with Karl's help he had completed a collection of his essays on poetry which would be published as *The Common Asphodel* the following year; he was putting in order 'all my short stories, plays and miscellaneous essays (of any interest)' for another possible volume;[223] and he had seen through the press his *Collected Poems: 1914–1947*.

Once again he had gone over his previously published work with a critical eye, liberally discarding and revising. The most notable additions, apart from the whole of his recent *Poems: 1938–1945*,[225] were a group of poems related to *The White Goddess*, including 'The Battle of the Trees', 'The Song of Blodeuwedd', and the haunting 'Nuns and Fish', which runs:

> Circling the circlings of their fish
>   Nuns walk in white and pray;
>   For he is chaste as they,
>   Who was dark-faced and hot in Silvia's day,
> And in his pool drowns each unspoken wish.[225]

By the beginning of June 1948, Graves was writing the final chapters of *Watch the North Wind Rise*. By this stage of the book, Edward Venn-Thomas faces serious conflicts of loyalty. It has been easy enough for him to decide that he loves the 'good' Antonia far more than the 'evil' Erica; but his situation is complicated not only by his feelings for Sapphire, but also by the presence in New Crete of Sally, a witch with the same sexual allure as Erica. She wants him so badly that when he rejects her, having, he declares, 'finished with that for ever',[226] she outwits him and lures him into bed by impersonating his wife.

Graves solves Venn-Thomas's dilemma as best he can, first by engineering Sally's death, and then by making Sapphire return with Venn-Thomas to the twentieth century, where she is to be reborn as his daughter. A kind of loyalty to Antonia has been preserved; and yet this part of the novel feels very contrived. The emotional truth is that Graves was subconsciously tiring of a domesticity which he sensed was inimical to his poetic genius; and in the final chapter he makes Venn-Thomas cry out: 'Blow, North wind, blow! Blow away security; lift the ancient roofs from their beams; tear the rotten boughs from the alders, oaks and quinces; break down the gates of the Moon House and set the madmen free ...' Which reads like a prophecy about the future of his own private life.

In the meantime, Graves was planning another visit to England, where Clarissa and their mother were now staying with Rosaleen, so that Amy could receive 'X-ray treatment' at a hospital in nearby Exeter. It had been discovered that she was suffering from 'a classical, obvious cancer of a slow-growing type';[227] and Robert, who had already offered to come up to Erinfa for two days in July,[228] now wrote to tell Amy that he wished her to meet 'his children and Beryl' while it was still possible.[229]

CHAPTER 7

At London Zoo

Amy Graves began her X-ray treatment at Exeter hospital on 9 May 1948;[230] and two weeks later, after six of a proposed fifteen treatments, Rosaleen reported that she was making good progress. Not only was the cancerous lump 'softer and smaller', but a chest X-ray showed that there were no secondaries in Amy's lungs; the doctors were, if anything, more worried about an enlarged thyroid which was displacing her windpipe.[231] Clarissa believed that Amy was not only 'standing the treatment & the rush & bustle of Rosaleen's world, remarkably well', but (having wanted to be a doctor herself when she was young) was thoroughly enjoying 'the medical atmosphere & talk of medical symptoms'.[232]

It was only when the fifteen treatments had been safely completed that Amy began to suffer from unpleasant side-effects. These included depression,[233] occasional vomiting and 'a troublesome jerk of her right arm' which made writing difficult and led her to 'feel suddenly old'.[234] Clarissa was not much better: the permanent loss of her home in Palestine had come as a shock so severe that, as Susan had already noticed, it had upset her always delicate mental balance.[235]

However, by the end of June both women were fit enough to travel up to London, where Robert, accompanied by Beryl and their three children, was due to arrive at Croydon airport on the evening of 30 June.[236] It had been arranged that he and his family should stay at '108 Clifton Hill NW8 (near Alma Square)' with his niece Sally Chilver;[237] and the following day there was a family meeting at London Zoo.[238]

'What an inspired place to choose,' Clarissa wrote afterwards to Robert, 'the London Zoo, where with monkeys pelicans & lions nobody could feel shy or ill at ease.'[239] In a later letter she explained that she herself had deliberately 'sat back & hardly said a word to you', since she realized that it might be his last meeting with their mother.[240] Robert and Amy spent two hours in conversation. 'It was such a pleasure to see your dear face again', Amy wrote on returning to Erinfa, '& to make the acquaintance of Beryl', whom she had found 'wonderfully bright & kind to the children, under difficult circumstances'. She had also been excited to meet three new grandchildren; but most thrilling of all was Robert's news that Beryl was 'so soon, we hope, to be made your legal wife'.[241]

Sam had recently finished at Cambridge,[242] and so Nancy had been able to put her fears of scandal to one side. Hearing of Amy's possibly terminal illness, and knowing how strongly she felt on the matter, may also have been a consideration. At any rate, as she herself told Amy when the two women met at Erinfa later that month, she had not only withdrawn her opposition to a divorce, but had positively instructed her solicitors to procure one 'if possible'.[243]

The next few weeks were spent in what Robert described as 'a wonderful whirl', whose 'high spots' included:

> supper with our friend Philip Harben, the Television cook ... Cricket at Rotten End ... where I batted not discreditably and did not miss any catches ... lunch with Agatha Christie; and the same day with T. S. Eliot ... Supper with Beryl's parents at the National Club – ourselves and nine Bishops – like an anti-room in a very shabby Protestant heaven ... Pottering round antique shops, and buying good clothes with dollar vouchers and no coupons, like rich Americans.[244]

They also saw Rosaleen,[245] dined at the Café Royal with George and Joanna Simon,[246] and were visited by Dorothy Simmons. She and Montagu were shortly to move to Kneesworth near Cambridge, where he was to run 'an experimental school for the most intelligent young delinquents'; and she told them that Wabasso already seemed 'like a bad dream of 100 years ago'.[247]

Finally, on 2 August, after a week's holiday at Oulton Broad in Norfolk, they flew home again to Majorca, where Robert settled down to work on his 'novel about the Solomon Islands and the Woman Admiral in 1595'.[248]

CHAPTER 8

The Isles of Unwisdom

As he began writing *The She-Admiral* in August 1948, Robert Graves skilfully set up dramatic conflicts between the greedy Dona Ysabel de Barreto and her saintly but largely ineffectual husband General Alvaro; between General Alvaro and Colonel Don Pedro Merino, the senior military officer of the expedition; and between those who wish to convert the natives of any colonized territories to Christianity, and those who simply wish to exploit the new lands for their precious metals.

But despite these conflicts, and despite occasional erotic asides (such as the fantasy of 'the blind girl of Panama', who feels her way over a soldier in uniform until she finds a 'concealed weapon' which he tries to explain away as 'a prime Bolognian sausage'), the first six chapters of Graves's narrative fail to catch fire. They were still lively enough to anger his collaborator Dr Kubler, who 'became temperamental and dissatisfied with the way Graves was handling the material', and 'took himself off'.[249]

With Kubler's departure, the quality of Graves's writing improved dramatically. When Alvaro founds a settlement on the island of Santa Cruz, the inevitable clash between the natives and the settlers is superbly described; as are the human follies which doom the settlement to failure.

Sadly however Dona Ysabel herself, despite her blue eyes, her wheat-coloured hair and her powerful personality, ultimately failed to capture Graves's interest, and she therefore fails to dominate the novel as he had intended. Ysabel de Barreto does not become admiral in her husband's place until the settlement is on the point of failure, and the novel is three-quarters complete; and when she finally obtains power, she uses it to little purpose: so that after a while Graves very sensibly changed his title from *The She-Admiral* to *The Isles of Unwisdom*.

By the beginning of December 1948 Graves was writing the final chapter of *The Isles of Unwisdom*;[250] the proofs of *Watch the North Wind Rise* had been dealt with (John Aldridge had once again agreed to do a jacket design[251]); and Rene had given birth to her first child by Karl: 'a very pretty, fat baby', Beryl told George and Joanna, 'who seems to me to be altogether perfect'. Robert added a postcript saying that although *The Isles of Unwisdom* was 'very carefully historical and lots of bloody and bawdy and exciting things happen', he was not at all sure about its overall success. 'Still', he concluded, 'it was a nice voyage'; and in any case, there was no time to discuss the matter further, as: 'I must fly – bath-time for … little Juan – Love Robert'.[252]

There followed a tedious dispute with Laura Riding. By the start of 1949 *The Common Asphodel* was already in page proof with Hamish Hamilton, who had offered sheets to Creative Age Press for an American publication. But unfortunately Graves had included a number of extracts from articles and books on which he had collaborated with Laura Riding; and although Riding had verbally surrendered her rights in all such work at the time of her separation from Graves (and Hamish Hamilton had accepted this), Eileen Garrett of Creative Age Press 'thought it "morally right" to ask Laura if she minded'. The result, as Graves explained to Alan Hodge, was that:

> Laura sent a long *megillah* – a good Jewish word for an immensely long tedious hair-splitting tract – saying that she wouldn't mind, if I used only excerpts from the books and printed them in an appendix in small print, with all sorts of promises and undertakings about the copyright (which would have been invalid in any case).[253]

At Garrett's request, Graves wrote personally to Riding; but she would not relent, and sent him what he described to Karl Gay in July as a 'nasty, complicated, silly letter'.[254] 'What a commander of a submarine she would have made!' commented the vice-president of Creative Age. 'I really can't see how either to get through her or around her.' The result was that there was no American publication of *The Common Asphodel*; and with this final exchange of letters, all direct communication between Robert Graves and Laura Riding ceased for ever.[255]

While Graves was embroiled in this dispute with Riding, he became engaged in another and much more fruitful correspondence which also took him back to the days when he had been living with her at Canelluñ.

It was generally agreed by classical historians that Claudius (the hero of Graves's most famous historical novels) had been murdered at the instigation of his wife Agrippina; and the three principal accounts of the crime all begin with the emperor being given a plate of poisoned mushrooms. From two of the sources, it appears that he saved himself 'either by vomiting or a great evacuation of the bowels', only to be given a second poison 'either by a gruel or enema'.

It was a story which fascinated both R. Gordon Wasson (a Wall Street banker with an expert knowledge of mushrooms) and his Russian-born wife Dr Valentina Wasson (a paediatrician). Together, as a labour of love, they were preparing a great work which would eventually appear in print as *Mushrooms, Russia and History*; and, for a separate paper, they were currently 'investigating Claudius's death from the mycological angle'.[256]

Dr Valentina Wasson therefore wrote to Robert Graves at the end of January 1949, suggesting that the dish of mushrooms given to Claudius probably consisted of the wholesome *Amanita caesarea*, with a small addition of the deadly poisonous *Amanita phalloides*, which would have caused symptons very similar to the ones described in the classical texts. Did the author of *Claudius the God* have any views on the subject?[257]

Yes, he had. At the end of his novel Graves had quoted Seneca's satire *The Apocolocyntosis of Claudius* which (*apocolocyntosis* being a word which combines *apotheosis* or deification, with *colycynthos* meaning a pumpkin), he had translated as *The Pumpkinification of Claudius*. However, Graves believed that 'Pumpkinification' was misleading, and he replied to this effect. In Greek, *colycynthos* also means the wild gourd, 'a useful purge in minimal doses', but also 'a powerful alkaline poison', and he thought it likely that Claudius had been poisoned by wild gourd which had been added to his mushrooms.[258]

After a further exchange of letters, in which Gordon Wasson joined, it was agreed that Claudius had first been poisoned by *Amanita phalloides*, whose symptoms, described in repulsive detail, tallied with some of the historical accounts,[259] and then 'finish[ed] ... off with a colocynth clyster [an enema]';[260] and in March Gordon Wasson declared that 'the Claudius episode will appear as Appendix 1 to our paper. We are proud to add to our theory your brilliant suggestion concerning colocynth.'[261]

However, this was only the beginning of their correspondence. There was evidence that the eating of special mushrooms was a vital part of initiation into the mysteries of ancient religious cults; and both Graves and the Wassons shared a fascination for this subject which led to a friendship lasting for almost twenty years.

In February 1949 there was sad news from England. A letter from Amy announced that Robert's half-sister Molly had died on 13 February at the age of seventy-one. Amy enclosed a letter from John with details of the funeral, and told him that the Sister Supervisor had said of Molly: 'She

was a good Christian woman & glad to be called home.'[262] Robert had
seen little of Molly in recent years, chiefly because of her ill-health; but
she had been a loyal and affectionate correspondent, and he had never
forgotten that when he had been a child at Red Branch House in
Wimbledon, Molly had loved and tended him like a second mother;[263] so
now he sent Amy a long letter saying how much he had always loved Molly
in return.[264]

The following month there was another death which touched Robert
closely: that of Juan Marroig Más, Gelat, the delightful rogue who had
been a friend and ally (of a kind) for the better part of twenty years.[265] The
whole of Deyá was at his funeral, not to mention bus-loads from Palma
and Valldemossa; and Beryl reported that 'Three masses were said, which
had a very soothing effect on the relatives; but then the whole
congregation had to file past and offer condolences which of course
reduced them all to tears again.'[266] More seriously, as Robert told Cecily
Gittes:

> Before Gelat died they gave him a lot of morphia so he didn't quite
> know what he was saying and persuaded himself that I had given him all
> that land below the house ... at any rate, he bequeathed it to his wife for
> her lifetime and then to the daughters. I can't bring myself to
> disillusion the wife that he gave her what wasn't his ...[267]

Which left Robert's ownership more tenous than ever.

Money remained tight; but there was encouraging news in March from
America, where *Watch the North Wind Rise* was published to very good
reviews.[268] And by that time, having completed *The Isles of Unwisdom*,
Graves was doing more work with Karl on a volume of stories, plays and
miscellaneous essays, which he had decided to call *Occupation: Writer*. He
was also helping Ricardo Sicré with *The Tap on the Left Shoulder*,[269] the
novel based closely upon Ricardo's war-time experiences; and he was
seriously considering a very much more scholarly work, as a follow-up to
King Jesus.

Joshua Podro, now back in London, had sent him a number of detailed
criticisms of that novel; and the result was that the two men were thinking
about collaborating upon a major piece of historical research into the life
of Jesus, whose 'real story' they both considered had been thoroughly
obscured in the New Testament.[270]

CHAPTER 9

The Nazarene Gospel Restored

Robert Graves and Joshus Podro arranged to meet in London in July 1949 to discuss their ideas; but Robert had already written a sample analysis of one of the New Testament parables, and he was carrying it with him in June when he and Beryl took their children to Portofino, the fishing village which Mussolini had declared a national monument.[271]

This was not just a holiday, but a reunion with family and friends. Tom and Julie Matthews' sons were staying in an hotel on the village square; while Robert and Beryl and their children occupied a house about halfway up the headland, at whose highest point, some nine hundred feet above the sea, Tom and Julie themselves were staying with Jenny and Alex in the Castelletto. Described by Tom as 'surely one of the most beautifully placed houses in the world', the Castelletto overlooks:

> Portofino's miniature harbour and the hillsides behind it, the Bay of Rapallo and the whole sweep of sea towards Spezia on one side and San Fruttuoso and Genoa on the other. Most of the house itself is carved out of the solid rock, with two turret-like rooms – an octagonal living room and a spare bedroom –emerging from the walled terrace that is also the roof of the house below.

For the three days of Tom and Julie's visit, there was:

> a continuous round of lunches, cocktail parties and dinners. Robert was in great form. He announced happily that this was the first time he had ever been in Italy – in spite of all he had written about the Romans – and that he liked it.

However, there was a serious aspect to the holiday.

After one of the lunch parties, Robert asked Tom to read the analysis of a parable that he had brought with him; and Tom took it back to his room. 'I think, but can't be sure', he wrote later, that the parable in question was the one about the unjust steward; I do remember that Robert had recast it so that the moral was just the opposite of what it had been. Robert's assertion was that he had *restored* the parable to its original and proper form; that the reason why it had come down to us in a corrupt version was that some enemy had tampered with the original manuscript and had turned the meaning of Christ's words upside down.

Tom was privately a little alarmed by the prospect of Robert bringing his idiosyncratic brand of scholarship to bear upon the Christian faith. *King Jesus* had been acceptable as a novel; but the project which Robert was now contemplating would need to be taken seriously by the academic world, and it stood little chance of that, however brilliant its insights, if Robert was determined to apply his 'analeptic thought' to filling the numerous gaps in the evidence. However, Tom had no wish to damage his friendship with Robert, so when asked his opinion of the sample material, he confined himself to saying that: 'I preferred the original version.'

Later, as Tom records, when he and Julie and their children were being given a farewell lunch, and:

the whole party [were] sitting at a long table on the piazza in front of the Nazionale ... I sat next to Robert, who was not feeling well and had little to say. But at one point he turned to me with his characteristic sigh and said,

'I don't think you could ever do anything I would really mind.'

Tom was 'surprised and touched. "Why, Robert," I said, "what makes you think that?" ' To which Robert replied characteristically: '*I* don't know.'

After the Matthewses had left, there was a brief visit from Charles Graves, who learned that his brother had turned down 'a year's job at Princeton, U.S.A.'[273] – perhaps Tom had been trying to divert him from his work on the Gospels; Robert also went over to Rapallo 'to see Max Beerbohm whom I hadn't seen since 1919 and we renewed our conversation from that point';[274] and then at the beginning of July Robert and Beryl and their family moved on to London. There they rented, from some friends of Sally's,[275] 21 Maunsel Street, 'a nice little house not far from Westminster School' with 'a tiny back garden',[276] and within walking distance of the River Thames.[277]

As on their visit to London the previous year, they managed to see many of their friends, including George and Joanna Simon, who now had a second daughter, Julia, a big healthy baby born on 13 March 1949.[278] Sally was a frequent visitor; and Martin Seymour-Smith was 'invaluable';[279] but, as Robert complained to Karl and Rene, there were 'Too many people to see: talk, talk, talk all day'; and a 'frightful heat-wave worse than any in Majorca because of the dirt and the impossibility of having sea-bathes or going about naked'.[280]

While he was in London Graves also recorded a wireless broadcast in which he read seven of his poems, and analyzed the Parable of the Talents;[280] and subsequently, he had what he described to Seymour-Smith as 'a wonderful evening with [Podro] who's enthusiastic about working with me on the Sayings of J[esus]'.[281] This was followed up by a meeting with T. S. Eliot, whom he was hoping to interest in publishing the proposed work.

Oddly enough, he took nine-year-old William with him. Eliot, warned in advance of William's visit, had bought a horse-racing game for the occasion, and became so involved in it himself that for a while he seemed to have forgotten that Robert was waiting to talk to him. When the serious conversation began, 'Eliot immediately expressed his amazement at the power he found in *The White Goddess*, and praised the poem "In Dedication".' He then expressed particular admiration for the poem beginning: 'Circling the circlings of their fish,/ Nuns walk in white and pray', rising from his chair and exclaiming:

> That's certainly real poetry, the real thing! But what does it mean, and how on earth did you do it?
>
> Graves, pleased, shrugged his shoulders modestly and muttered, 'Don't know, don't know. It's there. I saw it.'[283]

However, Eliot 'seemed anxious to turn aside any discussion about Graves's forthcoming Jesus book ... commenting sardonically that he would of course be interested to read it – and that he hoped it might be rather 'dry' 'if the Faith were to survive'.[284]

On Monday July 1949, Robert caught the night train for north Wales. To his sorrow, he went alone. He had been hoping to introduce his second family to Harlech; but although it was clear that his divorce from Nancy would be going through very soon, Amy felt unable to have Beryl and the children under her roof until everything was settled.[285] Robert retaliated by refusing to come up for his fifty-fourth birthday, as Amy had asked;[286] and by staying only from Tuesday morning until twelve noon on Thursday.[287]

It was not an easy visit, as Amy found Robert 'far from well',[288] and reported to John that he:

> had a tooth drawn the root of which was worrying him still & he was continually working at with a tooth pick, & in his last half hour with pliers, as I had not the toilet pincers he asked me for & the nail scissors only cut off a bit of loose bone. This was enough to spoil any visit, but he had some good sleep & said he had a good time here & 'felt fine'. We could not give him a bath in the house [because of a drought] and his cough prevented his bathing in the sea.[289]

Robert had also brought a good deal of work with him; Amy found him 'rather difficult to understand for his speech is hesitating'; and she was a little offended when he insisted on 'see[ing] Susan and Kenneth *alone*'.[290] However, before leaving he told her that she was 'looking better than last year', which cheered her up; and he also presented her with a good ham, which had arrived in the post while he was at Erinfa, as a present from one of his American publishers.[291]

At the beginning of August, Robert and Beryl spent a few days with Dorothy and Montagu Simmons at Kneesworth Hall,[292] from where Robert wrote an encouraging letter to Joshua Podro, thanking him for his recent hard work, and adding:

> I don't know how our collaboration will work, but I'm sure that we'll come to a firm conclusion on details since we agree in principle. This is a job that should have been undertaken long, long ago. If properly documented it is bound to make itself felt as an influence in separating the idea of Jesus from the idea of the Man-god-ethics in fact, from myth.

Graves concluded that there was 'a place for both in this world, but not confused together as in the Gospels'.[293]

A few days later,[294] Graves and his family returned to Deyá, where he threw himself into full-time work on what he had provisionally entitled *The Hand of Simon Magus*: because, as he told Cecily Gittes, 'the gospel editor who tampered most with the story was evidently a Samaritan, like the wicked Simon, mentioned in Acts VIII, ii.'[295] First he 'soak[ed] [him]self in the subject', to 'get ... a clearer picture of the technique of distortion';[296] and then he began his more detailed investigations. He found it 'intensely interesting', declared that 'the great thing is to write as dispassionately as possible', and told Podro movingly that his ambition was 'to stop Jesus from writhing endlessly on that Cross; to give his spirit rest'.[297]

Undertaken with the best of motives, pursued with a rare insight into so many obscure crevices of scholarship that its findings would often be confirmed years later by more orthodox scholars, it was nevertheless a sadly misconceived task; it involved intensely hard work ('nearly eight hours a day', he told Eliot in May 1950 when a first draft had been completed[298]); and it occupied Graves for much of the next two years.

The closing months of 1949 saw Beryl having another minor operation, this time for the removal of an ovary,[299] 'after which', as Robert told several correspondents in September, she was 'promised good health in perpetuum'.[300] The doctors were right about the improvement in her health. For the first time since she and Robert had begun a family, Beryl was able to play a full and energetic part in family life. This, in Karl's view, had profound consequences, for it released Robert from enough of his domestic burden to give him a margin of freedom in his private life.[301] Ironically, this happened just at the time when, with Robert's divorce from Nancy finally coming through on 18 November 1949,[302] Robert and Beryl were at last able to think seriously about getting married.

In the wider family, these months saw the birth of a fourth child and second son, Robert George, to Catherine Dalton;[303] they saw Dick, with whom Robert had been enjoying an occasional correspondence, taking up a new appointment in the administration of the international zone in Tangier;[304] and they saw John, now with two sons, three-year-old Richard and two-year-old Simon, preparing for a move to Sandroyd School, in the heart of Cranborne Chase. There, if all went well, he could look forward to becoming Assistant Headmaster, though this knowledge would be kept secret at first from the other members of staff, and Amy wrote to Robert begging him not to address envelopes to his brother with any special title which might give the game away.[305]

Tragically, these months also brought news that Julie Matthews was dying of cancer:[306] news which, as the philandering Tom would later record with searing honesty, brought out all her courage and all his guilt;[307] and which inspired Robert to write his poem 'Counting The Beats',[308] which ends:

> Counting the beats,
> Counting the slow heart beats,
> The bleeding to death of time in slow heart beats,
> Wakeful they lie.[309]

Julie died in December 1949; and then early in 1950 came more bad news: Amy's breast cancer had flared up again, so that in March she had to stay with Rosaleen for a further course of treatment at Exeter.[310] Of late, she and Robert had been writing very tenderly to each other. 'Dearest Robert,' she began on one occasion,

> Your last letter gave me great pleasure, for in it you told me that you thought of me, one way or another, every day, as you supposed I did of you. Yes, you are right. I may have told you so too. Motherhood is a very strong bond.[311]

And she was very much cheered when Robert told her that he and Beryl would be getting married at last on 11 May. 'It was a particularly nice wedding at the Consulate', Beryl wrote shortly afterwards. 'Lake was very sweet and married us in a firm and dignified way I hadn't expected of him. We had lots of flowers and two bottles of champagne.' Norman and Gretl Cameron were the witnesses; and those present included Karl and Rene, the Podros, who had arrived from England that morning; and some other friends who had sailed to Palma in their own yacht. So the wedding was followed by a party 'on board the yacht Rosalind which was lovely and we then adjourned to the fish market and had a large fish paella followed by strawberry and cream ices at the Bar Formentor'.[312]

That summer there was another brief holiday in Portofino.[313] Robert and Beryl stayed in the Castelletto, while the children boarded with a local family; and their stay was memorable because of their meeting with Jenny's novelist friend Selwyn Jepson (working on one of his thrillers in Jenny's garden shed) and his Russian wife Tania, a remarkable woman who as a girl had been rescued from the Russian Revolution by a diplomat, risen to be headgirl of Cheltenham Ladies' College, and finally built up a small but successful antiquarian book business.[314] They also overlapped for a couple of days with Diccon and Frances Hughes, and Diccon was in fine form, playing the kind of apparently dangerous games which frightened parents and made children adore him, such as getting Juan to jump into the water without asking whether he could swim.[315]

The Graveses' visit to Portofino was followed by a month in England, where at first they stayed with Rosaleen.[316] Robert was disappointed that Amy had not remained in Devon until their arrival, but when her course of treatment had begun to make her feel really unwell, she had hurried back to Harlech.[317] There her nervous depression was slightly alleviated when, on doctor's orders, she began drinking a large tablespoon of sherry each day after lunch;[318] and there she was visited by Robert.

Jenny had driven him up to north Wales on Tuesday 11 July, and had dropped him off at Erinfa shortly after midnight. 'I was packed off to bed as usual', Amy reported to John,

> but just saw [Robert] … Jenny [went on to stay] with Diccon Hughes & his wife. She had asked to stay here at the last, but Clarissa took the call & said we could not. I was much ashamed, but it would have been difficult, with [Fred Taylor, a tramp whom Clarissa had temporarily installed in the garage] colour-washing the end room & Mrs. Janet [the cook] feeling too busy. No one could have been sweeter than she (Jenny) was when she came to lunch on Wednesday with us & her father …[319]

On Wednesday, she and Robert were invited to tea by Diccon and Frances, who were presented with a copy of Robert's recently published *The Isles of Unwisdom*.[320] On Thursday Jenny came to lunch, after which, as Amy continued in her letter to John, Robert and his daughter:

> left … to get to London that night & to meet his wife & 3 children on the day following. I had a very nice time with Robert, discussing his aramaic discoveries of the life of Jesus … Yr. brother Robert is far from irreligious …[321]

To Robert himself she wrote not long after his departure: 'I was glad to see that some of your Biblical studies have made you see still more of the beauty and wisdom of the words of Jesus, our Lord.'[322]

Robert for his part had been pleasantly surprised to find Amy outwardly so well; but, as he wrote to Rosaleen shortly afterwards, he was shocked by the extent to which Clarissa appeared to have taken control. Rosaleen, after making a short visit of her own to Erinfa, replied that their mother's general health was certainly good; but the cancer had now spread to at least four outlying colonies, so her days were numbered. As for Clarissa:

> I told her she must relax more and get more sleep – interfere less with Mother's house (she took down and rearranged all Mother's pictures at 8.30 a.m. one day) & clutter her life less with lame dogs. Claree certainly dominates Mother …

But to that Rosaleen saw 'no remedy … Even if we could find a suitable nurse-companion whom Mother could boss … where could Claree go?

At the beginning of August 1950, Robert Graves and Joshua Podro went to see T. S. Eliot.[323] It was a meeting which had been pencilled in back in May, when Podro had been working with Robert Graves in Deyá, and Graves had written to Eliot about:

> [my] collaboration with my learned Talmudic friend Joshua Podro on the book I promised you – the recension of the Gospels ... I have been writing at the Graeco-Roman end; he at the Aramaic-Hebraic-Syraic end. Our findings dovetail exactly. It is a very long, very readable, very strange book [*margin note*: I have had to abandon a good deal of what I wrote in *King Jesus*, which was a novel not a historical work] and we claim to have solved on sound historical lines, with every sentence documented, all the outstanding Gospel *cruces*.

Graves had admitted that this was 'a very large claim'; but assured Eliot that they were proceeding 'from what is historically certain to what is certainly un-historical', that all was being done 'in close argument', and that Podro would soon be checking 'meticulous Talmudic points with Dr. Epstein, the translater of the Talmud in English'; while 'Dr. Patai, the head of the Department of Folklore and Ethnology of the Hebrew University at Jerusalem, now in New York, is checking a few specialist chapters concerned with the Nativity and Baptism'.

Graves had then challenged Eliot to a meeting at which he should produce some Church of England dignitary:

> armed with certain knotty questions about, say, three selected texts. If the solutions to these set questions contained in our book can be shown erroneous, inadequate or historically unsound, then obviously you'll not want to publish; but if they stand up to scrutiny, even though heretical from a Catholic point of view, you'll probably want to publish.

And if Eliot could not 'decide in a two hours' test whether or not it is a *Faber* book, then we'll go elsewhere ... Is this fair?'[324]

Eliot had been cautiously interested, which had unfortunately led Graves to assume that publication by Faber was assured;[325] but now, in the course of his meeting with Graves and Podro, and in subsequent correspondence after Graves had returned with his family to Deyá, he explained that he would need to see the entire text and submit it to experts 'capable of judging the scholarly value of the work' before he could come to any definite decision.[326]

Graves realized that this might be a stumbling block. ' "Scholarly value" ' he replied, 'is of course a double-edged expression ... But at least no single sentence is undocumented, and if this is what is meant by scholarship, then there you are.'[327]

Uncertainty about the future of a work over which he had already laboured, without an advance, for the past fifteen months, helped to make it a difficult autumn. There was more bad news from England, where Amy's condition deteriorated to such an extent that she needed another set of X-ray treatments. There were also domestic worries about the children's education: now that William was already eleven years old, Robert decided that he should be prepared for the Common Entrance examination (usually taken at the age of thirteen), which would enable him to study at an English public school. For this, a tutor was needed; and Robert's first choice was W.S. or 'Bill' Merwin, a handsome twenty-two-year-old graduate of Princeton who 'contributes to the *Hudson Review* a lot',[328] and had published a poem in the *New Yorker*. Merwin was now installed by Robert in the Posada (his magnificent property by the village church) with his wife Dorothy, a delightful Irish–American redhead who had worked as a secretary to put him through college.[329]

There were also barely noticeable but nevertheless important alterations in the relationship between Robert and Beryl. These stemmed first from Beryl's improved health, which made her less physically dependent upon Robert in their ordinary domestic routine; and second, from their wedding which, as is usual when two people marry after living together for many years, had affected them more strongly than they had expected. Everything was so much more secure and settled: which did not suit Robert at all. Like Venn-Thomas, part of him was crying out: 'Blow, North wind, blow! Blow away security; lift the ancient roofs from their beams'; and he was already beginning to search out the 'other woman' upon whom he knew that his creativity depended.

Earlier in the year, Robert Graves had briefly taken a slight interest in a young widow of twenty-four who had been introduced to him by the local midwife;[331] then in September Jacquetta Hawkes, the author and archaeologist (now Mrs J. B. Priestley), had visited Deyá, and had left 'with a heart stirred – only very gently but', as she wrote to Robert afterwards, sending him a selection of her poems, 'the stirring somewhere rather deep!'[331] But in neither case had Robert's heart been seriously touched.

However it was now November, that 'rawest of seasons' in which Graves had set 'In Dedication'; and his words of devotion to the White Goddess suddenly had about them a touch of prophecy. At the time of the full moon a beautiful seventeen-year-old American girl called Judith Bledsoe arrived on the island of Majorca; and suddenly 'the next bright bolt' of which he had written in his poem was about to fall.

BOOK FOUR

JUDITH
1950–53

CHAPTER 1

Flawless Blade[1]

Judith Bledsoe was a tall, slender, graceful girl with reddish-brown hair, magical grey-green eyes, a provocative mouth and a smile of searing warmth. On the day that she first met Robert Graves, she was wearing a long skirt embroidered with bands of yellow, red and turquoise like a Russian gypsy skirt, a conch belt round her waist, and turquoise bracelets on her wrists. At their meeting, as Robert later recalled,

> a shock passed between her and me of the sort usually explained in pseudo-philosophic terms as 'we must have met in a previous incarnation.' Psychologists postulate 'compatible emotion-groups'. I am content to call it 'Snap!' Indeed, as it proved, [Judith] and I could converse in a joking verbal shorthand, which meant so little to anyone else, but for us expressed a range of experience so complex that we could never have translated it into everyday language.[2]

This moment of recognition was not unexpected.

By the summer of 1950, Graves both desired and dreaded the arrival of a new poetic muse. 'The Ghost in the Clock' is eloquent of this:

> About midnight my heart began
> To trip again and knock.
> The tattered ghost of a tall man
> Looked fierce at me as in he ran,
> But fiercer at the clock.
>
> It was, he swore, a long, long while
> Until he had had the luck
> To die and make his domicile
> On some un-geographic isle
> Where no hour every struck.

'But now, you worst of clocks,' said he,
    'Delayer of all love,
In vengeance I've recrossed the sea
To jerk at your machinery
    And give your hands a shove.'

So impotently he groped and peered
    That his whole body shook!
I could not laugh at him; I feared
This was no ghost but my own weird,
    And closer dared not look.[3]

In 1929, when he had first moved to Deyá with Laura Riding, Graves had rejoiced in living in a timeless land that he named 'Somewhere Nowhere'; but then he had been living with his muse, so there had been nothing to impede the flow of his poetry. Now he had a wife again, no longer a muse, and this, as his weird or other self fully recognized, spelled his creative death as a poet. But now the ticking of the clock had begun again. Judith had arrived on the scene; and in her he recognized the source of poetic inspiration for which he yearned.

Judith Bledsoe had been born in 1934 to a forceful French-speaking beauty from New Orleans who loved literature, and made her living as a violinist. However, Judith's Irish–Italian father (a writer, teacher and translator) had deserted his family very early; while Judith's mother not only showed her very little affection, but deprived her of any roots by moving house with such frequency that by the time Judith was thirteen she had already lived in California, New Orleans and New York. They then returned to California, where Judith met her father for the first time, and he gave her the conch belt which she was wearing when she met Robert.

However, the meeting with her father had come too late. Judith had already begun to compete with her mother for male attention and, for obvious reasons, was particularly drawn to much older men. She was also highly imaginative, romantic, and artistically gifted. On leaving home at the age of sixteen, by which time she and her mother had moved from California back to New York, she became an art student; while at the same time becoming fiercely attached to Marvin, a large not very attractive man of thirty,[4] whom she had met in California three years previously.

Years later, Judith would talk of having been the Cathy to Marvin's Heathcliff; and their relationship was so stormy that in the autumn of 1950, soon after they had become engaged to be married, Judith left him and worked her passage to Europe by taking a job as nanny to the children of the American film star Alan Ladd and his wife.[5] At the back of her mind was the idea that she might be able to make her living as an artist either in Paris or, still better, in Vienna, a city to which she was romantically attracted. Questioners were simply told that she wanted 'to take a look at Europe before it blows up'.[6]

When her job with the Ladd family ended, Judith wandered through France and Spain before crossing the sea to Majorca: where, one November afternoon, she was stopped in a Deyá street by Karl Gay. To her astonishment, he invited her to supper, telling her that Robert Graves would like to meet her.

Judith accepted at once, though it had surprised her to hear that Robert Graves was still alive. She had vaguely heard of him as a popular historical novelist, but knew nothing of *I, Claudius*, believing instead that he had written *Ben Hur*.

The evening began tamely enough in a drink with Karl and Rene; then Beryl and her three children appeared; and only later did Robert arrive looking, in Judith's words, 'wild, shaggy, and a little awesome'. By this time the drink had gone a little to her head; but she sensed at once that Robert liked her very much; and she found the days which followed both extraordinary and perplexing.

Robert was clearly an exceptional man, who seemed to be on first-name terms with many famous people; and yet he was taking a close personal interest in her, and had soon made it clear that she was someone of central importance in his life. In some ways he therefore appeared to be living in a crazy world at a complete tangent to normal reality; and at first Judith was self-protectively cynical about this sudden friendship, writing to a friend back in America (according to one story) that she had met an old guy who seemed to be dotty, but who also had money and influence.[7]

However, she and Robert were soon taking long walks together; and when she was actually in Robert's company, Judith was aware that something wonderful was happening. She answered directly and honestly when Robert, in his quiet precise voice, asked her lovingly about her hopes and fears; and as he also told her about his poetry, instructed her in mythology, and explained that she had become his source of inspiration, she was flattered and allowed herself to be drawn more and more closely into the private world of his poetic imagination.

Robert particularly admired Judith's directness, which contrasted so noticeably, so far as he could tell, with the 'false' voice of her mother. Judith seemed to him to be wild, in the sense of acting in the authentic manner of a real woman, but essentially innocent; and before long he was literally running to Judith with the final draft of a poem which he had entitled simply:

THE PORTRAIT

She speaks always in her own voice
Even to strangers; but those other women
Exercise their borrowed, or false, voices
Even on sons and daughters.

She can walk invisibly at noon
Along the high road; but those other women
Gleam phosphorescent – broad hips and gross fingers –
Down every lampless alley.

She is wild and innocent, pledged to love
Through all disaster; but those other women
Decry her for a witch a common drab
And glare back when she greets them.

Here is her portrait, gazing sidelong at me,
The hair in disarray, the young eyes pleading:
'And you, love? As unlike those other men
As I those other women?'[8]

In writing these lines, Robert Graves felt a sudden and invigorating sense of renewal. Once more he was a poet, treading the circle of his fate within the sacred grove of the White Goddess of Pelion.

For this privilege, Graves believed that it was his moral duty to risk the most serious personal difficulties: so that in 'To a Poet in Trouble' he wrote uncompromisingly:

Cold wife and angry mistress
And debts: all three?
Though they combine to kill you
Be grateful to the Goddess,
(Our cruel patroness)
For this felicity:
Your poems now ring true.[9]

Fortunately for him, Beryl's initial feelings were ones of considerable relief, very like the feelings which Nancy Nicholson had experienced when Laura Riding first appeared on the scene and realized that she would have some help in coping with Robert's complex emotional and spiritual needs.[10] In any case, Beryl had learned from *Watch the North Wind Rise* of Robert's belief that a poet could entirely separate the world of his inspiration from that of his domestic routine; so she bravely added Judith to the circle of her friends, and carried on with family life as normal.

As Robert learned more about Judith, whom he described to a friend as 'a tall American footloose beauty … who goes about in long black trousers, and paints',[11] he decided to encourage her artistic ambitions, and suggested that they should collaborate on a 'holiday task' which he had set himself as a diversion from *The Nazarene Gospel Restored*, as *The Hand of Simon Magus* had now become. It involved:

> solving the secret of the first four chapters of Genesis which, as primitive myth, stink to High Heaven yet contain all the ingredients of the corresponding 'Orphic', i.e. Libyo-Thracian creation story and sequel. Shall make a little book of the real story, with pictures, beginning with 'Eve's' sexual dance with the North Wind (which resulted in the Cosmic Egg) and ending with 'Lamech's' killing of his brother 'Cain' …[12]

Robert's idea, to which Judith agreed, was that he should write the text, and that, after he had done some rough sketches, showing what was required, she should draw the necessary thirty-six illustrations.[13]

Talking one day to Judith about her own imaginative world, Robert discovered that (perhaps because of her liking for Keats's 'On first Looking into Chapman's Homer', with its well-known line: 'Silent, upon a peak in Darien') she had privately given the name 'Darien' to the artistic endeavours in which she hoped to succeed.[14] Hence the title of the poem which he wrote for Judith to explain how 'Darien' would be born from their love, even if that love necessarily involved his own destruction:

DARIEN

It is a poet's privilege and fate
To fall enamoured of the one Muse
Who variously haunts this island earth.

She was your mother, Darien,
And presaged by the darting halcyon bird
Would run green-sleeved along her ridges,
Treading the asphodels and heather-trees
With white feet bare.

Often at moonrise I had watched her go
And a cold shudder shook me
To see the curved blaze of her Cretan axe.
Averted her set face, her business
Not yet with me, long-striding,
She would ascend the peak and pass from sight.
But once at full moon, by the sea's verge,
I came upon her without warning.

Unrayed she stood, with long hair streaming,
A cockle-shell cupped in her warm hands,
Her axe propped idly on a stone.

No awe possessed me, only a great grief;
Wanly she smiled, but would not lift her eyes
(As a young girl will greet the stranger).
I stood upright, a head taller than she.
'See who has come,' said I.

She answered: 'If I lift my eyes to yours
And our eyes marry, man, what then?
Will they engender my son Darien?
Swifter than wind, with straight and nut-brown hair,
Tall, slender-shanked, grey-eyed, untameable;
Never was born, nor ever will be born
A child to equal my son Darien,
Guardian of the hid treasures of your world.'

I knew then by the trembling of her hands
For whom that flawless blade would sweep:
My own oracular head, swung by its hair.

'Mistress,' I cried, 'the times are evil
And you have charged me with their remedy.
O, where my head is now, let nothing be

But a clay counterfeit with nacre blink:
Only look up, so Darien may be born!

'He is the northern star, the spell of knowledge,
Pride of all hunters and all fishermen,
Your deathless fawn, an eaglet of your eyrie,
The topmost branch of your unfellable tree,
A tear streaking the summer night.
The new green of my hope.'
                                        Lifting her eyes,
She held mine for a lost eternity.
'Sweetheart,' said I, 'strike now, for Darien's sake!'[15]

In showing this poem to Judith, Robert gave her the clearest possible ideal of the role that she was expected to play; but it was an enormously demanding role; and then it became clear that a group among the expatriate community was so hostile towards her that Robert began talking angrily of a 'witch-hunt', and later declared that he would have 'thrown [the ringleader] out on his ear for the lies he told if I'd not been sorry for [his wife]'.[16] Within a few weeks of meeting Robert, the emotional pressure on Judith had become so great that she began to feel that she was dying. At the same time, she was seized by the romantic notion that before her death she would don a black dress and dance a waltz in the city of Vienna.

Judith confided her ambition to a Jewish fellow-American named Irwin, a young, slightly built student[17] who was wandering around Europe working on a thesis for a master's degree in English; and he offered to accompany her. They set off together in mid-December, leaving Robert uncertain whether he would ever see Judith again; and in his next letter to James Reeves he explained that:

The Goddess has been plaguing me lately, very cruelly, and I have managed to satisfy her by two or three poems written in red arterial blood; she appeared in person in Deyá during the last full moon, swinging a Cretan axe, but is now away again. Put into historical terms the story isn't really interesting; no liaison dangerous or alteration of the local ebbs and flows.

What seemed most important was that he had written several fine new poems; and Graves told Reeves categorically that: 'their publication in my new collection [will be] the only impingement of poetic on historical truth'.

Not long after Judith's departure, the Graveses celebrated Christmas in the traditional manner; although, as Beryl wrote to James Reeves, 'every year we curse ourselves for having started the whole thing – nobody else in the whole village does anything but go to midnight mass'. While in Canelluñ they were 'slav[ing] away with turkey and mince pies & stockings & all the rest, & worst of all a Christmas Eve party …'[19] Then towards the end of January 1951, while Graves was still busily working on 'this damned Gospel book', as he described *The Nazarene Gospel Restored* to George and Joanna Simon,[20] a letter arrived from Rosaleen. Dated 24 January, it began with the words: 'My darling Robert, Mother died at 1.20 yesterday afternoon.'[21]

CHAPTER 2

Death of a Matriarch

After Amy Graves's series of radiation treatments at Exeter in October 1950, she had returned to Harlech in a cheerful frame of mind;[22] but before long she was beset by fresh worries.

First an action for libel was brought against her son Charles. It was, as Clarissa commented, 'sheer bad luck'.[23] A Mr Martinez having been convicted of some crime, Charles had subsequently commented on the matter in print – but then the trial was annulled, and in a fresh trial Martinez was declared innocent. Charles's statements could now be regarded as libellous, and he had to appeal to Amy for £500 to settle the case which was brought against him. She was able to raise the money, arranging that it should come from his ultimate share of the estate; but only by selling stock, which at the age of ninety-three was a source of great anxiety.[24]

Amy was further alarmed by the news that Rosaleen was taking her three sons (seventeen-year-old Dan, fifteen-year-old Roger and thirteen-year-old Paul) on a winter sports holiday, which she felt certain would result in broken arms or legs or something even worse;[25] and then at the very beginning of January 1951 came depressing news of the unexpected death at the age of fifty-seven of her niece Maria von Faber du Faur,[26] a citizen of Munich who had shown 'uncompromising hostility to Hitler and all his works' in the years leading up to the Second World War.[27] Maria had died 'alone and untended at a hospital in the night', and Amy began to fear that she too 'might die alone in the night'.[28]

Amy had already suffered from a mysterious 'bout of twitchings' in late November, long after her course of treatment at Exeter was over;[29] and now those unpleasant symptoms began to recur. By 15 January, as Clarissa reported to John, their mother was:

so alarmed at her own condition ... that I have made up my bed so as to be in her room, & close at hand. Her involuntary movements are now so severe that she wishes to see no-one, & has asked to see no visitors ... [She is] no longer capable of reading or writing, & eating is a messy & difficult business.[30]

As Amy's physical condition deteriorated, the local doctor wrongly assumed that she was suffering from a nervous breakdown induced by her family worries; and Clarissa wrote along these lines to Robert, adding: 'Just now I went up to get a message for you & she said "Say: I often think of him. Give him my love & say I hope to get better & to see him in the summer." '[31]

Rosaleen, who had become increasingly worried by the news from Erinfa,[32] eventually reached Amy's bedside on the night of Saturday 20 January. As she later reported to Robert, she found their mother: 'mentally quite clear & thinking only of us', but also suffering from 'frightful convulsions of her whole body – face, head, arms',[33] in agony, and clearly in a terminal state of exhaustion.

Clarissa, still detesting conventional medicine, and relying on Christian Science to effect a cure, had lost her head and become utterly unable to cope; and Rosaleen was shocked by the apparent lack of any love or sympathy in her attitude towards their dying mother. Immediately assuming control, she packed Clarissa off to a guest-house,[34] and injected Amy with sedatives 'that quietened her tormented body'. Rosaleen had hoped, as she told Robert, to bring Amy back to a level of quiet consciousness,

> but before she was really conscious the terrible twitching started again & I had to put her to sleep again ... Her amazing heart was regular & strong to within ¼ of an hour of her death ... I held her dear hand till her pulse ran out.

Rosaleen added comfortingly: 'You have given her no worries, darling, or not for a long time'; and concluded that: 'I should never have known what a saint she was, if I hadn't seen her enduring her misery with such unselfish courage. "Faithful unto death" certainly applies to her.'[35]

Later, the cause of Amy's death would be established by a neurologist as a secondary cancer in the hypothalamus, or mid-brain: a rare and invariably fatal condition, from which sufferers usually die in about three weeks, worn out by the violence of their convulsions.[36]

But first came the funeral of this formidable matriarch, who for so many years had been the linchpin of her extensive family. Dick, who was still working in Tangier and therefore unable to be present, sent Robert a letter of sympathy in which he wrote that:

Your Mother was always very good and perfectly fair to us elder children & I personally always regarded her as one of my best friends ... I felt it was rather an asset to her that she never became really English. She preserved her personality better in that way and retained through her life an old-fashioned and conventional virtue which I found very endearing, though I didn't always agree with her. Requiescat in pace.[37]

Robert was also unable to be present; but two of his children, Jenny and Sam, attended the funeral of their beloved grandmother, after staying overnight with Diccon and Frances Hughes at Môr Edrin; and Robert received a full account from Jenny of the day's events, from the moment when:

Uncle John came to fetch us with Roz in his little car. Roz was in the most collapsed state. Tear-rolling weary. Uncle John came out best – as you shall see. He was wearing a frightful false bear coat, the matching half of which had been patched by Grandmother with black velvet. He was all the time quiet, good-natured and sensible.

At Erinfa Claree was in the drawing-room admiring her funeral hat in a glass. She swung round with sickening cheerfulness: 'Don't you think I look just like Greer Garson?' Then she turned to Roz and commanded her brightly 'You can't wear that terrible wool thing for Mother's great day Rosaleen.' Roz says 'Oh dear can't I' vaguely and leaves the room. Claree turns to us and says: 'I simply can't understand Roz behaving in such a curious way – she must surely be used to this kind of thing.' And then cries gaily: 'Here you are Sam. Like to have anything in this room? I'll give it to you with great pleasure.' John says peaceably: 'Now Clarissa, you ought not to touch anything till after the will's read.'

Rose Gribble [a family friend from childhood] comes in. Uncle Charles breezes in and failing to find any audience for the sales account of Peggy's book on slimming, tells a risky golfing story to cheer everybody up. He says Peggy will be down to luncheon. Rose Gribble asks coldly: 'Peggy not up yet? I hoped she would help me arrange the flowers on the coffin.' Uncle Charles looked rather sheepish. Rose Gribble had given them both hell earlier on because they had (can you believe it) ordered their breakfast in bed.

Sam and I were still stunned that Grandmother was dead. It seemed so dreadful and unreal. The drawing-room smelled just the same. The same gong in the hall and Grandfather looking out at the generations of golf-sticks and buckets with sand in the bottom. I went into the kitchen. Mrs Janet and Mrs Good were both struggling with the family lunch and sniffing. I helped and they were so grateful …

We got through lunch with, for once, all the Graves more or less silent except for Claree trying to decide out loud which of many exciting futures she would now choose. After luncheon John read out Uncle Bones's obituary which was 2,000 words long and hopeless and the family all made quarrelsome amendments.

Then the parson and the curate came and while the coffin was carried down the stairs past Clarissa's water-colours they read prayers to the assembled family and servants in the drawing-room. The thing was that evening prayer fitted Grandmother. She was such a very good woman. And the parson and the curate were really sad and read every word as if they meant it

As the procession went slowly along everyone came to the cottage doors with hankies. The day was unbelievably brilliant. The sea sparkled, the sun warmed, Snowdon stood snow-capped against a cloudless sky. The sun slanted almost like a revelation onto the coffin in the church, your telegram sticking out of a wreath of daffodils. A tiny bunch of anemones from Mother, a branch of mimosa from Alex, Claree's dismal heather wreath with its label 'To my Mother – who taught me patience.' Roz and Sam were in convulsions of weeping. Uncle John and Uncle Charles did not trust themselves to repeat the responses. Peggy looked as if she was going to faint … Claree sang all the hymns as if they were children's songs in the German songbook on the Erinfa piano in rousing piercing soprano. The church was full. Outside the sheer marvellousness of the day made the grave seem more tragic. I cried then. I did wish she wasn't dead.

Afterwards, Jenny went round to see Susan, 'who was feigning flu in order not to go to the funeral and meet Claree'; and then the will was read by Susan's husband Kenneth Macaulay, whose sight was failing, and who had therefore sat 'on the drawing-room window-sill holding it to the light with a magnifying glass'.[38]

Snowdon, snow-capped against a cloudless sky … it was a sight which Robert could vividly recall from his childhood; and one which after Amy's death he would never care to see again. As he laid Jenny's letter down in his study in Canellun, and thought of how much Amy had meant to him for the past fifty-five years, and all the difficulties that had arisen between them as a result of his living with Laura Riding, he could at least remind himself that he and his mother had latterly been on good terms: a fact, as he learned from John, co-executor with Kenneth of Amy's will, reflected in:

> a characteristic note on the 1/7th share of her estate which was originally to have been yours, but which she left direct to your children when you went abroad. After you were reconciled she hardly liked to go back on the new arrangement of which your children already knew, but when David had been presumed dead she passed his share back to you.

'I could not leave him out of my will altogether', Amy had written, 'though the share will be so small as to be only a gesture.' In fact, John told him, the overall value of the estate was so large that he would be receiving at least £500, a very useful sum when he had spent so long on a project which, as he had already complained in a letter to the poet and critic Derek Savage, would bring him in no more than a few months' living expenses.[39]

But financial matters seemed comparatively trivial when Robert contemplated the profound influence which Amy had exerted upon the whole course of his life.

From the days of his earlier childhood when, as he records in *Good-bye to All That*, he and his brothers and sisters had 'spent a great deal of our time on self-examination and good resolutions', Robert had been brought up by Amy to be a strong moralist. It was his feelings of moral outrage against his fellow Carthusians which had, at first, made Charterhouse the hell from which he found relief only in the writing of poetry. It was his feelings of moral outrage against the Germans which had led him to join up at the start of the Great War, since 'France is the only place for a gentleman now.' Subsequently, Robert's conviction not only of the past existence but also of the future necessity of matriarchal rule says a great deal more about Amy's influence upon her brilliant but so often tormented eldest son.

Even when Robert had lost his Christian faith, he still needed to feel that he was a good man; and in due course he had established the tenets of an alternative personal religion based upon worship of the White Goddess, to whose service he remained utterly dedicated for the rest of his life; while at the moment of Amy's death this profoundly religious man was still, through his work on *The Nazarene Gospel Restored*, seeking to come to terms with the Christianity which had so dominated the first twenty-four years of his life. Amy had also taught Robert that 'Work is far more interesting than play': a great lesson whose rigorous application had sustained him through numerous personal and financial crises; though sadly she had also taught him, quite inadvertently, to confuse cleverness with moral worth.

'Mother's death came as a great shock to me', Robert wrote to Sam in the spring of 1951 (congratulating him on a new job in an architect's office). 'She was a very good woman, & far more talented than she realised, especially as a writer.'[40] And when Judith Bledsoe unexpectedly returned to Deyá in March, Robert had a good deal to tell her about his saintly, indomitable mother: Amy Graves, who had once, as Amalie von Ranke, wanted to be a medical missionary, until her father had said 'then we shall try to forget you'; who had instead married an Irish poet with five children; and who had then had five more of her own: none of whom would ever hear the slightest word said against her for the rest of their lives.

CHAPTER 3

Volcanic Emotions

One spring morning in 1951, as Robert Graves would later remind her, Judith Bledsoe, with 'a rather guilty smile' on her face, 'came up the drive unexpectedly', looking as though she anticipated being 'flogged with a cat-o'-nine-tails. But Heaven knows why', wrote Robert lovingly, 'because you are our darling and always will be even if you play truant.'[41]

Her story was this: she had tried to reach Vienna with her student companion Irwin; but their train was snow-bound at Innsbruck for several days, so they had abandoned it, and travelled down through Italy as far as Rome. There Irwin, whose presence had given Judith a feeling of security, had left her staying with a friend of her mother's, a film director who promised to give her a screen test at the famous Cinecitta studios. However, Judith had been scared by this prospect and, in her own words, 'cleared out'.

She had then travelled back as far as the Balearic Islands, but to Ibiza this time; until, emotionally exhausted by so many men pursuing her, she had decided that she would return to Deyá and throw herself on Robert and Beryl's mercy. Robert was overjoyed by the return of his Muse; and, with Beryl's approval, he immediately invited her to recuperate at Canelluñ, where she was given a bed in an upstairs room. Later Judith would recall that she had come to Europe looking for a new mother and father; and that in Robert and Beryl she appeared to have found them.

Potentially it was an extraordinarily difficult situation. Earlier in the year, telling George and Joanna Simon of the 'sudden visitation of the Goddess', Robert had mentioned that 'all honest wives dread her shadow on the door';[42] but Beryl, whatever her private feelings, showed Judith every care and consideration; while Robert was kindliness personified. Each morning he took Judith up a tray laden with good things, so that Judith could enjoy a 'wonderful breakfast' in bed; and once she was dressed, he happily allowed her to interrupt him in his study at any hour of the day or night.

When Judith began to feel more rested, she and Robert resumed their long walks of the previous November; and he talked to her at length about his current projects. In particular, he would soon have the page proofs of *Poems and Satires 1951* to show her; while his major prose work, *The Nazarene Gospel Restored*, was at last virtually complete.[43]

Beyond that, the future was uncertain. Robert was hoping to edit the contemporary manuscript life of Bunyan which he had heard was among the family papers;[44] but if so, it perished in the epic bonfire of such papers over which Clarissa is said to have presided with almost manic glee. She had recently been wondering, as she told Robert, whether or not she and a male friend to whom she was obsessively attached were in fact already angels; and when Robert suggested gently that this might be interpreted as 'spiritual pride' on her part, it was a reproof which she could not fully accept.[45]

Besides telling Judith about his work, Robert ranged over the most important events of his early life, talking a great deal about Amy, and telling Judith how he had 'died and come back to life again' during the battle of the Somme. In Robert's company, Judith felt wonderfully protected; and when he told her about his mythological discoveries, she seemed to understand everything, just as one might do in a dream, and yet afterwards found herself unable to repeat anything that he had said.

Sometimes, however, the dream edged towards nightmare, and Judith would become aware of volcanic emotions waiting to erupt from the surface of Robert's protective charm. Once, they were standing on a high rock above the sea when he suddenly asked her to jump. 'Tremendously' wanting approval, she did so; and came to no harm, though the experience had been terrifying.

Another time, the two of them were walking down a darkening road not far from the sea. As Graves later recalled, they were 'exchanging our usual nonsense', when he decided to ask her 'to tell [me] something really frightening'. In reply, she clutched his arm, and said:

I ought to have told you, Robert, days ago. It happened when I was staying with my grandmother in New Orleans ... I guess I must have been twelve years old, and used to ride off to school on my bicycle about half a mile away. One summer evening I thought I'd come home by a different route, through a complicated crisis of cross-streets. I'd never tried it before. Soon I lost my way and found myself in a dead end, with a square patio behind a rusty iron gate, belonging to an old French mansion overgrown with creepers. The shutters were green too. It was a beautiful cool, damp place in that heat. And as I stood with my hand on the latch, I looked up, and there at an attic window I saw a face ... It grinned and rapped on the glass with its leprous white fingers and beckoned to me ...[46]

Robert was chilled by this description, since it immediately brought to mind a similar experience from his own past.

It had been in January 1919, when as the shellshocked Captain Robert Graves of the Royal Welch Fusiliers he had been stationed in Limerick in southwest Ireland while awaiting demobilization. Several times, he had visited the shop of an antique dealer named Riley from whom he had bought a number of oddments; but then he had become 'haunted and frightened' by 'a nightmarish picture hanging in the shop entrance', the portrait of a man whose skin was 'glossy-white', and whose eyes were 'Mongolian', with

> their look imbecile. He had two crooked dog-teeth, a narrow chin and a billycock hat squashed low over his forehead. To add to the horror some humorist had provide the creature with a dudeen pipe painted on the front of the glass, from which a wisp of smoke was curling.[47]

It was exactly the face that Judith had seen in New Orleans ... And when he had told her about it, they 'broke into a run of perfect terror, hurrying towards the nearest bright light'.[48]

Later, back at Canelluñ, an American friend burst into the house in a state of nervous collapse. And when Robert asked coldly: 'What's new?'

> 'I've had a most horrible experience', he gasped, 'give me a drink will you? I took a car to Soller this afternoon. The heel had come off my walking shoe and I wanted to get it fixed ... You know Bennasar the shoe-maker, off the market square? I was just about to go in when I happened to look through the window ...'[49]

At that point, Robert and Judith 'glanced at each other. We both knew what [he] was going to say. And he said it: "I saw a frightful face." ' Which made them both feel more scared than ever.

This story is symptomatic of the way in which, day by day, Robert's passionate interest in Judith was driving up the emotional pressure. Soon he had reminded her about her promise to work on his Genesis project; and once he had made thirty-six rough sketches, she began working on the final drawings.[50] But as Robert's obsession with his Muse seemed more and more exclusive, an unhappy atmosphere began to pervade

Canelluñ. Karl recalls a supper to which he and Rene had been invited. First the children all refused to sit next to Judith; and later, when Beryl began to speak, Robert told her bluntly to: 'Shut up! I want to hear Judith.' Beryl, to Karl's astonishment and dismay, did not appear to react at all.[51]

However Beryl was acting more wisely than Karl knew. When she judged that the right moment had come, she took Judith out to lunch alone, and quite calmly asked her whether she wanted Robert or not.[52] To which Judith could only protest, quite honestly, that she loved Beryl and Robert more than her mother and father, and that she had no intention of doing anything to injure their marriage.

Under this additional pressure, Judith is said to have veered in the direction of William's tutor, the good-looking blue-eyed Bill Merwin. This made Robert furious.[53] He had already decided that Merwin was 'not a great success', and had been sounding out a possible replacement;[54] and now he began privately accusing him of the worst possible behaviour.[55]

The situation was further complicated in the third week of April when Marvin, Judith's former American fiancé, turned up unexpectedly at Canelluñ, after walking there all the way from Palma.[56] Telling Judith contemptuously that she had become 'Robert Graves's woman', this large, slightly deranged-looking man demanded that she break with Robert at once. Marvin's emotional hold over Judith remained so strong that she obeyed, meekly following him to Lluc Alcari, a little hamlet which lies just above the sea about a mile to the north of Canelluñ.

There, on Marvin's insistence, Judith burnt a whole series of 'extraordinary' letters that Robert had written her. However, Marvin allowed her to preserve the nine or ten drawings which she had made for the Genesis project. He could see that completing the series would be an important step forward in her career. But it was to be done, he told her as 'a matter of business' only; and those were the words she used when they returned together to Canelluñ in order to discuss the matter with Robert.

The predictable result was a thoroughly unpleasant conversation. Robert had taken an instant dislike to Marvin;[57] and Judith was horribly aware of Robert's feeling that she was betraying both him, and her own better self. It was like a stab at her heart when Robert replied pointedly to Marvin's assertion that the drawings were 'a matter of business', 'that between J and us there were no business conditions, only love'.[58] At the same time, Robert's open hostility only made Marvin seem more attractive to Judith, as she had always liked him most when he seemed most isolated and rejected.

Unable to make up her mind between the two men, Judith spent two days at Lluc Alcari of such agonizing indecision that it later seemed like a fortnight. Then she returned alone to Canellun, for a further conversation with the Graveses. After which, as Robert later recalled, she 'decided to go away & decide whether she really loved [Marvin]. But she had no money. So we lent her £50 to go direct to England.' There it was planned that she 'would work on the book until we came, and then either resume life with [Marvin] or return with us to Mallorca'.[59]

It was an enormous relief for Robert to have separated Judith from Marvin, whom he described as a 'monster';[60] but he was worried about her being alone in London. So on 5 May, not long after her departure from Deyá, he wrote to the Jepsons as follows:

My dear Selwyn and Tania,

A girl named Judith Bledsoe who for some unaccountable reason has become what the Majorcans call 'worse than family' to us – i.e. attached to us by stronger bonds than those of blood, and a sort of daughter-of-the-house – is on her way to London today where she knows nobody and naturally we are anxious on her account until we arrive there in July.

Beryl and I both ... independently ranging in our minds round London for a rock of security to which she could be belayed, reached the conclusion that you were the rock in question. She has had a very difficult time and anyone less destructible than she would be in a private asylum by now; but nothing is wrong, twisted or missing, and her health is good.

Robert added that Judith had money; and that when she had worked in New York as a textile designer she had been 'making a very good income, so she is no problem. But she needs friends and you are our friends, and so please love her and look after her.'[61] He also wrote to Norman Cameron and to others, telling them that he had given Judith their telephone number, and asking them to be kind to her.[62]

Robert was right to be anxious about Judith. She was not yet strong enough to function alone. When her train reached Paris, she remembered that the studious Irwin was now living there, and that she had his address. Breaking her journey, therefore, she went round to see him; and Irwin, who had come to love Judith, was glad enough to welcome her in.

CHAPTER 4

A Disappointing Answer

After Judith Bledsoe's departure from Deyá in May 1951, the household at Canelluñ settled back into its normal routine; and Robert worked furiously hard on his final revisions to *The Nazarene Gospel Restored.* But occasionally a poem began forming itself unbidden in Robert's mind, as he tried to explain to himself the nature of his love for Judith – and not always in mythological terms.

In 'Dialogue on the Headland', for example, HE/Robert and SHE/Judith discuss their relationship in a way which shows how important it is; and yet how it is ultimately bound to be unsatisfactory for both of them, and especially for Judith. 'Whatever happens', HE/Robert declares,

>   … this goes on.
> SHE: Without a future? Sweetheart, tell me now:
>   What do you want of me? I must know that.
> HE: Nothing that isn't freely mine already.
> SHE: Say what is freely yours and you shall have it.
> HE: Nothing that, loving you, I could dare take.
> SHE: O, for an answer with no 'nothing' in it!
> HE: Then give me everything that's left.
> SHE: Left after what?
> HE: After whatever happens:
>   Skies have already fallen, seas are slime,
>   Watersnakes poke and peer six-headedly –
> SHE: And I lie snugly in the Devil's arms.
> HE: I said: 'Whatever happens.' Are you crying?
> SHE: You'll not forget me – ever, ever, ever?[63]

Disconcertingly, there was no news of Judith from any of their friends; and then, as Robert reported to Betty and Ricardo Sicré, 'That mad Marvin … suddenly went off in pursuit of Judith without money, addresses or prospects.' Robert had no idea whether Judith was in France or England, 'or whether he caught up with her; and if he is run over by a Paris taxi-cab we won't shed a tear, but we hope she escapes'.[64]

In the meantime, Beryl was reaping her reward for having avoided any direct confrontation over Judith. Robert was greatly relieved that Beryl had been so understanding; and years later, when writing of his special rapport with Judith, he added that with Beryl he enjoyed 'the less spectacular but more relevant rapport that comes of having all friends in common, four children, and no secrets from each other'.[65]

When *The Nazarene Gospel Restored* was finally completed in mid-May, the two of them spent a few days in Madrid 'to celebrate the end of two years' work'.[66] By 23 May the typescript had been posted to Farrar, Straus & Co, who had 'swallowed up' the Creative Age Press; and Robert had also sent a copy to T. S. Eliot, with a covering letter in which he asked him to decide whether 'the book is as scholarly and temperate as the subject requires'. So confident was he of a favourable reply, that he foresaw the restored Gospel, which was 'printed in sequence in Part III', being 'one day printed by itself in a popular edition, and translated into one hundred-and-fifty-three languages'.[67]

While waiting for a response, Graves took his family for a brief holiday with Jenny and Alex in Portofino. Since the end of the previous summer it had been known that Alex was suffering from Hodgkin's disease, a cancer of the lymphatic system which was usually fatal; and he and Jenny were now to be found living not in Italy, but in their fashionable London apartment, Albany K5. However, they had kept on the Castalletto; and with Alex's cancer in a period of natural remission for some months, they were able to share another holiday at Portofino with Robert's second family.[68]

On their return to Deyá towards the end of June, Graves found a disappointing answer from Eliot, who acknowledged receipt of the manuscript of *The Nazarene Gospel Restored*, but warned him 'that it was a book he and his colleagues at Faber would have to "think twice about" before publishing'.[69] This was not surprising. Alongside the most exacting and often illuminating scholarship were passages in which Graves and Podro had made assumptions, admittedly in the light of their own highly developed critical intelligence, for which there could not possibly be any proof.

To take an example entirely at random: there was an occasion documented in Luke ii. 47–50, when the twelve-year-old Jesus is said to have been found:

in the temple, sitting in the midst of the doctors, both hearing them and asking them questions. And all that heard Him were astonished at His understanding and answers. And when they saw Him, they were amazed: and His mother said unto Him: 'Son, why hast Thou thus dealt with us? behold, Thy father and I have sought thee sorrowing.' And he said unto them:

'How is it that ye sought Me: Wist ye not that I must be about My Father's business?'[70]

And they understood not the saying which He spake unto them.

Graves and Podro write of this, in part, that:

a twelve-year-old child, however brilliant, would hardly have been allowed to intervene in a doctoral dispute. Neither, if he was so well versed in the Law, would he have dishonoured his parents by the rude rejoinder, quoted in *Luke* ii.49; this detail seems to reflect the manners of the Gentile Christian period, when the family peace was often broken by the conversion of a son or daughter. Some explanation of his failure to notify Joseph that he wished to stay behind must have dropped out, and also an antecedent remark which would explain 'my Father's business'.[71]

When the passage is rewritten, therefore, Jesus is found:

in a porch of the Temple, where the doctors expounded the Law, sitting in the midst of their disciples.

Now, the doctors were astonished to find such love of learning in so young a child; for he had asked them many questions as they entered into the porch where they taught.

But Mary said unto him: 'Son, why hast thou thus dealt with us? Behold, thy father and I have sought thee suffering.'

And Jesus fell at their feet and desired their forgiveness, but he asked them: 'How is it that ye sought me?'

For one of his kinsfolk, having business to perform in Jerusalem, had undertaken to plead with Joseph and Mary that Jesus might tarry with him there for certain days, and afterwards return to Galilee in his company.

And when they asked further: 'But wherefore didst thou desire to tarry here, not being also a merchant?' he answered: 'Wist ye not that I must be about the Father's business?'[72]

This is a superbly imaginative reconstruction, based upon an intimate knowledge of the period, and may even be very close to the original truth; and yet there is too much conjecture for Eliot or any biblical expert to treat it as serious scholarship.

Fortunately Graves was never pedantic (or there would have been no *The White Goddess*); and he immediately replied to Eliot's letter by agreeing that *The Nazarene Gospel Restored* was indeed:

> a book to think twice about before publishing; but only for reasons of private or public policy which can be decided only at a F&F board meeting. The argument is documented throughout and where it cannot be checked merely by flipping over the pages of the Old and New Testaments, demands the services of a Talmudic scholar.

'Joshua Podro', he went on, 'who has the largest private library of Hebraica in England ... would be pleased to take down the relevant tomes from the highest shelves and put his finger on the justifying quotations.' In the meantime Graves himself would be in London from 4 July for a month; and he asked whether Eliot could 'give me a decision by July 24th ... it would give me a week to find another publisher before I return here'.[73]

Beside Eliot's letter about *The Nazarene Gospel Restored*, there was also a letter from George and Joanna Simon which at last gave Robert Graves some up-to-date news about Judith. She was evidently leading a highly independent life; but there seemed every reason for Graves to suppose that, like Eliot's final decision, she would be waiting for him in London.

CHAPTER 5

'Rather a *Boring* Saint'

After breaking her journey in Paris early in May 1951 and moving in with Irwin, Judith Bledsoe had enjoyed a brief period of tranquillity. This was soon broken when Marvin tracked her down and once again demanded that she return to him. This time, Judith refused; and in due course Marvin sailed away across the Atlantic, and was heard of no more.

With Irwin at her side, Judith then travelled to London, where she began contacting those friends of Robert's whose names had been given to her before she left Deyá. She made a particularly good impression on George and Joanna Simon, who reported to Robert that they had found Judith 'a wonderful person'; although they were a little concerned that after visiting them, she had 'gone off with a young man [presumably Irwin] to Cornwall Torquay and Edinburgh and we await her return before we can get to know her better.'[74]

Other brief glimpses of Judith that summer: at one time, she can be found staying with Irwin in an Oxford flat; at another, she meets Robert's protégé the poet Terry Hards who, much to Robert's fury when he learns of it, falls madly in love with Judith and wants to run away with her: but the attraction is not mutual.

Several of Hard's poems had just appeared in the first two numbers of *Quarto*, a quarterly broadsheet of new poetry edited by James Reeves. Graves had contributed two poems to the summer number: 'To a Poet in Trouble'; and also 'Queen Mother to new Queen', in which sexual fidelity in men appears to be condemned, on the ground that it makes a wife the man's 'only whore'; and so the 'new Queen' is told that she must:

> … act the wronged wife if you love us.
> Let them not whisper, even in sport:
> 'His Majesty's turned parsimonious
> And keeps no whore now but his consort.'[75]

Quarto also included poems by Norman Cameron, James Reeves and Martin Seymour-Smith, the last of whom would soon be playing an important part in the Graves ménage.

Robert and Beryl and their three children reached London on 4 July, and settled into a small flat in Hampstead.[76] Clarissa was briefly a near-neighbour, and called on them full of family news. Erinfa had been on the market for several months, but was still unsold; she herself was to begin teaching art at a girl's school in Shropshire that September;[77] Dick had returned from Morocco 'in a very poor state of health', and had 'been in bed ever since';[78] while John had become Headmaster of a preparatory school in Berkshire, and was living there with his wife and three children, Richard, Simon and Elizabeth, in an attractive Norman Shaw mansion known as Holme Grange and set in seventeen acres of grounds.

Another visitor was Judith Bledsoe, wearing a beautiful silver pendant which Robert had given her. This seemed a token of her spiritual attachment to him, far more important, Robert believed, than her current physical relationship with Irwin, who irritatingly accompanied her everywhere. However, Judith's arrival immediately transported Robert into the magical world that he hoped to share with her; and over the next few weeks he also introduced her to a number of interesting and potentially useful contacts, including the artists Max Beerbohm and Ronald Searle; and the actor Peter Ustinov.

As for Irwin: Robert could not help disliking him, and described him to the Jepsons as 'a gentle spiv with eyes rather too close together, but affectionate and a bad writer', for whom he had 'no particular use'. The kindest thing Robert could say was that, with luck, this relationship was no more than 'a sort of convalescence after the last one ...'[79] But once again, Robert drove Judith further into his rival's arms by displaying such blatant hostility. On one visit, for example, Robert had been showing Judith and Irwin:

> a book of portraits of saints. Judith came across Esdras, and muttered: 'Why, that's just like [Irwin]!'
> 'Yes, yes,' said Graves in his most mincing tone. 'Rather a *boring* saint, Esdras, I've always thought!'[80]

Irwin, as Seymour-Smith observed, 'never stood a chance in this sort of contest. But instead of admiring Graves, Judith pitied [Irwin] the more ...'

At about this time Norman Cameron, recognizing how Robert

Graves's life had become dominated by the poetic theme about which he
had written in *The White Goddess*, was inspired to send his friend a warning
poem on the subject. Ironically entitled 'That weird sall never daunton
me', it contains the lines:

> If thou a weird wilt rightly woo,
> Kiss not, and hush thy mirth,
> For firstly must thou undergo
> The very pangs of birth.
>
> Thy resurrection then is hers:
> She showeth another face,
> A woman still, but unawares
> And dowered with magic grace.

But finally:

> She'll daunton thee and drag thee down
> In worship and despair,
> In sorry self-negation
> Hating thyself in her.[81]

Cameron described this to Graves as 'so much your own work – although
you probably will strongly disagree with it – that I perhaps shouldn't call it
mine. Perhaps it can pass as a Scotsman's dissimilar view of your theme.'

For the time being, Graves had better luck with his business affairs than with
Judith. Although it was disappointing when T. S. Eliot wrote 'a strange letter
turning … down' *The Nazarene Gospel Restored* with the words 'if it had been
duller and dryer, I should have published it', an offer was already on its way
from elsewhere. Eliot's reluctance was ascribed by Graves to the malign
influence of his close friend and 'crippled *malus angelus*' John Howard; and
when he wrote to a friend on the subject, it was to commiserate with 'Poor
Eliot', who had 'made a brave effort to do right, but could not. However, a
quarter of an hour after getting his letter I was able to ring him up … and tell
him that Cassells would be delighted to publish it.'[82]

Much more important from the financial point of view, Graves had
arranged with Viking Press to write a substantial work, *The Greek
Myths*. This was a potentially lucrative project which would keep him
busily occupied for the next two years. However, as Martin Seymour-
Smith recalls, Graves realized at once:

that he would need help in assembling, and sifting, the huge amounts of available material. An assistant would need facility in Latin and Greek.

My [blonde partner Janet de Glanville, usually known as Jan, had] read Greats at [Somerville College,] Oxford, and was willing to do the job. If she could do the myths job, why shouldn't I teach William? The arrangement killed two birds – if not with one stone, then with two that were tied together.[83]

Having agreed that Jan and Martin should follow them to Majorca later in the summer, Robert and Beryl took William, Lucia and Juan down to Devon, where they stayed with Rosaleen and enjoyed what Robert called a 'superlative' week's holiday.[84]

Not only was it a week of birthdays, with William's eleventh and Lucia's eighth on 21 July, and their father's fifty-sixth three days later, but also, as Rosaleen reported to John, 'the children loved the beach, the pier, the grass (they have none at home, it seems) the English fruits. Robert liked the quiet – & did a lot of writing; Beryl is a kind mother & liked the freedom.' And afterwards, they were 'in London till August 8th – then back to Spain'.[85]

Before leaving for Majorca, however, there was another meeting with Judith. Robert already knew that she had done no work at all on the Genesis drawings since leaving Deyá; and now, when he asked her about them again, she could only say 'that she had no time … because she had arranged to go with friends to France and Southern Spain. But she would, of course, finish the book with us that winter.'[86] And with that, Robert Graves had to be content.

CHAPTER 6

'Thank You Always & For Ever'

With the arrival of Martin Seymour-Smith and Janet de Glanville in the late summer of 1951, Robert and Beryl Graves had succeeded in finding the tutor they wanted, and Robert had also secured valuable assistance for his work on *The Greek Myths*. However, they also wanted the younger children to receive the best schooling that Majorca had to offer; and since the standards in Deyá were very low, this would mean spending each term-time in Palma where, as Robert had already written,

> there is more going on and where the sun strikes more genially ... We are not quite sure yet of the economics of this plan, but it has obvious advantages and would, for example, be a good deal cheaper than sending even one of the children to school in England.[87]

In September, therefore, Robert moved Martin, Jan and his own family into Palma. There was a brand new block of flats at Guillermo Massot 69, near the northern edge of the city in an area known as the Ensanche, and Robert took two of them, one above the other.[88] Robert, Beryl and their children had the more spacious lower flat, which was on the first floor, cost them only £4.15 a month, and had a dining room, sitting room, kitchen, bathroom and four bedrooms – one of which was occupied by their maid Francisca; while Jan and Martin had the upper and smaller apartment on the second floor, where William received his tutorials, and where Robert had a workroom overlooking the narrow, dusty, quiet street in front.[89]

It was an unfashionable area; but they were not far from where the Deyá bus came in. This was important, not only because they had no car, but also because it was their principal source of communication with Karl, who had stayed behind at C'an Torrent where he continued to do all the typing and other secretarial work. Each morning, the early bus from Deyá would arrive at 8.30, and it was William's job to collect from the driver an old brown leather briefcase[90] into which Karl had placed his previous day's work together with any important post; and which would be returned by the 2.30 p.m. bus with whatever Robert had written or revised since he had last filled the briefcase (or 'diplomatic bag' as it came to be known), together with a short covering letter.[91]

The Graveses were also close to 'good shops and adequate schools'; and a ten-minute walk was enough to take them either right into the city centre, or right into the countryside: indeed, the area had been built over so recently that the terraces at the back of the flats in Guillermo Massot looked out over a farmhouse where turkeys ran loose.

Robert and Beryl had both been 'highly apprehensive' about the move;[92] but after a month Robert wrote very cheerfully to Selwyn and Tania Jepson, telling them that:

> Here we are pretty good … We have a dog track two minutes off, no entrance fee and sixpenny bets, and brandy at 3d. and no big money or rich swindlers, and the dogs are faster (Martin says) than any outside the White City. We return to Deyá at week-ends and on fiestas which are many.

He added that he 'like[d] a bit of urban life', and since they were living in the unfashionable part of the town, he had no visitors to disturb him. As for his work: he had written 'three or four poems and two or three articles', and was two-thirds of the way through the first draft of his *Greek Myths*. At the same time, he was

> working with Jan on a translation of Lucan's *Civil War* for Penguin. And Beryl is translating Alarcon's *Nino de la Bola*, an 1800-ish Spanish novel; and I'm in on that a bit. And Martin is writing a novel about Zuleika Dobson in modern Oxford, and doing an edition, definitive, of all the Robin Hood ballads, because he's found some good obscene unpublished ones . . .

As Graves commented, their two flats were 'a hive of industry'.[93]

But what he wanted to know from the Jepsons, he went on, was 'how and where is Jenny?' Three weeks earlier, he had received an alarming letter in which she had written 'bitterly … about Alex's illness … and I wrote at once. But no answer. And now I hear that Diana [Dick's daughter] has seen Alex and says he looks bad and doesn't seem to care whether he lives or not.' Alex was indeed dreadfully ill; and at the end of October Robert would receive a further letter from Jenny telling him that

'Alex's lungs have been filling up with liquid. He's in hospital. They seem to think they can squeeze him through to another remission but he's certainly very bad this time.'[94]

There was also news about Judith Bledsoe: strangely, her mother had established herself on Majorca, where she had rented a house in the town of Soller, just a few miles to the north of Deyá; while Judith herself had returned with Irwin to Paris, where she was 'living a sort of Trilby life',[95] as Robert described it, and being 'bombarded', as she recalls, with his letters.

In these letters, Robert was growing increasingly excited about the imminent publication of his *Poems and Satires 1951*. For this new volume he had written another forceful introduction, which began:

> Nine poets out of every ten are content to die young; the mortality rate is highest when they leave their Universities to take up careers. Many of the survivors who do not turn playwrights – which, however, is to temper poetry with rhetoric – try to prolong their lives by philosophical or ecclesiastical studies or the writing of occasional verse; continuing moribund until the time comes to rally their strength for a poetic testament, or until physical dissolution mercifully overtakes them.

'Thus', he declared,

> popular imagination conceives of the poet as either a doomed gallant struggling in the toils of romantic love; or a blind, white-bearded prophet; or, if he is ever middle-aged (as I am now), a paunchy Horace-Herrick, jocosely celebrating the trim servant-girl who carries the drinks out to his garden retreat.

Then, reminding his readers that he had 'once suggested that no poet could hope to write more than twenty pages in his life-time that were really worth preserving', he commented on the fact that his 1947 *Collected Poems* still contained:

> an ambitiously large number, and here are more. 'Do I contradict myself?' I ask, and cannot answer with Walt Whitman: 'Very well, then, I do contradict myself', because truth and tidiness are both debts owed by a poet to his readers. So I try to remember for whom I meant that those twenty pages might be worth preserving. Was it for posterity? I must have been thinking of myself as the posterity of certain posterity-conscious heavy-weights of the last three centuries, who have always

bored and depressed me. Personally I have little regard for posterity ...
Whatever view they may take of my work, say a hundred years hence,
must necessarily be a mistaken one, because this is my age, not theirs,
and even with my help they will never fully understand it ... I write for
my contemporaries.

A volume of collected poems, he added, should form a sequence of the
more intense moments of the poet's spiritual autobiography, 'moments
for which prose is insufficient'; and he concluded that such an
autobiography 'does not always keep chronological step with its historical
counterpart: often a poetic event anticipates or succeeds the corresponding physical event by years'.[96]

His own new volume certainly contained not only poems written for
Judith, such as 'Darien' and 'The Portrait'; but also poems written in
anticipation of her arrival on the scene, such as 'Conversation Piece' (with
its 'Two long stemmed glasses,/One full of drink', which watch 'how the
moon trembles on the crag's brink'), and 'The Ghost in the Clock'. *Poems
and Satires*, which was finally published in November 1951, also included
the best version of the poem 'In Dedication' with which Graves had
prefaced *The White Goddess*.[97]

Reviews were excellent, and Graves was suddenly in the news again.
The *Times Literary Supplement* devoted its entire leading article to an
assessment of Graves's poetry, though he was amused, as he told James
Reeves, to see that they quoted 'mainly from my suppressed poems – and I
am haunted, and in perpetual retreat they say. God bless my soul!'[98] On 5
December Christina Foyle of the famous London bookshop reminded him
that 'Every year my father gives a prize of £250 to the author of the finest
volume of poetry published'; and asked him whether 'you as one of the
greatest poets would be a guest of honour' when the winner of the first
prize for 1951 was announced at their January literary luncheon.[99] And
two weeks later Ricardo Sicré commented: 'I see that you're a well-known
poet again this week – the *New Yorker* paying tribute to your loss.'[100]

Robert Graves continued to correspond 'regularly' with Judith
Bledsoe;[101] and shortly before Christmas 1951, he wrote to her as
follows:

Darling –
    Your letter ... arrived today ... Yes, myths are still clustering thick
around my table ... I won't try to send you my poems to Austria but wait
until you go back to Paris; anyhow you have seen the book in proofs, I

think. *Darien* and *The Portrait* seem to make many readers' eyes brim with tears; which is only fair, considering their history, and I am still as proud about Darien – him, not the poem – as about anything that has ever happened to me; and thank you always & for ever.

He added that: 'This is going I hope to be a good New Year for us.'

For one thing, Selwyn and Tania Jepson were planning a visit to Deyá in February. For another, ('isn't this nice?'), two of Robert's friends who had already met Judith and liked her would be returning to the island;[102] while other visitors would include Bill Moss (a young Englishman who was a friend of Jenny's, [103] and had been 'one of the two English officers who were dropped in Crete during the war and kidnapped the German general commanding the forces in Crete'); and 'also, perhaps, Robert Kee [then known as the author of *The Impossible Shore*] ... who would make a whole letter in himself, and who is the only person besides yourself in whom I can forgive a taste for opera. Anyhow, you don't know him, so what the hell?'

Robert added family news and Deyá gossip; and then, on a more personal note, he told Judith that:

Your handwriting is so regular and pretty that I am most relieved with your state of health – gassy though your diet and chilled your back – though it is leaning backwards a little more than usual and even your beautiful capital l's point to 11.30, not midday, now: showing your increased reluctance to put primary obligations before your secondary – or so the graphologists put it.

There followed a long digression on the subject of Santa Claus, described by Graves as

a bit of a beast in real life. As a child he was so holy that he caused his mother frightful inconvenience by abstaining from the nipple every Friday – and she had to draw the milk off with one of those nasty German breast-pumps – and in age he was so violent that when he took part in the famous Council of Nicaea where the Arian heresy was aired, about Jesus being only a man after all, he gave Arius such a box on the ear that he sent him spinning across the hall into the lap of the Archbishop of Scythopolis who was too aged for that sort of horse-play. Santa Claus is *really* what God the Father has come down to being. When Father Gods get senile and dribble, as usually happens after a millennium or two, they have a tendency to 'go the way of all flesh' ...

So be sorry for the greasy old bastard with his mince pies & plum pudding & dirty red dressing-gown, He has seen better days.

Then, writing again in a more personal vein, Robert tells Judith that Beryl is 'active and pretty'; that they have 'given each other antelope-skin wind-cheaters for Christmas, though it is too hot to wear them at present; the sun is terrific'; and, most important of all, that they are 'both sad about … the telescope lens through which we have to look at you'. Robert knows that he must accept 'what has to be'; but he asks miserably 'how have we erred?' And then, after a curious section about consulting a fortune-teller, who gives a broad hint that Judith should come to Deyá again in May, Robert concludes his letter lovingly: 'Anyhow as I write this, the telescope lens fades away and there's you in your black trousers and black shoes, with cold-nipped nose and a rather guilty smile … you are our darling and always will be …

X Robert X[104]

There is much anguish in this love-letter; and the darker side of Robert's feelings for Judith appears on the Christmas card which he and Beryl had sent to friends and relatives. It was inscribed with Robert's new poem, 'Cat-Goddesses', which runs:

> A perverse habit of cat-goddesses –
> Even the blackest of them, black as coals
> Save for a new moon blazing on each breast,
> With coral tongues and beryl eyes like lamps,
> Long-legged, pacing three by three in nines –
> This obstinate habit is to yield themselves,
> In verisimilar love-ecstasies,
> To tatter-eared and slinking alley-toms
> No less below the common run of cats
> Than they above it; which they do for spite,
> To provoke jealousy – not the least abashed
> By such gross-headed, rabbit-coloured litters
> As soon they shall be happy to desert.[105]

CHAPTER 7

Absence

Robert Graves had bravely predicted to Judith Bledsoe that it was going to be 'a good New Year for us'; but in practice uncertainties about their relationship with her combined with family and financial worries to give a depressing tinge to the first few months of 1952.

As Judith's continuing absence preyed on Robert's mind, he wrote another poem, 'The Straw', in which he describes walking through a 'wild valley' and suddenly feeling, as the result of telepathic communication with the woman he loves, that all is not well between them. 'Peace', it begins.

> Peace, the wild valley streaked with torrents,
> A hoopoe perched on his warm rock. Then why
> This tremor of the straw between my fingers?
>
> What should I fear? Have I not testimony
> In her own hand, signed with her own name
> That my love fell as lightning on her heart?

But the poem ends gloomily:

> Were she at ease, warmed by the thought of me,
> Would not my hand stay steady as this rock?
> Have I undone her by my vehemence?[106]

In the midst of this anxiety, it may have been comforting for Robert to remind himself that he had been hearing for some months about another potential Muse.

It was in the early summer of 1951 that Robert had first seen some verses by Jay MacPherson. After which he had reported to James Reeves that he had discovered:

a new woman poet ... I tried to find something wrong with her poems but could not; you know how grudging I am of praise, but these were the real thing, though from Canada. [She is said to be] brilliant at classics, hates Canada, is utterly lonely and also beautiful: what troubles lie ahead for that girl! I think of Laura.[107]

Later that year Jay MacPherson had moved to England, where she lived with her father in Well Walk, Hampstead,[108] and began studying at London University.

Then in January 1952, Jay called on George and Joanna Simon. Subsequently George wrote about her in the most glowing terms, telling Robert that she was:

indeed like a messenger from the Mediterranean. Dark sensitive unhappy and then like quicksilver a flow of words all in your language. She is indeed visited perhaps one should say inhabited by the White Goddess ... I think it most important that she should see you and be guided by poetic contact with you.

George added that he 'would willingly buy her a ticket but her extreme sensitivity and laudable independence make her refuse'.[109]

In any case, Graves was now highly impressed. In February he told the Jepsons that: 'the spirit of the *White Goddess* is heavily entrenched in her, poor child';[110] and in June he paid for Jay MacPherson's *Nineteen Poems* to be published under the imprint of the Seizin Press.[111]

Family worries concerned Beryl's mother, who in November 1951 had had to be operated on for cancer at the Middlesex hospital;[112] and Alex Clifford, whose condition continued to deteriorate. In January 1952, when his latest course of treatment was over, Jenny managed to take him as far as Kitzbuhel in Austria; but in addition to suffering from Hodgkin's disease, Alex was now extremely ill with radiation sickness,[113] and it began to look as though he had only a short time to live.

Financial worries added to Robert's emotional burden. In January 1952 he told Derek Savage that *The Nazarene Gospel Restored* was 'being hung up while Cassell argue transatlantically with Farrar Straus about the printing expenses'; and that it had been 'silly of me (to speak in a wordly sense) to spend two solid years on the Gospels without hope of any return for at least another two years'. At least *The Greek Myths* was 'doubly commissioned, and I'm also writing a modern sex-novel on the side, so all will be well I trust'.[114] It was some extra comfort that, with a relaxation in

exchange controls, the German edition of *I, Claudius* was 'at last paying ...
a proper dividend';[115] and there was a letter from John Graves enclosing
Robert's share of the royalties which still came in each year from the
performance of their father's songs, and which had gone to Amy until her
death.[116] 'Many thanks for your cheque', Robert replied, 'which I feel
rather bad about taking, somehow, but which will come in handy.'[117]

As it turned out, the 'modern sex-novel' was not really to Robert's taste:
his genius was for embellishing what had really happened, rather than for
pure invention, and he never completed it; while by the beginning of
March he had realized that *The Greek Myths* was 'getting a bit out of hand
– twice as long as I expected', he told Joshua Podro in March, 'and now I
am stuck with the proofs of the amended *White Goddess*'.[118] That month
he also wrote gloomily to Ricardo Sicré, who replied:

> It was nice to have your letter although I was sad after I read it. You
> sounded rather depressed and seemed to have an accumulation of
> worries in your head. Your letters are usually the opposite. This is an
> additional reason for you to come to Madrid at least, if you cannot come
> to Sevilia.

'Do not worry about the expense of it', Ricardo told his friend. 'If you are
short of money ... ask me for it without hesitation.'[119]

Shortly after receiving this generous offer, Graves began to be troubled
by portents. First, a hearse galloped past the block of flats. Next, two
undertakers with a tape measure came to the front door 'enquiring if we
had a corpse'; and later the same day,[120] Robert heard from Jenny that
Alex had died on 13 March at the age of forty-two. She had been in the
room with him, she told her father,

> when he drew a last shallow breath. He was in no pain and absolutely
> himself – himself on a remote romantic plane – till the end. Heavens.
> How much one has to be grateful for ... I have tried more than once
> during the last two years since I have known to make myself
> independent of him to make the end bearable.

'But he didn't let me get away with it', Jenny declared, 'because he knew
that after him anyone would be second-best.'[121] Robert immediately sent
an obituary to *The Times* praising Alex's 'integrity', his 'staggering talent',
and above all the stoicism with which he had accepted the news of his fatal
illness. 'He always took a long-term view of problems', Robert concluded
the obituary, 'and politely assumed that his friends would not allow

themselves to be any more emotionally involved in his early death than he was himself. In this, for once, he was wrong.'[122]

Tom Matthews had also been saddened by Alex's death. 'I cannot understand and never shall', he wrote to Robert, 'why Julie died at 46 and Alex at 42';[123] and early in May he made a pilgrimage to Deyá, which he had last visited when his wife was still alive.[124]

In the meantime, Graves had been conducting an occasional correspondence with the Wassons, who were still examining the role of mushrooms in ancient religion. From time to time Graves would come across information which he thought might be relevant; and in April he sent them details of an Etruscan mirror upon which a mushroom had been engraved, which gave them a valuable last-minute addition to their text.[125]

Other distractions from work on *The Greek Myths* included an occasional bull-fight; meetings at the nearby greyhound racing track (where Martin Seymour-Smith remembers seven-year-old Juan showing 'uncanny' skill in forecasting 'the order in which the first three dogs would come in');[126] unsuccessfully campaigning for Max Beerbohm to be publicly honoured on his eightieth birthday;[127] and coping with a steady stream of visits from admirers.

One such visitor was the twenty-one-year-old bisexual American artist Charles Corbett, a devotee of Graves's work since the age of twelve, when his father had given him a copy of *Welchman's Hose*.[128] As Corbett recalls, he had:

hung around Palma for a month or more but was too shy to introduce myself to Robert. Like a lover I learned his routine and lurked about at The Formentor Café where he occasionally came in for a drink. He [must] have noticed, peering at him from across the room, a rather odd looking blonde boy, a type not seen too often in Mallorca in those days.

When at last Corbett 'summoned the courage to knock at the door of [Graves's] Palma flat', he expected a maid to answer, as

Everybody had maids then. [Graves] answered the door himself and said 'Yes?', I was startled and said, 'I love you' and he said 'In that case you had better come in'. He was holding a copy of Laura Riding's book *A Trojan Ending*, keeping his place in it with a finger.[129]

First Robert introduced him to Beryl; and then 'we went into his workroom where we had a long conversation ... He was very kind to me and I love him still.'[130] Beryl was now several months' pregnant with her fourth child. 'Got caught rather the same way you did', Robert told a friend; 'but there are advantages in it as with a Spaniard in the family we'll be able at last to own house and land here.'[131]

Another distraction was trawling through the Palma antique shops where, one spring afternoon, Robert 'came across a seahorse nicely mounted on a small plinth, with a neat lid to the whole'. Deciding that it would make a good present for Judith, he sent it to her accompanied by this poem,[132] in which he told her that he was aware of the pain that their relationship must be bringing to her, as well as to him; and that she should try to be as indomitable as the seahorse which he was giving her.

THE SEA HORSE

Since now in every public place
Lurk phantoms who assume your walk and face
You cannot yet have utterly abjured me
Nor stifled the insistent roar of the sea.

Do as I do: confide your unquiet love
(For one who never owed you less than love)
To this indomitable hippocamp,
Child of your element, coiled a-ramp,
Having ridden out worse tempests than you know of;
Under his horny ribs a blood-red stain
Portends renewal of our pain
Sweetheart, make much of him and shed
Tears on his taciturn dry head.

Judith continued to haunt Robert's waking hours; but the spring came and went without any tangible sign of her return.

CHAPTER 8

The World's Delight

Financially and professionally, the situation remained so dark in May 1952 that Robert Graves told the Jepsons that: 'Portofino is off on all counts, even if we could balance our budget.' His further reason: that he was still being 'plagued by this damned mythology book which won't be finished by July & the US Publisher is clamouring for it'.[133]

Then, quite unexpectedly, a few gleams of light appeared from a totally unexpected source. Graves was contracted by Forrest Judd and Will Price, who suggested (in what Seymour-Smith describes as 'the usual excited telegrams') that Graves should write a script for *The World's Delight*, a film to be based upon a story from the Arabian Nights. They also 'expressed willingness to come to Deyá' for detailed discussions; and although Graves had no wish to repeat his earlier unhappy experiences with the film world, 'he did not feel in a safe enough position to turn them down flat', and agreed to their visit.[134]

Besides, both Judd and Price had interesting track records. Only the previous year, Judd had been in India working as an assistant producer on Jean Renoir's film *The River*; while Price had taken 'what he called "a youthful hand" in *Gone with the Wind*'; and in 1939 he had married the film star Maureen O'Hara.[135] His career had then been interrupted by the Second World War;[136] but on his return to Hollywood, Price had directed, produced or co-produced numerous films: one of which, *The Sands of Iwo Jima*, made in 1949, owed much to his own experiences in the Pacific (the battle scenes were said by *Variety* to be 'terrifyingly real'[137]) and had been a great popular success.

When Robert Graves met Forrest Judd and Will Price, he found that Judd's role would be limited to finding financial backing for *The World's Delight*. Judd immediately offered him:

what was then a handsome sum in dollars – half now and half when the script was delivered – and suggested that Price and Graves get together

and do the writing by the end of September. This was almost too good
to be true: the money offered was worth it to Graves even if the film was
never made ...[138]

But in Seymour-Smith's view it was not so much the money which
induced Graves to accept Judd's offer, as the fact 'that he liked Will
Price'.

It turned out that Price had served in the American Navy with
enormous distinction, winning 'a special Navy medal from an extraordinary feat of courage and endurance in the Pacific'.[139] However, his
wartime service had left him emotionally scarred, something which
Robert could well appreciate after his own years of shellshock. Eventually,
heavy drinking bouts had given him a bad name in Hollywood, and had
led very recently to the break-up of his marriage, which Will found
especially distressing since Maureen O'Hara had been given sole custody
of their daughter, upon whom, Robert commented sympathetically, 'he
dotes'.[140]

At any rate, an agreement was made, though no money was paid over on
signature, as the agreement stipulated;[141] and in June Will Price returned
to the island, where he established himself in an hotel at Lluchalcari.
Unfortunately for all concerned, what followed, as Seymour-Smith tells
the story, was pure farce. Will had brought with him:

> a young girl he had encountered in London: called 'Kitten' by him, she
> was the scion of an ancient and noble family – [the Howards, leading
> house of the English Catholic nobility] ...
>
> Kitten became a problem. She drank triple brandies, and many of
> them; often she would order them by house telephone while lying stark
> naked on the bed in the room she shared with Will, causing
> considerable agitation to the waiters (most of whom were young men
> unfamiliar with such matters) ...

When Robert and Will tried working at Lluchalcari, 'Kitten kept
interrupting them'; and when they moved to the Posada, the situation was
almost as difficult, for in their absence Kitten became bored, and was then
quite likely 'to concentrate her attention on a male guest, or even a male
waiter – and this caused commotions'.[142]

Five weeks after her arrival, Kitten was finally persuaded to leave the
island; and not long afterwards, on 14 July, Robert and Beryl also
departed for their annual journey to England, where once again they took
a flat not far from Beryl's parents in Hampstead.[143]

On their return, Robert resumed work with Will Price. But Will had reverted to his alcoholic ways and, as Beryl explained to a friend, she and Robert were 'always having to rescue him and get him to bed and try to prevent trouble and gossip – not easy here. It wouldn't have mattered', she went on, 'if we hadn't liked him so much – but it really is a hell of a problem, and a whole time job while it last[s].'[144]

At least there was good news from Jenny. 'Hurray! Getting married again', she wrote excitedly from Rome.

> You must trust me that I will not do it on a rebound, out of the awful loneliness ... He is getting an annulment from his wife hoping that I will marry him ... What he lacks in Alex's greatness he makes up for with a genius for humanity. I won't describe him because I wouldn't get it right. You'll have to make do with his nationality which is Somerset Irish, his age which is 36 his upbringing which was South Africa, Florence, his school which was Downside his job which is head of the Reuter's bureau here, his war which was mostly prison-camp ... his wealth absolutely nil and his name Patrick Crosse.[145]

The wedding took place almost immediately, to the narrow-minded scandal of some, especially Jenny's former mother-in-law, who were disgusted that Jenny should marry again so soon.[146]

Robert for his part was delighted that his daughter had been lucky enough to find happiness. But by this time, almost everything in his mind had been displaced by the news that Judith Bledsoe, with whom he had recently been out of touch, had been seen with Irwin and her mother walking down a street in Palma.[147]

CHAPTER 9

Your Naked Name

'When spotted', one August afternoon in 1952, Judith Bledsoe is said by Martin Seymour-Smith to have 'looked annoyed'; and Robert Graves certainly 'lost no time in establishing contact'. This was simple enough, as she and Irwin were staying with Judith's mother in Soller; and superficially all went well during their early meetings.

The underlying tensions, however, were acute: not surprisingly, as Irwin was now determined to marry Judith, to whom he was now engaged; while Robert was equally determined that they should part, and that Judith should find someone more 'suitable'. Indeed, Seymour-Smith recalls that 'a consideration of who would be the "right" man for Judith' had been 'one of the chief topics of conversation at Canelluñ that summer': Robert Kee, who had visited Deyá the previous summer to write a story on Graves for *Picture Post*, was apparently regarded as the most suitable of the various candidates proposed.[148]

Graves had also written a poem in which Irwin's love for Judith was ridiculed as the attachment of an 'ignorant, loutish, giddy blue-fly' to a particularly delicious peach. One particularly savage verse runs:

> Magnified one thousand times, the insect
> Looks farcically human; laugh if you will!
> Bald head, stage-fairy wings, blear eyes,
> A caved-in chest, hairy black mandibles,
> Long spindly thighs.[149]

Judith herself does not wholly escape, as Graves ends his poem resentfully with the line: 'Nor did the peach complain.'

However, Graves still regarded Judith as his Muse. Before long he had brought her up to date with his current news (which involved explaining that Beryl was now almost five months' pregnant); and he also introduced both Judith and her mother to his collaborator Will Price. And since

Judith's mother had been raised in New Orleans, which had also been one of Will's family 'stamping-grounds', she and Will 'were soon discussing third and fourth cousins'.[150]

As the underlying tensions became more acute, the subject of the evil-looking face was reopened. It was Judith who told the story, as she and her mother and Irwin and Will Price and Robert sat outside a café under a hot early September sun. Afterwards, as Robert would later recall,

> Her mother gasped and shook her roughly. 'Darling, why in heaven's name didn't you tell me about it at the time?' 'I was terrified.' 'I believe you're making it up from something I told you sweetie. I saw the same face myself before you were born and the rusty iron gate and the creepers and the shutters.' 'You never told me anything of the sort. Besides I saw it myself. I don't have other people's visions.'[151]

For a while, the truth of the matter seemed more elusive than ever.[152]

But then Will Price came up with a solution which Robert found utterly convincing. He told them of a rare condition known as 'hereditary ectodermal dysplasia', whose victims in the southern United States of America were once known as 'turtle men' because they lacked proper sweat glands, and in very hot weather kept on having to dunk themselves in water. They also had very few teeth and other deformities, so that a sufferer's face was 'highly terrifying to any but a physician who could look coldly at it and characterise it as a facies'.[153]

There was no reason, Robert came to believe, why Judith's mother should not have 'stumbled across the same old house in New Orleans, and seen the same turtle man peering through the attic window twelve years previously'. Robert himself might well have seen the portrait of a turtle man in that Limerick antique shop; while their American friend's vision in Soller could be simply explained in terms of his 'remarkable receptivity for the emotions of people at a distance, and the trick of converting them into waking visions of his own'.[154]

But no explanation could rob the story of its sinister tone: a tone which resonated in the tortured emotions of several of those present. Already, Robert Graves's frustration over Judith Bledsoe's continuing close relationship with Irwin meant that he had begun to live more and more in a world of portent and nightmare, which spilled over most memorably into his poem 'The Foreboding'.

> Looking by chance in at the open window
> I saw my own self seated in his chair

> With gaze abstracted, furrowed forehead,
>   Unkempt hair.
>
> I thought that I had suddenly come to die,
>   That to a cold corpse this was my farewell,
> Until the pen moved slowly upon paper
>   And tears fell.
>
> He had written a name, yours, in printed letters:
>   One word on which bemusedly to pore –
> No protest, no desire, your naked name,
>   Nothing more.
>
> Would it be tomorrow, would it be next year?
>   That the vision was not false, this much I knew;
> And I turned angrily from the open window
>   Aghast at you.
>
> Why never a warning, either by speech or look,
>   That the love you cruelly gave me could not last?
> Already it was too late: the bait swallowed,
>   The hook fast.[155]

And besides writing haunted poems like this one, Robert began pressuring Judith to finish her book illustrations.

Judith once again promised to complete the work; but she would only do it 'by correspondence'. This did not please Robert at all. He wanted her working by his side in Deyá, not far away with Irwin's 'long spindly thighs' in their Parisian apartment. He told her that he must be 'at hand to check the drawings', and reminded her 'that she was still morally bound to fulfil her original obligation, whatever difficulties might be put in her way'.[156]

In the meantime, Graves tried to concentrate on his collaboration with Will Price. Their script of *The World's Delight* had been completed by 13 September – though there had also been 'an ominous failure [by Forrest Judd] to pay the first two instalments contracted for';[157] and before Price left Majorca later in the year, leaving Graves to continue work on *The Greek Myths*, the two men had also written 'a play based on a pet idea of Will's, the story of Susannah and the Elders'.[158]

However, Robert could not do his best work while the situation with Judith remained so unsatisfactory; and when it became clear that she was inflexible about doing the drawings elsewhere, he became angry and confused. Irwin's influence was blamed; and finally, one afternoon, Robert could stand it no longer, and 'went to Soller to "have it out": ostensibly', as Seymour-Smith recounts, 'about the drawings, but really to settle matters with the "blue-fly" '.[159]

Finding that Judith and Irwin had gone to the cinema for the afternoon, Robert followed them there. The next thing they knew, as Judith vividly recalls, was that Robert 'came blustering in, hitting Irwin and trying to drag him out'. Judith quickly grabbed Robert's arm, and tried to prevent a full-scale fight by telling him sharply that Irwin was 'not going to attack a man of your years'. But by this time Robert had already caused a considerable disturbance, and a policeman had been called in. Robert rapidly calmed down, and was allowed to leave.

On returning to Deyá, he explained that he had told the policeman, in Spanish, that Irwin was 'an American idler', who had been 'making an affray'; and that Irwin had then been:

> led ... away to gaol ... 'People who love one another' [Robert had concluded, when he told his side of the story to Martin Seymour-Smith], 'should stick together.' When someone suggested that he might at least have got [Irwin] out of Soller gaol he replied that this was where he naturally belonged.[160]

Graves's account was partly wishful thinking: he would readily admit that although his 'protestant conscience' restrained him 'from inventing complete fictions', he was 'Irishman enough to coax stories into a better shape than I found them'.[161] In any case, as soon as the truth of the matter had been established, Irwin had been allowed home.

The chief result of Graves's outburst was that it strengthened Irwin's hand against him. Judith, though she would have liked to maintain her friendship with Robert, found that she could no longer plead his case without risking the loss of her future husband: so she desisted, and communication between the poet and his Muse came to an abrupt end.

Although there is an important sense in which Judith had only conformed to the pattern of the 'Belle Dame Sans Merci' in which he had so scrupulously instructed her, Robert felt utterly betrayed by Judith's total defection; and he wrote several extraordinarily bitter poems on the subject. In one of them, 'Reproach to Julia',[162] he remonstrates with her for sacrificing 'Love to pity, pity to ill-humour'; while in another, he dreams that 'Julia' tells him that she still loves him.

I answered: 'Julia, do you love me best?'
'What of this breast,'
She mourned, 'this flowery breast?'

Then a wild sobbing spread from door to door,
And every floor
Cried shame on every floor,

As she unlaced her bosom to disclose
Each breast a rose,
A white and cankered rose.[163]

By the beginning of December 1952 Graves decided that he had enough poems for another 'slim volume', and he made up a package for Cassell in which he included another iconoclastic foreword. After asking whether a foreword was 'really necessary', since poems, if they were 'any good, ought to tell their own story. If they are not, why publish them?' Graves attacked the practice of listing the periodicals in which each poem had first appeared, since grateful though one might be to editors, 'the copyright does not remain theirs, and to boast of having caught their interest is not quite seemly.

> Is a foreword really necessary? [he repeated] Even as an assurance that the poet can express himself decently in prose? And though I have written more poems in the last two years than in the previous ten, must I apologise for having been more than usually plagued?[164]

And after posting this package, Graves wrote a letter to James Reeves telling him that his new volume 'was ... dripping with heather honey and black gall'; and that it marked 'the close of an epoch'.[165]

In mid-January 1953 Graves wrote again, telling Reeves that the birth of the new baby was expected daily. Beryl had moved into the upper flat, which Jan and Martin had vacated by moving into another flat nearby; and at the age of fifty-seven, Robert was finding it:

> rather like going back in history this business of cots and baby-clothes and napkins but as my sister Clarissa solemnly says: 'Every baby finds its welcome' ... so good luck to it![166]

Maria, the midwife from Deyá, had been installed for the birth;[167] and two weeks later, on 27 January 1953, Beryl produced her fourth and Robert's eighth child, whom they named Tomas.

Some months later, when they were all back at Canelluñ, Beryl 'pleaded' with Judith that she should 'come to the house and make friends again'; but Irwin predictably refused to let her go. Judith felt anguished; – but settled for security. In due course, she and Irwin were married; and for many years she and Robert altogether lost sight of each other. However, a handful of poems about the love between this muse and her poet survived Graves's occasional culling, and went on to form a distinctive and sometimes unsettling part of the 'emotional auto-biography' of his final *Collected Poems*.

In the meantime, although it would be more than six years before Robert Graves discovered another muse, a pattern had been set for future encounters involving Graves, his wife, and whatever mouthpiece of the White Goddess might be the next to arrive in Deyá and inspire him with poetry.

BOOK FIVE

AMBASSADOR OF
OTHERWHERE
1953–60

CHAPTER 1

No Holidays for a Writer

Apart from the birth of his son Tomas, the early part of 1953 was a gloomy time for Robert Graves and his family.[1] There was little money in the bank, but a great deal of ill-paid work to be done on *The Nazarene Gospel Restored*, whose galley proofs had just arrived for checking; and *The Greek Myths* was still unfinished. Graves's financial position was further weakened by a betrayal of trust. It was almost exactly four years since Gelat's death when Marcus, one of his sons-in-law, 'let slip that "Señor Graves's land in Deyá" belonged to his brother-in-law Juan'.[2]

Marcus was referring to the land which lay in a wide strip on either side of the road which Robert Graves and Laura Riding had built to the sea. Robert had been receiving a share of the olive oil from this land each year; but now, as Seymour-Smith recalls,

> Marcus explained: 'That's not your land. That's our land. Who do you think's been tending it?'
> Graves immediately went round to protest to Gelat's widow – now living in Palma. But she confirmed it. She was ashamed, but asserted that her late husband had lovingly looked after Graves's houses in his absence of ten years, and that it was his land because of 'his sufferings in the war'.[3]

Since the land was not officially in his name, there was nothing that Robert could do about this blatant theft; except that in due course, using Ricardo Sicré as his intermediary,[4] he arranged to buy back almost half of it, this time making sure that he had a proper title.

In the meantime, Robert and Beryl were holidaying in Seville with the Sicrés and Tom Matthews in May 1953, when they heard that Norman Cameron had died late the previous month. For several years it had been known that he was suffering from high blood pressure;[5] and not surprisingly it was a stroke which carried him off.[6]

Subsequently, Tom Matthews wrote to Robert to suggest that Norman's poems 'should be collected in one book. And you'd be the person to write an introduction.'[7] Alan Hodge, who had been left Norman's copyrights, welcomed this idea;[8] and the two men agreed to discuss the matter further when Robert and Beryl paid a short visit to England in the summer.[9]

In mid-April there was cheerful news from Jenny. She and Patrick had been enjoying a few spring days 'in the wilds of Calabria'. There, much to Robert's excitement, they had discovered Bagnara, a village on the coast opposite Messina,

> where matriarchy is tradition. Men stay at home and look after the children and do the housework, women (marvellous, proud, in splendid costumes) travel all over the Continent trading fruit and fish and olives, doing all the commerce and finance etcetera etcetera.

'The only place in Italy', Jenny concluded, 'where women are not treated as if they had no souls ... '[10]

Later that month Robert also heard from two young writers who were living on Majorca, one in Deyá, the other in Soller, and who hoped to visit him.

The first, who was twenty-nine, introduced himself as 'a naturalised American negro born in Panama', and a devotee of *The White Goddess*.[11] This was Alston Anderson, a writer of some originality who had seen active service during the Second World War in the US Army, and had studied philosophy first at Columbia University and then at the Sorbonne. He had then moved to Deyá where, as the only black person living there, he was considered by the locals to be good luck.[12]

The second writer, then equally unknown, enclosed three poems 'in the hope that you will have the time to look at them', and announced that he had been living at Puerto Soller for the past three months, and was just finishing the last draft of a novel called *The Deserters*. He was twenty-five years old, he came from Nottingham, he had been 'pensioned off some time ago by the RAF after being out in Malaya', he felt 'guilty of having taken your time', and he signed himself 'Yours sincerely, Alan Sillitoe.'[13]

Graves wrote back asking him 'to come over to Deyá one Sunday to have tea. So on the first fine weekend of spring', Sillitoe recalls, 'I borrowed a bicycle and pedalled off up the mountain road.' On arriving at Canelluñ, he helped Graves pick some lemons for lemonade,

> tugging fruit from trees and filling a straw basket. 'Some of your poems

are good,' ... said [Graves] ... 'At least you end them well. So many people get off to a good start, then fizzle out half way through, coming in lamely at the end.' He was a big man, with grizzled hair, a broken nose ... full lips, a vigorous head; he wore sandals, blue jeans, and a brown open-necked shirt – a well-built middle-aged sixty.

When they went into the house, Sillitoe asked whether Graves 'was busy of a Sunday'. At which his host thoughtfully 'poured two glasses of lemonade and sat at the large table covered with books and papers', where he began:

signing limited editions of his poems, a light labour that enabled us to talk through the scratching of his signature. 'I'm always busy,' he replied. 'There are no holidays for a writer, especially when he has a large family.'

Later, when Beryl had returned from the Cala with her children, Alan Sillitoe stayed for tea; and later still, after some encouraging words from Graves about his writing, he 'sat for some time drinking *coñac*, a fiery Spanish brandy that later helped me on my way back to Soller – flying round the hairpin bends with more speed than wisdom'.[14]

By the end of May 1953, having finally posted his typescript of *The Greek Myths* to Penguin, and page proofs of *The Nazarene Gospel Restored* to Cassell, Graves had begun thinking seriously about his next major project. The most important thing was that it should make as much money as possible; and so he decided that he should write a novel.

His agent Bill Watt was delighted by this news; and soon wrote back to say that he had discussed the matter with Desmond Flower of Cassell, who hoped that Graves would write one of his 'big historical novels as soon as possible. He feels that this is what the public is really waiting for.' Flower's suggestion was that Graves should capitalize on the enduring success of the *Claudius* books by writing 'a novel dealing mainly with life on the Roman wall, though with some of the scenes at any rate laid in Rome itself'; and Watt commented that 'this would be a magnificent subject treated as you would treat it. I wonder whether it appeals to you?'[15]

It did not: principally because Robert Graves knew that in order to do his best work as a novelist, he needed the stimulus of an actual set of events, preferably involving some as yet unsolved historical conundrum. He was already considering two possibilities. The first concerned 'Queen

Salote of Tonga's Great-grandfather (from 1797–1893)'; while the second involved going 'to Sicily in 900 BC about',[16] and solving the problem of who had written the *Odyssey*.

July found Robert and Beryl staying with the Chilvers in London.[17] Rosaleen came up to see them from Bishopsteignton;[18] and she and Robert spent an evening discussing family matters,[19] especially the loss of their half-brother Philip, Sally's father, who had died peacefully in Ireland in his eighty-fourth year and was much missed.[20] Another evening, Robert and Beryl dined with Tom Matthews, who had 'decided to throw in my lot at least for a year with *Time* in Britain'.[21]

Before they flew back to Majorca on 16 July, Robert and Beryl had excellent news about an offer from Doubleday for *The Nazarene Gospel Restored*. After Selwyn Jepson had taken a hand in the negotiations,[22] this involved plans for a print run of 20,000 copies, and 'a pleasantly large advance'[23] which, as Robert reported to James Reeves, would make him 'solvent again – isn't that nice'.[24]

Returning to his study in Canelluñ, Graves thought some more about his two possible novels, and came down in favour of the 'Homeric' story, which appealed to him because it involved solving an historical problem.

CHAPTER 2

Blind Homer's Daughter

August 1953 found Robert Graves at Canelluñ 'dreadfully busy with visitors & clearing my desk of odd jobs before I start the Homeric novel'. These 'odd jobs' included 'translating poems by Juana de Arbaje the 17th c. genius who took huff and turned nun';[25] and his visitors were Dick Graves's thirty-five-year-old daughter Diana and her son Simon Gough, a lively, goodlooking boy who celebrated his ninth birthday on the fifteenth of the month.

Diana had been on the stage for many years, but was now finding it difficult to get parts.[26] She was also a fully fledged hypochondriac with a rich, throaty voice who drank heavily, smoked incessantly, and whose love of life was intensified by the conviction that she was dying. The slightest irregularity in her heart beat would be classified as a 'heart-attack'; and to guard against sudden death she insisted on being carried all the way to and from the Cala on the back of an ass.[27]

Another visitor that summer was the twenty-seven-year-old Scottish poet Alastair Reid. He and his wife had stumbled on Deyá quite by chance, having no idea that Robert Graves lived there; but more than thirty years later Reid would 'recall with a kind of lunar clarity the Deyá of those days', when 'Mallorca still lived ... by the agrarian round, the turning of the fruitful seasons. Villages maintained a rough self-sufficiency ... Nobody had much money, and indeed there was little to buy.'[28]

Reid is said by some to have given 'the impression of studying [Graves] from a distance' on this first visit; he was certainly intrigued by the older man; and indeed they had much in common. Both were sensitive and highly intelligent (Reid, a graduate of St Andrew's University, was currently teaching at Sarah Lawrence College in New York); both were poets (Reid had 'published one book of verse, *To Lighten My House*, with a small American firm called Morgan and Morgan';[29] both had seen wartime service (Reid had served in the Navy); both had been keen sportsmen (for two years, Reid had been 'a Rugby Blue who had played in Scottish trials'); and both had rebelled against a 'fiercely puritanical' upbringing, Reid having been 'the son of a poor minister and', in Robert's words, 'brought up the hard way'.[30]

As Reid spent more and more time with Graves, he noted with interest that when Robert 'emerged from his workroom, his writing preoccupations would spill over into conversation'; and this was 'particularly' the case with the new historical novel[31] which Robert had begun writing by the third week in August.[32]

As a young man, Graves had been deeply influenced by Samuel Butler's *The Way of All Flesh*; and now he drew his inspiration from some theories elaborated by the same author when he had been translating the *Odyssey* in 1891. Butler had deduced not only that the *Odyssey* was set in Sicily, but also that the poet was a woman, who had lived at or near Trapani, and who had written herself into the poem as the beautiful Princess Nausicaa.[33]

Butler's supporting arguments had never been taken seriously by classical scholars; but when Graves was researching for *The Greek Myths* he found them conclusive. He therefore came to believe that the *Odyssey* had originally consisted:

> of a straightforward Homeric saga about the return of Odysseus from Troy, only to find that his wife had been unfaithful – to which (after the first eighty lines) has been added a fairy-tale, unconnected with it, about a hero called Ulysses who escaped various kinds of ritual death.

But when these two separate elements had been removed, there remained, as Butler had realized, what Graves described to Selwyn Jepson as:

> a substantial mass of realistic modern novel-writing which reflects a domestic and political crisis in a Sicilian court about the year 730 BC. I have worked this story out and it makes a very exciting drama full of suspense: centred around the Princess Nausicaa

'of whom', as Graves commented, 'such a charming portrait is given in Book VI of the *Odyssey*.'[34]

Selwyn Jepson was now regularly negotiating on Robert Graves's behalf; and so Graves explained to him that besides working on his 'Homeric novel' he had also been 'shortening & tightening up' his and Beryl's translation of Alarcon's *Nino de la Bola*, and working on his short book 'summarizing the sources of the Genesis creation story'.[35]

This latter task involved Graves in one final attempt to persuade Judith Bledsoe to complete the series of drawings that she had promised him. The point was that Arnold Fawcus of the Trianon Press had said that he would publish the Alarcon 'if he could also have the Creation'; and so Graves, not quite daring to write to Judith herself, asked her mother to write about the drawings on his behalf. She did so, and after a short interval Judith duly replied; but 'Her answer', as Graves complained to her mother on 10 September,

> no longer acknowledges her moral obligation, or even a legal one. She is so far from remembering what kind of people Beryl & I are that she has been persuaded – the words once more do not seem to be hers – that I would give her drawings to a commercial artist and say 'please do another 27 in the same style'. All I am asking, since it seems that she cannot keep her word, is that she either returns me my original drawings or lets me have her drawings to reduce to squiggles again – because I spent a good deal of time working on the set-up, & do not want to have to do it again.

He concluded in a somewhat Olympian fashion that Judith 'has our continued love, and remind her that Beryl and I will always tell her the truth'.[36]

In the event the Trianon Press took both books, as they had promised. But the 'Creation' book, which was published as *Adam's Rib*, contained none of Judith's work. Instead, there were 'seventy-two wood-engraving illustrations' by an artist whom Graves described to James Reeves as 'our local genius Jim Metcalf':[37] he and his wife Tommy were friends of Cecily Gittes and her husband, and have been living on the island since the summer of 1951.[38]

Besides negotiating on Graves's behalf, Jepson had also begun offering his friend some sound advice on promoting his career, which appeared to them both to be at a critical turning point. Earlier in the year, recognizing the improvement in his status, Robert had written 'From the Embassy', in which he introduced himself as:

> I, an ambassador of Otherwhere
> To the unfederated states of Here and There
> Enjoy (as the phrase is)
> Extra-territorial privileges.

With heres and theres I seldom come to blows
Or need, as once, to sandbag all my windows.
And though the Otherwhereish currency
Cannot be quoted yet officially,
I meet less hindrance now with the exchange
Nor is my garb, even, considered strange;
And shy enquiries for literature
Come in by every post, and the side door.[39]

And by September, he could tell Jepson that most of his newer poems had 'appeared in the *New Yorker, Atlantic Monthly, Poetry, Hudson Review*, etc.', and that 'no anthology which includes poems by English authors ventures to omit me now.'[40] Graves added that he had already 'written about a quarter' of his new novel, and that: 'A title has just been put into my mind doubtless by the Goddess Athene: BLIND HOMER'S DAUGHTER. All right.'[41]

The following month Selwyn Jepson declared that he was aiming for Graves to earn enough money:

> to let you write your novels not faster than one every eighteen months, of which at least four should be spent deciding whether to write it at all instead of some other story you've spent another three months rejecting the notion of; and when you do start writing the one you finally choose it should be the only thing apart from Beryl of course in your heart and mind.

He added bluntly that it was 'absolutely no cop at all' being a genius, if he remained unable to 'enjoy every moment of it for worrying about feeding you and yours'.[42]

Robert admitted on 4 November that he had been 'too busy writing to think much about marketing'. But although he agreed 'about not overproducing books capable of a large sale', he also pointed out that he found it 'impossible not to work all the time at something. Occupational neurosis. But there are a great many things I can work at which don't interfere with the money-making ones': for example, his incidental articles, his 'Creation book', and his translations: including just then both the Alarcon, and a 'coming translation for Penguin Classics of Lucan's *Pharsalia*'.[43]

Nor did poems 'interfere'; and Robert reported incidentally that his *Poems 1953* were 'having a fantastically good press: meaning that people have decided that it is time I was recognized'.[44] Published in October

1953, it was certainly an impressive volume, which included not only 'The Foreboding', 'Cat-Goddesses', and other poems about his relationship with Judith; but also incidental verses such as 'The Blotted Copybook', in which Graves, wondering about the effects of increasing fame, asks himself:

> Will he at last or will he not,
> His yellowing copybook unblot:
> Accede, and seriously confess
> A former want of seriousness
> Or into a wild fury burst
> With: 'Let me see you in hell first!'[45]

October had also seen the publication of *The Nazarene Gospel Restored*: there had been no reviews as yet, so Graves liked to imagine that the theologians were 'stunned and wildly thumbing their exegetical cribs'; and Robert had been visited by Gordon Wasson,[46] who later wrote to thank him for 'a glorious weekend'.[47]

Partly on the strength of information passed on by Robert about the existence of hallucinogenic mushrooms in Mexico,[48] Gordon had recently visited Mexico with his wife Valentina. Their visit had been a great success: they had 'taken part' in a divinatory mushroom session in a backward Indian tribe', and 'brought back the mushrooms in formaldehyde for identification by Paris savants'.[49]

Not long after Wasson's visit, Graves was excited by a request from Trinity College, Cambridge. Overcoming his temperamental dislike of 'the other place', and on the strict understanding that all six lectures could be delivered within a three-week period in the autumn (when he hoped that William would be starting at Oundle), Robert agreed to give the prestigious Clark Lectures for 1954. His subject would be 'Professional Standards in English Poetry',[50] and the composition of these lectures made his burden of work still heavier.

Graves's main task continued to be *Homer's Daughter* (he had soon dropped the 'Blind'); and his new novel would be dedicated 'To Selwyn Jepson, of course'. This was partly because Graves had once described Princess Nausicaa as 'a sort of Ionian Eve Gill': Eve being the heroine of several of Jepson's highly entertaining thrillers;[51] and partly because the light and easy manner in which Graves told his story owed much to Jepson's influence. Gone were the long passages of background information with which Graves had to some extent disfigured his most recent historical novels *The Golden Fleece* and *King Jesus*. Instead, he had concentrated on plot and character. The result was one of his most readable novels: sadly under-rated chiefly because it is unlike anything else Graves wrote, and critics as well as readers prefer consistency in their authors.

The story is set in context and given a distinctive 'voice' by a prologue in which Nausicaa introduces herself as a Princess of the Elymans, 'a mixed race living on and about Eryx, the great bee-haunted mountain which dominates the westernmost corner of three-sided Sicily and takes its name from the heather upon which countless bees pasture'. From the age of fifteen she has brooded on death, and grown melancholy, and 'reproached the Gods for not making me immortal and envied Homer'; and she declares that this preoccupation with death:

> excuses, or at least explains, the most unusual decision I have recently taken: of securing for myself a posthumous life under the mantle of Homer. May the Blessed Gods, who see all, and whom I never neglect to honour, grant me success in this endeavour, and conceal the fraud.

'Phemius the Bard', she adds, 'has sworn an unbreakable oath to put my poems in circulation: thus paying the debt he incurred on that bloody afternoon when, at the risk of my own life, I saved him from the two-edged sword.'[52]

The story proper begins with the departure from Drapanum of Princess Nausicaa's brother Laodomas. But he leaves in mysterious circumstances; and some months later the King goes in search of his missing son, leaving Nausicaa's Uncle Mentor as regent. Nausicaa now discovers that there is a conspiracy against the royal house. Laodomas has been assassinated; the King's ship is to be ambushed, and he too is to be murdered; and in the meantime the company of conspirators descend upon the royal palace in the guise of suitors for the Princess Nausicaa's hand. Their plans include 'mak[ing] free with the Palace flocks, herds and wine',[53] provoking Nausicaa's brother Clytoneus to violence as an excuse for killing him; and marrying off Nausicaa to one of their leaders.

First, however, the conspirators dispose of Mentor. Clytoneus, Nausicaa and Aethon, the Cretan archer with whom Nausicaa falls in love, are then left with only three others, including the swineherd Eumaeus, to face 'one hundred and twelve suitors, and a score of their servants'.[54] There follows a gripping tale in which love and loyalty triumph in the face of overwhelming odds, and against a background of savagery so unbridled that by the end of the story the palace is heaped with corpses, and Nausicaa comments in a matter-of-fact tone of voice that 'the pailfuls of dark red water drunk that day by the quinces and pomegranates were acknowledged three months later in a bumper crop of fruit'.[55]

While Graves was busily writing *Homer's Daughter*, reviews of *The Nazarene Gospel Restored* began to appear. He had once expected the book to be 'a bomb of great power',[56] which would destroy or at the very least substantially undermine the Christian faith in its present form;[57] but in the event, the book was both a critical and a commercial failure.

In January 1954, Robert told his brother John that *The Nazarene Gospel Restored* had been 'vulgarly abused' by the Church, 'but nobody has yet succeeded in finding a historical flaw to invalidate the argument'.[58] The reviewers were indeed 'mostly members of the clergy', and were 'with very few exceptions, very hostile, some to the point of hysteria … content to denounce the book as "a farrago of rubbish" (*Church Times*) or complain that Graves and Podro had "reduced the story to the plane of pure history" (*Observer*)'.

Robert answered each reviewer, extracted an apology for libel from the *Manchester Guardian*,[59] and later told Selwyn Jepson that it had all been 'great fun'.[60] But it was galling to find that his theories received so little serious attention; and in February he complained to Basil Liddell-Hart that many newspapers, including '*The Times*, *Telegraph*, *News*, *Sunday Times*, etc.', had 'funked any notice at all. It is all very interesting.'[61]

After an interval of several years, Graves and Liddell-Hart had resumed their correspondence because of the shared interest in T. E. Lawrence which had first brought them together in 1935. Liddell-Hart had written first, to tell Graves about the forthcoming publication of Richard Aldington's *Lawrence of Arabia: A Biographical Enquiry*, a malicious account which is interesting chiefly as a classic example of how a biography can be meticulously referenced, yet thoroughly misleading. Having learned of Aldington's principal charges against Lawrence, in particular that he was a liar and a homosexual, Liddell-Hart wanted to know whether Aldington had bothered to consult Graves or not; and what could be done about preventing publication.[62]

'This is the first I have heard of Aldington's interest in T.E.', Graves assured Liddell-Hart on 19 February 1954. Whatever he had checked in Lawrence's stories had 'always proved true or even understated'; and the suggestion of his being a homosexual was 'absurd and indecent'. Sadly, there was no law of libel to protect the dead. Indeed, the 'only punitive action' they could take, apart from action in defence of copyright, would be 'to publicly strike Aldington and plead the book as provocation. This', declared Graves, 'I should be glad to do myself were I in New York, Paris, or wherever Aldington hangs out.'[63]

In the meantime, Graves had been working as hard as ever. He had recently posted copies of the completed *Homer's Daughter* to Cassell in London and Doubleday in New York;[64] there would soon be proofs of *The Greek Myths* to be dealt with; and, as he had told Selwyn Jepson earlier in the year:

> To keep wood in the stove & charcoal in the brazier I have been sending things to *Punch*: Muggeridge accepts them all, which is very nice, because I can earn his 35 pounds in four hours, & that is 3,500 pesetas, my secretary's wages for a month.

Other news was that Jenny was attempting 'to match Tom Matthews with Martha Gellhorn', the distinguished journalist who had incidentally been Ernest Hemingway's third wife, and who was described by Jenny as 'the nicest woman she had met in years'.[65] In due course, Jenny's efforts would prove successful; but first there was a marriage much closer to home.

CHAPTER 3

Under Fire

At the beginning of March 1954, Robert Graves's thirty-year-old son Sam announced that he was engaged to Anneliese Hildebrandt, a warm- hearted children's nurse whom he had known for just over twelve months.[66] Sadly, Robert was deluged with work; but he said that he looked forward to hearing about the wedding, which would be in some four months' time, and he invited Sam and Anneliese to spend their honeymoon in Deyá at his expense.

In the meantime, Robert's labours included coaching William for the scholarship examination to Oundle,[67] since Martin and Jan Seymour- Smith had 'left suddenly and in rather a muddle';[68] there was another new project: the translation of George Sand's *Winter in Majorca*,[69] and correspondence about T. E. Lawrence dragged on through March and April.

Graves eventually decided, after being shown the Aldington biography when it was still in half-galleys[70] that:

on the whole, it had after all better be published, <u>because</u> it is perverse and sneering and contains all the muck that an industrious rogue could rake together in three years; and should certainly not be corrected or modified by you or anyone else to modify its nastiness but left to its critical fate. A 'debunking' was obviously due one day:

'Better that it should come now, and in its most unpleasant form', he told Liddell-Hart, 'while it can be dealt with faithfully by survivors who know the facts.'[71]

Graves added that within the past few years he had shown one of T.E.'s letters to a graphologist, who had told him that Lawrence's writing was 'that of a man who has been made impotent by some great shock and, instead, enjoys fantastic sexual orgies in his mind'.[72] And in due course, Graves would write reviews in which he stated his belief that 'the clue to

T.E. was that as a result of physical impotence and degraded feeling produced by the flogging at Deraa, T.E. had very vivid, waking fantasies (diabolical even) which he could not always control'.[73]

While 'defending' Lawrence from Aldington in this curious manner, Graves continued to defend his own reputation from critical attacks upon *The Nazarene Gospel Restored*: and this came to seem less and less amusing. 'I have just had to spend valuable time stink-potting nasty clerical dons in *XXth Century* and *Theology*', Graves told Jepson on 10 March 1954. 'Jesus Christ, how ignorant and how dishonest!'[74]

Still more time-consuming was an altercation with the *Times Literary Supplement*. It had begun with a hostile and anonymous review by M. J. C. Hodgart of Pembroke College, Cambridge. On 5 March the TLS printed Graves's reply; and there the matter might have ended. Unfortunately, the TLS then printed a further statement by Hodgart,

> who was incensed by Graves's portrait of St. Paul (he had described him as 'a Syrian Greek opportunist with no regard for factual truth and mainly responsible for the Christian misrepresentation of Jesus's acts and beliefs') and accused Graves and Podro of 'unethically camouflaging the true text of Galatians 4, 14', which concerned Paul's famous 'thorn in my flesh'.[75]

The editor had then declared the correspondence closed.

However, Graves discovered that Hodgart had been 'using a secondary reading abased on the worst manuscripts', and demanded the reopening of the correspondence on the grounds that the reviewer's comment was defamatory. When the editor refused, Graves consulted a solicitor; and on 29 June he told Basil Liddell-Hart: 'I shall know this week whether the *Times Literary Supplement* are going to apologize for libel or prefer to be sued. My lawyer has taken Counsel's advice and reports our case is cast iron.'[76] No apology was forthcoming; and both sides began preparing for litigation.

Homer's Daughter and *The Greek Myths* also caused Graves some anxiety that spring and summer. At first Ken McCormick of Doubleday would only say of *Homer's Daughter* that it was 'a very provocative book', and Graves gloomily imagined that 'Professor Tush of Columbia and Professor Bosh of Harvard are bellyaching about Homeric scholarship. But I have taken expert advice', he explained to Selwyn Jepson towards the end of March, 'and there's nothing in the world *against* my reconstruction: and every nice Vassar girl will feel flattered that she could have written the *Odyssey* herself. How University Professors hate me!'[77]

At the same time there was bad news about *The Greek Myths* from America, where Viking Press, who had been due to publish a hardback edition, 'got scared ... and turned it down'.[78] Or, as Graves put it in a further letter to Jepson, they had 'showed the book to Professors Tush and Bosh', who say 'it is most unscholarly and we can't recommend it to our students'.[79]

Selwyn Jepson tried to calm Robert's fears, suggesting that Doubleday were only trying to decide whether *Homer's Daughter* was a commercial proposition; while if Viking had 'turned down *The Greek Myths* the best thing to do' was 'to sit on it for the time being at least until the Penguin is out'.[80]

Before Graves received this advice, his anxieties had been intensified by news of the general opinion at Doubleday that *Homer's Daughter* was not 'of the same stature as *Claudius*'. Graves immediately wrote to Doubleday to point out that T. E. Lawrenc once 'rightly observed' that:

'R.G. was born without a reverse gear' – meaning that he never writes the same book twice ... *I, Claudius* and *Claudius the God* made a big book of some 340,000 words long; full of barbarous late Roman detail. This is a sweet, exciting, early Greek love story of 80,000 words. It is as different from *The Claudius* books as *The Nazarene Gospel* is from either ... Your editors must understand that whenever I write a book they ought to judge it as though it were an imponderable first novel by an unknown author; it will never be the same mixture as before.[81]

Jepson thought this letter most unwise; but in any case Doubleday decided in favour of *Homer's Daughter*, which they planned to publish in an edition of 12,500 early the next year.

As for *The Greek Myths*: Graves continued to have trouble selling the American hardback rights; but by the end of March 1954, a clever manoeuvre by Jepson had secured an American paperback. He had asked Allen Lane of Penguin Books for a set of proofs of *The Greek Myths*, telling him that he needed one to try to secure an American publisher; and Lane's 'reaction to my request ... was an immediate desire to buy the rights himself, to penguinise it also over there'.[82]

Work on *The Greek Myths* continued until mid-June, when Graves was busily compiling an index; a tedious chore from which he stole a few minutes to write to a beautiful young film star who had a flat in Madrid, and had become a close friend of the Sicrés.[83] 'I am not a Greek scholar or an archaeologist or an anthropologist or a comparative mythologist', Robert wrote to Ava Gardner, but I have a good nose and a sense of touch, and think I have connected a lot of mythical patterns which were not connected before. Classical faculties will hate me, and I will get a lot of sniffy reviews. But people like you and Sally [Chilver] and her other friends will I think know that a good deal of it makes sense;

'and anyone', he concluded, 'is welcome to take over where I leave off and make even better sense.'[84]

Soon afterwards Sally and Richard Chilver arrived in Deyá for their summer holiday;[85] and then came the long-awaited news of Sam's wedding to Anneliese at Caxton Hall Registry Office.[86]

The wedding had been followed by a splendid reception in the House of Lords in a room directly overlooking the River Thames. Clarissa reported to Robert that: 'Anneliese seems a splendid wife for Sam, & I hear Nancy is pleased';[87] and a few days later, the newly-weds arrived in Deyá for their honeymoon: an act of generosity on Robert's part which later led to his being severely attacked by Jenny.

The storm blew up in an unexpected quarter. Eleven-year-old Lucia had been studying ballet for several years,[88] and this was the summer when she successfully 'got on her points'; after which Robert wrote to Jenny suggesting that it would have been kind of her to congratulate Lucia on this event. Jenny immediately sat down and wrote her father a long letter on the subject of his own treatment of his first family.

'It seems to me', Jenny began comparatively mildly, 'that by some law of reverses your children get more and more adult as they appear'. She was 'only just reaching the age of reason'; while Tomas was:

doubtless a professor. And you (and Mother) still need a lot of bringing-up …

Sam's terribly happy letter from Majorca said one or two things which wounded me on his behalf and I think for the sake of your upbringing … you should know. Your *attitude* to both of us as your children is painfully unfatherly. You get on with me all right but for unfatherly reasons. And your friendship supplants fatherliness so I'm all right and don't notice. But Sam who is your son is coming to show you his new wife. You should really have made a ceremony out of it. I do think you might have put them in the romantic Posada instead of in a fisherman's cottage.

And I do think you might have had a wedding present ready for them all excitingly packed. And when you went to Palma – if you were going to give Beryl (who a million per cent deserves a swiss watch if anybody does) a present – you might have done it without their seeing, having *not* given them a wedding-present. There! Now I've said it.

Jenny made it clear that there had been no complaint from Sam – she had 'found these things in his letter'. She said that she had already

been pretty angry actually when I heard that Betty and Richard were going to be with you at the same time. I hope they weren't. You should really have cleared the decks for Sam. They were nervous enough about how they were going to carry off the meeting jointly as it was.

And now her 'between the line detection' had been

quickened by a letter from you suggesting that I should have done something the day Lucia got onto her points. I would like to remind you quietly that the day I got on my points, and for that matter the day I got my first job went totally unremarked even by my father.

In her view, Robert's 'second lot of children' were 'damned lucky in the life they have and the attention they get – one doesn't want to overdo it'; and even if, 'in the welter of life here [in Rome], she had 'found a minute for a postcard of congratulations for Lucia … the attention that needs making up is to Sam and Catherine.'[89]

While under such heavy fire not only from academics, critics and publishers, but also from his eldest daughter, Robert Graves found much relief in the company of his friends. His 'money shortage … timely arrested', as he told James Reeves, 'by an extraordinary cheque for £600 from Czecho Slovakia (*Golden Fleece*) and some *Punch* acceptances',[90] that summer he presided over a huge party at Canelluñ. Alan Sillitoe, who was now living in Soller with the poet Ruth Fainlight, wrote afterwards that it had been:

Magnificent. We enjoyed it so much that we hardly noticed the walk back to Soller until waking up next morning. We swayed happily along the pitch-black road, me singing dirty songs. I'm paying for my sins now choc-a-bloc with pills and punctures, only for a short time though. I think yours was the best party I've ever been to.[91]

Another guest was Alastair Reid. He had recently returned to Deyá where he was in the process of becoming Robert's closest and most trusted friend.

CHAPTER 4

Ambassador of Otherwhere

Noticing how Robert Graves 'presided over the village as its attendant spirit and custodian', Alastair Reid gradually came to think of Deyá 'as a private landscape of Robert's, almost a geographical projection of the inside of his head'; and as an observer he was well-placed. Before seven o'clock each morning, Reid would arrive at Canellun, where he usually found Graves 'watering the garden before the sun climbed'; after which the two men would wind their way:

> down to the nearest sea for an early-morning plunge and swim, before panting our way back up, always locked in conversation, to make breakfast, as the children straggled in from sleep. After breakfast, Robert would rise, stretch, and disappear into his workroom.[92]

There he was 'desperately busy' during July and August, 'with seven books about to come out ... proofs pouring in', and his six Clark lectures to be written.[93]

Graves had already decided that in his role as 'Ambassador of Otherwhere' his principal aims would be to defend the poetic tradition as he understood it, and to speak out firmly against apostates from that tradition. This meant attacking a large number of established reputations. 'How difficult it is', he wrote to James Reeves on 25 July, 'to be undull and honest without giving offence!'[94]

Alastair Reid recalls Robert Graves sitting in his study while he was working on the Clark lectures, 'his essential books and tokens at hand, dipping his steel pen intermittently into the inkwell and writing, writing, always on the back of old typescripts'. Graves 'wasted no time, nor ever seemed to pause for thought'; and it was Karl Gay who:

> made Robert's furious pace possible, and kept up with it. Once Robert had finished a passage of a few pages and then gone back over them,

crossing out and adding in the margins, he would put the pages to one side, and Karl would come over from C'an Torrent ... and bear them off. They would reappear, typed, on Robert's desk later in the day, ready for further mutilation and possibly another two typings.[95]

Lunch came at 1.30; after which Robert would enjoy a twenty-minute siesta, before returning to his study for another two hours of work, a second swim, and tea.[96] After which, in the early evenings, 'ritual dictated a walk to the village to collect the mail'. Opening the mail was done in the café, 'where the sprinkle of foreigners from that time generally gathered'.

One of the strangest foreigners that summer was Bynum Green, an American alcoholic who blamed his drinking on a bizarre wartime experience. At the end of the Second World War, he had been an officer in Shanghai, where:

one of his duties was repatriating Japanese prisoners and sending them back to where they came from, and somehow ... he lost five or six hundred Japanese prisoners, and every time he got drunk he'd tell the story – he'd lost them and couldn't get over it and claimed that was why he drank so much.[97]

In the late summer he disappeared for a few days; only to reappear during a mass in the village church, when he fell out of the choir loft in which he had been hiding. Subsequently he was removed to an asylum in Barcelona, where Robert heard that he had 'been shocked into a sort of semi-sanity, but still has delusions'.[98]

Other café regulars included Bill Waldren, a tough and athletic American photographer and painter who spent most of the year in Paris with his French wife and their daughter; and Mati Klarwein, the tall, thin good-looking young Israeli artist who wore a Panama hat, played the guitar, and painted hyper-realist landscapes and still lifes.[99]

Any newcomer whom Robert liked would soon, as Alastair observed, be assimilated into 'his private Universe'. For Robert would rapidly 'create, out of a few essential facts, a whole identity, holding it out as though it were an overcoat, for the person's arms to be slipped into the ready-made sleeves'.[100] One young English secretary, for example, was introduced as 'the fastest typist in England'; and Alastair would later comment that while Robert 'clearly meant well, others were less keen on having their essential selves reconstructed'.

After a spell at the café Robert and Alastair would return to Canelluñ for the evening watering; and then, as Reid recalls, they:

invented supper, cooking on charcoal, which always involved activity ... and, since Robert always seemed to prefer the food from the plates of others to his own, meals turned out to be raucous occasions. Robert would quite often go back to work after supper, to catch the last of the light, for we were wired to an electric plant that, just before eleven, would dip three times,

which sent them 'scuttling for candles and matches before it turned itself off'.

William set out in mid-September for Oundle;[101] where the following month Robert gave a talk on poetry to the sixth form,[102] and where he also had an unexpected encounter with an old friend.

It happened like this. Robert Graves was standing outside the Headmaster's study, when the door opened and out stepped Siegfried Sassoon, whose son George was a pupil at the school. Having quarrelled over Laura Riding's influence on Graves, it was more than a quarter of a century since these former comrades-in-arms had met each other face to face;[103] and some days later they saw each other again in the chapel of King's College, Cambridge. Afterwards, Sassoon wrote that 'all the years and misunderstandings had melted away'.[104] Although their friendship would never be fully resumed, Graves too was pleased by the encounter; and when in January 1955 Sassoon gave him a copy of *The Tasking*,[105] a privately printed edition of his recent verse, Graves's only recorded comment was one of 'great relief that there was one real poem in the bag'.[106]

Robert Graves's own reputation as a poet had been steadily growing during the early 1950s, especially among fellow writers such as the thirty-two-year-old Kingsley Amis, another St John's man, who had just published his highly acclaimed first novel *Lucky Jim*. Amis had recently sent Graves an amusing letter about one of Graves's articles for *Punch*;[107] and on receiving a friendly reply, he declared that he now had 'some excuse for saying what I had often wanted to say', which was that, for Amis's money, Graves was:

the best poet now writing in English if you'll pardon the expression. I know you know that all poets like your verse best, after their own of course, but I thought I'd just confirm it from my own corner of the battlefield. All my friends agree on how good you are, including some who don't write any verse themselves.

'Reading you', he concluded, 'has done such poems as I've written a power of good ... That's right, have a good time at Cambridge and tell them what is what.'[108]

Graves also appealed to university students fascinated by his *White Goddess* theories; and after giving his first Clark lecture on Monday 11 October, he was able to tell James Reeves that 'hordes of devoted students' had been 'turned away at the door'.[109]

In the lecture, Graves had emphasized that it was the 'crowning privilege' of every true English poet to receive the 'silent benediction' of 'the Muse, their divine patroness'.[110] Telling his audience that what he had to offer for their scrutiny were 'personal principles, deduced for my own guidance from a long study of poems and poets',[111] he also commented that he had 'never been able to understand the contention that a poet's life is irrelevant to his work ... If it means that a poet may be heartless or insincere or grasping in his personal relations and yet write true poems, I disagree wholeheartedly.'[112]

Graves then sketched the history of poetry in England from the earliest days to the defeat of Charles I at Naseby in 1645; and stated that professional standards in poetry were 'founded upon the sense enjoyed by every English poet since the time of Chaucer, that he forms part of a long and honourable tradition'. His first lecture ended with a brief account of Pope's 'apostasy', as he saw it, from that tradition.

Pope had managed to persuade his contemporaries that 'nothing of consequence' had happened in English poetry until the 'French style' was introduced by Denham and Waller; and Graves not only condemned him for this but also declared forcefully that:

Today we are threatened by a new apostasy from tradition; which has been my main reason for accepting the College's generous invitation. I am not a born lecturer, nor even a very willing one; but it seems to me that someone has to speak out, and nobody else seems prepared to do so.

He added that his 'own preferences among the poets, and my reasons for making them, will be clearly given'. And he concluded: 'If, in the course of this lecture, I have said anything out of order, pray forgive me. I am a stranger here.'[113]

On Friday that week, Graves gave his second lecture. 'The Age of Obsequiousness', in which he discussed the disastrous effects of the 1660 Restoration. Charles II's court had been so dominated by French culture that 'no poet could follow the central English tradition':[114] hence Dryden and Pope – and with carefully chosen examples of the worst of their work, Graves proved both Dryden's repulsive lack of taste and Pope's technical incompetence.

These iconoclastic lectures were immensely popular with the undergraduates; and in the meantime there was excellent news about Graves's dispute with the TLS. A notable theologian had found 'that the text which I have been favouring, and which *The Times* regards as hopelessly "bad", is in fact one hundred years older and far superior to the one they call me unscholarly for not accepting'.[115] This meant, Graves believed, that 'their case will break down and not even (I think) go into court'; and so it proved, though it was not until July 1955 that the *Times Literary Supplement* finally printed an apologetic editorial, and agreed to pay Graves's legal costs.[116]

On Monday 18 October 1954, Graves gave his third Clark lecture 'The Road to Rydal Mount',[117] in which he principally contrasted the careers of two early nineteenth-century poets: Clare, the servant of the public who, with his growing sense of what poetry demanded, ended as a devotee of the Goddess; and Wordsworth, who reversed that process.[118] Then the Graveses briefly decamped to London, where on Wednesday evening, Robert gave a broadcast on the Home Service.[119]

Taking as his subject 'The Poet and his Public', Graves explained that true poems are written not for the public, but for a personal Muse; and that therefore readers should 'not make a public figure' of a poet, 'but rather, if they please, a secret friend'; and he begged young poets not to send him their poems. 'If they are true poems', he explained, 'they will know this themselves and not need me to say so and if they are not, why bother to send them?'[120]

Back in Cambridge again, Graves delivered his two most technical Clark lectures. In 'Harp, Anvil, Oar', he discoursed chiefly on the origins of different types of metre (with Irish verse, for example, matching 'the rhythm of the smith's hammers', and Anglo-Saxon poetry 'based on the slow pull and push of the oar'); on the use of rhyme; on rules and the deliberate breaking of rules; and on 'the heresy of free verse'.[121] Then in 'Dame Ocupacyon', he inveighed against impressionist, futurist and surrealist techniques, together with what he described as 'Lycophronic verse', in which lines are full of over-erudite references whose chief purpose appears to be to make the reader 'humbly ashamed of the gaps in his education'. He then talked for a while about the difference between the few 'necessary' poems and the many unnecessary ones; and about the preservation of poetic integrity.[122]

Graves's sixth and final lecture, delivered on Friday 29 October, was ironically entitled 'These Be Your Gods', and begins with the words:

I was never one to stroll down the street with a catapult and break windows just for the fun of hearing the tinkle of glass and seeing furious faces peering out as I scuttle away. But to break windows *from the inside* amounts, at times, to a civic duty ...[123]

As he had promised in his first lecture, Graves was about to speak out against 'the new apostasy from tradition'. There was no space for more than a few words about 'sick, muddle-headed, sex-mad D. H. Lawrence' or for 'poor tortured Gerard Manley Hopkins';[124] but he launched full-scale attacks, backed in each case by carefully chosen quotations, upon five contemporary idols: W. B. Yeats, Ezra Pound, T. S. Eliot, W. H. Auden and Dylan Thomas.

Yeats, given credit for the promise of an 'early copper period'[125] in which he wrote poems like the one beginning 'Who dreamed that beauty passes like a dream', is attacked for having renounced his adherence to the Muse. Instead, influenced by Ezra Pound, and with nothing of his own left to say, 'unless one counts the literary ballads written for the Irish War of Liberation',[126] he had collected all kinds of material ranging from 'rubbish borrowed from the planchette'[127] to snippets from 'the *Vedanta* and the *Mabinogion*',[128] and tried to alchemize them into poetic gold. However, comments Graves, the alchemists never succeeded in making gold out of anything but gold; and he dissects Yeats's poem 'Chosen' to expose both the imprecision and the intellectual nonsensicality of his new-model verses.

The previous year, in his essay 'Dr. Syntax and Mr. Pound', Graves had successfully exposed Pound's gross incompetence as a translator.[129] And now he attacks Pound's anti-Jewish obsession, and finds it 'an extraordinary paradox that Pound's sprawling, ignorant, indecent, un-melodious, seldom metrical Cantos ... with illiterate Greek, Latin, Spanish and Provençal snippets ... are now compulsory reading in many ancient centres of learning'.[130]

T. S. Eliot is at first treated more sympathetically. Graves admires him for having been 'once, however briefly, a poet. I refer to the haunting blank verse passages in *The Waste Land* – and if he found the demands of the Goddess too severe, who can blame him?'[131] He is given credit for having been 'the only publisher in London with the courage to print my long *White Goddess*';[132] and if he was 'as polyglot as Pound: Greek, Latin, French, German, Indian, Sanscrit tags alternate in his poems', then at least 'he took decent care to check their accuracy, and had a far better ear for verse.' However, Graves wishes that Eliot had not been 'encouraged by Pound to voice the anti-Jewish obsession';[133] and that he 'had stopped at *The Hollow Men*, his honest (and indeed) heart-breaking declaration of poetic bankruptcy, to the approved Receiver of poetic bankruptcy, the Hippopotamus Church';[134] in support of which, Graves quotes Eliot's lines beginning:

> We are the hollow men
> We are the stuffed men
> Leaning together
> Headpiece filled with straw. Alas!
> Our dried voices, when
> We whisper together
> Are quiet and meaningless
> As wind in dry grass
>
> ...
>
> For Thine is the Kingdom ...
> Life is very long ...
> For Thine is the Kingdom ...

Auden, told that his real talent is for light verse (Graves quotes his Phi Beta Kappa poem as a *tour de force* in the field) is reminded that he borrowed 'half lines and whole lines' from Laura Riding's *Love as Love, Death as Death*;[135] and is informed that his borrowed inspiration makes him 'as synthetic as Milton', with a style 'compounded of all the personal styles available'.[136]

As for Dylan Thomas: he was 'drunk with melody, and what the words were he cared not. He was eloquent, and what cause he was pleading, he cared not'; though 'a central thread of something like sense makes the encrustations of nonsense more acceptable'; and Graves quotes the stanza beginning 'If my head hurt a hair's foot' as an example of 'nonsense ... but Dylan's golden voice could persuade his listeners that he was divulging ineffable secrets'.[137]

Fortunately, Graves declared, there was still 'a small, clear stream' of living poetry:

> To take only the United States: Robert Frost, e. e. cummings, John Crowe Ransom, Laura Riding, have all written living poems in their time. I refrain from invidiously singling out their English counterparts still alive ... But I do find it remarkable that the extraordinary five years

of Siegfried Sassoon's poetic efflorescence (1917–21) should be utterly forgotten now.[138]

Finally, Graves thanked his audience for their 'continued patience' and concluded, in a reference to the words he had used at the end of his first lecture: 'If, in the course of these lectures, I have said anything out of order, pray forgive me doubly; I am no longer a stranger here.'

Before Robert Graves left England on 3 November (with the applause of most of the undergraduates and the disapproval of most of the dons still ringing in his ears) he had recorded his part of a tribute to Thomas Hardy which was broadcast by the BBC early the following year;[139] and he had collected commissions for two new translations.

CHAPTER 5

Golden Hopes

During the winter of 1954–5, Robert Graves was chiefly working for Penguin on Lucan's *Pharsalia*, which he was translating at the rate of two thousand words a day; and on Suetonius's *Lives of the Twelve Caesars*,[140] for which he had engaged Alastair Reid to produce a rough draft.[141] Christmas was spoilt by bronchitis;[142] but early in the New Year of 1955, Robert told his brother John of a:

> Delightful surprise: I was elected without my knowledge (or engineering) a Fellow of the Royal Anthropological Institute. The only letters I can put with my name except B. Litt – I must have them embroidered on my pyjamas and socks, in Gothic characters, and tattooed on my shoulders.[143]

In February 1955 *Homer's Daughter* and *The Greek Myths* were both published; and towards the end of March Robert noted that 'both seem to be selling well enough in England; & the first of them very well in U.S.A.'[144]

The Greek Myths had been received less than rapturously by a number of academic critics; but *Homer's Daughter* won excellent notices on both sides of the Atlantic.[145] Jenny was so impressed that, in April, she persuaded her father to send a copy of *Homer's Daughter* to Ingrid Bergman.[146] This beautiful actress, star of such classic films as *Casablanca* and *Spellbound*, had been forced to leave Hollywood five years previously after her love affair with the film director Roberto Rossellini had caused an international scandal. Her first husband divorced her, and she was now living in Italy and married to Rosellini; but the films in which he directed her had been box-office disasters, and she longed for a role to restore her fading career.

As she read Graves's novel, Bergman was enormously attracted to the lively, intelligent character of the Princess Nausicaa; with the result, as

Jenny reported to Robert in mid-June, that she spoke 'for hours' one evening with Patrick 'about making a film of *Homer's Daughter*. That's how she sees herself and how Rossellini sees her.'[147]

Towards the end of the month Ingrid Bergman wrote to Graves herself. 'You kindly sent me your book *Homer's Daughter*', she reminded him,

> saying it was not for the movies. Now having read it and told the story to Roberto (he tried to find a French or Italian copy but didn't) we think it would make a very good movie. We really would like to know if you would give Roberto an option on this story and how much you want for the movie rights on *Homer's Daughter*.

Rossellini would then 'immediately try to find the suitable set-up to make this picture'.[148]

A few days later, on 2 July, Jenny and Patrick drove along the coast to have lunch with Ingrid Bergman. Jenny subsequently described her to Robert as 'one of the most charming women presently on the face of the Globe and she's absolutely determined to play Nausicaa if she and Roberto can rustle up the money'. Apparently Ingrid Bergman had explained that she would first:

> have to go to France to make a Renoir film. Rossellini has suddenly run out of ideas she says which means he can now make other people's. If true this may yet save her career ... She wants you to come over and write with Roberto technically advising the script.[149]

Jenny was still writing this letter when Ingrid Bergman telephoned to say that she and Roberto Rossellini had been 'up early discussing *Homer's Daughter*', and that she wanted Jenny's help in drafting a telegram to Watt in reply to his asking £5,000 for the film rights. When the telegram was sent, it read:

> AGREE IN PRICIPLE GRATEFUL YOU SEND URGENTLY DRAFT CONTRACT

When the contract arrived, Rossellini would then begin 'rustling up the money-lenders. So far', wrote Jenny, 'so good.'

Robert Graves was once again desperately short of money, so the thought of Ingrid Bergman playing Princess Nausicaa was particularly exciting; and within the next few days he had sent her two further letters on the subject.

Then, on 19 July, Ingrid Bergman wrote to Robert telling him that 'of course' she wanted 'to play Nausicaa. I wouldn't let any younger and more beautiful actress take it away from me'. However, she was committed not only to the Renoir film, but also to a possible stage play; while Roberto Rossellini was travelling to India 'to discuss a picture to do later in the season' and would then be going on to France. So the earliest that *Homer's Daughter* could go into production would be next spring or, failing that, next autumn – 'as in the summer we plan to go to South America with our opera Jeanne d'Arc ... Please believe me', she reassured him, 'we are very serious about *Homer's Daughter*, but it will take some time.'[150]

Bergman's letter arrived shortly before Graves's sixtieth birthday celebrations, at which, as he told James Reeves, 'at least 60 guests were present':[151] including Robin Blyth, an ex-inmate of Kneesworth Hall, and a wealthy twenty-one-year-old with dark hair, quizzical eyes and a large sensual mouth. Dorothy Simmons had sent him out to Majorca at the start of the year,[152] shortly before he inherited a fortune of £45,000, in the hope that Robert and Beryl would be a good influence on him.

Robert liked Robin very much, attributing his reckless and occasionally violent moods to the fact that he came from 'one of the most gifted families in England – the Legges, Earls of Dartmouth. Hates restraint, born 350 years too late.'[153] And although Robin was highly impulsive, his first major purchases after he came into his money were reassuringly practical: first he imported two canvas-topped Land Rovers, one of which he gave to Beryl, who had learned to drive the previous year; and then he bought himself Sa Guarda, a small property in Lluchalcari, on the hillside above Robert's boathouse.

Robin Blyth's purchase of Sa Guarda had soon led to a new custom which lasted for almost twenty years. Each Sunday during the summer the Graveses and a number of their friends would gather there in the heat of the late morning with the ingredients for a large picnic lunch, to which everyone was expected to bring a contribution. While the picnic was being assembled in the coolness of the house, some of the party would walk down a steep path to the jetty by the boathouse; and there they would sunbathe or swim, while Robert struck out for the rocky outcrop some thirty yards out to sea, on which he gathered rock samphire and sea salt. Later, having climbed back up to Sa Guarda, where bathers had the salt hosed from their bodies, they collected a selection of food and a glass of the local Binisalem, and sat together in the dappled shade of vine-covered trellises to enjoy their picnic lunch. After which the party broke up, and Robert walked back to Canelluñ for his usual short siesta before resuming work.[154]

Once Graves had completed the Lucan, he undertook, for a third share of the royalties, to rewrite the psychiatrist Dr William Sargant's *Battle for the Mind*, to which he promised to contribute a chapter on brain-washing in ancient times.[155] At the same time, thoughts of making large sums of money from film or television work were rarely far from his mind. He continued working on ideas with Will Price, who had reappeared on the scene;[156] and not long after Graves's sixtieth birthday, he wrote a letter to Alex Korda in an effort to revive plans to film the *Claudius* novels.[157]

Six weeks later, he had heard nothing from Korda; and then, shortly before Robert set out for his annual visit to England,[158] the disappointing news arrived that Roberto Rossellini had failed to raise enough money to buy the rights to *Homer's Daughter*, the filming of which was therefore postponed indefinitely.[159]

Robert Graves was in London for the publication of his translation of Lucan's *Pharsalia*, and of *The Crowning Privilege*, which included his Clark lectures, ten essays on poetry, and sixteen poems written or amended since his 1953 collection.

The *Pharsalia* was generally well received: even the great E. V. Rieu (translator of the *Iliad* and the *Odyssey*) could not fault the translation, though he complained that Graves had made a personal attack on Lucan in his preface. About which Graves commented: 'Haven't I a right to, after months of sharing a shaving-brush and razor with the yellow bastard?'[160]

As for the Clark lectures: they had already been attacked for 'perverse' or 'eccentric' opinions by academic critics such as Herbert Read and Donald Davie,[161] and now, as Graves observed, their publication in *The Crowning Privilege* 'made a lot of people cross. Even Martin had his little yap.'[162] For once, however, Graves resisted the temptation to strike back. 'As you know,' he explained to Alastair Reid,

I make a point every few years of blotting my copybook by doing or saying the wrong things. Those Clark lectures ... are indeed the wrong thing; they show quite clearly that the ball game I play has a very different set of rules from the one played by the other chaps ... I'm afraid of getting caught up in literary society and obliged to perform; so I said what I thought and am grateful to you for abetting me.[163]

There is a reason why this explanation sounds oddly self-conscious. Shortly after Graves's return to Deyá at the end of September, he and Alastair Reid had begun a formal correspondence intended for publication: from which this is an early extract.

October brought with it Robert Harling of the *Sunday Times*, who had come to gather material for an article on 'Robert Graves in Majorca'. 'Graves is a tall, big man', he began his portrait,

> and moves easily and well. In profile he has the head of a Roman senator on an ancient coin. The high-bridged, broken nose, firm chin and grizzled hair could be a coin-maker's delight. Full-face, there is something of the air of an eighteenth-century bare-fist fighter about him.

But Harling also noticed that Graves spoke nervously,

> mumbling, standing up, moving around, rubbing at his stubbled chin, seeming to throw out words, scarcely making sentences. Much of his conversation consists of his casting forth ideas and the outlines of ideas:

'the result', Harling observed, 'of his restless curiosity'.

For much of the interview, Graves amused Harling with a familiar blend of witty but slightly eccentric scholarship. Mentioning, for example, that he had nearly completed his translation of Suetonius's *Twelve Caesars*, Graves described it as 'One of the most informative books in the world', and explained that he had been 'entranced' that very morning:

> by Suetonius's dry comment on the Emperor Caligula's amateur performances as singer, dancer, chariot-driver, elocutionist and solider: 'yet with all these varied gifts he could not swim a stroke!' This makes one more addition to my list of famous non-swimmers: Lycidas, St. Peter, Blackbeard the Pirate and the Knave of Hearts ...'

Only occasionally did Graves strike a more personal note.

Once, for example, they were talking about modern English painting, when, 'as a thought for discussion', Graves said that painters seemed to do their best work when they were unhappy. 'What about writers?' Harling enquired. 'I'm happy now', Graves replied.

'Personally happy, that is. I'm not at all happy about the world we live in. One's personal life flattens out. I suppose – like me – you were a manic-depressive when you were young. That side of life makes a graph. It's always up and down when one's young.' He shapes a hollow in the air. It is quite a dip. 'After thirty-five or so the curve begins to flatten out. We can both look forward to a reasonable old age.'

Harling let this go; but he recognized that by suggesting 'a parallel life of hectic ups and downs in his visitor', Graves had subtly discouraged further investigation into his own private life.[164]

This was not surprising. For what Graves really wanted was not a 'flattening-out' in his emotional life, but the arrival of another muse, as he recognized most notably in his poem 'The Face in the Mirror':

> Grey haunted eyes, absent-mindedly glaring
> From wide, uneven orbits one brow drooping
> Somewhat over the eye
> Because of a missile fragment still inhering,
> Skin-deep, as a foolish record of old-world fighting.
>
> Crookedly broken nose – low tackling caused it;
> Cheeks, furrowed; coarse grey hair, flying frenetic;
> Forehead wrinkled and high;
> Jowls, prominent; ears, large; jaw, pugilistic;
> Teeth, few; lips, full and ruddy; mouth, ascetic.
>
> I pause with razor poised, scowling derision
> At the mirrored man whose beard needs my attention,
> And once more ask him why
> He still stands ready, with a boy's presumption,
> To court the queen in her high silk pavilion.[165]

Money was still in short supply, and when on 8 November Robert Graves wrote to James Reeves mentioning the *Sunday Times* profile ('Quite decent, as these things go') he added that: 'We are still not rich, but still have golden hopes, which cost nothing except incidental postage.'[166]

By the beginning of December, as he told Sally, there was nothing further to report about those golden hopes; although by then he had 'cleared off' his Suetonius; together with 'a volume of stories … and the final versions of Will Sargant's book'. Now there only remained 'a school book of ballads done to please dear James Reeves'; and a 'very exciting' book about Jesus.[167]

The latter work, entitled *Jesus in Rome*, was the result of a fresh collaboration with Joshua Podro. Offered as 'historical conjecture', it assembled all the evidence that Jesus had survived the crucifixion; soon after which, according to Graves and Podro, Jesus had realized that:

> he was not the Messiah, nor was the end of the world imminent and that by trying to 'force the hour', i.e. by trying to fulfil all the Biblical and Apocryphal prophecies he had led his disciples into sin ... [And so] he admitted his error ... disappeared across the border to Damascus ... [and] travelled widely in the East ...

Finally, having lived to a ripe old age, Jesus had been 'buried in Srinagar, Kashmir, by his disciple Thomas Didymus, not later than AD 72'.[168]

However, *Jesus in Rome* was just the kind of book which could be guaranteed a poor sale; and it made Ricardo Sicré even more concerned about the enormous disparity between Robert's work load and his earnings. Chiding him for his unbusinesslike approach to his career, Ricardo told him, when he and Beryl were spending a week in Madrid, that he must learn to enjoy periods of leisure. He also introduced him to Ava Gardner, who took a great liking to him;[169] and afterwards the poet commented that it was 'the first week in which I have done no writing for ... can't remember if it's five years or twenty'.[170]

On returning to Palma, Robert Graves found waiting for him an excited letter from the composer Peggy Glanville-Hicks, who announced that she had 'just finished reading your novel *Homer's Daughter* and I am writing to ask you *immediately* – to forestall all others! – to ask if you would give me permission to make an opera libretto from this novel?' She also enclosed a publicity leaflet, from which it appeared that she had studied at the Royal College of Music under Vaughan-Williams; that her main stage work to date was an opera with a libretto by Thomas Mann;[171] and that she had recently been awarded a Guggenheim Foundation.[172]

Graves replied that he was all in favour of an opera being based on *Homer's Daughter*, provided that it raised no contractual problems when he came to sell the film rights. He also insisted that the libretto should be written in collaboration with his friend Alastair Reid, who had recently had some experience in the field.

Graves was still hoping to hear better news from the Rossellinis about their proposed film of *Homer's Daughter*; and at length, in a final attempt to stir them into action, he sent Ingrid Bergman a copy of the Swedish edition of *Homer's Daughter* as a Christmas present.[173] Not even this drew any response; but the project was briefly displaced from the centre of Graves's mind by two unexpected developments: a lucrative invitation to lecture at Princeton University; and a suggestion that he might wish to stand in the coming election for the Professorship of Poetry at Oxford.[174]

After some thought, Graves turned down the Princeton offer. It would have involved him in 'six weekly lectures this Fall for $5,000' but, as he told Gordon Wasson on 24 February 1956, it would also have meant 'being away from home for four months ... and I haven't been away for more than a week since 1939!' He added that his decision displeased Ricardo Sicré, who had recently been 'plotting' with Gordon to secure him a grant, and knew that regular lecturing would make a major difference to his finances.[175]

Robert had already explained to Ricardo that the fundamental reason for his having declined the Princeton offer was neurasthenia:

> Probably you don't realise how neurasthenic I get when not firmly fixed; especially when a lot of talking goes on in which I am expected to join. After a few days I'd be on a stretcher. The neurasthenic pension I still draw from World War I is deserved.[176]

He added that in any case he still had 'golden hopes' in connection with both Will Price and Ingrid Bergman.

None of this satisfied Ricardo, who replied that Robert must not allow neurasthenia to be a limiting factor: it was possible to be a neurasthenic yet lead a perfectly normal life. He also declared that Robert was too much of an idealist to see things clearly; that he himself had no faith in Will Price (to whom Robert and Beryl had now lent substantial sums of money); that there was very little hope of *Homer's Daughter* ever being made into a film, as Ingrid Bergman had recently signed with Twentieth Century-Fox, where her first task would be to play the title role in *Anastasia*: and that if Robert was serious about making money he should either lecture, or write books in the same vein as his most popular successes.[177]

On 11 February Graves drafted a reply to Sicré, in which he acknowledged his views on neurasthenia, while explaining that his own was no longer evident only because he was so very careful to avoid any situations in which he might be seriously affected. He also commented that he had been permanently influenced in the direction of idealism from his earliest childhood, and could not change now. True, he had stopped believing in Father Christmas until recently when Ricardo had given him fresh hope. Still more bitterly, Graves added that he had foolishly assumed until recently not only that he must labour from dawn until well beyond dusk, but also that he should entertain freely, and be generous to those who had fallen on hard times. Ricardo had made him think again . . .[178]

As for some of Ricardo's other points: Robert explained that he and Beryl were gambling on Will Price, and liked him well enough to take that risk, come what may. And although hopes of *Homer's Daughter* were at a low ebb, they should remember that a determined woman – in this case Ingrid Bergman – could work miracles, if she really wanted to get the film made.

The question of his lack of earnings touched Robert more closely. He drafted a sentence cursing himself as an idiot, before crossing it out and telling Ricardo that he should not try to change his habits at this stage in his life; and he threatened in some years time, when Ricardo had reached Robert's current age, to force *him* to go lecturing the length and breadth of the U.S.A.[179]

However, the letter was never sent in this outspoken form. Instead two days later, Graves posted a rewritten version in which there was no implied criticism of Ricardo, and the main body of the letter had been pared down to a very few lines about his dislike of lecture tours and his neurasthenia.[180]

As for Graves's possible candidature for the Professorship of Poetry at Oxford: this was in the air by the beginning of January;[181] but then came what Robert described as:

> a technical snag. When I got a B. Litt in 1926 I was 'deemed to have taken a B.A.' but the Professorship of Poetry demands an M.A. and the machinery for deeming that I was still deemed to have taken one was cumbersome & costly.

'So', he explained to John Graves, 'my supporters had to let it go.'[182]

It was a particularly cold, unpromising winter. Towards the end of January, a letter came from John telling Robert that their half-sister Susan had died. 'Sad for dear Susan, whom I had learned to love in recent years', Robert replied. 'We wrote often and her shrewd touches always pleased me.'[183] The following month saw the death of Beryl's mother,[184] and more snow and frost. 'Our lemon trees', wrote Robert, lost their leaves in the second cold spell and the fruit turned white and pulpy and had to be pushed on the compost heap ... Valldemossa was cut off from Palma for three days by snow-drifts ... an old man froze to death in his hovel at Alcudia; the Inca road was strewn with abandoned Cadillacs and Chevrolets; and a Frenchman skied through Deyá![185]

On the sixteenth Robert reported '10 degrees of frost';[186] and a few days later he received bad news which temporarily blighted his 'golden hopes'.

Ingrid Bergman wrote to apologize for not having acknowledged Robert's gift of a Swedish edition of *Homer's Daughter*, and to explain that the shooting of *Anastasia* had been postponed; that in the autumn she was:

> going to do *Tea and Sympathy* on the Paris stage for six months – that is if it runs that long. So you see I am not very free, not for some time. I still and always will love to do *Homer's Daughter*. The only thing is I'll be a pretty *old* daughter ...

'Please forgive us for the waiting and wondering that we have made you go through', she concluded; 'sincerely Ingrid.'[187]

Ironically enough, the only film money to reach Robert Graves during these months had arrived from an altogether unexpected source. At the end of January, when Robert received his annual royalty cheque from his father's estate. It was significantly 'more substantial ... than usual', since APG's song 'Father O'Flynn' had been sung on film; and this had brought in a windfall of more than £500.[188]

CHAPTER 6

They Hanged My Saintly Billy

'I ought to write for the masses', Robert Graves had told his brother John in mid-February 1956; 'but it would embarrass me too much.'[189] However, financial needs continued to be pressing. *English Ballads*, which he had finished back in January,[190] could never be expected to make much money; nor could *Jesus in Rome*, a completed draft of which he sent to Joshua Podro on 1 March;[191] nor could *Battle for the Mind*, which was also virtually finished; nor could his translation, in collaboration with Beryl, of *El Embrujo de Sevilla*,[192] 'a bullfighting story by the Uruguayan novelist Carlos Reyles (1868–1938)'.[193] So Graves began casting about for a suitable subject for another popular historical novel.

Graves was distracted from these concerns when Betty Sicré rang up from Madrid to tell him that she was sending Ava Gardner to Palma: partly for a much-needed rest and partly, as Robert later recalled, so that she could 'study Spanish grammar, swim daily, and consult me about how to finish her random education by a crash-course in English poetry'.[194]

It was in the late afternoon of Thursday 8 March that Ava Gardner arrived at Palma airport, where she found Robert, Beryl, Lucia and Y-Grec the poodle waiting for her; and where, in Robert's words, she 'came rushing across the tarmac to us taking good care to get wrapped in a close family embrace – which was her only way of throwing off the Spanish wolf who was pursuing her with amorous yelps'.[195]

For the next five days Robert had the 'fantastic experience' of 'getting caught in Ava's spotlight'. She found little time for resting, and none for Spanish grammar;[196] but Robert interested her in the idea of starring in a film version of *El Embrujo de Sevilla;*[197] and on Sunday she went out to Deyá with the Graveses to join them in their picnic lunch at Sa Guarda. By then the weather was too cold for bathing, but:

bathe she did. She also asked me about poetry, and how she should start reading it. I reassured her that there was so little really worth reading, and so much that was wrongly supposed to be worth reading, that she had better not start without being sure she wasn't wasting her time.[198]

'Poems are like people', Robert told her. 'There are not many authentic ones around.'[199]

On Monday night, after an evening with friends, and a 'brief tour of midnight streets'[200] Ava Gardner asked Robert Graves for a signed poem. He chose 'She speaks always in her own voice', which he had written for Judith Bledsoe, but which seemed wholly appropriate; and as he had expected, the verse beginning 'She is wild and innocent, pledged to love/ Through all disaster', went 'straight to her heart'.[201]

It was during Ava Gardner's visit that Graves had an idea for a new novel; and as soon as she had left, he began to read whatever he could find about Dr William Palmer, the notorious poisoner who was hanged in 1856 for the murder of fourteen people.[202]

The story of the murders was dramatic enough; and Graves told James Reeves that he was writing the book 'for fun & other people's fun; & money';[203] but he also intended, as he explained to Selwyn Jepson, to correct what he believed to be an historical injustice, and 'to get Palmer out of the Chamber of Horrors as an impostor ("He never done it")'.[204]

After several days of careful study, Graves was ready to begin writing; by 20 March he had already drafted the first three chapters of what he had provisionally called *Palmer*. However at that point, realizing that he needed to read a great many more relevant books if he was successfully to re-create Palmer's world, he laid his draft chapters to one side for the time being.[205]

Soon afterwards, a letter arrived from Vincent Korda about the rights to *I, Claudius*.[206] He had unearthed 'two of the existing [Charles Laughton] reels ... It looks so wonderful', he reported, that:

Seeing now again what we did in 1936, and remembering the books I am sure a wonderful film could be made now with the new large screen and modern techniques. Naturally we cannot use any of the old material as we must have an entirely new cast and it must be made in cod colour with completely new conception.

So he told Graves that he 'would like very much to meet you and discuss all these things which I am sure could be arranged with advantage to you and London Films'.[207]

Graves knew that he had 'only moral rights in more money', but he hoped that Korda might 'respect them (as a fellow-artist)'; and a meeting was held on 25 April, when he and Beryl were passing through Paris on their way to England.[208] Over dinner at the Mediterranée,[209] Korda spoke enthusiastically about *I, Claudius*, and told Robert that he had Alec Guinness in mind to play the title role.[210]

A further meeting was held five days later in London. Clips from the Laughton *I, Claudius* were shown;[211] after which, as Graves reported to Alastair Reid, Korda told him that 'he wants me to do the script again. This time, it won't be messed-up by Hungarian rewrite men, he promises.'[212]

Robert Graves was also given tickets to see Alec Guinness in the farce *Hotel Paradiso* at the Winter Garden, 'and went round to his dressing-room afterwards, and he is mad keen to play Claudius'.[213] On 18 May, shortly after his return to Palma,[214] Graves wrote to Guinness to tell him that their meeting had been 'great fun' and that, once he had 'the all clear' from Korda, he intended to rewrite the *Claudius* script 'with an eye to your particular talents, giving Claudius a dry, comic but generous wit'. He also mentioned that he had sent him, under separate cover, 'The *World's Delight* script ... partly as a reassurance to you that I can manage the technical side of the Claudius script ... chiefly in the hope that you may get excited by it'.[215]

The result was that on 13 June Graves received this encouraging telegram:

VERY MUCH WANT TO DO WORLDS DELIGHT IF CONTRACTUAL DIFFICULTIES CAN BE OVERCOME WHICH I THINK POSSIBLE LETTER TO YOU IN POST ALEC GUINNESS[216]

However Beryl, 'never fooled by golden dreams', had already said that she would not believe in any of Korda's promises until the money was safely in the bank;[217] and by 26 May, when his reserves were so depleted that he had only £7 left in England and $100 in the United States,[218] Robert had returned to work on *Palmer*:[219] taking his 'old-fashioned wooden pen-holder with its old-fashioned steel nib', and earning his 'next year's money the hard way, scratching laboriously on the back of old typescripts'.[220]

To begin with, as he told James Reeves, Graves found that his 'book about Palmer the Poisoner' was 'almost too eery to write';[221] but he persevered, and by mid-August, having completed a first draft of the entire novel, he wrote to Reeves again, telling him that he was 'very pleased with my luck in getting a subject on which I can use my detective capacity and in which all the seven deadly sins parade so splendidly. It will be a "Book of the" with any luck.'[222]

It was certainly an extraordinary story; and one of the strangest things about Graves's version was its title, for which he had settled upon words uttered by Palmer's doting mother: '*They Hanged My Saintly Billy.*' This is strange because even Graves's partisan account cannot disguise the fact that Palmer, far from being saintly, was extremely villainous.

This does not necessarily make him a murderer: as the Attorney-General says at Palmer's trial: 'A man may be guilty of fraud, he may be guilty of forgery; it does not follow that he should be guilty of murder';[223] and Graves reveals glaring deficiencies in the evidence relating to the death of John Parsons Cook which actually sent Palmer to the gallows. Graves also gives us grounds for sympathy with Palmer by presenting him, initially, as a naive seventeen-year-old whose first crime is committed for the best of motives. We are told that his landlord's:

red-headed daughter Jane, who was William's senior by two years, decoyed him into her bed. She thought William a pretty good catch, having heard that he possessed seven thousand pounds of his own, and was determined to lay her hands on it. After a few weeks had passed she pretended to be with child and, coming to him wth eyes red from weeping, begged that he would marry her.[224]

William protests that this is out of the question; but very soon she pretends that she has stolen money from her father's strong-box to pay for an abortion, and to protect her honour he is forced to raise the money: first by gambling on the race course, and then, when that fails, by a series of thefts.

From then on, Palmer careers downhill into a life of gambling, fraud, seduction and murder. Time and again, Graves provides alternative explanations for the serial poisonings in which Palmer indulges himself; but eventually, as so many of those close to him die agonizing deaths (in two instances, shortly after Palmer has taken out huge amounts of insurance on their lives) the weight of circumstantial evidence becomes overwhelming and we realize that, even if Palmer did *not* deliberately murder John Parsons Cook, he had deliberately murdered many others, and by the standards of the day he certainly deserved to hang.

Graves's agent, Watt, was reluctantly amused by the sheer intellectual perversity which Graves had exercised in *They Hanged My Saintly Billy.* 'You do run true to form, don't you?' he wrote to him in July. 'I might have known from the moment you started on Palmer that he had not poisoned. Are you going to tell us who did, or were the victims an illusion like the crime?'[225]

As Graves worked on *They Hanged My Saintly Billy* that summer of 1956, the news from the film world was decidedly bleak. Hopes of Ingrid Bergman persuading Twentieth Century-Fox to film *Homer's Daughter* had faded to vanishing point; Ava Gardner had been unable to find anyone interested in filming *El Embrujo de Sevilla*; there was 'Not another peep or cheep from Vincent Korda about *I, Claudius*';[226] and on 27 June Alec Guinness wrote to say that the script of *The World's Delight* had been 'going the rounds here during the past fortnight and there is no encouragement *at all*'.

Guinness had 'let three producers read it and they all say the same thing that they find it charming and amusing … but that the canvas is too broad for the substance of the story for it to be economically possible …'[227] The one remaining hope appeared to be that Sir Michael Balcon of Ealing Studios, for whom Guinness signed a contract in October to make four films, would take an interest;[228] but, as Graves recounts, it was Balcon who gave him 'the last rebuff', in a letter telling him that 'the script [of *The World's Delight*], though charming, is unlikely to interest Alec Guinness.'[229]

One of the few highlights of Graves's summer was the arrival of Marnie Pomeroy, a tall, fair-haired American writer in her mid-twenties, who had been sent to meet Robert by Alastair Reid. Years later, as she once told Robert and Beryl, Marnie would remember:

how damned kind you were from the moment I first arrived in Palma … and a towering seer-looking man opened the door, (to whom one just wouldn't say 'Is your master in?') And you took me to the beach and made me feel part of the family right away.[230]

Robert installed her in the Posada in Deyá until the Matthewses arrived to take her place on 15 July;[231] but she stayed on in the village for several months, and often attended the Sunday picnics that summer: which continued to be held at Sa Guarda, even after it had unexpectedly changed hands.

What had happened was that its owner, Robin Blyth, had found it necessary to leave the island. An increasingly colourful character, often seen in Palma sporting a Spanish hat, a cape and a silver-knobbed cane,[232] he had begun taking part in public bullfights;[233] and he had also bought himself a Jaguar painted a flamboyant yellow. Unfortunately, while driving the Jaguar, he was involved in two road accidents: one of them in Barcelona in the autumn of 1955,[234] and the other on the island of Majorca in June 1956. It was after this second accident that he came for help to Robert, who 'arranged to mortgage Sa Guarda for him for 80,000 pesetas; which will allow him to get off [the island] on the launch'.[235]

Robert was left with the title deeds as collateral and a power of attorney so that he could sell the property himself if the money was not returned;[236] and Robin decamped to Brussels for a while.[237] At the end of August he reappeared, only to tell Robert that he had no money;[238] in October he was thrown into jail 'for breaking into a yacht & having a loaded gun in his car';[239] and soon afterwards, after Robert had secured his temporary release,[240] he left Majorca permanently.[241] As for Sa Guarda: that was bought by Ricardo Sicré,[242] who allowed Robert and his friends to continue to use it for their Sunday picnics.

A more sedate visitor was Peggy Glanville-Hicks, who arrived on 3 August to begin collaborating with Alastair Reid[243] on *Nausicaa*, as they were calling their operatic version of *Homer's Daughter*;[244] and a week later she was there to enjoy Robert Graves's 'official' sixty-first birthday party, at which there were more than eighty guests, a play written and produced by Marnie Pomeroy, and a ballet danced by Lucia and one of her friends.[245]

Shortly afterwards, Robert's daughter Catherine also arrived with her husband Cliff Dalton (now Chief Engineer of the Australian Atomic Energy Commission) and their five children;[246] and the Daltons briefly overlapped with Robert's sister Rosaleen, on her first visit to Deyá.

Despite these visitors, Robert Graves had been working hard all summer, making a selection of his poems for a Penguin edition, writing two or three articles, reviewing T. E. Lawrence's translation of the *Odyssey*,[247] and finally, on 20 September, putting the last touches to the foreword of *They Hanged My Saintly Billy*.[248] This left him free to deal with a request from the American publisher Doubleday that, some twenty-seven years after its first publication, he should revise his classic autobiography *Good-bye to All That* for publication under their Anchor Books imprint.

It was a curious coincidence that on the very day when Robert became free to work on *Good-bye to All That*,[249] he and Beryl should be lunching in a Palma restaurant with Ralph Vaughan-Williams, the famous Old Carthusian composer, who was holidaying on Majorca with his wife Ursula. It was the first time that Graves and Vaughan-Williams had met since 1912; they 'talked fondly', as Graves recalls, 'of Max Beerbohm (who had been in the same form as Uncle Ralph at Charterhouse)';[250] and then, as a thunderstorm broke directly overhead,[251] the two men 'suddenly found ourselves singing the *Carmen Carthusianum* in unison'.[252]

Robert Graves had briefly asked himself 'how far is a man of my age justified in rewriting his earlier books? Some would say that they have passed out of my jurisdiction.' But this doubt was soon banished, on the grounds that he had 'dictated most of *Good-bye*, late at night, hurriedly and in a state of great emotional tension'.[253] Soon he was commenting to James Reeves that he had found the original 'very badly written', but that it would still make 'a good story when some of the nonsense is cut out and some of the things restored that I had to cut out in 1929'.[254]

Unfortunately, the alterations Graves now considered necessary were extensive enough to give a markedly different flavour to *Good-bye to All That*, and to remove it from the only context in which it can be fully understood. For cutting out 'some of the nonsense' meant cutting out both Riding's poem at the front of the book and Graves's 'Dedicatory Epilogue' to her at the back. Riding is not even mentioned in the new Epilogue, in which Graves boldly declares that little of outstanding autobiographical interest has happened since 1929.

Graves also cut out a number of passages from the main body of the book which reveal the enormous mental strains under which he had laboured during the years immediately after the First World War. He also carried out what he described as 'a general editing of my excusably ragged prose',[255] which meant in practice that virtually every paragraph was tidied up just a little; and by these alterations Graves robbed his masterpiece of the painfully raw edge which had helped to make it such a powerful work.[256]

Graves, his 'past life ... flashing by me',[257] was completing his revisions to *Good-bye to All That* when, on Monday 5 November, he received an invitation from Mount Holyoke College, Massachusetts, who offered him $1,400 to give a single lecture in February 1957.[258] Having been so short of money earlier in the year, this offer was extremely tempting. So he called in Alastair Reid; and then, as Reid recalls,

he and Beryl and I had a kind of summit meeting ... in the Graves flat in Palma. I was shortly to be leaving for New York, and could make travel arrangements, and arrange for other readings to be fitted in around the Mount Holyoke occasion. I had an apartment in the city, besides, which Robert could use as headquarters, and I could promise Beryl that I would travel with Robert, and make sure that his socks matched, and that he did not mislay his manuscripts.[259]

With Reid as his companion, and the prospect of being home in Deyá after only a fortnight, Graves decided that he could cope. He wrote at once to accept the invitation from Mount Holyoke; and he told James Reeves that he was 'now in a holiday mood, no more proofs expected for a few months and all my contracts completed'.[260]

Not long afterwards, leaving Marnie Pomeroy to look after Y-Grec, Lucia and Juan, while Tomas stayed with some other friends, Robert and Beryl took a week's holiday in the south of France;[261] and when they returned to Palma, Robert began work on his American lectures.[262]

CHAPTER 7

Dreams and Lectures

Robert Graves had almost completed the first of his lectures when, on 28 November 1956, he received a letter from Jenny which revived his dreams about the filming of *I, Claudius*. Jenny reported that she had seen Alec Guinness,[263] who was passing through Rome on his way to Ceylon to film *The Bridge on the River Kwai*; and not only did he have the two *Claudius* books with him but also he told her that he was 'fearfully anxious to play the part', if it could be played 'as a palace tragi-comedy, not as a spectacular'. Jenny had then telephoned Vincent Korda, who had promptly decided to renew his option on a script written by Robert; and they had discussed the possibility of persuading Anna Magnani to play the part of Messalina.[264]

On hearing this, Graves wrote directly to Anna Magnani;[265] and soon received an enthusiastic reply, thanking him for the honour of having thought of her.[266] Armed with this, he wrote a long letter to Korda beginning:

Dear Vincent,
    As you are in England and Alec Guinness is in Ceylon and I am in Spain and my daughter Jenny is in Italy and so is Anna Magnani, the realisation of Jenny and mine Alec Guinness's and Anna Magnani's hopes which I hope coincide with yours may be a little difficult to organise, but let's try.

Explaining that Anna Magnani ('the best actress in Europe, we think') had already told Jenny that Alec Guinness would be the perfect Claudius ('so that's all right), he added that she had made it a condition

that I wrote the script, which as you know I should be very glad to do. But, since it is important to get the mostly highly-polished actable script – Anna too as you see has the right idea on the subject – I ought to get a really capable professional assistant such as Bridget Boland, whom I know and admire and with whom Alec likes working.

All that remained, in Graves's view, was for Korda to find the money. 'Please Vincent,' he concluded, 'don't leave the soap in the water as my father-in-law William Nicholson used to say, but get going while Alec and Anna and I are still excited about the scheme.'[267]

By Christmas Graves had written two more lectures; but there had been no reply from Korda.[268] Then, immediately after Christmas, an enthusiastic letter arrived from Alec Guinness, reporting that his agents had asked whether he was prepared to do *Claudius* with Gina Lollobrigida: to which he had 'replied promptly', telling them that:

> there was nothing I wanted more than to do *Claudius* ... I was prepared to do it in 1958 but knowing of Magnani's interest I would infinitely prefer to do it with her rather than with Lollo, pretty and clever though the latter is. The only stipulations I made were approval of script and director, so that all looks as if it has taken a step forward in the right direction.[269]

However, when a letter from Vincent Korda finally reached Graves in late January 1957, everything once again began to seem vague and indefinite. Korda had clearly secured no financial backing for *I, Claudius*; he was uncertain whether Guinness really wanted to play Claudius; but in any case Guinness would not be free for some time, which 'will give you the chance to prepare a wonderful script'.[270]

Graves replied by return of post that Guinness was 'extremely anxious to play Claudius and will be free early in 1958'. He added that he himself was 'thoroughly ashamed of what I served up originally as a script and have since learned how to write scripts, so I don't think you need worry on that score especially if I have a good technical assistant'.[271] To which Korda replied that, as he now understood it, Alec Guinness was under contract to Mr Robert Dowling of New York, and had no wish to make *Claudius*. Perhaps Graves could meet Dowling while he was in New York to clear up the mystery?[272] And there the matter rested when, on Sunday 3 February, Graves flew to Madrid on the first leg of his journey to the United States of America.

On the eve of his departure, Robert Graves had been extremely nervous about the lecture tour. 'Why am I writing so small?' he had asked in a letter to Martin Seymour-Smith. 'Probably because at 7 a.m. tomorrow I fly to the States, and am not feeling particularly extrovert at the prospect. But the money's all right, if I can stick it out for a fortnight.'[273]

At 8.30 in the evening of 4 February 1957, after lunching in Madrid with Ricardo Sicré, Graves boarded another plane which took him on to Lisbon, the Azores and Gander in Newfoundland.[274] There his lecture tour almost came to grief before it had properly begun, because it was discovered that he needed a vaccination before he could complete his journey into the United States of America. And even after being vaccinated, he flew on the 'bumpy' last leg of his journey knowing that, according to all the rules, he should be kept in quarantine for seven days after his arrival in New York. But very fortunately, after touch-down in New York at 11.25 on Monday morning, 'the health officer didn't notice how recent my vaccination certificate was so I got through'.[275]

Having cleared immigration and customs with nothing worse than the confiscation of the oranges and sobresada he had brought with him ('both confiscated as unclean imports'[276]), Robert was met at the airport by Alastair Reid, who 'found him in fine spirits, if still a trifle wary',[277] Alston Anderson, 'and a nice girlfriend of Alastair's called Susan Greenberg who's a photographer', Robert told Beryl, 'and cured my tiredness with some lovely china tea'. Alastair's apartment, though small, 'isn't too small for us two. I have a very comfortable bed, a sofa by day, and there's perfect heating and a bath and a telephone and everything's fine.'[278]

That evening they had supper with Robert's old friend Len Lye, the film-maker, who was a close neighbour of Alastair's. Several other people were present, but Robert was very much the guest of honour; and Alastair noticed that Robert relaxed, 'seemed to decide to enjoy the attention lavished on him, and became the best of company'.[279]

Tuesday was busy. First came a 'crowded hour' at Doubleday discussing Graves's books 'past and future'; then an equally 'crowded hour' at the *New Yorker*, who 'want me to review books for them (soon)'; there were 'phone calls from all over the place', plans for reducing Graves's tax liability, and a meeting with Will Price, 'in very good shape indeed and *very* helpful ... I must say', Robert added in the letter he wrote to Beryl that evening. 'New York is a very nice city if one can stand the pace and lots of people can and I keep warm.' After completing his letter, he would be 'off to a quiet supper with Alastair at a Spanish restaurant'; and he concluded that: 'Alastair's absolutely splendid. Lots of love from him and even more from me. Will write after first lecture.'[280]

On Wednesday Graves and Reid travelled by train and car to South Hadley, Massachusetts where, at eight o'clock that evening, Graves lectured in a packed auditorium to the girls of Mount Holyoke College on

'Legitimate Criticism of Poetry'.[281] It was a well-judged and thoroughly entertaining talk, flattering the knowledge and intelligence of the audience, poking fun at Milton's 'L'Allegro' and Wordsworth's 'Solitary Reaper', praising the two American writers Robert Frost and John Crowe Ransom, and attacking 'the modern careerist' writer,

> who doubts whether he can make his name by traditional writing, yet shrinks from becoming a whole-hearted abstractionist. He will commit himself neither to a metre on which he can make his individual variations, nor to precise images and an accepted syntax; but takes Eliot's irresponsible advice and teases the critic by constantly approximating to sense and rhythmic pertinence, and then constantly withdrawing into deliberate nonsense.[282]

Finally, Robert begged 'you younger people to preserve your critical integrity'. They should never accept shoddy work offered them as 'great', 'however dearly you may love the donor or the author. Keep tight hold of the critical cold-chisel and strike it home without mercy: on my work too, if you please.'[283]

After the lecture, so many students wanted to take part in the further discussion which had been arranged in a smaller hall that 'it wouldn't contain the audience so', as Robert told Beryl, 'we had to go back and fill the main hall again'. He was writing to her on Thursday morning, having 'got up at 7 a.m. ... for a walk through the snow'; and he added that: 'My whole attention is given to the details of this tour and to bringing back the most honours and the fewest accidents. Won't pretend that it's not great fun but I'm glad I'll be back to you so soon.'[284]

That afternoon,[285] Graves and Reid travelled by train to Boston, where they spent the next two nights with Cecily Gittes, the family friend who had been so helpful in Palma at the time of William's accident. Then on Friday evening, after meeting his fellow-poet Robert Lowell, Graves gave a poetry reading at the Massachusetts Institute of Technology (M.I.T.).[286] As Cecily Gittes reported to Beryl, Robert:

> carried off the evening in high style. Everyone says that he has the right touch, and that if he returns and is given better publicity (that wasn't too good) there is no limit to what he could do. They like his humour and informality, also his unorthodox opinions.[287]

Alastair Reid later recalled that 'crowds had to be turned away', and this was a pattern which would be repeated at future readings, with the result that Robert 'began to realise how much more his work was read than he had imagined, and to expand perceptibly'.[288]

On Saturday evening, after flying back to New York, Graves gave his lecture on 'The White Goddess' at the Y.M.H.A. Poetry centre. He used the occasion partly to defend himself from the criticisms of the American poet Randall Jarrell who, as Graves reminded his audience, 'has generously declared that I write good poems; but holds that what I say about the White Goddess is grotesque nonsense, a personal fantasy of my own ... adding that my world picture is a projection of my unconscious on the universe'.[289]

To counter Jarrell's assertions, Graves ran over the historical background to his theories about the White Goddess; but he was at great pains to point out that his discoveries about neolithic and Bronze Age religious faith were 'not essential to my central theme – namely the persistent survival of this faith among what are loosely called 'romantic poets'.[290] After which Graves described some of the 'chain of more than coincidence' which had haunted him throughout his life; explained that superstitions were 'magical beliefs which (as the word conveys) *survive* from some banned faith';[291] and admitted that he himself never failed:

> to bow to the new moon, disregarding the scientific presumption that the moon is merely a dead satellite of Earth; for the moon moves the tides, influences growth, rules the festal calendar of Judaism, Islam and Christianity, and possesses other unaccountable magic properties, known to every lover and poet.[292]

Later on, after deploring the subordinate role of women in societies governed by Protestant dogma, Graves commented that:

> Some of you are looking queerly at me. Do I think that poets are literally inspired by the White Goddess? That is an improper question. What would you think, should I ask you if, in your opinion, the Hebrew prophets were literally inspired by God? Whether God is a metaphor or a fact cannot be reasonably argued; let us likewise be discreet on the subject of the Goddess.

All that could be known for certain was that:

> the Ten Commandments, said to have been promulgated by Moses in the name of a Solar God, still carry religious force for those hereditarily prone to accept them; and that scores of poems written in the Muse-

tradition still carry the authentic moon-magic for those hereditarily prone to accept that.[293]

Finally, after a dramatic version of his story about the differing fates of the publishers who had, or who had not accepted *The White Goddess* for publication, he declared that 'A poem which is moon-magical enough to walk off the page' was 'more-than-coincidence at its most miraculous. And Solar Apollo, for all his new thinking-machines and rhyming dictionaries and analytic courses in poetry-writing, can't begin to imitate it.'[294]

The lecture had been a sell-out; and, as Robert told Beryl, he 'got through [it] with popular acclaim and had to go back and curtsey three times'.[295]

The next day, Sunday 10 February, it had been arranged for Robert Graves to appear with John Mason Brown and the famous stripper Gypsy Rose Lee on a half-hour television quiz programme on the meaning of English words.[296] After which he told Beryl that he had 'got through [it] without disgrace (didn't say Hungary when I meant Yugoslavia)';[297] but according to Martin Seymour-Smith he also felt that he had been a little too scholarly. On explaining, for example, that the word lady 'had originally meant "a woman who kneads bread" ' he had been just about to ask Gypsy Rose Lee punningly 'if she had ever kneaded any, when "the eloquent John Mason Brown" "robbed [him] of the ball" '.[298]

Once the programme had been recorded, Graves and Reid flew down to Baltimore, and were then driven to Maryland where they had 'a heavenly night with [Betty Sicré's parents] the Lussiers',[299] who entertained them to turkey and corn fritters and blueberry pie.[300] On Monday 11 Graves gave a poetry reading at the Library of Congress;[301] and on Tuesday morning there was a meeting with Robert Richman who, in Alastair Reid's words, 'took him through the tax office'.[302] The result was that Graves was listed, for tax purposes, 'as a cultural missionary'[303] and later that morning he was able to write to Beryl on the plane back to New York that:

Everything is better and better ... It's so easy when Alastair handles all the money and tickets and times. I can concentrate on being happy and putting on the good shows expected of me. The thing that will please you most (except that I am having a very nice time and not feeling overworked) is that I am getting the whole thing free of tax and since expenses are negligible (about $200) this means something like £1,250.

He added that he was 'taking great care not to miss you: but on the other hand am very anxious for you to come out here next Feb with Tomas for a month for an even more profitable raid'.[304]

There had only been one night when Graves's 'neurasthenia' had threatened to get the better of him; and then, as Alastair Reid recalls, he had 'decided that he must see the moon, not always easily accessible in Manhattan. We walked all the way to a west side pier before we found it, and he breathed more easily. It was Deyá that he had been looking for.'[305] When Alastair wrote to Beryl to tell her how well things were going, he declared that:

> Robert has done the lectures brilliantly, and has had great ovations. We've done all the things we had to – no mishaps and really had terrific fun. Robert's been talking about mushrooms to strangers and has even been good about his teeth hasn't got tired or fussed and has been in the greatest good humour.[306]

On the evening they arrived back in New York, the two men went to a party given by the mushroom experts Gordon and Tina Wasson, whose work had come to fascinate Graves more and more.

It was eighteen months previously, in August 1955, that Graves had received an astonishing letter from Wasson, who had recently spent five weeks in the mountains of southern Mexico. There, in his own words, he had 'attended three all-night shamanistic performances where ... mushrooms were used to bring the divine powers into our presence'; and on one occasion Wasson had eaten the mushrooms himself, and could:

> testify of my own knowledge that their effects ... are breathtaking. In a way that it will be hard for you to understand, we retained our full presence of mind, our ability to speak to each other lucidly and comment on what was going on, while having visual hallucinations, in colours, of the richest splendour ...

'We seemed to be disembodied,' he recalled, 'viewing ourselves as among the objects in the room. We saw distant lands and great palaces.'[307]

When Wasson had visited Palma over Easter 1956,[308] Graves had been shown 'coloured transparencies taken during an oracular seance', and had been 'promised a taste of the celestial food – apparently the mushrooms keep their potency when dried', Graves had reported to Reid, 'because the mushroom deity is the oldest and most powerful in the whole pantheon'.[309] More recently, Graves had been conducting an ingenious correspondence with Wasson on the nature of ambrosia;[310] and now he enjoyed what he later told Seymour-Smith was 'the most exciting occasion' of this tour.[311]

Not only were 'the sacred mushrooms ... put on show and a tape-recording played of the *curandera's* (local priestess's) chanting'[312] during the 'ritual of [the] divine mushroom'; but also there were slides of the ceremony (including one showing 'Gordon in [a] trance'); and Graves was allowed to see an advance copy of the Wassons' two-volume *Mushrooms, Russia and History*.[313] In this, as he later discovered,[314] he had been given 'full credit for his part in their discoveries of the exact circumstances of Claudius's death ... of the sacred mushroom cult in Mexico, of the role of narcotic mushrooms in ancient history and the thesis that mycophobia, the irrational fear of mushrooms felt by a great part of mankind, is the survival of an ancestral religious awe or taboo'.[315]

On Thursday 13 February, Graves and Reid went by train to New Haven, where that afternoon Graves gave the third of his lectures at Yale University, on 'Diseases of Scholoarship Clinically Considered'. This was another highly entertaining talk in which, after listing the virtues of the true scholar, Graves discussed such difficulties as 'creeping pedagogitis', and made much of the academic xenophobia which had greeted his and Podro's *The Nazarene Gospel Restored*.[316] There was, as Reid recorded in Graves's diary, a 'large crowd and loud applause'.

Afterwards, Graves and Reid caught a train back to New York, where they spent the evening at 4 Patchin Place 'laughing much and chattering' with e. e. cummings[317] and his photographer wife Marion Moorhouse. This, according to Graves, was the 'most memorable' meeting of his tour: the one 'longest looked forward to, and even happier than I expected'. It was more than twenty-five years since Graves had first introduced cummings's *Enormous Room* to the British public; and now, as Graves later described the event in one of his formal letters to Alastair Reid, 'Nothing was said, of importance, but little needed to be said; we weren't doing business together, just humorously communing.'[318]

During the remaining few days of his lecture tour, there was one final poetry reading, at the University of New York.[319] Apart from that, Graves concentrated upon finding more work; and soon after his return to Palma on Sunday 17 February,[320] laden down with 'whacking great boxes of chocolates and nylon night-gowns and ... wads of 1000 peseta notes bought on the free market',[321] he told Selwyn Jepson that he had secured:

all sorts of rich commissions, such as reviews for *New Yorker* and work

for *Atlantic* and *N[ew] Y[ork] Sunday Times*. Am getting an option on
writing a stage version of *Mrs. Milton*, and took the *I, Claudius* film
negotiations one stage further ... Briefly (between you and me) the
main obstacle is Vincent Korda who's a sweet, sentimental, lazy slob
and from whom somehow I've got to recover the rights in the film for
secret sale to United Artists ... [322]

This had to be done, he explained, without Korda learning that anyone
was interested. In the meantime, Graves was hoping to hear shortly from
Max Youngsteen of United Artists, to whom he had been introduced by
Will Price[323] on his last Friday in New York,[324] about a definite offer.[325]

Once again, however, his hopes were ill-founded; and at the beginning
of April, Youngsteen wrote to 'deeply regret that we are not able to put the
Claudius film into work. I tried but it was impossible under present
conditions.'[326]

This was disappointing news, but no longer critical for by then Graves's
American tour had completely transformed his financial position. 'Lots of
money and commissions keep rolling in', he had written to Jepson on 7
March. All his debts were paid, and he had approximately £25,000 in the
bank.[327] At the same time, Graves was receiving requests for a further
visit to the States from Americans such as Elizabeth Kray of the Poetry
Center in New York, who told him that 'A great clamour has arisen in all
parts of the country – from Chicago to Texas, from Texas to California,
for you.'[328]

The triumphant success of his first American lecture tour was a
turning-point in Robert Graves's professional career. He himself wrote to
Alec Guinness that it was 'almost frightening ... – I hadn't realised I was a
public performer';[329] and Alastair Reid recalls that from this moment on,
Graves's life became:

much more public. He accepted invitations to travel, to give lectures
and readings, and to write magazine pieces. I do, however, remember
with some poignance a moment during one New York walk when
Robert stopped suddenly, absent, tuned-out, something I had grown
used to in him, that temporary absence of thought. 'Don't much like
that chap!' he said shaking his head.

When Reid asked whom he meant, 'the chap turned out to be himself, at
the previous night's reading, in a jovial public guise about which he was
having misgivings'.[333]

On his return from the USA in mid-February 1957, Robert Graves was soon awaiting publication of:

> Norman [Cameron's] poems, a Poetry Society recommendation, out in April ... if not sooner. My *Suetonius* also, any day. And the *Ballads*; and in May my *Palmer* book. Heavens! And in the autumn Cassells are publishing *Good-bye to All That* in a revised edition; and a handsome revised *Greek Myths*. Too Much![331]

Those revisions[332] together with a children's version of *The Greek Myths*, occupied Robert for most of March and April;[333] but he also found time to make a new friend.

This was Esteban Frances, the Catalan post-Surrealist painter who had been working since 1946 as designer and decorator for the New York City Ballet.[334] He and his companion Anne Heather took a house in Deyá that spring with their children Mike and Miranda,[335] and liked it so much that they began returning year after year. Esteban was a solid man, not tall, but broad, with a large slightly lugubrious face surmounted by short curly hair, and large hands with which he gestured as he spoke; and he had firm opinions and a great contempt for anything second-rate.[336] At a time when Robert was becoming more and more the object of unthinking adulation,[337] Esteban Frances was one of the few men in the inner circle at Canelluñ whom Robert could respect as being someone of his own intellectual size: so it was an important friendship.[338]

At the end of April,[339] the Graveses set out by Land Rover[340] for England. When they arrived at Sally's house, Robert found waiting for him an advance copy of *They Hanged My Saintly Billy*. There was also a covering letter from his agent, passing on the news from Cassell that on the morning of 23 May, publication day:

> there will be two sandwich board men stationed outside Madame Tussaud's carrying this message by arrangement with the author:

REMOVE DR. PALMER

from

THE CHAMBER OF

HORRORS

UNJUSTLY HANGED AS

A POISONER

See THEY HANGED MY SAINTLY BILLY

by ROBERT GRAVES – Cassell & Co.[341]

During his stay in London, Graves was also interviewed, alongside Malcolm Muggeridge, for the BBC wireless programme 'Frankly Speaking';[342] and he received a letter from 10 Downing Street telling him that the Prime Minister, Harold Macmillan, had it in mind:

> to submit your name to the Queen with a recommendation that Her Majesty would be graciously pleased to approve that you be appointed a Commander of the Order of the British Empire.
>
> Before doing so, the Prime Minister would be glad to be assured that this wish of Her Majesty's favour would be agreeable to you.[343]

Graves declined, on the grounds that his writing of poetry was a private pursuit not done in hope of public honour; and on 14 May he received a sympathetic reply from Macmillan, who wrote:

> Fortunately we have been able to enjoy the results, or some of them, of your private pursuit. I suppose it is in the recognition of the pleasure, in the widest sense, that is given by the communication of poetry ... that honours are offered and accepted. This seems to me to be reasonable – and all creative art ... is primarily a private pursuit.
>
> But you know best what is right for you as a poet.[344]

The highlight of Graves's visit to England was a meeting with Robert Frost, who arrived in London in the third week in May and who, attributing his English fame to Graves's influence, had asked if Graves would 'be the first to see him (after the Embassy folk)'.[345] On 20 May, when the poets talked alone at the Connaught Hotel for two hours or more,[346] Graves found Frost 'exactly as I expected him: wonderful man'; and the two of them 'agreed about everyone'.[347]

On their way back to Majorca, the Graveses stayed for a few days in Geneva. There they met Jenny, who had not looked 'so blooming for years'; and they 'arrange[d] for Lucia and Juan (now 13 and 12) to attend the International School at Geneva in September'.[348]

In view of these changes, which Robert intended to finance by further lecture tours in America,[349] the Graveses had decided to leave Palma, vacating one of the flats but keeping the other as a pied-à-terre,[350] and make a permanent return to Deyá.

First there were the proofs of the revised *Good-bye to All That* to deal with;[351] and in mid-June there was a friendly visit from Stephen Spender and his wife, with whom Robert and Beryl enjoyed one of their Sunday picnics at Sa Guarda.[352] There followed a frantic period of packing and moving; and on Friday 28 June when Robert and Beryl finally 'cleaned [the bottom] flat, & gave up key',[353] they brought to an end a period of almost six years during which they had lived principally in Palma.

Before they left, a letter arrived from Alec Guinness telling Robert of a 'sudden interest' in *Claudius* from Sir Michael Balcon, who had promised to contact MGM immediately, 'as they are doing *Ben Hur* again in Rome next year and might be intrigued to do two Roman pictures at once'.[354] It was only a few weeks ago that Bridget Boland had told Graves of Columbia having refused *I, Claudius* 'on the grounds that togas is out':[355] so Guinness's letter was most encouraging; and Robert's dreams of success in the film industry were once again revived.

CHAPTER 8

More Dreams and Lectures and Cindy Lee

Returning to Canelluñ in the summer of 1957 was principally a practical move; but it was also an attempt by Robert Graves to return to his poetic roots. Since the end of his attachment to Judith Bledsoe in the autumn of 1952, the quality of his inspiration had deteriorated to such an extent that one family friend had commented: 'the poems I read of his nowadays seem a bit sad, clinging too hard to something that's no longer there, perhaps'.[356] Robert himself was very much aware of this, and later he would tell James Reeves that he had begun 'wondering whether I had reached my menopause ... Not that it matters stopping, but it is very enjoyable to work on a poem and get it right.'[357] In the meantime there was a lecture tour to be arranged for the following year; and a distressing letter from Jenny to be answered.

Earlier in the year, asked by the *Spectator* to cover a socialist congress in Venice, she had written an article which described how the British delegation, consisting of Nye Bevan, Morgan Phillips and Dick Crossman, had 'puzzled the Italians by their capacity to fill themselves like tanks with whisky and coffee'; and she added that 'Although the Italians were never sure if the British delegation was sober, they always attributed to them an immense political acumen.' This was a good-humoured allusion to the fact that the three British delegates had been hopelessly drunk. Fifteen years later, the brilliant Dick Crossman 'was happy to boast to a party of journalists' in the hearing of Auberon Waugh 'that he and Bevan had both been as pissed as newts'; but at the time, he and the others had reckoned that it was a golden opportunity to damage the right-wing *Spectator*, even if it meant telling lies in court; and so they decided to sue. This decision astonished the then editor of the *Spectator*, Sir Ian Gilmour;[358] and it terrified Jenny, who told Robert that the onus was on her to find witnesses, but that in her view this was 'Impossible. The British Consul and British First Secretary cannot, the journalists dare not, the socialists don't wish to, the hotel barmen would not risk losing their best customers – the English. Pray for me.'[359]

At the end of July, Alec Guinness arrived in Deyá with his lovely wife Merula and their son Matthew;[360] and two days later there was a delayed sixty-second birthday party for Robert to which a vast number of friends were invited, including Esteban Frances, Alastair Reid, Alan Sillitoe, Ruth Fainlight, Alston Anderson and Mati Klarwein. Forty-eight rockets were 'heroically despatched' followed by three hot air balloons; there was dancing to gramophone and guitar; an ensaimada was duly clothes-pegged to a line and shot at with a bow and arrow; and there was a series of entertainments including a play by Alston entitled *Godot Missed*. After which Robert went to bed, as he noted in his diary, 'with cold and slight hangover from seven glasses of Binisalem. It was a great success.'[361]

The visit by the Guinnesses also went well. It was now more or less understood between Robert Graves, Alec Guinness and Bridget Boland that Guinness would be starring in a film of *I, Claudius* to be made in September 1958; and although as yet there was no backer for the project, Robert and Bridget had made plans to meet later in the year to work together on a screenplay.[362] Guinness was therefore treated as an especially honoured guest; and shortly after returning to England on 20 August, he sent Robert and Beryl a letter telling them that he was:

now so unwound that I wonder and don't much care whether the mainspring will ever be got taut again. It was so lovely having a holiday in a house and not in a hotel. And with that view. And the morning glory.[363]

He had especially enjoyed 'just being able to be one's dull self and not having to make an effort – bowing and smiling at the concierge, catching the eye of passing waiters etcetera etcetera and etcetera'.

As the Guinnesses flew out of Palma, James Reeves flew in, with his wife Mary and their daughters, one of whom, nineteen-year-old Stella, had just left school, and was quite remarkably beautiful. They were soon settled comfortably in the Posada by the church;[364] and during the next few weeks, in between many hours of work on his lectures, Robert spent a great deal of time with them. Together they enjoyed suppers out, sing-songs at the Posada, picnicking and picking almonds at Sa Guarda, where Marnie Pomeroy also appeared; and by the time they left the island on 11 September a new academic year had begun, and Beryl had departed with Lucia and Juan for the International School at Geneva.[365]

After a fleeting visit from Rosaleen, Robert and four-year-old Tomas followed Beryl to Geneva on 13 September;[366] and a few days later Bridget Boland arrived from Rome, and she and Robert spent four days dissecting the *Claudius* novels, 'cutting out unnecessary characters', and completing a ' "treatment" in rough'.[367] Bridget thoroughly enjoyed working with Robert; but not long after they had parted, and he had returned to Deyá with Beryl and Tomas, she sounded a warning note, suggesting possible trouble with the front office.

> What, no Livia poisonings, what no Capri orgies! I'm not doing my duty as the film-racket-knowing-partner if I don't stress again that it is professional madness on such a subject to spend time on a screenplay before the treatment has been approved.

And she added that although she was prepared to risk her own time, since she had set aside twelve months 'for having fun', Robert should 'consider if there is anything else you could be writing in November, whether it would not be more sensible to get that out of the way'.[368]

However, Graves was not to be deterred. By 9 October he had despatched eighty-four pages of an *I, Claudius* treatment to Boland; and then spent the rest of the month on 154 pages of another speculative film script which he named *Binimusa*. He also did a great deal of gardening; and he had now become so proud of his compost heaps that he had started naming them after his visitors. On 30 October, for example, when Gordon Wasson was due for a brief visit, Graves noted in his diary that he had 'Finished Alston's compost heap. Started "Gordon Wasson" one.'[369]

During November, Bridget Boland wrote twice from Rome with encouraging news about *I, Claudius* negotiations, which now involved the possibility of Juliette Greco playing Messalina instead of Anna Magnani;[370] but by the end of that month there was bad news from Alec Guinness. He told Robert plainly that he had written to Bridget:

> saying I didn't like the *Claudius* treatment, which read to me like a multi-million-dollar epic and not what I expected or hoped at all ... I will read it all again. But I know in my bones that what she, and you, or both of you have done together is not good *sales* material – and to me it conveys nothing of the book.[371]

However, Bridget Boland remained confident enough in what she and Graves had written to send a copy of the treatment to Twentieth Century-Fox; and there the matter rested for the time being.[372]

Meanwhile, Jenny Nicholson's libel case had finally reached the courts and at length, on 22 November, after much false evidence from Nye

Bevan, Morgan Phillips and Dick Crossman, a High Court jury awarded each of these three outrageous liars the sum of £2,500 in damages. Jenny, feeling that her reputation as a freelance journalist had been irrevocably damaged, 'burst into tears in court'.[373] Fortunately Patrick was a great support; and he helped her to arrange a family Christmas in Rome.

Robert, who had been in a very cheerful mood since the beginning of December, when he had 'finished a poem about walking around a mountain, which I think is so-called typical Graves',[374] was very excited by the prospect of visiting (or perhaps revisiting) Rome. For Graves believed that when he had been writing *Count Belisarius* his use of analeptic thought had in a very real sense propelled him back into the past, and so he told Selwyn Jepson that he had 'never been in Rome since around 540 A.D.'[375]

Rome was just as exciting as Robert had hoped, and much more welcoming than he had expected. He and Beryl and Tomas had 'arrived to the noise of cameras whirring and were met by the whole family and a lot of newsmen ... Italy is treating me rather as America did', he told Karl, 'and as England never has and never will.'[376]

On Christmas Day, the Graveses received 'the old Pope's general blessing' from a corner of the Vatican Square; and then called on Ingrid Bergman and Roberto Rossellini, who were briefly back together again after a long spell apart.[377] Subsequently, Robert made a special 'Visit to Shelley & Keats house';[378] and, as he told the Sicrés, he also:

> threw a great party in a private Palazzo lent me by a Princess; and all the Ambassadors and intellectuals attended – including even the British Ambassador & the head of the the British Council, but of course they were brought along by the head of the American Academy because I'm not at all V.I.P. in the U.K.
>
> This was only one of a lot of parties, in most of which my five children took part. Jenny indefatigable; William very handsome & at ease in a scarlet Royal-Opera Arcade waistcoat; Lucia the belle of the ball; Tomas delighted quiet and imperturbable ... [379]

On leaving Rome at the beginning of January 1958, Robert, Beryl and William travelled to Lubliana in communist Yugoslavia, where Robert used some of his embargoed earnings to buy 'wild-swine boots and a dormice hat';[380] and after four days they went onto Lech in Austria, where they rejoined Patrick, Jenny and the rest of the family for a skiing party. It was the first time that Robert had been on skis since a family holiday in January 1914;[381] but it took only a little coaching from Patrick for him to enjoy several days of 'pottering about' on the snow; and one morning, seeking inspiration perhaps, he rose early to walk by moonlight.[382]

After a brief return to Canelluñ, Robert Graves flew to New York to begin his second American lecture tour, and 'earn enough to pay a year's school fees for Lucia and Juan'.[383]

Arriving in New York early in the morning of Saturday 1 February, Graves took a taxi to Alastair Reid's flat, where he went over the programme of lectures, poetry readings and personal appearances which Reid had arranged for him. The rest of the day was spent catching up with old friends: lunch with Gordon Wasson was followed by supper with Len Lye; and it was in Lye's company that Graves first met Jess McNab,[384] a 'serious, unflighty, warm, beautiful young woman'[385] who worked for the Metropolitan Museum of Modern Art, and had soon become one of the inner circle of his New York friends.

On Sunday, Graves and Reid caught a train to Washington, where on Monday evening Graves lectured at the I.C.A. on 'Sweeney Among the Blackbirds'. This was partly an entertaining ramble through differing visions of the after-life, most of them with 'no individual love, no grass, no trees, no birds or animals', and therefore 'disastrously dull'. Graves also examined the differences between major (unsound) poets such as Ezra Pound and minor (true) ones such as the 'nameless' poet who had recently declined a CBE 'on the ground that politicians have no right to distribute poetry prizes'; and there were further autobiographical asides about the impossibility of separating poetry from the state of being in love, and the need for poets to live in the countryside if they are not to risk their 'poetic flame ... being snuffed out by a city-bred miasma'.[386]

On Tuesday, Robert Graves flew to New Hampshire in 'a little provincial aeroplane,' and was driven to Dartmouth, 'where I ... was given a beautiful hand-made hunting knife', and where he delivered the second lecture which he had prepared for this tour: 'What Food the Centaurs Ate', his highly idiosyncratic investigation into the nature of ambrosia.

Wednesday found him in Boston where he was reunited with Alastair Reid and where, before giving a poetry reading at the Hebrew University of Brandeis, he wrote to Beryl telling her that he fully expected 'to clear that $3,000 quite apart from getting new jobs etcetera'. He added reassuringly that he had not had:

a moment to think of anything in a brooding or contemplative way. The rule is telephones telegraphs travelling talks tucking-in tickets toilets etcetera ... This is all my unreserved and fanatic love for you. But I shall be careful not to miss you too much until it's time to come back.

'That's done', he concluded, 'by going to sleep as soon as I put out the lights. The beds are all hard and the rooms are all warm ...'[387]

Thursday saw a return to New York, where Graves appeared on television, gave three lectures in four days, lunched with Marnie Pomeroy, talked late into the night with e.e. cummings, and drank tea with his old enemy W. H. Auden.[388] Afterwards he reported with some satisfaction to Tom Matthews that Auden's hands had trembled, but that he himself had 'behaved gently and affably'.[389]

There followed a week of criss-crossing the country, attending numerous parties and receptions, giving poetry readings at Wayne State University and the University of Michigan, and lecturing both at the University of Indiana, on its Bloomington campus, and at the University of Texas in Austin. Even with Reid's constant support, this was a considerable strain; and towards the end of his tour Graves was running a temperature of 101 degrees, and needed 'a heavy shot of penicillin' two days before his final lecture at Austin on the evening of 17 February.[390]

Before returning to Spain, Graves visited Dallas, where he attended a masquerade ball as a domino clown; and there was more partying in New York;[391] but by the evening of Sunday 23 February, Robert Graves was back in his study at Canelluñ, reading through the large pile of mail that awaited his return.

The most exasperating letter came from Bridget Boland, who had finally heard from Twentieth Century-Fox about her *Claudius* treatment. Fox had pointed out that in the film *Demetrius and the Gladiators*, a sequel to *The Robe*, the main characters apart from Demetrius had been Messalina, Claudius and Caligula. Boland's treatment, in which Claudius, Caligula and Messalina were the chief protagonists, therefore risked an injunction from Fox if it was ever made into a film. 'I am sorry', wrote Bridget. 'It's a thing I should have known existed.' She now proposed to write a new script based mainly on the first part of the story, with Livia as the leading woman.[392] (A more robust letter from Jenny on the same subject would suggest suing Fox for having shamelessly plagiarized *I, Claudius* in *The Robe*, and *Claudius the God* in *Demetrius*, but caution prevailed.[393])

There was also correspondence about an invitation to visit Israel to take part in the celebrations marking the tenth anniversary of the Jewish State. Robert had already been sounded out by Dick, on behalf of the Israeli ambassador in London; and he had told his half-brother that the invitation was 'the greatest public honour I have ever been paid', and that if Beryl would accompany him, he would 'go like a shot'.[394] Beryl agreed, provided that she could take Tomas; and in due course it was arranged that they should visit Israel the following January.[395]

In the meantime, the *Claudius* saga rolled on and on. Towards the end of April 1958, Alec Guinness wrote to Robert Graves to tell him gloomily that the last script was 'a vast improvement, I thought, on the treatment – was clever, but a bit clumsy and above all, I fear, and don't know how to say, finally dull'. He added that he was '*not* committed beyond the end of August ... so if *Claudius* could really be got right I could do it.' But this would never happen 'until the right producer and/or director gets wholeheartedly interested'.[396]

Robert immediately wrote to Jenny to ask whether Bridget Boland would travel to Deyá:

> if we paid her expenses? And would it be a good idea if she first sent me the script, which I haven't yet seen, and if then I tend to put my finger on the dull patches and then *she* came and I worked at it under her eye?[397]

As he told Jenny, he was 'beastly busy' (since 16 March; he had been working for Cassell on a new prose and verse translation of Homer's *Iliad* [398]); but he would give priority to the *Claudius* script, because Bridget had 'committed herself to the risk and I feel responsible for her losses'.[399]

The script duly arrived on 9 May;[400] and less than a week later[401] there was a further letter from Alec Guinness with the exciting news that Sam Spiegel was:

> interested in *Claudius* and has asked for the script which I am delivering to him tomorrow. I told him I think it is a no-good-thing of a script but what he is most interested in is to know whether you would work on it (or rather on another script, I imagine) yourself. I have said I KNOW you would. Anyway, there we are – and as he is a genuine besotted fan of yours maybe something will come of it.[402]

Working at enormous speed, Graves had posted a redrafted *Claudius* script by 19 May; and he also wrote to Ricardo Sicré telling him how promising things looked.[403]

Ricardo was impressed by Robert's news; but he was anxious about whether Robert would be treated properly. 'What financial arrangements have you made?' he asked him.

This is most important. The reason is as follows – the prizes paid for scripts today *are fantastic* – Sam Spiegel is one of the highest-paid directors in the business. Also his productions are of the *highest budget* … This must be a good chance for you to make enough money for the rest of your life – but you must be for once business-like.[404]

Ricardo promised to 'handle your business in this case if you appoint me'; but there was then a lull in proceedings; and apart from a flattering letter from Bridget at the end of May,[405] it was months before Graves heard anything more about *Claudius* from anyone.

In the meantime, he continued with his lively translation of the *Iliad* (to be published the following year as *The Anger of Achilles*); in mid-May he enjoyed a brief visit from Tom Matthews;[406] he sat for a portrait by Mati Klarwein;[407] and with the help of two new friends: Margery Terrassa, a New Yorker, and her Mallorcan husband Ramian, Graves arranged for an Aga to be installed in the kitchen at Canelluñ: something which would make an enormous difference to the quality of domestic life.[408]

In the meantime the village filled up with its crowd of summer residents; there was an interview, arranged by James Reeves, with the artist Edward Ardizzone, who would later illustrate several of Robert Graves's books for children;[409] and Robert also met for the first time Ralph Jacobs and Cindy Lee, two highly unusual characters with whom he would be closely associated for many years to come

Ralph Jacobs was a teacher and a homosexual Jewish New Yorker who, in the days when the contest was rigged, had won a jackpot on the television quiz show 'The $64,000 Question'. A relaxed, understanding, genial man, with a smile on his bespectacled face, a twinkle in his eyes, and a constant stream of witticisms pouring from his lips, he was a good friend to women, and, perhaps to balance his comparatively mundane career, there was nothing he liked better than living a little dangerously. With the money he had won on television he could afford to travel; and he had arrived in Deyá with a highly sexed thirty-two-year-old woman companion named Cindy Lee. The story that Ralph had been something to do with television soon spread; and when he was therefore called in to help with rehearsals for *Round The World In Fifteen Minutes*, the summer play in which Robert took the part of Passepartout,[410] his wit and good humour soon won him a place as an accepted family friend.

Cindy went with him everywhere: so that she was by his side when he dined at the Posada with Robert, Beryl, Alastair and Alston on 15 August;[411] and a fortnight later, when Robert had invited Ralph to accompany him into Palma one morning, she went along for the ride.[412] At first, she remained quietly in the background, observing, and posing no threat to anyone. However, the fragmentary glimpses which survive of her earlier history suggest that this was highly uncharacteristic.

Cindy was no newcomer to the island. Robert's admirer Charles Corbett had first met her in Majorca back in 1952 when, at the age of twenty-six, she had been living with her American husband Owen Lee in Terreno; and Corbett found her 'breathtaking'. He recognized that her beauty 'wasn't the type that everyone would appreciate', for despite 'beautiful skin' and 'lovely teeth' she had 'almost the mask of a fox'. Cindy was also:

> very slim, and tall-ish … with a wonderful face: great made-up eyes with lots of kohl around the eyes, short curly black hair, dressed a good deal in black, wore wonderful … very slim high-heel shoes which someone told me she had made for her by Capriccio in New York. She loved to dance at night-clubs and when she danced she would take her shoes off and almost invariably leave them behind her.

She 'drank excessively … we all did', he recalls, but her drinking was 'unique even in those days', and she had 'the Jekyll and Hyde personality of an alcoholic'.

One day, for example, Charles Corbett and Cindy were walking down a street in Terreno, accompanied by 'a little blonde woman an actress, her name was Dorothy Londoner'. The three of them 'had stopped off in the afternoon and had a couple of martinis somewhere', and were on their way to another bar,

> when suddenly for no reason that I could ascertain Cindy threw a right hook that caught Dorothy right on the jaw and knocked her cold in the middle of the street. Nothing led up to it: it was just out of nowhere and I realised that among other things she was very dangerous.

Indeed, Owen Lee told Corbett that after their parties in Terreno, he would take Cindy's clothes away from her and 'lock her in the chicken coop behind the house and the maid would come in the morning and let her out. Because he was afraid (when she had been drinking heavily) to be in the same house with her and be asleep.'

As it turned out, he had good reason to be afraid: one night Cindy escaped from the chicken coop, and went at him and stabbed him with a large knife and damned near killed him. He got out of the house and went down the hill to a friend of his ... called Bill Brothers and fell in the door covered with blood. Brothers took him to a clinic in Palma in the middle of the night.

An emergency operation saved Owen's life, but only just: one of the stab wounds in his abdomen had been 'so deep that they took the appendix out before they closed it up', and he was left with 'scars all over his belly'.

Besides being beautiful and dangerous, Cindy was also mysterious. Even her nationality was uncertain. Owen Lee said that she was Puerto Rican, while she herself declared that her father had been French and her mother Moroccan. Later on she would claim to be Mexican, which, as Corbett says, 'may have been true but somehow I doubt it'.

Some months later, Charles Corbett found that the Lees were fellow-passengers on board the *Rheindam*, a Dutch liner out of Le Havre bound for New York. Owen explained privately that he had decided to return to the States so that he could divorce Cindy; and when Corbett ingenuously asked him why, he replied: 'Because she damn near-killed me, that's why!' Later in the same voyage, Cindy, who seemed to be unaware of her husband's plans, showed Corbett 'some photographs – theatrical 8 by 10 glossies. They were rather amazing, with Cindy posed as a harem girl in pantaloons and breast-plates: no veil but there should have been; some kind of head-dress'; and Cindy explained that she had once been a model in Chicago.

Corbett had then lost touch with the Lees for several years. Owen, as he later discovered, had returned to Majorca, where he had come to know Robert Graves after interviewing him for a possible magazine article. Still later, he had left the island to sail with the underwater explorer Jacques Cousteau, after which he wrote a definitive work on skin-diving. As for Cindy: she appears to have remained in New York, where one warm summer afternoon in 1955 or 1956, Corbett had been walking down Seventh Avenue when he bumped into her in the street.

Corbett soon discovered that Cindy, now aged twenty-nine or thirty, 'had a one-roomed apartment on Charles Street in the village about one block away'; and 'somehow', as he recalls, the two of them 'wound up in bed together drinking rye whisky out of teacups: she didn't have any glasses'. The sequel was bizarre.

After a couple of hours in bed, Cindy decided she was hungry so we went down the street to a place called Louis' Tavern, now torn down but quite well-known in its day, where a lot of actors hung out ... It was five or six in the afternoon and the place was crowded ... We knew a lot of people there and said hello to a bunch of them. I went up to the bar to get us a couple of drinks and I gave one to her and I had one and I turned round and talked to somebody and she wandered off in another direction, and it seemed that within a couple of minutes a fight broke out of which she was the centre.

Corbett could hardly believe his eyes: 'people were throwing punches at each other ... and I thought it would be a pretty good idea for me to go home at that point. So I finished my drink while the furniture was flying and left in a hurry.'[413]

There was no sign of this wild behaviour in Deyá in the summer of 1958. Indeed, in her capacity as Ralph's companion, Cindy soon became accepted as a minor character on the fringe of the Graves's inner circle. No one could possibly have guessed that she would later play a starring role in the most troubled Act of Robert and Beryl's married life; and on 2 September, the eve of their return to New York, she and Ralph were treated to a farewell steak supper at the Posada.[414]

As the summer visitors began to depart, Robert Graves was still working on *The Anger of Achilles*, a task which would take him to the end of the year since he had so much other work in hand, including the choice of poems for a 1959 Collected Edition; the proofs of *Steps* (a miscellany which Cassell published that autumn); an introduction to an encyclopaedia of mythology; numerous articles for the press; and lectures for his forthcoming visit to Israel. Many hours were also spent in correspondence; and Graves particularly enjoyed writing to Alan Sillitoe to congratulate him on the success of his first published novel, *Saturday Night and Sunday Morning*.[415] It was a success for which Graves could claim some responsibility, having earlier told Sillitoe that if he wanted to produce something publishable, he should write from his own experience.

That autumn also saw another dramatic episode in the *Claudius* saga. Quite unexpectedly, the following cable arrived from Alec Guinness:

SIR MICHAEL BALCON MAKING BID FOR CLAUDIUS WITH IDEA OF PRODUCTION ROME NEXT SUMMER WITH ME STOP BALCON WILL WRITE TO YOU SHORTLY STOP IF LONDON FILMS WILL SELL AT REASONABLE PRICE HE IS PREPARED TO INVEST CONSIDERABLE MONEY IMMEDIATELY TO OBTAIN SATISFACTORY SCRIPT AND SERVICES OF DIRECTOR OF INTERNATIONAL REPUTE STOP WILL WRITE MYSELF WHEN LESS BUSY AFFECTIONATELY ALEC[416]

In his subsequent letter, Guinness explained that Rizzoli, a big Italian producer, had suddenly said to Sir Michael: 'Why don't you do *I, Claudius* with Guinness?' For a while, this seemed like a real possibility. True, Guinness had lost confidence in Bridget Boland's work; but he told Jenny that he still wanted Robert to be connected with the script; and that he also wanted him to play the part of Tiberius. Robert retailed this news to James Reeves, telling him: 'I'll have to join Equity and pay 200 dollars; but worth it. Hope to qualify as the world's best bad actor.'[417]

In practice, Rizzoli backed out; and the film of *I, Claudius* was never made;[418] but by mid-September Graves was aware of another potential money-spinner: this time, not for the silver screen, but for the stage. The Broadway producer Alexander Cohen wrote to Graves telling him that he wanted him to write the 'book' for a musical based upon the story of Antony and Cleopatra;[419] and six weeks later he called on Graves's London agent Bill Watt, to tell him that he was still thinking in terms of a musical, but now wanted it to be about Solomon and Sheba.[420]

Having settled on a subject, Cohen moved fast. He had already talked to the singer Alfred Drake, a recent success on the London stage in *Kismet*, and said to be 'enthusiastic' about playing Solomon;[421] he had also retained the services of the producer Tyrone Guthrie[422] (then widely respected as one of the most brilliant theatrical producers of his day);[423] and in November he told Graves that the composer Dimitri Tiompkin wanted to do the music.[424] The following month Graves reported to James Reeves that:

> This Broadway musical project seemed a sort of joke but appears to be perfectly serious. And I am now asked to write lyrics as well as 'book' & they have the best stars & composers laid on, and so if I don't look out I'll be disgustingly rich.

Negotiations, he added, were 'in full progress'.[425]

A crucial factor would be whether Graves and Guthrie would be able to collaborate successfully. Graves did not think this would be a problem. 'Dr. Guthrie is an Irishman', he pointed out to Watt, 'so am I. He lives on an island and leaves it only when he must: so do I. He is very busy until December 29: so am I.'[426] A further coincidence was that in January they were both due to be in Israel; and so they arranged to meet in Tel Aviv.

As for Graves's untried ability as a writer of musicals: he would later explain to James Reeves that Cohen's 'odd choice of me as the writer of the "musical" was due to his being a devoted reader of my poems. (Who says poetry don't pay, eh?)'[427] And to his agent he commented:

Yes: I have written three or four film-scripts which have passed muster, and a play which is OK but too outrageous for the stage;[428] and dramatic dialogue passim in my novels and short stories, but a musical not yet. On the other hand I know most of the historical and legendary stuff about Solomon from Josephus, The Koran, the Abyssinian Scriptures, the 1001 Nights, the Bible and the Jewish Haggadah.

'[Solomon] is an old friend of mine', Graves concluded, 'and I have a good many ideas about him.'[429]

CHAPTER 9

Sheba, Lawrence, and
Magic Mushrooms

Although *The Anger of Achilles* was still unfinished, Graves spent one Sunday in mid-December 1958 making a start on the lyrics of *Solomon and Sheba* for Alexander Cohen.[430] He had been encouraged to do so by a recent letter from Cohen, telling him that:

> ... we see this as a Broadway musical not as a musical drama or as a play with music ... the focus is essentially a love-story between two people with different environments and points of view. On Broadway it would be nice to have a witty intelligent literate musical instead of the commercial stuff we have been getting.

Cohen added that it would be 'exciting theatre to have a negro and a white on stage in an historical truth without the necessity of commenting on it'.[431] For besides having recruited Alfred Drake as Solomon, Cohen had managed to interest Lena Horne in the role of Sheba.

Graves replied enthusiastically;[432] and a few days later, he wrote again, to say that it was not the biblical Solomon, but the Solomon of Arab, Jewish and Abyssinian legend who would make the best theatre. 'This means', he explained,

> that I should like to introduce magic, in the person of the Devil Asmodeus (he is Scriptural, of course) who stole Solomon's magic ring, usurped his throne and sent him out penniless into the world – so that he first came to meet Sheba as a wanderer in her own black territory, and cooked in her kitchen.

Using this story would help 'to get our black scenes alternating with the white, and so keep Lena Horne and Alfred Drake constantly employed'. He added that he was 'trying *not* to think about *Solomon and Sheba* while finishing *The Anger of Achilles*' and writing lectures for Israel; but '*Sheba* intrudes and scenes keep sliding into my head unasked.'[433]

Robert, Beryl and Tomas set out for Israel on 9 January 1959. After a flight to Barcelona and a train journey to Marseilles, this involved them in a three-day voyage through the Mediterranean on the SS *Theodor Herzel*. Robert left the ship at Naples for a few hours so that he could visit the Roman ruins at Pompeii; but that was almost the only relaxation he allowed himself, and by the time the ship docked at Haifa on Thursday 15 January, he had sketched out the whole of the first Act of *Solomon and Sheba*.[434]

The Graveses found themselves honoured guests. For their first three days, they were taken to visit not only tourist attractions such as the Lake of Tiberias and Mount Carmel, but also several of the communal settlements or kibbutzim, by which they were both much impressed; and on Sunday 18 January Robert had what he described in his diary as 'a very useful talk' with Tyrone Guthrie on the subject of *Solomon and Sheba*.

Then on Monday, while Beryl and Tomas stayed with a writer friend at Caesarea, Robert Graves began the more public part of his visit: meeting the press, lunching at the British Embassy in Tel Aviv, and dining with the Israel and British Commonwealth Association, to whom he lectured that evening on 'What it feels like to be a Goy'. His lecture was in part an ironical look at his own Protestant background. Graves made much of the way in which the Hebrew scriptures had:

> passed into enemy hands; with the eventual result that Christian *goyim*, who cannot even pretend to be the sons of Abraham, claim the God of Israel as their God and the Scriptures as their own Holy Writ: denying you stiff-necked and rebellious Jews any hope of the eventual salvation that your own Prophets had held out to you![435]

He then commented on the absurdity of Jesus being depicted 'as a blond, fair-skinned Anglo-Saxon wearing a Greek robe'; and of the equal absurdity of the English 'squire and his lady, the village worthies and their wives ... identifying themselves with the Israelites of old, and boasting of God's help to them in Egypt and the Wilderness'.[436]

Later on, Graves spoke of his awe that Israel was a nation once more; and that Hebrew was 'again a living spoken language'. And in his conclusion, he reminded his audience that Israel was 'the first nation to make brotherly love and mercy head the list of moral virtues'.[437] The lecture was well received, though the loudspeaker system had been far from perfect, and an official later apologized for the fact that 'owing to the rain, the powerful amplifier attracted other wavelengths from abroad, and occasionally even Cairo came through'.[438]

During his remaining week in Israel, Graves lectured both on Homer's *Iliad* and on contemporary poetry. He also lunched with Golda Meir (then Minister of Education); but his most memorable meeting was with David Ben-Gurion, the Prime Minister of Israel.[439] Early one morning, the two men walked alone together for an hour, after which the statesman presented the poet with a gift from his own kibbutz: a rug which Graves used for the rest of his life.[440]

Before leaving Israel, Graves visited King Solomon's mines at Elath, from where he brought back 'copper, slag & pottery' partly 'as a memento' of his visit;[441] and partly as a source of inspiration for his *Solomon and Sheba*. From Rome, where he visited Jenny on his way home, he brought back something rather more important: a promise from his daughter that she would help him write his musical. Robert was delighted by this, telling Betty Sicré that Jenny had 'been in with Jerry [Jerome] Robbins [the famous choreographer] on *West Side Story* ... knows all about timing and what isn't funny ... [and] doesn't mind letting me know when what I write *stinks*'.[442]

Jenny Nicholson arrived at Canelluñ on 19 February;[443] and that very evening she and her father began a sustained bout of hard work on *Solomon and Sheba*, closeting themselves in Robert's study for up to ten hours each day.[444] After a week of this, they decided that it would be easier to write 'the whole book with lyrics',[445] than to give Cohen the 'rough outline' for which he had asked.[446] And by Tuesday 3 March, after a particularly gruelling session which had not ended until 11.30 at night, their first draft was complete.[447]

Jenny returned to Rome on Wednesday, leaving Robert to revise *Solomon and Sheba*; and with Karl's help he had completed and posted a second draft of 151 pages by the following Monday.[448] By then, Jenny had already written to her father, telling him that she had seen:

for the first time and fully what a plum peach apple from the top of the tree you have in Karl. His puckered brow and small mesh-sieve apparatus through which all your work is forced is more valuable for any writer than Solomon's heart. His approval is worth the blood in which it is written.[449]

However, when Jenny received her father's revised version of *Solomon and*

Sheba, she was highly dissatisfied with what he had done, and sent him a telegram 'protesting at "damaging" minor changes'.

Cohen took a different view, sending Graves an ecstatic telegram on 16 March saying 'MAGNIFICENT, BRAVO, BRAVO, BRAVO!'[450] and following this up with a letter in which he declared that 'We are all enormously pleased and think it the best first draft of a book we have ever read.'[451] In the meantime Tony Guthrie had flown out to Majorca where he had spent a day and a half helping Graves to make a further set of minor revisions;[452] so everything was beginning to look distinctly promising.

The beginning of April saw the arrival of Huw Weldon and a camera crew from the BBC television arts programme 'Monitor'. They spent a week making a twenty-minute film about Robert Graves, in which the most memorable scene shows him shaving while, as a voice-over, he recites his poem 'Face in the Mirror'. But although this attention was flattering, Graves was increasingly conscious of a general sense of unease.

This unease was heightened by a series of minor accidents: a broken finger, a badly bruised chest, after tripping over a wheelbarrow in the dark, and a cricked back; so that by 9 April Robert recorded in his diary that he was feeling like 'a wreck'.[453] However, that was also the day when he began another bout of work with Jenny on *Solomon and Sheba* (in the course of which they amended the title to *A Song for Sheba*); and then on 20 April Robert and Beryl and Tomas flew to England.[454]

On his first morning in London, Robert Graves visited Watt, from whom he learned that the *Claudius* film was finally off; but this disappointment was outweighed later that day by a long talk with Cohen, whom Graves presented with the revised 'book' of *A Song for Sheba*. In return, Cohen gave him tickets to *West Side Story*, to which Robert took Beryl and William that evening; and the next day (after being photographed by his old friend Douglas Glass), he went to a matinée performance of *My Fair Lady*.[455]

This time, Robert took six-year-old Tomas with him; and to make up the party, he had also brought along the two Simon girls: his god-daughter Helena, just five weeks short of her twelfth birthday, and her ten-year-old sister Julia.[456] Robert had always had a special affection for Helena, the beautiful and highly intelligent child over whose conception he had presided like Merlin presiding over that of King Arthur; but after her birth, to protect her from the jealousy of the gods, he had warned her parents 'to appreciate her as an ugly unwanted little thing and if you put on her socks inside out by mistake, don't change them':[457] which may have made her more vulnerable. Her younger sister Julia, by contrast, was 'a flamboyant creature all emotions and movement with tremendous zest for everything'.[458]

By 10 May, Graves was back at his desk in Canellun, busily answering some of the fifty letters which had accumulated during his absence.[459] Among them was one from Cohen suggesting that in *A Song of Sheba* Graves had 'underemphasised the royal conflict', to which Robert replied simply: 'It seems likely you are right … but it may be that in rehearsal you will find that the acting brings it out without much more emphasis.' However, by the time Cohen received this letter on 18 May, he had shown the revised book of *A Song for Sheba* to a number of people whose lack of enthusiasm had severely shaken his own initial confidence.[460]

This was not at all surprising, although the book contained some real show-stoppers. In the very first number Amina, a beautiful Egyptian girl, is being taken by her avaricious father from Heliopolis to Jerusalem where he hopes to sell her 'into the harem of King Solomon the great and wise'. At each place where they pause to embellish Amina's beauty, she sings a verse of a song which begins:

> We pitched that night in Rinocolura,
> A fly-ridden town
> By the Mediterranean sea,
> Where my father bought crayfish and oysters and scallops,
> And lobster and crab and doree:
> For sea-food's the best for encouraging Zest,
> If the King's to take pleasure in me.

> Next day we came to Philistine Gaza,
> Where Samson got shaved,
> (*Then* what a poor lover was he!)
> My father bought scarlet and purple apparel,
> And paid an astonishing fee –
> Though I said that undress might have surer success
> If the King's to take pleasure in me.

> We pitched one night near the well of Beersheba –
> It was Abraham's pride –
> In the shade of his tamarisk tree.
> And my father said: 'Daughter, go wash at that well,
> May its charm confer beauty on thee!'
> For my eyes must shine bright in his chamber at night:
> If the King's to take pleasure in me.

> Last night we slept at Bethlehem city
> Where King David was born,
> From the perils of travel now free;
> And my father bought rouge, belladonna and henna.
> I begged him, 'No more, let it be!
> I must enter bare-faced with my bosom unlaced
> If the King's to take pleasure in me.'[461]

This is not the only production number which could have been staged as a highly entertaining set-piece; and yet the book as a whole contains very little plot, and almost no character development.

'We want a musical', Cohen complained, 'not an opera.' In opera, he pointed out, one could go 'from production number to production number with small bridges of recitative'; but a musical needed 'individual scenes which develop characterisation within people, and dialogue which is then heightened by the musical numbers'. Graves had certainly provided the production numbers; but this, wrote Cohen, was 'not enough. You must do the essential primary creative job of writing the scenes from scratch for people to act.'[462]

Graves found this letter 'disturbing'.[463] In effect, he was being asked to do a major rewrite 'for nothing'; and he wrote for advice both to Selwyn Jepson, telling him that Cohen's letter was 'stupid and bloody';[464] and to Tony Guthrie, suggesting that the next step was to find a composer. Early in June, both men replied at length.

Jepson wrote sympathetically about the difficulties of working on a Broadway musical with 'the football-team size group of professionals' which would soon collect:

> round the dead-looking if newly-born child, the script of the man who wrote it in the first place. They start moiling over it with poorly-expressed, ignorant diagnoses and worse prescriptions for its continued life. That it sometimes survives and grows to millionaire maturity, however, is *always* and *entirely* due to the indestructibility of its basic vitality, and that in its adult and public state is quite unrecognizable to its fond parent – as in the case of most children grown-up – is of no significance to anyone but himself.

So he advised Robert to go along with Cohen so far as he could, though he should put on 'an Olympian air', and, 'like any other God, let the mortals do most of the talking'. Cohen and his cronies could reasonably be expected to 'talk themselves out of the worst errors and come sacrificially to you for approval and the deft touch of divinity that will turn their dross to the gold they covet'.[465]

Guthrie was more hard-hitting. He believed there was substance in Cohen's criticisms 'that the dialogue is under-written, that the psychological situations are under-prepared, and that, with the exception of Solomon, none of the acting parts would at present attract any player who is getting other offers'. On the other hand, he also believed that Graves was right to insist that 'the next step is to *hire a composer*. His views are now not only relevant, but essential, if I were you I wouldn't write another line until the composer is agreed, and consulted.'[466] Later that month, Guthrie wrote with equal force to Cohen, telling him that it was unreasonable to expect Graves to do another rewrite without 'an absolutely clear and specific set of suggestions'. The next step was to find a composer with whom Graves could collaborate; and 'if such a composer can't be found,' he concluded, 'then the project should be regretfully abandoned.'[467]

But by this time, Cohen was becoming increasingly discouraged. Lena Horne had seen the script and disliked the lyrics so much that she was no longer interested in playing Sheba;[468] and although Cohen offered Graves a contract for a further option on *A Song for Sheba*, Graves decided on 19 July not to sign,[469] believing that he would do better with a different producer. In any case, he could afford to wait a little, as he had recently accepted an offer from the State University of New York at Buffalo, who were willing to pay $30,000 for the manuscripts of his poems.[470]

In the meantime, extracts from *A Song for Sheba* were presented under the title *Show of Shows* at Robert's birthday party on 24 July that summer in front of an audience of some 130 guests, with Mati Klarwein playing the part of Solomon, and Robert himself in a minor role.[471] It was a successful party, with the usual rockets and fire-balloons; and the following day Robert went with Ricardo Sicré to a bullfight in Palma, after which Ricardo entertained both Robert and the leading toreador on his yacht.[472]

These were pleasant diversions; but quite apart from the general sense of malaise which had been afflicting him for months, Robert had begun to suffer from specific symptoms of some physical disorder; and when he therefore consulted Dr Llobret of Palma on 29 July, he was given a thorough examination which 'hurt like hell'. The evidence was unmistakable: Robert was suffering from an enlarged prostate. On being advised that a prostatectomy was essential, he made arrangements to fly alone to London at the beginning of September to consult Mr Mempriss, a Harley Street specialist, after which, if necessary, he would be admitted to St Thomas's Hospital for an immediate operation.[473]

It was necessary; and on the morning of Monday 7 September Mempriss performed a prostatectomy.[474] However, this was not the end of the matter. On Thursday, Robert suffered from a haemorrhage which required attention; and so a second operation[475] was performed by Mempriss, and followed by a series of blood transfusions.

To begin with, Robert appeared to be making a rapid recovery: by Sunday he was already 'tottering around [the] ward'; by Monday he had started work on some proof-reading; and during the next few days he entertained a stream of visitors including Jenny, Dick, and Alec Guinness who, learning of Robert's blood transfusions, later sent him 'four bottles of hooch to alcoholize the new stuff'.[476] Beryl flew out to join him on Friday 18 September; and the following Tuesday he woke up 'feeling fine' for the first time since entering hospital.[477]

Later that very day, however, Robert suffered a second, more severe haemorrhage and intense 'memorable' pain.[478] 'Something', he wrote later,

> Something occurred after the operation
> To scare the surgeons (though no fault of theirs)
> Whose reassurance did not fool me long.
> Beyond the shy, concerned faces of nurses
> A single white-hot eye, focusing on me,
> Forced sweat in rivers down from scalp to belly.
> I whistled, gasped or sang with blanching knuckles
> Clutched at my bed-grip almost till it cracked:
> Too proud, still, to let loose Bedlamite screeches
> And bring the charge-nurse scuttling down the aisle
> With morphia-needle levelled ...
>   Lady Morphia –
> Her scorpion kiss and dark gyrating dreams –
> She in mistrust of whom I dared out-dare,
> Two minutes longer than seemed possible,
> Pain, that unpurposed, matchless elemental
> Stronger than fear or grief, stranger than love.

Robert was rushed to the operating theatre; and one of the house-surgeons staunched the bleeding.

There followed a much more gradual recovery. It was not until 10 October, after several more episodes of bleeding (attributed by a specialist to a rare blood condition), that Graves was allowed to leave St Thomas's and move in with Sally and Richard Chilver. However, far from relaxing during his final fortnight in hospital, Graves had become involved in several new projects for stage and screen.[480]

Two of these involved Graves's old friend T. E. Lawrence. The first, a possible film, had been brought to his attention by Ricardo Sicré, who had conducted Sam Spiegel to his bedside on 29 September. The following afternoon the film director David Lean also visited Graves for 'a long talk' about Lawrence; and eventually, thanks largely to Ricardo Sicré's bargaining skills,[481] negotiations ended with Robert being promised at least $10,000 for the film rights to his 1927 biography *Lawrence and the Arabs*.[482] He was also asked whether he would 'help in an advisory capacity, though the exact nature of his function, and the payment he was to receive for it, were both kept vague'.[483]

In the meantime, Graves had received the script of Terence Rattigan's *Ross*.[484] This was a play about T. E. Lawrence (who had once enlisted under the name of Ross in the Royal Air Force); and it had been sent to him by the stage producer Hugh Beaumont at the insistence of Alec Guinness. He had agreed to play the title role, and hoped that if Graves liked the play, he might persuade T.E.'s brother A. W. Lawrence to take a favourable view.[485]

Beaumont had merely told Robert Graves that A. W. Lawrence had asked for his opinion, which Graves found 'fishy', because when he read the play, he felt that 'Ross' had been unfairly portrayed as 'a sadistic, vain, unbalanced queer'.[486] So he contacted A. W. ('Arnie') Lawrence, who visited him at Sally's house,[487] and explained that at one time, thinking Rattigan's play unstoppable, he had indeed suggested to Beaumont that Robert shoud vet the play for him, 'and try to make it less disgusting'. However, since then he had 'discovered accidentally that the Lord Chamberlain had told Beaumont that the family if they objected strongly enough could stop the play altogether'. To make such an objection was now his intention; and Robert did his best to help, by preparing a wholly adverse report.[488]

But while opposing the Rattigan play, Robert Graves had done Sam Spiegel a good turn, since he had discussed Spiegel's proposed film with Arnie Lawrence, who had concluded that, as Graves reported to Karl,

'If Spiegel wants to make some sort of Western, that's fine. The public deserves it. But no psychological slants or libels. The trouble is one can't control the script-writer and director.' So I said: 'Who can't? I can. Tell Spiegel you want me to guard the decencies and everything's fine.'[489]

It was this successful intervention on Spiegel's behalf which had enabled Sicré to bargain from a position of strength, and to secure Graves a sum of money which eventually amounted to $20,000.[490]

As for the play: Robert Graves wrote both to Merula Guinness (Alec being away in New York) and to Terence Rattigan, suggesting that *Ross* gave a very false view of his old friend. Merula simply replied that Alec had read her much of the play, which she had found 'very moving';[491] while Rattigan, in a 'curiously emotional' letter, made it clear that if the Lord Chamberlain succeeded in banning *Ross* from the London stage, he would put it on in New York instead. However, he was generously prepared to make whatever 'changes, cuts and emendations' Graves suggested, so long as these were 'compatible with the play's theatrical life'.[492]

Guinness was momentarily annoyed with Graves for having bothered his wife with 'all these goings-on', though he made it clear that he wanted 'no part of any denigrating of a great man';[493] but before long Graves's machinations had become irrelevant. Basil Liddell-Hart persuaded A. W. Lawrence not to try to ban *Ross*, but to ask for alterations; and in due course preparations for the production went ahead.[494]

Several other schemes had been brought to Graves's attention while he was lying in St Thomas's, all of them based upon his published work. Jerry Robbins brought Chinese lilies to his bedside, and talked about choreographing a ballet from *Watch the North Wind Rise*; William ('Bill') Morris visited Graves to discuss the possibility of making a film out of *The White Goddess*;[495] and there was a burst of correspondence about the opera based on *Homer's Daughter*.

Nausicaa, with music by Peggy Glanville-Hicks and a first-class libretto written largely by Alastair Reid, was nearing completion when Graves was disturbed by a report that Peggy and Alastair had quarrelled. When he wrote to Peggy about this, she replied that she was 'bewildered' by his letter. The last time she had seen her collaborator was at a party in her New York home, when he had been 'his usual charming and provocative self'. He had been accompanied by Mary, who since then had become his second wife and given birth to their son Jasper; and he had certainly said 'something in a ragging manner about leaving his name off the score of *Nausicaa* but I didn't really pay any attention as I thought it a whimsy of the moment'.[496]

Robert Graves then wrote to Alastair Reid asking why he wished his name kept off the credits; and, in a confidential letter, Alastair replied that he had personal reasons which he would never divulge under any circumstances.[497] Instead of letting the matter rest there, Robert wrote

A 1938 portrait of Beryl (*née* Pritchard), who was then married to Alan Hodge, but would set up home with Robert Graves in October 1939.

Robert Graves in the mid-1940s, when he and Beryl were living at Galmpton in Devon.

Robert and Beryl Graves with their children Lucia, William and Juan in 1949 at Kneesworth Hall where they were visiting their friends Dorothy and Montagu Simmons.

Robert Graves's mother Amy at Harlech in 1949, with his brother John and nephew Richard.

An early portrait of the artist Judith Bledsoe, who became Robert Graves's Muse in November 1950.

The only surviving letter from Robert Graves to
Judith Bledsoe, written in December 1951.

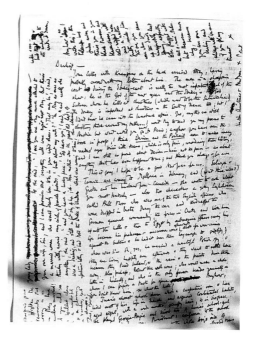

Robert Graves in 1951 with his friend Tom
Matthews of *Time* magazine.

The composer Peggy Glanville-Hicks in Deyá in 1955 with Robert Graves, whose *Homer's Daughter* she was using as the basis for her opera *Nausicaa*, and with her collaborator, Robert's close friend Alastair Reid.

In Deyá in 1959 with Martin Amis, Hilly Amis, Tomas Graves and Kingsley Amis.

Margot Callas in June 1960, when she became Robert Graves's Muse. This is a still taken from a film by Mati Klarwein in which she and Robert both took part.

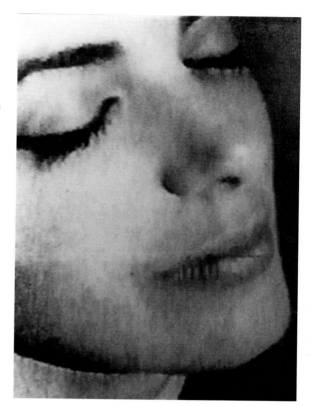

Robert Graves and his daughter Lucia on a beach in Greece in 1961 with Eleni, the Greek sculptress who became Robert's 'spiritual sister'.

With his daughter Jenny Nicholson, with whom he had been collaborating on the musical *Solomon and Sheba*, in 1963.

With his daughter Lucia in 1962.

At *The Indigo* in Palma in 1963. On Robert Graves's left (and wearing his hat) sits 'Cindy' Lee, later known as Aemilia Laraçuen, who became Robert's Muse in July 1963. On his right is his friend Ralph Jacobs. Across the table sit Beryl and Lucia with their friend Helen Morningstar, while Ramon Farran, Lucia's husband, sits at his drums in the background.

Robert Graves in 1964 with his niece Sally Chilver, who had often helped him with his researches. The title *The Mob* was given to the snap by Aemilia Laraçuen.

THE MOB

A play rehearsal in the summer of 1965 in the theatre below Canelluñ: Ralph Jacobs, Esteban Frances and Robert Graves, with Tomas Graves on guitar.

Robert Graves's sister Clarissa Graves in 1968.

Robert Graves in Deyá on 27 July 1968, walking with his god-daughter Helena Simon, on his way to be made an adoptive son of the village.

Robert Graves in 1969 with Juli Simon, who had become his Muse in October 1966.

Giving a poetry-reading.

With the Sufi philosopher Idries Shah in 1970.

With his friend Ava Gardner.

With his daughter Catherine Dalton in 1978, when his memory was already severely impaired.

Robert Graves leaning on one of the olive trees on his land below Canelluñ.

to Peggy suggesting that, if she showed love and understanding, her differences with Alastair would be resolved, and his name could then go back on the credits.

Alastair was furious when he heard from Peggy about Robert's letter. How dare Robert tell her that 'love will vincit absolutely omnia. This makes me so angry',[498] he told Robert, 'that I don't know what to say ... I will write to Peggy and tell her that you utterly misled her, and assumed things that were not true without knowing the truth ... please don't do things like that.'[499]

Their quarrel was of short duration. Within a month or two, Alastair was once again writing to 'My dearest Robert'. However, it left a permanent mark on their friendship, as it exposed a fundamental difference in temperament between the two men, one of whom lived as openly as possible within the circle of his intimate friends, while the other had a private life which he preferred to keep entirely to himself.[500]

By the beginning of November 1959 Robert and Beryl were safely back in Deyá, where Robert chose a selection of his poems for *The Penny Fiddle*, a children's book containing 'mostly romantic 1820-ish pieces, with more salt than honey in them', and superbly illustrated by Edward Ardizzone. He also prepared for a third American lecture tour, which was due to begin in January 1960.

This time it was to be his daughter Jenny who acted as Robert's companion while he was on American soil; and by the evening of Friday 15 January the two of them were comfortably installed in Gordon Wasson's New York apartment.[501] 'Darling', Robert wrote to Beryl, who was in London with Tomas,

> Safari sagoodi. We had to land at Boston because of bad weather over New York. There we wired Sam Spiegel's office to go in a Cadillac 320 miles to New York instead of by train; so got here at 8.30 in time for supper ... I was given a room here overlooking the East River where liners and naval vessels and barges go by; but Jenny took it – it had more cupboards – and I now have a smaller room instead, overlooking the Fifth Avenue bus route, but with a bath and study attached.

He told Beryl that he had been deluged with 'all sorts of letters and messages from all our friends'; that 'You're here with me in a very real sense', and that 'I spend all my leisure reminding myself how much I love you and how much you'd be enjoying yourself if you were here.' But his most momentous news was that Gordon Wasson 'has some mushroom crystals and <u>maybe</u> he and I will take them. All quite safe', he added reassuringly, 'and the dose exactly calculable by weight.'[502]

In fact there was no knowing whether it was entirely safe or not; so Wasson had arranged that the experiment (which Robert Graves hoped would provide him with the spiritual illumination granted in ancient times to participants in the Eleusinian mysteries), should wait until shortly before Graves's return to Europe.

In the meantime, Robert Graves was caught up in a frantic rush: seeing Alastair Reid, lunching with Jerry Robbins, discussing his *Lawrence* contract with Sam Spiegel's lawyer, and attending a dinner at the Waldorf Astoria, where Robert Frost presented him with the gold medal of the National Poetry Society of America.[503]

Although Graves was subsequently disappointed to find that the medal was not gold but electroplated bronze, the evening was a great success. 'Robert Frost was at my elbow', Graves told Betty Sicré:

he'd come up a day earlier especially to see me and was in wonderful form. Meeting him again was worth the whole visit. Anyhow I was suddenly called on to speak for 25 minutes *impromptu* and with a radio transmitter sticking into my face & flash bulbs flashing; and no drink in me.

'But what with Robert Frost cracking dirty jokes at my elbow & Jenny grinning encouragingly from down below the dais', he concluded, 'I got through all right.'

There were also lectures and poetry readings;[504] and on Saturday 30 January Graves enjoyed a special 'Deyá lunch', at which those present included Esteban Frances, Gordon Wasson, Len Lye, Jess McNab, Marnie Pomeroy and Ralph Jacobs, who was accompanied as usual by Cindy Lee.[505] It was the evening after this 'Deyá lunch' that the 'great experiment' took place, with Robert Graves, Gordon Wasson and a few close friends sampling the Mexican hallucinogenic mushroom Psilocybe Heimsii.

Jenny Nicholson joined Gordon and her father for the mushroom-eating on 31 January 1960. Robert had also invited Jess McNab to be there; and Jerry Robbins was present, since he had asked Robert Graves 'to explain the paintings in the *Women's Mystery* house at Pompeii, because he wants to do a ballet of the Mysteries'; and Robert had told him, 'Bring them along and look at them when we eat mushrooms together.'[506] Richard Hammersley of M.I.T. made up the number;[507] and, as Graves later wrote, the six of them 'gathered in Gordon Wasson's apartment overlooking the East River, prepared to set out for Paradise under his guidance'.[508]

Wasson had advised them 'to fast beforehand, drink no liquor, and try to achieve a state of grace'. At seven-thirty he gave them the mushrooms 'in crystalline form washed down with water'; and then at eight o'clock he 'began turning out the lights one by one, while we settled down in easy chairs'. By that time, Graves had begun to feel 'a numbness in my arms, and a pricking at the nape of my neck'.

In the half-light that filtered through the shutters, Graves saw coloured dots, which shone more brightly when he closed his eyes. He began to shiver, his pulse slowed, and Gordon's daughter, Masha Wasson brought in blankets. Since she was a trained nurse and had twice made this journey herself, Graves welcomed the reassuring presence of her hand. At that moment he was remembering a warning quotation which ran: 'You are going where God dwells; and will be granted all knowledge ... Whoever nurses evil in his heart sees hideous demons and nameless horrors, more proper to Hell than to Paradise, and wishes he had never been born.'

Graves kept his eyes closed, while he anxiously considered his motives for taking the mushroom; and then he was aware that while his 'corporeal self' was still sitting fully conscious in a chair, 'exchanging occasional confidences with friends', there was greenish water lapping round about him.

I entered a marble grotto, passing a pile of massive sunken statuary, and found myself in a high-roofed tunnel lit by brilliantly coloured lamps. The sea lay behind ... Still worrying about the demons, I glanced up at the roof. Thousands of pink green or yellow faces, like carnival masks, grimaced horribly down; but I dismissed them with a wave of my hand, and they obediently vanished.

A turn in the tunnel then brought Graves 'to the domed Treasury, without which no Paradise is complete'. Before him lay:

diadems, tiaras, necklaces, crosses, breast-plates, goblets, ephods, cups, platters, sceptres, blazing or twinkling. But, even richer than these jewels, were the royal silks spread out for my inspection in blue, mulberry and white: vast lengths. miraculously brocaded with birds, beasts, flowers ...

Reaching for a notebook, Graves wrote: '9 p.m. Visions of ... ' But he got no further. After a while, he heard himself saying: 'I have seen enough treasure for a life-time. Is there no human beauty in Paradise?' And then, all at once, the treasure vanished; and instead Graves saw:

> a row of lovely, live, naked Caryatids ... lined along the wall, as if supporting the dome. Their faces were shrouded. Yet I hesitated to indulge in erotic fancies, lest the Caryatids turned into filthy, deformed devilkins ... Blushing, I dismissed them too, and came out from the tunnel into daylight.

All around him lay 'a mountain-top Eden, with its jewel-bright trees, its flowers and its pellucid streams'.

Here Graves experienced 'not only the bliss of innocence, but also the "knowledge of good and evil" ... a universal understanding of all things'. His mind had suddenly become:

> so agile and unfettered that I felt capable of solving any problem in the world; it was as if I had immediate access to all knowledge everywhere. But the sensation of wisdom sufficed. Why should I trouble to explore it?

By now, Gordon Wasson was playing a tape-recording of the singing of a Mexican curandera, invoking the god Tlaloc. 'I fell wholly under her spell', Graves would later recall,

> and presently enjoyed the curious experience of *seeing* sound. The song-notes became intricate links of a round golden chain that coiled and looped in serpentine fashion along jade-green bushes: the only serpent I met in Eden ... Each song was followed by a pause, and always I waited in a lover's agony for her to begin again, tears pricking at my eyelids.

Towards the end of her singing, the curandera sang 'a cheerful song of creation and growth', during which it seemed to Robert that the notes 'fell to earth but rose once more in green shoots which soared swiftly up, putting on branches, leaves, flowers'; and his spirit 'followed after, gazing down on cornfields, fields of poppies, and the spires of a heavenly city'.

When the singing was over, and the effects of the mushroom had begun to wear off, they moved to the kitchen where they turned their attention to cold turkey sandwiches while comparing notes about their drug-induced experiences. For one of them, at least, it had been a terrifying ordeal: he had looked at his hand, and watched it 'turn corpse-like and slowly disintegrate into a dusty skeleton'. But for Robert it had been 'pure delight'[509] both at the time and immediately afterwards: for 'a curious bond of affection had been established' between himself and the other mushroom-eaters which was 'so strong that I felt nothing could ever break it'.

Finally at two o'clock in the morning of 1 February they parted; and only six hours later, Robert Graves was on his way to the airport, where he was seen off by Jenny and Alastair.[510] As he flew to England, Graves felt 'profoundly refreshed' in spirit by his mushroom-eating; and he would soon be telling Gordon Wasson that he had

> no doubt at all but that the mushroom should be restored among Europeans and people of European descent to its original (presumed) position in religion: first of all as an initiation ceremony to religion at puberty; then as a heightening of the marriage rite ...

It was even possible, he speculated, that the mushroom could be used 'as a *viaticum* – so that when the door of heaven opens one really enters and sees those one has loved'.[511]

Graves's visit to America had also earned him a great deal of money, so that in his various banks in London, Geneva and New York he now had funds somewhat exceeding £18,000;[512] and it had greatly enhanced his reputation. His gold medal acceptance had been broadcast live to some five million radio listeners;[513] and he became still more of a celebrity two months later, with the screening of an appearance on Ed Morrow's popular television programme 'The Small World' which had been recorded while he was in New York.[514]

Back in Deyá Robert Graves found waiting from him a moving letter from Tom Matthews. 'Dear Robert,' began his old friend, 'I have owed you this letter for about 36 years'; and then, after briefly recounting the history of their friendship, Tom declared that:

> quite apart from my personal fondness for you, you are a good and true poet, and you have made my life more alive. Your poetry is astringent to false tears but sometimes breaks my bloody heart. How could I not thank you for that? I don't care how much of an artful dodger you are (so is Robert Frost, who presented you with that medal); you haven't dodged the point where art and agony meet.

'Many, many people', he concluded, 'and I am one of them, are grateful to you for meeting that point head on.'[515]

Within a few days of his return, Robert had also received a lengthy telegram[516] from Christina Foyle of the famous London bookshop which bears her name. She told him that she very much admired his *Collected Poems 1959*, not to mention his forthcoming translation of the *Iliad*, and that she hoped to present him with an award at a luncheon to be held on 3 March at the Dorchester. Robert accepted; and was then infuriated to receive a letter from his brother Charles, telling him: 'I think I have fixed for you to receive the £250 Foyle Poetry Award.'[517]

Hating the idea that he should owe Charles anything, Robert sent him an angry letter saying that the award had absolutely nothing to do with any outside intervention. To which Charles replied equably:

> All right, all *right*
> Ramasse-toi la chemise.
> So I didn't fix it. All that happened was that Christina came up to me at Kettners the other night, asked me dubiously about the idea, wondered how to broach the subject to you, and asked for your Majorca address.

'By the way', Charles added, 'C. P. Snow wants to meet you again & Dick wants to come to the function. The latter I *am* fixing.'[518]

The lunch was a glittering occasion: among those present were Sybil Thorndike, Julie Andrews, the impresario Val Gielgud and the ambassadors of five countries; and Graves made an entertaining acceptance speech in which he declared that he was 'only a peasant', and described the gods of Olympus as 'a bunch of lecherous old squares'.[519]

The event was widely reported, and for a while Graves was much in the news. He appeared live on the popular current affairs television programme 'Tonight';[520] on 10 March *The Anger of Achilles* was published to generally favourable reviews; and he also figured in the correspondence column of the *Observer*, where his Clark Lectures had recently been dismissed by John Wain as an instance of the 'absurdly eccentric in criticism'.[521]

When Graves protested, Wain declared in print that he was full of admiration of Graves's poetry, and never missed 'an opportunity to praise it and try to win it new readers'; but that he found Graves's literary criticism 'aggressive and unbalanced'.[522] As one of his examples, he cited Graves's description of Ezra Pound as 'an ignoramus who didn't get his Latin verbs right'. Before long, however, Wain probably wished that he had remained silent, for Graves publicly referred him to *Dr Syntax and Mr Pound*, a critical comparison of Pound's Propertius translation with the original, in which he had convincingly demonstrated that Pound's Latin was 'distinctly below O-level in *all* parts of speech'.[523]

The rest of March was spent chiefly in making amendments to *The White Goddess* for a revised edition; and then in April, Alastair Reid returned to Deyá. By this time Alastair had sampled both mushrooms and mescaline, and was loud in their praise, declaring that he liked them much better than whisky;[524] and he and Robert had lengthy discussions about mushrooms and religion.[525] They also discussed *A Song for Sheba*, and ideas for filming *The White Goddess*

The previous October, *A Song for Sheba* had been pronounced 'a wonderful piece of writing' but 'un-producible' by a professional in the field; and Ricardo Sicré had advised forgetting about it.[526] However, in January 1960 Robert and Jenny had persuaded Jerry Robbins to choreograph some ballet scenes for the musical; and Jerry had suggested that Robert should write about the composition of the necessary music to Benjamin Britten.[527] He did so; and in April Britten replied that he was 'extremely interested'. He felt he must point out that he had 'never been associated' with the world of musicals. 'but I presume you and Robbins would not have approached me unless you felt that my gifts might be suitable. Anyway, as I said, I would much like to see your script if you could ask your daughter to send it to me ... '[528] However, this offer was never followed up, chiefly because filming *The White Goddess* had begun to seem a more attractive proposition.

In the meantime, the University at Buffalo had been preparing for a Robert Graves exhibition, and Robert and Beryl had been invited to the official opening in mid-May. They accepted, combining their journey with a visit to London (where Robert paid a farewell visit to Dick Graves, who was lying terminally ill in the London Clinic); and a visit to New York City, where Robert was hoping to eat magic mushrooms a second time.

Gordon Wasson explained that unfortunately the remainder of the real mushrooms had been stolen from his icebox;[529] but Robert and Beryl, and Esteban Frances, who also wanted to eat the mushrooms, were welcome to take part in an 'experiment with synthetic psilocybin'. They agreed, and the experiment took place on Friday 6 May; but it was a great disappointment.

Beryl saw only 'a cheap roundabout', and suffered from headaches and nausea which 'lasted until well into the next day'; while Esteban saw nothing at all, and 'experienced only the slightest psychic effects: a dizziness and apparent lightness of weight'. As Gordon noted two days later, only he and Robert found that the psychic effects were 'consider-able'; but they were also:

> confused and hard to remember afterwards ... We did not enjoy the sense of complete clarity of perception, of thought, of the unity of all the senses. We played the recording of Maria Sabina's voice and it was beautiful, but it lacked the enchanting quality that we had known in January.
>
> Above all there was not that overriding sense of emotional unity binding those present in a holy communion, which had distinguished the gathering in January.[530]

Robert, suffering from a headache and a severe stomach-ache which lasted until he took a large swig of whisky at eight on Saturday morning, wrote to Karl telling him that the synthetic psilocybin had been 'all wrong: a common vulgar <u>drug</u>, no magic, and followed by a nasty hang-over'.[531]

By midday, Graves was well enough for a working lunch on the subject of filming *The White Goddess*. First he talked to Bill Morris; and then they were joined by Jerry Robbins,[532] who had been persuaded back in January to read *The White Goddess* 'in terms of a picture'.[533] In the course of a lengthy discussion, Graves won their approval for an idea which he had already discussed with Jenny:[534] that Alastair Reid should be asked to write a draft screenplay.[535]

On Monday there was another business meeting, this time with the Hebrew scholar Dr Raphael Patai,[536] who had checked some of the draft chapters of *The Nazarene Gospel Restored*. The two men now agreed to collaborate on *The Hebrew Myths* – a companion volume to Graves's earlier *The Greek Myths*, and one which they must have hoped would be equally profitable.

Later that week came a train journey across New York State through a beautiful snow-covered landscape to Buffalo,[537] where on Sunday 15 May Robert and Beryl were guests of honour at a reception in the Lockwood Memorial Library which now housed many of Graves's manuscripts. As Robert later told Richard Hughes, it was a strange experience seeing his own work on display: 'I felt I had been dead a quarter century', he wrote, 'looking at the glass cases and the yellowing.'[538] However he rose to the occasion with a good-humoured speech; and the following day he gave a poetry reading and was interviewed by a local television network.[539]

On Tuesday 17 May, the eve of their departure for Europe, Robert and Beryl returned to New York, where they met a group of their friends at *The Lion's Head* in Greenwich Village. Ralph Jacobs was there, as was

Cindy Lee, and a young man whom Robert described as 'her poet ([Howard] Hart)'. Len Lye was also present, and introduced Robert and Beryl to the musician John Benson Brooks of the so-called 'Twinkle Publications & Nothing Music Company'. They took an instant liking to him, after discovering that he had greatly admired *The White Goddess* and from *The Lion's Head* they went on to his apartment.

There Benson Brooks played them some of his compositions; and Robert began discussing the possibility of his writing the music for Bill Morris's *White Goddess* film. Benson Brooks was delighted; and a few days later, he wrote to Robert telling him:

> It seems incredible you were sitting in this very chair – soon again I hope! But now my warmest to Beryl (who Cindy later assured me really *liked* the music or she wouldn't have said so seeing that in these matters she is naturally 'as cold as ice.')[540]

Robert, who must have been intrigued by Cindy's observation, replied that he believed:

> in cosmic coincidence as the only way that things happen properly; so that evening made sense. If Bill Morris is as serious as he says, about making *White Goddess* into a picture, and if he has the same sort of recognition of your music as Beryl and I and Len had – yes, she really likes very little of anything, as I do too – things may happen ...'[541]

And very soon he had heard from Alastair Reid, who confirmed that he would like to write a treatment of *The White Goddess*,

> because as you know I have a strong weird feeling about the book, confirmed by our recent adventures (*Menos* your synthetic experiences) into hyper-consciousness. When these things have happened to us before (poems and your WG experience) they have had an incontrovertible validity, since there has been no pill or agent to claim the credit. So I expect that when I hear from William Morris I will spend the next two months doing it with the greatest gusto.

*

A Song for Sheba had now faded into the background, and would never be professionally produced. However its central theme, that of a man who is bored with the ritual of his domestic life, remained highly personal to its author. When Solomon complains:

> Who is my love of loves? Where does she stand?
> In what thronged city or what lonely land?

it is Graves's voice that can be heard lamenting the comparative poetic sterility into which he has been cast by his lack of a Muse.

Graves still put everything to one side if there was the slightest chance that a poem 'threatened'; but when he did this on 8 June, for example, it was only to revise *The Simpleton*, an anthology piece describing how his friends borrowed money and never paid it back, and to write eight drafts of *Nightfall at Twenty Thousand Feet*, a depressingly second-rate six-line verse about the inevitability of death.[543] However, as Graves/Solomon had sung,

> Patient I am, nor shall I yet despair,
> For this is sure: that suddenly, somewhere,
> She will be there!

And only two days later, at a supper given by Alston Anderson to celebrate the acceptance of one of his pieces by the *New Yorker*, Graves met a young Canadian of beauty, warmth and grace with whom he felt an immediate rapport. Her name was Margot Callas; and Graves had soon recognized her as a fresh incarnation of the White Goddess.[544]

BOOK SIX

MARGOT AND 'INEXORABLE NEED'
1960–63

CHAPTER 1

'Lyceia'

Margot Callas, though a Canadian citizen, was half-Greek and half-Irish, with a shapely figure, long legs, dark hair, and challenging grey eyes. She moved with pride and grace; she also had a wild streak; and she was equally capable of aristocratic hauteur, and passionate warmth.[1] Having lived in Ibiza for a while, she had first crossed over to Majorca in the summer of 1959, when she had worked briefly as a barmaid at C'an Quet, a small hotel just above the main road, about half a mile before it winds into Deyá from the south. She and Robert had not met that summer; though he must have heard stories of the stranger who was so beautiful, it was said, that men fought over her;[2] and he may even have glimpsed her in the distance.

After returning to Ibiza for the winter, Margot had accepted Mati Klarwein's invitation to star in an 8-millimetre film which he intended to shoot in Deyá. This had brought her back to the village, where she was once again staying at C'an Quet; and where she and Mati attended Alston Anderson's celebration supper on Friday 10 June 1960. It was there, over roast chicken, strawberry shortcake and champagne,[3] that Robert and Margot talked to each other for the first time.

Margot's combination of beauty, warmth, pride and high spirits was irresistible; and when Robert learned that she was involved in Mati's film-making, he rapidly agreed to take a minor role himself. The result was that two days later, on Sunday 12 June, he found himself acting opposite Margot in a scene shot in the garden at Canelluñ.[4] Leaping down from one terrace to another, looking fit and healthy and far more like a thirty-year-old than someone approaching his sixty-fifth birthday, Robert converses eagerly with the lovely Margot in the shade of an olive tree; and there is another scene in which they are at an open-air party together, and she comes up to him very seductively, and for a few moments her lips are so close to his that it looks as though they are about to kiss, before she smiles and whirls away again into the crowd.[5]

Just over a week later, on Monday 20 June, Robert was on his way to the sea for an early-morning swim, when he found Margot 'posted/Under the pine trees' by the side of his path.[6] She looked as though she had stepped straight out of the magical world of poetic myth about which he had written in *The White Goddess*; and it was at this moment, when he became fully aware of the dramatic, wild and untameable element in Margot Callas, that Robert Graves fell absolutely in love.

It seemed to Robert that Margot was aware of his love, and welcomed it. They walked on side by side, Robert talking in his quiet, precise, affectionate manner; and then they swam together in the cool waters of the sea. By the time they parted, with Margot explaining that she would be away from Deyá for a while, the balance of Robert Graves's life had been decisively altered.

True, Robert returned to Canelluñ to begin serious work on *The Hebrew Myths* (which he found 'full of dry Rabbinic humour'[7]); Beryl went into Palma to do some shopping; and superficially, things went on as before. But before the week was out, Robert had written a poem clearly announcing that Margot Callas had become his Muse.

LYCEIA

All the wolves of the forest
Howl for Lyceia,
Crowding together
In a close circle,
Tongues a-loll.

A silver serpent
Coiled at her waist
And a quiver at knee,
She combs fine tresses
With a fine comb:

Wolf-like, woman-like
Gazing about her,
Greeting the wolves;
Partial to many,
Yet masked in pride.

The young wolves snarl,
They snap at one another

Under the moon.
'Beasts, be reasonable,
My beauty is my own!'

Lyceia has a light foot
For a weaving walk.
Her archer muscles
Warn them how tightly
She can stretch the string.

I question Lyceia,
Whom I find posted
Under the pine trees
One early morning:
'What do the wolves learn?'

'They learn only envy,'
Lyceia answers.
'Envy and hope,
Hope and chagrin.
Would you howl too
In that wolfish circle?'
She laughs as she speaks.[8]

Margot was away until 9 July;[9] and during her absence Robert revised some previously discarded poems, in one of which he wrote of being plagued by 'dreams of doubt'. Had he just imagined what had occurred between himself and Margot? Or was it really true

That love rose up in wrath to make us blind,
And stripped from us all powers of heart and mind,
So we were mad and had no pulse or thought
But love, love, love, in the one bale-fire caught?[10]

As soon as Margot Callas returned, these doubts evaporated: especially when Margot definitely claimed to be associated with the White Goddess, casually commenting on the fact in Robert's hearing.[11]

Enjoying her new relationship with Robert, Margot declined to take any further part in Mati's film, and successfully discouraged her poet from doing so;[12] but she agreed to play the role of 'Beautiful Spy' in Robert's birthday play *Lawrence and the Wetbacks*, whose central conceit was that Lawrence of Arabia had reappeared in Texas, and was attempting to liberate Mexican 'wetbacks' from their Texan oppressors.[13]

A fortnight of rehearsals followed, during which Robert Graves fell more and more deeply in love. By 21 July he had drafted a poem which, in its revised state, would be entitled 'Symptoms of Love', and which runs:

> Love is a universal migraine,
> A bright stain on the vision
> Blotting out reason.
>
> Symptoms of true love
> Are leanness, jealousy,
> Laggard dawns;
>
> Are omens and nightmares –
> Listening for a knock,
> Waiting for a sign:
>
> For a touch of her fingers
> In a darkened room,
> For a searching look.
>
> Take courage, lover!
> Can you endure such grief
> At any hand but hers?[14]

Three days later, on Sunday 24 July, two hundred guests joined in the birthday celebrations; and the play, as Robert told Betty Sicré,

> was sensational, with a lot of guitar music, songs, acrobatic dancing, explosions and jokes. I was a Texan barman ... Lucia a wetback dancing girl ... Mati as Lawrence and Margot Callas (an Irish-Greek girl from Vancover, who danced with Katherine Dunham) as 'Dynamite Margot', Lawrence's rival spy.[15]

The play had ended with a hugely comic scene in which Lawrence, suffering from an identity crisis, asks: 'Who am I? Will nobody tell me? Am I Alec Guinness? Or Marlon Brando? Who? Who? Who?' To which Margot replies by bombing him with a fire-cracker, while calling out triumphantly:

> I'm dynamite Margot
> And I'll have you know
> I create CHAOS
> Wherever I go.[16]

Among the enthusiastic audience was Alastair Reid, who had just arrived in Deyá with his wife Mary and their son Jasper.[17] He had come to resolve a number of disagreements with Robert Graves over his *White Goddess* treatment;[18] and he soon found to his surprise that Robert intended to involve Margot in their discussions. First she was tentatively invited to 'assist'; and within a day or two she was actively collaborating – and at the same time learning about the proper relationship, as Robert understood it, between a poet and his Muse.[19]

Margot learned quickly; and Robert had soon begun handing her his latest poems 'for consideration';[20] but when on Saturday 30 July he was laid up in bed with a heavy cold, Robert began 'brooding', as he wrote in his diary, about the current turn of events. He had fallen in love; and the result was that he was once again writing real poetry. But what of Beryl? Realizing that the only way forward lay in being utterly truthful, Robert confided in her, and awaited her verdict.[21]

Fortunately for him, Beryl was wholly understanding. As had happened when Judith had appeared on the scene, there was an element of relief that another woman was prepared to share the burden of meeting Robert's complex emotional needs; and in the light of past experience, there seemed no reason for supposing that Robert's relationship would present her with any long-term threat. The romantic knight-at-arms always found himself, before long, abandoned by the Belle Dame Sans Merci 'on the cold hill's side'; and so she 'reassured' her love-sick husband; and he sat up in bed much more cheerfully, and began writing Margot another poem.[22]

Now that Beryl had approved of his liaison with Margot, the following day, as Robert noted was a 'Day of decision'. By chance, he met Ricardo Sicré in Palma, and persuaded him to lend Sa Guarda to Margot whom, as he told Betty Sicré a few days later, 'Beryl and I love dearly and so would you.'[23] The result, by the end of the day, was that Margot, who in any case had said that she wanted to leave C'an Quet, had agreed to be installed in Sa Guarda as Robert's guest; and so he could write in his diary: 'no troubles found'.[24] Lyceia's question: 'Would you howl too/In that wolfish circle?' had been answered with a decisive 'Yes!'

CHAPTER 2

'The Starred Coverlet'

With Margot Callas as his acknowledged Muse, Robert Graves found that August 1960 was a magical time. Early each morning they swam and then breakfasted together; and Robert wrote a poem in which he declared that although he could not 'hope to dwell apart' with Margot 'on Apple Island', he refused to:

> ... fear your element, the sea,
> Or the full moon, your mirror,
> Or the halved apple from your holy tree ... [25]

Margot had to leave Sa Guarda when Ricardo Sicré arrived on Friday 5 August for a short visit to the island; but two days later she was sharing a most unusual Sunday picnic with the Graves family at C'an Floque. She was the only guest; and Robert spent the afternoon writing 'The Visitation',[26] a tender poem in which he asks why he should have been lucky enough to win her love.

> Drowsing in my chair in disbelief
> I watch the door as it slowly opens –
> A trick of the night wind?
>
> Your slender body seems a shaft of moonlight
> Against the door as it gently closes.
> Do you cast no shadow?
>
> Your whisper is too soft for credence,
> Your tread like blossom drifting from a bough,
> Your touch even softer.

You wear that sorrowful and tender mask
Which on high mountain tops in heather-flow
Entrances lonely shepherds;

And though a single word scatters all doubts
I quake for wonder at your choice of me:
Why, why and why?[27]

Margot's effect upon Robert was so profoundly devastating that all other considerations flew out of the window. On Monday 8 August 1960, for example, the day when Margot returned to Sa Guarda, Robert received a telegram from Sam Spiegel asking him:

COULD YOU POSSIBLY JOIN DAVID LEAN MIKE WILSON AND ME FOR A FEW DAYS OF CONFERENCES ON SCRIPT IN SWITZERLAND ROUND FIFTEENTH AUGUST STOP IF YOU CAN PLEASE CABLE MY LONDON OFFICE AND WILL MAKE ALL DETAILS AND PLANS BEST REGARDS SAM SPIEGEL[28]

Graves would normally have jumped at the chance of working on the *Lawrence of Arabia* script; but at this stage of his involvement with Margot Callas, he could not bear to leave her. So he cabled Spiegel's London office telling him that if any help was wanted, it would have to wait until the autumn, when he was planning to be in London;[29] and he followed this up with a letter explaining more fully that he could not leave Deyá in the summer when it was full of family and friends; and that, in any case, 'I can't think in Switzerland; I've tried it.'[30]

On Tuesday 9 August, James Reeves and his family flew in to Palma. Robert had generously paid for their flights back in March;[31] and they were welcome visitors, especially to Beryl, who collected them from the airport and invited them to supper at Canelluñ for each of the next three evenings.[32] But it was not until Sunday, when they happily took part in the usual Sunday picnic at Sa Guarda,[33] that the Reeveses were introduced to Margot, and suddenly realized how large she loomed in Robert and Beryl's life. Stella noticed that Beryl tended to fall silent in Margot's presence; while Robert followed her 'every movement ... like a love-sick teenager'.[34]

Beryl may have been silent; but she never sulked, and always retained her dignity.[35] This was made easier by her understanding of the highly idealistic nature of Robert's love for Margot. Later that very day, for example, he completed 'The Starred Coverlet',[36] in which he wrote:

> A difficult achievement for true lovers
> Is to lie mute, without embrace or kiss,
> Without a rustle or a smothered sigh,
> Basking each in the other's glory.
>
> Let us not undervalue lips or arms
> As reassurances of constancy,
> Or speech as necessary communication
> When troubled hearts go groping through the dusk;
>
> Yet lovers who have learned this last refinement –
> To lie apart, yet sleep and dream together
> Motionless under their starred coverlet –
> Crown love with wreaths of myrtle.[37]

Under these conditions, Beryl could even be Margot's friend. On Tuesdays, they drove into Palma together to go shopping; and they helped each other in the kitchen when Margot came to supper at Canelluñ, or when she invited them to join her at Sa Guarda.[38]

However James Reeves, who was very fond of Beryl, was exasperated by Robert's behaviour; and although he said nothing to him for the time being,[39] he was sensitive enough to be well aware that for once Robert was not at all pleased to see him. 'The Reeveses are sweet, but a dead weight on us', Robert was then writing. '[They] expect to have their noses wiped and their mouths filled … [and] apart from Stella, show no manners or mercy.'[40] As for Stella: she found it difficult to fathom how Margot could possibly enjoy being at Robert's beck and call. Indeed, there was so little conversation between the poet and his Muse, that it sometimes seemed to Stella that Margot's chief function was simply to be adored.[41]

There was some truth in this, and before long it would be a real difficulty: because few women can cope for long with being set on a pedestal. Yet Margot had learned her role well; and when Robert appeared to want more than a platonic relationship, she radiated, to begin with at least, considerable displeasure. This was curiously satisfying to her poet, who had become accustomed to being reproved by Laura Riding for his sexual desires; and when on 23 August Margot and Beryl had gone into Palma together to do some shopping, he stayed behind and wrote:

Almost I could prefer
A flare of anger
To your dumb signal of displeasure.

Must it be my task
To assume the mask
Of not desiring what I may not ask?

On a wide bed,
Both arms outspread,
I watch the spites do battle in my head,

Yet know this sickness
For stubborn weakness
Unconsonant with your tenderness.

O to be patient
As you would have me patient:
Patient for a thousand nights, patient![42]

Four days later, in 'The Falcon Woman', Robert wrote about the difficulties of a poet with his Muse, saying that:

It is hard to be a man
Whose word is his bond
In love with such a woman,

When he builds on a promise
She lightly let fall
In carelessness of spirit.

The more sternly he asks her
To stand by that promise
The faster she flies.[43]

But by then he had been restored to favour, and had enjoyed a midnight bathe with Beryl and Margot;[44] and so he concluded sympathetically:

But is it less hard
To be born such a woman
With wings like a falcon

> And in carelessness of spirit
> To love such a man?

On 30 August Beryl took the Reeveses to Palma for their flight home, while Robert spent the day at Sa Guarda where, after a shower of rain, he began writing 'Turn of the Moon'. Using the moon as a metaphor for Margot, who could not be ruled, he described her as being:

> ... prone to delay the necessary floods,
> Lest such a gift might become obligation,
> A month, or two, or three; then suddenly
> Not relenting but by way of whim
> Will perhaps conjure from the cloudless west
> A single rain-drop to surprise with hope
> Each haggard, upturned face.

The poet, Graves tells us, must learn to accept this situation; and 'if one night she brings us, as she turns,/Soft, steady, even, copious rain', then this gift, 'Neither foretold, cajoled, nor counted on', will be 'woman giving as she loves'.[45]

'Turn of the Moon', taken together with 'The Death-Grapple', written a few days later, and beginning 'Lying below your sheets',[46] strongly suggest that Robert and Margot had become sexually very close. Margot must certainly have felt enormous gratitude to as well as affection for the man who had become convinced that she should play the title role in the film of *The White Goddess*, and had therefore arranged for her air tickets[47] to New York, where she was to be interviewed by Bill Morris. Robert in his turn had learned more of Margot's history, and especially that before moving to Ibiza she had been living unhappily in New York with a husband to whom she was still married; although now, thanks to Robert's generosity, she would return to him and ask for a divorce.[48]

It was on 4 September, the day after Robert had completed 'The Death-Grapple', that Margot left the island 'in a thunderstorm'. And some minutes later, which magically confirmed, so far as Robert was concerned, the supernatural nature of their love 'a waterspout hit the Cala from the direction of Margot's plane'.[49]

CHAPTER 3

The White Callas

With Margot Callas on her way to New York, Robert Graves spent several days selecting poems both for a new slim volume for Cassell, and for a *Collected Poems 1961* for Doubleday. He also wrote to Jenny, who had handled the early negotiations with Bill Morris for *The White Goddess* film,[50] to tell her about Margot being perfect for the starring role.[51] 'About the white Callas', Jenny replied on 15 September 1960,

> Gosh yes if she's typecasting let's sell her but I fear ... that Morris's associates will want a star ... Though this is up to the money-boys and producers and they may decide to simply do a terrific publicity stunt on her ... the search for her ... running her to earth living with panthers in a primeval forest or some such!!! Anyway since the White Goddess is the most difficult to snare ... I think it terrific that she simply walked in.

Which, as Jenny reflected, would be an even 'better publicity story'.[52]

On 16 September, Robert and Beryl set out by boat from Palma on the first stage of another journey to England. 'No letter from M. yet', Robert noted in his diary when they had reached Barcelona that evening; and when they reached London, after a week spent travelling through France and Switzerland, there was still no news.[53]

Then on 26 September they heard from Bill Morris that he approved of Margot Callas for the part of the White Goddess. A letter from Margot herself arrived 'at last' on 1 October; by which time Robert had spent several days with Alastair Reid on the treatment of *The White Goddess* film, and had begun checking over the *Lawrence* script for Sam Spiegel.[54]

As for family and friends in England: sadly, Dick had died in the London Clinic as recently as 15 August, only a few months after the death of his estranged and melancholic wife Eva; but Robert went to see Alec Guinness in *Ross*[55] (his performance was so impressive that Graves sent him an original T. E. Lawrence letter as a thank-you[56]); he also saw the film première of Alan Sillitoe's *Saturday Night and Sunday Morning*;[57] he had tea with his thirteen-year-old god-daughter Helena Simon and her family;[58] and he visited his old friend Douglas Glass, in whose company he met Laurie Lee of *Cider with Rosie* fame, and Isla Cameron, a folk singer from Newcastle with a wonderfully pure voice and 'a bubbling sense of fun',[59] who gradually became a close friend.

One Saturday, Robert and Beryl also visited Holme Grange School, Wokingham for lunch with John and Mary Graves and their three children:[60] fourteen-year-old Richard, an imaginative child for whom Robert had a special affection; thirteen-year-old Simon, a brilliant classical scholar who had just followed his elder brother to Charterhouse; and nine-year-old Elizabeth, with her long plaits and her independent turn of mind. But instead of being the happy family occasion everyone had hoped for, lunch in the Headmaster's House was a disaster. Beryl said little, while Robert appeared more and more ill at ease.

It was one thing to correspond with his brother; but another to visit him in this citadel of traditional values, over which, like Amy in her heyday, John presided so lovingly, and yet with such an iron grip. The very room they sat in was like a corner of Erinfa. Over Richard's head, Robert could see the family bookcase, with the tin case in which the family coat-of-arms was preserved; while on the wall beside him were the gold medals won in the 1830s by Bishop Graves and his brothers at Trinity College, Dublin. It was an uncomfortable reminder of the moral oppression of his youth; and when at length Robert was able to escape, his happiest memory was of Elizabeth daring to be rebellious.

Returning to London, Robert took part in a radio broadcast of the 'Brains Trust' (on which his fellow-guests included Alan Bullock and Marghanita Laski);[61] and he appeared on the television programme 'Bookman',[61] in which he was generously introduced by John Betjeman as 'the greatest living poet': 'which made me laugh', Graves told Selwyn Jepson, 'because I'm not competing except with myself'. He added that he had been heavily engaged upon 'a long sequence of new poems about the symptoms, delights & trials of love – Honi soit qui mal y pense'.[63]

The trials were uppermost in his mind just then. It was not until 17 October that Robert received a second letter from Margot;[64] and then it was chiefly to complain about her treatment when she went to cash one of his cheques at Gordon Wasson's bank in New York. Graves rushed blindly to her defence, considerably annoying Wasson, who wrote crossly: 'Margot Callas's account of her visit to Morgan's sounds out of character. Our paying tellers are the most courteous of people. Why didn't she ask for me?'[65]

A still longer period of silence followed; and when, on 6 November, Robert went down to Chalfont St Giles to see James Reeves,[66] it was immediately evident to his old friend that Robert was suffering terribly. At length, knowing that he risked their friendship, he asked Robert as tactfully as he could whether or not he was deluding himself over Margot? This question struck Robert so forcibly that instead of being angry with James, he spent much of the next three days trying to clarify his own thoughts in draft after draft of 'Troughs of Sea',[67] which begins:

> 'Do you delude yourself?' a neighbour asks,
> Dismayed by my abstraction.
> But though love cannot question love
> Nor need deny its need,
>
> Pity the man who finds a rebel heart
> Under his breastbone drumming
> Which reason warns him he must drown
> In midnight wastes of sea.
>
> Now as he stalks between tormented pines
> (The moon in her last quarter)
> A lissom spectre glides ahead
> And utters not a word.

Robert also sent Margot an anguished letter asking why she had been silent for so long.[68]

When Margot's 'cable of reassurance' arrived on 17 November, Robert was busily drafting a further poem in which, comparing the differing virtues of the wife who is 'good as bread,/Bound to a sturdy husband'; and the muse who is 'rare as myrrh,/Bound only to herself', he finds that although he greatly admires his wife, he cannot resist being fatally attracted to his Muse: upon whose breast the 'pale rose-amethyst' has 'such a garden in it/Your eye could trespass there for hours,/And wonder, and be lost'.[69]

At the end of November, Robert Graves read some of his latest poems to an appreciative audience at the Festival Hall;[70] and then in December he began another stretch of work with Alastair Reid, who had returned to London after a spell in Madrid.[71] Jerome Robbins, who had been working on the film of *West Side Story*, also reappeared for talks about the film of *The White Goddess*.[72] But nothing further was heard of Bill Morris's plans; and there was no further news of the potential star of the film until a

letter arrived from Ralph Jacobs, who could only say that he had met the
beautiful Margot and her husband in New York, and that Margot had
apologized for not having written.[73]

This was highly unsatisfactory; but Alastair Reid, who had already
arranged to fly to New York on 13 December,[74] agreed to contact both
Bill Morris and Margot Callas as soon as he could, in an attempt to move
things forward. In the meantime, on the eve of his departure, Alastair was
involved in an unpleasant incident with Ricardo Sicré.

The details are now disputed but it happened something like this.
Robert believed that he and Alastair Reid had been fellow-guests at a
party given by Ricardo in a London night club.[75] Reid disputes this. But
in any case, Ricardo was one of those[76] who instinctively distrusted
Alastair; and at some stage he said or wrote something to him which
Alastair found so upsetting that he complained to Robert soon afterwards.
He would not repeat Ricardo's words; but they somehow concerned
Robert, Margot and himself.[77] Most likely, their disagreement had
something to do with Ricardo's unpalatably right-wing political views.[78]

At any rate, the matter remained unresolved when, on 21 December,
Robert and Beryl finally set out for Majorca; and the first of Alastair's
letters to reach them from New York said nothing on the subject. Instead
Alastair told them that he had:

> Met Margot and delivered things. She seems very frazzled by New
> York and was moving from one house to another that day, but I will see
> her properly on Monday, after I come back from seeing Bill [Morris]. I
> only had about half an hour with her. She looked very cold and
> puzzled ...

He added that he was determined to 'give the film the time it requires';
and he would ensure that Margot, who was 'very anxious to get to work',
met Jerry Robbins as soon as was possible.[79]

In practice, this would not be for several weeks, because Robbins was
out of town over Christmas. Reid's first important meeting about the film
came at the very beginning of January 1961 when he saw Bill Morris, who
was enthusiastic but also, at times, disconcertingly eccentric: talking, for
example, about 'the Catholic menace'. As for Margot: Reid reported to
Graves that she sounded 'a little shrivelled' after being in bed with flu for
five days; but she had 'a rare humour, and we have very amusing
conversations on the telephone'.[80]

Alastair himself was 'still very upset about the Ricardo thing'. Robert
had clearly written a letter trying to reconcile Alastair to Ricardo; but as

Alastair pointed out, 'you have no idea of the kind of thing Ricardo did say, and I have sworn myself never to tell. He was certainly not trying to protect your family life from a dangerous woman.' However, Alastair concluded, he was prepared to let the matter rest. He merely added: 'I hope that Ricardo never crosses my path again.'[81]

The following day, there were discussions between Alastair Reid, Bill Morris and Jerry Robbins; on Friday 6 January, Alastair and Margot were invited by Bill Morris for supper,[82] over which they wrote a joint letter to Robert, thus providing him, incidentally, with the first words that he had received in Margot's own hand for almost three months;[83] and on the following Wednesday Alastair took Margot to Jerry's apartment where, as he reported to Robert, they ate a Japanese dinner together,

> sitting cross-legged and laughing. When Jerry saw Margot come through the door he gulped and choked and when I went on with him to the ballet he whistled low and cool all along the street. So you need not worry about how they see eye to eye, nay nose to nose.[84]

Soon afterwards, Jerry too wrote to Robert, telling him excitedly:

> You are absolutely right, [Margot] *is* the White Goddess. Naturally tests would have to be made to see how she filmed, and I'd like to find out what her acting and dancing abilities are like. But just on meeting her she has such a wonderfully attractive and mysterious and out-of-this-world quality. I fully understand your enthusiasm for her.[85]

However, there would be no screen test for the time being, for just when things were looking promising, Margot decided that she had had enough of New York. Alastair was sailing to Europe on board the *Leonardo da Vinci*; and she would sail with him. From that moment, the idea of a film of *The White Goddess* began to fade.

'We can play ping-pong all the way across', Alastair reported nonchalantly. He added that Margot's husband intended to procure a divorce in her absence, while Margot herself was 'very keen to be in Spain', and had made 'no plans beyond leaving New York'.[86]

CHAPTER 4

Baraka

Alastair Reid and Margot Callas sailed from New York on 17 January 1961. That was also the day on which Robert Graves went into Palma to keep an appointment with Idries Shah,[87] a thirty-six-year-old Afghan philosopher who had written out of the blue asking to meet him. In his letter, Shah had explained that he had 'written various books on the diffusion of magical practices, published in Britain and elsewhere'; and that at the moment he was 'studying ecstatic religions', and had been 'attending ... experiments conducted by the witches in Britain, into mushroom-eating and so on'.[88]

No doubt Shah had read Graves's miscellany, *Food for Centaurs*, published the previous year by Doubleday, and had calculated correctly that the mention of mushroom-eating would be enough to intrigue this distinguished author. When they met, Shah also had with him Dr Gardiner, a Manxman who was deeply interested in magic;[89] and the three men spent the whole day together.

Afterwards, Shah wrote to Graves thanking him for 'giving me so much to think about'. He added that he was 'intensely preoccupied at the moment with the carrying forward of ecstatic and intuitive knowledge, and I have learned a great deal from you.'[90] This flattering letter led to a further meeting between Shah, Graves and Gardiner at Canelluñ on 22 January; and then Shah and Graves met alone on the 23rd.[91] Shah was an expert listener; and once he had learned enough about Graves, he was able to reflect back to him a version of his own beliefs, and an interpretation of his experiences, impressively heightened by a liberal dash of Sufi mysticism. In this way Shah very rapidly established himself as one of Graves's most trusted and most influential friends.

In particular, Shah introduced Graves to his own interpretation of the Islamic concept of 'baraka', meaning 'the sudden divine rapture which overcomes either a prophet or a group of fervent devotees ... whom it unites in a bond of love'.[92] This tallied perfectly with Graves's first experience of mushroom-eating, when the bond of love had been so strong that he was about to receive the first of many letters from Jess McNab on the anniversary of their joint spiritual 'birthday'.[93]

It was also agreeable for a man who had turned his back upon the mass production and materialism of modern civilization to know that baraka could also be applied to hand-made objects, with their 'certain glow of life';[94] while in literature and the creative arts it was 'of the utmost importance', as it was that 'quality of life' which was 'never granted to a man more concerned with selling than with making'.[95] Above all, Graves learned that his own definition of true poetry made excellent sense in terms of Sufi philosophy: for 'a poem can have baraka, inspired by the Muse; and the Moslem Sufis, surprisingly enough, own to a female Muse'.[96]

While Robert Graves revelled in these new insights into the crucial importance of his own work and way of life, Margot telephoned from Algeciras saying that she would be shortly arriving in Deyá;[97] and when she did so, on 1 February, Robert began a blissfully happy fortnight spent largely in her company.[98] She gave him a Cordoban hat with an inscription on the band;[99] while he was able to show her a copy of a recent *Observer* in which a group of poems written in her honour had been prominently displayed;[100] and then on 9 February there was an official announcement in the Oxford University *Gazette* of his candidature for the Oxford Professorship of Poetry.[101]

W. H. Auden's five-year tenure of the professorship was rapidly drawing to a close; and Graves had been approached about taking his place back in November 1960, though he had kept the matter extremely secret, mentioning it only to one or two of his closest friends such as James Reeves.[102] Despite the considerable academic opposition to his Clark Lectures, Graves was now recognized by many as 'one of the most influential and rewarding of poets now writing in English';[103] and he was nominated by no fewer than 123 MAs, including Dame Janet Vaughan, Principal of Somerville, and the heads of five other colleges,[104] together with such distinguished names as John Wain and Kingsley Amis of St John's, Sir Isaiah Berlin of All Souls, A. J. Ayer of New College, C. B. Ricks of Worcester and John Bayley of New College.[105]

Graves's opponents were Enid Starkie of Somerville (whose sixty-two nominations included the heads of five colleges); Helen Gardner of St Hilda's (whose fourteen nominations included Sir Maurice Bowra, Warden of Wadham, Hugh Trevor-Roper, Fellow of Oriel and Lord David Cecil, Fellow of New College); and Professor F. R. Leavis of Cambridge, with only eight nominations.[106] Despite Enid Starkie's popularity within the university, Helen Gardner's academic distinction and F. R. Leavis's unique position in English literary criticism, the voters decided that a practising poet was what they wanted, and on Thursday 16 February Graves was elected to the professorship by a comfortable majority.

Curiously enough it was in Madrid, where he and Margot were staying that Thursday night with Alastair Reid, that Robert Graves first heard the news of his election victory: after which his lack of the necessary MA was rectified by a special university decree.[107]

Robert and Alastair had been on better terms since Robert, still not knowing what had been said, had written to Alastair guessing that Ricardo had been trying to destroy their friendship. 'I agree about Ricardo', Alastair had replied. 'He would splinter us all apart, if he could.' And then, feeling much more certain of his own position, Alastair had declared that Ricardo 'would now always be the supplicant', and told Robert: 'Never get into any position of depending on him for anything, even a telegram.'[108]

In the same letter, knowing that Margot intended to come to Madrid after her fortnight in Canelluñ, Alastair invited Robert to come over with her for a few days: 'just', he had said casually, 'to celebrate life'.[109] Robert had naturally accepted this invitation, and had arrived with Margot on his election day; but there was a great deal of emotional tension between the three of them (Mary and Jasper seem to have been away for a few days); and the next morning Margot decamped to an hotel, while Robert (despite his election victory), felt so ill that he went to see a doctor.[110]

The doctor told Graves that although his health was basically fine, he was in an extremely 'nervous condition'. The trouble was clearly that Margot and Alastair were on the verge of falling in love. Robert was sensitive to this; and although he could not bring himself consciously to recognize what was happening, it is interesting that he dined at the Jockey Club that evening with Alastair's current *bête noir*, Ricardo Sicré.[111]

Several meetings with Margot followed over the weekend; but they were not at all satisfactory; and when Robert returned to Canelluñ on the following Tuesday, he immediately began 'In Trance At A Distance',[112] a poem in which he writes of experiencing 'a cold fear/Of never again here, of nothing good coming'; and asks himself:

> It is no longer – was it ever? – in your power
> To catch her close to you at any hour:
> She has raised a wall of nothingness in between
> (Were it something to be known and seen, to be torn apart,

You could grind its heartless fragments into the ground);
Yet, taken in trance, would she still deny
That you are hers, she yours, till both should die?

Graves's personal anxieties could be intermittently forgotten while he
dealt with the torrent of congratulations which had poured into Canelluñ
to applaud him on his election victory;[113] and he found that he had also
been honoured by a request from the President of the American Academy
of Arts and Letters to attend their ceremonial meeting in New York City
on 24 May, and to deliver a twenty-minute speech as the fortieth, and
highly prestigious, 'Blashfield Address'.[114]

However, Robert was in an unbalanced state of mind over Margot; and
when he heard a rumour that his brother Charles had 'lost me 50–60
votes by espousing my cause at Oxford',[115] he reacted violently, and wrote
Charles an extremely severe letter reproaching him for his lack of
principle and sensitivity.[116]

Charles, in typical fashion, met blow with blow. 'You've now done the
unforgivable thing', he told Robert. 'You've started to bore me. In fact', he
went on,

I was so enchanted by Enid Starkie that I told all and sundry, including
her, that if it had not cost me £26.10 to pay my answers as an M.A. I
would certainly have voted for her. This is probably what got you in.

As a *coup-de-grâce*, he added that his wife Peggy, whom Robert knew to be
an aristocratic lady of the highest principles and warmest heart, 'says she
never thought she would live to see the day when she would read a letter
from you which was pompous and impertinent'.[117]

Robert left this letter unanswered, though he later complained to John
that he could not expect their brother 'to act with decent formality', and
could only beg him 'not to meddle with my concerns for the sake of a few
lousy guineas'.[118]

For the past ten days or so, Robert had been working hard on his
Blashfield Address, for which he had chosen the title 'Baraka'; and when
it was finished, on 8 March,[119] he telephoned Margot, 'who was being
vaccinated'; and persuaded her that she should visit him once again in
Majorca towards the end of the month. She agreed; but her attitude was
not what he would have liked.

It was not long since Robert Graves had told Ava Gardner, who had
met and liked Margot, that his Muse was 'the only one of her kind in

existence, as I think you'll discover';[121] but now, in another new poem, he wrote of a Muse who had once invited him to 'Do as you will tonight'; but had subsequently placed him in the position of 'Knowing-not-knowing that such deeds must end', and who 'would be gone one night/With his familiar friend'.[122]

In the meantime, the only further news of Margot came from Idries Shah, who was rapidly making Graves's friends his own, and who reported that he had been in Madrid, where Alastair had been 'good enough to give me lunch and the benefit of his ideas and experiences of Mescalin'; while 'Margot was very kind, and took me around a bit.'[123] Not long afterwards, Robert's growing resentment against Alastair was fuelled by a letter from Peggy Glanville-Hicks. Writing from Athens, where *Nausicaa* was due to be premièred later in the year, she told Robert that she had been 'deeply hurt' by Alastair, who had told her that he wanted his name removed from the production.[124] What had actually happened was that, quite by chance, Alastair had heard Peggy give an interview on the radio, in which, talking of her hopes for *Nausicaa*, she had claimed that the libretto had been written by Graves, and had altogether omitted Alastair's name. It was at that point that he had decided to sever his links with the production.

Robert's diary shows that he was now working partly for Doubleday on an edition of *The Comedies of Terence*; and partly for his great-nephew Martin Freeth, one of Molly's grandchildren and a schoolboy at Marlborough College, on *The More Deserving Cases*, a limited edition of eighteen previously discarded poems.[125] But after Margot had arrived in Deyá on 25 March,[126] his diary for the next fortnight is almost entirely blank.

When Margot left again on 9 April, saying that she was on her way to Provence,[127] Robert was in an extremely unhappy frame of mind. On the day after her departure, he began working on a poem[128] in which, as the 'Lion Lover' of the eventual title, he endures 'Cruel ordeals', including 'Springing a trap baited with flesh: my own.' However, he is reconciled to his own suffering,

> Though by the Moon possessed
> I gnaw at dry bones in a lost lair
> And, when clouds cover her, roar my despair.
>
> Gratitude and affection I disdain
> As cheap in any market:
> Your naked feet upon my scarred shoulders,

Your eyes naked with love,
Are all the gifts my beasthood can approve.[129]

At the same time, Graves wrote to Alastair Reid accusing him of a general lack of openness. Reid replied that he simply had that 'sacred respect for privacy' which Graves both lacked and, in Reid's view, resented.[130]

Graves, who received this letter on 17 April, found it 'Unsatisfactory'.[131] The following day, after writing Margot a long letter, his spirits rose and he noted that he 'Felt free again';[132] but this feeling was not to last. 'Trouble' appears in pale red chalk as Graves's diary entry for Friday 21 April and, often repeated, as the only entry for the whole of the next three weeks. For on that day he learned that Alastair Reid had joined Margot Callas in France; and Robert Graves could only do as he had predicted, and 'roar his despair'.

CHAPTER 5

'Beware, Madam!'

The defection in April 1961 of Robert Graves's two closest friends from his carefully constructed imaginative world into a private idyll of their own left him feeling so distraught that for a while he could hardly eat, and he had very soon lost almost a stone in weight.[133] Once he had discovered their address (they had come to rest in a water mill at Navarra in the Basses-Pyrénées), Robert wrote to Alastair and Margot asking them for an explanation.

Margot wrote nothing; and what Robert received from Alastair was a masterpiece of casuistry. Couching his letter in the most affectionate terms, Alastair explained that his betrayal was no betrayal; that Margot's inconstancy was no inconstancy; that although everything had changed, nothing had changed. 'Dearest Robert', he began,

> Thank you for writing. I write back, not to explain anything, but just to say that to me nothing has changed. We all have several selves; some of them connect, others do not. No relationship eliminates others. There is the Margot that *you* know who is and will remain constant. She I will never know, because I am not you. The relationship between her and me is quite separate and different. The two relationships do not affect one another, except with respect to time.

Alastair went on to explain modestly that neither he nor Margot had taken any positive action – 'it was just the mutual recognition of something that had come to exist, almost without either of us realising it'; and he concluded lovingly that:

> Whatever of your life I hold in my hand, I will guard it well, as I would my own. The misunderstandings of the past month were just crosswinds, that have blown themselves straight. Whatever anxieties you have about Margot, you must realise that her wellbeing and her

true being are my deep concern too ... She is writing you herself, as she always will, as I always will.[134]

A howl of rage was the only appropriate answer to this letter; and Graves's hatred of Reid began to assume the epic proportions of Laura Riding's hatred of her former lover Geoffrey Phibbs. Like Phibbs in 1929, Reid was now equated with the devil. But what of Margot's role?

The letter which Alastair had promised on Margot's behalf never materialized but on 13 May she sent Robert a cable, which he found so reassuring that he commented in his diary 'As we were'.[135] Three days later, therefore, flying to Brussels on the first leg of his journey to New York, Graves was able to tell James Reeves 'no damage done', despite something 'rather horrible', which could not be put into a letter, but which involved the 'discovery of treacherous behaviour in an old friend well known to you'.[136] So while Alastair remained wholly black in Robert's eye, Margot was allowed to be the innocent victim of Alastair's machinations.

Graves's American tour was, in his own words, 'terrific'.[137] He successfully delivered his address on 'Baraka' to the American Academy and Institute; gave poetry readings 'to three audiences in Pennsylvania, New York and Washington';[138] and discussed their progress on *The Hebrew Myths* with Raphael Patai.[139] On his way home, he also spent several days in London, where he saw the recently married Idries Shah and was introduced to his wife,[140] who was another link between Shah and Graves because, by a curious coincidence, Cynthia (soon to be renamed Kashfi) had been brought up in the Oxfordshire village of Islip where Graves had lived in the 1920s.[141]

Shah further endeared himself to Graves by his combination of hostility towards Alastair Reid and kindliness towards Margot Callas; and soon after his return to Deyá, Graves would once again explain to Reeves that there were 'no hearts/bones broken', although he and Beryl had been 'equally surprised and horrified' by a certain person's 'Satanism and devious lying'. He added that he had written 'several more poems, including one beginning "Beware Madam, the Witty Serpent" which will make the hair rise on some lovely necks'.[142] This poem, drafted the previous day on the flight home from London,[143] would eventually begin:

> Beware, madam, of the witty devil,
> The arch intriguer who walks disguised
> In a poet's cloak, his gay tongue oozing evil.

> Would you be a Muse? He will so declare you,
> Pledging his blind allegiance,
> Yet remain secret and uncommitted.
>
> Poets are men: are single-hearted lovers
> Who adore and trust beyond all reason,
> Who die honourably at the gates of hell.

While the devil, by contrast,

> ... is capable of seducing your twin-sister
> On the same pillow, and neither she nor you
> Will suspect the act, so close a glamour he sheds.[144]

'Beware, Madam!' had a vengeful last line accusing Margot of being 'no more a Muse' than Alastair was a poet; but three days later, on 31 May, Robert Graves wrote another poem, 'The Golden Anchor',[145] in which Margot, though said to be 'consorting/With lovelessness and evil' is restored to her role as his undoubted Muse. Speculating that she cannot wield the axe against him, being 'warned by a voice what wide misfortune/Ripples from ill faith', Graves asks:

> What should I say or do? It was she chose me,
> Not contrariwise. Moreover, if I lavished
> Extravagant praise on her, she deserved all.
> I have been honest in love, as is my nature;
> She secret, as is hers. I cannot grieve
> Unless for having vexed her by unmasking
> A jewelled virtue she was loth to use.

By now, Idries Shah had explained to Graves (who was more receptive to ideas of this kind after his mushroom-eating experiences the previous year) that:

A Sufi feels superior to normal restraints and, being spiritually and physically at one with the woman who has accepted his devotion, claims a certitude that allows him to face every danger and bring seeming impossibilities to pass.[146]

So when Margot announced that she intended to return to Deyá very soon, her decision could plausibly be ascribed by Graves to his own 'certitude' in her respect; and this induced an increasing sense of euphoria.

On 10 June, Graves noted that it was the anniversary of his first meeting with Margot Callas;[147] and twelve days later he wrote to Martin Seymour-Smith, telling him:

> I've been plagued by poems lately: one of those awful periods that come every seven years or so, and sear the heart while gilding the name. But all's well. Deyá is still Deyá, Beryl is wonderful, we have a Landrover and an Abyssinian cat, and two poodles. The garden has never been so fruitful.

In the meantime, as he explained, he had completed his *Terence* translation, and was 'busy on *Hebrew Myths* and the Oxford lectures'.[148]

Two of these lectures would soon be completed, and they covered what was becoming well-worn ground. In the first, 'The Dedicated Poet', Graves took John Skelton as his chief example of the dedicated Muse poet; while in the second, 'The Anti-Poet', he dealt with Virgil as an example of 'the Apollonian poet, his precise opposite'.[149]

Then on 6 July Idries Shah and Kashfi arrived in Deyá, followed two days later by Margot;[150] and Robert's euphoria became more and more pronounced. By Friday 21 July, he was recording in his diary that it was the 'Happiest day of the year'; and on Saturday, when he celebrated his sixty-sixth birthday two days early, he wrote that he was 'even happier'.[151] Nor was this surprising, for Margot had taken him to one side, and told him to bear in mind that her devotion to him would remain constant.[152]

On Sunday morning, Margot Callas left Deyá and went back to Alastair Reid and their mill in the Basses-Pyrénées. Fortunately for Robert's peace of mind, she had promised to return towards the end of August;[154] and in any case Idris Shah was still at hand to place an encouraging interpretation upon everything that was happening. While he waited for Margot's return, there were friendly visits from Isla Cameron and his 'spiritual sister' Jess McNab;[155] and he began writing his third Oxford lecture, this time taking as his subject 'The Personal Muse'.

Asserting that 'true possession by the Muse ... does occur sporadically to this day among dedicated poets', Graves recapitulated details of 'the main theme of her worship' about which he had written in *The White Goddess*; and then discussed 'The Ugarit Epic, discovered at Ras Shamra in 1926' which 'supplies one ancient text of the Theme'. The story is of two demi-gods, Aleyan and Mot, who fall in love with the Goddess Anatha:

Aleyan is the Bright Twin, Mot is the Dark Twin ... Anatha encouraged Mot to murder his Bright Twin Aleyan, and then went off with him. As a result, all grass and herbs languished and a universal lamentation arose. Anatha then thought again, and avenged Aleyan's death by the destruction of Mot, whose body she ground in a mill, leaving the remains to carrion birds. Finally she harrowed Hell, rescued Aleyan, and set him on his throne again.[156]

This story, declared Robert Graves, could be seen:

not only as an ancient seasonal myth, but as a prophecy of [a] new, not yet fully explored, poet-Muse relationship. Anatha may well discipline Aleyan for showing signs of marital possessiveness: may betray him with his cruel, destructive twin as a means of asserting her personal freedom. But if Aleyan survives the ordeal, after dying cheerfully for her sake, she will surely – he tells himself – raise him up again and destroy his rival.[157]

This is clearly autobiographical: Anatha/Margot disciplines Aleyan/Robert for being too possessive, and betrays him with Mot/Alastair; but with any luck, she will then grind Mot's body to death in that mill-house in the Basses-Pyrénées, before returning to Aleyan, 'the poet as Sacred King', who 'cannot avoid a love-ordeal which puts his sense of certitude to the supreme test'.

Oddly, it is while working on this lecture about the Muse that Graves heard news of Laura Riding. According to Tom Matthews, she and Schuyler Jackson had 'broken out of Wabasso and headed north, "to see people" ... Like Lee's raid into Pennsylvania', Tom commented, 'and as hopeless'.[158] Robert replied that although he had 'no desire to meet Laura and Schuyler myself', he now knew a great deal more about the Muse, and was better able 'to separate the mythic from the personal ... I feel now that I failed Laura no less than she failed me – not that I blame either of us – we were premature'.[159]

In mid-August 1961, Robert Graves set out with eighteen-year-old Lucia for a few days in Greece, where he was to present 'a TV programme for CBS on Greek Myths',[160] and to attend the première of *Nausicaa*. Idries Shah had prophesied that Robert's journey to Greece must be 'for a very special purpose'; and this seemed to be confirmed when on Saturday 19 August, the day of the première, Robert met a Greek sculptress called Eleni.[161]

A woman of intuition and understanding, Eleni was separated from an English husband, and lived with her two daughters and her mother on the island of Aegina, less than an hour by boat from Piraeus, the port of Athens. Robert had soon poured into Eleni's sympathetic ear all that there was to say about himself and Beryl and Margot and Alastair, about his friendship with Idries Shah, and about how Sufi wisdom was intimately connected with poetry and moon magic. He also told Eleni that he loved her like another spiritual sister (he would soon inform Idries that 'our number has increased by one at least');[162] and on returning to Canelluñ he sent her a letter declaring: 'How brave of you to seek me out; and how discreet of you to leave the rest to me!'[163] He also enclosed this poem, written on his plane journey home:

OUZO: AT NONACRIS

Here is ouzo (she said)
Better not mixed with water,
Better not chilled with ice,
Nor sipped at cautiously,
Nor toped in secret –
Drink it down (she said) unclouded,
At a blow, this tall glass full,
But keep your eyes on mine –
Like a true Arcadian acorn-eater.[164]

Robert explained that these nine lines were 'in Selene's honour ... as you know Nonacris is her seat above the Styx'. He added that he was about to drink champagne in honour of Lucia's examination results (she had crowned two years at the Lycée Français in London with a set of excellent A-levels); and that evening there would be a 'farewell party under the moon' to celebrate the fact that twenty-one-year-old William had finished his geological studies at London University, and was shortly to set out for Texas to learn about the oil business.[165]

As for Margot: there had been no letter or news of her for a month, although she was:

supposed to arrive today. But I've decided not to worry, or take any more steps to bring her where she wants to be. I conjure up your protective smile and your hand-clasp; and the number thirteen loses its sinister connotation. Patience: and humour! And assurance! For yourself too equally.

– How big the moon is tonight! Anything may happen.[166]

This letter was completed but not yet sealed in its envelope when news
came from Margot; and so Robert added a postscript:

> Just had a letter from Margot – to say that 'All is well' – she 'loves me
> and that's all that matters.' But it's a false letter written in a wavering
> handwriting and when she comes here on September the 7th we'll see
> how things are ... I have told her about you now ... Poor girl: how she
> injures herself! But I suppose it has to be got through. I wish she had
> your certainty and kindness. But there are different sorts of love and
> each has its rules. Ours is very simple. I hope I get a letter from you
> soon: please write just as you feel, it will match what I feel for you, be
> sure. Robert[167]

This particular letter was misaddressed and so never reached Eleni; but
other letters followed, and she remained a friend and confidante of
Robert's for many years.

Soon after the beginning of September, when Robert was counting the
hours to Margot's arrival, he received a letter from Alastair which ran:

> Dear Robert,
>   The misunderstandings have become murderous. For which I am
> most bitterly sorry.
>   Anyway, I would like you to be clear about one thing, and to have it
> direct from me –. I love Margot utterly and truly, and am wholly
> committed to her. The love that is between us happened with a
> terrifying suddenness. Never because of, or in despite of, you – utterly
> apart from you, in itself entirely. Otherwise, it could never have been.
> That it is true and clear between us, time will let you see.
>   Ever
>   Alastair[168]

There was also a note from Margot, saying nothing about her promise to
join him on 7 September, but telling him instead that she and Alastair
were planning to travel to Barcelona, and then on to Tangier.[169]
For a few days, Robert deluded himself into believing that Margot
would come to him from Barcelona, allowing Alastair to travel on to
Tangier alone.[170] When she failed to arrive, he wrote an anguished letter
to Idries Shah, who replied that although Alastair might persuade Margot

for a while that he needed her, their relationship could not endure. In the meantime, 'If we regard evil as a negative force', then he and Robert:

must reinforce the positive force. I see this as being done in a two-fold way: LOVE and ACTION ... You and I are on linked but slightly oblique angles of the prism: this is the very best way, because we can reinforce one another thus. For my own part, these past few days have seen some very striking examples of the coincidences and certainties which mark the beam's path.

He added that 'something constructive' was developing; but in case of trouble, Robert should 'drop me an immediate note', for then it would be a question of putting 'Plan 4' into operation ...[171]

Nine days later, after a further letter from Robert, Shah had no more positive advice to give. 'Plan 4' had been dropped, and instead he wrote darkly about 'the struggle of ... positivity certainly against negation. And A seems to me to monopolise the anti-forces, to cultivate them.'[172]

Shah seems to have been chiefly interested at this time in persuading Graves to collaborate with him on a rewriting and 'decoding' of *The Book of the Thousand Nights and One Night*, the true meaning of which he claimed to have understood with an insight gained 'largely through reading GREEK MYTHS which you have reconstituted'.[173] But at the beginning of October, realizing that Graves could think of little but Margot, he advised him:

The most that you can do, as you have said, is to point out the truth. Time and again I have seen you offer the truth, and act in accordance with it. This is yakina (certainty that you are right or that a certain thing is right) ... I think that there will now have to be a fermenting period in which what you have done and said will work in the minds of the other people concerned ...

In Margot, this would mean 'a reconstitution of the personality which can only take place when the yeast has been implanted'; while in Alastair, 'the yeast will almost certainly cause an explosion, sooner or later'.[174]

CHAPTER 6

The Personal Muse

'My stock is rising geometrically', Robert Graves wrote in the summer of 1961, 'and everything of mine being paperbacked – including a 100,000 edition of *Jesus in Rome*!' Since his election as Professor of Poetry at Oxford, Graves's reputation had soared; and his *More Poems: 1961* had been a critical triumph. 'These quiet, firm poems confirm his truth and his position', wrote Anthony Thwaite in the *Spectator*; 'The major note in [his] poetry is unmistakable', declared the *Poetry Review*; 'This represents Graves at his unsurpassed best', trumpeted the *Guardian*. Graves accepted this recognition modestly. 'It happens', he told Kenneth Allsop,

> A kind of law operates – a vacuum occurs and someone is pushed up to fill it. It seems to be my turn.
>
> I haven't changed my way of writing or way of life in the past 40 years, and shan't now. Simply that the time comes when people begin to take notice.
>
> It makes no difference at all. It may embarrass my children, but not me![175]

However, there were annoying consequences of his new status, one of which was that Charles Graves continued to make copy out of him.

On 6 October for example, two weeks before Robert was due to give his first lecture at Oxford as Professor of Poetry, the London *Evening Standard* ran a substantial feature in which Charles wrote that:

> … As [Robert's] full brother, I feel it is time to present this engaging, egregious chap in his true colours – immensely self-sufficient in his own craft, haunted with a gouty complex about his private life induced by our very religious early upbringing, completely charming when he feels you are with him, a fantastically hard worker with all the

courage in the world, horrified at the mere thought of patronage, a literary perfectionist, a mixed-up grown-up kid.

Charles added that Robert was unduly sensitive to criticism ('the slightest slighting comment and he is once again yelping blue murder'), which made him 'one of the world's leading unpaid letter writers to the papers'; and he described his brother as being:

> tremendous value as the Picasso of authors, as the rebel Irish writer, as the hermit of the Balearics, as the cantankerous old gentleman of English letters ... but the public must face it, he has no abiding sense of good humour.

However, Charles thought it a distinct possibility that Robert would 'ultimately be awarded the Nobel prize for literature ... He was certainly on the short list in 1960. It might well happen.'[176]

The professorship which had brought Robert Graves so many column inches in the press carried with it a remuneration of only £300 a year, far less than his travel and other expenses; but at least he had been allowed to minimize his losses by concentrating his three annual lectures in the Michaelmas term; [177] and St John's provided him with an elegant set of rooms in college, even though he and Beryl actually lived in what he described as a 'Charles Addams flat on Boar's Hill'.[178]

Robert's first lecture, given at 5 p.m. on 20 October 1961 in the Playhouse Theatre in Beaumont Street, was a huge success. John Graves and Rosaleen Cooper were both in the audience (Rosaleen 'on the platform among the VIPs'); and they were among the lucky ones.[179] 'As I warned the Univ. authorities,' Robert told James Reeves with some satisfaction, '2000 came and there was room for only 650.'[180]

Interest in the new Professor of Poetry continued to run high. The undergraduates were entranced both by his savage attacks on the established literary pantheon, and by the honesty with which he told them of his own trials in the service of the Muse; while the professional academics admired his poetry enough to 'welcome [him] home as something of a returned prodigal'.[181] Within a week of his first lecture, Robert would report that he was 'having great fun here, especially as the Vice-Chancellor & the Merton professor of English were both under-graduates with me, and I knew the manager of the best local pub as a school boy on Boars' Hill'.[182]

By the time of his second public lecture, given on 10 November in the Examination Schools, Robert had been involved in such a frantic but stimulating round of professorial engagements, including addresses to various undergraduate societies, that there was little time for friends or family: though one weekend he and Beryl visited Lucie Aldridge,[183] now sadly divorced from John, who had fallen in love with Norman Cameron's widow Gretl.[184]

Nor was there much time to worry about Margot Callas; although on 1 December, when delivering 'The Personal Muse', his third and final public lecture for the year, Graves recited a recent poem in order, he said, to remind his audience that 'A poet may ... be mistaken in his Muse; she may prove unworthy of continued trust':

IN HER PRAISE

This they know well: the Goddess yet abides.
Though each new lovely woman whom she rides,
Straddling her neck a year, or two, or three,
Should sink beneath such weight of majesty
And, groping back to humankind, betray
The headlong power that whitened all her way
With a broad track of trefoil – leaving you
Her chosen lover, ever again thrust through
With daggers, your purse rifled, your rings gone;
Nevertheless they call you to live on,
To parley with the pure, oracular dead,
To hear the wild pack whimpering overhead,
To watch the moon tugging at her cold tides.
Woman is mortal woman. She abides.

James Reeves (now almost completely blind) was present at this lecture and wrote afterwards that he had 'liked the talk in Oxford for many things', though he disagreed with his old friend about Donne, whom Graves had accused of using love poems simply as a means of seduction. 'I am sure you are wrong', wrote Reeves, 'and will find your point of view hard to justify to the critics when the lectures are published.'[185]

The day after his 'Personal Muse' lecture, Robert was about to set out with Beryl on their journey back to Deyá, when he received this wonderful tribute from his defeated rival for the professorship Enid Starkie, who wrote:

I am glad that you have enjoyed your first year of office and I am only sad for my sake as well as for that of the whole of Oxford, that your stay has been so short. You have been, as you must have felt, a great success and have been much appreciated. Your availability and kindness to everyone, your helpfulness, have been received with pleasure and gratitude.

'I hope', she concluded, 'that you will not have felt it all too much a waste of precious time.'[186]

On returning to Canelluñ, Robert and Beryl enjoyed an extremely busy Christmas holiday. Visitors included Ramon Farran, a gifted Spanish musician with whom Lucia had been in love since the previous summer; Len Lye's daughter Yancy, a lovely girl who 'caught onto Deyá at once';[187] and Stella Reeves; and Robert mentioned in his diary that 'We have had anything from 10 to 15 people at every meal.'[188]

In the meantime, Margot Callas had continued to be constantly in Robert's thoughts. He sent her a New Year letter; and in his poem 'The Wreath'[189], which would appear in the June *Encounter* and win high praise from Tom Matthews,[190] he declared:

> A bitter year it was. What woman ever
> Cared for me so, yet so ill-used me,
> Came in so close and drew so far away,
> So much promised and performed so little,
> So murderously her own love dared betray?
> Since I can never be clear out of your debt,
> Queen of ingratitude, to my dying day,
> You shall be punished with a deathless crown
> For your dark hair, resist it how you may.

To some of Robert's friends, his continuing obsession with Margot was highly distressing. James Reeves had already voiced his displeasure, and on 25 January 1962 Alston Anderson, writing from Paris, told Robert bluntly that he was mad. 'I must say Robert,' he went on, 'that Beryl is one of the most beautiful women I've ever seen.' Then, prefacing his remarks with the words 'if you'll forgive me saying so and I know full well you won't,' he launched into an attack upon Margot. He qualified this attack by adding: 'I like her as I've told you before. But then Robert darling I like all pretty girls or most at any rate'; and he remarked (in words which echo one of Alastair Reid's insights into Robert's habit of reinventing his friends): 'All the properties that you attribute to M are the ones that you gave her. I told you that before too ... '[191]

When Robert remonstrated with him, Alston replied: 'I meant everything I said about Margot';[192] and in a further letter he added: 'Robert love you're *so* innocent,' and suggested that Margot had regularly been smoking marijuana: 'Why do you think she went to Tangier for God's sake?'[193]

January also saw disturbing news about Robert's daughter Catherine. Her husband Clifford Dalton, Chief Engineer of the Australian Atomic Energy research establishment, had died the previous summer at the age of forty-five. He had died of cancer; but Catherine had become convinced that some enemy had given him a carcinogenic drug, and that her own life was in danger.[194] 'Is she going a bit dotty?' Jenny wrote to their father on 28 January 1962 from New Delhi, where she was doing some work for Reuters. 'Could she be suffering from persecution mania or has there really been an attempt on her life?'[195]

By the end of January, Margot and Alastair had left Tangier; and Margot had turned up alone in London. However, Idries Shah (whom she visited several times) reported that Alastair was to follow her in a few days; and in the meantime she had found a flat for them to share in Hampstead.

Early in February, Alastair joined Margot; and shortly afterwards he wrote angrily to Robert telling him that he had no intention of ever seeking a reconciliation, and would shortly destroy the manuscript of *Quoz*, the curious title Robert had given to their formal correspondence. He also complained that he still came across

> traces of your vindictiveness, and only hope it has served its purpose for you. One thing however – you have apparently told people that I owe you money. I don't. But if you believe this to be true, and can substantiate it, then I will put it right at once. Details, please.[196]

Robert described this accusation as 'odd and unfounded'; and later in the month he told James Reeves that Alastair seemed to be 'pursued by ill-luck of his own making. I can't be either glad or sorry; but my friends refuse to see him, and he's consumed by self-pity, I hear.' As for Margot: 'What [she]'s at, I don't know. She doesn't write to me but cultivates my friends still.'[197]

Although Margot had not answered any of his letters since the beginning of the year,[198] Robert bravely maintained his 'certitude' that all would eventually be well between them. He was given some grounds for hope when on 17 March he heard from Isla Cameron that Margot was 'happy & well', while Alastair appeared to be 'bloody sad'; and that day Robert started writing 'The Unnamed Spell',[199] which begins:

Let us never name that royal certitude,
That simultaneous recognition
When first we stood together ...

And ends by praising Margot's 'headlong wisdom'.[200]

By mid-April, however, hope was once again fading, and Robert wrote the lines:

To beguile and betray, though pardonable in women,
Slowly quenches the divine need-fire
By true love kindled in them. Have you not watched
The immanent Goddess fade from their brows
When they make private to their mysteries
Some whip-scarred rogue from the hulks, some painted clown
From the pantomime – and afterwards accuse you
Of jealous hankering for the mandalot
Rather than horror and sick foreboding
That she will never return to the same house?[201]

By this time, worries about Catherine had increased the emotional pressure on Robert, with the arrival of a thirty-page report from Jenny, who had flown out to Australia to see the situation for herself.[202] The report made disturbing reading. She had learned from Catherine that Clifford had latterly been both mean and violent;[203] and that after his death, one difficulty had followed another. Catherine had quarrelled with Mr Timbs, the man appointed by Clifford to be his executor, and now believed that he was plotting her death. There was no evidence for this, but someone had tried to run her off the road; and a trusted adviser had died suddenly.[204]

Jenny's 'instinct' told her that her sister had 'got it all wrong'; but there was some doubt in her mind, and in any case it was clear that Catherine was in need of a good deal of support.[205] So Robert sent her £500 to help her through her immediate financial difficulties;[206] and later on, Nancy Nicholson flew out to Australia, where Catherine found her 'a wonderful help'.[207]

Having relieved Catherine's financial difficulties, Robert once again heard some encouraging news from London. Idries Shah wrote to tell him that in his view Alastair Reid was close to a breakdown, having telephoned so angrily that (Shah claimed, most improbably) he had felt it necessary to request the authorities to intercept any further calls.

There was no further news for a month; but Robert felt very much more confident about the future; and by 5 May he could report to Sally Chilver that he had completed 'about 3/4 of the *Hebrew Myths*: a useful book, I think, and written some more poems'; he had also drafted the text for the Creweian Oration, an address (in Latin) which he had to deliver as part of his professorial duties; and he told Sally that he hoped to stay with her in late June when he was over for the Oxford Encaenia (the annual commemoration of founders and benefactors) at which it was to be delivered. He added that his own life was 'serene', and he commented: 'What a lot of sheer unhappiness there is around: I feel ashamed to be so well-placed, and especially to watch people whom I have loved try to trick fate by doing what they know carries a curse.'[208]

Only five days later, Robert's serenity was disturbed by some utterly contradictory news about Margot. From Isla came a letter saying 'that M has turned out well and finished with A'; but the same post brought a letter from another friend, telling Robert 'that A is on his way to set up house with her at Barcelona'.[209]

The following month, Robert drafted a letter to Margot in which he told her that, having heard nothing from her for half a year, he thought that it was reasonable for him to insist that their relationship should be clarified. Should Margot wish to receive no further letters, should she in fact intend to avoid him on a permanent basis, on the grounds that she was too deeply entangled in another relationship, one which Robert believed to be utterly devilish, then he would clearly have to come to terms with her decision. However, if she had decided to honour her promise of eternal devotion, then he would go on patiently waiting for her return. And he reminded her that whatever her decision, she should remember that he was ready to be called upon if needed, and would expect nothing in return.

If, however, he heard nothing before the end of June, he would be forced to conclude that everything was over between them. In which case, he would back away: and Margot would lose the magical shielding from harm with which she had been endowed by their mutual devotion.[210]

In the meantime, there was an interesting exchange of letters with Gordon Wasson. On 30 May, Graves wrote to tell Wasson that Idries Shah, who would be in Deyá on 14 June, had reported:

that he's got new exciting information for you about the mushroom-eaters. Isn't it strange how I seem to act like a lightning conductor for these things on your behalf? I don't believe in coincidence, only in a scientifically inexplicable serendipitous nexus of thought between a few people who are aware of certain problems and recognize one another as of that sort.

He added that his interest in hallucinogenic mushrooms was 'mainly historical'. Having once experienced that 'full use of the imaginative senses', he did not really want it again, though 'It certainly has heightened my poetic powers by making me aware of sound and colour and texture as never before since my late childhood.'[211]

Wasson replied with a new theory that soma, the 'legendary divine intoxicating drink celebrated in Vedic hymns and poems' was in fact the mushroom *Stropharia cubensis*. 'I suggest', he wrote, 'that the cow is sacred in India because their excrement carried the sacred mushroom, the mushroom of the Rig-Veda hymns.' The only possibly fatal drawback to this theory, the fact that the *Stropharia* had never been sighted anywhere in India, was explained by the fact that 'gathering the *Stropharia cubensis* from cow-pats, if done diligently in response to a voracious demand, would (I think) wipe the species out, since it can only be spread by the dissemination of the mature spores'. Wasson completed his letter with a warning about the dangers of his idea being pirated, and begged Graves to 'keep this idea between us ... do not even tell Idries Shah'.[212]

However, that was just what Graves did, as he explained to Wasson in a letter which begins:

> My dear Gordon: *Exciting News!*
> You won't believe me, but it's true: Idries came here yesterday and, at the end of 24 hours' talk about poetry and other important things, came to mushrooms. He says he has an Indian cousin, whom he has sent as an undercover man to study this subject on your and my behalf in India among the Brahmins, impersonating a Brahmin himself.
> *Soma is still made* from *Stropharia*, in cowpats ritually offered to the Gods, and the urine of the priest who has eaten it and gone into ecstasy is drunk by the lesser devotees as 'cow's urine'. Idries told me this without prompting and says he's *not at all interested in publishing the material himself:* it's a friendship's offering to you and me.

Graves added that 'It was only when he had told me everything that the cousin reported that I felt empowered to read him your letter'; after which, Shah had apparently commented: 'How brilliant of Wasson to come to this conclusion by intuition! Tell him that we already have a man in the field.'[213]

At a much later date, Wasson realized that 'soma could not have been the *Stropharia* mushroom after all';[214] and in the meantime, the truth of Shah's highly improbable story could not be tested, because, as the increasingly guillible Graves explained to Wasson in a further letter,

'You'll never get the Brahman's secret acknowledged: it was stolen by Idries's cousin as Prometheus stole fire – *perhaps the same sort of fire?*'[215]

A lesser excitement that month was the inauguration, on land which Robert owned on the other side of the road just below Canelluñ, of an open-air 'Theatre of the Three Seasons'. This had been built principally by Robert's great-nephew Simon Gough (Diana's son and Dick's grandson), who had been staying at Canelluñ since early April. As a trained actor, he had realized that 'an irregular area at the foot of the rock face' was 'a natural theatre in miniature'; and he had set about improving it with 'a few tiers of concrete benches across a recess in the rock, and a circular concrete stage'.[216] Thirty people were invited to an inaugural party on 18 June at which two sheep were roasted, after Simon and Lucia had given a performance of *Prometheus Vinctus*, an entertainment, loosely based on Shelly's *Prometheus Unbound*, which had Simon bound to a convenient outcrop of rock not far from the new stage.[217]

A week later, on 25 June, Robert flew to London, where he stayed with Sally for a night before being driven down to Oxford by Isla Cameron. There he lunched with Kingsley Amis, and attended a Gaudy (a graduate reunion) at St John's. The following day, clad in the long black gown and scarlet cap of an MA, he donned the mortar-board which Auden had told him must be raised 'at any mention of the Deity, semi-divine personages, i.e. the Queen, the Chancellor, the Vice-Chancellor the Proctors and the dead',[218] and delivered the Creweian Oration to an audience which included Dean Rusk (then American Secretary of State), Charlie Chaplin, Graham Sutherland and Yehudi Menuhin.[219]

On Graves's return to Deyá there was still no word from Margot, and the end of the month was rapidly approaching. However, on 30 June Esteban Frances brought extremely welcome news: a 'good report of M. at Barcelona', where she was now living alone, having parted from Alastair about a month previously.[220] And then on 24 July came Robert Graves's sixty-seventh birthday. It was celebrated by another play in the new theatre, and a visit from Ava Gardner, who turned up late with Ricardo Sicré[21] and, as Robert noted, 'was soon making love to the Guardia Cabot. It was a beautiful sight', he told a friend, 'and now we can smuggle and murder all we please.'[222] Far more important to Robert, Margot had finally broken her months of silence.

Margot Callas had telephoned Robert Graves with the news that she might visit Deyá in September.[223] But it was only a possibility; and so a few days after her telephone call, Robert drafted a letter in which he began by making it clear that she was very dear to him. He added that he had prepared a careful analysis of the situation between them. Whether it would be useful or not, he could not tell, but he would send it to her all the same.

As Robert saw things, Margot had searched for him, and then, having found him, had undertaken to play the part of the White Goddess, just as he had outlined it in his book of that name. She had performed her role carefully and precisely; and it was entirely because of this, that both she and Robert had had to endure all the trials and torments of the past eighteen months.

He had entrusted her, he wrote, with the key to his soul; and her subsequent actions were a necessary working-out of the story of the Goddess Anatha, and the two demi-Gods, Aleyan and Mot. He believed that she had battled with evil powers, and had at last begun to triumph. He himself had been preserved by his enduring faith and devotion to her cause.

Graves added that masculine loving differed from the feminine variety, in that it depended upon a man being honourable and generous. He expected neither of these qualities from Margot. They were excellent attributes in a wife, not in a muse. However, he knew that if she was to recover her happiness, she must be aware that the bond between them was unbreakable, and must be ready to offer herself to him with no reservations. Nor was it only Margot's happiness which was in the balance: if Robert was right, then upon Margot's recovery of her essential self – that highly individual self to which people responded with either great love or great hatred – depended the outcome of great events in the wider world. And he concluded mysteriously that the result of making poetry his vocation was that he had acquired prophetic powers.[224]

After drafting this letter, however, Robert Graves decided that Margot might need some more practical inducement to come out to Majorca. It so happened that at the end of June he had purchased Son Coll, a semi-derelict property on the mountainside above the road to Soller;[225] and when he rewrote his letter, Robert offered it to Margot as a present. She accepted almost immediately, and wrote telling him that she would definitely come out to Deyá early in September.[226]

It was now merely a question of waiting; and on 9 August Graves wrote a poem on the subject,[227] in which he advised himelf to be patient, and 'Dabble [his] nerveless fingers in the shallows;/A time shall come when she has need of them'.[228] In the meantime, he received a disturbing letter from Jenny; and he was interviewed by Kingsley Amis.

Until very recently, Robert Graves's standard biographical note had included the fact that one of his children was 'Jenny Nicholson, the well-known foreign correspondent'.[229] And then he suddenly removed her name: which came to her as such a tremendous shock that she wrote him a long letter in which the pent-up resentments of many years poured out. 'The funny thing was', she told him,

> I hadn't realised that I was no longer anything until I saw you'd taken my name off the back of your Penguins ... but I guess you are right. In fact the shock of the realisation that you no longer thought of me as anything is what gave me the final OK to stop trying. It was the greatest possible relief ...
>
> I know you only like success and want us all to be successes: I know you don't think I am and are disappointed. Not half as disappointed as I am, let me tell you. I was cursed with too much at birth. I was cursed with a tradition of rigid standards of creation which has made it impossible to get going except in levels discounted as too low for measurement such as the stage and journalism, derogatory terms. I was cursed as David was with a blinding eye for shape colour and people being able to see clearly through the flint exteriors. A door in the wrong place, an ugly dress, lollocks of any kind and ugly characters can distress one out of all proportion ...
>
> You didn't want to hear about Alastair when you were in love with him – I use the word love as you used it in this sense – and by this time I had learned to be polite, though I have never been very good at being polite about Ricardo have I ...
>
> When it suits him and it may suit him forever Ricardo will be friendly. It's no good my saying any more than that because you fly into a rage. You are wrong to. You believe in Ricardo more than you believe in me. I don't hope that you will ever believe in me ...

'Maybe one of these fine sunny days,' she concluded despairingly, 'when spring is all over everything I'll do something which you can recognise as something you can be proud of ... '[230]

Kingsley Amis arrived with his wife Hilly and their three children on the moonlit night of 14 August, just in time to catch the tailend of a farewell party for Isla Cameron, and to be regaled in Simon Gough's new theatre with 'pizza, hot dogs, and local red wine'. Graves had offered to put him up at the Posada for nine days, while he gathered material for an article for *Show* magazine (an American glossy); and the following day he arrived at Canelluñ, where he found Graves in his study, and:

noticed that, like some other genuine writers I know, his expression and demeanour constantly altered; grim one moment, gay and warm the next, abstracted and alert by turns, his talk fluent and hesitant. He will range from an anecdote about one of his children to a sharp but never churlish comment on some inflated contemporary reputation, from a piece of erudition about the Odyssey to a Welsh dialect story. He can dress up adequately to go out to dinner, but his working rig is shirt, shorts and slippers, with perhaps a day or two's growth of beard.[231]

Graves enjoyed the visit, during which the two men made marmalade, while singing comic songs to the tune of 'The International';[232] and he described Amis to James Reeves as 'very sane, very decent', with 'a generous heart, and a sense of vocation'.[233] Amis in his turn, as he wrote many years later, found that 'all that Muse and Moon Goddess and White Goddess stuff ... inspired uneasiness'. But he could still admire Graves as a poet, since in his view Graves's most successful poems, such as 'The Cuirassiers of the Frontier' and 'Love in Barrenness', avoid such themes.[234]

At the time, Amis was also very much attracted by Graves's rejection of some aspects of modern civilization, writing of:

the care he lavishes on his garden, the speed and efficiency with which he makes a salad, his hatred of ball-point pens and insistence on steel nibs and ink-pot as the only decent way of getting words on paper. (He was quite shocked when I told him I did most of my own stuff at the typewriter.)

Amis therefore saw Graves as 'a living refutation of the sentimentalists' view of the poet as one who inhabits some cloudy idealised world of the imagination. On the contrary', he concluded, 'such a man moves in a severely tangible and concrete world, one in which he is not insulated from reality, from things, by the civilised devices of packaging, canning, machinery, synthetics.'

The Amises were still at the Posada when Graves wrote to James Reeves telling him of Margot's imminent arrival, and explaining that she was

no longer with Alastair who now accuses her of ruining his life ... The strange thing is that I can find nothing to reproach Margot with, and owe a great deal to her, & that all my family ... remain deeply attached to this strange primitive being. She's been on her own for about three months, clearing her mind: though unpredictable, she's not impossible and I now expect a lot from her in a constructive sense.

Graves added that it was 'easy to see' why Margot could be 'treated as … heartless …; that is a natural social interpretation; but I see her in a different context where she makes better sense. The fever has ended, I hope & believe; but the bond between us remains.'[235]

On 21 August, the day of the Amises' departure, Graves completed his revision of *The Hebrew Myths*, and received another telephone call from Margot Callas. 'Everything all right at last, as was plain in her voice', he recorded in his diary.[236] A few days later came a 'good letter from M';[237] then on 11 September, 'Margot arrived – thin but all right'; and was soon established in the Posada.[238]

CHAPTER 7

Margot in Attendance

On Wednesday 12 September 1962, the day after her arrival in Deyá, Margot Callas was taken by Robert Graves to view the Son Coll ruins. At first she was extremely uneasy and reserved, so that Robert would later recall that it had not been easy for her to understand that his only real concern was that she should be happy, and that she should fulfil her potential. He explained that he did not want to own her. He wanted only to enable her to become herself in the truest and most exalted manner possible. But sadly (as Robert saw it), Margot's lack of confidence in him meant that she went on testing him in a number of ways, and especially by silence, by evasiveness, and by making unreasonable requests.[239] The silences and evasiveness were wholly understandable: for by this time, Margot was not only worried by Robert's possessiveness, but was also feeling 'very sensitive'[240] about Beryl.

Never betraying the slightest jealousy, Robert's wife had continued to act with enormous dignity. She treated Margot with unfailing kindness (though Robert noticed that they never talked together about anything but trifles[241]); and on 18 September, the Tuesday after Margot's arrival, Beryl calmly set off for England in advance of Robert, who would later be following her to deliver his second series of Oxford lectures. She took with her both seventeen-year-old Juan (who was to begin working for a London photographer) and nine-year-old Tomas (on his way to an English school), and so Robert and Margot were left alone together to sort out their private difficulties unhindered by her presence.[242]

It was only then, as Robert reported to Beryl two days after her departure, that

Margot finally talked to me. She's completely and utterly through with [Alastair], and has changed in a number of ways: especially in suddenly having women friends she can gossip with, and in her great consideration for other people. You can stop worrying about my devotion to her: it continues, but without fear of any more trouble. She hopes to come to London soon, and ... get work.

Robert added that Beryl had been 'beyond all reproach in this long business; and will be repaid'.²⁴³

Two more letters to Beryl followed in rapid succession. On the 23rd, Robert wrote:

> I hope my last letter made sense: you know I love you you you with all the natural warmth of my heart and with all the gratitude and admiration and devotion you could ever demand and still more so because you do not grudge me this other strange thing with M. It is absolutely impossible now that this will go wrong again: especially as she is now keeping me at a careful distance. She's your friend for always.²⁴⁴

On the 25th, he wrote again with news of an annoying accident. Margot had been about to drive off to Palma 'to sign for [Son Coll]', when 'Ramon and I mistook petroleo for gasoline and filled her car with it. It broke down, of course, and in draining off the petroleo somehow it caught fire and burned up.'²⁴⁵

That night, there was a fearful storm; and the following day, Robert wrote a further letter telling Beryl that he would have to lend Margot money so that she could buy a new car before her insurance claim was processed.²⁴⁶

Just a few days later, on 1 October, Robert Graves flew to London; and before long he and Beryl and Juan and Tomas were comfortably established with their Spanish maid Antonia in a flat in Montagu Square, from where Robert intended to commute to Oxford for his lectures and other official engagements. Lucia joined them, before setting off to begin her studies at St Anne's College, Oxford; and the news of William was that he had landed a well-paid job with an oil company in the Sahara.²⁴⁷

After three weeks of unusually happy family life, Robert Graves went down to Oxford where, on 23 October, he gave his first of that year's principal lectures. He had decided to concentrate chiefly on technical matters; and in 'Some Instances of Poetic Vulgarity',²⁴⁸ he effectively and wittily demolished poems by Robert Browning, Tom Campbell and Rudyard Kipling. He also accused Byron of having:

> adored no muse but acted as male Muse to scores of infatuated women

who, like Lady Caroline Lamb, knew that he was 'mad, bad and dangerous to know', adding: 'his beautiful face is my fate.' I pair Byron and Nero as the two most dangerously talented bounders of all time.

The savagery of this attack means that Graves must surely have had Reid in mind; and on an equally personal note he declared that:

No poet has yet solved the main problem: how to maintain the gift of certitude. Always to be in love: that is one recommendation. To treat money and fame with equal nonchalance, is another. To remain independent, is a third. To prize personal honour, is a fourth. To make the English language one's constant study, is a fifth … Yet lightning strikes where and when it wills. No-one ever knows.

'It is easy', he concluded, 'to take up a pen at random and plead: "I'm just keeping my hand in." But nine-tenths of what passes as English poetry is the product of either careerism, or keeping one's hand in: a choice between vulgarity and banality.'

The day after the lecture, Margot Callas rang, to say that she had arrived in London, where she was living at an address in Ladbroke Road;[249] and she was soon the most favoured member of the Graves entourage. On Sunday 28 October, when Beryl drove Robert and Margot down to Oxford, it was Margot whom Robert showed round the St John's College library before lecturing on superstition to the Oxford Humanists.[250] The following Thursday, when Sam came up to London to visit his father, he found Margot in attendance;[251] and on the Saturday, when Robert, Beryl and Tomas were invited to supper by the Jepsons, Robert insisted on taking Margot with them.[252]

It was a tense evening, largely because Tania Jepson reacted to Margot like 'a congenital wife who sees a husband-stealer in every good-looking young woman. She can't help it', Selwyn apologized to Robert afterwards, 'and her perception is totally unreliable. But I daresay you spotted all that.' He himself had been chiefly struck by Margot's underlying strength and independence; and he told Robert never to worry about her 'capacity to survive the worst of messes: she may even make them in order to prove to herself she can climb safely out on the other side'.[253]

Robert's second principal lecture, on 6 November, was attended by Beryl, Margot, Betty and Ricardo Sicré, Tom Matthews, and Helen Morningstar,[254] a lively young actress from New York who had abandoned her career, settled in Deyá and rapidly become a family friend. Graves spoke specifically on 'Technique in Poetry',[255] and his lecture was memorable for its witty line-by-line demolition of Tennyson's famous poem 'The Eagle'. 'To present him as close to the sun', Graves declared at one point, 'is hardly fair. What are a few hundred feet compared with 92 million miles!'

Four days later, Graves lectured at Burlington House to the Institute of Linguists on the subject 'Moral Principles in Translation';[256] and on 20 November came his third principal lecture at Oxford, 'The Poet in the Valley of Dry Bones'.[257] For every dictionary, he asserted, was:

> a valley of dry bones. The poet is inspired to breathe life into them (as Ezekiel did when he prophesied), and to convert them into language. You will remember the rattle and shaking, and how the bones came together into skeletons, every bone to its bone, and put on sinews and flesh. That is a matter of craftsmanship. Then the four winds blew upon them, and they stood up, in fighting companies; which is how poems come alive. Technique takes one no further than articulating the skeletons with wire, and plumping them up with plastic limbs and organs.

He himself still consulted the large *Oxford English Dictionary* 'at least four or five times a day: never letting a doubtful word go by – I need to know its derivation, its first occurrence, its change of meaning down the centuries, and the sort of people who used it in different contexts'.

His lectures over, Graves remained in London for another month; and the press of social engagements continued. Tom Matthews came to dinner, and sat next to Margot, whom he would later remember as 'tall, coldly handsome, dark-haired ... She hardly spoke, and we did not exchange a word, but afterward Robert reported happily that she liked me.'[258] Another day, Robert talked to James Reeves, and had got as far as accusing Alastair Reid of homosexuality, and reminding James that Beryl had suggested Margot as the 'White Goddess', when they were interrupted. James found this highly unsatisfactory; and so a few days later he dictated a long letter in which he told Robert that he had:

> raised several things which I would have liked to go on about. Let us start with Alastair, though that is rather marginal, as it happens. What you call his homosexuality is neither here nor there. We are many of us that, in less or greater degree. It is what we do or don't do in consequence that matters. If his effect on women is as you say, he is to be blamed for that, not for what he 'is'. Many men have been homosexual and saints ...

More seriously, he pointed out that 'every true poet' had some 'vision of order' at the back of his mind; and he believed that Robert's vision had been 'disturbed by your obsession of the past two years or so'. He did not see how Beryl could be happy about this, and could not understand why Robert had again insisted on Beryl having suggested Margot as the White Goddess, 'unless it is to persuade yourself that anything that has resulted from this suggestion must be regarded as her responsibility. Surely you know it can't.'

James also asked Robert to remember, when he told people 'that Margot has the capacity to deflate you when you need it and steer you away from the temptations put in your way to be phoney', that he had friends who had known him 'longer and perhaps better, who are equally fond of you'. He realized that Robert might accuse him:

> of moral rectitude and draw a picture of a puritan chewing sour grapes and spitting out the pips. But I am not one to preach, and you are not one, as you said clearly in talking of Alastair, to be indifferent to morals. Take this as the beginning, if you will, of a conversation I hope we can have the chance to continue ... [259]

The result of this letter was that on 4 December Robert Graves caught a train down to Lewes, where James Reeves had been living since the beginning of the year,[260] and the two poets went for a walk, during which they somehow resolved their differences. 'It was such a relief', Robert wrote to James afterwards, 'having that long talk with you along the roads of Lewes, and finding that nothing was wrong between us.'[261]

But whatever had been said, there was no alteration in Robert's devotion to his Muse. When he flew back to Majorca on 21 December, Margot remained in London; but she had already been 'equipped for her next sortie'.[262] First, as Robert told Selwyn Jepson, she would be 'visiting her parents in Vancouver from where she ran away at the age of 16, & hasn't been back since';[263] and then she would travel on to New York where, perhaps emulating Juan, for whom she had a warm affection, she was hoping to learn photography. In the early spring she would visit Canelluñ;[264] and in May she might accompany Robert back to the USA,[265] where his itinerary would include a lecture in Boston, and a poetry reading in New York.

All this was to be accomplished by Margot with the aid of a substantial £370 loan, which created a good deal of awkwardness. Robert had said nothing to Beryl about the considerable financial support that he had been giving Margot for the past two-and-a-half years; but his agent had recently withheld some £3,500 of his earnings pending the settlement of a tax dispute, so he was temporarily short of money, and the only way in which he could raise the £370 was to ask Beryl to advance it from a recent legacy. Beryl agreed, having been assured by Margot that the money would be repaid, that she had finished with Alastair Reid, and that from now on her relationship with Robert and Beryl would remain harmonious;[266] but it alerted her to an aspect of her husband's relationship with Margot which hitherto had been successfully concealed.

In the meantime, Robert Graves's New York circle had been devouring Kingsley Amis's article in the December issue of *Show* magazine, and one or two of them, including Cindy Lee, had been searching their consciences over Robert's remarks that: 'there is an expatriate colony of a sort, mainly Americans, most of them semi-impoverished, doing a bit of painting or writing. Quite a few neurotic casualties. This is a dangerous place – there's no inspiration here.'

CHAPTER 8

Neurotic Casualties

The winter of 1963 was so severe that England was blanketed in snow for months on end. New Year's Day saw Lucia snowed up in a West Country village with Ramon and his band, Los Valldemossas; and the bad weather spread so far south, through France and into Spain, that on 3 January Robert noticed that in his garden at Canelluñ the wind and snow had 'destroyed all but a few shoots of the mimosa'. Despite this, an extension to the dining room was 'rising fast'; while Robert was busily revising the poems he had written in London, he was also writing an introduction for Idries Shah's book *The Sufis*, and he would soon be starting work on his Boston lecture which, since he was to deliver it to the students at M.I.T. – the Massachusetts Institute of Technology, he had decided should be 'about Poetry and Science'.[267]

A silver chain arrived from Margot on 10 January, accompanied by a long letter telling Robert that she had 'been snowed-in a lot' since their last meeting,[268] announcing that she was sailing for America on the 20th, and giving him, as he told Selwyn Jepson, 'lots of commissions against her return'.[269] Several of these involved further expense; and the next day, lying in bed with a cold, Robert noted rather crossly in his diary that he had 'answered all the dull letters piled up; and Margot's with a cheque'.[270]

Later that month, Robert went into Palma to pay the rent on Margot's Barcelona flat up to the end of May;[271] but he received no thanks for his help; and it was galling when he realized in due course that she had set sail without even sending him an address.[271] In the circumstances, a good-humoured letter from Ralph Jacobs was a welcome distraction.

'The "neurotic casualties" New York edition', Ralph had written, 'miss the Graves even though they do say those nasty things about us in *Show* December issue'. Cindy, he declared, had assumed that:

Robert was talking about all of us except her. I told her he definitely had her in mind. She sulked in the corner, wouldn't drink the cheap wine I'd bought her and kept muttering: 'Do you think he really meant me, do you really?' When I told her she probably inspired the term she was so pleased her hope now is to return to Deyá this summer and make the scene again.

'This time', Ralph emphasized, 'she wants credit. She says she doesn't want to be grouped with a lot of sick people she doesn't even know.'

Ralph added that since the thirty-seven-year-old Cindy was 'between men', her fate was 'a little uncertain'; but she had written to Bill Waldron asking about renting a particular house in Deyá, and Ralph himself 'would definitely like to have it whether Cindy comes or not'. He also talked of securing Robert an introduction to the White House so that he could meet President Kennedy; and he relayed news of Esteban Frances, who had undertaken to design *Don Quixote* for Balanchine.[273]

Robert Graves's attention the previous summer had centred on Margot Callas; but he recalled that Cindy Lee had been in Deyá with Howard Hart, her devoted but somewhat uninteresting lover; and so when on 24 January he replied to Ralph's letter, he told him: 'Cindy's not a neurotic casualty. Howard was a bit out of his depths here, that's all. Cindy's fine.' As for meeting the President: Graves remarked that Kennedy had 'quoted a poem of mine in the Cuba crisis so maybe he's not so dumb'; but he was much more interested in telling Ralph: 'If you see a girl called Margot in New York anytime this spring it is she. That sort only come in a single model.'[274]

Margot remained silent for the whole of February. Robert was hard at work for much of the time on 'a BBC Sound Version of the Iliad in 3 one-hour stretches';[275] but her silence placed him under intense emotional pressure. His stomach became bad, an old neck injury flared up, and he wrote fifteen drafts of 'A Last Poem',[276] one of his most despairing pieces, which runs:

> A last poem, and a very last, and yet another –
> O, when can I give over?
> Must I drive the pen until blood bursts from my nails
> And my breath fails and I shake with fever
> Or sit well wrapped in a many-coloured cloak
> Where the moon shines new through Castle Crystal?
> Shall I never hear her whisper softly:
> 'But this is truth written by you only,
> And for me only; therefore, love, have done'?[277]

In his correspondence, Graves managed to be more philosophical. 'I'm glad you met [Margot]', he told Selwyn Jepson, 'and realised that there's nothing one can do with her except wonder and let her go her own way; with love, if one is that sort of person; with suspicion if one isn't.'[278]

At last, on 2 March, an envelope arrived in Margot's handwriting and with a Vancouver postmark. Opening it with trembling hands, Robert found to his enormous relief that all was well, and she would soon be on her way to New York. His neck was still so bad that he had to have a series of injections to quieten it down.[279] The radiologist told him that it had been technically broken, 'some forty years ago, or maybe more' (perhaps when he almost lost his life during the Battle of the Somme back in 1916); and Robert wrote Margot a whimsical poem on the subject, concluding with the lines:

> For though I broke my neck in God's good time
> It is in yours alone I choose to live.[280]

He also sent Margery Terrasa a letter to be handed to Margot when she arrived in New York; and he was pleased when he heard that the letter had been delivered, and that Margot 'seemed relieved to be through the Canada trip and optimistic about things ahead. Esteban had introduced her to people and is being otherwise attentive.'[281]

With Margot safely under the protection of one of his closest friends, Robert could concentrate more easily on his work, writing a preface to a collection of his short stories,[282] and preparing an 'Oration' on the subject of money for the London School of Economics.[283] He also enjoyed the company of Kingsley and Hilly Amis, who had decided to emigrate to Majorca in the near future, and had got as far as renting themselves a house,[284] and on 2 April he watched the masons break through the wall of the dining room at Canelluñ into the new extension.[285]

The following day, Esteban Frances arrived in Deyá with more news about Margot. Apparently she was about to fly to London, where she would be staying for a few days at the Savoy Hotel; and then, instead of coming on to Majorca, she would be returning to New York, where she hoped to welcome Robert on his arrival at the end of the month.[286]

Robert was so disturbed by the possible implications of this news that on Friday 5 April he spent three and a half hours in the village trying to get through to Margot by telephone. When he finally succeeded, she would give him no explanation, though she confirmed that she would be flying back to New York again at the weekend. So on returning to Canelluñ where even Beryl's patience had been strained by his lengthy absence, Robert could only explain the mystery by recalling that Esteban had mentioned Margot's close friendship with Bobby, whose boyfriend was said to be wealthy, and by suggesting to Beryl that Margot was at the Savoy because Bobby had invited her there. Accepting what Robert had told her, Beryl simply said that Bobby appeared to be in funds, and left it at that.[287]

Eleven days later, a cable arrived from Margot, who was now back in New York. Unfortunately for Robert, as it later turned out, Beryl opened it first, and discovered that Margot had asked whether the key to Wasson's vault was available. Beryl passed the cable to Robert, who said that Margot was obviously running short of money, and who therefore replied: 'UNO "GRANDE" LIBRE MANDANDOTE MITAD': meaning that he had a 'grand' (or a thousand dollars) banked with Wasson, and that she could take half.[288]

The fact that Margot still needed his money was reassuring to Robert as he began preparing to set out on his latest American lecture tour. Esteban had aleady told him that Margot had no job as yet, and that she had rejected the chance of using an apartment owned by a man-about-town since obligations were involved:[289] so Robert and Beryl both assumed that she was free and unattached, and would be available to help Robert with his labours as soon as he arrived in New York.

Although Robert's bad stomach had been even worse since his telephone call to the Savoy, and he was losing weight as a result,[290] the thought of being alone with Margot had begun making him extremely happy. On Tuesday 23 April, two days before leaving Deyá[291] he wrote a new poem in Margot's honour:

THE THREE-FACED

Who calls her two-faced? Faces, she has three:
The first inscrutable, for the outer world;
The second shrouded in self-contemplation;
The third, her face of love,
Once for an endless moment turned on me.[292]

On Thursday, Robert Graves flew to London, where on Friday he lunched with the producer Sam Wanamaker.[293] The idea of *A Song for Sheba* had been revived, this time as a film. Wanamaker had already written to David Lean about directing, and suggested that Irwin Shaw might work with Graves on a screenplay;[294] and for a while, much to their excitement, it seemed to Robert and Jenny as though their collaboration might at last come to fruition. Robert also saw Idries Shah,[295] who had begun to suspect that Robert's involvement with Margot was nearing its end, and cannily warned him of the dangers of Margot 'using her infallibility as a Goddess for other ends, and ... losing *baraka* and her whole being'.[296]

Then on Sunday 28 April Robert Graves flew to New York. There was no one waiting for him at the airport; but after he had reached Gordon Wasson's apartment, where he had arranged to stay,[297] Margot telephoned and came round.[298] She greeted him 'with every evidence of perfect love',[299] and handed him a loving letter which she explained that she had written to him, but never posted.[300]

That evening Robert wrote in his diary: 'Things couldn't be better';[301] and on Monday night, after speaking at Sarah Lawrence College,[302] he was so elated that he wrote a poem beginning 'Not to sleep all night long, for pure joy'.[303] This he described to James Reeves as 'one of the few poems of utter happiness ever written'.[304] On Tuesday, soon after completing it, he lunched with Margot; and that evening they went to a 'Deyá party'.[305]

This was a buffet supper to which Gordon Wasson had invited many of Robert's friends,[306] including Jerry Robbins, Margery Terrasa, Len Lye, Jess McNab, Ralph Jacobs and Cindy Lee.[307] Robert was far too exhilarated to be consciously aware that Margot was not as happy to be in his company as he was to be in hers; but Cindy noticed that something was wrong; and in the course of the evening she staged a 'mock-fight'[308] with Margot, whom she may suddenly have begun hoping to replace as Robert's muse.

The day after the party, Graves flew to Boston, where he was entertained by some of the M.I.T. professors.[309] Afterwards, he remarked that he had been 'filled with such a sense of joy and eloquence' that his effect on them had been 'frightening'; and on Thursday he wrote to James Reeves telling him, 'As a matter of record: I have never been so happy in my life as now: all the unhappiness of three years has peeled away.'[310] However, on Friday he flew back to New York;[311] and the events of the next thirty-six hours would bring his euphoria to a very sudden end.

CHAPTER 9

The Black Goddess

Robert Graves was overjoyed when, on Friday 3 May, he was reunited with Margot Callas; and at first he took it in his stride when she told him about her friendship with Mike Nichols, soon to be described by him as 'young, sweet, honest, industrious: a rich successful New York Jew in show-business'. Graves was certain that he had nothing to fear from Nichols, especially when Margot gave him 'her passionate assurance that everything was absolutely all right and that she was doing a cure on him'.[312] Margot then asked Robert to talk to her 'patient' over the telephone; and when he did so, it was to be told by Mike Nichols that his knowledge of Margot, as revealed by the poem 'She Is No Liar', was so profound that he was alarmed.[313] The poem runs:

> She is no liar, yet she will wash away
> Honey from her lips, blood from her shadowy hand,
> And dressed at dawn in pure white robes will say,
> Trusting the ignorant world to understand:
> 'Such things no longer are; this is today.'[314]

And at first Graves was flattered by Nichols's praise.

Later the three of them met in Mike Nichols's luxurious penthouse apartment,[315] where it soon became clear to Graves that their host was 'utterly captivated' by Margot;[316] and Saturday found them travelling together to New Hope, Pennsylvania.[317] Curiously enough, this was just five miles north of the hamlet of Brownsburg, where in that nightmarish autumn of 1939 Laura Riding had left Robert Graves for Schuyler Jackson; and by a chilling coincidence, it was here in New Hope that Margot Callas chose to tell Graves that she and Mike Nichols were living together. She added that it was as Mike's companion that she had been staying in the Savoy the previous month.[318]

Robert was shocked to learn that Margot Callas had established such an apparently ultimate relationship with Mike Nichols; and since it was still unthinkable for him to blame her for anything, he immediately began revising his opinion of her new partner. Mike's remark that Robert's understanding of Margot alarmed him was now seen as evidence of his cowardice: something confirmed, in Robert's view, when he began talking about his 'Jewish inheritance',[319] asked Robert why the German Jews had submitted so meekly to being herded into the German gas-chambers during the war, and added that every descendant of the Jewish race was probably just as submissive.[320] Jumping rashly to the conclusion that Nichols was '*not a real man*', Graves began acting contemptuously towards him.

The following day, he telephoned Margot, who made it clear that she had forgiven him for his outburst against her lover.[321] Not surprisingly, however, Graves still had a 'gnawing sense of something that has gone wrong'; and on Monday 6 May, as he flew from New York to Boston, he wrote to Idries Shah telling him that he had warned Margot of the dangers she faced if she deserted him; and that Mike Nichols was 'an innocent who has strayed into a furnace and begun picking flames as if flowers; when he realises, he will be scorched to death'. As for Margot, she 'thinks no ill of herself but only of me for displaying my true colours in his company'.[322]

In a draft of the letter which he had outlined to Idries Shah, Graves had told Margot that he was pleased that she had decided not to end their relationship, because as a source of inspiration (or White Goddess) she needed someone whom she could inspire; while as a writer of poems, he needed someone by whom he could be inspired. Whose quest was most difficult, Graves was uncertain. All he could say definitely was that the writer was bound to worship his Muse, and to be honest; while his Muse could do exactly as she pleased.

Graves added his current adage that as a poet he was also a prophet, and declared that it was important to him to be able to reconcile the different aspects of his life: the prophetic, and the poetic and the private. He felt strongly that he should not have had to endure the anxiety of not knowing what was really happening when Margot had been staying at the Savoy; and pointed out that her lack of trust had made him ill. What seemed unfair was that once she had made him ill, she then became annoyed with him for his illness, and began to accuse him of being possessive, and hoping to tie her to a property in Majorca.

Robert protested that this was not so. 'Seldom Yet Now',[324] the poem in which he had long ago written 'Seldom the encounter/The presence always,/Free of oath or promise', was, he declared, how he had been accustomed to view the way they loved each other. And then Robert referred to another more recent poem to Margot, in which he had written of 'Time, Love's gaunt executor!' a being who, Graves declared, would be seen to have recorded the fact that nobody could ever replace him in Margot's life.[325]

Once he had set it all down in writing, the position seemed so clear to Graves that he was somehow able not to notice what was really happening, and during the next few days, as he commuted between Boston, New York and Washington, attending receptions and giving poetry readings,[326] he felt almost as joyful as he had done before Margot's revelations. He certainly observed on Friday 10 May, when he was briefly in New York, that it was Cindy who had taken the trouble to shop for him.[327] But as he drafted and redrafted his next letter to Margot, he could still tell her that things were occurring in the most extraordinary manner. Or rather, that her influence upon him was altering his manner of thinking in every possible area. His complete devotion to Margot, his faith in her essence as a human being, could (he told her) be compared to a blazing torch which devoured everything in its path. He no longer, he promised her, had any interest in either his reputation or his magical strength; but he was experiencing things that were far beyond the normal. In view of this astonishing transformation, he wondered whether she could visit Boston when he gave his M.I.T. lecture (on the 14th) and witness at first-hand the weird things which were bound to happen as soon as he began addressing his audience.[328]

In his M.I.T. lecture, Graves spoke at length about the relationship between a poet and his Muse, suggesting that it had first been introduced into Europe during the early Middle Ages 'from Sufi sources in Persia and Arabia'; and pointed out that:

> the poet-Muse relationship can never be a domestic one, nor need it be sexually consummated; since, despite all the symptoms of romantic love, it belongs to another order of experience – which, for want of a better term, we must call 'spiritual' and which is usually characterised by remarkable telescopings of space and time and by cosmic coincidences.

Coincidences which, 'though rationally inexplicable', had 'clearly been created by the power of thought'.

Graves concluded that intellectual arrogance had sunk humanity into a morass; and that there could be 'no release from the present impasse' until there was 'a personal understanding' between the male mind and the female mind. This alone would enable the development of 'the so-called supernatural powers of which both sexes are capable'.[329]

The next day Graves flew back to New York; and although Margot had not answered his summons to the M.I.T. lecture, she was still fascinated enough by Robert and his ideas to attend his appearance that evening at the local Y.M.C.A.[330] There she heard him publicly debate the points which Mike Nichols had raised about Jewish courage, or the lack of it. He declared forcefully that many Jews had unfortunately 'taken the cowardly Jacob as their ancestor', but that others were spiritual descendants of 'two or three Edomite tribes including Kadem and Kenaz, who were *men* and fought like hell'. (Afterwards he drafted a letter to Nichols telling him that he had clearly chosen the wrong path; and that Margot, far from being like one of the more submissive Jews, was an incarnation of that Great Goddess who destroyed nearly everyone, and was loathed by Jeremiah.[331])

Margot Callas, having seen Robert acquit himself so well in the debate at the Y.M.C.A., was temporarily drawn back towards her poet. On the next day, Thursday 16 May, when he was due to leave for Europe, she went with him to the airport to see him off;[332] and there she was reconciled with him in a way which, in his words, 'left her fundamental truthfulness and love in no doubt'.[333] Before saying goodbye, Robert felt generous enough towards his apparently defeated rival to call him a sad fellow and ask Margot to pass on his love.[334]

On returning to Deyá, Robert Graves found himself confronted by an unhappy nephew and, when he had told her as much as he dared about Margot Callas and Mike Nichols, by an almost equally unhappy wife.

The nephew was John's fifteen-year-old son Simon. His fellow Carthusian hash-pros (scholars), considering 'Graves mi' to be 'too clever by half' in what remained a lamentably philistine school, had encouraged one of their number to 'beat him up' on a regular basis. This had driven him into a nervous breakdown; and Robert and Beryl had kindly agreed that he could spend a few months recuperating at Canelluñ.

The effect was encouraging. In the liberal Deyá atmosphere, Simon was able (briefly) to flourish, and by 20 May Robert could write to John telling him that: 'Simon is *absolutely all right*, in my prejudiced opinion ... he's happy here and everyone likes him and he'll see a lot of people here whom he'd not otherwise meet and who will be educative'. He himself liked his nephew so much that he added: 'I seem to be Simon's *avunculus* not *patruus* despite genealogical evidence.'[335]

As for Beryl: on 21 May Robert noted in his diary that she was 'ill and dispirited'.[336] This was hardly surprising. When Beryl had asked about Margot, he had had to explain, as he told Margot in one of his numerous draft letters, that she was sharing an apartment with a wealthy comrade; and unfortunately, the comrade had taken a dislike to him, so that he had seen very little of Margot until his final twenty-four hours in New York, when the comrade was temporarily absent. Beryl's reaction to this news was that Margot should not have been cabling Robert for dollars when she was living with someone else. Worse still, Margot had borrowed cash with a view to learning how to become a professional photographer, and on the understanding that she would be selling her French property before the beginning of May. But neither of these requirements had been met, and now it seemed that Margot had not even helped Robert when he was in New York.

The result was (as Robert continued in this draft letter to Margot) that although *he* understood why Margot had acted as she had, Beryl did not, and it was up to Margot to write to Beryl and repair the damage she had done to their friendship. Because there was no doubt that Beryl was thoroughly shocked by what had happened.[337] When, on 20 or 21 May, a letter from Margot arrived and Robert asked Beryl whether she would like to read it, she replied that he should show it to her only when she had more time. Robert did not offer the letter again, nor as he told Margot in a letter drafted on 22 May, did she ask for it.[338]

In the same letter, Robert told his Muse that he understood why she had become involved with Mike Nichols: they had both been lonely, and Mike had been unbalanced by the departure of some other woman. Naturally, Robert continued, Margot wanted to help Mike; however, she had been compelled to distance herself from him, since he could not possibly share her inner living. And because of that, there was no hope of Mike being totally reformed unless Margot was prepared to allow herself to be destroyed.

By this time, exhausted by the 'unpredictable vagaries'[339] which are an integral part of romantic love (and therefore of the way in which the White Goddess treats her poet), Graves was groping towards a fresh synthesis of his thinking both about the nature of an ideal relationship between the sexes, and about the nature of poetic inspiration. For he had come to believe that although most men find traditional marriage an inadequate arrangement, romantic love with a succession of 'other women' brings so much pain and suffering in its wake that it can only be tolerated as a stage upon the road to something infinitely more satisfying.[340] In groping towards that elusive state, Graves recalled what he had learned about 'the Sufic tradition of Wisdom as blackness',[341] and told Shah that 'The real point is when and how the White Goddess ... will become the Black Goddess of wisdom'.[342]

Graves was now writing his third set of Oxford lectures; and in one of them he would explain that the White Goddess, when she went under the name of Ishtar, 'did not rule alone. At Hierapolis, Jerusalem and Rome, she acknowledged a mysterious sister, the Goddess of Wisdom, whose temple was small and unthronged. Call her the Black Goddess ... ' According to Graves, this Black Goddess, who 'represents a miraculous certitude in love', has ordained that the poet who seeks her 'must pass uncomplaining through all the passionate ordeals to which the White Goddess may subject him'.[343] He added that the title 'Black Goddess' was:

so far hardly more than a word of hope whispered among the few who have served their apprenticeship to the White Goddess. She promises a new pacific bond between men and women, corresponding to a final reality of love, in which the patriarchal marriage bond will fade away. Unlike Vesta [Goddess of domesticity], the Black Goddess has experienced good and evil, love and hate, truth and falsehood in the person of her sister; but chooses what is good: rejecting serpent-love and corpse-flesh. Faithful as Vesta, gay and adventurous as the White Goddess, she will lead men back to that sure instinct of love which he long ago forfeited by intellectual pride.

Unfortunately, Graves was uncertain what this would mean in practice. 'It is idle,' he wrote, 'to speculate what poets will then become, or whether the same woman can, in fact, by a sudden spectacular change in her nature, play two diverse parts in one lifetime.'

Robert Graves was clearly thinking of Margot when he wrote of a woman playing 'two diverse parts in one lifetime'; and he drafted several letters coaching her in her new role. In one of them, he tells her that the surface appearance of their relationship, in which they met very infrequently, and then almost always in company, had absolutely nothing whatever to do with what was really happening between them. In reality, their relations were those most appropriate to a poet and a woman who has ceased to be his White Goddess, but is moving on to a role of far greater importance in his life. Robert added that he knew that Margot understood this, although she said little on the subject. And he begged her not to allow people who were rich or famous to syphon off her inner virtue. Instead, she should recall those who truly cared for her: for it was in their company that she truly belonged.[344]

By this time, however, Robert was aware that Margot might be unable to play the part of the Black Goddess, and this disturbed him. 'I can't see an alternative to Margot, not even Eleni', he complained to Idries Shah as early as 20 May;[345] and later on, when Margot seemed unwilling to join him in Majorca to discuss their future, Graves told Shah that, 'In New York [Margot] was on the brink of a decision; but seems now to have fallen away again, perhaps to a further point than before'; and he added that if a meeting with Margot should prove to be impossible, then he would 'have to re-route my [spiritual] journey with your help'.[346]

This 're-routing' might possibly involve Eleni; and Robert Graves had also been very touched in recent months by Cindy's sympathetic interest. As he told Idries Shah, she and Ralph Jacobs had both been 'greatly concerned' by his difficulties with Margot, and that Cindy in particular had

> come to a decision about ranging herself with *us*, and being all that she can be; and she is a wonderful girl, and very close to Margot, and shocked at what Margot has been recently doing to herself and to me. Cindy writes that Margot's main preoccupation, she thinks, is how she can possibly face Beryl, with whom she has broken a sacred bond.[347]

On the strength of Cindy's decision to 'range herself with us', Robert had arranged to pay for her journey to Deyá that summer; although what he had heard from Ralph Jacobs about her being 'between men' was not quite true. Margery Terrasa, who approved of Robert's generosity, wrote to tell him that Cindy still had 'very mixed feelings' about having left Howard. 'They get along so poorly', Margery told Robert, 'yet don't seem able to break off completely.' She added that Ralph was 'looking forward to Deyá like a child to Christmas and Cindy going on the same flight as his "wife" has topped it all'.[348]

Cindy and Eleni were not the only possible candidates for the role of muse, or 'post-muse'. There was also Mary Allen, who had previous experience as the muse of the Canadian poet Frank Prewett, a friend of Robert's back in the early 1920s. After Prewett's recent death, Graves had written an introduction to a volume of his poems;[349] and soon after Mary's arrival in Deyá on 25 May,[350] she had won Robert's confidence, and he was telling her the most intimate details of his private life.

On her return to England, Mary went to see Idries Shah, with whom she reported she had 'clicked instantly'. They had discussed the sorry state of Robert's relationship with Margot at some length;[351] and the following month, Mary would tell Robert of the happy hours she had spent listening to a recording of him reading his poems. 'It looks', she wrote hopefully, 'as if Frank prepared the ground and sowed the seed and now something is beginning to stir. He would have been very pleased.'[352]

In the meantime, Robert's attitude towards Margot had been veering wildly to every point of the emotional compass. His only fixed belief appeared to be that unless she fell in with his wishes, her beauty would fade, and her health would fail. On Tuesday 4 June, he wrote to her most severely, telling her that she had now hurt so many people, and had so many fences to mend, that he could not see how she could progress, short of making a completely fresh start, and dedicating herself whole-heartedly to her most important role. Should she prove unworthy of this task, Robert continued in his draft letter, then she should depart, and go back to the sphere of normal reality.[353]

On Wednesday, his mood changed completely. The reason was that a friend of Eleni's came to Canelluñ, bringing with her a black Mycaenean bead as a present from Eleni, together with the news that Eleni herself would soon be on her way to Deyá. The result was that Robert wrote a letter to Margot which, apart from a sinister reference to her health in the first line, was far more tender and loving than the one he had written the previous day.

Robert began by hoping that Margot was not being overcome by illness. But he added that everything would ultimately be all right: her personal transformation would begin at the appropriate moment. The period of waiting which they both had to endure gave them time first to experience and then to discard each and every wrong course of action; and he realised that for a while, at least, he would simply have to trust in the future.

Robert went on to tell Margot that Eleni would soon be arriving in Deyá. He explained that they loved each other, but that was all; and their love was like a lamp in the current darkness of his life. Eleni had the knack of writing to him at the very moments when he particularly needed to be comforted. He added that Eleni knew and approved of his special relationship with Margot; and fortunately, despite being extremely good-looking, she did not have an ounce of jealousy in her body.[354]

At the close of his letters to Margot, Robert had begun drawing occult signs: usually of a pentacle with five dots around it. No doubt this was intended as an aid to telepathic communication: for Wednesday's letter, like Tuesday's, remained unposted.

On Thursday, Robert wrote again. In Wednesday's letter, he had mentioned to Margot that he would not ruin his communication by detailing those financial matters which she would have to sort out on her arrival;[355] but having since then taken to his bed 'with a cough & a virus & temperature',[356] he had become so obsessed with Margot's debts to Beryl that in his new letter he enclosed an amended verse from his 1920s poem 'Myyrhina', which he evidently believed could now be applied to Margot:

Then shall Myrrhina groaning say
She knew not there were debts to pay
    For city beauty,
But pay she must and on the nail,
Giddied with tears, distraught, death-pale –
    This done, there's room for beauty.[357]

While he lay ill in bed, Robert was further depressed by bad news from
Jenny about *A Song for Sheba*: apparently David Merrick (who had seen
their script several years previously) had announced that he would be
putting on a musical comedy called *Solomon and She* in 1964; and Jenny
and Robert both felt that this 'dreadful news'[358] finally put an end to their
own hopes, at least in their present form.[359]

However it was about his relationship with the muse that Graves was
most concerned. When, on 12 June, he was finally well enough to get up
from his sick-bed, there was still 'No news from M'; and he began work
on this melancholy poem of farewell:[360]

I WILL WRITE[361]

He had done for her all that a man could,
And, some might say, more than a man should,
Then was ever a flame so recklessly blown out
Or a last goodbye so negligent as this?
'I will write to you,' she muttered briefly,
Tilting her head for a polite kiss;
Then walked away, nor ever turned about …

Long letters written and mailed in her own head –
There are no mails in the city of the dead.

This was not quite the end of the story. For the next fortnight, Margot
Callas continued to be as elusive as ever; but then on 28 June she finally
sent Robert a cable, in which she talked of coming to Deyá with her
mother, and then leaving her mother behind while she went on a private
holiday: possibly to Greece.

This threw Graves into a two-day paroxysm of letter-writing. To begin
with, he wrote draft after draft of a letter to Margot. In part of what
appears to be the earliest surviving version, Robert tells her that her
telegram had told him virtually nothing that he wanted to know. Why was
this? Had all his letters to her gone astray?

In any case, he begged her not to arrange to leave her mother in Deyá as she suggested. If she did so, she would be treating Beryl unfairly. Margot's first task must be to sort things out with Beryl. Indeed, Margot had allowed everything to get into such a mess that she could only make things better by abandoning herself whole-heartedly to being a loving and trusting human being.[362]

Then Robert began again, with a new approach, telling Margot that he had no desire to compel any particular course of action upon her. It was just that the troubles of the past three years had developed his abilities as a prophet. He was therefore in a position to reveal that she had arrived at a critical moment in her life.

He would not forget that she had been quite superb in the role of the White Goddess; but times had moved on. Now she must decide whether (as she was entitled) she would undertake the role of the Black Goddess, or whether she would allow another person to play the part instead. Not, he added hastily, that a woman so well qualified for the part sprang rapidly to mind.

Robert added that in her heart of hearts, Margot had decided to undertake the new role; and that he and his intimate circle counted on her to do so within the next three months.[363] And then Robert drew another pentagram with dots around it.

Then this approach too was abandoned, and on 29 June, Graves drafted a letter in which he told Margot that her coming to Deyá would mean that she was prepared to settle matters completely and finally with everyone in Deyá who loved her. She should therefore, Robert told her, avoid making any plans for the next few months: for plans might interfere with the only really important task of the summer.

Should matters be settled between them, Robert added, then all would be 'top-hole' once more, and miraculous events would occur. His only desire, he concluded, was that she should come to a final decision about whether or not to play the part of the Black Goddess.

However, the next person in Deyá to hear from Margot Callas was not Robert Graves, but Helen Morningstar. She received a telegram from Margot asking if they could meet on 20 July at the Phoenix Hotel in Palma. There Margot announced that she had married Mike Nichols; but she could not bring herself to tell Robert. Would Helen do so on her behalf?[365]

When Helen agreed, Margot explained that there was an added complication. Robert wanted her to return the house which he had given her at Son Coll. She was most unwilling to do this; but her new husband had insisted that she should. Could Helen think of a compromise?

'You love Juan', said Helen. 'Why not give it to him?'

'I love it', Margot replied enthusiastically. 'It's a great idea!'

As it happened, the very next day Helen Morningstar was invited by Beryl to meet her and Robert for lunch at a Deyá restaurant. It was there that Helen told Robert of Margot's marriage to Mike Nichols. Robert threw down his napkin in disgust. 'That does it', he said angrily, and rose from the table and walked hurriedly away.[366]

One of Robert's next acts was to write to Mary Allen telling her of Margot's 'betrayal'. He expressed himself forcefully, and in due course she replied that she was:

> appalled at the nature of the blow you have suffered. None of this detracts from the unique quality which Margot possessed ... Poor girl. She is to be pitied. As I see it, she is not able to carry the weight of her divinity and nobody, not even you, can prop it up. She has taken the only step open to her in the circumstances ... That is her tragedy and your pain. I have met this situation before. To the betrayed it seems the final disillusionment. I have learned that it isn't. Perhaps I can help you, Robert, in this crisis. Indeed I 'both feel and know' I can ... Furthermore I both felt and knew this before I came to Majorca.[367]

However, if this was a bid for the position which Margot had vacated, it was already too late.

Helen Morningstar had been taking part in one of the rehearsals for that year's birthday play, humorously entitled (by Beryl) *The Timelessness of the Long-distance Professor*. It was only three days after Robert had heard the news about Margot's marriage but, much to Helen's astonishment, she noticed that Cindy Lee was already 'falling into the role of Margot: and with such ease'.[368]

BOOK SEVEN

CINDY AND POETIC TRUTH
1963–66

CHAPTER 1

'Gift of Sight'

When Cindy Lee arrived at Deyá in the summer of 1963, she shared a cottage with Ralph Jacobs a little to the east of the main village beside the road to Valldemossa; but she had come at Robert Graves's expense, and with the hope of becoming his Muse. Even before news came of Margot Callas's marriage to Mike Nichols, Cindy had taken to introducing herself with a flourish: 'I'm just Queen of the Beats, honey', she said to those like Simon Graves who had never met her before. 'They call me Cindy. It's a title'; and for her role in *The Timelessness of the Long-distance Professor* (in which she explained to a prospective partner that she needed 'M-O-N-E-Y money, honey. Otherwise we're splitting'), her short, dark, curly hair was crowned with a wreath of myrtle.[1]

Now in her mid-thirties (she was eight years older than Margot), Cindy had lost none of her provocative sexuality; and although she still had the wild streak she had displayed in her early twenties, in general she was far more controlled; and alongside what some observers saw as a capacity for manipulation (so that Seymour-Smith, for example, writes that she 'treated old men like, and thought of them as, sugar daddies'[2]), others perceived her as having a highly developed intuition, a quick intelligence, a considerable understanding of human nature, and a compelling need both to love and to be loved.[3]

It was Cindy's need to be loved which attracted her to Robert, just as much as his fame; her intuition enabled her to undertake the part of Robert's Black Goddess; and her understanding meant that she could sustain the role, so that after knowing her for more than a year Robert would still be praising her 'fantastic delicacy of moral judgment'.[4] Cindy's presence certainly reconciled Robert to Margot's absence. By mid-August, he was already telling James Reeves that Margot's departure had left him 'sound in head and heart';[5] and by late September Selwyn Jepson was informed:

that Margot, who had the choice between the real and the unreal, fell for the latter: married for money and unlove, and I fear will never recover from the violence she has done herself. I'll always be grateful to her; and hope she becomes just ordinary, not actively ill-fated. But our patterns have divaricated.[6]

Robert added that he himself was now genuinely happy.

Part of the reason for this happiness was not only that Robert Graves had found a new source of inspiration, who was prepared to enter the world of myth and magic which he had gradually been creating around himself ever since his return to Deyá in 1947; but also that at the age of sixty-eight he had attracted a sexually experienced mistress more than thirty years his junior. For Cindy had always had a healthy sexual appetite; and she was also a generous and deliciously abandoned lover.[7]

Robert, after two wives and a number of other intimate relationships, was no sexual ignoramus; but he had never altogether thrown off a puritanical disgust for the pleasure of the flesh: Laura Riding had found it comparatively easy to persuade him that 'bodies have had their day'; and so Cindy's uninhibited delight in a wide range of sexual practices must have been a revelation.

Not that Cindy could possibly have been satisfied by Robert alone; and among her other conquests that summer was John de St Jorre, a handsome twenty-seven-year-old who was in the British Foreign Service on his way from Africa to the Lebanon. He had been invited to Deyá by George McDowell, a friend of his who worked for the United Nations; and soon after his arrival in Deyá at the beginning of August, he met Cindy and began an affair with her. John had a wonderful time in the hands of this older and much more sexually experienced woman. It soon became clear that she could be wild and unpredictable; but she also seemed to him to be very worldly wise.[8]

On one occasion, for example, George, Cindy and John de St Jorre went to Palma on the morning bus, began bar-hopping and consorting with friends and strangers alike, and missed the bus back to Deyá, after which Cindy and John stayed in Terreno for a couple of days. When they finally returned to Deyá one afternoon on the 2.30 bus, they found a reception committee waiting for them, with an anxious-looking Robert at its heart. The sun was blazing down, there was almost complete silence except for the ticking of the cicadas, and the atmosphere was extremely hostile. As John de St Jorre stepped out of the bus, Robert wagged his finger at him and exclaimed: 'You are a wicked, wicked boy!' In the circumstances, as de St Jorre relates, Cindy was 'magnificent'. Following him out of the bus as though she had not a care in the world, she seemed surprised when Robert asked her anxiously: 'Cindy, Cindy, are you all right?'

'I'm fine', she replied casually, instantly defusing the situation; and then, while John de St Jorre slipped away, she sauntered off up the street on Robert's arm. However, she had already told John that she would 'sort it out'; and for the remainder of his month in Deyá she managed to see him quite regularly, despite spending most of her time with Robert Graves.

Cindy had now become important to Robert for yet another reason. Like Judith Bledsoe, she had trained as an artist; and there was something in the clarity of her visual perception which seemed to Robert, when he was in her company, to cleanse his own vision, as he explained in 'Gift of Sight':

> I had long known the diverse tastes of the forest,
> Each leaf, each bark, rank earth from every hollow;
> Knew the smells of bird's breath and of bat's wing;
> Yet sight I lacked: until you stole upon me,
> Touching my eyelids with light finger-tips.
> The trees blazed out, their colours whirled together,
> Nor even before had I been aware of sky.[9]

Cindy also took a keen interest in two of Robert's current projects: the establishment in Deyá of a village museum;[10] and in Palma of a jazz club, which was intended as a home for Ramon Farran and the Valldemossans. On Robert's return from America earlier in the year, he had given Ramon a substantial sum of money to get the club under way;[11] and by the end of the summer the Indigo was so popular that attendance figures continued to climb even when most tourists had left the island and gone home.[12]

Cindy had always loved jazz;[13] and a memorable photograph shows her at the Indigo, sitting on the far side of Robert, who looks extremely happy, and staring provocatively into the camera while she tries on one of his broad-brimmed hats. Ralph Jacobs sits on Robert's near side, looking bored; Lucia and Beryl are also present, both smiling; and in the background, Ramon sits at his drums and cymbals.

Simon Graves is absent: he had gone back to England in the first week of August, seeming very much better for his months at Canelluñ,[14] where he had played the part of Apollo in the summer play, delivering a speech in Ancient Greek from the top of the cliff face above the theatre. Robert, horrified by Simon's stories about Charterhouse which showed 'that the bloodiness of Writing School, Studies & Hall has defied the passage of 50 years',[15] had begun calling him 'Glaucus' to give him a new and more 'real' identity. Robert also enjoyed discussing 'fine points of Latin' with him;[16] and after his departure, Robert told John Graves, who had asked whether Simon would be ready for school in September, that:

> in some ways I think of him as the father (Bulstrode?) in Anstey's *Vice Versa* forced to be a schoolboy when already adult ... With a bit more knowledge of the Classics and an adult voice he would make a good Classics don at any Oxford College: the trouble is bridging the next ten years.[17]

Then on 13 September Robert wrote directly to 'Dear Glaucus', asking what he had decided to do, and telling him the latest news: Beryl was about to take Tomas and Antonia (Catherine's daughter) to school in England; Juan was to travel with them, having 'decided to go to a crammer's for 3 O-levels'; and the Museum was shortly to open 'with a showcase full of ... the long- extinct Balearic gazelle of which there is no example in the Natural History museums of England or U.S.A. Bill [Waldron] dug them up. And lots of other exhibits of earlier and later date'.[18]

The 'fabulous' opening'[19] was attended by Jenny Nicholson, who had been in Deyá for several weeks on a working holiday. Part of her task was to help her father 'to work out the GRAVES AT THE KITCHEN SINK for Border TV';[20] and she and Robert also discussed whether they could salvage anything from the months of work they had both done on *A Song for Sheba*, eventually deciding that Robert should turn it into an historical novel. Sadly, their time together was not as harmonious as usual. 'I didn't enjoy the work part much', Jenny told Beryl afterwards;[21] but the real problem was Jenny's dislike of her father's obsession with Cindy.[22]

In mid-October, after a few weeks without either Beryl or Jenny to distract him from his Black Goddess, Robert Graves wrote to Ralph Jacobs telling him that Cindy was 'all you ever said she was and more'. He himself was 'Just off to St. John's College'; and Cindy, who had been delayed by such things as 'her need of clothes ... and her modista's mother-in-law', would soon be following him to England.[23]

Graves added that Cindy was not his Muse: for 'Muse [in her White Goddess aspect] connotes cruelty and suffering. The Muse always goes back to cohabitation with serpents and eating corpse-flesh. Cindy', he said firmly, 'is not that sort and we see perpetually eye-to-eye and only good comes of our new bond of understanding.'[24]

When Cindy arrived in London, Robert was there to meet her; and, since she had nowhere to stay, he telephoned Tom Matthews, who recalls that the conversation 'went something like this':

'Will you do me a favour, Tom?'
'Of course, Robert. What is it?'
'Well, I'd like you to put up a friend of mine.'
'Yes, sure. But you realize there's no one in the house but me. No cook or anything.'
'That's all right. We'll be there in ten minutes.'
And very shortly arrived at my door Robert and [Cindy], both wearing Andalusian hats, rarely if ever seen in London, and making them look, I thought, like a family act in a circus; and Robert's daughter Jenny, by now an old friend of mine. Jenny gave me such a look! And I returned it. I knew we would both have given a good deal to be able to voice our thoughts. Robert was brisk and businesslike, [Cindy] all silence and smiles.[25]

Tom gave Cindy a latchkey, and 'that was just about the last I saw of her'; a few days later he found a message from her saying that she had 'found some friends of her own age living in Chelsea ... and was moving in with them'.

In the meantime, the 'bond of understanding' between Robert and Cindy had been considerably strengthened. Not long after their meeting with Tom Matthews, Robert and Cindy had visited Idries Shah in his London home. Idries had asked Cindy why she perpetually hid her true identity from view; and Cindy, rising to the occasion, explained that her real name was Emile Laraçuen.[26] She said she was of Mexican-Italian-French descent[27] (the Moroccan mother about whom she once told Charles Corbett now became – and perhaps always had been – Mexican); and with a romantic flourish she added that many of her ancestors had been put to death by the Mexican guerrilla leader Pancho Villa.[28]

Just as Robert had seen his nephew both as 'Simon' (his 'false' identity as a broken-down schoolboy), and as 'Glaucus' (his 'true' identity as a potential classics don); so he now saw his mistress both as 'Cindy' (her 'false' identity as a fun-loving alcoholic junkie) and as 'Emile' (her 'true' identity as an incarnation of the Black Goddess); and he immediately began using her 'real' name.

Following the naming of 'Emile', she and Robert 'made a pact, or "vow" ... witnessed by Shah'. She was then ' "adopted" as Shah's spiritual sister in a solemn ceremony';[29] and on 14 October, writing from

St John's to the Jepsons, Robert told them that: 'This year I hope Emile Laraçuen will come down; she has already made the right sort of choice, and so the visit will be a simple confirmation: though anyone less English is hard to seek. Whoever loves her, loves me.'[30]

CHAPTER 2

Death of a Daughter

Robert Graves's first Oxford lecture in the autumn of 1963 was given on 23 October,[31] to an audience which included Beryl, his daughter Jenny, and his sisters Rosaleen and Clarissa.[32] Tom Matthews was also there, and he noticed Emile, who was sitting 'on the other side of the hall, but we spotted each other, and waved'.[33]

Almost immediately after the lecture, Robert flew out to Greece, where, as he had told his nephew Simon Graves, he was due to 'go for a week to Epidaurus to do a T.V. show in the theatre there ... I have to explain Greek Drama to 27 million knowledge-thirsty Americans. In 10 minutes flat.'[34] In the event, he travelled not to Epidaurus but 'to Delphi and brought back a shepherd's hat and crook and an increased reputation as a ham actor';[35] and he learned that his television programme would be 'shown on seven New York stations. So watch out', he told Ralph Jacobs, 'for my white hair and black eyebrows.'[36]

On 1 November, Robert returned to England, where he and Beryl were now sharing 'digs' in the Oxford suburb of Headington with Lucia and their Spanish maid.[37] By this time, Cindy/Emile had already left London for New York, from where she wrote him an extremely loving letter.[38] It contained no real news, but this hardly mattered to Robert, who had become convinced that he and Emile were in regular telepathic communication, and that from time to time they were actually present in some incorporeal form in each other's immediate surroundings. In a fragmentary draft of a letter written in his room at St John's early one evening, Robert tells Emile that now he has completed his correspondence, and improved one of the lectures which he proposes to deliver early the following year in America(where he hopes that she will be one of the audience), she has entered his room and is soon sitting on his knees. She says not a word, he tells her, apart from the odd moan of pleasure as she warms herself by his fire. She remains on his knees, he goes on, and he is completing this letter to her with his writing-paper leaning upon her body, close to her neck.

And now he tells her to stay where she is. There is nothing to worry about. She is invisible to everyone but him, so that no unexpected guest bursting into the room would be surprised by her presence. But then he recalls that it is almost time to return to his Oxford suburb, for dinner with his grand-daughter's landlady. Very well, he concludes. After some kissing and hugging, it is time for Emile to be off . . .[39]

Robert was planning to see Emile in the flesh towards the end of February, when he would be spending a week and a half in New York, 'to lecture and recoup the expenses of our Oxford visit'.[40] In the meantime he completed his course of lectures, the third of which, on 1 December,[41] was his dissertation on the subject of the Black Goddess; and, as he told Simon Graves, he also gave a largely impromptu talk:

at the Classical Association's annual bun-fight. I thought it would be only a formal three minutes but was expected to go on for 40! In the middle of it Pres. Kennedy was assassinated, but the news wasn't brought into the ... hall for fear of interrupting my extemporizations (which were not helped by the unsolicited presence of your aunt Clarissa wearing a coquettish hat and slowly drinking tea in time to my Ciceronianisms![42]

While he was in London, Robert also saw Margot Nichols, who sent him 'a mysterious telegram in French from the Savoy suggesting lunch at the Café Royale'.

When they met, as Robert reported to his son William, Margot told him that she was 'having a baby', and:

... Has the most beautiful apartment in New York – Mike has had a big Broadway success – but hates NY and loathes show-business ... Admires me more than any man she knows, but resists the temptation to love me *or* anyone else.

'She was very elegant', Robert concluded, 'but had lost her beauty. Still on an even keel, but bound nowhere ... '[43]

By the evening of 11 December Robert and Beryl were back in Canellún,[44] from where Robert continued to send Emile regular instalments of 'a journal-letter' giving her his 'ordinary news'.[45] In return, Emile sent Robert occasional letters and postcards telling of her progress. After Christmas, she had travelled to Phoenix, Arizona;[46] and then she had gone on to Mexico where, as Robert reported to William, she had 'found a whole lot of wonderful cousins who practically own the province of Senora'.[47] Then in mid-Janury 1964 she returned to New York, where she was said to be 'magnificent and getting on with her painting'; and where she received a further present from Robert Graves, a copy of Idries Shah's newly published *The Sufis*.[48]

Reading Shah's words in cold print was a very different experience from hearing him talk, and to begin with Robert could not help being professionally disappointed by the poor quality of the writing, 'as if I found the village carpenter using an out-of-date and awkward hand adze instead of an electric plane'.[49] To which Shah replied that had it been his aim to project a personal image, or to make a plausible case for Sufism, he would naturally have done 'a suitable processing job on the material, making it both more acceptable and "better written" '. But of course his purpose had been to 'decondition' people, and to prevent their 'reconditioning'. So he had had to avoid writing too 'well'.[50]

Graves so much wanted to believe Shah that he swallowed this explanation; though he did so with some difficulty, as it went against a lifetime's devotion to the craft of writing,[51] a devotion shared by an old friend with whom he had recently been spending much time. Diccon Hughes (whose *The Fox in the Attic* had been an international best-seller[52]) had been staying with his wife at the Posada since 13 January; and 'most afternoons' had been walking up in the mountains 'with Robert for 2–3 hours; and Sundays [we] go further afield'.[53]

Robert Graves had good reason to be grateful to Diccon for the attention he had lavished on Robert's children by Nancy Nicholson; and the two men were equally devastated when Robert received the worst possible news about Jenny. On Wednesday 5 February, when staying with friends in Wiltshire, she had suddenly collapsed. She was rushed to hospital, but died on Thursday without regaining consciousness.[54]

Jenny's death sent a shock wave through a wide circle of family and friends-journalists. Martha Gellhorn for example (on the verge of a divorce from Tom Matthews), would write from Kenya to tell Robert:

> it's all wrong, that people who have so much life should untimely die. You must be sick with grief; I cannot think of anything worse than having one's child die before one, and such a child too. Oh Robert, what is there to say; I can't imagine anything consoling, Jenny was life-loving and life-giving and a pride and joy to you, and now she is gone, and there's nothing anyone can say to make that easier to bear.[55]

Patrick Crosse flew back from his current assignment for Reuters in South Africa;[56] and Rosaleen arranged for the funeral service to be held in a 'little ancient chapel, attached to the mediaeval almshouse' in Salisbury. As she reported to her brother John,

> Nancy was terribly shaken. But we all felt it a blessing that her (congenital) cerebral aneurysm hadn't burst in Africa – or somewhere equally remote – nothing could have saved her – but at least we know she had every possible care & knew nothing of death. She had packed her 45 years so full, that she'd lived more than some people of 80.[57]

She added that: 'Robert's passport was out of date, so he couldn't come; but I don't think he could have faced it anyhow. He didn't come to mother's funeral you remember.'

William was present as Robert's representative both at the funeral and, the following day, at the memorial service held in London at St Bride's, Fleet Street. One of Jenny's former colleagues paid tribute to her 'special and golden talent for being able instantly, yet always with grace, to get near to any human being with whom she came into contact ... As a reporter', he added,

> she had immense *attack*: when she went to cover the illness of Satchmo Armstrong the trumpeter, she wasn't content to remain outside waiting with rival reporters; she at once became Satchmo's Press Officer. When she covered a communist coup d'etat in the republic of San Marino inside Italy she at once became personally involved with the fate of each of its 13,000 inhabitants: she made personal friends with its leaders: one can be quite sure that neither the Captains-General who governed it nor the Communist guerrilla leader, a stonemason called Hercules, would have dreamed of making a move without first letting her know.

'In the Rome office', he went on, 'her enthusiasm for what she was doing was irresistibly infectious. It caught up those around her, especially the young, and gave them the courage to give their best, as she did. She always put astonishing vigour into all she did. She staked all at every throw.'[58]

Jenny had certainly triumphed over the very considerable troubles of her early life. Her father would say that she had been a good woman: a just comment; and in the course of writing this biography I have come very much to regret never having known this cousin who suffered so much, and became so wise.

As a memorial to Jenny, Robert decided to start work on transforming *A Song for Sheba* into an historical novel, as he and Jenny had planned. The idea particularly appealed to him because, as he told Idries Shah: 'the story is so very close to all that I have been thinking about, with Emile and yourself, about the ideal relations between real man and real woman, which the present ethical set-up delays and distorts'. He intended 'to make it ... as close to your own traditional Sufi thought as possible ... I am certain that the Moslem legends of the Soloman-Sheba relationship are of the utmost importance'.[59]

In the meantime, however, Robert had a lecture tour for which to prepare; and in the third week of February he set out for New York. For once he had no idea where he was going to stay. Not with Gordon Wasson, who the previous year had found it hard to understand Robert's emotional problems with Margot, and even harder to cope with his Sufi mysticism. Nor, for some reason which remains obscure, with Len Lye. But no matter: Robert counted on Emile being in New York and, as he told Shah, 'your sister will find me a pad somewhere'.[60]

CHAPTER 3

Talk of Leaving

When Robert Graves arrived in New York on 22 February 1964, he was met by Aemile Laraçuen: she had added the A to her first name after her recent journey to Mexico.[61] She had also arranged for Robert to stay with John Benson Brooks, the musician whom he had met back in 1960, and who would have composed the music had *The White Goddess* film ever been made. John and his wife Peggy had just moved into a house in Greenwich Village, and were 'happy to offer [Robert] our small spare room', where he stayed for the next nine days.[62]

Aemile's presence made it an exceptionally happy time for Robert. She looked on admiringly as he lectured to 'wonderful audiences'[63] at the City College, and appeared on radio and television programmes: for one of which he and Raphael Patai were jointly interviewed about *The Hebrew Myths*, which was due to be published in March. Aemile was also introduced by Robert to Alec Guinness, whom they saw more than once;[64] and through John Benson Brooks, the poet and his Black Goddess not only attended a jam session, but also met and 'made friends with the top-ranking, wildest and therefore shabbiest-looking jazz musicians'.[65]

Robert was now ecstatically in love. He had already written a poem in which he and Aemile enter 'the seventh heaven':[66] which turns out to be:

> a green castle
> Girdled with ramparts of blue sea
> And silent but for the waves' leisured wash.
> There Adam rediscovered Eve:
> She wrapped him in her arms.
>
> An afterglow of truth, still evident
> When we had fallen earthward,
> Astonished all except the born blind.[67]

And he would soon be telling Idries Shah that he and Aemile 'have had extraordinary experiences of the strange healing power that seems to affect people when we enter a room together'. He added that it was 'a sobering experience, because we can't claim to know how it happens or even to take credit for anything except the strength of our personal bond'.[68]

That bond seemed of such overriding importance to Robert Graves that for the first time in the twenty-five years since he had fallen in love with Beryl, he began seriously to contemplate leaving her. His lengthy discussions with Aemile[69] were the prelude to an article on 'Real Women' which he wrote for the *Ladies Home Journal*, in which he declared:

> The most important historical study of all, utterly dwarfing all economic and political ones, is for me the changing relationship between men and women down the centuries – from prehistoric times to the present moral chaos in which both sexes have become equally confused about their roles.[70]

He still believed, as he had stated when writing *The White Goddess*, that modern civilization was travelling down a blind alley towards its destruction, and that 'a calamitous collapse' was necessary 'before a new start can be made – from the point where the sex war was first declared and women's conservative instinct as the guiding force of humankind repudiated'.

Graves added that womanhood remained incomplete without a child, and therefore most real women would marry. The fact that they preferred 'simple, affectionate husbands who cannot understand them' was not, however, a renunciation of real love, since they agreed with the thirteenth-century Countess of Narbonne that: 'Conjugal affection has absolutely nothing in common with love. We say "absolutely", and with all consideration, that love cannot exist between husband and wife.'

Fortunately, in view of this chilling dictat, Beryl Graves had maintained an inviolable sense of her own private identity,[71] and a secret inner life comparable to that of Gamel Woolsey, author of the lines:

> You twist and shape me to your will,
> I bend to all the moods that pass;
> But I am proud and secret still,
> And but more truly what I was.[72]

Understanding Robert as well as she did, Beryl nobly overcame any natural feelings of anger or jealousy, dealt privately with whatever pain Robert caused her, and managed to survive and keep her family together. She understood the forces which drove Robert's life as a romantic poet; and she knew that it made no sense to describe his actions in terms of a Christian morality to which he no longer subscribed. In his own terms, he had remained a deeply moral human being; and until he lost his heart to Cindy, her own position was never under threat. Now however (with her youngest son still only eleven years old,) she knew that she faced a major crisis.

On their way back to Deyá at the beginning of March, Robert Graves and Aemile Laraçuen stayed in Madrid with Ava Gardner. 'What a splendid-mad and crazy-fine time', Aemile wrote afterwards,

> Four days of go-go & booze & flamenco. [Ava]'s kind-hearted as hell and I don't know who's got more energy she or I but it was all night life at its swingingest. Robert dropped 40 years and moved with us. Landing here was a thud for both of us. We're still trying to adjust to sheep bells. Also *COLD* ... so I'm getting progressively more surly.[73]

Aemile had been installed in the house that she had shared with Ralph the previous year. Twice a day, Robert would join her either there or at the café; and before long, as she explained in a letter to Ava Gardner on 19 March, she was beginning to feel in an extremely awkward position. 'I don't know what is going to happen', she wrote when she was alone one afternoon:

> Robert keeps talking of leaving Beryl – and is getting *more* in that direction. But somehow it pains me because it would mean his giving up a lot of roots – 30 years – and I know I wouldn't take the good and excellent care of him that she does. I've told him and all he says is that he doesn't want to grow old the way she wants him to & so on. He should pay more attention – *all* attention to her – and she might bloom ...[74]

But then Robert arrived, all charm and loving concern; and only an hour later Aemile wrote Ava a second letter, in which she announced that she was sitting by the fire, 'awaiting a roast chicken Robert has prepared. Oh hell – I simply can't write today but my heart keeps impelling me to do so ... I've been so bored and depressed here except when Robert comes walks into the room. He's sun – verdad.'

By now, Robert had decided that he and Aemile were at the forefront of a revolutionary change in the relationship between men and women; and in 'Iron Palace' he wrote:

> We stood together, side by side, rooted
> At the iron heart of circumambient hills,
> Parents to a new age, weeping in awe
> That the lot had fallen, of all mankind, on us;
> Now sealed as love's exemplars.

As for Aemile: when she was alone, she continued to be depressed: with the result that she was frequently high on dope or LSD; and then she would tell her friends that her relationship with Robert meant nothing to her.

However, there was also a great 'striving and yearning' in her 'for higher things';[75] and when Robert was present, she found life so exciting, with so many amazing vistas opening up, that she longed to share it with him for ever; and at length, knowing how much he wanted to live with her, she even talked to him about the possibility of their being married. This led to Robert's poem 'Batxoca', which begins with a formal description of Aemile:

> Firm-lipped, high-breasted, slender Queen of Bean-stalk Land,
> Who are more to me than any woman upon this earth
> Though you live from hand to mouth, keeping no certain hours,
> Disguising your wisdom with unpracticality
> And your elusiveness with hugs for all and sundry,
> Flaunting green, yellow and scarlet, suddenly disappearing
> In a whirlwind rage and flurry of skirts, always alone
> Until found, days later, asleep on a couch of broom
> And incommunicable until you have breakfasted ...

But although Graves too is tempted by marriage, he knows that this would destroy what is for him the most valuable part of their relationship; and so he writes:

> By what outrageous freak of dissimilarity
> Were you forced, noble Batxoca, to fall so deep in love
> With me as to demand marriage, despite your warning
> That you and I must on no account be seen together –
> A Beanstalk Queen, no less, paired with a regular man!
> Did you wistfully, perhaps, expect me to say 'no'?[76]

The complications multiplied; and Aemile must have been relieved when after a few weeks the time came for her to fly back to New York, where she had arranged 'to show her mother the World Fair'. The plan was for her to come back to Deyá in May;[77] but as soon as she had left Robert's side, all her doubts about their relationship intensified. She stopped answering his letters, and made no plans for her return flight.

At first, Robert had no idea that anything had gone wrong; and in any case he was busily occupied with writing his next set of Oxford lectures: 'using the Oxford Book of English Verse as an example of the current views of poetic craftsmanship', he told Diccon Hughes on 30 April. 'And brother, *does* it stink.' He also had a new building project in hand. Earlier in the year he had bought two derelict houses just opposite the new museum, and now Bob 'Waldron and four indigent painters' were hard at work on their restoration.[78]

The Hugheses had been superseded at the Posada by Alan Sillitoe and Ruth Fainlight, who had briefly coincided with Aemile;[79] Mary Allen had reappeared for a brief visit and was said to be 'wholly with us'; while Graves believed that one or two of his new poems had 'a quality of compactness and certitude' which stemmed from his love for Aemile. Because although 'on the everyday level' Aemile was 'unpredictable and even scatty, on the durable level she's as firm as a rock; so I don't worry about how and what and when'.[80]

There was still no news from Aemile towards the end of June when, as he told Ava Gardner, Graves was 'just off to give my ridiculous [Latin] Oration at Oxford';[81] but while he was in England, he managed to get through to her on the telephone. Without specifying exactly what had happened, she told him that she had been through a bad time, but that she would fly out to Palma the following week. 'She will never hurt me', Robert reported to Ava Gardner, 'now that she knows where she is; has hurt herself too much when she doubted the inevitable.'[82]

Shortly after returning to Canellun, Robert Graves received a letter from Idries Shah which pleased him, since he took a quotation in the letter as 'a telepathic comment' on his earlier distress about Aemile's silence; and in the same post there was a loving letter from Aemile to whom, as he told Shah, he therefore cabled the quotation 'as your blessing'.[83]

However, a second letter from Shah made him realize that he had been wrong about the first. The fact was that Shah, recognizing that Robert's relationship with Cindy/Emile/Aemile Lee/Laraçuen was almost certainly doomed, had begun to distance himself from the whole affair. His two letters to Robert were therefore utterly bland; and to the second,

Robert replied testily: 'No: I don't want news-letters or formal letters about *The Sufis* book ... You answered my letters without answering them; silence would have been better.'[84]

Aemile had clearly made an appeal to Idries for help or advice which had fallen on deaf ears, for Graves added that she had been 'in great distress, and if you had stood by her as was your duty as a brother you would have saved her and me from a great deal of pain'. He also told Shah, who had obliquely reproached him for courting popularity, that he had 'recently decided to cut out of my life everything that is no longer alive and sound; it will be a long process'. So if he went to Oxford to deliver his lectures that autumn, it would be 'only in case there are a few live people there; I went there once as a young man and have a debt to pay. Soon it will be paid.'[85]

At this stage, Robert Graves still imagined that Aemile would be arriving back in Deyá within a few days. Instead, she remained in New York; and to his anger and dismay he heard early in July that she had returned to her former lover Howard Hart, and that they were seriously thinking of getting married.

Graves immediately issued 'an ultimatum: that she must honour her sworn pact with me and break this suicidal re-affair with Howard, or never be able to make magic again or paint or face herself in a mirror'; and he wrote to John Benson Brooks telling him:

> It's funny, but all the five women I have loved in my life all betrayed me, in turn, in favour of a third- or fourth-rate poet! Because, I suppose, they could not live up to the responsibility of the truth they themselves conceived. I still trust Cindy to break the pattern. She is my greatest & last love, & she knows it.

'Poets', he added, 'die honourably at the gates of Hell; but I had thought I had died enough in my long life. Cindy was the first woman who ever loved me wholly; & still does. Why do they *do* these things?'[86]

Only two days later, Graves's optimism was once again in the ascendant, and he wrote a further letter to John Benson Brooks, telling him: 'Something seems to have happened yesterday, Saturday, to change the Cindy situation. Don't know what, but I feel calmer & more confident that she will come through, & not destroy herself.'[87] He also made overtures to Idries Shah, telling him that he felt 'very close to you again from being laid up with a twisted back and reading *The Sufis* undisturbed'.[88] The village was full of friends; and the play that year was *To The Lighthouse*: nothing to do with Virginia Woolf, but a murder mystery based on the assassination of Ringo Starr, and including among its suspects Bill Waldron and William Graves, who sang:

> I'm a Sufi, Aren't we all?
> Goofy Sufi on the ball
> In our mystic dreams it seems
> That wisdom comes to call.[89]

Graves told Shah with some relish about the 'couple of Goofy Sufis whose caricature you would like';[90] and before long his good humour was completely restored by a letter from Cindy/Aemile in which she made it clear that Howard was no longer around; that she was sorry to have missed Robert's birthday party; and that she hoped to be joining him in Deyá in the near future.[91]

First came a visit from Ken Tynan. A former drama critic, Tynan had been appointed Literary Manager of the National Theatre by Sir Laurence Olivier the previous year;[92] and now he broached the idea of Graves 'revising the text of *Much Ado* for the National Theatre, replacing dead similes, archaisms and words of changed meaning with living Elizabethan words and images'.[93]

Despite having once revised Dickens and received a critical beating for his pains, Graves showed real interest in revising Shakespeare; and on 20 August, having returned to London, Tynan reported that he had:

> discussed this at length with Olivier. He likes the notion, though he wishes the play were one of the less intelligible Shakespeares so that you can rewrite the whole thing! Before signing a contract he wonders if you will consider revamping a specimen act for him to look at. In the hope that you will, I am enclosing a script in which I've marked the bits I personally find dead and/or unclear … [94]

Tynan's other news was that, after only fifteen months of marriage, Mike Nichols was 'separated from Margot', who was left with the responsibility of looking after their baby daughter, and 'sends you his best'.

This news was rapidly overshadowed by a letter from Aemile: a letter which, as Robert described it to Ava Gardner, was 'stained with tears'. After booking her flight to Palma three times, she:

> now says she can't: doesn't want to break up my life here and feels that she is too impractical and unpredictable to make our permanent togetherness a success because – she says – I am a perfectionist and like

a routine she can't easily provide. This doesn't *hurt*, because she admits that she remains inseparably bound to me in soul; & I have told her now that I can't accept this separation until she has come here & faced things personally.[95]

In a letter to Ralph Jacobs, Graves added that Aemile had flown to Nice instead of Palma, though why it should have been Nice, he had no idea, and had since 'gone to a village called Moulinée Alpes Maritimes'.[96]

Ralph replied that 'Emile or I should say Cindy' had gone to Nice simply because the plane had landed there. 'From what I could learn up until the time she left', he went on, 'she had intentions of going to Deyá. Being torn and confused she could not tell you that it was with Howard.'[97]

CHAPTER 4

The Trouble with Howard

When Ralph Jacobs told Robert Graves in September 1964 that Aemile Laraçuen had once again returned to Howard Hart, he attempted to soften the blow by adding that:

> Pity in its various disguises can often be stronger than love at least temporarily. I have no doubt she will be in Deyá soon to make it right with you. A right decision never carries with it the anguish Emile has suffered. Visiting cathedrals and hurried night-calls to priests [Howard was a Roman Catholic] is not the meat of which she is carved, but it may be one of the un-needful experiences she must have before redemption.

'Money' he concluded, 'can often keep a weak situation together but not for long. What will happen when the gin money runs out?'[98]

Ralph's view was confirmed to some extent by a further letter from Aemile, who wrote miserably telling Robert 'about her unavailing efforts to ditch Howard, the fights the violence. Nevertheless', Robert reported to Ralph on 13 September,

> she insists on [Howard's] perfectibility and can't make up her mind to return here. She hasn't collected my letters and cables from Nice wonders whether I wrote … Oh well we continue to hope but I have told Emile she is close to the point of no return. In her letter she says she would curl up and die if she thought we would never be together.[99]

To which Robert Graves had 'cabled c/o American Express Nice that in that case we had better act quickly'.

However, there was no reply either to this cable, or to the stream of further letters and cables which Graves sent to Nice during the last two weeks of September; and it occurred to him that Margot had 'done a great deal of mischief in representing the very different time between herself and me to Emile. At first Emile did not trust her', he told Ralph; but 'lately she has come out in her defence.' The result of this anxiety, he added, was that he had gone through a 'psychosomatic period', during which he had fallen and injured his knee; and had also developed a cyst on his elbow. The knee injury had been minor; but the cyst had required an operation, which had left him feeling 'sick and incapacitated'.[100]

Robert had also suffered from nightmares 'of violence ... with curiously accurate detail. Lilac dress. Emile. Howard with a big knife screaming.' In the circumstances it had been impossible for him to write any poems, though he had 'forced myself to work on my lectures for October'. He concluded that Aemile's 'spiritual struggle seems incurable'; and if she reappeared in the States, Ralph should 'tell her that she has a lifetime to make amends in, and will need all that, if she hopes for grace and peace'. However, he hoped that she would remain in Europe for the time being: in which case, all might still 'be settled for the best'.[101]

In the meantime, Isla Cameron had spent a week at the Posada with her friend the brillant young actress Maggie Smith who, like Ken Tynan, worked for Olivier at the National Theatre. 'I can't believe that a whole week has passed', Maggie Smith wrote afterwards,

> but it certainly has. Getting back to work has been hideous. Too many plays to work on and all at once ... I'm looking forward to seeing you in Oxford. We will be at the New Theatre when you are there so perhaps you will have time to see the plays. I think it's *Master-Builder* which is a bit stodgy and *The Recruiting Officer* which is great fun.[102]

Tynan himself had written on 16 September, after receiving a sample of the revised *Much Ado About Nothing*, to say that he was 'bursting with gratitude for the speed and thoroughness of your response. What a play-doctor you would make';[103] and then six days later he reported that 'Larry has now read your *Much Ado* and I'm glad to say that he agrees with me. We'd both like you to go ahead and finish it. If I may, I'll hang on to your text for a day or two, because Franco Zeffirelli – who's directing the play – wants to look at it.'[104]

At the beginning of October, Robert heard at last from Aemile, who had finally visited the American Express offices in Nice and collected a huge bundle of his letters and cables. In her reply, as Robert told Ralph Jacobs, she 'sounded more paralysed than ever; but she insists that she must be rid of her incubus'. Robert wrote again, suggesting that she should 'cable a rendezvous' for mid-October, when he and Beryl would be passing through Paris on their way to London, and enclosing money.[105]

This had the desired effect. Before long there was a friendly cable from Aemile.[106] When Robert and Beryl reached Paris on about 13 October,[107] she telephoned them; and a little while later, as Robert reported to John Benson Brooks, 'there she was. We had of course so much to say that we didn't: it wasn't necessary. Anyhow, felicity is here.'[108] After this reconciliation between her husband and his Muse, Beryl went on to England alone, leaving Robert and Aemile to spend a few days together in Paris.

Robert was happy again; Aemile was 'looking marvellous'; and the two of them spent much of one day discussing their future with Idries Shah's brother Omar Ali-Shah, another Sufi who was then in Paris. 'No plans made', Graves explained afterwards to Ralph Jacobs, 'except that we don't intend to plan, but to play by ear and be careful to keep the same people.'[109]

On 19 October Robert and Aemile travelled to London, where Aemile was installed at the house of Sonja Guy, an attractive air stewardess in her twenties, who had lived in Deyá in her late teens, and had gradually become one of Robert's confidantes.[110] Robert then went to Oxford, where he and Beryl shared a flat not far from St John's;[111] and where on Tuesday 27 October he delivered his first lecture of the season,[112] a closely argued dissertation on the subject of poetic craft.[113]

Just over a week later, however, Robert Graves was back at Sonja's from where, in a letter to Ralph Jacobs, he damned his lectures as 'totally unimportant'. It was Aemile who was 'the centre of my thoughts', and he knew that 'nothing will ever separate us not even time and distance'. He added that Beryl was 'great';[114] but in fact, as he explained to Selwyn Jepson, their relationship was more troubled than ever.

The problem, as Graves saw it, was 'the natural discrepancy between poetic and historic reality'. He was 'fated to be a poet', but the nearer he came to what he really meant,

> the greater the opposition from those who love me in another sense altogether; such as my immediate family. And even those who refuse to take sides, do so really. It's no fun for anyone. But I can't let go.

His new poems were 'all they should be'; but he knew that:

> this can't very well be offered in mitigation of what seems to others shameful behaviour on my part – Beryl of course doesn't agree with the

judgment but she and Aemile can't meet on sisterly terms having nothing in common except what divides them; and the same basic goodness. I have to keep the two lives separate, which is difficult. And both women behave blamelessly, which allows me to make no choice.

He added that Aemile 'has too good a heart, rather than too grudging a one'; and that she was 'embarrassed, annoyed, surprised, and infuriated sometimes to find that she and I both get sick and paralysed and psychosomatic whenever we try to break this fatal bond between us – which is rarely sexual and then only because one can't cheat the body'.[115]

Aemile for her part found that their days in London together were highly stimulating. 'Any disguises', she told John Benson Brooks,

were taken off and we *really talked* & I don't mean irrelevant earnest conversation but of speaking from the very core of one's world, Freedom, and so you can see that it was wonderful and that we won't roast one another with demands. It's amazing how *much power* flowed and still does and will continue. The last few days we were double-winged birds.

They also had 'good celebrations': especially on Hallowe'en night, when Aemile wore 'a jazzy black chiffon from the 20s' which Robert had bought for her in Portobello Road; while Robert himself:

felt so good that he painted his face black, filled a small box with bones, got a wand and cast spells. He got everyone relaxed in the candle-light by saying since it was Halloween they might as well have witches' names, 'good witches', he added – then since they had witches' names they should practice pretending ...

And before long, 'you never saw so many witchy people': one of whom was soon so far gone that she 'had turned into her broomstick'.[116]

In more serious moments, Robert persuaded Aemile to design a dust jacket and four full-page illustrations for the 250 copies of *Love Respelt*. This little volume, containing facsimile copies of the manuscript of thirty-two of Graves's latest poems, was to appear the following summer in time for his seventieth birthday. Each poem was about Robert's relationship with Aemile; and several school her in her duties. In 'Son Altesse', for example, Robert tells her that:

Alone, you are no more than many another
Gay-hearted, greedy, passionate noblewoman;
And I, alone, no more than a slow-witted
Passionate, credulous knight, though skilled in fight.

Then if I hail you as my Blessed Virgin
This is no flattery, nor does it endow you
With private magics which, when I am gone,
May flatter rogues or drunken renegades.

Name me your single, proud, whole-hearted champion
Whose feats no man alive will overpass;
But they must reverence you as I do; only
Conjoined in fame will we grow legendary.

Should I ride home, vainglorious after battle,
With droves of prisoners and huge heaps of spoil,
Make me dismount a half-mile from your door;
To walk barefoot in dust, as a knight must.

Yet never greet me carelessly or idly,
Nor use the teasing manners learned at Court,
Lest I be ambushed in a treacherous pass –
And you pent up in shame's black nunnery.[117]

The emotional pressure was once again building up, and Aemile developed an attack of eczema on her hands.[118] Then early in November, she set out at Robert's expense for Paris, ostensibly on her way to begin a working holiday in southern Spain, and therefore supplied with much fresh painting gear.[119] Robert himself withdrew to Oxford, where on Tuesday 10 November he delivered his second principal lecture of the season.[120]

Later that week Robert and Beryl took a party of family and friends, including their daughter Lucia, in her third year at St Anne's, and their nephew Richard, in his first at St John's, to the New Theatre. There they watched Sir Laurence Olivier in George Farquhar's classic comedy *The Recruiting Officer*. It was a memorable evening. Olivier owned the stage from the moment he set foot upon it; and afterwards he and his wife Joan Plowright, together with Maggie Smith and several other members of the cast, joined Robert and Beryl and their guests for a buffet supper.

Graves and Olivier clearly recognized each other as equals. Disdaining the use of chairs, they sat down side by side on the floor, and began an animated conversation. Olivier looked utterly relaxed. ('He's utterly relaxed' murmured an aide in a dark suit, who had been fussing round Olivier before being politely shooed away.)

Later on, Sir Laurence entertained the party with stories of his theatrical life: such as the occasion when he had been due to make a speech at a reception in Moscow. Well in advance, he had told the official interpreter that he wanted to say a few words in Russian:

'I want to thank you all' – quite simple – the fellow looked rather surprised, but he coached me parrot-fashion. Then came the reception. A glittering occasion. I made my speech, and said the words in Russian. Total silence – then riotous applause! A tremendous success! Couldn't understand why.

Then he found out: 'The fellow hadn't understood me, do you see. I hadn't said 'I want to *thank* you all. I'd said 'I want to take you all to bed!'

Graves's third lecture, given on 24 November, was attended by two more guests. 'Ava Gardner, J. R. R. Tolkein', said Robert as he introduced the famous actress to the author of *The Lord of the Rings*. 'I'm afraid you won't have heard of each other': which was true. The lecture itself was chiefly interesting for its revisionist view of Keats and his muses. Now that he preferred the Black Goddess to the White, Graves had decided that the most important Muse in Keats's life was no longer Fanny Brawne but Isabella Jones, an earlier source of inspiration of great 'beauty, character, judgment and taste', who was also 'wise and generous'; while Fanny was decried as 'a coquettish *Belle Dame Sans Merci*, who gave him little but pain'.[121]

Afterwards, there was a party with Ava Gardner at a Chinese restaurant. 'What fun we had!' Robert Graves told her a few days later. He added that Aemile had 'vanished again as she has a habit of doing at full moon – gipsy-like, much affected by the season – and may now be back in N.Y. But we remain always on each other's hooks.'[122] In fact, unknown to him, Aemile had remained in Paris, where she had resumed her affair with Howard Hart. It was only when this too ran into difficulties that she consulted Omar Ali-Shah who, as Graves reported to Ralph Jacobs, sent her back to London at the beginning of December 'with frayed nerves'.[123]

Aemile's reappearance was made all the more satisfactory when she explained that the trouble had been her sense of loyalty to Howard; but that 'in the end', as Robert explained to John Benson Brooks, Howard had come through and unselfishly approved her union with me. She still grieves for him as a lonely have-not; while knowing that another attempt to live with him would be disastrous. The I-Ching [a Chinese book of divination] warned her so often this summer, but she would not listen; now she realises that she can't avoid her fate.[124]

Robert was persuaded to write Howard a letter 'apologising ... for having thought ill of him';[125] and he soon found himself in the 'high, careless, felicitous mood', in which on 6 December he recorded an episode of the BBC television series 'Muses with Milligan'.[126] This was a show in which Spike Milligan 'appeared between various poets and singers':[127] so Robert Graves read out some poems; and then his song 'Mend Them Fences' was sung by Annie Ross in a jazz setting[128] by John Benson Brooks.[129]

After the recording, Robert Graves and Aemile Laraçuen dined with Spike Milligan and his wife Paddy at the Matelot restaurant in Pimlico. Robert later recalled that Aemile 'rather spoilt things' at one point 'by getting high and refusing to leave';[130] but he and Spike Milligan immediately became the best of friends.[131]

'To think', Robert wrote to Spike just a few days later, 'that I nearly turned down that *Muses* TV show on the ground that I need neither fame, nor money, nor voice practice.' Getting to know Spike and Paddy had been 'a GREAT EVENT in world (or other-world) history; so Aemile and I agree'. He added that he was about to fly back to Deyá; but that he and Aemile would be reunited in February in New York; and he ended with an open invitation to stay at the Posada, saying that previous booking was usually unnecessary: 'if I'm there – I'm learning from Aemile to be unpredictable, so maybe will be in Mexico or Afghanistan if you don't look out'.[132]

This enigmatic remark carried a definite meaning. In a recent poem, 'Between Hyssop and Axe', Robert Graves had written:

> To know our destiny is to know the horror
> Of separation, dawn oppressed by night:
> Is between hyssop and axe, boldly to prove
> That gifted, each, with singular need for freedom
> And haunted, both, by spectres of reproach,
> We may yet house together without succumbing
> To the low fever of domesticity
> Or to the lunatic spin of aimless flight.[133]

And Robert was now seriously thinking about leaving Beryl and 'housing together' with Aemile in Mexico. On 14 December, he wrote to John Benson Brooks with the news that:

> What happens next I don't *exactly* know but the plan is to go off somewhere together where we can live sensibly & undisturbed and think out the problems of love & poetic reality together: and record our findings. Beryl raises no obstacle.[134]

The same day, Graves asked Selwyn Jepson a little plaintively, 'Why was I born so *thrawn?* Certain things make no possible sense; but like the impossible (statistically) chance, these things befall me; nor am I dishonourable in my ways'; and he added that after his forthcoming visit to America, 'Dr Nostradamus, peering through his two-way mirror, merely remarks "O".'[135] But then once again (after professing 'complete togetherness up to the last moment')[136], Aemile completely disappeared from view.

Robert Graves had bought Aemile Laraçuen a ticket so that she could fly to the USA on 16 December 1964. The plan was that she should go on to Mexico for Christmas, and then return to New York, where her mother would stay with her in her Charles Street apartment until Robert arrived.[137] But towards the end of the month, Robert told Ralph Jacobs that Aemile had been 'playing fast and loose for almost a year now. The closer we come in spirit, the more erratic her movements become.' He had written a great many letters to her New York address, 'but no reply. She may be in Mexico or still in Europe.'[138]

Then at the beginning of January 1965 Robert heard, and he told a mutual friend that the news had shocked him severely,[139] that immediately after his departure from London, Aemile had asked Howard to follow her to London and stay with her at Sonja's.[140] Soon afterwards came reassuring news from Aemile herself: she wrote to Robert telling him that she had rejected Howard again, and that she would soon be in New York.[141] Once again, however, silence followed.

This behaviour, as Robert complained on 15 January 1965, was typical! When Aemile behaved in this manner, he told a friend, she felt so guilty that she could not write to him, let alone let him know where she was. It was devilish! He had no idea of her whereabouts, but supposed that she was at Howard's side. What was so dreadful, he went on, was that Aemile knew that Howard's company harmed her, and that her actions were giving pain to Robert himself. But her self-protective response was to pretend that it was somehow his own fault! The whole situation was also deeply painful to those who cared for them both; and Robert concluded miserably that it was all quite insane, since Aemile so often admitted that he was her greatest *amour* – as Aemile was his.[142]

But within three days of writing this despairing letter, Robert Graves heard from Aemile once again. Apparently she had experienced her 'final flare-up' with Howard, and was now in Paris where she was 'recovering from things'. She added that before leaving London she had been enrolled as the 'spiritual sister' of Alan Sillitoe and Ruth Fainlight; and she told Robert that he had been a witness, since she had 'signed' with a Byzantine ring that he had given her.[143]

Robert, who had 'been pretty low for weeks' until receiving this letter, wrote excitedly to Alan and Ruth telling them: 'A corner has been turned at last and I think now I understand exactly what's remained unsettled between (Aemile] and me ... Anyhow, we find that our bond resists even atomic explosions. Like the beer on Christmas Island.'[144]

Ruth Fainlight went over to Paris for a few days to visit Aemile: 'They get on well', commented Alan Sillitoe, 'and find lots to talk about';[145] and then on 24 January Aemile flew to New York.[146]

CHAPTER 5

To Seek Felicity

Robert Graves was delighted to hear from Ralph Jacobs of Aemile Laraçuen's safe arrival in New York; and on 29 January 1965 he sent Ralph a long letter in which he told him:

> The historic facts are unimportant and the great thing is to keep historical or factual truth from getting mixed up with poetic truth. The poetic truth is that Aemile and I get closer and closer; the factual truth has been that mistiming impatience and external accident has long kept us apart except for a few miraculous occasions.

He explained that Howard has 'written me that he's now utterly through with "Cindie" and thinks that I'm the only person who can do her any good'; and, far more important, that;

> Beryl accepts the fact that her and my ordinary husband and wife life can never be resumed and urges me to seek felicity in Aemile's company ... For both Aemile and me, Deyá is a holy place, necessary to us. Yet Beryl has never really felt its enchantment and would be just as happy elsewhere – but for the animals and for the use of Canelluñ as a centre for our children! She neither likes nor very much dislikes Aemile, who loves her ... I love her too but with the steady affection she shows me; not with the miracle-working love which joins Aemile to me at our highest level, and which when thwarted by separation becomes a poltergeist –
>
> My closest friends assure me that all will be well, that Aemile (now that she is free at last from Howard) is sure to find the solution; and that whatever it is, everyone will accept it as the right one. I am worse than useless to Beryl as things are; she is ready to do whatever makes me really happy – though naturally dubious of Aemile's power to keep me so. –

Graves added that he had 'been sick for a month and was 'anxiously awaiting Aemile's letters'; but he was also 'confident that our love must eventually be proved in a permanent togetherness; and any time she wounds me, she wounds herself equally'.[147]

More news of Aemile reached Deyá early in February from James McKinley, an American historian who had become friendly with Graves, and who now told him that he had visited Aemile in New York, where she appeared to be in good health, and emotionally on an even keel, though she talked a little strangely about Spain and Morocco.[148] Robert replied that he had heard from Aemile about their meeting. Her strange talk was easily explained: neither of them felt happy if they were away from Majorca for too long; while it was in North Africa that Idries Shah thought of establishing a community. Graves added that he hoped to arrive in the U.S.A. not long after McKinley received his letter.

Graves then explained that although he was lecturing,[149] his chief aim was to spend some time together peacefully with Aemile. He realised that they had lost contact with each other as ordinary human beings, even though they could not help remaining close together in some more extraordinary realm. He had no idea how they would manage to live together in practice; but the experiment must be made, as they could not live apart. He added that when Aemile had learned to harness the blazing, golden quality which was in her, she would produce something remarkable.[150] His other news was that his adaptation of *Much Ado About Nothing* was to go ahead as planned at the National later in the year; but sadly it was ahead of its time, and not at all well received.[150]

Then on 10 February[151] Robert Graves flew to New York,[152] leaving Beryl feeling extremely uncertain about whether he would ever return.[153]

Graves was still in New York when he told Karl Gay that: 'My life is so changed that I don't know how to write, really.' He then explained that he was 'not going to write any more books,' so he had no more need of a secretary; but he intended to provide Karl with enough capital:

> to work elsewhere, either in Spain or England ... *Don't worry*; just think well of me and consider *yourself* and your family. There's no hurry! An epoch has ended and what comes next is bound to be good if we realize that we are all in each other's hands, in a way.

Besides delivering this bombshell, Graves told Karl that he was:

going with Aemile ('Cindy') to Mexico for a fortnight. Difficult for me to mention her name to you, because though you at first liked her, her friend Ralph insulted you, so you sheared off; and perhaps had other reasons. Anyhow, our fortunes, hers and mine (as you must have realized) are curiously linked together ... if it were a simple love-affair I should agree with everyone that I'm a fool. But it's not that in the least. Patience! ¡*Calma*!

'How this will affect my life in general', he concluded, 'I don't yet know; but we are each on the other's hook and any attempt to unhook causes psychosomatic trouble.'[154]

Exactly what happened next remains shadowy; but Robert Graves and Aemile Laraçuen left New York together in mid-March,[155] and travelled down to Mexico.[156] Later that month, Robert sent a postcard to Peggy and John Benson Brooks from Puerto Vallarta, telling them:

From waiting in the sleet for a cab 15 minutes on 7th St. to this ambience is more than 7 flying hours: a whole lifetime. We had a mad time in Mexico City and are now getting brown on the Gulf ... No plans but unceasing felicity.[157]

Then on 9 April he wrote to them again, this time from Mexico City, saying that Aemilia (as she had now become) had remained in Puerto Vallarta, with 'something to find out still'; and that she and he were 'closer than we ever were, but ... on such a high plane that our 2 bodies are left way behind, which distresses both of them'. He added that he 'must make my peace with Beryl & see if we can start again as new people'; and two days later, on 11 April, he reappeared alone in New York.[158]

Spike Milligan was informed simply that 'the story is horror-fiction ... the necklace broke, the beads spilled';[159] But Ruth Fainlight, as Aemilia's 'sister', received a fuller account. She learned from Robert that Aemilia: 'went wild and behaved scandalously ... At least I saved her from running off with a delinquent young enough to be her son (easily)'. At one point, when Aemilia had:

gone off to a place where there was no mail, and did not answer my letters when she returned and had decided to marry another, rather sweet man (but another *perdido*) – who promptly went off elsewhere with someone else's wife.[160]

Robert had then received a cable from William announcing that he was about to be married, and asking whether the Posada was free. The Posada had of course been promised to Aemilia; but in her absence Robert replied simply asking William whom he was marrying, and agreeing that he could use Aemilia's house. He then wrote to Aemilia telling her what he had done; and soon afterwards, leaving her 'wads of cash among the group of American expatriates always high on pot – not', he told Ruth, 'that I have aught against pot', Robert 'came quietly away'.[161]

From New York, Robert Graves wrote on 14 April to Karl, telling him that he seemed to be 'beyond' writing; and that, although it was 'impossible to explain', his 'preoccupation' was not a love affair, but 'something so way-out there's no definition possible. It ends my literary life. What happens next I'm waiting to see. I'm returning to Deyá alone.' He added that he had not 'turned mystic. Nothing vulgar like that: only an extraordinary awareness of reality and a sort of prophetic and therapeutic possession. Sane as ever.' And in a postscript, he wrote: 'My life at Deyá was beginning to stink. I had to get out and think.'[162]

Two days later, Robert set out for Majorca.[163] Curiously enough, he was seen off at the airport by Margot Nichols, who told him that she had been 'tailed by detectives for the last year by her husband, who doesn't want to pay her too high an alimony … If … she showed … [more] … generosity', Robert declared, 'how happy she could be! But her father', he added unkindly, 'was a peasant from the S. Peleponnese.'[164]

When Robert Graves reached Deyá, Beryl greeted him casually, and with no recrimination, as though his absence had been quite unremarkable, and his return fully expected.[165] 'Mexico was a furnace fire', Graves would write to Spike Milligan, 'and here I'm back in the domestic frying pan once more: but it's a kindly one: most kindly.'[166]

But despite Beryl's kindliness, it was not long before Robert Graves had begun to believe that he and Aemilia Laraçuen might still have a future together. On 5 May he told Ruth Fainlight that 'if (as motor-cyclists say) she can get out of her "roll" and back on the highway, it will be a miracle. Nevertheless, miracles occur';[167] and shortly afterwards, writing to Spike Milligan, Graves told him that it was 'just possible' that by the summer, 'Aemile will have recovered from her Mexican craziness … and be here, clothed and in her right mind. Alas, I miss her cruelly.'[168]

All Robert's correspondents were sympathetic, and none more so than Ruth Fainlight, who told him that:

just about the time when you were in fact leaving Mexico … [I] dreamed you had left Aemile in order to save yourself. Since that dream I have had several others: that is, not dreams so much as Aemile herself, her desolation and unhappy presence, manifesting to me ... I am glad you have come out alive.

She added, 'I cannot accept that she is lost forever. Lost to herself, I mean.'[169]

CHAPTER 6

Lure of Murder

Early in June 1965, Aemilia Laraçuen suddenly reappeared in New York City. Spike Milligan, who at Robert Graves's request had written to her address in Charles Street,[170] received 'eight explosive pages in which one could almost *hear* the writing', telling him that she had 'managed to get nailed on a narcotics charge (all a mistake of course)', and had 'spent time in some lousy jail in Mexico'.[171]

Now that she was free, Aemilia also reopened her correspondence with Robert, and sent him a letter encouraging him 'to get up and out'. However, as Robert explained to Alan and Ruth, he replied that he was 'no Tolstoy to die at any railway station':[172] Canelluñ remained his home and he urged Aemilia to visit him in Deyá in July to celebrate his seventieth brithday.

Partly because she was short of money, and partly because she still yearned for the spiritual enlightenment which, as the Sillitoes had observed,[173] she hoped that her poet could provide, Aemilia agreed. This put Robert in a cheerful frame of mind: as Philip Toynbee found when he arrived in mid-June to write a profile of him for the *Observer*.[174]

Their sessions together were not very productive. 'It's [Toynbee's] chance to get drunk', Graves explained to Selwyn Jepson, 'and when he's drunk he forgets my answers to his questions.' But what did it matter? Graves was too happy to care;[175] and one morning he told his guest that:

'I'm enjoying myself all the time. I'm always in love; there's never been a moment when I wasn't in love. Look at this photograph!' The girl was very beautiful. 'That's the girl I'm in love with just now; and I've written all my last poems to her … I'm writing a fantastic amount of good poetry just now – must keep it up.'[176]

The following day, Toynbee went with Graves into the village, where most of the '100 foreign artists of one sort or another' appeared to accept:

Señor Grav-és as the legitimate emperor of the place and pay him a fitting tribute. He receives this gaily, and enjoys it. A few of the colonists, as I learned later, are a little resentful of the imperial atmosphere – perhaps because they themselves had received too little favour from the Emperor; perhaps, as they claim, because they are too proud to bend their knees.

At any rate, Toynbee felt certain that Graves was 'a real poet who has lived for his poetry and not for any tribute which may be paid to him because of it'. And if his court 'were to evaporate tomorrow', Graves 'would miss them for their company and feel, for a moment, a little sad at the loss of their tribute'. But 'then he would go on writing poetry'.

Everything connected with Graves continued to be news; and towards the end of June, BBC Television screened 'The Epic That Never Was', Bill Duncalf's enthralling documentary, narrated by Dirk Bogarde, in which the surviving rushes of Alexander Korda's film of *I, Claudius* were pieced together. The genius of Charles Laughton in the title role was amply demonstrated, while Graves himself, who had been filmed in New York looking astonishingly youthful, commented that 'a beautiful dream was ended because Claudius just didn't want it'.[177]

July saw the publication of Graves's *Love Respelt* with Laraçuen's drawings;[178] and when James Reeves wrote asking Robert whether, at the age of seventy, he had learned what poetry was all about,[179] Graves replied that he knew more than he did:

namely the impossibility of reconciling the solar with the lunar calendar though every hundred years (if one is lucky to see it) a full moon exactly coincides with the Summer Solstice: or almost. Those coincidences are all that really matter; plus the refusal to die while still alive, or to fudge and fluff when seized by a poem. Or to pity oneself, or deny oneself faith in the coincidence.[180]

And as evidence that he himself was still alive, he enclosed a new poem. *Loving True, Flying Blind*, in which he asks with some satisfaction:

> How often have I said before
> That no bland 'if', no 'either-or'
> Can keep my obdurate male mind
> From loving true and flying blind?

> – Which, though deranged beyond all cure
> Of temporal reason, knows for sure
> That timeless magic first began
> When woman bared her soul to man.
>
> Be bird, be blossom, comet, star,
> Be paradisal gates ajar,
> But still, as woman, cleave you must
> To whom alone endures your trust.[181]

A day or two later Aemilia arrived in person to obey this summons;[182] and so at the beginning of August she was present at the wedding party for Lucia Graves and Ramon Farran.[183] John de St Jorre was also there; and during the festivities Aemilia asked him to join her for a talk with Robert. So they walked through Canelluñ and into his study, where they found him sitting at his desk.[184]

St Jorre found something magical about what followed. Aemilia appeared 'very wise and sensitive' in the way she handled Robert; and this in turn 'brought something out' in Robert: some quality of unselfish and very loving concern. 'She was marvellous', St Jorre would say, still recalling the scene vividly after almost thirty years, 'and he was gracious.' St Jorre found what it was like to be welcomed, however briefly, into Robert's innermost circle, and it was a heady experience: not least because he and Aemilia were encouraged to talk at length about themselves: something that was particularly valuable to John, since he had recently quit the Foreign Service, and was uncertain about the future direction of his life.[185]

However, emotions had already been running dangerously high in Mexico. It was now difficult, perhaps even dangerous, for Robert and Aemilia to be at close quarters for too long. Ruth Fainlight had been justifiably relieved when Robert had 'come out alive' from Mexico; and Robert had recently written one poem, 'Strange Jewel', in which he asks:

> What do you fear: My hand around your throat?
> What do I fear? Your dagger through my heart?[186]

And another, 'Lure of Murder', part of which runs:

> I crouch among rocks, scanning the gulf, agape,
> Whetting my knife on my horny sole.

Alas for the lure of murder, dear my love!
Could its employment purge two moon-vexed hearts
Of jealousy more formidable than death,
Then each would stab, stab, stab at secret parts
Of the other's beloved body where unknown
Zones of desire imperil full possession.[187]

In the circumstances, it was not surprising that Aemilia's presence in Deyá caused little but trouble.

First with Beryl. She said nothing openly, but she could not help blaming Aemilia, justifiably or not, for the fact that Robert had returned from Mexico carrying marijuana. Had he been caught, it would have had a serious effect upon his reputation. She had also realized for some time that, although Aemilia was good company and liked helping people,[188] she was also the first muse who had seriously threatened Beryl's own position at Canelluñ.

Next with William. Although Robert Graves had been happy for William and his new wife Elena to move into the Posada on a temporary basis at the time of their wedding, he had always intended that the Posada should be Aemilia's home. But when he suggested that they should stay on as Aemilia's guests, Elena was outraged. 'I'm not living in the same house as my father-in-law's mistress', she told William;[189] and he in his turn told Robert first that they had no intention of being Aemilia's guests, and second that they were not going to leave the Posada.[190] Robert therefore began to feel as though William and Elena had misappropriated his property.[191]

Since they were in possession, there was little that he could do about this; but he began coming into the Posada and telling his daughter-in-law that several items of furniture (two in particular) really belonged to Aemilia. At length Elena, an intelligent woman who was deeply scandalized by her father-in-law's behaviour, put a table and a few chairs out into the street, where they sat unclaimed for several days until she retrieved them again.[192]

Such open hostility, as Robert later recalled, made 'trouble between Beryl & me & Ae';[193] and one disagreeable incident led to another.

For example: because Aemilia could not move into the Posada, she stayed instead with the Waldrons, and told them how William had, in her view, mistreated her. So one evening William and Elena were dining with some friends at a café in the village, when a drunken woman friend of Aemilia's staggered up to William and told him: 'You son of a bitch: you'll pay for this!' To which he replied calmly: 'I think you've been drinking too much. We'll talk tomorrow.' But the next morning, it was Robert who came round to the Posada at eight in the morning to tell his son that he would have to ask forgiveness. Not surprisingly, he met with a firm refusal.[194]

The situation at Canelluñ became increasingly impossible. William and Elena would go round for afternoon tea, and find that Robert and Aemilia were downstairs while Beryl was upstairs lying on her bed, determined not to come down from her siesta until Aemilia had left the house.[195] 'It was war', William and Elena recalled years later. 'We turned our back on [Aemilia] if we saw her. The marriage was close to breaking-point.' And, in their view, Beryl was hanging on 'because of Tomas'.[196]

On top of these severe personal difficulties, Robert heard that he had 'been (temporarily at least) ruined by the arrest of my Swiss agent (for counterfeiting) who controls all my copyrights & money and owes me about £7,000. That's a laugh', he commented philosophically in a letter to his nephew Simon Graves on 30 August. 'One shouldn't have so much for a man to embezzle.'[197]

'You got away just in time: money-wise I mean', Robert told Karl Gay, who had now found fresh employment as Curator of the Poetry Collection at the University of Buffalo. 'When I can repay you I will – BUT not only have I been robbed of 30,000 bucks but I can't get any new money in, because it legally still has to go through International Authors, although this company has no funds and its sole director is in jail and unable to sign anything.'[198]

In the meantime, Aemilia was once again finding that the emotional strain of being Robert's Muse was almost unbearable; and after a while she could only cope by reverting to the excesses of her days as Cindy: which involved becoming increasingly unpredictable, taking a great many drugs, and giving wild parties.[199]

A month later, however, Graves and Laraçuen were once again the best of friends; and while he worked at his final series of Oxford lectures, she sat 'on the other side of [his] inky table'[200] drawing portraits of him, and writing to Peggy and John Benson Brooks to tell them that 'Everything has been up and down – that's life – right now it's UP!'[201]

To celebrate the improvement in their relationship, Graves (who thought of himself as 'Sun-like in his maleness and heroic pride', while Laraçuen was 'ruled by the Moon'[202]) wrote 'The Near Eclipse':

Out shines again the glorious round sun –
After his near-eclipse when pools of light
Thrown on the turf between leaf shadows
Grew crescent-shaped like moons – dizzying us
With paraboles of colour: regal amends
To our own sun mauled barbarously
By the same wide-mouthed dragon.[203]

And when on 12 October Aemilia flew to London to stay with Sonja, Robert could tell Selwyn Jepson that 'all our troubles and tensions had completely disappeared. No practical solution either found or looked for; but that doesn't really matter. We are tied in a Staffordshire knot together.'[204]

With Aemilia's departure, the atmosphere at Canelluñ lightened a little, and Beryl told Cecily Gittes: 'It's been difficult to write this year – everything has been difficult in a way and I feel as though I've been walking on a tight-rope for too long. Anyhow we survive one way and another and there have been some good things.'[205]

But then on 18 October, Robert and Beryl followed Aemilia to London, where Beryl completed her preparations for a journey to Moscow, and Robert saw something of his Muse before she flew to New York. There Aemilia intended to resume her painting, and also to prepare a drawing for the title page of Robert's latest project, a limited edition of *Seventeen Poems Missing from 'Love Respelt'*.[206]

Once both Aemilia and Beryl were safely on their way abroad,[207] Robert travelled to Oxford, where on 26 October he delivered the first of his final set of lectures as Professor of Poetry at Oxford.

CHAPTER 7

Sagacious Friend

Professor Graves had discussed the delivery of his lectures with Aemilia Laraçuen earlier in the year; and he later explained that it was on the advice of 'a sagacious Mexican friend' that he had decided to give his last three lectures 'as conversational talks': a change to which he attributed the way in which his audience swelled 'from four hundred to six, to twelve'.[208]

But it was not so much the conversational nature of these final lectures which attracted larger and larger audiences, as their content. Here was a world-famous poet who was clearly speaking from the heart about his most personal experiences. The result, despite Robert's flat and un-polished delivery, was that the respectful silence which greeted the start of one of his lectures would deepen and intensify to such an extent that the slightest amusing aside would be greeted with roars of appreciative laughter.

In his first 1965 lecture, Graves spoke at length about the nature of the poetic muse; and he was clearly talking about Aemilia Laraçuen when he did so. 'Poetic love', he declared,

> is uncalendared, and a woman's capacity for Musedom cannot be measured by her ethical virtues, or by her intellectual powers, or by any of the qualities that make a good wife, mistress or secretary. The sole proof will be that the poet has responded to a magic of her own without which his poems would have remained sterile.

And since all social virtues were now associated with complicity in the anti-magical State, the Muse was most likely:

> to have had 'a difficult home background' where patriarchal control has broken down. She will be passionately proud of her womanhood and of her latent powers, ready to bestow love, but unwilling to risk

humiliation at the hands of any would-be husband, and wildly shying away from the least threat of male possessiveness.

As for her poet: he was likely to be reproached for:

celebrating someone without constancy of direction, tenderness of conscience or recognised social background, rather than standing by a nobler, more predictable, other woman whose fixed devotion to duty should earn her the highest eulogies.

'But solid virtues', Graves lamented, even when 'tempered with intellect and loyalty to social convention, yield no poetic inspiration.'

He added an autobiographical aside: that the poet's service to his Muse was governed by the same pride:

of 'bearing it out even to the edge of doom' that sustains a soldier in the field ... It is not masochism, or even stupidity, but a determination that the story shall end gloriously: a willingness to risk all wounds and hardships, to die weapon in hand.

For a poet this defiance was, of course, 'metaphorical: death means giving in to dead forces, dead routines of action and thought'.

Sadly, there was 'no solution in time, to the problem of love; only in timelessness'; and true love was 'often discovered after one of the lovers, or both, has become involved in marriage, or taken a religious vow, or become otherwise inaccessible.' In that case, as he knew from his own experience, each would be 'tempted to accuse the other of not sacrificing everything to their single cause'; and 'the miracle of true love – the *duende* that heals and enlightens any company into which a fortunate pair of lovers strays' would become 'a dangerous poltergeist that causes physical sickness and accidents'.

However, hope remained. The *duende* could be sustained in its healing aspect, provided that the lovers' home never became 'a mere machine for living ... It must at least', he told his audience, 'be a centre where other lovers come calling with their excitements, troubles and discoveries. And if the married pair can, by some miracle, preserve each other's freedom of action, avoiding any drudgery of planned routine, neither face need fail to light up at the sight of the other's after the briefest absence.'[209]

Graves returned to these themes in his second lecture;[210] but in his third and final lecture, given on 23 November, he roamed through very different territory, giving his views on, for example, pop-art, pop-poetry, the effect of drugs, and the nature of heaven and hell. Pop-art and pop-poetry were both savaged: pop-art because standards had 'collapsed when non-figurative expressionism helped the art dealers to impose fictitious values on whatever wares they could buy cheaply, sell dearly, and the output of which they could control';[211] and pop-poetry for its reliance upon readings to mass audiences. The poems recently declaimed by a group of Beat Poets at the Albert Hall were described as 'deliberate acts of rebellion against the rules or principles that control written verse'; and Graves declared that such 'ultra-modern poetry' was written 'under the influence of marihuana, alias "pot" ' which, though 'occasionally beneficial in its effects', had nothing to do with genuine creativity.

By contrast, LSD and other psychedelic drugs could stimulate creativity; and Graves's opinion was that 'a single "trip" – and the hallucinogenes are not habit-forming – can under proper medical control be most informative'. However, psychedelic drugs needed to be chemically pure; and should only be taken 'in a state of grace, which is a state of love; otherwise the mind may find itself naked and lost, out of touch with native circumstances, and frequently suicidal'.

Finally, Graves declared that although he could not 'honestly deny' an interest in the survival of his poems, he had no hope or wish for an afterlife. Scientifically, he understood that 'the one eternity acceptable to the brain' was 'the very last second of human consciousness – because the mind cannot consciously put an end to it'. This last moment, 'which one either dreads or longs for', must therefore be 'the sole endless Heaven or Hell'; and if he himself died in a state of grace, his own 'timeless paradise' would be 'the secret garden of the woman I love best'.

It had become customary after Robert Graves's Oxford lectures for him to give a drinks party for forty or fifty friends in St John's. The previous year one of these parties had been graced by the presence of the beautiful thirty-three-year-old Irish novelist Edna O'Brien, who had met Robert through their mutual friend Isla Cameron; and after Graves's final lecture, the principal guest, apart from College and University dignitaries, was Richard Hughes, looking with his red face and grey beard very like a retired sea captain.[212]

Beryl was still in Russia; while Robert himself, as he would soon be telling Pam Matthews, Tom's third wife, was chiefly conscious of the presence of his 'sagacious Mexican friend'. He and Aemilia, he explained to Pam, were separated by the Atlantic, But Aemilia knew:[213]

> that after the lecture there would be a party for him, and she [had] made him fix the precise time when he would be lifting a glass of

champagne to drink her health, promising that she would do the same. And at that very instant, said Robert, a glass leapt from the table and shattered itself on the floor.

'What power!' he marvelled. 'With 3,000 miles between us. Imagine what the air must be like when we are face to face!'

CHAPTER 8

Withering Heights

Flying back to Majorca on Thursday 2 December 1965,[214] Robert Graves carried with him an interesting new commission: the rewriting of *The Unquiet Mind*, the autobiography of the same Dr William Sargent whose *Battle for the Mind* Graves had rewritten some ten years previously. 'Never', Robert told his niece Sally Chilver, with whom he had been staying while in London,

> was such good material so grossly mishandled; but it will turn out a real whacking book & sell 1/2 million copies. The effect will be to give the young people something to *march* against – especially in the U.S.A. – namely the diabolic treatment of the deranged in modern mental hospitals.[215]

Robert also informed Sally that he had become a grandfather again, with the birth on 6 December of William and Elena's son Philip. He added that Beryl was 'enthusiastically a grandmother. We fadge together well, & sleep contentedly alone: a new phase, which allows me transcendental dreams untroubled by scratching & whining poodles and the use of my own cooling & heating system.' As for Aemilia: she had 'written nearly twice a week – a record – very calmly, very amusingly, very lovingly and has done a cover for my new poem book which Selwyn is looking after; & will be busy working in a men's shop for the Christmas rush'.[216]

Graves had not yet recovered his copyrights, so money was still short and by Christmas, as he told Selwyn Jepson, he had decided that he must sell the two semi-derelict houses that he had bought in Deyá the previous year. This was extremely awkward: partly because Bill Waldron had done a good deal of repair work on both, and was actually living in the one which had been converted into a library, and so would have to be compensated; and partly because William also wanted 'the money from the sale of the houses for buying him a partnership in Majorcan Wimpy

Bars!! No Graves has ever gone into trade!' Robert protested, 'Besides I owe half the money (or more) to Karl ... '[217]

Robert added that he was continuing to have difficulties with William, whom he complained was 'playing the heavy father since the birth of Philip & accusing me of corrupting the village!' However, William soon dropped the Wimpy Bars idea; and Robert told Selwyn Jepson that he was comforted by Aemilia's letters – and by his discovery that her name 'means *Work* in the sense of poetic enchantment not only in Arabic but in ancient Irish – Odd, A?'

Selwyn Jepson replied on 1 January 1966 with the encouraging news that 'the *17 Poems* project' was 'being very adequately and honestly handled by [Anthony] Rota and the Stellar Press. You will see that it should give you £400 clear.' The only difficulty was that Aemilia's decoration was

> only reproducible in photogravure which just wouldn't on a title-page or anywhere else match the rest of the format in design or price for that matter so I have written to her today asking if she can contrive a line drawing instead that can have a block made of it, at the same time explaining the technical difficulty of the first one.

Jepson believed that Aemilia would take this in her stride, since in her letter accompanying the drawing he had sensed 'some dissatisfaction ... I think she feels it is over-solid for the idea she was after: a fragmentising sun design which could also be stars', and branch out 'into moon, night, dreams, earth'.[218]

Graves, on the contrary, feared that Aemilia would be seriously disturbed by the request for a new drawing. 'It nearly killed her to do it', he told Jepson.

> and she may be too upset to attempt another. She was sure I'd like it. Oh hell – I'm afraid she'll fly off the handle ... If this leads to another nervous upset, I'd rather not publish it at all ... The money side is of infinitely less importance to me than her [state of mind] at this juncture.

He explained that Aemilia 'has been riding out a very difficult situation in N.Y.; and any deterioration in her condition naturally affects me'. However, Graves had hit upon a possible medical explanation for Aemilia's mood swings, and he declared that he had:

> diagnosed Aemilia's case as one of *hypo-glycaemia*: when within four or five hours of a meal one's blood-sugar-level falls below the necessary

level and in the resultant imperfect control of one's mood one does thoughtless and violent things of which one has only a patchy memory afterwards.

The remedy, he had learned, was regular meals; but although Aemilia was 'dimly aware of this she can't be bothered and the worst excesses come late at night when supper is long over; and she *always* wakes in the morning with a foul temper. I have told her about it now.'[219]

Selwyn Jepson replied on 12 January that he had 'halted the project' at once, pending further news from Aemilia; but he also asked Robert whether he might not be:

worrying too much about her health? Her letter to me was one quarter about the drawing and three quarters about food and cooking, asking for recipes and saying she was trying her hand at wholemeal bread baking ... You may well be right however about a degree of hypo-glycaemia. It's extremely common and we all suffer from it more or less ... I would say that Aemilia's interest in food is a healthy reaction to her particular share of the deficiency.[220]

Fortunately by 16 January Selwyn had received a 'happy letter' from Aemilia, 'with a new drawing which she says she likes better than the first one – it certainly looks technically more easily reproducible (one sixth of her letter is concerned with it, the other five-sixths with food and cooking)'.[221] Robert replied that he was 'immensely relieved' by this news, especially as Aemilia 'had just sent me one of those self-destructive letters, but it was soon followed by a repentant cable pleading fallen sugar-level'.[222]

At the beginning of February, Graves wrote again to Jepson, to tell him that despite having just spent a week in bed, he was quite cheerful, having received three letters from Laraçuen which were:

all splendid and noble. One day we will learn to be as present in each other's company as *in absentia* ... Our mutual readiness to die for each other at the drop of a hat hasn't yet enabled us to live with each other at the raise of a hat; which is odd.

In the meantime, he had decided to make 'no plans at all for the year, but try instead 'to fix my principles still more firmly'.[223]

Making no plans went against the grain; but Graves was determined

not to frighten Aemilia away. 'Though constantly invited to go over to the
States to lecture', he told Ralph Jacobs,

> I don't want to seem in pursuit of Aemilia – and she must have time to
> do some *work*, which cures people, so long as it's work nobody else in
> the world can do: she and I are such snobs about that! And so proud of
> each other too!'

Robert added that he had 'never been so at ease in my life'; and he was
certainly feeling relaxed enough to repair another of the friendships
which had been broken during his years with Laura Riding.[224]

It happened like this: Edmund Blunden, with whom Graves had
quarrelled over the factual truth of *Good-bye to All That*, had been elected
as the new Professor of Poetry at Oxford, having defeated Robert Lowell
by 477 votes to 241.[225] Shortly afterwards, Graves was infuriated by a
letter in *The Times* of 8 February, in which Stephen Spender declared that
he was glad of Blunden's election, but that Lowell was 'the most brilliant
and original and serious poet of his generation'; and that, as the inheritor
of the modern tradition initiated by Eliot and Pound, Lowell would have
been elected had the undergraduates been allowed to vote.[226]

Incensed by this defence of a modernism which he had spent so long
trying to discredit,[227] Graves, whose letter was published on 16
February, declared that 'Mr. Robert Lowell is a personal friend of mine,
but Dr. Enid Starkie gauged the University's feelings accurately in
sponsoring Mr. Edmund Blunden's candidature.' The 'modernist revolution', 'directed mainly by American expatriates in London and Paris
against the English poetic traditions', had been entirely misconceived;
and where Mr Lowell's work was tainted with 'modernistic overtones',
Mr Blunden always kept 'close to the English tradition which is still
infinitely diversifiable'.[228]

Graves also sent a personal letter of support to Blunden, who replied
that he was:

> moved and gladdened by a letter from you. That I was so editorial ages
> ago about your war chronicle has not pleased me much in later days.
> But I must beg for one thing: do not finally condemn your war poems of
> the 1915–16 vintage. I think I have said this in print.

'They do not seem to me to coalesce into a protest', Blunden added, 'but
they are most original.'[229]

In the meantime, Robert Graves was conducting a voluminous

correspondence with Aemilia Laraçuen; but as the weeks went by, the difficulties of conducting a long-distance relationship with someone so volatile began to make Robert feel ill. 'Our bond is so unreasonably & excessively powerful', he told Selwyn Jepson on 21 March,

> that it confuses all ordinary relationships, and she does her best to make it as impossible as she can, and she feels correspondingly guilty. She loves to expend sweetness on you as her true friend without committing herself to me.

'I have no idea', he concluded miserably, 'when she and I shall meet again, and refrain from making any plans.'[230]

By now, Graves was suffering from an 'acid stomach';[231] and by 9 April his diet had been reduced to 'mainly rice & shredded apples & magnesia', though he declared to Jepson that he still felt 'very happy ... mainly because something nameless happened between AE and me, at a distance (we don't know quite what) that solved all our problems – though leaving us without any plans!'[232]

Eventually Graves became worried enough about his ill health to have some X-rays of his stomach taken and sent to George Simon in London; but Joanna replied from Drayton Gardens that her husband could see no organic disease, though he had suggested that someone should do a gall bladder X-ray.[233] 'I wish it would stop', Graves told Jepson: 'really I suppose it's suppressed tension caused by AE.'[234]

This tension can only have been increased by a letter from John Benson Brooks. 'Requested and commanded' by Robert Graves to take Aemilia Laraçuen out to lunch and report on her condition, John wrote on 6 May that after agreeing to meet for lunch one Thursday, Aemilia had actually arrived 'late Friday afternoon (having just gotten out of bed)'; and although she was looking 'better than I have ever seen her', she was also talking 'about a re-birth and LSD'. Worse still, she had declared that her reason for not travelling to Mexico was that 'Howard is so great now.'[235]

Although 'plunged' into 'gloom', Graves was soon convinced by further letters from Aemilia and 'from others close to us both'[236] that she was continuing to behave 'well'; and he was carefully giving her every incentive to do so. For example, she was continuing to write at least two letters a week: but was that entirely due to her love for Robert and her thirst for enlightenment? 'Half my writing', Robert Graves had told Selwyn Jepson on 20 April, 'is letters to Aemilia: one day they'll be printed. I've given Aemilia the copyright and she'll use it honourably.'[237] So although Aemilia may not have been aware of this, every time she colonized Robert's heart with another declaration of love, a highly profitable trade was following the flag.

Another major incentive stemmed from Graves's negotiations with Southern University, Illinois for the sale of some manuscripts. At first they had refused to buy, since he had included no poetry; but, as he explained to Sally Chilver, when he also offered them 'the work-drafts of my poems to AE for about six months [500 sheets], this raised another 8000 dollars! *And* sold the prose.' And with this extra $8,000, he bought a house in the village for Aemilia[238] – who had soon announced her intention of travelling to Deyá sometime in the summer.[239]

When Graves told Selwyn Jepson of his purchase, claiming that it was perfectly fair to lavish money on Aemilia 'since all the poems were addressed to her', he added that it was a house which Aemilia already knew and loved,

> and she's so happy she can hardly sleep. And her work is going on marvellously ... so when she takes possession as a householder, not as a vacationer-tenant, her whole attitude to Deyá will necessarily change, as getting into her *real* work is at last made possible.[240]

He did not foresee any serious problems with his family. Ralph Jacobs had already been told that:

> All love, if it's real, is reconcilable with other loves, so long as one doesn't give away what belongs to someone else or take what belongs to someone else. The only problem is *exactly what belongs to whom*. It's so easy to claim semi-ownership of a person while forfeiting the right to do so by a refusal to love acceptably; and so hard for the other person to dispute the claim without seeming mean.[241]

Robert believed that Beryl would 'wait & see what happens'. The only potential difficulty, in his view, was that William and Elena treated Aemilia 'as a leper-colony of one person'.[242]

However, Robert was determined 'not to go to war' with them. Their latest project was to become local hoteliers; and so on 14 May, their opening night at C'an Quet[243] (the hotel-restaurant where Margot had once worked), he brought along 'nine people ... including Ramon & Lucia & the Sillitoes & Simon Gough, and had to pay ... This I did', he told Sally Chilver, 'without a flinch; but my Irish reaction was at once to cancel all Lucia & Ramon's debts to me for the original *Indigo* set-up,

because they have always entertained me free *and* my friends with true
FLAHOOL'.[244]

In mid-June, Graves flew to London, where he stayed with Sally while he
made several public appearances. The first of these, billed as 'a New
Moon Carnival', was the very type of event which he had ridiculed in his
final Oxford lectures the previous year. However, he had put his trust in
Jonathan Boulting, a charming young poet who had flown to Majorca
specifically to ask him to 'open the celebrations';[245] and he was pleased to
hear that Spike Milligan had also been persuaded to take part.[246]

But when Graves and Milligan arrived at the Royal Albert Hall on the
evening of Saturday 18 June,[247] they found 'a hopelessly confused
situation backstage ... and the ensuing show was a shambles'.[248] The
audience (described by Michael Horowitz, one of the poets taking part, as
full of 'demoniac energy'[249]), began barracking. Christopher Logue,
another performer, later protested that it was 'very moderate barracking';[250] but Graves, who was accustomed to respectful audiences,

> startled everyone by challenging them to either shut up and go home,
> or meet him round the back. 'I may be in my seventies, but I can take
> the pair of you on, if you like,' he said ferociously. Astonished, they
> quietened down immediately and the concert, such as it was,
> continued.[251]

Graves read a few more poems 'to a most attentive audience';[252] but then
listened with 'obvious contempt' to those who followed him;[253] and he
was still more annoyed when he woke up on Sunday morning to find that
the press had labelled him 'Leader of the English Beat Poets'.[254]

On Sunday evening, there was an occasion far more to his taste. The
previous autumn, Bernard Miles had written deferentially to 'Professor
Graves' asking whether he would care to use The Mermaid Theatre 'to
do what you like with whom you like ... We could I am sure find beautiful
actors to read, singers to sing, players to play and even give you a little
cheque at the end of the day';[255] and soon they had agreed on a suitable
Sunday.[256] Spike Milligan, his wife Paddy and Isla Cameron were
recruited; as was Robert's thirteen-year-old son Tomas,[257] once Robert
had explained to Spike that Tomas was a guitar-player who had 'twice
sung talking blues to huge audiences of his own.'[258]

Graves was less certain about his own contribution. 'What can I do?' he
asked Spike Milligan. 'I have about 600 songs and a carrying voice. I can
tell stories, recite crazy poems, my own included, hold an audience by my

magnetic presence … BUT hate rehearsing or learning a part.' He added that Aemilia was 'agog to be present in the audience … but I don't know if she can make it in time from N.Y.' Milligan replied affably that Graves could 'Talk, read your own verse, sing any song you know or takes your fancy – read excerpts from your books, tell a joke, or just sit there drinking rose hip cordial '47 … Most certainly we won't rehearse!'[259]

On the night there was no Aemilia; but the show was an unqualified success. Graves, looking splendid in a startling brocade waistcoat with diamond buttons, and a red spotted neckerchief slotted through an ancient ring, sang 'Abide With Me' word perfect, in ragtime, and danced as well. Paddy sang light opera, Isla sang folk, Tomas played on his guitar, and then Milligan and Graves read selections from their poems. Adlibbing went on throughout the hour-long performance, which was then stretched to an hour and a half when the audience sat firmly in their seats absolutely refusing to leave.[260]

The following Thursday, Graves attended a Gaudy in Oxford as the guest of the Canon of Christ-Church;[261] and on Friday he flew back again to Majorca, where he continued to improve Aemilia's house, C'an Susanna; and to long for her arrival.

Soon after Robert's return, there was an unexpected visitor to Canelluñ: his nephew Richard, who had been hitch-hiking through Spain until, finding himself in Valencia, he had impulsively caught the night ferry to Palma. During the next few days Richard accompanied Robert several times to C'an Susanna. Usually his uncle seemed quite cheerful and business-like: there was china to be left, a solid wooden table to be placed in the dining area, and decorations to be decided upon; but once he looked very melancholy, and appeared to want just to sit in the empty house and savour its atmosphere.[262]

C'an Susanna remained empty that summer; and Ralph Jacobs nicknamed it 'Withering Heights' because of the thwarted passion which it seemed to him to represent.[263] 'At the last moment', Robert Graves explained to Selwyn Jepson on 30 July,

[Aemilia] got cold feet about coming – not wishing to face Beryl's 'it's none of my business I don't care one way or the other' attitude or William's frankly hostile one. She's got her own work to the 'bang-on' point, which is all that matters, & went to Mexico to mend her fences there … [264]

Robert added that he was 'Expecting her here soon'; and in the meantime (though this was a closely-guarded secret which not even Jepson was allowed to know for some months), he had borrowed money to buy Aemilia a cottage at Puerto Vallarta on the Pacific Coast.[265]

Graves continued to be plagued by ill health; and George Simon, who was in Deyá that summer with his family, became more convinced than ever that his friend had gall bladder problems. However, on returning to London, he wrote saying that he was personally opposed to the operation for which Robert was now pressing, as it was one 'from which haemorrhage can be fatal';[266] and Graves was pondering this advice when at the beginning of September he heard that Laraçuen too was ill, lying in St Vincent's hospital in New York[267] with what appeared to be hepatitis.

Graves immediately sent her funds so that she could take a special cure of which he had heard;[268] but it soon appeared that the problem was not hepatitis after all, but 'damage done her liver by some wrong tablets she took for sleeplessness'.[269] While Aemilia lay ill, Robert's gall bladder problems worsened; and on 17 September he told Selwyn Jepson that 'constant nausea nauseates me by its reminder of pregnancy'. He added that he was finding it 'very difficult to keep on an even keel when one is ill, and when one has too close a vibratory connexion with someone else at a distance, also ill, whom one loves'.[270]

As for the future: he was unable to see it clearly, but he recognized that the current situation could not be sustained:

> I can't remain like Issacher in Holy Writ – an ass between two loads of hay ... I think Aemilia has been trying to tell me that we must neither of us allow ourselves to be poisoned by the past: so her analogy between Howard & Beryl, though unfair in most ways, has some sense – Neither of them can change nature.

Graves concluded that it was 'all very "saddd"; as [Aemilia] says'; and the very next day he wrote to Sally telling her that he had definitely decided to have his gall bladder removed; and, more important, that his marriage had virtually broken down.

Robert conceded that Beryl was 'naturally worried' about him; but she could never bring herself to refer to Aemilia,

> in whose presence I live continually, and who lives in mine and shows no sign of marrying or choosing any other substitute to me and writes twice a week as a rule though she mails letters every ten days only. The animals get more numerous, demanding, and disagreeable and interrupt every plan or easy adventure.

'It is coming to a break', Robert concluded, 'for Beryl's sake really.'[271] But also for his own: Aemilia had admitted that she was once again 'seeing a lot' of Howard; and although she professed to feeling 'rather guilty about it',[272] Robert had realized that his time was running out.

On 26 October, Robert Graves flew from Palma to London, where he had arranged to stay with Sally Chilver for a few days before his operation;[273] and on the 28th, he telephoned Aemilia, who was out of hospital and back in her New York apartment. A curious conversation followed. At first, as Robert reported to Ralph Jacobs, Aemilia appeared to be 'so overcome by my phone call she could hardly answer'.[274]

Then he gathered that she was on her way to Mexico, and that she had written him a letter 'which *settles* everything ... her need of me all the time is apparent; so I'm going to her', he wrote from his hospital bed in St Thomas's the following day,

> and Beryl says that this should have happened long ago. Beryl has been suffering terribly from the waiting and sorrow and tension; as we all have. This will clear up everything; Beryl is really wanting to start being something on her own, not a mere housekeeper unpaid.[275]

Robert's adoration for Aemilia was now so great that it had merged in his mind with his adoration for his mother, whom he had begun to refer to not as Amy or Amalie but as Aemilia Graves.[276] He had also given Laraçuen one of Amy's brooches; and he was planning that after his American lecture tour in November, he would join her in Mexico 'where, she says, her house is eternally mine'.[277]

Soon afterwards, Aemilia Laraçuen's letter arrived. Written the day before she and Robert had talked on the telephone, it did indeed 'settle everything'. But, to Robert Graves's horror, it settled everything in what was, in his view, the worst possible manner.

CHAPTER 9

Closing Accounts[278]

The letter which Aemilia Laraçuen wrote to Robert Graves on 27 September 1966 told him that she was once again back with Howard Hart; yet in some ways it seemed to Robert to be 'very loving and romantic'. She wished, she told him, that they were separated by only twenty or at the most thirty years of age. She reproached him for not having run away with her, as he had once run away with Laura Riding. She also told him how much her mother loved Howard; and she added that she would still be Robert's, but for the accident of her having become ill in New York just when she had been about to set out for Deyá.[279]

In a state of shock, Robert picked over some of the details of her letter. Her comments about the age gap annoyed him, and he pointed out to Ralph that it *was* only thirty odd years which separated them; 'and the French law of marriages is half the man's age plus seven years i.e. 35 and a half plus seven equals 42, only two years too many. In four years' time it will be exact, and I'm seven years physically behind my real age.'[280]

About a week later a further letter from Aemilia announced that she was now in Mexico, where she was living with Howard in the very house in Puerto Vallarta which only a month ago she had told Robert was 'eternally' his. She added, as Robert told Selwyn, that Howard was, in her view,

the inspiration of her new work (it was myself who helped her when she wrote before) and that he is *fabulously* renovated and the first of all for her.

So I won't go to Mexico, but sit it out once more; this is the 4th time she's done it. Clearly this adventure will end again either in violence or jail or severe illness; but she lies beyond my protection until she realises what she is doing to herself. I should not like to be Howard ... when the combined thought of her friends concentrates on him.

Robert added that he had 'long dimly but unbelievingly suspected that this would happen'; that he found it 'rather macabre' in view of his having bought Aemilia the cottage when he had no money; and that it had been easy to write to tell her very gently that it would be a long time before she saw him again. 'Oddly enough', he remarked, 'I cannot give her up: my own soul would be in jeopardy ... all will end well.'[281] And John Benson Brooks was told 'Cindy has brief victories over Aemilia but this will be the last, I know.'[282]

Robert Graves's gall bladder was successfully removed on Monday 10 October; and he came round from the anaesthetic to find a sympathetic letter from Selwyn Jepson, who told him that he would wake up:

weak and no doubt somewhat miserable, but your sun still shining brightly, the moon gone [only] temporarily into the night where she belongs ... Proceed, therefore, to return to your accustomed good health as speedily as your will can drive you:

'which if I know anything about it', he concluded 'should be at a reasonable gallop.'[283]

Graves did indeed make a rapid recovery (though he was still nauseous for several weeks);[284] and he was soon sitting up in his blue hospital bedjacket,[285] and working on his latest project: a new translation into English verse of the *Rubaiyat* of Omar Khayyam.

Since there was already a memorable translation by Edward Fitzgerald, which had been well loved ever since it appeared in 1858, this was a risky undertaking. But Graves had been persuaded to undertake the work by his trusted friend Omar Ali-Shah, who told him that Khayaam, far from being the atheist Epicurean of popular belief, was a great Sufi poet and teacher; that Fitzgerald's translation was not only highly inaccurate, but also based upon questionable manuscripts; and that he could provide Graves with 'a crib' of an original manuscript which had been in his family since the twelfth century, and was called the Jan Fishan Khan manuscript after his great-great-grandfather.[286] Omar added casually that it had been 'available to Sufic students in Afghanistan since shortly after Khayaam's death'.[287]

It was about ten days after his operation, when Graves was hard at work on the *Rubaiyat*, that a further letter reached him from Laraçuen.[288] He described it to Ralph Jacobs as 'confused, loving, defensive, [and] carefully pacific'. In it, she declared that 'Howard was rehabilitated and wonderful, and had been responsible for her regeneration at work etc etc that she didn't want to hurt me but that I would be cruel to deny her this happiness'.[289]

This letter, though not very different from Aemilia's previous two letters, was the one which allowed Robert to bring their impossible relationship to an end. Writing to Selwyn Jepson on 23 October (the day that his stitches were removed), he explained that after Aemilia's letter (and with the support of Sally Chilver) he had felt obliged to tell her:

> that our outstanding accounts could now be settled – she could keep all that I had given her, though she would not now be wanting the Deyá house (for which payment is not yet made) and which I would reserve for her friends – I didn't say 'former friends' but it amounts to that – that if she was ever in great trouble she could ask me for help and it would be regarded as a further gift from the past ... That Howard was evil and her frequent returns to him had always been conducted with deceit and cruelty to me, and followed later by loneliness. That I believed in miracles, but not in *that* sort; nor had she given me the least evidence of any change in him. On the contrary, her timing of this default was particularly cruel ...

Robert added magisterially that if Aemilia ever wanted to return to him, 'it will be I who directs her; and as a teacher not as a husband or whatnot'.[290]

With his letter to Aemilia, he had enclosed what he described to Ralph Jacobs as 'a frighteningly Irish poem about the seven wards of Hell that she had laid open for herself by disowning the heaven she has so long shared with me.'[291] In it, he had written of the wards of horror which lay stretched before her,

> To brand your naked breast
> With impious colours,
> To band your thighs.

And he had asked:

> How can I discharge
> Your confused spirit
> From its chosen hell?
>
> You who once dragged me
> From the bubbling slime
> Of a tidal reach,

Who washed me, fed me,
Laid me in white sheets,
Warmed me in brown arms,

Would you have my cede
Our single sovereignty
To your tall demon?[292]

This is a recollection of both love and lust; but it conveys little of a deserted lover's anguish.

Indeed, in his letter to Ralph, Robert wrote very cheerfully about the 'wonderful' time he had experienced in his hospital ward with the 'sweet intelligent nurses', the 'wise walking patients', the hours spent on Omar Khayyam, and the visitors who had come armed 'with flowers, fruits and chocolates and champagne'. He added that he was not allowing himself to find a new focus: 'though, as you can guess', wrote this seventy-one-year-old, 'dozens of women are waiting to pounce on me when I am disengaged'.[293]

These and subsequent letters by Graves about his 'closing accounts' with Aemilia Laraçuen would sound, in the circumstances, quite uncharacteristically cheerful and robust to anyone who was unaware of a major and most unexpected change in his private life.

It had happened like this. Graves had been visited by the Simons: George, deaf and delightful; Joanna, warm and admiring; and their children Helena, Julia and Christopher. They had brought various gifts with them: apart from nineteen-year-old Helena, who had known so many happy hours in Robert's company that she had assumed her presence would be enough. When Robert cried out: 'What – my god-daughter hasn't brought me anything!' she felt humiliated and wretched. The spotlight of Robert's warmest interest moved elsewhere, as he turned to Helena's seventeen-year-old sister Julia, and gladly accepted her bunch of flowers.[294]

Julia, or 'Juli' as Robert called her, was sweet and attractive, but had constantly been overshadowed by Helena, who was both more intellectual and more classically beautiful; and now the sudden warmth of Robert's attention was overwhelming. The very next evening, she returned alone. A close family friend takes up the story:

She was seventeen, a student at the Royal Ballet School, innocent, inexperienced and beautiful.

Robert looked enquiringly at her. She said, 'I have fallen in love with you.' Robert was somewhat taken aback, but very moved. Some years later, he [recalled]: 'I said to her, well, I happen to be very sad at this moment because a woman I trusted and loved has behaved badly; perhaps it is intended that you are to be my muse.'[295]

Not long afterwards, Juli left the hospital feeling so full of powerful emotions that tears were running down her cheeks.

So by the time Robert Graves wrote that cheerful letter to Ralph Jacobs, he had already been 'pounced on', as he put it. And although his tumultuous relationship with Cindy/Aemilia was by no means over, the remainder of Graves's life as a poet would come to be dominated more and more completely by a young woman who would become the longest-serving and most benign of all his Muses.

BOOK EIGHT

JULI
1966–75

CHAPTER 1

Tousled Pillow

After their recognition of each other as muse and poet in a hospital ward at St Thomas's in October 1966, Juli Simon swore Robert Graves to secrecy about their new relationship;[1] but he was soon writing about her appearance on the scene in his poem 'Tousled Pillow', which runs:

> She appeared in Triad – Youth, Truth, Beauty –
> Full face and profile whispering together
> All night at my bed-foot.
> 					And when dawn came
> At last, from a tousled pillow resolutely
> I made my full surrender:
> 'So be it, Goddess, claim me without shame
> And tent me in your hair.'
> 					Since when she holds me
> As close as candlewick to candleflame
> And from all hazards free,
> My soul drawn back to its virginity.[2]

After leaving hospital on 25 October, Robert Graves spent ten days recuperating with the Jepsons at The Far House in Liss near Petersfield; and then he travelled to Deyá for a brief visit home, before flying to New York for the start of another successful lecture tour.

On his return to Canelluñ Graves wrote to Ruth Fainlight telling her that he was 'feeling well at last', and (more important), that Juli wrote to him regularly. Their love for each other, he told Ruth, was:

very strange: she has never lost her virginity. Of course there are two sorts of virginity – the physical and the spiritual. She has kept both. I have tried to keep the spiritual sort all my life so her feelings for me are a great blessing and are what helped to get me out of my combat-shock in hospital; and what sustain me now.

However, Robert understood very well how the conventional world would be likely to misinterpret his relationship with Juli; and so he added fiercely: 'Let anyone call me a dirty old man who dares.'[3]

Despite Graves having 'closed accounts' with Aemilia Laraçuen, she had continued to send him 'romantic, joking letters';[4] and then on Christmas Eve, she cabled him for $500, telling him that Howard had gone, and that it was an emergency. He sent her the money without question. 'I supposed prison, hospital or some other emergency', he told Ralph Jacobs, 'but no, (when she wrote full of bubbling gaiety), she just had run out of cash.'

Apparently Howard had left her with 'nothing but a decayed tooth on the window-ledge';[5] and (having felt 'a certain horror, instead of joy' before opening her letter), Robert was not altogether surprised when Aemilia also told him of 'wonderful Californians who want to marry her',[6] and of her plans for 'going to Las Vegas as a schill'. This, as he explained to Selwyn Jepson, was 'a beautiful young lady who eggs on gamblers to gamble at the tables ... What a waste!'[7]

Robert's reply to Aemilia, written on New Year's Eve, was very firm. This was her usual Second Act, he told her; and she would have 'to go through a bit more' before she could finally get rid of [Howard]'.[8] When, however, she responded by returning $350 of the money she had borrowed from him, explaining that the $150 was 'needed for an urgent visit to her mother, Robert began to believe, as he told Selwyn Jepson, that:

> there *are* signs of a change in climate with 'Aemilia' ... this is the first time that she has admitted that she has behaved badly and also that I was right about Howard. Remember she is not a tricksteress, only a girl who has got herself into an impossible situation by proudly trying to help a man whom everyone else thought unhelpable; whereas under his influence she caught ... something quite uncharacteristic of her ...

'Don't worry!' he concluded. 'I'm all right. And so is she, eventually.'[9]

In mid-January 1967, Aemilia wrote again from her mother's home in El Paso, Texas, with a declaration of unconditional love. 'I always have and always will love you, whatever you do', she told Robert; and she went on to apologize for her 'temperament' and to explain that when she was in an over-wrought state, he should not take everything she said too seriously.[10]

Despite recent warnings from Selwyn Jepson, who had told him that 'I don't believe for a minute that [Aemilia] is parted from Howard, even temporarily', and that 'You won't get her to believe in even the front line under your accounts until you say no',[11] Robert could not help being touched. In his reply, he assured her that she 'had no cause for jealousy' over his relationship with Juli Simon; and then, as he told Selwyn, he:

reiterated my belief in her eventual complete integration ... after all, I am still enormously in her debt; and I have finished with her only in the sense of not wanting to share her boisterous life in Mexico, Brazil or the African jungle. But there is only one Aemilia in this poor, confused world.

'No, I am not weakening', he concluded, 'but neither can I forget her basic goodness.'[12]

February 1967 saw the birth of Lucia and Ramon's daughter Natalia; and later that month, C'an Susanna, which Graves had once hoped would be Aemilia's home, was 'inaugurated' with eleven bottles of champagne and a party for all those who had worked on it, including masons, carpenters and electricians. Graves had renamed the house the Torre de Susanna; and told Selwyn Jepson that it was 'now not [Aemilia's], nor mine, but its own: for friends'; that it 'shone'; and that the Sillitoes were 'the first occupants & [had] brought feather pillows and Chinese lamp shades, the only furnishings unobtainable here'.[13]

Aemilia continued to write; but in March, as Graves reported to Ralph Jacobs, she mentioned that Howard had:

turned up, by coincidence ... 'to buy a new car' at El Paso. She couldn't be uncivil to him in front of her cousins, (she wrote) but she would go off a day earlier to avoid scenes.[14]

Next, as he told Selwyn Jepson, Graves received:

a coruscating love-letter from Aemilia at Puerto Vallarta with a small sentence put in at haphazard among minor items: 'Howard drove here' – meaning I suppose from her previous letter from El Paso that she could not face the train journey with all her luggage so asked him to help her with his new car.

O.K. but I have asked if she remembers that I stopped writing to her last Nov. because of his presence down there; repeating that I cannot change my view of him, so that I hope he is gone by now. Also that I can at best regard him not as evil, but as her incurable, if registered, mental patient.[15]

To soften this message, Robert had sent Aemilia, whom he knew was a Cancerian, 'a silver-mounted lion-claw' together with a few lines of verse which ran:

> Gentle Crab, accept this claw
> Plucked from the lion's patient paw.
> It will propel her forward who
> Ran sideways always hitherto.[16]

Presently, however, Aemilia wrote another letter telling Robert 'how wonderful [Howard] was once more, and wasn't I <u>happy</u>?' So, as Robert explained to Ralph Jacobs, he replied once again 'closing accounts', and telling her that:

she was not to write to me again except in an emergency: hunger, prison or jail – but before she got *that* letter she had written me one saying how wonderfully happy she was, couldn't I sense it? And she was 'foundationed in Puerto Vallarta' and he was no trouble, and I needn't worry about *him*; but she couldn't come here because of *work* being so important – 'Picasso wouldn't go wherever people said he was needed' – now would he?

At this point, Robert 'wrote a lot and tore it up'; but then came a tear-stained letter from Aemilia with the news that her mother was dying.

Robert immediately told Aemilia that if she could reach to El Paso in time, he would pay her fare. 'But I fear', he informed Ralph,

it's too late. Also her – and my – best friends [in Mexico] Jungle Jim and his wife Jo are in trouble. Police swooped on him – he's a pot smoker – and took him off to jail. He'll be fined and extradited. So may she. I can't see Aemilia again or write to her now until [Howard] goes for good. I have told her that the order is Remorse, Penitence, Regeneration, Amends, Real *Work*. You can't skip the first two steps. And that Picasso is a thief and a rogue [and] I have long refused to meet him.

'Please don't be depressed by this', he concluded. 'It gave me a migraine or two – but I am not alone – in fact I am more surrounded by real friends than ever before.'[17]

June brought an unexpected public engagement. Robert Graves's former landlord John Masefield, Poet Laureate since 1930, had died on 12 May 1967; and the Society of Authors wrote asking Graves to give an address at the memorial service in Westminster Abbey.[18] He did so, 'preaching from the pulpit';[19] and afterwards received enthusiastic letters both from Alan Hodge, who was pleased that Robert had praised Masefield's much-neglected narrative poems;[20] and from John Betjeman, a future Poet Laureate, who wrote to him: 'Dearest and best of poets, That was a splendid address you gave on Masefield today, affectionate humorous fair personal and loyal.'[21]

Before leaving England, Graves also read some poems at a literary festival; and this resulted in a letter from another future Poet Laureate, Ted Hughes, who told him:

> I have been intending to write to you for years, to thank you for your poems and for *The White Goddess*, which I regard as the chief Holy Book of my poetic conscience (confirmed again, after this Festival). Somebody gave me a copy when I was 17.[22]

Graves himself had no wish to succeed Masefield as Poet Laureate (and in any case Cecil Day-Lewis would be the Government's choice). For a number of years he had deliberately refused all public honours on the grounds that 'membership would put me under a certain moral constraint if I ever felt tempted to blot my copybook'.[23]

In July Graves returned to Westminster Abbey to take part in a lunchtime poetry reading with Isla Cameron;[24] and he stayed for a few days with the Simons at 12 Drayton Gardens,[25] which had become his principal London home.

From the street, a flight of steps led up to an imposing front door which opened onto a long hallway: at the back of which, on the left, was the twin-bedded room which became known as Robert's. One wall was a solid mass of books; and there was a convenient desk beneath the window, through which (when he raised his eyes from his work), he could look out over the garden, with its small pond surrounded by shrubs and flowers, its huge horse chestnut, and its pretty little crab apple which had been planted to celebrate Juli's birth. Robert became so fond of this garden, which he nicknamed 'Drayton Great Park', that he enhanced it with a pair of stone 'Guardian Lions'; and celebrated it in verse.[26]

On 21 July, Robert flew back to Majorca accompanied by the Simons, who were to be his guests at the Torre; and soon afterwards he received a letter which cast one of the very few shadows across what would be an unusually happy summer.

The letter was from Lucia's Oxford friend Stephanie Sweet, a woman with a keen intellect, an hour-glass figure and a mass of blonde hair, who had found herself in trouble with the law after subletting a farmhouse near Oxford in which cannabis had been smoked. Although she 'had no knowledge of what was going on', managing premises in which cannabis had been smoked was 'a technical offence' for which she was to be prosecuted,[27] with every likelihood that she would be found guilty. Stephanie had therefore written to ask whether she could borrow money to fight the case;[28] and while Robert was pondering the matter, she followed her letter to Deyá, one of the numerous visitors who flocked to the village that summer, and found themselves in an extraordinary world.

CHAPTER 2

Summer of '67

By the summer of 1967, the so-called 'alternative culture' of the sixties (with its free love, marijuana, and those terrible long-drawn-out silences during which everyone waited in vain for a word of illumination) had become deeply engrained in Deyá's expatriate community. The artists, actors and remittance-men who had arrived in the village full of ambition, and had somehow been left high and dry drinking their 'Cuba Libres' in the village bar, were now equally likely to be passing round joints while listening to exotic music in darkened rooms.

Earlier in the year an American expatriate, David Solomon, had been fined and sent to prison for a while after having unwisely included a guardia's daughter in a pot-smoking session in Palma.[29] After his return to Deyá, he and his two young and attractive daughters seemed to keep open house for the floating population of pleasure-seekers who descended on the village each summer. Many of these visitors spent as much time as possible getting 'high' on drugs; and for some of them the experience was especially powerful when combined with cheap rum, a beautiful mountain setting, and the mythology of Robert Graves's *The White Goddess*.

Graves himself was visible very regularly, wearing an open shirt, shorts and a battered broad-brimmed sun hat, and carrying a Majorcan basket over one arm as he strode down to the Cala for his early-morning swim, or into the village to collect the day's post. He was still a handsome man, whose rugged profile could well have adorned an imperial coinage; and wherever he went, he carried with him what one of his friends and admirers would later describe as 'the atmosphere of the ancient world'.[30] Under gnarled olive-trees, in the presence of this high priest of the White Goddess of Pelion, it seemed natural to adopt his beliefs, and to offer up a prayer to Isis or to Ishtar: especially on a clear night, when a full moon rode over the high mountains by which Deyá was almost encircled.

Robert Graves's nephew Richard, who stayed at Canelluñ for the whole of August, would later be suspicious of those who described that year without having experienced it at first hand for more than a few days. Invariably, in his view, they had 'got it wrong'. But when asked to be more specific, he fell back on analogy: 'Did you ever read John Fowles's *The Ebony Tower?*' he would ask.

> It was filmed with Laurence Olivier as an elderly aritist living in the south of France, and Greta Scaachi and Toyah Willcox as the beautiful young women who inspire his work and look after him in bed. A young art critic arrives to interview Olivier, and ends up falling for Greta Scaachi and wanting to rescue her. But he's got it all wrong: she's happy to be there. The point is, that the artist has invented his own world, with his own set of rules. It's an enchanted, magical world; and yet in an important way it's more 'real', more 'true' than the conventional world outside.

For Richard, and for many others, it was like being in a waking dream, very vivid and very intense, in which the normal rules had ceased to apply.

As for Robert: whenever he was with Juli Simon, the two of them radiated such happiness that they touched other people's lives with warmth. Juli herself seemed transformed; while her more conventionally beautiful sister, by contrast, exuded misery and even despair. Juli may have especially appreciated Robert's trust in her since, as Robert explained to Idries Shah on 2 August, she had:

> been turned out of the Royal Ballet School on various pretexts, the truth being that she is too good a dancer and too independent-minded for a Prussian drill-school. I am helping her write a long piece about it: because the same attempt to militarize any so-called art or craft is found everywhere in England ... [31]

Robert felt that he had returned 'to the gentle age of innocence, with most of my problems solved', and remarked that he was 'very close indeed' to Juli, but that 'publicly she keeps her distance with an assumed negligence which is really remarkable. Ours', he concluded, 'is really a constructive alliance rather than an old-world love-affair. I am the unicorn who lays his narwhal-horn in the pure virgin's lap, as in medieval tapestries.'

Although Beryl was relieved that Juli was so much easier and so much less threatening than Aemilia, her position continued to be uncomfortable. Robert was aware of her suffering: but, as he told Sally Chilver, he believed that his relations with his wife were 'as good as possible in the circumstances'. He was, he declared, 'affectionate, loyal, & no cad. But I can't give her what she does not want and has not for many years, nor do I want to offer it, after so many rebuffs. And I *hate* animals.' He added that he was 'on a perfectly steady keel now because of that relationship which you disapprove of because you don't know what it's all about and try to put it into a more familiar but irrelevant pattern. Until you do know', he concluded, 'I shall be at cross-purposes which is very sad. I am a poet not a dirty old man.'[32]

Memorable events that summer included an evening when Robert gathered a younger group, including Juli Simon, Stephanie Sweet and Martin Good – his student factotum for the summer – walked with them to one of the cottages on the high ground above the Cala, and read them his completed translation of the *Rubaiyyat* of Omar Khayaam by candlelight.

For those who had been brought up to love Fitzgerald, it was at first deeply disappointing to find, for example:

> A Book of Verses underneath the Bough,
> A Jug of Wine, A Loaf of Bread, and Thou
> Beside me singing in the Wilderness –
> Ah, Wilderness were Paradise enow!

altered into the far less memorable:

> Should our day's portion be one mancel loaf,
> A haunch of mutton and a gourd of wine
> Set for us two alone on the wide plain,
> No Sultan's bounty could evoke such joy.[33]

However, as the reading progressed, a combination of the candlelight, the company, and the hypnotic rhythm of Graves's lines worked a certain magic; and any doubts were temporarily allayed.

That summer also saw a play which used *The Frogs* by Aristophanes as a loose framework for a series of cabaret acts and comic scenes; each Sunday, there were picnics at Lluchalcari; and each night, after sunset, there were parties (scrupulously avoided by Robert Graves) at which the air was full of the sweet sickly scent of hashish.

CHAPTER 3

To Avoid Drowning

Robert Graves claimed to be no longer in love with Aemilia Laraçuen;[34] but on 25 September 1967 he was enormously heartened when, as he told Ralph Jacobs, he received from her the very letter:

> which I have been waiting for these three years now – a letter of real penitence and an admission of guilt, explaining that she has been terrified of … Howard for some time. She now says she's really afraid of him … She's going to clear out of P[uerto] V[allarta] and sell up.

'It was a really good letter', he went on; 'and I can't *not* respond with joyousness and congratulations. She is even earning good money by portraits! She doesn't want Howard to know her whereabouts … she'll be restored to us at last.' He added that he had been 'upset about her of course and haven't been very well for some time – colds and migraines etcetera – but Juli writes regularly'.[35]

At the same time, there was bad news both about Stephanie Sweet, and about the publication of the *Rubaiyyat*.

Stephanie was found guilty of allowing her house 'to be used for the smoking of cannabis or cannabis resin while concerned in its management'; and less than a fortnight later she received a letter from the Department of Education threatening her with expulsion from the teaching profession.[36]

As for Graves's translation of the *Rubaiyyat*: it was a critical disaster. The poetry was considered to be 'flat', and doubts were raised by Persian scholars both about Omar Khayaam's credentials as a great Sufi teacher, and about the very existence of the so-called Jan Fishan Khan manuscript; while a former translator of the *Rubaiyyat*, Major J. C. E. Bowen, having read two references in Graves's introduction to Omar's *Rubaiyyat* as 'a poem', ventured to ask 'whether Mr. Graves has fully understood the complexity of his task'. For *Rubaiyyat* was merely the plural of the Persian word *ruba'i*, meaning quatrain; and it was 'well known that every *Diwan*, or collection of Persian poetry, is arranged so that each poem is grouped with others having the same letter-ending in the first line. This arrangement by letters rules out the possibility of any significance being attached to the sequence.'[37]

As the controversy raged on, the impression grew that Robert Graves had been guilty, at best, of extreme gullibility, and his popular reputation was severely damaged. Graves's friends wished that Karl Gay had still been working at his side: surely Karl would have demanded, at the very least, some independent proof of the existence of the Jan Fishan Khan manuscript? Graves's enemies, of whom there were many throughout the scholarly world, rejoiced.

Robert Graves himself, lunching with his nephew Richard in a Chinese restaurant in Oxford not long after publication, confided that he had 'just heard that someone in Persia has brought out a book, luckily in Persian, which more or less discredits the manuscript from which he worked'.[38] However, he could not allow himself to believe that the Shahs had deliberately deceived him; and he continued bombarding weak points in his opponents' arguments, while becoming increasingly aware that his own position was fundamentally indefensible.

In October 1967, Robert Graves flew south to spend a month in Australia.[39] His chief purpose was to visit his daughter Catherine Dalton;[40] and to pay for his journey, he had arranged a lecture tour which, as he reported to Sally Chilver, was 'embarrassingly triumphant', with 'all the largest halls and theatres sold out even in culture-numbed Tasmania'.[41] In the 'wild-roo-ridden parrot-haunted outback' of New South Wales,[42] he 'went opaling ... and brought back some beauts'; and at 'an official Canberra cocktail do', as he told Spike Milligan, he 'plumped down on the floor and made everyone else do the same. We ended with songs and outrageous stories. Couldn't do that in Washington, nor Buckingham Palace neither.'[43]

As for Catherine: she had continued to pursue her investigations into her husband's death. These had now widened into a study of neo-Fascist groups presumed by her to be threatening Australia's political stability;[44] and when she lost her job as a cook, and was replaced by a foreigner who spoke almost perfect English, she became convinced that he had been 'taught the English language under superior authority – probably in a Russian spy school'.[45]

After listening carefully to what Catherine had to say, and talking to a number of interested parties, Robert came to the conclusion that his daughter had been 'completely accurate in her statement and has one of the most extraordinary minds as well as the most enormous courage of anyone I have met for years'.[46] The result was that when Graves returned to Europe, he was accompanied by his granddaughter Caroline, whom he thereby hoped to rescue from any attempts upon *her* freedom or life.[47]

Robert Graves returned to Canellúñ to find an unhappy household. Beryl was feeling wretched;[48] while Juan was in the depths of one of the depressions which had severely affected him ever since an ill-fated expedition to Australia back in 1964–5.[49] And then came an angry letter from Aemilia.

Robert had misunderstood her, she complained; and their whole relationship had been based upon a lie. He had never truly loved her, as he had promised; and so his poems to her were also lies. Nor did she believe that he truly loved Juli Simon (who had been persuaded by Robert to write to Aemilia 'as a sister'). His poems to Juli were desperately weak; and if he and Juli really loved each other, how was it that Juli was still a virgin? Nothing made sense. It was time, wrote Aemilia, for them both to move on; and in due course she would return his mother's brooch.[50]

Robert's first response was to write 'a long very human letter'; but before posting it, he concentrated his thoughts by consulting the 'I Ching', from which he learned that he should avoid acting hastily. Later, therefore, he drafted another letter which he dated '22 December 1967 Juan's 23rd birthday'; and in it he told Aemilia that he did not propose to discuss the past with her, as they had agreed never to do that. What he could do, he said, was to proffer a new kind of loving, one freed from any encumbrance of passion: a kind of loving which it would be incorrect for her to spurn. There were no difficulties, he added, in his relationship with Juli; and he was glad to see that Juli could write to Aemilia in a sisterly fashion. He went on (I am required to paraphrase) in words to this effect:

I believe that you mistakenly regard me as English. Naturally, I am an Irishman, with a typically Irish understanding of romance: one demanding that the object of my desire should be both chaste and truthful.

Sadly, you and I, darling Cancerian, failed to understand each other. That has never been a problem between Juli and me. Certainly, the poetry I write to Juli lacks the intense quality which is plain in the poetry you received from me, but so much of that came from desperate suffering. However, that should not make you believe that I love Aemilia more, or Juli less.

It was with Juli's help, he went on, that he had survived being abandoned by Aemilia. And he suggested that to love someone was like being in a ship with an anchor. Should that anchor drag, so that the ship was in danger of being broken to pieces on a reef, it was necessary to drop a second anchor to preserve one's life ... Aemilia was being unjust to herself if she believed that what he had written for her was untrue. His eternal love was to be found in those lines of poetry, and it was she, not he, who was denying the wonderful experiences which they had shared. However, he could not blame her, and attributed her letter to her current difficulties.

Robert went on to re-affirm that the poems he had written for Aemilia were true poems, written from the heart. He was ready to burn her letter and put it out of his mind; and he asked her to be thankful that his relationship with Juli was so untroubled. The fact that Juli remained virginal did not mean that Robert lacked passion or had become impotent. What it meant was simply that he and Juli were lucky enough not to be tormented by sexual desire.

As for Amy's brooch, he now wanted her to keep it, since she had in an important way helped him to rediscover his mother: a wonderful accomplishment. He concluded that his poetry for Aemilia meant what it said, and was addressed to the essential woman in her, the being whom she had attempted to suppress, but who should now proudly re-assert herself. And he sent his love, marking two kisses beside his signature.[51]

This letter [52] evidently had the desired effect: for by mid-January 1968 Robert was telling Ralph Jacobs that Aemilia was 'all right again'. He added that Juli Simon had her first professional dancing appearance at Covent Garden Theatre in *Aida* on 21 January: in celebration of which, he had 'sent her a necklace that once belonged to Rudolf Valentino's wife', and was reputed to be 'from Tutankhamen's tomb'.[53]

Laraçuen's reconciliation with Graves (despite the fact that he continued to parade his love for Juli Simon in front of her) may have had something to do with his co-operation over her proposed sale of the four hundred or more letters which she had received from him during the past eight years. Selwyn Jepson had agreen to handle the sale; while Graves, as he told Ralph Jacobs on 16 February, had decided that:

her letters to me ... *must* be part of the deal because ... my letters by themselves make no sense, without hers and ... although I don't propose raking up the past, if it *is* raked up, I want the whole story, especially about Howard, properly told by her letters as well as mine.

He hoped that she would use the proceeds of the sale to 'buy an *annuity* and then earn her living *not* by business (which, since she proposes to make it illegal border-smuggling will only bring her bad luck), but by exercising her own craft of drawing, painting or designing'.[54]

Robert Graves's fears about Aemilia's proposed smuggling venture were fully justified: a note in Selwyn Jepson's hand reveals that she would later spend 'some time in gaol but RG pulled strings and got her out'.[55] But at the time, Robert was flattered when his generosity led to Aemilia having what he described as 'a flare-up of her original feelings for me'; and he was also relieved that she was 'careful not to seem wishing to detach me from my new centre'.[56] At one point, Aemilia even imitated Robert's recent gift to Juli, by sending her a necklace;[57] and she pleased Robert still more when in March she wrote to say that she had developed strong feelings for a mutual friend of theirs, a musician named George R——.Robert drafted a letter telling Aemilia that he thought George was a splendid man. Obviously, George would be nervous about meeting him; but everything would be fine, provided George realised that Robert would never think of him in terms of personal rivalry. So he asked Aemilia to inform George, should the opportunity arise, that no-one had truly comprehended the nature of the bond between them; and that in practical terms, nor had they: otherwise they would never have thought of attempting to live together as an ordinary couple, as they had done at Puerto Vallarta. (Aemilia, by deliberately behaving badly towards him, had wisely underlined that fact.) At last, however, their relationship was soundly based. Robert wished her the happiness she deserved; and he warmly invited her to bring George to Deyá in the summer.[58]

On 19 March Robert flew to London, where he stayed with the Simons, read some of his poems in the Festival Hall, and watched Juli dancing in *Aida*. 'Just back from Drayton Great Park as we call it', he told Aemilia on his return to Canelluñ.

That Juli gets better and better. Because of the great power and vindictiveness of the Royal Ballet School bosses she can't get a decent company job in England, so hopes to get to the best one in Continental Europe, the Norwegian, where she has a friend. This will be very lonely for her, but eventually she'll come back to England as a prima ballerina; as so often happens to RBC rejects. She looked lovely in your necklace, and a white lace blouse and a short black skirt last night.

He added that if Aemilia came to Deyá in the summer, he would not only pay the fare, but would lend her his 'retreat ['the sheep-hut'] high above Canelluñ for a studio. It is utterly unvisited, the only drawback is no electric light for night work.'[59]

In the meantime, life at Canelluñ had become more relaxed. It had turned out that Beryl's lack of *joie-de-vivre* had been caused chiefly by low blood pressure, for which, since Christmas, she had been receiving treatment.[60] At the same time Robert, with no major project in hand, had enjoyed writing a number of articles, including one on the current state of Stephanie Sweet's legal proceedings; and he was also preparing for his first sortie behind the iron curtain.

Following her conviction, Robert Graves had encouraged Stephanie Sweet to appeal; and when in March 1968 that appeal was dismissed, Graves wrote a biting article for the *Sunday Times* in which he explained that management of premises in which cannabis was smoked,

> though hitherto arguable, has now become an absolute crime, this seeming to the Judges of the Queen's Bench Division and to the Home Secretary the only possible means of stamping-out drug addiction.
>
> As a result, it has now even been suggested that merely by being the landlord of premises one becomes responsible at law for all sorts of offenses that might be committed, however gross.

'As a result', he concluded, *Sweet versus Parsley* has aroused a storm of protest among lawyers and politicians who fear further infringements of civil liberties.' And he added the verse:

PARSLEY V. SWEET

> Whatever Sweet might do was wrong
> Even if she did not do it
> Absolute crime is far too strong
> For felons not to rue it.
> So Parsley armed with the law's might
> Proves abso-bally-lutely right.
> Her case is closed in hell's despite –
> No Counsel can pursue it.

The then Editor of the *Sunday Times*, Harold Evans, sent a telegram to Graves on 13 April thanking him for his 'splendid' article, and promising to do all he could to help.

Publication was followed by a swift reaction from the Thames Valley Constabulary, who telephoned Michael Horniman of A. P. Watt badly wanting to interview Mr Graves and Miss Sweet with regard to 'the allegations against the police' contained in Graves's article;[61] by a flood of letters demanding justice; and by the filming of an episode in the BBC television programme 'Cause for Concern': which remained unscreened after being legally blocked by Lord Chief Justice Parker, since the whole matter was *sub judice* as a further appeal was in progress.[62] Eventually this appeal would be successful. An important legal principle was thereby established; and early the next year Robert would receive a grateful letter from 'the absolutely not criminal Stephanie'.[63]

In the meantime, Robert Graves had set out with Beryl on their first foray into eastern Europe. On 3 May they flew to Budapest, where Robert had been invited by the writer's organization P.E.N. to give a number of poetry readings; and where he thoroughly enjoyed meeting one of Raphael Patai's friends, the poet and classicist Gabor Devecseri who (besides making translations of Homer and Catullus), had translated several of Graves's poems into Hungarian.[64] Since Graves spoke no Hungarian, they tried talking to each other in Latin; and Devecseri would later stay with Robert and Beryl in Canelluñ.[65]

Margot Nichols, whom Robert had seen once or twice in New York, and who had managed the difficult change from being a muse to being a family friend, joined Robert and Beryl in Budapest; and before long the three of them had moved on to Moscow.[66]

After the liveliness of Budapest, Robert was disappointed by the Russian capital. He tried to relieve his boredom by arranging a meeting with the Russian poet Yevtushenko, despite having openly attacked him for his rhetorical public readings; but his efforts were fruitless. As Robert explained some months later to Martin Seymour-Smith, Yevtushenko

> couldn't come to the *rendez-vous*. He is a very interesting character & his visit to this island was hilarious. He was bedded up with a capitalist Banker's wife when cornered by the Press, but offered to write a poem in honour of Mallorca. He and I are at extreme ends of our common profession but I do not intend to quarrel with him.

'I only require that poets tell the truth', Graves concluded; 'and he doesn't always try.'[67]

Not long after the Graveses had returned to Canelluñ, Aemilia arrived in Deyá. She was alone (George R—— having been discarded); and at first she behaved beautifully, and Robert gladly lent her his cottage above the Cala. But then Juli arrived 'for a goodbye on her way to join the Royal Ballet at Oslo'.[68] Inevitably, trouble followed.

CHAPTER 4

Don't Hate Iago

It had been difficult enough for Aemilia Laraçuen to accept Juli Simon's relationship with Robert Graves at a distance; but when in June 1968 she saw with her own eyes how Robert shared with Juli so much of what he had once shared with her, she became a little unbalanced. The signs of this were evident. When Aemilia had arrived in Deyá, she had been 'looking very well'; but now she began drinking: and her liver was already so damaged that, as Robert noticed to his horror, 'a single glass sends her eyes yellow'.[69]

Drinking was not enough. Seeking out Juli, Aemilia felt vengefully 'impelled to disturb her mind', no doubt with stories of how difficult it was to be Robert's Black Goddess. And then, after Juli's departure from the island, Aemilia talked confidentially to Robert, and told him what he later described as a series of damaging statements about Juli 'which I believed'.[70] Hearing those lies (almost certainly about a sexual liaison with someone whom Robert detested) made him deeply unhappy; and things were no better when he decided that they were not true: for in believing them, even for a moment, Robert felt that he had shown an appalling lack of trust.

While he was tormenting himself over this 'betrayal', he telephoned Joanna Simon. Without naming Aemilia, he gave Joanna an outline of what had occurred, likening himself to another Othello deceived by a cunning Iago into killing Desdemona. He then asked whether he could put things right by coming over to stay at 'Drayton Great Park' for a few days before Juli flew to Oslo?[71]

Unfortunately there was a bad connection, so that Joanna could only hear part of what Robert was saying; but on 3 July she wrote a very wise letter reassuring her old friend, while discouraging him from making a special journey to London. 'I don't think one can blame Iago', she began:

He is only a symbol of the jealous outside world. The trouble was

Othello's gullibility and his immense over-riding emotions and the inability of Desdemona to defend herself ... I think you could rewrite the story with advantage. Don't hate Iago and don't kill Desdemona.

And although this particular dropped handkerchief seems to have been a concoction of someone's imagination, it was unlikely that Juli would remain perpetually inviolate as most of her circle had been going to bed together for ages. 'Please be happy again, darling Robert', she concluded. '... Do come and stay if it helps, but I think it might be rather disappointing, as Juli really has <u>MASSES</u> to do in order to get off to Oslo on July 25th, and you might find yourself sitting here alone ...'[72]

Robert took Joanna's advice and remained in Deyá, where he soon began veering back in Aemilia's direction, telling Selwyn Jepson on 12 July that although he could 'have no confident dealings' with her, 'I can't be *cruel*.'[73] It was at this point that his daughter Catherine Dalton made a decisive intervention.

Believing that she had been 'nearly killed in Sydney' earlier in the year, Catherine had returned to Europe 'to clean up the British end of the situation', while writing a book about her experiences.[74] After spending a little while in England, she had come over to Majorca, where she was horrified to learn that 'Cindy' (as all the Graveses but Robert persisted in calling her) had come very close the previous year to breaking up her father's second marriage.

Observing that Aemilia could still make Robert suffer, and deciding that she remained a potential threat to his marriage for so long as she was living in the village, Catherine decided to take matters into her own hands. Asking Aemilia to go for a walk with her, she led her along a precipitous path. Then she grabbed Aemilia's arm, and told her: 'If you don't promise to leave Deyá at once, I shall push you over the edge and kill you. And if you do promise, and then go back on your word, I shall kill you later. Which is it to be?'[75]

Aemilia, looking at the gleam in the eye of this large, powerful woman, knew that she meant what she said, promised to leave, and did so (flying to London[76]) without even daring to tell Robert exactly what had happened.[77] However, she turned the situation to her own advantage as well as she could. The result was that Robert commented at the time to Selwyn Jepson that 'things' had 'got a bit dangerous' for Aemilia; but he was persuaded that it was he who had had 'to send her away', after 'ma[king] peace with her first'.[78]

Before Aemilia left the island, there had been a reminder of equally dramatic events long past. A letter arrived from Tom Matthews announcing to Robert Graves that

> Your old enemy, my old friend Schuyler is dead. I thought you would like to know. He died in the evening of July 4th and his son and oldest daughter Griselda are going to Wabasso, presumably to see Laura and to attend his funeral. He would have been 68 on August 18th. I hope he left some money for Laura but don't know ...

'Here endeth one of the lives in our little chapter', Tom concluded. 'I hope yours still has a long way to go.'[79]

Emotional tension had led to Robert Graves becoming increasingly accident prone, and that summer he had suffered from a string of what he described to Selwyn Jepson as 'minor disabilities', having fallen '20 foot on my head, got 34 sea urchin prickles in my foot, [and] got 3 really poisonous jelly-fish stings, all in a month'.[80]

In the circumstances, it was a relief to retreat to his study and dabble in university politics. Learning that Edmund Blunden's ill health had forced him to resign the Professorship of Poetry at Oxford, Graves wrote to Enid Starkie, suggesting that she should stand in the coming election.[81]

Several pleasing things happened while he was waiting for an answer. First Margot Nichols arrived in Deyá; and Robert found her 'very collected, very busy, thoroughly reformed and generally beloved'. Margot had brought her young daughter with her: 'my god-daughter Daisy', as Robert called her, and 'a very bright kid'. Then Robert was invited by the Olympic Committee to read a poem at the Cultural Olympics in Mexico City later in the year; and finally, he was honoured in his own village.[82]

On 27 July 1968, in the presence of the mayor, the civil governor and the captain-general, Robert Graves was formally declared to be an 'Adoptive Son' of Deyá. Helena Simon walked with him to the ceremony, at which there were emotional speeches, and at which Robert was presented with a plaque and 'a parchment of eulogy'. Then Robert made the return gift of 'a 105-year-old mayoral staff from the village: almond wood decorated with orangewood inlay'; and there were free drinks for the villagers to celebrate this unique event.[83]

Early in August Enid Starkie (after congratulating Robert on his new honour) said that she would 'very much like to be' a candidate for the professorship; but 'of course, I would have to wait to be invited as one cannot put oneself up!'[84] Robert was still wondering whether or not to nominate her himself when, on about 19 August, he was astonished to receive a cable from Aemilia telling him 'HOLD EVERYTHING AM COMING'.[85]

Next a letter arrived, from which Robert Graves learned that Aemilia had found a new boyfriend (much younger than herself) named Peter Weismiller. Robert had met Peter in New York and, as he told Selwyn Jepson, had found him 'very sweet & guileless; & I'm glad that Aemilia and he are together. She's on the mend.' The only drawback was that Peter's mother disapproved of the relationship and had stopped Peter's allowance. Aemilia was in any event 'in two (three or four probably) minds about her association with him'.[86] At any rate, Catherine was no longer in Deyá, so it was safe for Aemilia to return; and before long she and Peter had taken up residence in Robert's cottage above the Cala.[87]

Aemilia's reappearance in Deyá once again increased the emotional tension; and Robert was also faced by a new set of family pressures. Sam, who had spent some years making a living doing up old houses, suddenly found that his business had dried up: there were no new orders, and Robert realized that he would 'have to support him awhile'. Catherine and her daughters were 'a further problem'; and William was hoping 'to borrow £6000 for enlarging C'an Quet'.[88]

One relief was the arrival in Deyá of John and Gretl Aldridge, who spent most of September living in the Torre.[89] John Aldridge had agreed to paint Robert's portrait; and since he had done no portraits at all since his head of the Emperor Claudius for the jacket of *I, Claudius* back in 1934, Robert asked him 'to paint me as if I was chalk and loam and gravel'. The resultant 'landscape portrait'[90] was a superb piece of work, in which Robert's craggy face reveals not only intellectual strength, but also the humanity born out of much suffering.

In between sittings for this portrait, Robert continued his correspondence with Enid Starkie. On 25 August he wrote that it was 'most important to get a candidate who *is* Oxford and (for a change) someone who is not a professional poet';[91] and by 28 September, after several more letters had been exchanged,[92] he told her: 'Dearest Enid: I have nominated you ... I hope this will work.'[93]

Shortly after writing this letter, Robert Graves began the long journey to Mexico City, which he reached on 2 October after nineteen hours of flying. He was much looking forward to seeing friends like Jimmy Metcalf; but his appalling experiences with Aemilia when last in Mexico had made him a little apprehensive, and shortly before setting out he had written to another friend whom he hoped to meet, asking her to treat him as gently as though he were a valuable piece of ancient porcelain.[94]

Robert's visit began badly, with a car crash, though fortunately, as he reported to Juan, he suffered nothing worse than 'a nice bloody bruise on my head'; and the opening of the Games was 'fantastic, with thousands of coloured balloons and also ten thousand pigeons released'.[95] As for the Mexican people: he found them '*alive* and noble-hearted. They take manslaughter lightly, and evil-wishing is a passport to prison.'[96]

Later, Robert Graves was awarded the Olympic gold medal for his Spanish poem 'Antorcha y Corona, 1968',[97] in which he described how 'Mexico was complementary to the Irish in me.'[98] However, he had won his medal in 'somewhat unusual circumstances'. Since Mexico City (like numerous cities in the world that summer) was full of rioting students, Graves was the only poet who had dared to accept his invitation. As he explained to Idries Shah, he had also single-handedly saved:

> the Cultural Committee's face by improvising a small, very small, stage-army of poets to form the great 'Reunion of Poets' advertised. I was the only one whom they had invited (of my two companions one was a Puerto Rican interloper, the other a Mexican who was rebelling against the Mexican poetic boycott of the Reunion!).

In the circumstances, he thought that his medal was 'well deserved ... especially as the audience had to be hauled in from the Olympic City restaurant, no public announcement having been possible. About 60 in all!'[99]

Among the letters which awaited Robert Graves's return from Mexico, there was one from C. Day-Lewis, the Poet Laureate, unofficially offering him the Queen's Medal for Poetry,[100] 'to restore its lost distinction'.[101] Graves, with his matriarchal ideas, liked the idea of being honoured by a Queen, and immediately accepted.[102]

There were also letters from Enid Starkie about the Professorship of Poetry.[103] Apparently there were now eight candidates, of whom the clear favourite was Roy Fuller. Graves tried to give a last-minute boost to Starkie's campaign, with a letter to the *Guardian* in which he stated that:

> Her election will decide whether Oxford intends to remain a serious University or to go all modern by the choice of a freak candidate ... In fact Oxford needs Dr Starkie: for her courage, learning and wit ...

'She is one of the Great Undefeatables', he concluded, 'and everyone loves her except the dull or mean-minded.'[104]

When she was in fact defeated, Starkie told Graves philosophically that although Fuller was 'a dull choice', the appointment 'could have been much worse'; and her only real regret was that 'I wouldn't say the things I could say, which I would have liked to have said and which I'll no longer have the opportunity of saying.'[105]

In the meantime there had been another flare-up of the Omar Khayaam controversy. Back in June, *Life International* had published a letter in which Graves fiercely attacked the reputation of one of his opponents, L. P. Elwell-Sutton, senior lecturer in Persian at Edinburgh University.[106] Graves was almost immediately compelled to retract a small factual error; but when in July two letters arrived from a London firm of solicitors demanding an apology 'in respect of the much more serious misstatements as to his scholarship', he unwisely ignored them both. On 5 November the solicitors wrote again to protest that any reader of Graves's letter would be bound to conclude:

> that our client was unable to make an address in ancient or modern Persian, and that he was unfit to retain his lectureship at Edinburgh University.
>
> This has caused serious injury to his reputation as a Persian lecturer, expert and scholar and of course it is untrue ... We are now to request that you forward to *Life International* an appropriate explanation, send a copy to us and make an offer to pay our reasonable costs.[107]

Advised by his own lawyers that his remarks could indeed be held to be libellous, and that if a writ for libel were to be issued before his arrival in England to accept the Queen's Medal, 'this might even prejudice the award',[108] Graves sensibly decided to 'make it clear', as he wrote to the editors of *Life International*:

> that I certainly did not intend to convey in my letter the impression that Mr. Elwell-Sutton is not an internationally-recognised authority on Persian language and literature with a fluent command of both spoken and written Persian. I deeply regret it if this was the impression created.[109]

This settled the matter.

Letters continued to arrive regularly from Juli; and on 8 November Robert was able to tell Selwyn Jepson that she had 'made a great success of her first solo part', and was 'all right; and so I am. I find absence as wonderful as presence if one is on the same temporal beam'.[110] Juli had also 'forgiven me for believing the lies'; and so Robert felt able fully to forgive Aemilia: who was still living in one of his cottages with Peter Weismiller, and who was soon found 'blowing smoke (not *fire*) over the workroom table'; though he described her as a 'silly – yes, no, all right, silly fool' for having 'removed the original early versions of the poems' from his letters to her.[111]

On 5 December, Graves flew to London, where he spent the night at 'Drayton Great Park' with the Simons,[112] before going to Buckingham Palace to be presented by Queen Elizabeth II with her Medal for Poetry. By a happy coincidence, the audience was filmed as part of Richard Cawston's ground-breaking television film about the royal family; and, as Martin Seymour-Smith points out, Graves's appearance would be 'one of the highlights of the show'.[113]

After staying a few more days with the Simons, Robert Graves flew on to Oslo, where he gave a poetry reading at the university, as an excuse for seeing Juli and giving her some Christmas presents. 'Her influence on me', he had recently told Selwyn Jepson, 'is wholly different from the others: she is not a Muse because she subjects me to no ordeals – I have had enough of those. She is simply a fixed star, vibrating.'[114]

Not long after Christmas, Beryl set out on her third journey to Russia. This time she took Tomas with her; and the third member of their party was Margot Nichols. Since Aemilia had also left Deyá (travelling with Peter Weismiller to Paris, where she waited for what Selwyn Jepson described as 'her $12,000 love-money' from the University of Victoria[115]), this left Robert very much alone, and increasingly depressed. 'Can't get well', he told Ruth Fainlight on 13 January 1969,

> – these last few months I've been sort of dragging around – stomach, head, throat – and my undefeatable spirit is still undefeatable but going through a sort of Black Period: weighing up the extent to which the forces of Evil have slowly pressed their conquests. Such a huge Bang it will have to be, before we are clear again; and by then so many crafts and magics will have been lost. It all started with the dethronement of women ...

He added gloomily that 'writing real English is on the way out except as a curiosity – like the hand-thrown pots or hand-woven satins that very rich people buy ... but there are still a few people who write and read poems even, for the right reasons. A?'[116]

A week later, Beryl returned from Russia, having unfortunately slipped on an icy Moscow pavement and broken her right wrist, which left her unable to type, drive or even use a can opener through February and March. Robert's gloom intensified. X-rays showed that he had 'no ulcer or cancer just acidosis' but he complained to friends that he could 'eat nothing with any trash and chew alkali tablets', and that he and Beryl 'never get away from here except on urgent business, separately. Russia is always urgent for Beryl.'[117]

It was true that Juli continued to write 'long and regularly',[118] but Robert was also receiving disturbing letters from Aemilia, whose private life was as complicated as ever. Peter had travelled to India,[119] while she stayed in Paris at an address in the rue des Beaux Arts where, as Robert reported to Sally, she was 'trying to start life again, but it's rather like warming up a car in winter. Fits & starts & acts of passion.'[120]

Towards the end of January, for example, Aemilia 'flew the handle', as Robert put it, 'about a coat which she had left at the Simons two years ago & never fetched & which Heli Simon only the other day had borrowed – and of course it got scorched!' Aemilia wrote a furious letter accusing Juli Simon of having taken the coat to Norway;[121] and the stress of hearing about all this placed a further strain upon Robert's health.[122]

At last by mid-February the sale of the letters had been completed, and Selwyn Jepson reported that:

> the remaining dollars, eleven thousand dollars, are on the way to [Aemilia's] New York Bank. I wish I could convince myself that she will do what she promised: invest the money and use the interest from it as a background to satisfy her daily needs in food and drink, sit still somewhere and get on with her work. In Europe.

He added gloomily that he would 'conceal surprise and thankfulness if there's any money left a year from now.'[123]

At this point Catherine, who had been in England for some while, became so anxious that she telephoned Selwyn Jepson, telling him that Robert was 'not at all well. Aemilia is writing to him at least twice a week and making him emotionally upset … can you do something about it?' Selwyn, as he immediately reported to Robert, 'took leave to doubt whether it was quite as bad as that, and she ran out of sixpences (for the pay telephone) and now I am worried. Are you unwell? Is it because Aemilia is upsetting you? Please reassure me.'[124]

'Don't worry about me and Aemilia', Robert replied on 25 February. 'She's all right – her boy friend went to India, didn't like it, said he was coming back, didn't turn up & now after all is still in India. She's going there now, to buy and sell in Europe semi-precious Indian jewellery.' He himself was looking forward to a more peaceful time. Juli was doing very well out in Oslo,[125] where she had been re-engaged for a further year;[126] and soon she would be coming out to Deyá with her 'magic touch' for a nine-day holiday in the Torre.

CHAPTER 5

Loss of Magic

By the time that Juli Simon arrived in Deyá on Sunday 30 March Robert Graves was in much better health: 'digging the garden about three hours a day', he wrote to Margot Nichols, 'and feeling fine again'. Beryl was also feeling better, and could drive again, though 'with certain difficulty with gears still';[127] and Robert's only real disappointment was with the quality of his recent poems. In February he had told Ruth Fainlight: 'my trouble is that I know too much of the *craft* of poetry, so that even non-poems read beautifully. But O how *bored* I can be, reading them a month later!'[128]

Graves was not yet alarmed by his increasingly frequent memory lapses, which sometimes made life difficult for other people. In mid-April, for example, he was in London for Sonja's marriage to Robert Page, and had arranged to meet the young poet David Sutton, whose work he much admired. When Sutton arrived at the appointed time, date and place, he found that Graves had not only entirely forgotten their arrangement, but had also:

> forgotten he was supposed to be going to a wedding reception at the Dorchester that morning, and the bridal party was just getting ready to depart as I turned up in my scooter clobber. No problem, he decided, it being established who I was: I could just come along, Sonja won't mind, will you, Sonja?

The bride nobly reassured Sutton that he was indeed welcome; and then 'Robert arrayed me in an old brown cardigan of his, and off we went.'[129]

David Sutton saw Robert Graves again in May, when Graves had flown to London for treatment after having ricked his back.[130] Sutton found him in considerable pain, lying on a couch, 'moving this way and that reflecting and reminiscing'. First he talked of the many strange things he had seen in his life: such as the lava streaming down the slopes of Stromboli; an oak tree 'struck by lightning fifty feet away from me, going up like tinder'; and, more recently, 'an iceberg, green, green as emerald'. And then, asked about how many of his poems would survive, he replied: 'five or six, perhaps, that's all one can really hope for, five or six in fifty years'.[131]

In June, there were difficulties with Aemilia. After several attempts to contact her, Selwyn Jepson wrote despairingly:

> No word yet from Aemilia with her copyright assignment lying around in New Delhi needing badly to be signed. She promised faithfully to let me know where she was all the time, knowing the documents were on their way from Canada. The University paid over the money to her, relying on her good faith and my assurance that she would complete her side of the deal.

'I daresay', he concluded, 'she'll come through in the end in this particular instance. In the meantime I am stalling with the people concerned.'[132]

'I am sorry Aemilia seems so untrustworthy', Robert replied on 10 June. To the best of his knowledge, she was now back in Paris, having 'in Nepal or somewhere met an unexplained holy man who put something on her head & said she'd never worry about money again. Perhaps that explains her delay in signing.'[133] To which Jepson replied that he very much hoped that when the holy man laid a hand on her head, 'he didn't in his next line in the dialogue add: "So you may as well give me what you have dear" and lay his other hand on it.'[134]

Nor did matters improve when Juli Simon returned to Deyá in July. Sonja and Robert Page were also staying in the village at Robert's expense; but already their marriage was in severe difficulties; and before long an attraction had developed between Robert Page and Juli Simon. This led to what Graves would call 'one of the most ghastly events of my life'.[135]

What Graves found particularly horrible was the fact that for some time he had been deliberately kept in the dark. As he saw it, Juli was not to blame. She 'had got into a mixed-up state and lost her magic touch with me (which meant everything to her) and didn't dare tell me what she was doing'.[136] But when Sonja had discovered what was happening, she had said nothing to her host, preferring to explain the situation to Juli's parents when they followed her to Deyá.[137]

By that time, as Juli afterwards admitted, she had been 'quite prepared to go off with [Page] at once, despite me, her parents' arrival next day, her dancing & everything'.[138] And when the news of her attachment finally reached Canelluñ, Robert Graves was so shocked that, in his own words, 'the eventual crisis and scandal nearly destroyed both of us'.[139]

In Robert Graves's private mythology, Page became another figure of evil, who had not only done him 'an unforgivable injury', by 'breaking five heavy taboos of hospitality simultaneously', but was also tainted with homosexual longings.[140] Sonja had also, in Robert's view, become 'implicated' in 'a conspiracy of evil ... through a failure to confide in me when things began to go wrong'.[141]

Somehow, the crisis passed, and Juli returned to the fold. By mid-August, Robert could tell Selwyn Jepson that:

> we are back again at Square One in perfect love and confidence. The magic is back. Juli has been taught a cruel lesson, spoilt her holiday and mine, and is in Oslo again, sober and hard-working, having re-assembled her broken pieces.[142]

He concluded somewhat querulously that his seventy-fourth birthday had also been spoilt, partly by 'Juli's detestable experiences', and partly by 'the profanation of the Moon', as he described the American moon landing on 20 July. This he regarded as 'the dirtiest most depressing act since Alexander cut the Sacred Jovian Knot to assert that the sword was mightier than the soul'; and he professed to be glad when it was 'pushed off the headlines by disgusting Teddy Kennedy'.[143]

At least Graves's difficulties with Juli had led to a new poem, 'Purification', which runs:

> 'He numbed my heart, he stole away my truth,
> He laid hands on my body.
> Never had I known ecstasy like that:
> I could have flown with him to the world's end
> And thought of you no more.'

> 'Wake, dearest love, here in my own warm arms,
> That was a nightmare only.
> You kept the wall-side, leaving me the outer,
> No demon slid between us to molest you.
> This is a narrow bed.'

> I would have brought her breakfast on a tray
> But she seemed haunted still

By terror that in nine short months, maybe,
A demon's litter, twitching scaly tails
Would hang from either breast.

And still she shuddered inconsolably
All day; our true love-magic
Dwindled and failed. 'He swore to take me
The round of Paris, on his midnight tours,
Fiddling for me to dance.'

Thus to have murdered love even a dream
Called for purification;
And (as the Great Queen yearly did at Paphos)
Down to the sea she trod and in salt water
Renewed virginity.

In mid-August, Selwyn Jepson announced that he had finally 'prised the assignment of copyright out of Aemilia', whom he found 'quick with suspicion and no less so in accusations of cheating ... Never mind, it's all over and done with now.'[144] Graves thanked him warmly for having been so 'extremely patient with Aemilia, on my account & I love you for it because otherwise she would have made things even worse with me. There is all this talk of her complete renovation and salvation; but she is trying hard not to hate me & still asking for money.'[145]

Later that year, Robert Graves would describe Aemilia to Ava Gardner as 'a woman twisted of two wholly dissimilar strands, not all of a piece like you & me';[146] and there was further disturbing news, to the effect that Aemilia had travelled with Peter Weismiller to California, only for Peter to suffer a severe mental breakdown. He had been cured by electric shock treatment of his 'Jesus Christ delusion';[147] but their life together, 'trying to establish a home and a business both at once in tight housing and business conditions' continued to be far from easy.[148]

At any rate, Graves was happy to believe that Juli was 'slowly recovering'; and towards the end of October, after a banquet at the Savoy,[149] he went to Oslo 'laden', as Joanna Simon put it, 'with tons or anyway stones of Juli's requirements. It was really touching of you', she told Robert, 'great man as you are!'[150] In Oslo, Robert found that Juli was doing no dancing, having temporarily strained a muscle in her foot; but she attended Robert's poetry reading at the university, and was introduced by him to a visiting British Ambassador.[151]

It was a cheerful visit: after which Robert told Ava Gardner that he was feeling 'younger than ever ... My bald spot has sprouted black hair & my wrinkles are smoothing out (Cause: love)';[152] and besides writing a number of poems for Juli, Graves had found an interesting job of work: a new translation of *The Song of Solomon*, often known as *The Song of Songs*.[153]

In his translation, Graves used the traditional form of the Hebrew pastoral drama performed at marriage festivals. This he had found preserved in the *Codex Siniaticus*, the earliest surviving Greek manuscript, which assigns parts to bride, bridegroom, bridesmaids and bridesmen; and the result is very pleasing. It begins:

Bride: Let his mouth shower kisses on me ...
Bridegroom: For your breasts are more to me than wine, and are fragant with the finest ointments.

And ends:

Bride: Only come away with me, my beloved; come away and become like a wild goat or a hart on my mounds of spice!

Working on this translation was one of the happiest parts of a year which had been generally depressing. Quite apart from Graves's other difficulties, there had been a dispute with the BBC over their filming a television play about Siegfried Sassoon, which included a portrait of Robert Graves in which he was made out to be anti-Semitic. Considering this to be 'highly libellous', Graves demanded the removal of several jokes, and compensation of £1,000;[154] and he eventually settled for £250 only, as he told Selwyn Jepson, because 'so many lies are told about me in the press & anywhere that I have decided not to care anyhow'.[155]

Another disappointment was the publication of Gordon Wasson's *Soma: Divine Mushroom of Immortality*, in which Graves's contribution to Wasson's theories received no acknowledgement. 'Any mention of my work in academic books', Graves complained in a review for *The Atlantic*, 'is so suspect as to detract from their sales value and general acceptance.' He added that since, scientifically, he did not exist, he had 'nothing against Wasson for failing to record our speculations about Soma'; but it was clear that he had been wounded, and his review was uncharacteristically severe.[156]

Wasson had indeed been backing away in recent years from Graves's more extravagant speculations;[157] but he in turn was upset by Graves's 'implied criticism', wrote to him asking to be forgiven,[158] and in due course the two men were happily reconciled.[159]

More serious was news of the death of Idries and Omar Ali-Shah's father, the Sirdar Ikbal Ali-Shah, killed in a car crash in Tangier. From Graves's point of view the timing could hardly have been worse. It came shortly before the publication in the *Sunday Times* of what is described by Seymour-Smith as 'a conclusive hatchet job, by a clever journalist'[160] on the claims made by Graves and Omar Ali-Shah in the introductory section of their translation of *The Rubaiyyat* of Omar Khayaam.

Graves did not even reply to this attack, largely because he had been under the impression that Ikbal Ali-Shah had been about to produce the disputed manuscript at the time of his death; and he was certain that it would not be long before his sons, being honourable human beings, directly descended from Mahomet and from the final true Persian monarch, would soon fulfil the paternal intentions.[161] In this, however, he was altogether mistaken.

CHAPTER 6

A Matter of Honour

During the first weeks of January 1970, when Robert Graves was working on *The Song of Songs*, he was plagued by more ill health. A doctor who was staying in Palma suggested 'that his trouble originates from somewhere connected with his nose';[162] and Robert told Juan (who was living quietly in London, where he was studying photography) that he had been 'ill for weeks', and was:

> now going to London on 9th February to see a real expert in Ear Nose and Throat aches and pains Dr. Bateman 55 Harley Street. Maybe the stomach is also hurting because of the same infection. I wake feeling like death warmed up, but that improves with olive-picking and orange-packing.

He would be staying with the Simons, 'or they'll know my address if not'; and his best news was that Juli Simon had been 'accepted as from August 1 for the English Festival Ballet and done her first solo with terrific applause at Oslo so she's okay'.[163]

Returning to Deyá after an inconclusive consultation with Dr Bateman, Graves gave a lengthy interview to Edwin Newman which was later broadcast on his American programme 'Speaking Freely'.[164] Newman began by asking Graves whether, when he sat down to write a poem, he had anybody in mind?

MR GRAVES: A poem is always written for some particular person. And I was asked this same question by Malcolm Muggeridge in a BBC interview.
MR NEWMAN: I know him.
MR GRAVES: Good! He asked me: 'Mr Graves, are the women to whom you write your poems real or imaginary?' And I answered:

'Well, Malcolm, if you want any telephone numbers, you're not going to get them.' That ended that.

The interview also ranged over many of Graves's current preoccupations: the 'shocking' moon-landing; the non-existence of time; old age being 'a pure illusion'; and 'the fact ... that for one reason or another homosexuality among men has gone so far that it's very difficult now for a woman to find a man who isn't in some way tainted with it'. He added eccentrically that it was 'partly due to heredity, partly to environment, but largely because men now drink too much milk'.[166]

In March 1970 it was Juli's twenty-first birthday. She had been 'longing to be officially of the age of responsibility',[167] and Robert persuaded Joanna Simon to fly with him to Venice, where they watched Juli 'dance-in her 22nd year', in 'Symphony in C'.[168] 'Venice', wrote Robert afterwards, 'is still wonderful, especially in the off season with no Germans about.'[169]

Three months later, Graves saw Juli dancing again, this time in London (where he had gone to be fitted for some new dentures);[170] and in August she came out to Deyá. Before her arrival, Graves had been writing gloomily to Jepson: 'I will soon be 75 for what good that may do me; I am not yet grown-up myself of course';[171] and soon after his birthday he told some other friends: 'O for that easy chimney corner in which I cannot settle.'[172] For a brief period, all that seemed to make life tolerable was the appearance on the scene of his friend Edna O'Brien.[173]

Edna looked beautiful and exotic. She sported an Indian caste mark on her forehead; and before Juli's arrival she sat for what seemed like hours on the terrace at Canelluñ, saying very little, but looking queenly and basking in Robert's attention. Occasionally, while the rest of the current set of courtiers looked on silently, hoping for illumination, they exchanged enigmatic morsels of conversation; and afterwards she wrote to Robert: 'I was, I am and I always will be delighted, and regaled, and warmed and made rich by the visit. I could listen to you for years and apart from that I think your life and your habits are on a very high scale and an exemplary one.'[174]

The Sunday picnics continued at Sa Guarda; where one of the chief topics of conversation that summer was the forthcoming publication (financed by Robert) of Catherine Dalton's *Without Hardware*, her account of the curious chain of events which had followed the death of her husband in 1961. There was much talk of plots and counter-plots, of clothes left on the beach, and of CIA agents; and the atmosphere of intrigue was often oppressive.

An increasingly credulous Robert Graves had already posted an extraordinary letter to Selwyn Jepson, in which he claimed that there had been an attempt upon his own life;[175] and he would soon be drafting another letter in which he told some unknown correspondent that his daughter Jenny had been assassinated. The assassin? Kim Philby, whom Robert now believed had 'eliminated' Jenny shortly before his defection to the Soviet Union. The reason? Jenny had been part of MI6, and had been about to expose him as a spy. The means of assassination? Philby had cunningly poisoned Jenny when she was in Salisbury. The occasion? An entertainment arranged by Lady Diana Cooper. Robert concluded, still more strangely, that press reports of the post-mortem had been deliberately falsified ...[176]

On Sunday 6 September, [177] Robert Graves was in London for a return visit to the Mermaid Theatre.[178] Much to Robert's pleasure, Jerome Robbins was in the audience; as was Vivien Holzer, an attractive young woman who had been his personal guide at the Mexico Cultural Olympics.[179] They had a long, intimate talk together; and later she wrote to him:

> ... really, Robert, you should try not to feel so sad because you get to see Juli so seldom. Just think, those few moments will be so full! One has to encompass so much in such a short time.

'You alone', she reminded him, 'were telling me how you have grown to be so close because of this cutting through time.'[180]

In October Graves returned briefly to London;[181] and that was also the month in which he made one last attempt to clear his name in the Omar Khayaam controversy, by asking Idries Shah to produce the Jan Fishan Khan manuscript of the *Rubaiyyat*.

Idries Shah, however, argued that production of the MSS would prove nothing, because there would be no way of telling whether it was original, or whether someone had washed the writing from a piece of ancient parchment, and then applied a new text using inert inks. In his view, it was 'high time that we realised that the hyenas who are making so much noise are intent only on opposition, destructiveness and carrying on a campaign when, lets's face it, nobody is really listening'. His father, he went on, had been so infuriated by the hyenas that he had refused to have anything to do with them;[182] and Idries was sure that his father had been correct. 'The manuscript, as you know, is not in my possession', he concluded. 'If it were, I would have no hesitation at all in refusing to show it to anyone under any circumstances at any time whatever.'[183]

Graves replied very forcefully that producing the manuscript was now 'a matter of family honour'. Publication of his translation had done him 'a great deal of harm, especially from continually renewed attacks on my reputation in the powerful *Sunday Times* and in leading American newspapers'. He would not have accepted the task so cheerfully had he known that he was putting his head into a trap from which the Shahs were unable to extricate him; and he still could not believe this to be true. In addition, he pointed out that Idries's letter completely contradicted two previous ones on the same subject, in which he had promised to produce the manuscript if necessary. 'The trouble is', Graves concluded,

> that what is now publicly considered to be my gross deception by the Shah brothers has cast doubt on all my historical writings. This smudge can be shown to have reduced the royalties drawn from these that keep my family alive. I have recently had to support, wholly or partly, about a dozen of them.

'So your decision', he concluded, 'for reasons of family pride, not to submit to scrutiny under any circumstances seem difficult to reconcile with either our personal or family friendship.'[184]

To this moving appeal, Idries Shah replied with no more than 'a brief, abrupt, business-like letter', thanking Graves for his 'most interesting letter of November 11th', and saying that he looked forward to discussing 'these and other matters when you come to England shortly'.[185] In practice, the manuscript was never produced; and after all these years it is difficult to believe, in view of the Shahs' numerous obligations to Graves, that they would have continued to withhold it *had it ever existed in the first place.*

CHAPTER 7

The Fifth Dimension

By November 1970, Robert Graves was once again feeling ill; and towards the end of the month, he travelled briefly to London in the hope of having an operation to clear his nose.[186] After a thorough examination however, it was decided to postpone the operation until the following year.

The intervening months were melancholy ones for Graves, especially as his pools of memory loss gradually broadened until they joined together to form a lake beneath which a substantial area of his past life was completely submerged. By February 1971, when he was still hoping to 'recover my health and memory, which is affected by the virus', he had to admit that he could not 'remember anything later than about 1956. Sad!'[187]

Then came news that his brother Charles had died suddenly of heart failure in the West Indies at the age of seventy; and on returning to Deyá after a spell in University College Hospital,[188] Robert heard from John that his wife Mary, and their children Simon ('Glaucus') and Elizabeth were all lying injured in hospital after a serious road accident. 'I've just come out of hospital myself', Robert replied.

> after what was called a major nose operation because it took the surgens two hours to clear away the damage of 1913 and allow nature to clean out the viral infection that has, for months, given me ear-nose-throat-eye-and-stomach ache. Will be well again in May they say. Yes – sad about Charles, but it was swift.[189]

Robert's most exciting news was that he had 'just been honoured' by St John's College, Oxford, who, much to his delight, had made him an Honorary Fellow. 'I refuse Honorary D. Litts and D.C.Ls', he explained, 'but St. John's has been good to me.'

Sadly, he experienced none of the promised improvement in his health; and when in May he was due to visit Hungary again, he undertook the journey to Budapest only because he had heard that his 'poetic friend', the translator Gabor Devecseri was dying of cancer.[190]

'There are, I believe', Graves began his 'Address to the poets of Hungary' on 28 May,

> only three countries in Europe where the name of poet is everywhere honoured rather than ridiculed. First comes Ireland ... Next Wales ... Finally Hungary. I am Irish by birth, Welsh by adoption, and Hungary has always brought me good luck, I suppose also because of its outstanding poetic tradition.

He went on to describe the poetic power 'to make things happen', which

> raises simple love-alliances to a point where physical absence supplies living presence ... these miraculous experiences can occur not only in the fourth dimension, where prison walls of the third dimension are easily cheated, but can also occur in the fifth dimension where time is ... easily manipulated, and where seemingly impossible coincidences and so-called 'acts of God' occur almost as a matter of course.

'In poetry', he concluded, 'the fifth-dimensional co-identification of lovers is truth rather than idealistic fancy.'[191]

As Graves wrote in his introduction to *The Green Sailed Vessel*, a signed limited edition of his latest poems which appeared in 1971,[192] he had become 'increasingly concerned with hidden powers of poetic thought, which raise and solve problems akin to those of advanced mathematics and physics'; and the 'fifth-dimensional' results of a poet's love for his muse were described 'however inadequately',[193] in such poems as 'Serpent's Tail', in which he wrote:

> When you are old as I now am
> I shall be young as you, my lamb;
> For lest love's timely force shoud fail
> The Serpent swallows his own tail.[194]

Or 'Quinque', the beautiful Latin poem for Juli which he loosely translated as:

Five beringed fingers of Creation,
Five candles blazing at a shrine,
Five points of her continuous pentagram,
Five letters in her name – as five in mine.
I love, therefore I am.[195]

Juli herself was on tour with the Festival Ballet in southern Europe. 'She gets all the gipsy parts', Robert commented; and she would be visiting Deyá on 25 July 1971, the day after his seventy-sixth birthday.[196]

There was also news of Aemilia. Earlier in the year, having parted amicably from Peter Weismiller, she had been seen in Puerto Vallarta looking 'fine' and wearing 'all those beautiful feathers';[197] and by July she was in Kathmandu, where she was planning to marry '*another* James McKinley' – not, in other words, the American historian whom Robert had now asked to write his biography, but 'a craftsman'.[198] Later, she sent one of Robert's friends a letter from Nepal, where she was 'in high spirits, but speaking about going to see some priest in order to heighten the spirit even more'.[199]

Still later, Robert heard from Aemilia himself: and it would be her final communication. She had run out of money on her way back from Nepal and had then, as Robert told a mutual friend, begged him to assist her. However, he could not transmit cash directly to Turkey. Besides, when he and Aemilia had met most recently ... at any rate, he had managed to return, and he supposed that she had found her way back.[200]

By this time, Robert Graves was feeling worse than ever. 'Have been ill and can't get well', he informed his brother John in October: 'after-effects of a nose-operation, plus psychosomatic worries'.[201] He had recently spent a further fortnight in hospital,[202] but the doctors found 'no symptoms ... of anything but unexplained nervous depression'.[203]

Despite this depression, Graves had managed to write a play 'about that crook Saul of Tarsus'; but he was definitely ill with a 'virus infection and emotional disturbances',[204] and he informed Seymour-Smith that the virus had led to 'bad effects on general health plus earache stomach & throat aches ... Worst is loss of memory and giddiness. Meanwhile', he concluded, 'I write poems (they are going way out into the fifth dimension).'[205]

In October 1971, there was news from Tony Richardson, who had been hoping to make a film of *I, Claudius* for several years. Earlier, he had explained his difficulties to Graves: numerous attempts at securing a satisfactory script, involving authors such as Edward Bond and

Christopher Isherwood had been a complete failure. 'Actually', he wrote as an aside, 'there is only one way to make Claudius: three films like the three parts of *Ivan the Terrible*'. Finally, he had:

> asked John Mortimer to come in and do a new script. I don't know whether you know his work. Alec Guinness is just playing his new play *A Voyage Round my Father* at the moment. He has produced at least a version which while still a way off has found the right style and irony for the dialogue which is a very good basis for a final screenplay.[206]

However, there was 'a prejudice against what the so-called industry calls a toga film'; and so now he and John Mortimer were considering turning it into a stage play first.[207]

Graves himself spent until February 1972 preparing a collection of essays and talks under the title *Difficult Questions, Easy Answers;* but from then on, the increasingly erratic nature of his memory meant that any sustained effort was beyond him. So he limited himself to writing poems, and giving poetry readings or very brief addresses.

CHAPTER 8

Loss of Memory

Robert Graves told his brother John in January 1972 that his best news was that after he had lived for so many years on Spanish soil, the Spaniards were at last 'translating 3 books of mine – the first ever'.[208] He was also excited about John's researches into the family genealogy.

Robert's interest was partly on behalf of their niece Sally Chilver: since she was now Principal of Lady Margaret Hall, Oxford, Robert felt that it was important for her to have proof of her descent, through Alfred Perceval Graves's first wife Janie Cooper, from John of Gaunt: which would make her a connexion of Lady Margaret Beaufort, after whom Lady Margaret Hall had been named. That proof had been easy for John Graves to supply; but Robert, who had been claiming for sometime to be descended from the Prophet Mohammed,[209] also wanted confirmation of his own descent from the Beauforts, which would enable him to prove his claim. And when this confirmation could not be supplied – because Robert was Amy's son, not Janie's – he simply ignored the evidence.[210]

In the spring, when Graves flew to England to take part in a series of festive occasions, one of them, on 20 April, was dinner with Sally Chilver at Lady Margaret Hall. Shortly beforehand, there was the Rawlinson Dinner at St John's,[211] which he now described as 'a home from home', adding that 'The new President Richard Southern the mediaevalist is wonderful';[212] and shortly afterwards Graves was present at the Shakespeare celebrations in London[213]

These had been arranged by the American director Sam Wanamaker, who was raising money with the intention of building a replica of Shakespeare's original Globe Theatre; and, for a token fee of £30, Graves had contributed a birthday poem which was set to music by Ramon Farran. At first there was little appreciation for the fact that he was the only one of the contributing poets who had provided the song that had been specifically requested;[214] but despite extremely limited rehearsal time, it was eventually sung in Southwark Cathedral 'with great success'.

It was also included in a signed limited edition of 100 specially bound copies of his poem and the many others that were read that day.[215]

In March, Tony Richardson sent John Mortimer's first draft of the *Claudius* play to Robert Graves,[216] who described it as 'a wonderful piece of work'; though he was worried that Mortimer had ' "chanced his arm" on small details of Roman matrimony, and I don't want to see him picked to pieces by over-clever critics'.[217]

The première of *I, Claudius* was on 11 July at the Queen's Theatre,[218] but it had closed by mid-September. According to Ralph Jacobs, it was one of the best plays he had ever seen, there had been a packed house, and David Warner had been superb in the title role. 'I just don't understand why it closed', he told Robert; 'other Americans who saw it while in London felt the same way I did.'[219] 'Yes', replied Robert, who had attended the opening night with Beryl.[220] 'The gallery and upper circles loved *Claudius*, the stalls (who pay the most) liked it the least. I hope it goes to the USA where they would not make the same mistakes.'[221]

Inevitably, there continued to be emotional ups and downs in Robert Graves's relationship with Juli Simon. Early in the year, he had enjoyed a week in England when he had watched her dancing.[222] But on 4 August Robert Edwards, a friend of Idries Shah who had visited Deyá several times with his wife, and had been helpful during the Southwark celebrations, mentioned Graves being 'in trouble' with his Muse.[223] Unfortunately, the poet could not help being jealous when any other man was close to her: hence, perhaps, such lines as:

> What she refused him – in the name of love
> And the hidden tears he shed –
> She granted only to such soulless blades
> As might accept her casual invitation
> To a loveless bed.[224]

Later that month, in any case, this particular difficulty had been resolved: for Juli wrote a friendly postscript to one of Joanna's letters to Robert, sending her love in advance of a September visit.[225]

In the meantime, Robert travelled with Beryl to the 'Hotel Claudius', in a part of Hungary that had once been conquered by the legions of that Emperor. Robert's health was poor, and his handwriting correspondingly feeble, when he reported to his brother John that he was signing:

hundreds of copies of *I, Claudius* (in Hungarian) because it is the favourite book in Hungary. It feels funny to be a celebrity. The hills here are an exact copy of the ones in Bavaria that I remember so well from my Grandfather's day – fruit, flowers, vegetables and all.

He added that he had not been well for some months, but was 'expecting a vaccine will be ready, when I get back tomorrow to Deyá to cure me'.[226]

The vaccine did appear to make a difference; but Juli's visit in late September was not altogether easy, and Robert reported to Ralph Jacobs that she had 'quarrelled a bit with me', although:

> in general all was fine and we went to see Calder the US painter having an exhibition at the invitation of Miro (whom she and I both love).
>
> The Cala was still batheable and I wrote three poems which she accepted.

'The papers', he added, 'say I'm too old for the poet laureateship.'[227] (C. Day-Lewis had recently died, and would be succeeded as laureate by Sir John Betjeman.) 'Should I burst into tears or just ugly laughter?'[228]

Honours of various kinds continued to come in Robert Graves's direction. Earlier in the year, he had 'persuaded the Spanish Government to protect the whole N.W. cost against touristic architecture: by decree', which led to the presentation of a Spanish Gold Medal 'for all I have done for Majorca'[229]; and in November, Sally Chilver passed on a message from Constantine FitzGibbon, asking whether he would accept election to the Irish Academy of Letters. 'Dearest Sally', Robert replied,

> The things that happen when one reaches the late Seventies! You could have knocked me down with a couple of feathers, left & right, when the invitation came through you for the Irish Honour, which it would be ungracious to decline.
>
> And your father, grandfather and great-grandfather would have frowned had I done so ... I have not been in Ireland apart from a single day's punitive visit to Sligo since I went there disguised as a Captain in the Royal Welch Fus. in 1918. So please tell them that I will gladly come next year in the Spring or summer.

'Meanwhile', he went on, 'hold your breath & register surprise'. At the invitation of the Burns Society, he was going to Glasgow on 24 January 1973 to make a fifteen-minute speech 'in Burns' honour at his Banquet'. Robert added that he was 'getting slowly cured, the vaccines etc. and my memory seems to be returning – Beryl claims to be losing *hers* now'.[230]

However this improvement was only temporary. Just over a week later, writing to his brother John, Robert admitted that his memory was once again 'shocking'; and indeed, he was becoming so muddled about which copies of his books he had already given away, that he began to believe that at least '10 copies of my two new books which I was going to send off to friends' had been stolen from him.[231]

Graves's eyesight was also deteriorating (in December it was so bad that Beryl typed a number of his letters[232]); and in the first few months of 1973, his memory continued to worsen. However, he managed to give his talk on Burns Night – encouraged by Juli Simon, who accompanied him to Glasgow,[233] where she was 'the only woman there in the assembly of the thirty most distinguished living Scots, plus the Russian ambassador';[234] and fortunately Robert's loss of memory had not yet affected his ability to write poems, of which, as he wrote, an unexpected flood had recently happened.[235]

Several of these had been inspired by Graves's realization that it was seven years since Juli Simon had become his Muse. In one of them, 'The Scared Child', he writes movingly of the pains and pleasures of the kind of idealistic love they shared with one another:

> It is seven years now that we first loved –
> Since you were still a scared and difficult child
> Confessing less than love prompted,
> Yet one night coaxed me into bed
> With a gentle kiss
> And there blew out the candle.
> Had you then given what your tongue promised,
> Making no fresh excuses
> And never again punished your true self
> With the acceptance of my heart only,
> Not of my body, nor offered your caresses
> To brisk and casual strangers –
> How would you stand now? Not in love's full glory
> That jewels your fingers immemorially
> And brines your eyes with bright prophetic tears.[236]

Graves's brave attempt to move on from the purely romantic love about which he had written in *The White Goddess*, towards some new and more appropriate relationship between men and women, was now foundering upon the rocks of his increasing senility. However, in his advocacy of matriarchal rule, he had been a powerful influence upon a number of 1960s and 1970s feminists.

One of these, Elizabeth Gould-Davis, first wrote to him in 1969 and then corresponded with him for several years while she was engaged in writing her ground-breaking work *The First Sex*. In December 1972, she pointed out that 25,000 copies of the paperback edition had been sold *in its first month*;[237] and in February 1973 she told him:

I suppose you know that you are the God of the new Movement here, the newest of the new women's movements, and you are the only male creature who is admitted to godhead in the movement. It has all sorts of names because it is not yet co-ordinated. Small groups from California to New York have formed to defy Christianity and all organised religion, to worship the female principle, and to bring back the Great Goddess.[238]

Despite Graves's numerous reservations about the reintroduction of Goddess worship, she believed that 'the time has now come, to judge by the fervency of the new women'. Tragically, Gould-Davis would later commit suicide under the pressure of increasing ill health; but not before she had also published *The Female Principle*, and completed *The Founding Mothers*.

Graves had also been a powerful influence upon Colin Wilson, who had been an instructor attached to the Mediterranean Institute of Dowling College when it was located in Deyá in 1969;[239] and who had subsequently sent Graves the second chapter of what would become his classic work on *The Occult*, in which he had written about *The White Goddess* at some length.[240]

Another of Graves's works, *Good-bye to All That*, had been receiving increased attention since the fiftieth anniversary of the outbreak of the First World War in 1914; and now the television documentary producer Paul Watson was hoping to film it 'at the back of Harlech with all the soldier actors supplied by the RWF depot'. A script was prepared by Watson and his script writer/collaborator Tim Jeal; and there was talk of Robert's sixteen-year-old nephew Charles Graves (John's youngest child) playing the part of Robert as a Carthusian schoolboy. However, the BBC did not have enough money – Robert was outraged when he heard that they were trying to secure the necessary finance from the Germans[241] and in December, after months of abortive work, the project was permanently laid to one side.[242]

In mid-February 1973, Robert had once again told John that he was 'ill with loss of memory and other symptoms';[243] but by April he was well enough to travel to London, where he had been invited by Eamon Andrews to contribute to a 'This is Your Life' programme in honour of Spike Milligan. As their mutual friend Pauline Scudamore tells the story, Robert 'was disinclined to go to the television studios so the television crew, producers and directors came to him'. He was staying, as usual, with the Simons; where he was 'very happy and co-operative and sat on a window seat, with the garden in the background'; and where he 'spoke almost exclusively about the joys and successes of the Mermaid evening'.[244]

Graves had often heard from Milligan about his efforts to preserve old buildings;[245] and while he was in London, his own help was enlisted (through Pauline Scudamore) by the Duchess of St Albans, in a fight to save the 100-year-old Albert Bridge from demolition. As the *Chelsea Post* records,

> Armed with a Regency table, an Edwardian tea urn, dozens of balloons and a few token bicycles the Duchess of St. Albans led her troups on to the bridge.
>
> Enthroned midway between Chelsea and Battersea they urged all passers-by to sign their petition to keep the bridge and turn it into a pedestrian precinct.

'Poet Robert Graves' declared that: 'The planners are ruining civilisation, let us witness a return to the bicycle';[246] the campaign caught the popular imagination; and in due course the bridge was saved.

By September 1973, Robert was again complaining to his brother John that he was 'unwell & struck by a nasty loss of memory which makes me feel a fool, but I get past, somehow';[247] and in October John Aldridge, visiting with his wife Gretl[248] noticed a severe deterioration in his old friend, who asked him whether this was his first visit to Deyá.[249]

Towards the end of March 1974, Beryl told a friend that: 'Robert spends most of his time picking olives as he can't do much writing because of his eyes';[250] and there were other difficulties. In particular, Robert's relationship with Juli Simon, which continued to mean much to him, became more and more difficult for her to cope with; and in May John Aldridge wrote to Beryl:

> Of course his relationship with Juli has become unreal and she must feel very constrained. But unless Robert can replace her with another Muse he will feel forlorn and what about her house in Deyá? I don't

expect she will want to give it up and if she still comes there Robert will be hankering with hopes.[251]

James Reeves was a visitor that summer, and noticed a distinct improvement in Robert's physical health: 'he seemed to me to be making progress during the fortnight', James wrote to Beryl. 'He couldn't have rushed up to the Posada and down to the Cala the day we arrived.'[252]

This improvement meant that it was possible for Beryl to accept, on Robert's behalf, an invitation from Bolek Taborski of the Warsaw Branch of the Polish Writer's Union to attend the so-called 'Warsaw Autumn of Poetry'. Accompanied by Beryl, Robert landed in Warsaw late on Friday 20 September 1974; and then, as Beryl records, 'All hell broke loose.'[253]

The contrast between the expectations which Robert Graves's presence aroused, and what he could actually deliver, was now so great that what followed has a surreal, comical and yet often touching glow, in which real difficulties were surmounted partly because even in his decline Graves was more impressive than many speakers in their prime; and partly because he had become a kind of 'Holy Fool', whose very innocence was capable of winning the day; but largely because of Beryl's constant support.

On their arrival, for example, Robert began telling anyone who cared to listen 'about the German sign he saw put up across the trenches in 1916 saying that Warsaw had fallen'; which caused complications, as it had actually fallen to the Germans the previous year. Then on Saturday, a Spanish-speaking Pole came to interview Graves 'about the significance of Greek myths on present-day life'. To begin with, he addressed Graves as 'maestro'; but when Graves seemed to find it difficult to answer his questions, he became first 'clearly disappointed,' and then no doubt somewhat baffled, for Graves changed the subject to LSD and mushrooms. 'Fortunately', Beryl commented drily, 'This was not recorded and I lent him ... our copy of *Difficult Questions* which has two articles on the subject.'

After lunch on Saturday, things became still more difficult. There was a book-signing session which, as Beryl records, was:

murder. As it had been advertised in yesterday's *Express* there was a tremendous queue of readers who applauded R on arrival. It wouldn't have been so bad if Irene Lason [of PEN International] hadn't kept interfering – or rather trying to help. Every time she spoke Robert got more annoyed. The trouble was instead of writing just his name he insisted on putting the date and the place both of which he kept forgetting and had to ask me nearly every time. After nearly an hour Bartleski one of the chiefs of the Writers' Union arrived and made matters worse by chattering to one of the ladies, until Robert threatened to leave! There was no visible end to the queue, Robert was exhausted and Mrs Lason didn't seem to know what to do so I suggested stopping when we reached the lady in the red jacket about six away ...

Sunday was enlivened by a brief visit from Eva Perhauska, 'a *White Goddess* enthusiast' whom Robert liked 'very much'; and then on Monday evening came the grand poetry reading in a small theatre near the old city.

Beryl joined Robert on the stage, where Robert 'sat on a sort of wooden throne in the middle', while Beryl 'sat next to him to help him find his glasses papers etcetera'. First Robert read some comparatively recent poems, which were also read in translation by Taborski; and then another poet declaimed Taborski's translation of Robert's much earlier 'The Persian Version':

> Truth-loving Persians do not dwell upon
> The trivial skirmish fought near Marathon.
> As for the Greek theatrical tradition
> Which represents the summer's expedition
> Not as a mere reconnaissance in force
> By three brigades of foot and one of horse
> (Their left flank covered by some obsolete
> Light craft detached from the main Persian fleet)
> But as a grandiose, ill-starred attempt
> To conquer Greece – they treat it with contempt;
> And only incidentally refute
> Major Greek claims, by stressing what repute
> The Persian monarch and the Persian nation
> Won by this salutary demonstration:
> Despite a strong defence and adverse weather
> All arms combined magnificently together.[254]

This brilliant satire on the use of propaganda by an imperial power was so obviously relevant to the experience of the Poles with Russian, that it received 'great applause, which was repeated when R read it in English'.

Events during the next few days included a visit to Chopin's birthplace, where they had to listen to 'an intense recital of Chopin's music from the front row' in the company of a drunken Swede who kept trying to amuse them with his collection of pornographic biros; several receptions; and a telephone call telling them, as Beryl noted, that:

> there was an urgent letter waiting for us at the Bank. Think of all the possible disasters that might be notified to us through the bank, but when we got there it turned out to be a letter from Richard Graves addressed to Robert Graves, poet travelling in Poland, asking for help on his projected book on T. E. Lawrence. What a relief.

Then on Sunday 29 September, Robert and Beryl left Warsaw and flew on to Budapest.

After a week in Budapest (where Robert met that year's winner of the 'Robert Graves Prize', and muddled everyone by insisting that he had been in Rome at the end of World War I), they flew to Warsaw, from where they were driven on to Cracow. There they had the good fortune to be put up by two young friends of theirs: the Scottish Rab Shiell and his pregnant Polish wife Barbara. Rab and Barbara both worked for the British Council, and had made several visits to Deyá, where Rab's good humour and sound intellect had combined with Barbara's considerable charm and wit (not to mention her sparkling eyes and raven-black hair) to make them a much sought-after couple. 'The flat consists of one large room', wrote Beryl,

> kitchen and bathroom. They let us have the bed rather a squash and they had the divans and we kept our clothes etcetera in the suitcases. They have a lovely pussy-cat ... after a delicious supper of borscht, duck and potatoes we went to bed early.

Rab had taken a week's holiday in order to have time to show Robert and Beryl around, and together they walked along the banks of the River Vistula, and looked up at the towering castle walls of Cracow. Rab and Robert enjoyed each other's company so much that Beryl was able to relax and tell herself 'What fun we are having here!' While Barbara's cooking was so good that, as she noted, 'we have no desire to eat elsewhere'.

On the evening of Thursday 10 October, there was a poetry reading at the university. Someone had predicted that very few would attend, 'but in fact the hall was full to overflowing'; and Robert was in such excellent form that he 'gave a very good reading without mishap'. When there were questions, and he was asked 'Do you have any regular hours for writing?' he gave such a scathing reply that his questioner was reduced to muttering: 'well some writers like to be regular'.

Friday morning was warm and sunny; and after visiting the market (where Robert wandered off and was lost for a while), Robert, Beryl, Rab and Barbara travelled to the village of Zakopane, not far from the Polish border, where they stayed in an unheated attic room with stunning views of the high Tatry mountains covered with snow.

By the following Wednesday, 16 October, they were back in Deyá. All in all, the tour had been a great success: but several times it had teetered on the edge of disaster, and it would be Robert Graves's last.

From then on, Graves would spend nearly all his time in the village which he had first made his home more than forty years before; and it was somehow appropriate that on his return from Poland he had found waiting for him a poem from James Reeves, who had written:

TO ROBERT GRAVES IN DEYÁ

After long search you came like Ulysses
To find your point of no departure here,
Where the gold houses in your valley grow
Like craggy olive trunks and walls of rock.
Taking the Valdemossa-Soller road,
Here you stepped off. You had no longer use
For any new direction or distraction.
Now between mopeds and percussive music
Cicadas drill the silences, and bells
Stumble about the slopes on unseen sheep.
Shutters repel the stifling afternoon.
Above the sheep, the olives and the houses,
The silences, the noise, the twelve stations,
You circle upward to the church-topped height.
Airs from the landlocked bay a mile below
Stroke the dry grasses, stir no memories
In the walled cemetery under the skies.
Old, new – old, young – live, dead are layered close
Between the swimmer's bay and the still summit.
About this centre turns your whole slow world
Future and past contracted to the present.
Here is your place who wrote no careless comma.
Whoever stands beside you here may share
The crowning privilege of your terraced valley.[255]

Early in December 1974 there was news that John Aldridge's first wife

Lucie had died;[256] but the news made little impact upon Robert. Nor did that of Diana Graves's death in February 1975. In her warm, throaty voice, Diana had so often told people: 'My dear, I'm *dying*' that they had ceased to believe it; and when she had been really dying of cancer, her hospital sick room, as her friend Peregrine Worsthorne wrote in *The Times*:

> was a veritable salon to the end, filled with writers, actors, artists (not to mention flowers and bottles) who never tired of listening to that throaty voice, known to millions through *Woman's Hour*, where she performed – there is no other word – with incomparable wit and humanity … As one who was lucky enough to enjoy a seat in the stalls.

he concluded, 'I grieve most bitterly that at last the final curtain has come down for ever.'[257]

In Canelluñ, another party had been in view since the previous March, when Robert Graves had told Spike Milligan that he would be celebrating his eightieth birthday on 24 July 1975 with 'a theatrical performance in my garden across the main road', and asking him to 'take general charge in company with Ronnie Scott who will bring his merry men'.[258] Spike had replied that he would certainly be there, barring any major work commitments; and there the matter had rested while Robert's memory spiralled downhill.

'Robert will be 80 this year', Beryl wrote on 13 March 1975, 'and is beginning to feel the weight of his years; his memory is awfully bad and he can't concentrate enough to do any writing. I suppose it may be some sort of self-defence as he's worked so hard all his life. So little is known about the workings of the mind.'[260] However, she was still determined to mark the occasion, as were many others.

Honor Wyatt's son Julian Glover, for one. Glover had prepared a one-man show on Graves, which he was to present at the Royal Court Theatre on Sunday 20 July, just a few days before the birthday.[261] The Royal Welch Fusiliers had greatly honoured 'Captain Graves' by making him their principal guest the previous year at the regimental dinner;[262] and St John's College had invited him to come to Oxford towards the end of June 1975 for a series of celebrations.

First, on Friday 27 June, came the College Gaudy, which included former undergraduates from the 1919–21 entry. This meant that one of Robert Graves's fellow guests was his brother John. The two men had not seen each other since Robert's last lecture as Professor of Poetry back in

1967, and so for John it was a melancholy meeting. When he knocked at the door of the President's lodging, it was opened to reveal not only Lady Southern, but a Robert who looked 'thin & old & unshaven ... wearing a blue suit, with one side of his collar undone and a completely faded flower in his button-hole'.[263]

When they went upstairs, hoping to watch a television interview Robert had given a day or two earlier, it never came on, and 'Robert sat saying "Blah! Blah!" to whatever appeared on the programme.' Later there was a special service in chapel to commemorate the College benefactors; and John saw Robert 'in a white surplice sitting opposite among the senior Fellows. From time to time he fixed me with a rather strange stare, as if he could not quite place me, though we had been conversing half an hour before.' Afterwards,

> Robert appeared to enjoy the dinner, at which he sat opposite the President. The meal was introduced by an Orator in Latin. In welcoming the guests, he noted with pleasure various pairs of brothers, mentioning among others:

> 'te, vates clarissime, Roberte Graves, cum fratre Ioanne';

which John Graves 'thought most courteous'.

The following day saw the official opening of the Sir Thomas White Building, a vast new range which provided much additional accommodation within St John's. It incorporated a special 'Robert Graves' room, in which Robert and Beryl were both present that day when John Wain, another distinguished member of the College, made a brief and amusing speech in Robert's honour, and then unveiled a splendid head by the Spanish sculptor Carmen Alvarez Feldman.[264]

Robert and Beryl then returned to their island home; where preparations were soon in full swing for Robert's eightieth birthday.

CHAPTER 9

It's Your Moon and My Moon²⁶⁵

Canelluñ: the afternoon of Tuesday 22 July 1975. A blazing sun. A small red hire-car turns in through the iron gates, and parks near the top of the narrow, sloping drive. Tomas Graves, who is now long-haired and twenty-two, and has just completed a typographical course in London, cheerfully greets the newcomers: his cousins Richard, Elizabeth and Charles. To one side of the drive, on the small, terraced lawn with the bay tree which Robert planted in 1929, two men are hanging lights for the party. On the other side the potter Colin Thompson, thin and wiry, is preparing an ice-cream cart for use as a drinks cooler, and remarks proudly that he has travelled all the way from the Outer Hebrides.

The cousins wander across the lawn, and sit on cane chairs in the shade of a carob tree hung with ripening beans. A moment later, Robert ambles along from the vegetable garden, wearing an old pair of white trousers, a blue shirt, and red braces. He has been gathering tomatoes; and on seeing the newcomers he flings some over, takes the rest into the house, and then finds a small green wheelbarrow which he steadily fills with dead leaves for his latest compost heap.

Later, Robert slips a casual blue top over his braces, dons a black flat-topped broad-brimmed Spanish hat, and he and Beryl join John and Mary and their family for supper at C'an Quet. Later still, they drink coffee back at Canelluñ. Richard Graves has just completed his book on T. E. Lawrence, and Robert takes him into his study to show him his Lawrence collection, and some of his other treasures: a small silver container, delicately fashioned, full of what look like small, black seeds; and a piece of fossilized wood, as hard as rock and at least three million years old. Walking out of the house again, Robert leans against the side of a car and looks up at the stars.

Richard asks him: 'Have you been writing any poems lately?'

Robert looks serious. 'As a matter of fact', he says, 'I wrote one yesterday, the first in over a year. One has to be in love, and that's difficult. Poems come on one.'

Headlights turn into the drive. Sam Graves has arrived. Robert joins him on the terrace, and greets him with evident affection, saying 'Boo!' and giving him a friendly pat on the shoulder. Then they join the others, and watch the moon rising above the mountains. After a long silence, John recalls a German song from their Wimbledon days. Robert, who has been pacing restlessly up and down, breaks into singing, and dances a few steps in the moonlight.

Wednesday morning. Robert, who has been talking to Beryl in the coolness of the central hall, walks out into the blazing heat of the verandah, where Sam sits with Juli Simon. Robert and Juli look at each other and smile. Juli gets up and kisses Robert on the cheek, and they wander happily down the garden together.

Later, Robert emerges from his study, carrying a small wooden writing-board, to which are attached the latest drafts of his new poem. He stands for a while abstracted, noticing no one. His poem is about love and the White Goddess; and its last line reads:

> There it shone in its infinite truth.

In the late afternoon, after his siesta, Robert walks into the village to collect the post. Then he climbs up the street of Ramon Llull to take tea with his friend the cabinet-maker Martin Tallents at the long wooden table which stands just inside his front door.

That evening, after supper on the terrace, Robert stays sitting at the table with Juli, Juan and Richard. Juli is wearing a long dress, and a necklace hung with brightly-painted China ornaments. She tells Juan that she would like to make jewellery, but that working in gold would require too much capital. Then she begins talking to Richard about the phases of the moon; and when she loses the thread of her argument, and comes to an abrupt halt, Robert smiles lovingly at her and says: 'Well, it's your moon and my moon, so it doesn't really matter.'

The next day, Thursday 24 July 1975, is Robert's eightieth birthday. In the morning a wooden stage is erected to one side of the terrace; paper decorations are hung on the trees; and Sam's daughter Georgina, a lovely young woman with a mass of red curly hair, sweeps the drive and sends up clouds of dust. Later, she joins Robert and other members of the family in C'an Torrent for a rehearsal of 'Widecombe Fair'. Robert, without his glasses, cannot read the words he has been handed, and begins to sing an alternative version. When John stops him, he says huffily: 'Oh well, then I'm not going to sing at all', and begins to walk out. Fortunately, Ramon smooths things over. Robert's glasses are found, peace with John is restored, and the rehearsal proceeds.

Dozens of birthday greetings have arrived, ranging from Edna O'Brien's warm-hearted, 'Dear Robert have a hale and happy birthday and abundant love', to the proud Latin of St John's College Oxford: 'Vatem Nostrum et Socium Salutamus Johannesses Octogenarium'.

Robert changes into a fawn suit, and a light blue shirt with red roses and green leaves embroidered on the lapels, He also puts on his St John's College tie, which he later replaces with the tie of the Royal Welch Fusiliers. He appears to remember nothing about what happened ten minutes ago; but the remote past is vividly recalled, and Robert remains intensely proud of both College and Regiment.

By eight o'clock that evening, Robert's sister Rosaleen has arrived. In her eighty-second year, she is as formidable as ever, has an insatiable appetite for new ideas, and announces that she has just started doing meals-on-wheels 'for the old folk'. Sitting on a bench beside the lawn, she holds court to an admiring circle. Nearby, a table is covered with bowls of olives and tomatoes, and all kinds of pastries. In the entrance to the garage a barrel of Binisalem has been broached; and guests, after being welcomed at the gate by Robert and Lucia, are pouring up the drive.

Eight-thirty. Robert, who is now standing by a pile of wood, takes up an axe and splits a log in half. A photographer tries to capture the moment, but misses her opportunity. She sighs and reports back to the man from *Newsweek*, who announces that he has 300 words and asks rather desperately whether any celebrities are coming?

Just after nine, a hot-air balloon with orange and yellow stripes is released from the balcony. Ralph Jacobs is among those applauding as it soars into invisibility; and Martin Tallents sits at the edge of the stage guarding a bronze head of Robert sculpted and cast by the beautiful Carmen Alvarez Feldman earlier in the year. It is getting dark, and the lights in the trees are switched on.

At ten o'clock, the 'Graves Family Singers' spread out in a line across the stage; and the audience falls silent as Lucia shines her torch on the words of 'Widecombe Fair.' Robert begins, in a clear, melodious voice:

Tam Pearse, Tam Pearse, lend me your grey mare ...

Led by John as Bill Brewer and Tomas as Jan Stewer, the rest of the family sing out the chorus. When Robert loses his place, and begins repeating one verse, Rosaleen starts calling out: 'No, darling!' but she is nudged in the ribs and told to keep quiet: just in time. Robert goes on singing:

> Of a sudden the old mare she shuddered and died
> Singing all along out along down along lea
> And Tam Pearse he sat down on a stone and he cried ...

There is prolonged applause, and Robert walks cheerfully to the far side of the terrace, where he sits with Georgina at his feet, while the Valldemossans sing 'On the banks of the Ohio'.

Later on, Lucia, accompanied by Tomas, sings a song about the shadow which a cedar tree casts in moonlight. The singer and the song are both hauntingly beautiful; and Robert smiles with pleasure.

Much later, Robert is standing beneath the orange tree on the lawn. He is tired; and when Beryl comes up, looking concerned, he says, 'I just want to see Juli.' She promises to look for her; but then Robert makes his own way up to the terrace, where he finds that sixty or seventy guests are standing in a ring, and watching Juli dance.

She has a partner, Dito, a friend of Juan's and a tough bearded Mallorquin. He dances well to the music, which has a loud, insistent beat – is that Tomas or Ramon on the drums? – but all eyes are on Juli. There is something both elemental and ecstatic about her dancing. Her body twists and sways. She achieves beauty. Robert, who is standing beside his nephew Richard, half turns towards him and whispers: 'She's terrific, isn't she.'

The dance comes to an end. The spell is broken. People begin to talk again. Robert goes up to Juli, says 'Well done, girlie!' and kisses her on the cheek. Then he begins to walk into the house; but Tomas calls him back; and, with Lucia holding her father's arm, everyone sings 'Happy Birthday!'

Beryl looks on enigmatically. The success has been her achievement; but already there has been a falling away. The celebrities among Robert's friends have been conspicuous by their absence. Soon, she knows, others will also desert. She, however, will remain steadfast and true.

BOOK NINE

DEATH'S NARROW SEA
1975–85

CHAPTER 1

Screening *I, Claudius*

Soon after Robert Graves had celebrated his eightieth birthday in July 1975, he and Beryl received two letters from Judith Bledsoe. 'It is now time', she told Robert, 'to stop telling your age and to start a new life, perhaps as a song-and dance entertainer.'[1] Robert could certainly manage a little singing and dancing: for numerous songs and dance-steps were stored among those memories to which he still had access. But with his current memory-span constantly shortening (by the end of the summer, it was no more than five minutes), any new work was beyond him. The poem he had written for Juli on his eightieth birthday was the last he ever wrote.

A few close friends remained loyal. In the autumn, John and Gretl Aldridge came out to stay at the Torre;[2] while Joanna Simon wrote with news of Juli, who had danced for a week at the ICA, before taking a small group on tour: a 'sobering experience', according to her mother, since she 'had the bulk of the organising to do, as well as the bulk of the dancing, and had to keep calm through every sort of crisis and near-disaster'.[3]

Robert's sister Clarissa died early in the morning of 14 January 1976. Already in her eighty-fourth year,[4] she had been telling Rosaleen for some time that she wanted to die: so now she had her wish and was at peace.[5] 'Darling Roz', wrote Nancy Nicholson,

I am *pleased* (or shall I say relieved) that dear Claree is safely out of all her illness and strain. She had such pluck. And I never once – in all her long letters – heard a suspicion of self-pity. It must be a sad relief to you. What a faithful sister you have been![6]

Robert heard of his sister's death with some astonishment: for the Clarissa whom he remembered was a young woman in her thirties; but the news caused him little pain, for it had soon been forgotten.

Then more cheerful news arrived. First, an option was taken out on the film rights of Graves's terrifying short story *The Shout*;[7] and then Selwyn Jepson wrote to tell Robert and Beryl of 'a gossip story in the *Daily Mail* – which I expect you will see today – it says BBC are planning to make a £50,000 a piece series of the *Claudius* books'.[8]

This was true; and although Robert had long ago sold the production rights of *I, Claudius* and *Claudius the God* to London Films, a television series would almost certainly revive the flagging sales of both novels. In July 1976, Robert and Beryl flew to London, where Robert took part for the last time in a public poetry reading, which he 'got through … fairly well';[9] and not long afterwards, he was taken to the set of *I, Claudius* to be photographed for the *Radio Times*.

This should have been an occasion for Robert Graves to savour; and yet, as Beryl reported to Rosaleen not long after their return to Deyá,

> he doesn't remember a thing about it now. We're just back from a swim. We go down by car now … the difficulty is to find enough things to do. Robert doesn't like gardening any more and is even losing interest in the compost! All he really seems to enjoy is going to the cafés and insists on supper in the village restaurant every night – so unlike he used to be.[10]

If nothing had happened for the past three or four minutes, it felt to Robert as though nothing had happened since about 1925; and if there was no café or restaurant open, to provide him with the constant bustle that he required, then he would disappear at odd hours of the day or night for long walks during which the changing landscape made his life seem less intolerably dull.

The BBC began screening *I, Claudius* on Monday 20 September 1976. At first, as Seymour-Smith observed, the critics were distinctly luke-warm.[11] Richard Last, for example, wrote in *The Times* that:

> The first ten minutes of *I, Claudius*, the B.B.C's £800,000 autumn epic, were full of Roman promise. A snake, symbol of poison and treachery, writhed across the tile mosaic. Claudius the Emperor, pale as wax, was discovered writing for posterity, just as in Robert Graves.

Unfortunately, the 'snappy modern dialogue, with its occasional humorous asides, prompted fears that the writer Jack Pulman, 'in his proper anxiety to avoid a stilted "period" speech', had 'fallen over into the opposite trap', and had 'reduced the rulers of the world to the status of characters in a newly-discovered soap opera'.

Last recognized however that 'there were good things, which might even become dominant good things'; George Baker as Tiberius had 'already begun to chart an arresting progress from misfit to psychopath'; and Last concluded that 'the greatest promise lies in Derek Jacobi's Claudius, so far seen only in his narrative role. He may yet eradicate the unfortunate impression of an epic we might have been better without.'

Derek Jacobi did indeed eradicate that impression, brilliantly supported not only by George Baker as Tiberius, but by Siân Phillips as Livia, Brian Blessed as Augustus, and Margaret Tyzack as Antonia; while in later episodes, there was a remarkable performance by John Hurt as the depraved Caligula. Above all, as episode succeeded episode, it could be recognized that Jack Pulman's dialogue had captured very precisely the spirit of Graves's original novels, in which Claudius had clearly stated at the outset that he wished his 'eventual readers of a hundred generations ahead, or more' to feel themselves 'directly spoken to, as if by a contemporary: as often Herodotus and Thucydides, long dead, seem to speak to me'.[12]

CHAPTER 2

Walking Back to Wimbledon

The serialization of *I, Claudius* was in full swing when Robert and Beryl returned to England in mid-October 1976. The chief purpose of their visit was to consult Rosaleen.[13] In those days few people had heard of Alzheimer's disease; and Beryl still nursed the hope that Robert's loss of memory was the temporary result of some curable illness.

First they stayed in London with the Simons; and occasionally things seemed relatively normal: as on 19 October, when they attended the publication party for Richard Graves's pictorial biography of T. E. Lawrence at the Woodstock Gallery. Robert could still pull himself together for a special occasion, and at the book-launching he appeared a little more absent-minded than usual, but otherwise all right. Within twenty-four hours, however, he was proving to be a very difficult guest at Drayton Gardens. He was still physically strong, and difficult to restrain; and one evening he disappeared and was lost for several hours.[14]

When eventually Robert was found, it was learned that he had been trying to walk back to Lauriston Road in Wimbledon; and it became heartbreakingly clear that in what was left of his consciousness, he had slipped back to the days of his youth. He was convinced that if only he could find Red Branch House, and knock on the door, it would be answered by his nurse Emily Dykes; and there in the drawing room he would find waiting for him Alfred, Amy, Clarissa, Rosaleen, Charles and John. The confusion of the past months would be swept away, and all would once again be well.

After this, Beryl hurried Robert down to Devon. Less than a week later, John received a distressing letter from Rosaleen. Beryl was in tears. Robert was 'dotty and violent', and the only way to keep him from wandering was to lock the doors and hide the keys.[15] Not long afterwards, Beryl took Robert back to Deyá.[16] But before leaving Devon, she bravely told Rosaleen that she was glad they had come: now at last she could accept the fact that Robert's condition was incurable and progressive.[17]

This meant that she faced the gloomiest of prospects. She would have to shoulder an increasingly exhausting burden for an indefinite period. Robert would need to be cared for and protected as he became more and more helpless; and she would have to deal single-handed with the flood of correspondence which continued to pour into Canellûn not only from friends and family, but also from literary agents, editors seeking articles which could never be written or interviews which could no longer be given; and (worst of all) from self-styled poets, half-baked thesis writers, and every other kind of literary pest.

Some requests could be dealt with rapidly. To the editors of 'The *Carthusian*, for example, Beryl replied simply:

> Thank you for your letter which I am answering for my husband who has given up letter writing.
>
> I'm afraid he has also given up writing altogether lately – so he won't be able to write an article for "The Carthusian". I'm sorry about this.[18]

Others were far more time-consuming: especially those from would-be biographers.

By the end of 1976, James McKinley, as Robert's accredited biographer, had spent a number of years patiently building up an archive of research material, and would soon be drafting his first five chapters.[19] However, Beryl had no personal loyalty to McKinley, and since Robert could no longer remember anything about his agreement 'nor even who McKinley is', she was happy to help a rival biographer in whom she had greater confidence.[20]

This was Martin Seymour-Smith, who announced in November 1976 that Hutchinson had invited him to write a biography of Robert Graves;[21] and the situation was further complicated early the next year when Beryl also heard that John Graves was at work on a family memoir which he had provisionally entitled *My Brother Robert*.

In the meantime, there had been a change for the worse in Robert's condition. In November 1976, be began reliving his terrifying experiences in the trenches during the First World War; and he was returned to the horror of shells bursting all around him, of dead and dying comrades, and of patrolling by moonlight through the shattered waste of no-man's-land.

CHAPTER 3

Under The Influence

By late November 1976, things had become so difficult at Canelluñ that Beryl Graves had decided to ask Catherine Dalton to fly all the way from Australia to lend a hand.[22] Not only was Robert immersed in the muddy battlefields of the Somme; but also his conscience troubled him; and in his more lucid moments he lamented that he had murdered many men. Martin Seymour-Smith, who was visiting Deyá early in 1977 at the start of his biographical researches, recalls memorably that on one of these occasions, when he had 'politely demurred: "That's hardly murder"', Graves had 'answered emphatically, in his confident and authoritative voice of thirty years back: "It is, you know." '[23]

Catherine was a tremendous practical help. Living in the Graves's flat in Palma, she went up to Deyá each weekend; and Beryl found it 'a relief to have someone to call upon if the need arises at any time'.[24] Gradually, Robert became quieter and less tormented;[25] and by 11 February 1977 Beryl could tell John Graves that his brother was 'fairly well – he complains how ill he feels but walks us off our feet'.

Later that year, Tom Matthews published his *Jacks Or Better*, which was subtitled 'Recollections of Robert Graves, Laura Riding and Friends', and would be published in England in 1979 as *Under The Influence*. Like most autobiographies, it is full of minor inaccuracies; and it ridicules Robert's relations with Margot and his subsequent Muses. Yet it also paints a convincing picture of the principal characters and incidents in the Robert Graves/Laura Riding/Schuyler Jackson imbroglio; and Tom Matthews courteously sent a copy for Robert's inspection.

Acknowledging Tom's gift on Robert's behalf, Beryl explained that Robert no longer read books, but that she had:

found it very moving and liked it very much. As you wrote it without fear of offending anyone, which makes most memoirs so dull, no offence taken – as far as I am concerned and I should think that goes for Robert too – in the long term anyhow.

She added that there were 'lots of mistakes as I suppose you know'; Tom had also been 'wrong in general about Robert's Muses', and it was a shame that the one he knew best, [Aemilia], 'was the only disaster Muse'. Margot had not been 'expunged' from Robert's history, as Tom had suggested; while Juli Simon was 'still one of our closest friends and after [Aemilia] we all thanked heaven for her!'[26]

The summer had recently seen the death of another principal player in the drama of Robert Graves's private life. On 15 August 1977, after being seriously ill for more than eight months, Nancy Nicholson died of cancer in Salisbury Infirmary.[27] A few days before her death, she had lapsed into semi-consciousness, and her end was peaceful. Sam and Catherine were both at the funeral: Catherine looking 'shaken and confused'.[28]

CHAPTER 4

'My Dear Old Friend'

During the summer of 1977, Robert Graves slipped still further back into his past. He would light candles, having forgotten about electricity; he would call out for his sisters Clarissa and Rosaleen; he would talk in German, a language that he had hardly used since he was a boy, on holiday at his grandfather's home at Laufzorn; and once, when it was time for bed, and his daughter Lucia had helped him to the foot of the stairs, he stood looking at them with some bewilderment, before asking plaintively: 'And what do I do now?'[29]

In the autumn, Julian Glover and his wife Isla Blair were invited to supper at Canelluñ. Afterwards Julian wrote to Beryl telling her that it had been 'so good to see you so unchanged, and Canelluñ too ... and Robert ranging about the place as he always did. We were, of course, initially disturbed by his almost constant state of amnesia ...'[30]

Beryl soldiered on, always treating Robert as though he could still understand what she was saying; reading to him when she thought that he was bored; and calmly noting the deaths of yet more of their closest friends. George Simon went in October 1977; and on 2 May 1978, Stella Irwin wrote to say that her father, James Reeves, had 'died yesterday after falling down stairs while carrying a tea tray', and had been 'found at the bottom of the stairs this morning by his cleaning woman'.[31]

Fortunately, the Herbert Wise television production of *I, Claudius* had been an international success, which had generated tremendous interest in the novels. As late as the spring of 1978, Ralph Jacobs wrote from the USA to Beryl to tell her that *I, Claudius* was first and *Claudius the God* was third on the American paperback best-sellers list.[32] Royalties poured in, and so at least Beryl had few financial problems.

In July 1978, she took Robert and Lucia to London to stay with the widowed Joanna Simon for a few days. Robert, who coped with the journey well, was said by Beryl, when she telephoned Rosaleen, to be 'a bit better',[33] and while they were in London he had his last meeting with

Tom Matthews. Afterwards, Tom wrote to Beryl, telling her that he had been:

> very glad to have seen Robert again, though it was sad to find him so absent. But he has become very handsome, hasn't he? A fine figure of an old man. I think he knew me ... When he said 'My dear old friend' I hope he meant it for me. I must admit it also made me feel guilty. For I know he wouldn't have liked some of the things I said about him in my book which now he'll never read.

'I don't suppose', Tom concluded, 'he and I will meet again. We're too old and live too far apart. Give him my love, whether he remembers me or not. And love to you too. He's lucky to have you.'[34]

CHAPTER 5

Heavenly Deyá

In July 1978, Julian Glover gave his 'Robert Graves' poetry reading in the theatre at Canelluñ;[35] and Juli Simon was also in Deyá for part of the summer. Afterwards, she wrote to Robert and Beryl to tell them that she was: 'so grateful yet again for the heavenly Deyá holiday'; although she admitted that she was finding it extremely difficult to adjust to life without Robert's loving support; and she hoped that one day she would have 'matured those qualities he tried to give me and be able to put them to good use, and hopefully help other people in distress.'[36]

Robert still seemed to enjoy Juli's company. 'He *knows* whom he is with', Lucia told Rosaleen later that year, 'and gives a tremendous value to feelings. He feels happy with his old friends and he just *adores* [her one-year-old daughter] Clarissa.'[37]

Sadly, Robert's physical co-ordination was now deteriorating, and in the late summer he fell on the front lawn and broke his arm.[38] Not long afterwards, Beryl heard that Tania Jepson had also fallen: but more seriously. She had broken her hip, and the shock, as Selwyn reported, had 'pushed her poor mind already losing touch with the realities of everyday life as we used to know it, into limbo … '[39]

CHAPTER 6

Death and Decay

The death toll of family and friends continued to mount. Perceval Graves, Robert's last surviving half-brother, went in March 1979 at the age of ninety-eight; and just over two months later, on 25 May, Alan Hodge died at the age of sixty-three.[40] Jane, his widow, wrote to Beryl:

Bless you for the nice card to Alan which he was just able to take in and happy to have. He died on Friday and we have to feel it was a blessing for him though he had been quite miraculously free from pain ...

She had been to see him the day before, taking with her 'the abridged *Reader Over Your Shoulder* [his collaboration with Robert Graves], which he looked at with a flicker of pleasure'.[41]

Ralph Jacobs had been in hospital the previous September, when Margery Terrasa had reported that 'Poor Ralphie ... started urinating blood. Tests have all been done, it's coming from the liver, as is to be expected.'[42] Ralph survived for just over another year; but then in October 1979 he was rushed to hospital in considerable pain after 'passing blood again';[43] and he died soon afterwards.[44]

Evening after evening in his windswept home on the Wiltshire downs, John Graves had pored with a magnifying glass over the almost indecipherable handwriting of his father Alfred's detailed 'page-a-day' diaries, copying out everything relevant to Robert's life between the years 1911 and 1931. Collecting material from this and other sources occupied much of his time; and he drafted numerous sections of *My Brother Robert*.

But then in the summer of 1979, John was struck down by the same kind of progressive memory loss as Robert. He could rally for an hour if there were visitors; but once they had gone, his mind wandered, and he became inaccessible. At one point, he clearly believed that he was back at Red Branch House, where Amy was nursing him through some childhood illness.

Shortly after Christmas there was a day when he was visited by several of his children and grandchildren, and for a short while it was as though he had climbed up from the bottom of a very deep well, and was once again able to understand and to communicate. Then he fell back again, and was lost; and he died just a few days later, on 7 January 1980.

John had always remarked that in old age all members of the Graves family begin to look alike; and his son Richard, after seeing him lying in his coffin, remarked that 'his finely moulded features, his high brow, his long handsome face and his acquiline nose exactly resembled those of the Bishop of Limerick'. This was fitting: like the bishop, his cool intellectual command and his patrician manner alarmed some people at first; but John was a devout Christian, a loving father, and a most honourable, unselfish man.

After John's death, Richard found heaps of papers in which recent bills, letters from the 1800s, extracts from *My Brother Robert* and ephemera collected on John's continental travels during the 1930s were mingled together in a confused and yet somehow deeply touching manner. Having recently enjoyed a critical success with a mildly controversial biography of the poet A. E. Housman, Richard was now heavily occupied with a biography of the Powys brothers. But he determined that, as soon as time permitted, he would build upon what his father had done, and ensure that the labours of John's old age should not have been in vain.

CHAPTER 7

Spell-bound

Paul O'Prey, who had read English at Oxford in the mid-1970s, had spent more and more time at Canelluñ since coming down in July 1977; and by February 1980 he was firmly established as part of the household, in which he dealt with much of the routine correspondence.[45] And while Martin Seymour-Smith laboured at Graves's biography, Paul O'Prey was preparing a first volume of letters.

By 1982, when Richard Graves (having completed but not yet published *The Brothers Powys*) came out to Majorca to begin his researches, Robert was almost completely absent. It was weird: like seeing the discarded outer husk of a man, still living and breathing. Robert could feed himself: when sat down at table, with a spoon or fork in his right hand, he would ladle it rapidly into his mouth. But he was capable of little else. He slept now in the press-room next to his study, in a kind of large cot. Once, on going to wake him in the morning, Richard saw a momentary awareness flicker across Robert's face, but then he was gone again, every trace of intellect wiped away from his ageing features.

Care was constant. Thanks to the *Claudius* royalties, Robert was looked after night and day by a team of youthful attendants, including Lyn O'Grady, a sturdily attractive nurse, with a good sense of humour, and her feet very firmly on the ground; and Suzy Townsend, a masseuse of great spirituality and rare beauty. But the remainder of the household seemed to be spellbound. It was confidently asserted that there was some purpose to Robert's present way of life. Apparently, when he appeared to be absent, he was actually flying around the world 'on the astral plane' doing work of global importance …

Visitors still arrived: some of them, people to whom Robert would have given no house room in the old days. Once, when he was sitting in his wheelchair waiting to be pushed out on to the terrace for his afternoon tea, a particularly ghastly trio entered the house. One of them, a woman, kneeled in front of him, held his hands, stared into his eyes and began talking to him as though he were a baby; while her companions looked on admiringly at this repulsive scene.

CHAPTER 8

Sad but Inevitable

Martin Seymour-Smith's *Robert Graves: His Life and Works* appeared in 1982. This pioneering work added little to what was known about Graves's earlier years by readers of *Good-bye to All That*. However, drawing chiefly upon material in the archives at Canellun it gave the most comprehensive account available about his subsequent life.

By the time of publication, Robert Graves (referred to in Seymour-Smith's book as 'often suddenly' interjecting 'a sharply appropriate remark into any conversation that may be going on around him'[46]), was in fact living the peaceful and virtually silent half-life of extreme senility; into which he would soon be followed by one of his oldest friends.

In the autumn of 1982, Beryl Graves had invited John and Gretl Aldridge to Deyá, but they were too ill to travel.[47] Then on 24 January 1983, Gretl sent a postcard to Beryl thanking her for a photograph, and telling her that:

> It's such a pity that John can't share the pleasure. As you will see from my handwriting we are going steadily down both of us. I hope it won't take too long. It's no fun any more. Still, dearest love from both of us to all of you Gretl.[48]

On 13 February, it was Gretl who died first,[49] while John was overwhelmed by senile dementia,[50] and died a few weeks later in the evening of 3 May, 'very peaceful and in no pain and so well and lovingly looked after'.[51]

Tom Matthews wrote to Beryl to tell her that he and his wife Pam would be attending the funeral at Great Bardfield. 'All gone', he commented. 'Norman, Lucy, Gretl and John. It's sad but inevitable.'[52]

For Robert Graves, the next three years were ones of slow but steady deterioration. By the summer of 1985, when there were muted celebrations for Robert's ninetieth birthday, he lay in bed for most of the time. His nephew Richard, who came out to stay at Canelluñ heard that during the past twelve months Robert had almost died more than once, but with his strong heart, good nursing, and a small course of antibiotics, he stayed alive.

CHAPTER 9

Death of a Poet[53]

During the early days of December 1985, Halley's comet blazed its way through the sourthern skies. This sign in the heavens seemed curiously appropriate to those who tended Robert Graves: for it was suddenly clear that he was very close to death.

It was on Wednesday 4 December that Robert first appeared to be sinking, and Elena Graves telephoned her son Philip and told him to be ready for the worst. Robert rallied again; and by Saturday morning, after sleeping well for the best part of three nights, he was fit enough to be sat up in his lounge-chair at the table in his bedroom.

Then William and Elena walked over, arriving at ten o'clock and staying with Robert and Beryl for about an hour. Soon after eleven, Beryl left the room to make some coffee. William followed her, while Elena remained behind, reading a letter. A few moments later, Robert sighed, his head began to nod forwards, and he was clearly on the verge of death.

Elena called William, and they helped Robert back into bed. Then Beryl came in, and held his hand, and said: 'Robert, darling'. And Elena touched his hand also; and after a while she said they had better call Xavier, the doctor, 'Is he gone, then?' asked Beryl. And Elena's answer was 'Yes'.

After the doctor had arrived, and Robert Graves had been certified dead, the village carpenter was summoned; and soon Robert had been dressed in his best suit, and laid out in a coffin with his black broad-brimmed hat on his chest. Lucia, after flying over from Barcelona, helped to garland his head with olive leaves, laurel and jasmine.

That afternoon, the men of the village made formal calls to pay their respects to Don Roberto; and that evening, they reassembled at Canellũn. Through the twilight (watched over by Spanish television cameras, for the news of Robert Graves's death had already been flashed onto television screens around the world), they carried their poet to church in his coffin:

with all the boys and able-bodied men taking turns to help, including Robert's sons William, Juan and Tomas.

Father Ignacio Montojo presided over a non-denominational mass; after which the closed coffin remained in the church all night, watched over by two of the guardia. In the morning, with Lucia there to observe, the coffin was lowered into the plot which William had secured: not in the pagans' corner, but in the main body of the churchyard.

Earth was packed in above the coffin (from which laurel and olive still protruded; and then two sandstone blocks were placed upon the earth, and cement was poured over the blocks. And while the cement was still wet, a simple inscription was written upon it:

Robert Graves
Poeta
1895–1985

The place was fitting: for it had once been a shrine to the White Goddess Pelion, to whom Graves had given faithful service for many years. That service had brought more suffering than joy both to him and to many of those close to him. Yet out of that suffering had come not only the classic work on what it is to be a romantic poet, but some of the finest love poems of the twentieth century. Graves's dedication to the Moon Goddess had also inspired him with a rare kind of understanding, which meant that at times (as Martin Tallents would often tell) he had seemed to bring with him a breath of the ancient world, and in his presence Deyá itself would sometimes appear to be a land of ancient days.

In the years of his decline, Graves had been granted a safe harbour by the woman who had once saved him from destruction, and had since remained loyal and true, respecting his poetic calling whatever sacrifices on her part that might entail. And when Graves ventured out upon his final voyage, who will dare to say that he was not singing, as he had once sung to Juli Simon, for him the last and most gentle incarnation of the Goddess:

With you for mast and sail and flag
And anchor never known to drag,
Death's narrow but oppressive sea
Looks not unnavigable to me.

AFTERWORD

And so the tale of my uncle Robert von Ranke Graves is told, from his birth at Red Branch House in Wimbledon on 24 July 1895 into a conventionally Christian family, to his burial in Deyá ninety years later on the site of a shrine sacred to the White Goddess of Pelion.

Graves had led an extraordinarily rich and productive life. Very little prose or verse outlasts the time for which it is written; and yet after more than sixty years in print the *Claudius* novels are still widely read and critically acclaimed; after more than sixty-five years, *Good-bye to All That* remains required reading for all students of the First World War; and it seems probable that *The White Goddess* will endure as long as romantic poetry continues to be written.

It is *The White Goddess* which, alongside a handful of Graves's poems, will from time to time have to be translated into more modern English, and will carry his name down the centuries into some remote future.

With that prediction, I resign my pen as Robert Graves's biographer after a labour of ten years, and say farewell for the last time (unless, as I hope, we meet again beyond that narrow but oppressive sea of which he wrote) both to Robert and to many others whom I love. Farewell, Robert. Farewell, dear Father. Farewell, Rosaleen, Clarissa, Charles and Peggy. And farewell also to that magical Deyá of my youth.

RICHARD PERCEVAL GRAVES
Shrewsbury 28 December 1994

ABBREVIATIONS

I *Unpublished Sources*

AUTHOR   The vast collection of family papers built up by Robert Graves's brother John Graves (1903–80) and now owned by John's son Richard, the present author. This collection has never been worked over before, except by John Graves, who made use of some items for his unpublished biography *My Brother Robert*.

BERG   Letters from Robert Graves to Selwyn Jepson in the Berg Collection at the New York Public Library.

BROTHER   The incomplete typescript of *My Brother Robert* by his brother John Graves.

DIARIES   The postwar diaries of Robert Graves, as transcribed by his widow Beryl.

INDIANA   Three collections of papers in the Lilly Library, Indiana University, at Bloomington, Indiana: (i) Nicholson MSS 1929–73 which contains correspondence between Robert Graves and his first wife Nancy Nicholson; (ii) Gay MSS which contains correspondence between Robert Graves and his friend and secretary Karl Gay (formerly Goldschmidt); and (iii) Hughes MSS, which contains correspondence between RG and his friend Richard Hughes (1900–76).

IRWIN   A typed transcript by James Reeves of letters from RG to James Reeves, now owned by James's daughter Stella Irwin.

LETTERS   Letters from Robert Graves to his brother John, together with handwritten commentaries by JTRG.

MAJORCA   The collection of family papers held by Robert Graves's widow Beryl Graves at her house in Deyá. These were studied previously by Martin Seymour-Smith for his biography (see MS-S below).

NYPL   Papers from the Berg Collection of the New York Public Library, copies of which were seen by the present author at MAJORCA as above.

QUOZ   The correspondence between Robert Graves and Alastair Reid, written for publication, but fortunately never published.

TRUST   The collection of papers relating to Robert Graves which is owned by the Robert Graves Trust and held at St John's College, Oxford.

VICTORIA   Letters from Robert Graves to Selwyn and Tania Jepson in the University of Victoria B.C. Special Collection.

2 *Principal Published Sources*

BAKER   Deborah Baker, *In Extremis: The Life of Laura Riding* (Hamish Hamilton 1993).

DALTON   Catherine Dalton [*née* Nicholson], *Without Hardware: Cases of Treason in Australia* (Ochre Press, Towamba, N.S.W. Australia 3rd edn 1980).

GTAT 29   Robert Graves, *Good-bye to All That* (Jonathan Cape 1929).

GTAT 57   Robert Graves, *Good-bye to All That* (1957 revised edition).

MS-S   Martin Seymour-Smith, *Robert Graves: His Life and Works* (Hutchinson 1982).

O'PREY (1)   Ed. Paul O'Prey, *In Broken Images: Selected Letters of Robert Graves 1914–1946* (Hutchinson 1982).

O'PREY (2)   Ed. Paul O'Prey, *Between Moon And Moon: Selected Letters of Robert Graves 1946–1972* (Hutchinson 1984).

SPIKE   Ed. Pauline Scudamore, *Dear Robert, Dear Spike: The Graves-Milligan Correspondence* (Alan Sutton 1991).

TAH   Richard Perceval Graves, *Robert Graves: The Assault Heroic 1895–1926* (Weidenfeld & Nicolson 1987).

TYWL   Richard Perceval Graves, *Robert Graves: The Years with Laura 1926–1940* (Weidenfeld & Nicolson 1990).

3 *Abbreviations of Names*

RG   Robert Graves. BG   Beryl Graves (*née* Pritchard, then Hodge). AG   Amy Graves. JTRG   John Graves, RG's youngest brother. NN   Nancy Nicholson. AH   Alan Hodge. RPG   the present author.

REFERENCE NOTES

*Book One   The Shadow of the
        Past   1940–43*

CHAPTER 1
A LETTER FROM LAURA RIDING

1 This is a chapter of introduction
for some, recapitulation for
others. Any unacknowledged
material is taken from TYWL.
2 BG is conv. with RPG Dec.
1993.
3 RG, *Collected Poems: 1914–1947*
(Cassell 1948) p. 196.
4 O'PREY (1) RG to Basil
Liddell-Hart 21 Nov. 1939
p. 289.
5 IRWIN RG to James Reeves n.d.
(prob. late 1934). The first
twelve words of the quotation
appear in BAKER p. 325.
6 MAJORCA n.d. (Dec. 1944) RG
to BG.
7 MAJORCA AH in Riga to RG
10 Sept. (1939).
8 Brian Bliss, 'Robert Graves:
Some Recollections' a nine-page
MSS sent by BB to RPG with a
letter of 14 Nov. 1986.
9 RG in *Work in Hand* with
Norman Cameron and AH
(Hogarth Press 1942).
10 As note 8 above. Bliss had
joined the Civil Defence in
London while waiting to go into
the Army.

11 MAJORCA RG from The Place
to Beryl Hodge Wed. nearly
lunchtime n.d.
12 O'PREY (1) RG to Karl Gay 26
Jan. 1940 pp. 290–91.
13 O'PREY (1) RG to Basil
Liddell-Hart 19 Feb. 1940
pp. 291–3.
14 O'PREY (1) RG to AH 14 June
1940 pp. 294–5.
15 RG and AH, *The Long Weekend*
(Faber & Faber 1940).

CHAPTER 2
THE VALE HOUSE

16 AUTHOR AG to JTRG e.g. 15
Jan. 1940.
17 Ibid. 5 March 1940. 'I have no
hope for the reconstitution of the
marriage after the strong terms in
which Jim expresses himself.' Ibid.
13 April and 25 May 1940 shows
that RG 'took up the cudgels' on
his sister's behalf in her dispute
with her husband; who soon
removed himself from the scene
by enlisting as an Army doctor.
18 TRUST RG to David Graves
n.d.
19 INDIANA (ii) RG to Karl Gay 2
April 1940.
20 RG explained that he was liable
to 'pay the guarantee on Laura's
poems in America and £80 to
Deyá etc.'

21 As note 8 above. Molly married Brian Bliss in Sept. 1941.
22 As note 8 above.
23 AUTHOR AG to JTRG 16 April 1940.
24 Catherine Nicholson in conv. with RPG 24 Aug. 1993.
25 As note 2 above.
26 MS-S p. 359.
27 As note 2 above.
28 As note 24 above.
29 As note 2 above.
30 BG in conv. with RPG 12 Feb. 1993.
31 Ibid.
32 INDIANA (i) RG to NN (late May 1940).
33 MAJORCA 7 April n.d. Jenny Nicholson to RG.
34 As note 32 above.
35 As note 23 above.
36 Ibid.
37 As note 32 above.

CHAPTER 3
THE BIRTH OF WILLIAM

38 As note 24 above.
39 AUTHOR JTRG to AG 23 June 1940.
40 AUTHOR AG to JTRG 26 June 1940.
41 AUTHOR Sally Chilver to RG n.d. (1940).
42 TRUST RG to David Graves 22 Jan. 1940.
43 As note 40 above.
44 Ibid. 19 July 1940.
45 Ibid. 6 July 1940. (On his way to see Nancy, David also spent a few days with some friends.)

46 MAJORCA Lucie Aldridge to BG 16 July 1940.
47 TRUST RG to David Graves n.d.
48 As note 44 above.
49 As note 24 above.
50 INDIANA (i) RG to NN 17 Aug. (1940).
51 INDIANA (i) NN to RG (? 19 Aug. 1940).
52 INDIANA (i) RG to NN n.d.
53 INDIANA (i) RG to Catherine Nicholson 7 Sept. 1940.
54 INDIANA (i) RG to NN 7 Sept. 1940.
55 Ibid. 16 Sept. 1940.

CHAPTER 4
WORK IN HAND

56 Karl Gay in conv. with RPG 8 Feb. 1993.
57 MAJORCA James Reeves to RG 14 Sept. (1940). The friend was Gordon Glover (now separated from Honor Wyatt, who had also visited Galmpton).
58 O'PREY (1) p. 295 RG to AH 23 Oct. 1940.
59 AUTHOR JTRG to AG 23 Jan. 1941.
60 RG, *Proceed, Sergeant Lamb* (Methuen 1941) p. 154.
61 TYWL pp. 285–303.
62 MAJORCA George Buchanan from the Harbour St Ives to RG 16 Jan. 1940.
63 MAJORCA David Graves to RG 29 Sept. 1940.
64 MAJORCA Sam Graves to RG n.d.

65 MAJORCA Lucie Aldridge to RG and BG 3 Sept. 1940.
66 INDIANA (iii) Richard Hughes to Frances Hughes 4 Oct. 1940.
67 AUTHOR AG to Charles Graves n.d.
68 As note 63 above.
69 Ibid. 21 Aug. 1940.
70 As note 63 above.
71 LETTERS Jan. 1941.
72 MAJORCA AH to RG 10 Oct. (1940).
73 As note 30 above.
74 As note 58 above.
75 MS-S p. 360.

CHAPTER 5
LAMENT FOR PASIPHAE

76 MATTHEWS pp. 214–15.
77 Ibid. p. 216.
78 MAJORCA Lucie Aldridge to BG 17 June 1940.
79 MAJORCA Dorothy Simmons from the White House, New Hope to RG and BG n.d.
80 As note 9 above.
81 Ibid.
82 Ibid.
83 Ibid.
84 Ibid.
85 LETTERS n.d. (Jan. 1941).
86 MAJORCA Bill Chapman to RG 12 Dec. 1940.
87 MATTHEWS p. 218.
88 INDIANA (i) RG to NN 30 Nov. 1940; MAJORCA Minnie Sullivan to BG 23 Dec. 1940 shows that she continued to do useful work for the Graveses, sitting up at night during the

air-raids knitting 'woollies' for them.
89 MAJORCA AH to BG 2 Jan. 1941 (misdated 1940).
90 INDIANA (i) RG to NN 20 or 30 May (1942).
91 LETTERS n.d. pmk Jan. 1941 Charles Graves, *Off the Record* (Hutchinson 1941) p. 86 shows that CG travelled back to London on 13 Jan. 1941.
92 When it was published, in April 1941, it made (as Charles Graves records in his *Off the Record* p. 129) 'the tenth written in one year by Robert, Philip and myself – a certain record for three brothers. Philip's are two of the *Quarters* [a Quarterly History of the War written for Hutchinson], *Briton and Turk*, and *The Life of Sir Percy Cox*. Robert's are two books about Sergeant Lamb and *The Long Weekend*; mine are *War Over Peace*, *The Pope Speaks*, and the new one.'
93 Jenny and Sam were also visiting, and the Sullivans' place in The Vale House had been taken by an RAF family of three.
94 LETTERS 12 Jan. 1941.
95 LETTERS 6 Feb. 1941.
96 Ibid. and as note 59 above.
97 AUTHOR AG to JTRG 20 Feb. 1941.
98 As note 95 above.
99 As note 96 above.
100 MAJORCA John Aldridge to RG 11 Feb. 1941.
101 MAJORCA Lucie Aldridge to BG 11 Feb. 1941.

102 MAJORCA Lucie Aldridge to RG 27 Feb. 1941.

103 MATTHEWS p. 218.

104 O'PREY (1) p. 299 RG to AH 20 March 1941.

105 AUTHOR AG to JTRG 30 July 1941.

106 RG, *Poems 1938–1945* (Cassell 1946) p. 26.

CHAPTER 6
NANCY'S CHILDREN

107 O'PREY (1) RG to AH 3 March 1941.

108 *Proceed, Sergeant Lamb* p. vii.

109 BROTHER.

110 AUTHOR AG to JTRG 8 March 1941.

111 As note 24 above.

112 INDIANA (i) RG to NN 11 March 1941.

113 As note 104 above.

114 QUOZ (quoted in MS-S p. 360).

115 As note 2 above.

116 As note 114 above.

117 As note 2 above.

118 O'PREY (2) p. 14.

119 TRUST Norman Cameron to BG and RG 19 April and 8 May 1941.

120 AUTHOR 8 June 1941 JTRG to AG: the broadcast was on this date.

121 MAJORCA AH to BG 18 June 1941. MAJORCA AG to RG 10 June 1941 shows that Amy listened to the broadcast; and was 'only sorry that you placed your upbringing entirely in the suburbs, while I think your constant visits to Harlech had a very strong influence on you & on the other children. I knew the merits of country life from Laufzorn and wanted you all to experience it also.'

122 Much of the story of this quarrel is taken from two n.d. letters MAJORCA Sam Graves to RG, the first of which has been heavily annotated by RG. Only material from other sources will be referenced in detail.

123 INDIANA (i) RG to NN 11 and 25 March 1941.

124 AUTHOR JTRG to AG 3 Aug. 1941.

125 AUTHOR AG to JTRG 7 July 1941.

126 Jenny Nicholson, *Kiss the Girls Goodbye* (Hutchinson 1944) pp. 7, 50.

127 AUTHOR David Graves to AG 29 June 1941.

128 MAJORCA Jenny Nicholson to RG n.d. (July 1941).

129 As note 125 above.

130 As note 128 above.

131 MAJORCA Sam Graves to RG n.d. (1941).

132 AUTHOR AG to JTRG 30 July 1941.

133 *Kiss the Girls Goodbye* p. 56.

CHAPTER 7
WIFE TO MR. MILTON

134 As note 2 above.

135 O'PREY (1) p. 302 RG to Basil Liddell-Hart 16 July 1941.

136 TAH p. 242.

137 MAJORCA Margaret Russell to RG 23 July 1941.

138 MAJORCA Tom Matthews to RG 8 Sept. 1941.

139 O'PREY (1) pp. 303–4.

140 O'PREY (1) p. 304 Alun Lewis to RG 4 Nov. 1941.

141 O'PREY (1) pp. 305–6 RG to Alun Lewis 6 Nov. 1941.

142 MAJORCA David Graves to RG 6 Nov. 1941.

143 MAJORCA Sam Graves to RG 16 Nov. 1941.

144 *Kiss the Girls Goodbye* pp. 56–8.

145 Mrs Maureen Pilling to RPG 17 Dec. 1986.

146 MAJORCA David Graves in Yorkshire to RG Nov. n.d. (1941).

147 MAJORCA David Graves in Lincoln to RG 2 Dec. 1941.

148 O'PREY (1) pp. 306–7 Alun Lewis to RG 15 Nov. 1941.

149 O'PREY (1) pp. 307–8 RG to Alun Lewis 15 Nov. 1941.

150 RG is referring to research for Laura Riding's book *Lives of Wives* (Cassell 1939).

151 O'PREY (1) p. 309 RG to AH 8 Nov. 1941.

152 Sir Walter Raleigh, *Milton* (Edward Arnold, 14th Impression) pp. 29–33 (orig. edn 1900).

153 RG, *On English Poetry* (William Heinemann 1922) p. 19.

154 Ibid. pp. 30, 124.

155 RG, *Wife to Mr. Milton* p. 176.

156 MATTHEWS p. 239.

157 RG, *Wife to Mr. Milton* p. 147.

158 Ibid. p. 177.

159 Ibid. p. 175.

160 Ibid. p. 270.

161 Ibid. pp. 291–2.

162 Ibid. pp. 239–40. Incidentally, MS-S p. 379 ridicules Matthews's idea on the grounds: i) that he respected Milton's gifts too much; and ii) that 'Besides, he had forgotten Jackson.' The first is a legitimate point of view; but the second is clearly nonsensical, since RG had only just received a letter from Matthews on the subject of Riding and Jackson.

163 O'PREY (1) p. 299 RG to AH 20 March 1941.

164 It seems that Anne Powell was entitled to her 'widow's thirds' on some property at Whatly which had belonged to her husband, and which on his death had passed into John Milton's possession; but when in the mid-1640s a fine of £180 was attached to the property (on the grounds that it had belonged to a Royalist sympathizer), Milton could not continue paying the thirds (£26-13-4d p.a.) without the property becoming an absolute liability. So he refused to do so, especially as the Powells still owed him Marie's agreed dowry or 'marriage-portion' of £1,000.

165 O'PREY (2) p. 196 RG to Tom Matthews 22 April 1960.

166 MAJORCA Eddie Marsh to RG 22 Feb. 1943.

167 Richard Hughes, *The Wooden Shepherdess* (Chatto & Windus 1973) p. 387.
168 *On English Poetry* pp. 134–7.
169 Ibid.
170 IRWIN James Reeves to RG 18 Dec. 1941.

CHAPTER 8
FAMILY AND FRIENDS

171 LETTERS 29 Dec. 1941.
172 Catherine Dalton (*née* Nicholson) *Without Hardware* (Ochre Press, Towamba, N.S.W. Australia; 3rd edn 1980) p. vii.
173 As note 171 above.
174 LETTERS ?2 Feb. 1942 – letter received by JTRG on 3 Feb. 1942 (see AUTHOR JTRG to AG 3 Feb. 1942).
175 LETTERS 5 Feb. 1942.
176 As note 174 above.
177 AUTHOR AG to JTRG 8 Feb. 1942.
178 As note 147 above.
179 AUTHOR JTRG to AG 23 Feb. 1942.
180 Ibid. 7 Feb. 1942.
181 INDIANA (i) RG to NN 27 Feb. (1942).
182 MAJORCA AG to RG 22 Dec. 1941.
183 Ibid. 11 Jan. 1942.
184 MAJORCA JTRG to RG 10 Feb. 1942 (misdated 1941).
185 LETTERS 12 Feb. 1942.
186 As note 181 above.
187 See e.g. AUTHOR enclosure Rosaleen Cooper to JTRG in a letter AG to JTRG 21 Feb.

1942, while RG was visiting their mother.
188 LETTERS 5 Feb. 1942.
189 O'PREY (1) pp. 310–11 RG to Alun Lewis 20 Feb. 1942.
190 O'PREY (1) pp. 311–12 Alun Lewis to RG 1 March 1942.
191 MAJORCA David Graves to RG 10 May 1942. John Graves and Lieutenant-Commander P. K. Kemp, *The Red Dragon: The Story of the Royal Welch Fusiliers 1919–1945* (Gale & Polden 1960) pp. 41–2 shows that the battalion embarked in the liner *Empress of Canada*, which set out to sea in a convoy on 15 April 1942, bound for Capetown and then Bombay.
192 LETTERS 4 May 1942.
193 Rene Gay in conv. with RPG 8 Feb. 1993.
194 As note 30 above.
195 See RG's Foreword to *Wife to Mr. Milton*.
196 Catherine Nicholson in conv. with RPG 24 Aug. 1993 says that Irene's hair 'was more copper than yellow'.
197 Karl and Irene Gay in conv. with RPG March 1989 and 8 Feb. 1993.
198 MAJORCA Francis Hemming from the Ministry of Home Security to RG 1 May 1942. Hemming was a great admirer of RG's niece Sally Chilver.
199 LETTERS 23 May 1942.
200 MAJORCA RG to Helen Waddell 25 July 1942.
201 See e.g. MAJORCA Helen

Waddell to RG 1 Aug. 1942. At
first Waddell refused him
permission, telling him that 'the
paragraph you have chosen to
paraphrase is obscure, in
isolation. It is abc to anyone who
has read with a mind awake . . .
the chapter of which it is almost
the colophon.' She then enclosed
'for comic relief . . . to the
Robert Graves of *Good-bye to All
That* 1929 aged 34 from the
Helen Waddell of *The Wandering
Scholars* 1927 aged 38' an extract
from the very first page of
Good-bye to All That, and critically
demolished it line by line.

202 MAJORCA David Graves to
RG 10 May 1942.

203 Ibid. 15 Sept. 1942.

204 INDIANA (i) RG to NN 19
Dec. 1946.

205 MAJORCA Sam Graves to
RG 23 July 1942.

206 MAJORCA AG to RG 4 Aug.
1942.

207 MS-S p. 366.

208 INDIANA (i) RG to NN 30
May 1942.

209 AUTHOR AG to JTRG 20
Oct. 1942.

210 MAJORCA Catherine
Nicholson to RG 18 Aug. 1942.

211 MAJORCA AH to RG 15
Aug. 1942.

CHAPTER 9
A DIVORCE IN THE FAMILY

212 As note 2 above.

213 Joanna Simon in conv. with
RPG 20 April 1993; supplemented by a telephone conv.
18 and 21 Oct. 1993.

214 Ibid. supplemented by BG in
conv. with RPG Dec. 1993.

215 Graves mixed a little business
with pleasure, lunching with his
agent in London on 20 Aug. (see
MAJORCA A. S. Watt to RG 14
Aug. 1942).

216 MAJORCA Falkland from
Brixham Yacht Club, Brixham to
RG and BG 28 Aug. 1942.

217 MAJORCA Tom Matthews to
RG 28 Aug. 1942.

218 MAJORCA AH to BG 6 Sept.
1942.

219 Ibid. 1 Oct. 1942.

220 Dr Maurice Newfield was
editor of the *Eugenics Review*.

221 MATTHEWS p. 228.

222 Tom Matthews' view was
confirmed by Lady Liddell-Hart
in a conv. with RPG in 1975.

223 MATTHEWS pp. 229–30.

224 IRWIN RG to James Reeves
n.d.

225 RG, *Poems: 1926–1930*
(William Heinemann 1931) p. 19.

226 TRUST Norman Cameron to
RG and BG 29 Oct. 1942.

227 AUTHOR AG to JTRG 12
Oct. 1942 encloses RG's letter
and mentions specifically, 'I have
answered it without referring to
Beryl.'

227 Ibid.

228 INDIANA (i) RG to NN 14
Oct. 1942.

229 MAJORCA NN 25 Bedford
Gardens to RG 4 Nov. 1942.

230 AUTHOR AG to JTRG 15 Nov. 1942.

231 MAJORCA Maurice [and Sigrid] Newfield at The Hall, Great Bardfield 27 Oct. 1942.

232 INDIANA (i) Parsons & Outfin solicitors of 3 Bolton Street, Brixham to NN 17 Nov. 1952.

233 INDIANA (i) RG to NN 18 Nov. 1942.

234 INDIANA (i) NN to 'Dear Sir' 19 Nov. 1942.

235 INDIANA (i) Waterhouse & Co. solicitors of Lincoln's Inn to NN 20 Nov. 1942.

236 MAJORCA NN to RG n.d.

237 Ibid. 23 Nov. 1942.

238 INDIANA (i) RG to NN (?25) Nov. 1942.

239 INDIANA (i) NN to RG (?30 Nov. 1942).

240 O'PREY (I) p. 315 RG to AH 6 Jan. 1943.

Book Two   The White Goddess   1943–46

CHAPTER I
THE GOLDEN FLEECE

1 All references in this chapter and the next to FLEECE are to Robert Graves, *The Golden Fleece* (Cassell 1944).

2 FLEECE p. 11.

3 Ibid. p. 20.

4 TAH p. 298.

5 This is speculative.

6 FLEECE p. 29.

7 Ibid. p. 28.

8 Ibid. p. 30.

9 Ibid. p. 31.

10 Ibid. p. 32.

11 Ibid. p. 33.

12 Ibid. p. 36.

13 Ibid. pp. 38–60.

14 St Matthew vii 20.

15 FLEECE p. 49.

16 TYWL p. 191.

17 FLEECE p. 71.

18 MAJORCA Ronald Bottrall to RG 10 Jan. 1943.

19 MAJORCA Sam Graves to RG 28 Dec. 1942.

20 TRUST Norman Cameron to RG 13 Jan. 1943.

21 AUTHOR AG to JTRG 26 Feb. 1943; Graves had even gained Churchill's permission to quote in a foreword the greater part of an admiring letter he had written about the book back in 1937, provided that he omitted a sentence in which Churchill had declared (inappropriately, he considered, now that he was Prime Minister), 'I delight also in the theological discussions which blend so amusingly with the easy morals.' (MS-S pp. 363–4).

22 MS-S pp. 379–80. For the story of how Creative Age Press acquired RG's *Wife to Mr. Milton* and subsequent works, see MAJORCA Robert Knittel of the Creative Age Press to RG 2 Jan. 1947. Knittel writes: 'Soon after I had left Doubleday to join Creative Age Press I heard from the grapevine that Robert Graves, always a favourite of

mine, had had a book turned down by Random House. My spies soon told me that the book was at Mackintosh Notice, the Agents. I rushed there, but since Creative Age was then none too well-known I had some difficulty in convincing dear Mrs. Abbot that she owed it to my enthusiasm for Graves to let me read *Wife to Mr. Milton*. Next I offered a contract, but on enquiring about an option for the next work I was told that Random House was to publish *The Golden Fleece*. Although we naturally would have published *Wife to Mr. Milton* without an option I did not like it. I therefore asked for an option on the works of Graves after *The Golden Fleece* which was granted. This however left Random House with the prospect of publishing one book after the appearance of *Wife to Mr. Milton* with Graves subsequently going back to Creative Age Press. If you know Bennett Cerf, his pride and ego, you know that he does not like to be on a spot like this. By this time I believe that he was sorry to have let Milton go. Realising this I had the Agents ask Random House to let us take over *The Golden Fleece* which they did reluctantly. It is therefore with great pleasure that I admit being responsible for bringing you to Creative Age Press.'

23 MAJORCA Eddie Marsh to RG 1 March 1943; quoted MS-S p. 380.

24 MAJORCA James Prydie to RG 4 March 1943.

25 MS-S p. 379.

26 MAJORCA Catherine Nicholson Camberley to RG 25 Sept. 1942 reports that: 'Nancy is looking well and happy and not more than 30 in her uniform which suits her well.'

27 MAJORCA Catherine Nicholson to David Graves 17 Feb. 1943.

CHAPTER 2
'MISSING, BELIEVED KILLED'

28 AUTHOR JTRG to AG 21 March 1943.

29 *The Red Dragon* p. 45.

30 Ibid. p. 46.

31 David Graves in the *Informer* Vol II No C 8 Aug. 1943.

32 *The Red Dragon* pp. 49–50.

33 AUTHOR Typed copy (in pages of JTRG's copy of *The Red Dragon*) of a report by Lt-Col. A. H. Williams of the Royal Welch Fusiliers headed: *Corps. Action for which commended.*

34 *The Red Dragon* pp. 52–3.

35 MAJORCA Under-Secretary of State for War to Capt. R. Graves telegram, received Brixham 3 April 1943.

36 AUTHOR AG to JTRG pc 23 March 1922 shows that David was born at 4.40 p.m. on 22 March.

37 IRWIN 31 May 1943.

38 AUTHOR Clarissa Graves to AG airgraph 4 May 1943.

39 TRUST RG to NN 4 April 1943.

40 MS-S p. 367.

41 Charles Graves, *Great Days* (Hutchinson 1943) p. 166.

42 MAJORCA Sam Graves to RG 6 April 1943.

43 MAJORCA Sam Graves to RG 6 June 1943.

44 As note 38 above.

45 MAJORCA Maisie Somerville (Gloucestershire) to RG 11 April 1943. She had heard the news from James (?Reeves).

46 MAJORCA Perceval Graves Hemel Hempstead to RG 19 May 1943.

47 MAJORCA Kitty Graves to RG 16 May 1943.

48 See e.g. TRUST RG to NN 14 April 1943, on hearing that David was not just 'missing', but 'missing, believed killed': 'This is not final of course but the margin of hope shrinks.' And then MAJORCA Sam Graves to RG 6 June 1943 'Mother . . . said that you sounded more cheerful as regarding David's chances . . .'

49 MAJORCA Francis Hemming to RG 3 May 1943.

50 MAJORCA AH to RG 24 March 1943 plans this visit – Easter was 20 April.

51 MAJORCA AH to BG 9 May 1943.

52 Ibid. 17 May 1943.

53 As note 49 above.

54 As note 37 above.

55 LETTERS 3 June 1943.

56 INDIANA (i) RG to NN 29 June 1943.

57 In *Collected Poems 1959* (Cassell 1959) p. 205.

58 MAJORCA Lt-Col. A. H. Williams to RG 5 Aug. 1943.

59 Ibid.

60 MAJORCA Wavell to RG 7 Sept. 1945 'I am afraid that, as you say, the hopes of his being alive are very slender.'

CHAPTER 3
MATRIARCHAL DAYS

61 O'PREY (1) p. 313 RG to AH 31 July 1942.

62 IRWIN n.d. (approx. 6 Aug. 1943).

63 O'PREY (1) p. 315 RG to AH 13 July 1943.

64 TAH p. 249.

65 Ibid. p. 299.

66 Ibid. pp. 78, 110, 191.

67 MAJORCA BG to George Simon Monday n.d. (July 1943).

68 IRWIN n.d. (approx. 12 Aug. 1943).

69 MS-S p. 384.

70 LETTERS 28 July 1943.

71 MS-S p. 394.

72 Ibid. p. 372.

73 Ibid. p. 384 (Aug. 1943).

74 O'PREY (1) p. 316.

75 O'PREY (1) pp. 317–18 RG to Mrs Rhys 1 Sept. 1943.

76 As note 69 above.

77 IRWIN 24 Nov. 1943.

78 MS-S p. 389.

CHAPTER 4
THE ANGRY SHEPHERD

79 RG, *King Jesus* (Cassell 1946) p. 352.

80 MAJORCA Sir Ronald Storrs to RG 21 Oct and 6 Nov. 1943.

81 BG in conv. with RPG Dec. 1993.

82 *King Jesus* p. 352.

83 As note 77 above.

84 O'PREY (I) p. 320 RG to Lynette Roberts 4 Dec. 1943.

85 *King Jesus* p. 353.

86 Ibid. p. 8.

87 Ibid. p. 51.

88 Ibid. p. 8.

89 Ibid. p. 9.

90 Ibid. p. 53.

91 Ibid. p. 55.

92 See also MS-S p. 393.

93 *King Jesus* p. 356.

94 Ibid.

95 Joanna Simon in conv. with RPG. George's divorce from Charlotte had gone through in Nov. 1943; and George and Joanna were married on 8 Jan. 1944.

96 AUTHOR RG to AG 6 Jan. 1944 has 'I . . . am working on . . . mostly the connexion of ancient Greek myths with the Babylonian ones.'

97 MAJORCA AH to BG 3 Jan. 1944.

98 O'PREY (I) p. 312.

99 RG, 'Foreword to the Poetry' in Alun Lewis, *Ha! Ha! Among the Trumpets* (1945).

100 MAJORCA Lieutenant A.

Lewis 6th Battalion South Wales Borderers India Command to RG.

101 As note 99 above.

102 Ibid.

103 As note 96 above.

104 RG's letter to his mother merely states that they were 'incomplete'; but since he had sent off a full set of maps to his publishers the previous summer, the likelihood is that they were in fact judged to be 'unsatisfactory' and in need of redoing.

105 MS-S pp. 383–5 appears to be quite wrong about the order of events. He has been misled by not knowing that Graves was indeed working on *The Golden Fleece* in 1944, though only for a brief period.

106 IRWIN 27 March 1944.

107 Quoted in RG, *The White Goddess* (Faber & Faber 1948) p. 17; RG's italics.

108 RG, Postscript to the 1960 edition of *The White Goddess* (Faber & Faber).

109 In RG's Postscript to the 1960 edition of *The White Goddess* he claims to have completed a first draft of *The Roebuck in the Thicket* within three weeks; but no doubt there was then much revision to be done, for IRWIN 20 June 1944 has, 'I took two months to write an inspirational sort of book called *The Roebuck in the Thicket*.'

110 O'PREY (I) p. 323 RG to AH 12 June 1944.

CHAPTER 5
THE ROEBUCK IN THE THICKET

111 As note 108 above.
112 *The White Goddess* (1948) p. 44.
113 Ibid. p. 45.
114 Ibid. p. 47.
115 Ibid. pp. 64–7.
116 O'PREY (1) pp. 322–3 RG to Lynette Roberts n.d. (but from MAJORCA Sam Graves to RG 24 May 1944 it can plausibly be dated to around 14 May 1944).
117 MAJORCA AH to RG 16 May 1944.
118 As note 116 above.
119 As note 110 above.
120 MS-S p. 395.
121 Ibid. p. 397.
122 QUOZ (quoted in MS-S p. 398).
123 MAJORCA Richard Church to RG 9 Nov. 1944.
124 MAJORCA Valentin Iremonger to RG 6 July 1944.
125 O'PREY (1) p. 367.
126 IRWIN 24 Aug. 1924.

CHAPTER 6
THE WINTER SOLSTICE

127 Karl Gay in conv. with RPG 8 Feb. 1993.
128 MAJORCA Catherine Dalton to RG 29 Dec. 1944.
129 MAJORCA AH to BG 20 Aug. 1944. Sadly, this cheerful mood evaporated a month later when he 'divided ways' with a woman friend, having 'found out that in some forgetful fit she married last Spring some chap in the forces whom she hasn't seen since and professes not to love' (Ibid. n.d. 1944).
130 MAJORCA Douglas Glass to RG 27 Sept. 1944.
131 The figure is taken from AUTHOR AG to RG 9 Dec. 1944.
132 AUTHOR AG to JTRG 4 Oct. 1944.
133 MAJORCA AG to RG 9 Dec. 1944. When she wrote enclosing the 10/6 she explained that, 'It must seem a drop in the ocean to you when you need £1300. But alas, I cannot at my present age, of close on 87, either give or lend it to you. All I have will be very little, with the terribly high death duties, & is all apportioned already. You & your children from Nancy will share your original portion of my estate. You can fancy how little that will be, as both girls [Rosaleen and Clarissa] are to get double portions & will, I fear, need them, both getting on over 50 & both without husbands.
134 MAJORCA AG to RG 3 Nov. 1944.
135 MAJORCA AH to RG Nov. 1944.
136 As note 127 above.
137 LETTERS 25 Dec. 1944.
138 AUTHOR RG to AG n.d. (?c.20 Nov.) 1944.
139 As note 134 above.
140 AUTHOR AG to JTRG 8 and

14 Oct. 1944 and MAJORCA
Clarissa Graves to RG 24 Nov.
1944.

141 MAJORCA Jenny Nicholson to
RG n.d. 1945.

142 MAJORCA RG to BG
Christmas Eve 1944.

143 MAJORCA AG to RG 9 Dec.
1944.

144 LETTERS 12 Dec. 1944.

145 O'PREY (1) RG to AH n.d.
p. 327.

146 As note 144 above.

147 AUTHOR RG to AG 8 Jan.
1945.

148 They were left with George
Simon's first wife Charlotte,
whom George and Joanna were
then visiting.

149 MAJORCA RG to BG Juan's
birthday 22 Dec. 1944.

150 MAJORCA RG to BG n.d.
(Dec. 1944).

151 TYWL pp. 294–8.

152 MAJORCA BG to RG Wed.
eve. n.d. (27 Dec. 1944).

153 *The White Goddess* p. 103.

154 *Poems 1938–1945* pp. 28–9.

155 MAJORCA BG to RG Fri. eve.
(?29 Dec. 1944).

156 MAJORCA RG to BG 31 Dec.
1944.

157 Ibid. n.d. (Dec. 1944). They had
agreed that 'the principal point of
Jesus's story, after all, turns out to
be his relation with women: his
attitude to sex and the mess it got
him into, trying to be chaste'.

158 As note 156 above.

159 MAJORCA AH to RG 1 July
1942.

160 As note 156 above.

161 Ibid.

CHAPTER 7
JENNY'S WEDDING

162 LETTERS 23 Jan. 1945.

163 As note 149 above.

164 Karl and Irene Gay in conv.
with RPG 8 Feb. 1993.

165 As note 162 above.

166 O'PREY (1) p. 327 RG to T. S.
Eliot 12 Jan. 1945.

167 O'PREY (1) p. 328.

168 O'PREY (1) pp. 328–9 RG to
T. S. Eliot 22 Jan. 1945.

169 As note 147 above.

170 AUTHOR AG to JTRG 16
Feb. 1945.

171 AUTHOR AG to JTRG 20
Feb. 1945.

172 MAJORCA Sam Graves to RG
3 April 1945.

173 As note 171 above.

174 MAJORCA AG to RG (quoting
his letter to her) 27 Feb. 1945.

175 Jenny Antonia Dalton was born
on 16 Jan. 1945.

176 AUTHOR JTRG to AG 9 Jan.
1945.

177 MAJORCA Catherine
Nicholson to Rosaleen Cooper 25
Feb. 1945.

178 AUTHOR AG to Charles
Graves 5 March 1945.

179 MAJORCA Jenny Nicholson to
RG 28 Feb. 1945. See also
INDIANA (i) RG to NN 3 March
1945, 'David's gunny- bale
arrived on the day Jenny married.'

180 As note 177 above.

181 Ibid.

182 Ibid.

183 Mary Graves in conv. with RPG 8 Nov. 1993.

184 *Poems 1938–1945* pp. 39–40.

185 INDIANA (i) RG to NN 3 March 1945.

186 MAJORCA Jenny Nicholson to RG 28 Feb. 1945.

187 MAJORCA Alex Clifford to RG 27 May (1945).

188 Ibid.

189 AUTHOR NN 14 Motcomb St. SW1 to JTRG 4 July 1945.

CHAPTER 8
CLARISSA AT GALMPTON

190 O'PREY (1) p. 329 RG to T. S. Eliot 18 March 1945.

191 IRWIN 8 June 1945.

192 MAJORCA Clarissa Graves to RG 20 May 1945; and AUTHOR AG to JTRG 29 Jan. 1945.

193 MAJORCA Clarissa Graves to RG 20 May 1945.

194 Clarissa Graves, *Seven Days and Other Poems* (Methuen 1927).

195 As note 193 above. This was followed up by a letter of 7 June asking about bus times.

196 MAJORCA AG to RG 15 June 1945.

197 AUTHOR RG to AG 5 or 8 Jan. 1945.

198 As note 196 above.

199 AUTHOR Clarissa Graves c/o Rosaleen Cooper to JTRG 14 June 1945.

200 MS-S p. 394 shows RG explaining this in another letter as 'a quotation from the Psalm Jesus quoted from the Cross'.

201 LETTERS 5 July 1945.

202 MAJORCA Sam Graves to RG 12 June 1945.

203 MAJORCA Clarissa Graves to RG 28 June 1945.

204 As note 201 above.

205 As note 203 above.

206 MAJORCA Clarissa Graves to RG 14 July 1945.

207 See e.g. MAJORCA AG to RG 21 July 1945, enclosing two linen bags, 'When you send off one bag you can be collecting in the other'; and ibid. AG to RG 7 Aug. 1945; and Ibid. AG to JTRG 30 Aug. 1945.

208 MAJORCA AG to RG 4 Aug. 1945.

209 MAJORCA (copy by AG) NN to AG 2 Aug. 1945.

210 As note 208 above.

211 AUTHOR AG to JTRG 30 Aug. 1945.

CHAPTER 9
THE WHITE GODDESS

212 IRWIN e.g. 23 Jan., 4 and 8 June and 3 Dec. 1945 shows that he had also made tentative plans with James Reeves to collaborate on a series of school anthologies of poems and prose.

213 O'PREY (1) p. 330 RG to Lynette Roberts 14 July 1945. Graves added that he kept 'making odd discoveries: yesterday's was that *The Tempest*

begins with exactly the same
dramatis personae as the *Mabinogi*
of Taliesin', with Tegid Voel
being Prospero, Caridwen being
Sycorax, Creirwy being Miranda,
Afagddu being Caliban and
Gwion being Ariel.

214 O'PREY (I) p. 331 RG to
Lynette Roberts 21 July 1945.

215 Ibid. RG to Lynette Roberts
and Keidrych Rhys 20 Sept.
1945.

216 MAJORCA AG to RG 9 Sept.
1945 and MAJORCA Clarissa
Graves to RG 20 Sept 1945.

217 MAJORCA AG to RG 9 Sept.
1945.

218 AUTHOR AG to JTRG 11
Oct. 1945.

219 Ibid. 23 Oct. 1945.

220 RG probably saw AH
(MAJORCA AH to RG 10 Oct.
1945), who had stayed with them
for a fortnight in the summer from
7 July (IRWIN 8 June 1945); and
RG lunched with John Graves
(now at the Ministry of Education)
on Friday 26 October. (AUTHOR
AG to JTRG 26 Oct. 1945 'I am
thinking of you lunching with
Robert to-day, with pleasure.')

221 AUTHOR AG to JTRG 26
Oct. 1945.

222 Ibid. 31 Oct. 1945.

223 Ibid.

224 Ibid.

225 MAJORCA Clarissa Graves to
RG 18 Oct. 1945.

226 As note 222 above.

227 MAJORCA AG to RG 31 Oct.
1945.

228 Ibid. 7 Nov. 1945.

228 On the fate of Amy's relatives
see e.g. AUTHOR AG to JTRG
31 Oct. and 6 Dec. 1945.

230 MAJORCA The War Office to
RG 16 Oct. 1945.

231 AUTHOR 1945 AG to JTRG
27 and 28 Nov.; Clarissa Graves
to JTRG 28 and 30 Nov.; AG
to Charles Graves 3 Dec.;
MAJORCA 1945 Clarissa Graves
to RG and BG 28 Nov.; Clarissa
Graves to RG 5 and 12 Dec.

223 TRUST RG to Sam Graves 31
Oct. 1945.

233 MAJORCA King George VI to
RG 12 Dec. 1945.

234 MAJORCA Robert Knittel of
The Creative Age Press to RG
2 Jan. 1947 admits that 'the
edition was not quite what it
should have been, particularly
with respect to the illustrations
and the maps'.

235 AUTHOR AG to JTRG 11
Nov. 1945 mentioning a letter
from Rosaleen to Clarissa on the
subject.

236 O'PREY (I) pp. 332–3 RG to
Karl Gay 8 Nov. 1945.

237 *The White Goddess* pp. 23–4.

238 Ibid. p. 338.

239 Ibid. p. 345.

240 Ibid. p. 346.

241 IRWIN 3 Dec. 1945.

242 O'PREY (I) pp. 334–5 RG to
Karl Gay 1 Jan. 1946.

243 IRWIN 11 Jan. 1946.

244 Ibid.

245 RG, 'In Dedication' in *Poems
and Satires 1951* (Cassell 1951).

The original runs as follows:
Your broad, high brow is whiter
than a leper's, / Your eyes are
flax-flower blue, blood-red your
lips, / Your hair curls honey-
coloured to white hips. / All
saints revile you, and all sober
men / Ruled by the God Apollo's
golden mean; / Yet for me rises
even in November / (Rawest of
months) so cruelly new a vision, /
Cerridwen, of your beatific love /
I forget violence and long
betrayal, / Careless of where the
next bright bolt may fall.

246 Irene Gay in conv. with RPG
8 Feb. 1993.

Book Three   Watch the North Wind   1946–50

CHAPTER I
A FLIGHT FROM CROYDON

1 MAJORCA AH to BG Whit
Monday 1945.

2 MAJORCA AH Flat 7, 30 New
Cavendish Street to RG Oct.
1945, 'I am supposed to be
starting life in the City next week
working for the combined
Financial Times and *News*.'

3 MAJORCA AG to RG 7 Aug.
1945.

4 AUTHOR AG to JTRG 12
March 1946.

5 *The White Goddess* p. 412.

6 Ibid. p. 410.

7 Ibid. p. 411.

8 *Poems 1938–1945*.

9 IRWIN 30 March 1946.

10 MAJORCA James Reeves to
RG 1 April 1946.

11 O'PREY (1) p. 344 RG to
Lynette Roberts n.d. (prob.
between 14 April and 6 May
1946).

12 MS-S p. 368 points out that
RG had been allowed to see little
or none of David's work.

13 MAJORCA Sam Graves to RG
27 July 1943.

14 MAJORCA NN to RG 2 Jan.
1946.

15 AUTHOR AG to JTRG 6 Feb.
1946.

16 MAJORCA Sam Graves to RG
4 April 1946.

17 Ibid. 8 April 1946.

18 MAJORCA This is the original
draft. MS-S p. 368 prints RG's
slightly amended version.

19 MAJORCA Hubert Ranke to
RG 1 Jan. 1946 and AUTHOR
AG to JTRG 2 Feb. 1946.

20 £50 was then one eighth of a
first-class teaching salary, and in
1995 terms it was worth at least
£2,000.

21 See TYWL p. 151.

22 O'PREY (1) pp. 337–8 RG to
Gertrude Stein 28 Jan. 1946.

23 Ibid. pp. 337–8.

24 O'PREY (1) pp. 338–40
Gertrude Stein to RG 4 Feb.
1946.

25 O'PREY (1) pp. 340–41 RG to
Gertrude Stein n.d.

26 MAJORCA Alex Clifford to RG
4 March 1946.

27 MAJORCA Clarissa Graves to
RG 1 April 1946.

28 Ibid.

29 AUTHOR AG to JTRG 10 Jan. 1946.

30 BROTHER.

31 MAJORCA AG to RG 13 March 1946.

32 O'PREY (1) p. 343 RG to Lynette Roberts 15 April 1946.

33 O'PREY (2) p. 23.

34 LETTERS 5 July 1945.

35 MAJORCA Ricardo and Betty Sicré to RG and BG 2 April 1946. For their meeting, BG in conv. with RPG Dec. 1993.

36 Karl Gay in conv. with RPG 8 Feb. 1993.

37 BG in conv. with RPG Feb. 1993.

38 MAJORCA Ricardo Sicré 436 West 20th St NYC to RG Wed. 3 Dec. 1941.

39 Ibid.

40 As note 37 above.

41 As note 36 above. Ricardo Sicré's *The Tap on the Left Shoulder* (Cassell 1950) has a superbly authentic account of life in the Resistance. See also Betty Lussier, *Amid My Alien Corn* (Lippincott 1958) p. 26.

42 Karl Gay in conv. with RPG 8 Feb. 1993 modified by BG in conv. with RPG Dec. 1993; and Betty Lussier, *Amid My Alien Corn* p. 22.

43 MAJORCA Betty Sicré to RG and BG 2 April 1946.

44 MAJORCA Wing-Commander Searle ('Crab') to RG 26 March 1946.

45 Ibid. 1 April 1946.

46 Ibid. 6 April 1946.

47 Ibid.

48 MS-S p. 411.

49 As note 31 above.

50 MAJORCA 18 March 1946 AG to RG LETTERS 19 March 1946 shows that in some cases Amy had split sets, and Robert, disliking this, arranged for a certain amount of redistribution.

51 O'PREY (1) p. 342.

52 Ibid. RG to T. S. Eliot 5 April 1946.

53 LETTERS 19 March 1946.

54 O'PREY (2) pp. 47–8 RG to George Simon 15 April 1946.

55 This turned out to be relatively simple: Sam asked for and was given the 'Windsor type armchair' which Robert had been using for his work; a pewter plate, and one of his two wireless sets, while Catherine took the rest of the furniture. MAJORCA Sam Graves to RG 8 and 16 April 1946; and O'PREY (1) p. 343 RG to Lynette Roberts 15 April 1946.

56 As note 36 above.

57 AUTHOR Rosaleen Cooper to JTRG 10 May 1946.

58 O'PREY (1) p. 344 RG to Lynette Roberts n.d. and Ibid.

59 As note 36 above.

60 As note 48 above.

61 O'PREY (2) p. 25 BG to James Reeves n.d. (11 July 1946).

62 MAJORCA Sam Graves to RG 16 April 1946 shows that he was planning to see his father in London.

63 As note 57 above and AUTHOR Amy Graves to JTRG 13 May and pc 17 May 1946 which has: 'this morning came a cable from Jerusalem "Both flourishing Graves" . . . Dick met Clarissa and looked after her . . .'

64 O'PREY (1) p. 345.

65 As note 52 above.

66 As note 48 above.

67 Karl Gay in conv. with RPG 8 Feb. 1993; supplemented by BG in conv. with RPG Dec. 1993. BG adds that Bebb was assisted by a navigator.

68 As note 36 above.

CHAPTER 2
RETURN TO CANELLUÑ

69 As note 61 above.

70 As note 48 above.

71 BG in conv. with RPG Dec. 1993.

72 As note 61 above.

73 Ibid.

74 O'PREY (2) pp. 25–6 RG to James Reeves n.d. (11 July 1946).

75 RG, 'The Phenomenon of Mass-Tourism' in *The Crane-Bag and Other Disputed Subjects* (Cassell 1969) p. 161. BG in conv. with RPG Dec. 1993 points out that they had sold the return fare from Palma to London to Ivan Lake, the British Consul at Palma, and his wife and child.

76 O'PREY (2) p. 295 n. 7.

77 As note 36 above.

78 O'PREY (2) p. 29 RG to MS-S 25 July 1946.

79 MATTHEWS p. 249.

80 As note 74 above p. 26.

81 Ibid.

82 O'PREY (2) pp. 27–8 RG to AH 29 June 1946.

83 MAJORCA Douglas Glass to RG 21 Nov. 1946.

84 'The Phenomenon of Mass-Tourism' as n. 75 above

85 As note 82 above.

86 As note 71 above. JB was a 'vague connection' of John Aldridge.

87 As note 74 above.

88 MAJORCA AH to BG June 1946.

89 As note 82 above.

90 O'PREY (2) p. 27.

91 As note 36 above.

92 TRUST BG to AH 29 June (1946).

93 As note 82 above.

94 As note 90 above.

95 As note 78 above.

CHAPTER 3
FAMILY, FRIENDS AND THE
QUEEN OF HEAVEN

96 MAJORCA AG to RG 19 July 1946.

97 Ibid. 22 Sept. 1946.

98 AUTHOR AG to JTRG pc 23 July 1946; and MAJORCA Rosaleen Cooper to RG 5 Sept. 1946.

99 O'PREY (2) pp. 30–1.

100 O'PREY (2) pp. 31–3 RG to Tom Matthews 29 Aug. 1946.

101 O'PREY (2) p. 34 RG to Julie Matthews 5 Sept. 1946.

102 As note 97 above.

103 As note 100 above.

104 MAJORCA Jenny Nicholson to RG and BG 13 Oct. 1946.

105 AUTHOR AG to JTRG 13 June 1946.

106 MAJORCA Peter Quennell to RG 14 Aug. (1946).

107 MAJORCA Lucie Aldridge to RG 21 June 1946.

108 As note 100 above.

109 RG in an introduction to *The Collected Poems of Norman Cameron* (Hogarth Press 1957) p. 21. See also MAJORCA AH to RG 8 Dec. 1946, 'Norman is in Vienna instructing the Austrians in democracy . . .'

110 MAJORCA James Reeves to RG 5 Sept. 1946.

111 MAJORCA AH to BG 13 June 1946.

112 TRUST BG to AH 29 June (1946).

113 MAJORCA AH to BG 27 Aug. 1946.

114 MAJORCA AH to RG 8 Dec. 1946.

115 MAJORCA BG to George and Joanna Simon n.d.

116 Ibid.

117 MS-S pp. 419–20.

118 AUTHOR AG to JTRG and Mary Graves 15 Oct. 1946.

CHAPTER 4
THE GOLDEN ASS

119 *The White Goddess* pp. 64–7.

The translation was by William Adlington.

120 RG, trans. Lucius Apuleius, *The Golden Ass* (Penguin 1950) p. 8.

121 Ibid. p. 9.

122 Ibid. p. 10.

123 MAJORCA Derek Savage to RG 23 Nov. 1946.

124 O'PREY (2) p. 38 RG to Derek Savage 16 Dec. 1946.

125 MAJORCA AH to BG 29 Dec. 1946.

126 MAJORCA Mrs Max Mallowan (Agatha Christie) to RG 3 Dec. (?1946).

127 As note 71 above.

128 MAJORCA Frances Knittel to RG Oct. 1947. She wrote again on 17 Dec. 1947 to say: 'I cannot tell you how often my thoughts wander to you both at this season of the year.'

129 MAJORCA Joanna Simon to RG and BG 15 Jan. 1947; and Ibid. AH to RG 17 Jan. 1947.

130 O'PREY (2) p. 40 RG to T. S. Eliot 19 Jan. 1947.

131 O'PREY (2) pp. 40–41 RG to Karl Gay 15 Feb. 1947.

132 MAJORCA Robert Knittel to RG 2 Jan. 1947.

133 As note 131 above.

134 AUTHOR RG to AG 11 Feb. 1947.

135 MAJORCA Clarissa Graves to RG 23 Jan. 1947 modified by AUTHOR Clarissa Graves to JTRG 26 Jan. 1947.

136 MAJORCA Clarissa Graves to RG 29 March 1947 and

AUTHOR Clarissa Graves to JTRG 5 Feb. 1947.

137 MAJORCA Molly Preston to RG 20 March 1947; and see also AUTHOR AG to JTRG 16 March 1947.

138 AUTHOR AG to JTRG 20 March 1947.

139 MAJORCA Rosaleen Cooper to RG 28 Jan. 1947.

140 MAJORCA JTRG to RG 18 April 1947.

141 MAJORCA Ricardo and Betty Sicré to RG 1 April 1947, saying that this was planned for 19 or 20 April.

142 O'PREY (2) p. 44 RG to Karl Gay 2 April 1947.

143 O'PREY (2) pp. 42–3, 43–4 RG to T. S. Eliot 23 March 1947 and RG to Karl Gay 2 April 1947.

144 *The White Goddess* (1961 version) p. 489. Robert attributes this work to the post-Jan. 1946 period; but O'PREY (2) RG to T. S. Eliot 23 March 1947 pp. 42–3 gives a rather different and probably more accurate story.

145 Ibid. pp. 392–3. I have followed MS-S pp. 403–4 in singling out this passage.

146 O'PREY (2) p. 297 n. 27; which I have preferred to MS-S p. 424.

147 MS-S p. 424.

148 MAJORCA AH to BG 8 May 1947.

149 *The Golden Ass* p. 229.

150 Ibid. p. 238.

CHAPTER 5
SILVER ISLAND

151 MAJORCA AH to RG 8 May 1947 has 'I also like the Utopia idea.'

152 As note 36 above.

153 Ibid.

154 Ibid.

155 The original anonymous report had been published in Madrid in 1876 by Don Justo Zaragoza under the title *Historia del descubrimiento de las regiones Austriales.*

156 RG, *The Isles of Unwisdom* (Cassell 1950) p. 7.

157 Their full address was 'Chez M. le Docteur Sicre, La Bestide de Seron, Ariège, France'.

158 MAJORCA George Simon to RG 28 June 1947.

159 Ibid.

160 O'PREY (2) p. 48 RG to George and Joanna Simon 15 April 1946.

161 Ibid. p. 49 22 July 1947.

162 As note 71 above.

163 As note 161 above supplemented by BG in conv. with RPG 9 April 1982.

164 BG in conv. with RPG 9 April 1982 and Dec. 1993.

165 As note 161 above.

166 MAJORCA George and Joanna Simon to RG and BG 28 April 1947.

167 As note 161 above.

168 Ibid.

169 MAJORCA RG to BG Wed. n.d. (Aug. 1947).

170 As note 161 above.
171 MAJORCA AG to RG 27 Aug. 1947.

CHAPTER 6
WATCH THE NORTH WIND RISE

172 MS-S p. 421.
173 AUTHOR AG to JTRG 26 Aug. 1947.
174 Ibid.
175 As note 71 above.
176 As note 169 above.
177 MAJORCA A doctor of 45 Cheyne Place SW3 to RG Tuesday 12 Aug. (1947).
178 As note 164 above.
179 MAJORCA RG to BG n.d. (Thurs. 4 Sept.) 1947.
180 TRUST RG to Archie & Cecily Gittes 4 Sept. 1947.
181 AUTHOR AG to JTRG 6 Oct. 1947.
182 Ibid. 14 Oct. 1947.
183 RG, *The Isles of Unwisdom* p. xiii.
184 RG, *Seven Days in New Crete* (in USA *Watch the North Wind Rise*) (Oxford University Press 1983) p. 14.
185 Ibid. p. 18.
186 Ibid. p. 19.
187 Ibid. p. 18.
188 Ibid. pp. 14–17.
189 Ibid. p. 247.
190 Ibid. pp. 11–12.
191 Ibid. p. 279.
192 Ibid. p. 25.
193 Ibid. p. 26.
194 Ibid. p. 25.
195 Ibid. p. 29.
196 Ibid. p. 30.
197 MAJORCA AH to BG 9 Sept. 1947.
198 Ibid. 19 Sept. 1947. Beryl's sister Evelyn had also been visiting.
199 As note 197 above.
200 MAJORCA RG to BG Tuesday morning Letter 10 I guess n.d. (Tuesday 16 Sept) 1947. For the sake of clarity, the sentence beginning 'Gaburro' has been inserted from later on in the letter.
201 MS-S in his excellent intro. to *Seven Days in New Crete* p. ix, to which I am much indebted.
202 *Seven Days in New Crete* pp. 66–7.
203 Ibid. p. 165.
204 AUTHOR AG to JTRG 1 Oct. 1947.
205 BG in conv. with RPG Dec. 1993 remarked that their recovery was hastened by visits from Ruth and Arnaldo Rosentingl, Jewish friends of the Gittes family. They had a son the same age as William, who was brought to the clinic to talk to him.
206 AUTHOR AG to JTRG 14 Oct. 1947.
207 TRUST RG to Ricardo Sicré 8 Dec. 1947.
208 MAJORCA Bill Chapman to RG 15 June 1948.
209 MAJORCA AH to RG 16 Dec. 1947.
210 O'PREY (2) pp. 50–51 RG to Joshua Podro 15 Dec. 1947.

211 MS-S p. 418. MS-S's dates are confusing. The letter from Creative Age dated 13 Jan. must have been 1948, not 1947. Their reply to Graves's response is dated on p. 419 as 3 March 1948; and Graves did not meet Dr Kubler with whom he collaborated on 'the novel about Isabella de Barretto' until much later in 1947. It was on 29 Oct. 1947 that Doubleday offered a $20,000 advance for an historical novel by RG in collaboration with Dr Otto Kubler.

212 Ibid.

213 QUOZ, quoted in MS-S p. 398 and O'PREY (2) p. 51.

214 RG, 'The White Goddess' (A Talk for the Y.M.H.A. Centre, New York, 9 Feb, 1957) in *Steps* (Cassell 1958) p. 105.

215 TRUST RG to Sam Graves 3 June 1948. 'I expect bad reviews', RG told his son, '. . . But bad reviews no longer affect my sales, which are always about the same: all the librarians buy and a few stalwart fans.'

216 MAJORCA Rayner Heppenstall to RG 19 March 1948.

217 MAJORCA AH to RG 16 June 1948.

218 MS-S pp. 416–17 H. D. Vursell to RG 17 Jan. 1949.

219 BAKER p. 402.

220 MAJORCA Margaret Russell to RG 11 March 1948.

221 MATTHEWS p. 226.

222 O'PREY (2) RG to James Reeves 13 May 1948 (O'PREY gives 1949, which from internal evidence alone is clearly inaccurate) p. 58. MAJORCA John Aldridge to RG and BG n.d. and 30 April 1948, and Ibid. Margaret Russell to RG 5 June 1948 shows that another disagreeable reminder of RG's years with Laura Riding followed the death of John Aldridge's mother. Early in 1948 the Trustees of her Estate began demanding from Robert repayment of the £75 that (on John's behalf) she had sunk into 'Luna', the imaginary company under whose banner Laura had planned to complete her road to the Cala, build an hotel, and begin various other commercial enterprises. As Margaret Russell commented when she heard that Robert had decided to settle the matter: 'Fancy you still paying LR's debts. The waste of money gives me the creeps. And nothing for it.'

223 O'PREY (2) RG to James Reeves 13 May 1948 (not 1949) p. 58.

224 In his Foreword to *Collected Poems: 1914–1947* RG writes that he has included 'forty-four poems from *Poems: 1938–1945*' which is curious, as that volume contained only forty poems.

225 *Collected Poems: 1914–1947* p. 238.

226 *Seven Days in New Crete* p. 175.

227 For Clarissa's reappearance

see AUTHOR AG to JTRG 27
March 1948. AG had received a
cable that morning from
Jerusalem: 'Am shortly leaving
Palestine. Both flourishing.
Writing Clarissa.' By 23 April she
was back home in England,
writing to JTRG from Erinfa; and
promising (as AG reported on that
date) to 'work' for AG's cure
through her Christian Science.
'So I have a double chance', wrote
AG 'but think I ought to see the
specialist.' For other details see
AUTHOR Rosaleen Cooper to
JTRG 29 April and 9 May 1948.

228 AUTHOR AG to JTRG 27
March 1948.

229 Ibid. 1 June 1948.

CHAPTER 7
AT LONDON ZOO

230 AUTHOR AG to JTRG 11
May 1948.

231 AUTHOR Rosaleen Cooper to
JTRG 25 May 1948.

232 AUTHOR Clarissa Graves to
JTRG 27 May 1948.

233 AUTHOR AG to JTRG 7 June
1948.

234 AUTHOR Rosaleen Cooper to
Peggy Graves 12 June 1948.

235 AUTHOR Susan Macaulay to
JTRG May n.d. (1948).

236 AUTHOR AG to JTRG 1 and
22 June 1948.

237 As note 223 above. However, a
week was spent at Lowestoft
towards the end of July with
friends.

238 AUTHOR AG to JTRG 22
June 1948.

239 MAJORCA Clarissa Graves to
RG 4 July 1948.

240 Ibid. 13 Sept. 1948.

241 MAJORCA AG to RG 4 July
1948.

242 TRUST RG to Sam Graves 3
June 1948.

243 MAJORCA AG to RG 15 July
1948.

244 TRUST RG to Cecily and
Archie Gittes 27 July 1948.

245 MAJORCA Rosaleen Cooper
to RG 8 Nov. 1948.

246 MAJORCA BG to George and
Joanna Simon 4 April (1949).
'We must at least have our
annual dinner at the Cafe Royal.'

247 MAJORCA Dorothy Simmons
to RG and BG 27 Sept. 1948.

248 As note 223 above p. 59.

CHAPTER 8
THE ISLES OF UNWISDOM

249 MS-S pp. 417–18.

250 MAJORCA Robert [unknown
correspondent] 17 Museum
Road Oxford to RG Friday 17
Dec. 1948.

251 MAJORCA John Aldridge to
RG and BG 25 Oct. 1948.

252 MAJORCA BG to George and
Joanna Simon 3 Jan. n.d. (1949).

253 O'PREY (2) p. 61 RG to AH
n.d.

254 O'PREY (2) p. 60 RG to Karl
and Rene Gay 14 July 1949.

255 MS-S pp. 425–6.

256 O'PREY (2) p. 52.

257 Ibid. pp. 52–3.

258 Ibid. p. 53 RG to Dr Wasson 26 Jan. 1949.

259 MAJORCA R. Gordon Wasson to RG 28 Feb. and 16 March 1949.

260 O'PREY (2) pp. 54–5 RG to Mr and Mrs Wasson 6 March 1949.

261 MAJORCA R. Gordon Wasson to RG 16 March 1949.

262 MAJORCA AG to RG 25 Feb. 1949 and AUTHOR AG to JTRG 26 Feb. 1949.

263 MAJORCA Molly Preston to RG 20 March 1947.

264 MAJORCA AG to RG 18 March 1949.

265 As note 223 above p. 59.

266 TRUST BG to Cecily Gittes n.d.

267 TRUST RG to Cecily Gittes 1 June 1950.

268 MAJORCA BG to George and Joanna Simon 4 April (1949).

269 Ricardo Sicré, *The Tap on the Left Shoulder* (Cassell 1950).

270 O'PREY (2) p. 62.

CHAPTER 9
THE NAZARENE GOSPEL RESTORED

271 TRUST RG to Cecily Gittes 7 Aug. 1949.

272 MATTHEWS p. 251–2.

273 AUTHOR JTRG to AG 4 July 1949.

274 As note 271 above.

275 O'PREY (2) p. 57 RG to James Reeves '23 April I guess, 1949'.

276 AUTHOR JTRG to AG 17 and 24 Aug. 1949.

277 As note 71 above.

278 Joanna Simon in conv. with RPG 10 Dec. 1993.

279 AUTHOR JTRG to AG 17 Aug. 1949.

280 O'PREY (2) p. 59 RG to Karl and Rene 14 July 1949.

281 Ibid.

282 MS-S p. 420.

283 Ibid. p. 432.

284 Ibid. p. 431.

285 AUTHOR AG to JTRG (pmk 15 Feb. 1949).

286 Ibid. (pmk 19 July 1949).

287 Ibid. 27 July 1949.

288 AUTHOR AG to Peggy Graves 2 Aug. 1949.

289 AUTHOR AG to JTRG 28 July 1949.

290 Ibid., 27 July 1949.

291 Ibid.

292 BG in conv. with RPG Dec. 1993 recalls that the boys at this reform school took turns to do the washing-up – and so one day Robert and Beryl found themselves displaying their own sense of communal responsibility by washing up for the entire school!

293 O'PREY (2) pp. 63–4 RG to Joshua Podro 3 Aug. 1949.

294 AUTHOR AG to JTRG 7 Aug. 1949 'Robert . . . leaves today for Spain.'

295 TRUST RG to Cecily Gittes 28 Aug. 1949.

296 O'PREY (2) p. 65 RG to Joshua Podro 17 Aug. 1949.

297 Ibid. pp. 68–9 23 Sept. 1949.

298 O'PREY (2) p. 73 RG to T. S. Eliot 14 May 1950.

299 MAJORCA James Reeves to RG 22 Oct. 1949.

300 O'PREY (2) p. 67 RG to AH Sept. 1949. See also MAJORCA Terence Hards to RG n.d. (1949). Terence Hards was a twenty-year-old poet who had written thanking RG for 'your valuable remarks about the poems'.

301 As note 36 above.

302 AUTHOR AG to JTRG 23 Nov. 1949.

303 AUTHOR Clarissa Graves to JTRG 17 Dec. 1949.

304 AUTHOR Dick Graves to AG 11 Dec. 1949.

305 MAJORCA Amy Graves to RG n.d. (1949/1950) MS-S's interpretation of Amy's letter on his p. 436 is not borne out by the evidence. Nowhere in her letter is there any mention of 'Dr' or 'Sir John' – or of 'MA', though JTRG was indeed an MA.

306 MAJORCA Tom Matthews to RG 10 Sept. 1949.

307 MATTHEWS p. 270.

308 As note 71 above.

309 RG, *Collected Poems 1975* (Cassell 1975) p. 165.

310 AUTHOR Dr Rosaleen Cooper to JTRG 21 and 27 Feb. 1959. See also AUTHOR JTRG Diary e.g. 31 March 1950 when he motored to Exeter for Amy's eighth treatment but Dr Hadden thought it unwise to continue, as her skin was beginning to show bad effects.

311 MAJORCA AG to RG n.d. (1950).

313 TRUST BG to Cecily Gittes 18 May 1950.

313 MAJORCA Jenny Nicholson to RG 28 April 1950 mentions their expected visit in the last days of June.

314 BG in conv. with RPG 11 Feb. 1993.

315 Ibid. Dec. 1993.

316 AUTHOR AG to JTRG n.d. (prob. Mon. 10 July 1950).

317 MAJORCA AG to RG 18 April 1950.

318 MAJORCA Clarissa Graves to RG 3 June 1950.

319 AUTHOR AG to JTRG n.d. (?14) July 1949.

320 MAJORCA Richard Hughes to RG 23 July 1950.

321 As note 319 above.

322 MAJORCA AG to RG n.d.

323 There has been confusion about Graves's meetings with Eliot. MS-S pp. 431–2 describes one such meeting, correctly attributing it to 1949, but wrongly describing it as 'their last meeting'. O'PREY (2) pp. 75–6 knows that Graves saw Eliot again in 1950, but wrongly attributes MS-S's story to that date, when he went not alone with William, but with Joshua Podro, see O'PREY (2) p. 95 RG to Eliot 23 May 1951 'since Podro and I saw you last August'.

324 O'PREY (2) p. 73 RG to T. S. Eliot 14 May 1950.

325 O'PREY (2) p. 75 RG to Gordon Wasson 10 June 1950.

326 O'PREY (2) passim pp. 76–8. The quoted words are taken from p. 77 RG to T. S. Eliot 10 Sept. 1950.

327 O'PREY (2) p. 77 RG to T. S. Eliot 10 Sept. 1950.

328 TRUST RG to Cecily Gittes 20 Nov. 1950.

329 As note 36 above.

330 Ibid.

331 MAJORCA Jacquetta Hawkes to RG 20 Sept. 1950.

Book Four Judith 1950–53

CHAPTER 1
FLAWLESS BLADE

1 Personal details in Book Four about Judith Bledsoe (unless otherwise attributed) are from her conv. with RPG on 12 Aug. 1993.

2 RG, 'The Whittaker Negroes' in *Five Pens in Hand* (The Books for Libraries Press 1970) p. 301. BG confirmed to RPG on 21 Dec. 1993 that the 'Julia Fiennes' of whom RG writes is in fact Judith Bledsoe.

3 *Poems and Satires 1951* p. 10.

4 The description of Marvin comes from BG in conv. with RPG Sept 1994.

5 Karl Gay in conv. with RPG 8 Feb. 1993.

6 'The Whittaker Negroes' p. 301.

7 As note 5 above.

8 *Poems and Satires 1951* p. 17.

9 Ibid. p. 33.

10 BG in conv. with RPG Feb. 1993.

11 TRUST RG to Cecily Gittes 20 Nov. 1950.

12 O'PREY (2) p. 105 RG to James Reeves n.d. (Dec. 1950/ Jan. 1951).

13 MS-S p. 442.

14 IRWIN 15 Dec. 1951 has: 'Why Darien? Because that was his name. Judith . . . had named him so prophetically even before I met her . . .'

15 *Poems and Satires 1951* pp. 18–19.

16 TRUST RG to Cecily Gittes 10 March 1951.

17 For Irwin's appearance, BG in conv. with RPG Sept. 1994.

18 O'PREY (2) p. 83 RG to James Reeves 14 Dec. 1950.

19 IRWIN BG to James Reeves n.d. (Late Dec. 1950; the remainder of the letter was written by RG and appears in O'PREY (2) p. 105.)

20 MAJORCA RG to George and Joanna Simon 21 Jan. 1951.

21 MAJORCA Rosaleen Cooper to RG 24 Jan. 1951.

CHAPTER 2
DEATH OF A MATRIARCH

22 AUTHOR Clarissa Graves to JTRG 23 Oct. 1950.

23 Ibid. 29 Nov. 1950.

24 AUTHOR JTRG to AG 7 Nov. 1950 and 10 Jan. 1951.

25 MAJORCA Clarissa Graves to RG 18 Jan. 1951.

26 AUTHOR Clarissa Graves to JTRG 11 Jan. 1951 pc. 'Mother, thanks to R's blue pill, had a better night. But she is still far from herself & seems to need a lot of rest to get over a time of strain. She seems to have felt the loss of Maria very much.'

27 AUTHOR JTRG to AG 3 Jan. 1951.

28 As note 25 above.

29 AUTHOR Rosaleen Cooper to AG 24 Nov. 1950.

30 AUTHOR Clarissa Graves to JTRG 15 Jan. 1951.

31 As note 25 above.

32 AUTHOR Rosaleen Cooper to JTRG 17 Jan. 1951. She had been detained first by her winter sports, and then by a locum having overturned her car.

33 MAJORCA Rosaleen Cooper to RG 24 Jan. 1951.

34 AUTHOR Rosaleen Cooper to JTRG 3 Feb. 1951.

35 As note 33 above.

36 As note 34 above.

37 MAJORCA Dick Graves to RG 28 Jan. 1951.

38 MAJORCA Jenny Nicholson to RG 20 Feb. 1951.

39 O'PREY (2) p. 84 RG to Derek Savage 3 Jan. 1951.

40 INDIANA (i) RG to Sam Graves 14 April 1951.

CHAPTER 3
VOLCANIC EMOTIONS

41 RG to Judith Bledsoe n.d. (late Dec. 1951 or early Jan. 1952). This letter, owned by JB, is the only one of his letters to her which has survived.

42 As note 20 above.

43 O'PREY (2) RG to Joshua Podro 25 March 1951; INDIANA (i) RG to Sam Graves 14 April 1951 shows that RG's miscellany *Occupation Writer* was out that month; O'PREY (2) RG to James Reeves 7 June 1951 shows that RG and Beryl were still working for Unesco on their translation of *Enriquillo* by the Dominican novelist Manuel de Jesus Galvan. It would eventually be published in 1955 as *The Cross and the Sword*.

44 LETTERS 19 April 1951.

45 MAJORCA Clarissa Graves to RG 18 and 29 Jan. 1951.

46 'The Whittaker Negroes' p. 301.

47 Ibid. p. 300.

48 Ibid. p. 303.

49 Ibid. The friend's name was Hank.

50 MS-S pp. 442–3.

51 As note 5 above.

52 BG in conv. with RPG Dec. 1993.

53 As note 5 above.

54 O'PREY (2) pp. 89–90, 92–3 RG to Derek Savage 2 March & 11 April 1951.

55 As note 5 above.
56 As note 52 above.
57 Ibid.
58 MS-S p. 442.
59 Ibid.
60 O'PREY (2) p. 102 RG to Selwyn & Tania Jepson 29 Oct. 1951.
61 VICTORIA RG to Selwyn & Tania Jepson 5 May 1951.
62 TRUST Norman Cameron to RG 7 June 1951.

CHAPTER 4
A DISAPPOINTING ANSWER

63 RG, *Poems 1953* (Cassell 1953) p. 284.
64 TRUST RG to Betty and Ricardo Sicré 1 June (1951).
65 'The Whittaker Negroes' p. 301.
66 O'PREY (2) pp. 94, 95 RG to Gordon Wasson 6 May and RG to T. S. Eliot 23 May 1951.
67 Ibid. p. 95.
68 MAJORCA Jenny Nicholson to RG 18 April and 17 (?May) 1951.
69 O'PREY (2) p. 97.
70 RG and Joshua Podro, *The Nazarene Gospel Restored* (Cassell 1953) p. 72.
71 Ibid.
72 Ibid.
73 O'PREY (2) p. 97 RG to T. S. Eliot 26 June 1951.

CHAPTER 5
'RATHER A *BORING* SAINT'

74 MAJORCA George and Joanna Simon to RG and BG n.d. (pre-July 5 when they go to Perpignan).
75 MAJORCA RG, 'Queen Mother to New Queen' in *Quarto* No. 2, Summer 1951.
76 AUTHOR Jenny Nicholson to JTRG 6 July 1951 pc. The flat was in Gardiner Mansions in Church Row.
77 AUTHOR Clarissa Graves to JTRG 6 Nov. 1951 shows that the school was Ruyton Hall School at Shifnal.
78 AUTHOR Clarissa Graves to JTRG 31 July 1951.
79 As note 60 above.
80 MS-S p. 445.
81 The poem was enclosed in MAJORCA Norman Cameron to RG 21 July 1951; and appears in NC's *Collected Poems*.
82 O'PREY (2) p. 98 RG to Gordon Wasson 10 March 1952.
83 MS-S p. 447.
84 AUTHOR Rosaleen Cooper to JTRG 1 Aug. 1951.
85 Ibid.
86 As note 58 above.

CHAPTER 6
'THANK YOU, ALWAYS & FOR EVER'

87 O'PREY (2) p. 93 RG to Derek Savage 11 April 1951.

88 As note 83 above.

89 Details from MS-S pp. 447–8;
William Graves in conv. with
RPG Sept. 1994; and O'PREY
(2) p. 102 RG to Selwyn &
Tania Jepson 29 Oct. 1951.

90 William Graves in conv. with
RPG Sept. 1994.

91 MS-S p. 448; see also O'PREY
(2) pp. 115–16.

92 MS-S p. 448.

93 As note 60 above.

94 MAJORCA Jenny Nicholson to
RG 27 Oct. 1951.

95 As note 60 above.

96 *Poems and Satires 1951.*

97 When printing this version
earlier in the book, I broke my
usual rule of printing poems
exactly as they appeared at the
time. In this case, Graves's
revisions had improved the poem
almost out of recognition. There
would be one more version (that
which, renamed 'The White
Goddess', appears in his *Collected
Poems 1959* and thereafter). But
in this, Graves weakened the
emotional force of the poem by
substituting 'Our' for 'My' and
'We' for 'I' throughout.

98 O'PREY (2) p. 103 RG to
James Reeves 15 Dec. 1951.

99 MAJORCA Christina Foyle to
RG 5 Dec. 1951.

100 MAJORCA Ricardo Sicré to
RG 19 Dec. 1951.

101 As note 60 above.

102 These were 'Greta and her
husband from Canada'. O'PREY
(2) p. 96 RG to James Reeves

7 June 1951 has RG describing
them as 'an Esthonian of English
descent married to a Swiss who
grows asparagus in the wilds of
Two Mountains'; and Greta had
apparently written 'to ask about
[Judith] most tenderly'. BG in
conv. with RPG Sept. 1994
comments that Greta used to be
a balloonist; and once wrote to
RG saying that she was living
with a dog at the bottom of the
sea; while her husband, Bob,
revolutionized RG's compost
heaps by introducing him to a
mixture which helped to break
them down faster.

103 BG in conv. with RPG Sept.
1994.

104 As note 41 above.

105 MAJORCA Dick Graves to
RG 2 Jan. and 8 March 1952.
The poem was first published in
RG, *Poems 1953.*

CHAPTER 7
ABSENCE

106 *Poems 1953.*

107 O'PREY (2) pp. 96–7 RG to
James Reeves 7 June 1951. The
verses were shown to him by
Jay's close friend Greta, the
woman who had so much liked
Judith.

108 VICTORIA RG to Selwyn
Jepson Feb. 1952.

109 MAJORCA George Simon to
RG 20 Jan. 1952.

110 As note 108 above.

111 O'PREY (2) p. 303 n. 116.

112 MAJORCA Ricardo Sicré to RG 19 Dec. 1951. Beryl visited her mother in hospital.

113 MAJORCA Jenny Nicholson to RG 29 Jan. 1952.

114 O'PREY (2) p. 104 RG to Derek Savage 21 Jan. 1952.

115 MAJORCA Clarissa Graves to RG 9 Jan. 1952.

116 MAJORCA JTRG to RG 22 Jan. 1952. The sum was £12-5–10, after tax of £11-2-7 on a sum of £23-8-5 – RG's share of the full £117-2-3 (about £1,500 in 1995 terms).

117 LETTERS 25 Jan 1952. In the same letter, RG mentioned his own financial difficulties; and JTRG responded with an offer to take William into his school Holme Grange to prepare him for Oundle; for which in LETTERS 3 Feb. 1952 RG thanked him, but declined, saying that William 'doesn't go merely to lessons with a single tutor. He also has an English Latin tutor, and goes to a Spanish school (with the ambitious name of 'University Studies') for lessons in French and Spanish literature, and gets a lot of miscellaneous teaching from Beryl and me . . . He also understands Catalan . . .'

118 O'PREY (2) p. 106 RG to Joshua Podro March 1952.

119 MAJORCA Ricardo Sicré to RG March 1952.

120 INDIANA (i) RG to Sam Graves 16 March 1952.

121 MAJORCA Jenny Nicholson to RG 14 March 1952.

122 RG in *The Times* Friday 28 March 1952.

123 MAJORCA Tom Matthews to RG 28 March 1952.

124 Ibid. May 1952.

125 O'PREY (2) pp. 107–10, inc. RG to Gordon Wasson n.d. (rcvd 8 April 1952); and Ibid. 15 April 1952.

126 MS-S p. 449.

127 TRUST RG to AH 'April 19 or so 1952'.

128 AUTHOR Tape of Charles Corbett Aug. 1993.

129 AUTHOR Charles F. Corbett to RPG 19 May 1993. Their meeting happened in about August 1952.

130 Ibid.

131 TRUST RG to Cecily Gittes 23 Aug. 1952.

132 MS-S p. 446.

CHAPTER 8
'THE WORLD'S DELIGHT'

133 VICTORIA RG to Selwyn and Tania Jepson 3 May 1952.

134 MS-S p. 450.

135 Ibid. p. 451.

136 MAJORCA *copy* RG to Alec Guinness 4 March (1957).

137 *Halliwell's Film Guide* 5th edn (Paladin Books 1986) p. 846.

138 As note 135 above; and LETTERS 13 Sept. 1952 shows that the sum agreed was $5,000.

139 As note 136 above.

140 Ibid.

141 MS-S p. 452 suggests that when the script was completed 'Graves could not get hold of the second instalment of the money, now due'; but LETTERS 13 Sept. 1952 makes it clear that (at that stage) the first instalment had not been paid either. RG was then expecting $5,000.

142 As note 135 above.

143 AUTHOR Clarissa Graves to JTRG n.d. and O'PREY (2) p. 109 RG to Gordon Wasson 15 April 1952.

144 TRUST BG to Cecily Gittes n.d.

145 MAJORCA Jenny Nicholson to RG 14 Aug. 1952.

146 MAJORCA Jenny Nicholson from Rome to RG 9 Oct. 1952.

147 MS-S p. 447.

CHAPTER 9
YOUR NAKED NAME

148 MS-S p. 453 wrongly recalls that Kee's visit was in the summer of 1952. It was in fact (see AUTHOR Robert Kee to RPG 6 Feb. 1994) in the summer of 1951.

149 *Poems 1953.*

150 'The Whittaker Negroes' p. 303.

151 Ibid.

152 Ibid. p. 304.

153 Ibid. pp. 304–9.

154 Ibid pp. 306–8. RG later checked the story with Tom Matthews, who found a medical column on the subject dating back from 1931.

155 *Poems 1953.*

156 MS-S p. 442 (RG to Judith's mother 10 Sept. 1953).

157 LETTERS 13 Sept. 1952.

158 MS-S p. 452.

159 Ibid. p. 454.

160 Ibid. p. 455.

161 'The Whittaker Negroes', p. 313.

162 RG, *Collected Poems 1959* (Cassell 1959) p. 290.

163 'The Window Sill' in Ibid. p. 295.

164 'Foreword' to *Poems 1953.*

165 O'PREY (2) p. 112 RG to James Reeves 11 Dec. 1952.

166 Ibid. p. 113 13 Jan. 1953.

167 William Graves in conv. with RPG Sept. 1994. Maria stayed with Beryl for a week before the birth, and two weeks after.

Book Five   Ambassador of Otherwhere   1953–60

CHAPTER I
NO HOLIDAYS FOR A WRITER

1 LETTERS 8 Feb. 1953.

2 MS-S p. 457.

3 Ibid. p. 458.

4 BG in conv. with RPG Sept. 1994.

5 O'PREY (2) p. 60 RG to Karl and Rene Gay 14 July 1949 has: 'Saw Norman; apparently the Life Insurance won't give him even a short term credit. High

blood pressure. He's scared.' In these circumstances, he had found spiritual solace in the arms of the Roman Catholic Church before he died.

6 O'PREY (2) p. 115 RG to James and Mary Reeves 14 May 1953. Graves wrote 'an appreciation' of Cameron's poetry for *The Times*, 'but', as he told James Reeves, 'they did not print it'.

7 MAJORCA Tom Matthews to RG 7 May 1953.

8 MAJORCA AH to RG 27 April 1953.

9 Ibid. 23 June 1953.

10 MAJORCA Jenny Nicholson to RG 17 April (?1953).

11 MAJORCA Alston Anderson from Deyá to RG 21 April 1953.

12 BG in conv. with RPG Feb. 1993.

13 MAJORCA Alan Sillitoe Villa Catalina Puerto Soller to RG 28 April 1953.

14 Alan Sillitoe, 'I Reminded Him of Muggleton' in *Shenandoah: The Washington and Lee University Review* Vol XIII No 2 Winter 1962 pp. 47–50.

15 MAJORCA Bill Watt to RG 9 June 1953.

16 O'PREY (2) p. 118 RG to James and Mary Reeves 15 June 1953.

17 O'PREY (2) p. 118 RG to James and Mary Reeves 15 June 1953 for the date of arrival, which was 3 July; and

VICTORIA 16 July 1953 has 'I am rushing back to Majorca this morning.'

18 AUTHOR Clarissa Graves to JTRG 19 July 1953.

19 Ibid. 19–20 April 1953. Erinfa had been sold for £1,500.

20 See e.g. AUTHOR Susan Macaulay to JTRG 3 July 1953 commenting: 'I didn't see much of Philip lately but we corresponded regularly . . . he became much more human and less detached in his last years . . . Kitty made him extremely happy . . . he was very fond of [his adopted son] George too . . .'

21 MAJORCA Tom Matthews to RG 17 June 1953 shows that such a dinner was planned for Thursday 9 July.

22 VICTORIA RG to Selwyn Jepson 16 July 1953.

23 IRWIN 9 Aug. 1953.

24 Ibid. 19 July 1953.

CHAPTER 2
BLIND HOMER'S DAUGHTER

25 Ibid. 9 Aug. 1953.

26 MAJORCA Dick Graves to RG 13 Aug. 1953.

27 VICTORIA RG to Selwyn Jepson 24 Aug. 1953.

28 MAJORCA Alastair Reid, *Remembering Robert* (Nov. 1985).

29 MS-S p. 462.

30 O'PREY (2) p. 157 RG to Gordon Wasson 6 Dec. 1956.

31 As note 28 above.

32 As note 27 above.

33 o'prey (2) p. 118.
34 o'prey (2) p. 119 RG to Selwyn Jepson 20 Sept. 1953.
35 As note 27 above.
36 ms-s p. 442 letter of 10 Sept. 1953.
37 irwin 28 Dec. 1953.
38 trust BG to Cecily Gittes 30 June 1951.
39 *Poems 1953*.
40 As note 34 above.
41 victoria for the word 'Athene' which is omitted in o'prey (2) p. 120 RG to Selwyn Jepson 20 Sept. 1953.
42 majorca Selwyn Jepson to RG 30 Oct. 1953.
43 o'prey (2) pp. 120–21 RG to Selwyn Jepson 4 Nov. 1953.
43 Ibid. p. 121.
45 *Poems 1953*.
46 As note 44 above.
47 majorca Gordon Wasson to RG 5 Nov. 1953.
48 o'prey (2) p. 145.
49 As note 44 above.
50 Ibid.
51 Ibid.
52 RG, *Homer's Daughter* (Cassell 1955) p. x.
53 Ibid. p. 56.
54 Ibid. p. 137.
55 Ibid. p. 194.
56 ms-s p. 450.
57 o'prey (2) p. 95 RG to T. S. Eliot 23 May 1951.
58 letters 20 Jan. 1954.
59 o'prey (2) p. 134.
60 victoria RG to Selwyn Jepson 16 Feb. 1954.
61 o'prey (2) p. 124 RG to Basil Liddell-Hart 19 Feb. 1954.
62 o'prey (2) p. 122.
63 As note 61 above.
64 victoria RG to Selwyn Jepson 22 Jan. 1954.
65 Ibid.

CHAPTER 3
UNDER FIRE

66 author Sam Graves to JTRG 7 March 1954.
67 As note 37 above.
68 majorca quoted in J. Williams from Connecticut to RG 16 June 1954.
69 irwin 9 March 1954 and see o'prey (2) p. 138 RG to Gordon Wasson 29 Aug. 1954.
70 o'prey (2) p. 134 RG to Liddell-Hart Holy Thursday 1954 (15 April).
71 Ibid. p. 132 n.d.
72 Ibid. p. 133.
73 o'prey (2) p. 140 RG to Selwyn Jepson '6 Feb 1955 I guess'.
74 Ibid. p. 126 10 March 1954.
75 o'prey (2) p. 135.
76 o'prey (2) p. 137 RG to Basil Liddell-Hart 29 June 1954.
77 o'prey (2) p. 127 RG to Selwyn Jepson 23 March 1954.
78 Ibid.
79 Ibid. p. 128 28 March 1954.
80 majorca Selwyn Jepson to RG 26 March 1954. o'prey (2) p. 127 RG to Selwyn Jepson 23 March 1954 shows that RG had suggested making it 'a mere college text-book of it in the US

by giving it merely the narrative part, and omitting the explanation'.

81 O'PREY (2) pp. 129–30 RG to Ken McCormick 28 March 1954.

82 MAJORCA Selwyn Jepson to RG 27 March 1954.

83 BG in conv. with RPG Sept. 1993.

84 MAJORCA RG to Ava Gardner 15 June 1954.

85 Ibid. has Sally and Richard arriving 'soon'; and AUTHOR Clarissa Graves to RG 20 Aug. 1954 has: 'I see you have Sally and Richard with you.'

86 MAJORCA has a document showing that the reception took place on 9 July 1954 followed by a 3.30 reception in the Houses of Parliament Room 6 Terrace level by courtesy of Lord Wilmot.

87 MAJORCA Clarissa Graves to RG 11 July 1954.

88 Tape of Charles Corbett August 1993 mentions that Lucia studied under Aina Johnson who had once danced with the Bolshoi, and was 'a very sweet young lady' of whom Robert was 'terribly fond'.

89 MAJORCA Jenny Nicholson to RG 18 Aug. 1954.

90 IRWIN 4 Aug. 1954.

91 MAJORCA Alan Sillitoe Lista de correos Soller to RG Aug. 1954.

CHAPTER 4

AMBASSADOR FROM OTHERWHERE

92 As note 28 above.

93 AUTHOR *copy* RG to Chuck Corbett 5 Oct. 1954.

94 IRWIN 25 July 1954.

95 As note 28 above.

96 William Graves in conv. with RPG Sept. 1994.

97 Tape of Charles Corbett Aug. 1993. RG worked this story into 'The Lost Chinese' in *Collected Short Stories* (Doubleday 1964) pp. 265–85.

98 AUTHOR *copy* RG in Palma to Chuck Corbett 5 Oct. 1954.

99 BG & William Graves in conv. with RPG Sept. 1994.

100 As note 28 above for this and following paragraphs.

101 VICTORIA RG to Selwyn Jepson 29 Aug. 1954.

102 O'PREY (2) p. 139 RG to James Reeves 15 Oct. 1954.

103 As note 96 above.

104 O'PREY (2) p. 306 n. 53.

105 MS-S p. 467.

106 O'PREY (2) p. 142 RG to Derek Savage 15 Feb. 1955.

107 MAJORCA Kingsley Amis to RG 2 Oct. 1954.

108 Ibid. 25 Oct. 1954.

109 O'PREY (2) p. 139 RG to James Reeves 15 Oct. 1954.

110 RG, *The Crowning Privilege* (Cassell 1955) p. 4.

111 Ibid. p. 5.

112 Ibid. p. 21.

113 Ibid. pp. 23–4.

114 Ibid. p. 25.
115 As note 109 above. The theologian was 'the great C. H. Dodd'.
116 O'PREY (2) pp. 142–3.
117 *The Crowning Privilege* pp. 45–69.
118 Ibid. p. 46.
119 As note 109 above p. 140.
120 *The Crowning Privilege* p. 191.
121 Ibid. pp. 72, 75, 85.
122 Ibid. pp. 97, 105.
123 Ibid. p. 112.
124 Ibid. p. 135.
125 Ibid. p. 119.
126 Ibid. p. 116.
127 Ibid. p. 117.
128 Ibid. p. 116.
129 RG, 'Dr. Syntax and Mr. Pound' (prompted by '*The Poet as Translator*', the *Times Literary Supplement*, 18 Sept. 1953) in Ibid. pp. 212–14.
130 *The Crowning Privilege* p. 123.
131 Ibid. pp. 127–8.
132 Ibid. p. 127.
133 Ibid. p. 126.
134 Ibid. p. 129.
135 Ibid. p. 130.
136 Ibid. pp. 130–31.
137 Ibid. pp. 132–3.
138 Ibid. p. 135.
139 O'PREY (2) p. 142 RG to Derek Savage 15 Feb. 1955 and p. 307 n. 54 showing that the broadcast was on the BBC Home Service on 20 Feb. 1955.

CHAPTER 5
GOLDEN HOPES

140 As note 73 above p. 141.
141 As note 28 above.
142 TRUST RG to Betty Sicré 11 Jan. 1955. RG attributed this to an infected tooth, which had to be extracted.
143 LETTERS n.d.
144 Ibid. 29 March 1955.
145 MAJORCA Selwyn Jepson to RG 28 Feb. 1955 and Ibid. J. Williams of Connecticut to RG 10 March 1955.
146 MAJORCA Ingrid Bergman to RG 9 April 1955. MS-S p. 472 followed by O'PREY (2) p. 307 n. 61 falsely claim that RG met Roberto Rossellini and Ingrid Bergman when visiting Jenny in Rome in 1954. All the evidence points a) to RG not having visited Rome in 1954 (thus MAJORCA Jenny Nicholson writing from Rome to RG June 1955 has 'perhaps at last we will see you here.') And b) to RG not having met RR and IB in 1954 (thus MAJORCA Ingrid Bergman to RG 19 July 1955 has: 'I am sure it will be a happy day when you and Roberto meet.') There is indeed a letter MAJORCA RG to Bill Watt 8 July 1955 in which RG claims to 'know the Rossellinis personally'. This should be taken as artistic licence: his daughter Jenny *did* know them personally; he did not; but to have brought in Jenny

would have unnecessarily complicated his letter.

147 MAJORCA Jenny Nicholson to RG June 1955.

148 MAJORCA Ingrid Bergman to RG 24 June 1955.

149 MS-S p. 472 has much of this letter. For the hitherto unpublished extracts, see MAJORCA Jenny Nicholson to RG 3 July 1955.

150 MAJORCA Ingrid Bergman to RG 19 July 1955.

151 O'PREY (2) p. 144 RG to James Reeves 27 July 1955. Among the guests were his daughter Catherine (whom he had not seen for eight years), her husband Cliff Dalton (now Chief Engineer in the Australian Atomic Commission) and their five children: twelve-year-old James, ten-year-old Antonia, eight-year-old Caroline, seven-year-old Robert and two-year-old Cordelia.

152 As note 96 above.

153 TRUST RG to Cecily Gittes 31 May 1955.

154 As note 96 above and personal knowledge, as this custom continued through the sixties when RPG was a visitor.

155 MS-S p. 476. AUTHOR RG to Sally Chilver 3 Dec. 1955 has RG having just 'cleared off . . . the final versions of Will Sargant's book'.

156 TRUST RG to Ricardo Sicré 30 July 1955.

157 MAJORCA *draft* RG to Alex

Korda (summer 1955 after RG's 60th birthday). RG reminded Korda that he had talked of selling 'the *Claudius* rights to anyone who offered' (while promising to pay Graves himself 'one third of the resale price'); and now he suggested that Korda should give him 'an option at a fixed price for the rights' which would leave him free to 'revive interest in the story through friends of mine', and might lead to the recovery 'of some of *your* investment losses and I get needed cash . . .' He added that if this arrangement did not appeal, 'no matter. You have always treated me so generously that I could have no reason to complain.'

158 They travelled separately: On 14 Sept. Beryl set out with William and Juan, by Land Rover and ferry; on 17 Sept. Robert, Lucia and Tomas followed them by air.

159 MAJORCA Roberto Rossellini to RG 5 Sept. 1955.

160 O'PREY (2) p. 150 RG to James Reeves 8 Nov. 1955.

161 O'PREY (2) p. 144.

162 As note 160 above.

163 QUOZ RG to Alastair Reid 3 Oct. 1955.

164 Robert Harling, 'Robert Graves in Majorca' in the *Sunday Times* 30 Oct. 1955 p. 8.

165 RG in *Steps* p. 239.

166 As note 160 above.

167 AUTHOR RG to Sally Chilver 3 Dec. 1955.

168 O'PREY (2) p. 151.

169 AUTHOR RG to Sally & Richard Chilver 25 Nov. 1955.

170 QUOZ.

171 *The Transposed Heads.*

172 MAJORCA Peggy Glanville-Hicks to RG 9 Dec. 1955.

173 MAJORCA Ingrid Bergman to RG 15 Feb. 1956.

174 O'PREY (2) p. 151.

175 O'PREY (2) p. 153 RG to Gordon Wasson 24 Feb. 1956.

176 TRUST RG to Ricardo Sicré 5 Feb. 1956.

177 Information deduced from MAJORCA *unposted* or *draft* RG to Ricardo Sicré 11 Feb. 1956.

178 Ibid.

179 Ibid.

180 TRUST RG to Ricardo Sicré 13 Feb. 1956.

181 IRWIN RG to James Reeves 6 Jan. 1956.

182 LETTERS 12 Feb. 1956.

183 Ibid. n.d.

184 MAJORCA Dick Graves to RG 26 Feb. 1956.

185 QUOZ RG to Alastair Reid 24 Feb. 1956.

186 IRWIN RG to James Reeves 16 Feb. 1956.

187 MAJORCA Ingrid Bergman to RG 15 Feb. 1956.

188 MAJORCA JTRG to RG 22 Jan. 1956.

CHAPTER 6
THEY HANGED MY SAINTLY BILLY

189 As note 182 above.

190 DIARIES 23 Feb. 1956.

191 Ibid. 1 March 1956.

192 Ibid. 25 Feb.–13 March 1956 passim.

193 MS-S p. 466.

194 RG 'A Toast to Ava Gardner' in *Steps* p. 52.

195 QUOZ RG to Alastair Reid 21 March 1956.

196 Ibid.

197 DIARIES 9 and 10 March 1956.

198 As note 195 above.

199 *Steps* p. 54.

200 DIARIES 12 March 1956.

201 As note 195 above.

202 DIARIES 13 March 1956.

203 IRWIN RG to James Reeves 19 April 1956.

204 VICTORIA RG to Selwyn Jepson 14 Aug. 1956.

205 DIARIES 15–20 March 1956.

206 Vincent's brother Alex, to whom Robert Graves had written on that subject the previous summer, had died in January 1956 without answering Robert's letter.

207 MAJORCA Vincent Korda to RG 26 March 1956.

208 IRWIN 19 April 1956.

209 DIARIES 25 April 1956.

210 MAJORCA RG to Juan Graves 27 April (1956).

211 DIARIES 30 April 1956.

212 QUOZ 6 May 1956.

213 MS-S p. 473.

214 DIARIES 16 May 1956 has the Graveses returning to Palma.

215 MS-S p. 473 Graves had recently heard from Will Price that he had recovered the rights to their *World's Delight* script

following the bankruptcy of the group who had originally commissioned it.

216 Ibid.

217 Ibid. (QUOZ 6 May 1956).

218 TRUST RG to Cecily Gittes 19 Feb. 1957.

219 DIARIES 26 May 1956.

220 MS-S p. 475.

221 IRWIN RG to James Reeves 29 May 1956.

222 O'PREY (2) p. 156 has all but a few words from IRWIN RG to James Reeves 14 Aug. 1956.

223 RG, *They Hanged My Saintly Billy* (Xanadu 1900) p. 7.

224 Ibid. p. 11.

225 MAJORCA Watt to RG 16 July 1956.

226 MS-S p. 475 (from QUOZ).

227 MAJORCA Alec Guinness to RG 27 June 1956.

228 Ibid. 5 Oct. 1956.

229 As note 226 above.

230 MAJORCA Marnie Pomeroy to RG and BG n.d.

231 DIARIES 1 and 15 July 1956.

232 As note 4 above.

233 TRUST RG to Betty Sicré 8 Sept. 1955. 'Robin is bull fighting tomorrow in the annual bull-fighter's beano in the Plaza at Palma.'

234 AUTHOR RG to Sally and Richard Chilver 25 Nov. 1955.

235 DIARIES 4 June 1956.

236 As note 96 above.

237 DIARIES 22 June 1956.

238 Ibid. 29 Aug. 1956.

239 Ibid. 5 Oct. 1956.

240 Ibid. 9 Oct. 1956.

241 Ibid. 20 Oct. 1956.

242 Ibid. See e.g. 30 Aug.; 6 and 13 Sept.; 2 Oct. 1956.

243 Ibid. 3 July 1956 show Reid arriving back on the island.

244 Ibid. 3 Aug. 1956.

245 Ibid. 10 Aug. 1956.

246 Ibid. 12 Aug. 1956. They had also visited the previous summer.

247 Ibid. passim Aug., Sept. 1956.

248 Ibid. 20–21 Sept. 1956.

249 The typescript of *They Hanged My Saintly Billy* was sent to England in the care of William, about to start his third year at Oundle.

250 *Good-bye to All That* (1957) p. 281.

251 MAJORCA Ursula Vaughan-Williams to RG 7 Oct. (1956).

252 As note 250 above.

253 MS-S p. 477 (extract from QUOZ).

254 O'PREY (2) p. 156 RG to James Reeves 5 Nov. 1956.

255 *Good-bye to All That* Prologue.

256 However, the original edition of *Good-bye to All That*, with annotations by RPG detailing Robert's later alterations, becomes available from Berghahn Books in 1995; and it is to be hoped that this edition will in time replace the 1957 version.

257 TRUST RG to Ricardo Sicré 22 Oct. 1956.

258 DIARIES 5 Nov. 1956; and as note 254 above.

259 As note 28 above.

260 As note 254 above.

261 DIARIES 9 Nov. 1956.

262 Ibid. 9–22 Nov. 1956. The Monte Carlo visit was on 12 Nov.

CHAPTER 7
DREAMS AND LECTURES

263 MAJORCA Jenny Nicholson to RG 25 Nov. 1956.

264 MAJORCA RG to Vincent Korda 10 Dec. 1956.

265 DIARIES 28 Nov. 1956.

266 MAJORCA Anna Magnani to RG 7 Dec. 1956.

267 As note 264 above.

268 DIARIES 25 Dec. 1956.

269 MAJORCA Alec Guinness to RG 15 Dec. 1956.

270 MAJORCA Vincent Korda to RG 24 Jan. 1957.

271 MAJORCA *copy* RG to Vincent Korda 25 Jan. 1957.

272 MAJORCA Vincent Korda to RG 28 Jan. 1957.

273 O'PREY (2) p. 159 RG to MS-S 2 Feb. 1957 and MS-S p. 478.

274 DIARIES 3–4 Feb. 1957.

275 MAJORCA RG to BG 5 Feb. (1957).

276 Ibid.

277 As note 28 above.

278 As note 275 above.

279 As note 28 above.

280 As note 275 above.

281 DIARIES 6 Feb. 1957.

282 RG, 'Legitimate Criticism of Poetry' in *Steps* p. 85.

283 Ibid.

284 MAJORCA RG to BG n.d. (7 Feb. 1957).

285 Ibid. shows that in the morning, Graves had given a free poetry reading to the girls of Mount Holyoke.

286 DIARIES 7–8 Feb. 1957. The reading was in the Kresge Auditorium.

287 TRUST Cecily Gittes to BG 10 Feb. 1957.

288 As note 28 above.

289 RG, 'The White Goddess' in *Steps* p. 94.

290 Ibid. p. 91.

291 Ibid. p. 93.

292 Ibid. p. 94.

293 Ibid. p. 101.

294 Ibid. p. 105.

295 MAJORCA RG to BG 12 Feb. 1957.

296 Ibid. 5 Feb (1957).

297 As note 295 above.

298 MS-S p. 480.

299 As note 295 above.

300 TRUST Vera Fleming Lussier to Betty Sicré 11 Feb. 1957.

301 DIARIES 11 Feb. 1957.

302 Ibid. 12 Feb. 1957 and MAJORCA Alastair Reid to BG (12 Feb. 1957).

303 O'PREY (2) p. 162 RG to Selwyn Jepson 22 Feb. 1957.

304 As note 295 above.

305 As note 28 above.

306 MAJORCA Alastair Reid to BG n.d. (12 Feb. 1957).

307 MAJORCA R. Gordon Wasson to RG 8 Aug. 1955.

308 DIARIES 30 March 1956.

309 QUOZ RG to Alastair Reid 20 April 1956.

310 O'PREY (2) p. 158 RG to Gordon Wasson 22 Dec. 1956.

311 MS-S p. 479.

312 Ibid.

313 DIARIES 12 Feb. 1957. In Alastair Reid's handwriting; 'Gordon's book' is mentioned, but whether RG saw an advance copy or whether they simply talked about it, is unclear.

314 O'PREY (2) p. 164 RG to Tina and Gordon Wasson n.d. (April 1957).

315 O'PREY (2) p. 163.

316 RG, 'Diseases of Scholarship clinically considered' in *Five Pens in Hand*.

317 DIARIES 13 Feb. 1957.

318 MS-S pp. 479–80.

319 DIARIES 15 Feb. 1957.

320 Ibid. 17 Feb. 1957.

321 TRUST RG to Cecily Gittes 19 Feb. 1957.

322 O'PREY (2) p. 162 RG to Selwyn Jepson 22 Feb. 1957.

323 MAJORCA *copy* of RG to Alec Guinness 4 March (1957).

324 DIARIES 15 Feb. 1957.

325 As note 322 above.

326 MAJORCA Max Youngsteen of United Artists to RG 4 April 1957.

327 VICTORIA RG to Selwyn Jepson 7 March 1957.

328 MAJORCA Elizabeth (Betty) Kray to RG 2 April 1957.

329 As note 323 above.

330 As note 28 above.

331 IRWIN RG to James Reeves 27 Feb. 1957.

332 DIARIES e.g. 23 Feb and 9 March 1957.

333 Ibid. e.g. 9, 26, 31 March and 4 April 1957.

334 *Thirty Years: Lincoln Kirstein's The New York City Ballet* (A. & C. Black 1979) p. 94.

335 DIARIES 20 March 1957.

336 This description is taken from RPG's memories.

337 AUTHOR RG to Clarissa Graves 3 June 1957 quoted in AUTHOR Clarissa Graves to JTRG 15 June 1957.

338 As note 336 above.

339 DIARIES 7 April 1957.

340 Ibid.: 26 April set out; 28 April Perpignan, Toulouse, Limoges; 9 April reach Paris; 1 May cross Channel from Dieppe.

341 MAJORCA Agent to RG 30 April 1957 saying that 'Bryan Gentry writes to me as follows'.

342 DIARIES 9 May 1957 and MS-S p. 482.

343 MS-S p. 482.

344 Ibid. p. 483.

345 O'PREY (2) p. 166 RG to James Reeves 21 May 1957; and IRWIN RG to James Reeves 13 July 1957.

346 DIARIES 20 May 1957.

347 As note 345 above.

348 As note 337 above.

349 Ibid.

350 As note 96 above.

351 DIARIES e.g. 31 May 1957.

352 Ibid. 16 June 1957.

353 Ibid. on relevant dates.

354 MAJORCA Alec Guinness to RG 20 June 1957.

355 MAJORCA Bridget Boland to RG 28 May 1957.

CHAPTER 8

MORE DREAMS AND LECTURES
AND CINDY LEE

356 AUTHOR Peggy to JTRG 21 Sept. 1957.

357 O'PREY (2) p. 172 RG to James Reeves 4 Dec. 1957.

358 Quoted in an article by Roger Berthoud for *The Times* n.d.

359 MAJORCA Jenny Nicholson to RG 9 June (1957).

360 DIARIES 31 July 1957.

361 Ibid. 2 Aug. 1957.

362 MAJORCA Bridget Boland to RG 24 July 1957 and n.d.

363 MAJORCA Alec Guinness to RG and BG 21 Aug. 1957.

364 DIARIES 20–21 Aug. 1957. They arrived on 20 Aug.

365 Ibid. passim 21 Aug.–11 Sept. 1957.

366 Ibid. 12–13 Sept. 1957.

367 Ibid. 17–20 Sept. 1957.

368 MAJORCA Bridget Boland to RG 30 Sept. 1957.

369 DIARIES 7 Oct.–7 Nov. 1957.

370 MAJORCA Bridget Boland to RG 13 and 19 Nov. 1957.

371 MAJORCA Alec Guinness to RG 27 Nov. 1957.

372 MAJORCA Bridget Boland to RG 29 Jan. 1958.

373 Alexander Chancellor to the *Spectator* 7 March 1981.

374 As note 357 above.

375 VICTORIA RG to Selwyn Jepson 20 Dec. 1957.

376 O'PREY (2) p. 173 RG to Karl and Rene 23–?26 Dec. 1958.

377 Ibid.

378 DIARIES 31 Dec. 1957.

379 TRUST RG to Betty and Ricardo Sicré 20 Jan. 1958.

380 VICTORIA RG to Selwyn Jepson 16 Jan. 1958.

381 TAH p. 98.

382 DIARIES 7–10 Jan. 1958.

383 LETTERS 25 Jan. 1958 Lucia and Juan were back in Switzerland; Beryl and Tomas went to London where Beryl was to stay for three weeks with her 'nonagenarian (but not yet retired) father, a treasury solicitor'. RG added: 'I should like to see your Richard again; felt a sympathy with him when he was very small.'

384 DIARIES 1 Feb. 1958.

385 O'PREY (2) p. 188 RG to Karl and Rene Gay 22 Jan. 1960.

386 RG, 'Sweeney Among the Blackbirds' in *Steps* pp. 109, 116.

387 MAJORCA RG to BG 5 Feb. 1958.

388 DIARIES 4–22 Feb. 1958.

389 MAJORCA Tom Matthews to RG 16 March 1958.

390 MAJORCA Alastair Reid to RG 31 Jan. 1958 'Itinerary for Robert Graves accompanied by Alastair Reid'; and DIARIES Feb. 1958.

391 DIARIES Feb. 1958.

392 MAJORCA Bridget Boland to RG 29 Jan. 1958.

393 MAJORCA Jenny Nicholson to RG 17 Dec. 1958.

394 MAJORCA Dick Graves to BG 19 Feb., and to RG 30 Jan. and 26 Feb. 1958.

395 MAJORCA Dick Graves to RG 5 March 1958; and DIARIES 8 March 1958.

396 MAJORCA Alec Guinness to RG 25 April 1958.

397 MAJORCA RG to Jenny Nicholson 28 April 1958.

398 DIARIES 17 March–8 May 1958 passim.

399 As note 397 above.

400 DIARIES 9 May 1958.

401 Ibid. 15 May 1958.

402 MAJORCA Alec Guinness to RG 9 May 1958.

403 TRUST RG to Ricardo Sicré 19 May 1958.

404 MAJORCA Ricardo Sicré to RG 21 May 1958.

405 MAJORCA Bridget Boland to RG 26 May 1958; DIARIES show that her letter arrived on 31 May 1958.

406 DIARIES 22–4 May 1958; see also MAJORCA Tom Matthews to RG 31 May 1958.

407 DIARIES e.g. 9, 19 June, 2, 4 July 1958.

408 Ibid. 19 May, 3 July, 29 Sept. 1958.

409 MAJORCA James Reeves to RG 7 July 1958; Ibid. Edward Ardizzone to RG 2 Aug. 1958; and DIARIES 18 Aug. 1958.

410 TRUST RG to Betty Sicré 12 Aug. (1958) and DIARIES 28 July 1958.

411 DIARIES 15 Aug. 1958.

412 Ibid. 29 Aug. 1958.

413 AUTHOR Tape of Charles Corbett Aug. 1993.

414 DIARIES 2 Sept. 1958.

415 O'PREY (2) p. 175 RG to Alan Sillitoe 17 Oct. 1958.

416 MAJORCA Alec Guinness to RG n.d. legible.

417 IRWIN RG to James Reeves 22 Oct. 1958.

418 MS-S p. 485.

419 DIARIES 11 Sept. 1958.

420 Ibid. 25 Oct. 1958.

421 MAJORCA Watt to RG 23 Oct. 1958.

422 MAJORCA Alexander Cohen to RG 27 Oct. 1958.

423 Tyrone Guthrie, b. 1900, had made his reputation as a producer at the Westminster Theatre (1930–31) and had been director of the Old Vic (1950–51).

424 MAJORCA Alexander Cohen to RG 24 Nov. 1958.

425 IRWIN RG to James Reeves 13 Dec. 1958.

426 MAJORCA RG to Bill Watt 25 Oct. 1958.

427 O'PREY (2) p. 178 RG to James Reeves 10 March 1959.

428 This was *But It Still Goes On*, written in 1930, with its candid treatment of homosexuality and lesbianism. See TYWL pp. 142–3.

429 As note 426 above.

CHAPTER 9
SHEBA, LAWRENCE, AND MAGIC
MUSHROOMS

430 DIARIES 14 Dec. 1958.
431 MAJORCA Alexander Cohen to RG 8 Dec. 1958.
432 MAJORCA *copy* RG to Alexander Cohen 11 Dec. 1958.
433 Ibid. n.d.
434 DIARIES 9–15 Jan. 1959.
435 RG, 'A Goy in Israel' in *The Crane-bag and Other Disputed Subjects* p. 104.
436 Ibid. p. 110.
437 Ibid pp. 113–14.
438 MAJORCA Alex Epstein of the Israel and British Commonwealth Association in Tel Aviv to RG n.d.
439 DIARIES Jan. 1959.
440 MS-S p. 486.
441 LETTERS 6 Feb. 1959.
442 TRUST RG to Betty Sicré n.d. BG in conv. with RPG Sept. 1994 adds that she and RG had once met Rex Harrison in Jenny's apartment, trying out songs for *My Fair Lady*.
443 MS-S p. 486 wrongly says that she arrived on 18 Feb.: that was when she was meant to arrive, but she forgot her visa and was stranded in Barcelona until the following day.
444 DIARIES Feb. 1959.
445 MAJORCA RG to Alexander Cohen 26 Feb. 1959.
446 MAJORCA Alexander Cohen to RG 20 Feb. 1959.
447 DIARIES 3 March 1959.

Jenny had been due to leave on Monday 2 March, but had changed her mind.
448 Ibid. 4–9 March 1959.
449 MAJORCA Jenny Nicholson to RG March 1959.
450 MS-S p. 487.
451 MAJORCA Alexander Cohen to RG 19 March 1959.
452 DIARIES 17–19 March 1959.
453 Ibid. March/April 1959.
454 Ibid. April 1959.
455 Ibid. 21–2 April 1959.
456 Ibid. 22 April 1959.
457 MAJORCA RG to George and Joanna Simon n.d.
458 MAJORCA George and Joanna Simon to RG 19 Dec. 1958.
459 DIARIES 23 April–10 May 1959.
460 MAJORCA Alexander Cohen to RG 18 May 1959.
461 MAJORCA has the script of *A Song for Sheba* from which this is taken.
462 As note 460 above.
463 DIARIES 23 May 1959.
464 O'PREY (2) p. 181 RG to Selwyn Jepson 28 May 1959.
465 MAJORCA Selwyn Jepson to RG 2 June 1959.
466 MAJORCA Tony Guthrie to RG 2 June 1959.
467 MAJORCA *copy* Tony Guthire to Alexander Cohen enc. in Tony Guthrie to RG 22 June 1959.
468 MS-S p. 488.
469 DIARIES 19 July 1959.
470 O'PREY (2) p. 182 RG to Selwyn Jepson 21 June 1959.
471 DIARIES 24 July 1959.

472 Ibid. 24–5 July 1959.
473 Ibid. 29 July, 3 Sept. 1959.
An enlarged prostate presses on the urethra, 'with progressive obstruction of the flow of urine, incomplete emptying, or ... dribbling of urine. The bladder is never totally emptied, however, and the remaining urine becomes stagnant and infection sets in. The stagnant urine may cause the precipitation of stones in the bladder; the bladder muscle thickens to overcome this obsctruction. If urine begins to back up in the kidney, progressive damage may ensue, which can lead to kidney failure and subsequent uraemia (the toxic effects of kidney failure).' *Encyclopaedia Britannica* 15th edn.
474 DIARIES Sept. 1959.
475 AUTHOR Rosaleen Cooper to JTRG 16 Sept. (1959).
476 O'PREY (2) p. 183 RG to Alan and Ruth Sillitoe pmk 21 Sept. 1959. So numerous were the visitors that RG begged Rosaleen not to visit, telling her: 'Don't come up. There are too many people eating my grapes already; and she then discouraged Clarissa also. (AUTHOR Rosaleen Cooper to JTRG 16 Sept. 1959).
477 DIARIES Sept. 1959.
478 Ibid. 22 Sept. 1959.
479 RG, 'Surgical Ward: Men' in *More Poems 1961* (Cassell 1961) p. 33.
480 DIARIES Sept./Oct. 1959.

481 See especially MAJORCA Ricardo Sicré to RG 19 Oct. 1959.
482 DIARIES 23, 28 Oct. 1959 shows that a preliminary *Lawrence* contract was signed on that day with Norman Spencer.
483 O'PREY (2) p. 184.
484 DIARIES 6 Oct. 1959.
485 MAJORCA Alec Guinness to RG 26 Oct. 1959.
486 O'PREY (2) RG to Karl Gay 13 Oct. 1959 pp. 184–5.
487 DIARIES 11 Oct. 1959.
488 As note 486 above.
489 Ibid.
490 MAJORCA RG to BG 22 Jan. (1960) and DIARIES Jan. 1960.
491 MAJORCA Merula Guinness to RG n.d. (Oct. 1959).
492 MS-S p. 497.
493 MAJORCA Alec Guinness to RG 21 Oct. 1959.
494 As note 492 above.
495 DIARIES 6 Oct. 1959.
496 MAJORCA Peggy Glanville-Hicks to RG 15 Sept. (1959).
497 MAJORCA Alastair Reid to RG Thursday n.d.
498 MS-S pp. 499–500.
499 As note 497 above.
500 MS-S p. 500.
501 DIARIES Jan. 1960.
502 MAJORCA RG to BG 16 Jan. (1960).
503 Ibid. 22 Jan. (1960) and DIARIES Jan. 1960.
504 RG lectures on 'Poetic Intuition' to the students of John Hopkins on 22 January; had two days' rest at the Lussiers' farm

(where he was joined by Ricardo Sicré; and moved to Washington where on consecutive evenings (as arranged by Robert Richman) he gave a poetry reading and a lecture on 'The Virgil Cult' at the Institute of Contemporary Arts. Returning to New York, there was another poetry reading and a further meeting with W.H. Auden at a party given by Jerry Robbins.

505 DIARIES 30 Jan. 1960.

506 O'PREY (2) p. 187 RG to Karl and Rene Gay 22 Jan. 1960.

507 DIARIES 31 Jan. 1960.

508 RG, 'The Poet's Paradise' in *Oxford Addresses on Poetry* (Cassell 1962) p. 122.

509 LETTERS n.d. (Feb. 1960).

510 DIARIES 1 February 1960.

511 O'PREY (2) p. 190 RG to Gordon Wasson 7 Feb. 1960.

512 As note 507 above. (RG's £18,000 represents well over £200,000 in 1995 terms.)

513 MS-S pp. 500–501 and RG, 'Poetic Gold' in *Oxford Addresses on Poetry* pp. 83–96.

514 MAJORCA Jess McNab to RG Wed. 6 April 1960 reports: 'I saw you in *Small World* on Sunday. You were jolly good, though I do hope you are wrong about things getting a lot worse before any better . . .'

515 MAJORCA Tom Matthews to RG 30 Jan. 1960.

516 MAJORCA Alec Guinness to RG 18 Feb. 1960 congratulates RG on his prize, regrets that he will be unable to be present on 3 March and adds: 'Christina Foyle's telegrams are so lengthy it's sad I have to reply to a two-pager with REGRET NO.'

517 MAJORCA Charles Graves to RG 11 Feb. 1960.

518 MS-S p. 503 quotes much of this; the rest is MAJORCA Charles Graves to RG 17 Feb. (1960).

519 MS-S pp. 503–4 and DIARIES 3 March 1960.

520 DIARIES 3 March 1960.

521 O'PREY (2) p. 193.

522 Ibid. pp. 193–4.

523 Ibid. pp. 194–5 RG to the editor of the *Observer* 5 March 1960.

524 MAJORCA Alastair Reid to RG 29 Feb. 1960.

525 DIARIES 6 April 1960.

526 MAJORCA Ricardo Sicré to RG 19 Oct. 1959.

527 MAJORCA Jerome Robbins to RG various n.d.

528 MAJORCA Benjamin Britten to RG 11 April 1960. (MS-S p. 489 has this letter, but with several misquotations, and without the reference to Jenny.)

529 O'PREY (2) p. 197 RG to Karl Gay 8 May 1960.

530 MAJORCA MSS by Gordon Wasson headed: '8 May 1960 Experiment with synthetic psilocybin'.

531 As note 529 above.

532 DIARIES 7 May 1960; though see Ibid. where RG to

Karl Gay declares 'Seeing Wm. Morris and J. Robbins today about the *White Goddess* film'.

533 MAJORCA Jerome Robbins to RG n.d.

534 MAJORCA pc Jenny Nicholson to RG 18 April 196?o.

535 As note 524 above.

536 DIARIES 9 May 1960.

537 As note 4 above. RG, having come to the USA without the necessary vaccination, had an extra jab, and suffered a bad reaction. After three days he had a high temperature, and so missed the excitement of visiting the Niagara Falls.

538 INDIANA (iii) RG to Richard Hughes 24 May 1960.

539 DIARIES 13–16 May 1960.

540 MAJORCA John Benson Brooks to RG 23 May 1960.

541 MAJORCA *copy* Mr and Mrs John Benson Brooks to MS-S 18 Aug. 1982 contains this extract from RG to John Benson Brooks 28 May 1960.

542 As note 524 above, 29 May 1960.

543 DIARIES 8 June 1960; and see RG, *More Poems 1961* pp. 34–5.

544 It must be said that no evidence whatever can be found for the belief both of MS-S and O'PREY (2) that Margot Callas first met RG in the summer of 1959. All the available evidence (including both eye-witness accounts and DIARIES 1960) points to a meeting on 10 June 1960.

Book Six Margot and 'Inexorable Need' 1960–63

CHAPTER 1
'LYCEIA'

1 Chiefly from RPG's observations based upon Margot's starring role in Mati Klarwein's film (seen Sept. 1994).

2 Karl Gay in conv. with RPG 8 Feb. 1993.

3 DIARIES 10 June 1960.

4 Ibid. 12 June 1960.

5 As note 1 above.

6 DIARIES 20 June 1960.

7 LETTERS 12 June 1960.

8 DIARIES show that RG began 'Lyceia' on 24 June, and completed it 'in about six drafts' on 25 June 1960.

9 Ibid. 9 July 1960 shows that RG was not absolutely certain that this was the day of her return.

10 'In Single Syllables', in *More Poems 1961* p. 15.

11 MAJORCA *unposted* RG to Margot Callas 30 July (1962); partly printed in MS-S p. 523.

12 Mati Klarwein in conv. with RPG Sept. 1994.

13 MAJORCA A copy of *Lawrence and the Wetbacks* marked 'MARGOT'.

14 'Symptoms of Love', in *More Poems 1961* p. 5. It was first drafted on 21 July as 'An Aching Head' (DIARIES of that date).

15 TRUST RG to Betty Sicré 3 Aug. 1960.

16 As note 13 above.

17 DIARIES 23 July 1960.

18 Ibid. 9 July 1960.

19 Ibid. 26–8 July 1960.

20 Ibid. 29 July 1960.

21 Ibid. 30 July 1960.

22 Ibid. The poem was 'To Myrto of Myrtles', a slight piece, which appears in *More Poems 1961* p. 25, but was later culled from his work: Goddess of Midsummer, how late / You let me understand / My lines of head, life, fate / And heart: a broad M brand / Inerasable from either hand.

23 As note 15 above.

24 DIARIES 31 July 1960.

CHAPTER 2
'THE STARRED COVERLET'

25 'Apple Island', in *More Poems 1961* p. 10.

26 DIARIES 5, 7 August 1960.

27 'The Visitation', in *More Poems 1961* p. 8.

28 MAJORCA Sam Spiegel of Horizon Pictures GB Ltd to RG 7 Aug. 1960 (telegram).

29 MAJORCA Miss Jean Menz secretary to Sam Spiegel to RG 11 Aug. 1960.

30 MS-S p. 498.

31 MAJORCA various e.g. James Reeves to RG 17 March 1960.

32 Stella Irwin, *née* Reeves, in conv. with RPG 29 April 1993.

33 DIARIES 14 Aug. 1960.

34 As note 32 above.

35 Ibid.

36 DIARIES 13, 14 Aug. 1960. The poem was at first called 'Coverlet of Snow'.

37 'The Starred Coverlet', in *More Poems 1961* p. 16.

38 DIARIES 16, 23, 18, 21, 25 Aug. 1960.

39 MS-S p. 492.

40 TRUST RG to William Graves n.d.

41 As note 32 above.

42 DIARIES 23 Aug. 1960; 'Patience', in *More Poems 1961* p. 16. The DIARIES entry shows that it was at first called 'Impatience'.

43 'The Falcon Woman', in *More Poems 1961* p. 11; and DIARIES 27 Aug. 1960.

44 DIARIES 25 Aug. 1960.

45 'Turn of the Moon', in *More Poems 1961* p. 21; and DIARIES 30 Aug. 1960.

46 DIARIES 2–3 Sept. 1960.

47 Ibid. 26 Aug. 1960 show that RG had certainly arranged everything as far as Paris.

48 MAJORCA Alastair Reid to RG n.d. (pre-12 Jan. 1961).

49 DIARIES 4 Sept. 1960.

CHAPTER 3
THE WHITE CALLAS

50 MAJORCA Jenny Nicholson to RG n.d.

51 RG had also written to William Graves, telling him that he and Beryl had seen Mati's film, and that (TRUST RG to William Graves 11 Aug. 1960) Margot

was 'even better when photographed than in three dimensions. Beryl says she ought to star as the White Goddess.

52 MAJORCA Jenny Nicholson to RG 15 Sept. 1960.

53 DIARIES 16–26 Sept. 1960. RG and BG had seen William, Juan, Sally and Richard Chilver in Geneva; visited battlefields at Bouchain and Perenne; and met Charles Graves at the casino in Le Touquet.

54 Ibid. 27 Sept.–1 Oct. 1960.

55 Ibid. 7 Oct. 1960.

56 MAJORCA Alec Guinness to RG 23 Oct. 1960.

57 DIARIES 26 Oct. 1960.

58 Ibid. 9 Oct. 1960.

59 Ibid. 8 Nov. 1960. See also MAJORCA 'Obituary Isla Cameron' by Shirley Abercair, who writes: 'She strayed into the Theatre Workshop when Joan Littlewood and her company were in Newcastle. She was helping out in the kitchen when our singer decided to leave the company to get married. We had no singer. One of the girls in the company said: "Just listen to that!" It was the purest voice we had ever heard. It was Isla singing in the kitchen. She stayed with the company doing parts and singing until the America folk-song collector Alan Lomax wooed her away to record some of those wonderful songs for the United States Library of Congress.'

60 DIARIES 15 Oct. 1960.

61 Ibid. 20 Oct. 1960.

62 Ibid. 1 Nov. 1960.

63 VICTORIA RG to Selwyn Jepson n.d. (post-1 Nov., pre-15 Nov., prob. 10 Nov. 1960).

64 DIARIES 17 Oct. 1960.

65 MAJORCA Gordon Wasson to RG 25 Oct. 1960.

66 DIARIES 20–21, 26–7 Oct., show RG writing two more poems for Margot: 'The Secret Land', and 'Seldom Yet Now'; and Ibid. 6 Nov. 1960 for when RG saw Reeves.

67 'Troughs of Sea', in *More Poems 1961* p. 12; and DIARIES 7–9 Nov. 1960, from which we see that the poem was first called simply 'The Trough'.

68 I deduce this, perhaps wrongly, from Margot's 'cable of reassurance' (DIARIES 17 Nov. 1960).

69 This was 'Two Women' (DIARIES 17 Nov. 1960); and it later became 'Ruby and Amethyst', *Collected Poems 1975* (Cassell 1975) p. 225.

70 DIARIES 29 Nov. 1960.

71 Ibid. 2–13 Dec. 1960.

72 Ibid. 4–5 Dec. 1960.

73 MAJORCA Ralph Jacobs and Margery Terrassa to RG air-letter pmk 2 Dec. 1960.

74 His business was principally negotiating a new contract with the *New Yorker* magazine.

75 DIARIES 12–13 Dec. 1960.

76 As note 32 above.

77 As note 48 above.

78 The friendship between Reid and RG was certainly intense; but no one who knows anything of RG's revulsion from what he called the 'pseudo-homosexuality' of his attachment to Peter Johnstone could possibly believe that RG had even a suspicion that it contained any homosexual element, until Ricardo Sicré put such a false suspicion into his mind at a later stage than this; and as for the 'full homosexual relationship' between RG and Reid which I have heard postulated in some quarters: it is quite simply absurd.

79 MAJORCA Alastair Reid to RG 16 Dec. 1960.

80 Ibid. n.d. (prob. about 4 Jan. 1961).

81 Ibid.

82 Ibid.

83 DIARIES 12 Jan. 1961.

84 MAJORCA Alastair Reid to RG 12 Jan. 1961.

85 MAJORCA Jerome Robbins 154 East 74th Street to RG 16 Jan. 1961.

86 MAJORCA Alastair Reid to RG n.d.

CHAPTER 4

BARAKA

87 DIARIES 17 Jan. 1961.

88 MAJORCA Idries Shah c/o wagon-lits Palma Mallorca to RG 3 Jan. 1961.

89 BG in conv. with RPG Feb. 1993.

90 MAJORCA Idries Shah to RG Monday (Jan. 1961).

91 DIARIES 22, 23 Jan. 1961.

92 'The Word Baraka', in *Oxford Addresses on Poetry* p. 99.

93 MAJORCA Jess McNab to RG 31 Jan. 1961.

94 As note 92 above p. 101.

95 Ibid. p. 102.

96 Ibid. p. 99.

97 DIARIES 25 Jan. 1961.

98 This may be deduced from the DIARY entries 1–6 Feb. 1961, which contain nothing more than Margot's name, followed by 'Etc.'

99 TRUST RG to Ava Gardner 22 Feb 1961. It is possible that Margot gave RG the hat when they were in Madrid immediately after this visit.

100 *Observer* 22 Jan. 1961.

101 Oxford University *Gazette Supplement* (1) to No 3071 Thursday 9 Feb. 1961.

102 MAJORCA James Reeves to RG 15 Dec. 1960 apologizes for having upset RG by mentioning the matter to his wife Mary.

103 Comment from *The Times* review of RG's *Collected Poems 1959*.

104 K. C. Wheare of Exeter, W. F. Oakeshott, of Lincoln, Sir Noel Hall of Brasenose, the Very Revd C. A. Simpson of Christchurch, and Lucy S. Sutherland of Lady Margaret Hall.

105 As note 101 above.

106 Ibid.

107 DIARIES 16 Feb. 1960; and MS-S p. 508.

108 MAJORCA Alastair Reid to RG 5 Feb. (1961).

109 Ibid.

110 DIARIES 17 Feb. 1960.

111 Ibid.

112 Ibid. 21 Feb. 1961: poem first called simply 'Trance'.

113 LETTERS 23 Feb. 1961 (more than 100 letters, and 40 telegrams).

114 This was an address on the Evangeline Wilbur Blashfield Foundation.

115 As note 113 above.

116 Ibid. 6 April 1961. I have speculatively treated what RG says to JTRG as being representative of what he wrote to Charles Graves.

117 MAJORCA Charles Graves to RG 3 March 1961.

118 LETTERS 6 April 1961.

119 DIARIES 1960 show RG working on this address from 27 Feb.–8 March.

120 Ibid. 8 March 1961.

121 TRUST RG to Ava Gardner 22 Feb. 1961. In this letter RG also gives AG magical advice about how to conceive a son: 'First the man. He must be *the* man, not just *a* man. Then the place: an upper room with swords and cutlasses about since you want a boy. Then the time: Friday night when the moon is approaching the full. The food: red wine and beef.'

122 DIARIES 10 March 1960 shows RG revising this poem.

123 MAJORCA Idries Shah 14 Chalcot Gardens London NW3 to RG 21 March 1961.

124 MAJORCA Peggy Glanville-Hicks to RG 12 March 1961.

125 DIARIES 22–5 March 1961.

126 Ibid. 25 March 1961.

127 Ibid. 9 April 1961.

128 Ibid. 10 April 1961 'POEM about Lion on shoulders'.

129 'The Lion lover', in *Collected Poems 1975* p. 233.

130 MAJORCA Alastair Reid to RG n.d.; and see MS-S pp. 509–10.

131 DIARIES 17 April 1961. It is however speculative that it was this particular letter from AR that was 'Unsatisfactory'.

132 Ibid. 18 April 1961.

CHAPTER 5
'BEWARE, MADAM!'

133 O'PREY (2) p. 202 RG to James Reeves 16 May 1961.

134 MAJORCA Alastair Reid to RG.

135 DIARIES 13 May 1961.

136 As note 133 above.

137 Ibid. p. 203 29 May 1961.

138 As note 133 above.

139 DIARIES 19–20 May 1961.

140 Ibid. 26 May 1961.

141 As note 89 above.

142 As note 137 above.

143 DIARIES 28 May 1961.

144 'Beware, Madam!' in *Collected Poems 1975* p. 243.

145 DIARIES 31 May 1961; and 'Golden Anchor', in *Collected Poems 1975* p. 232.

146 'The Personal Muse', in *Oxford Addresses on Poetry* p. 66.

147 DIARIES 10 June 1961.

148 O'PREY (2) p. 204 RG to MS-S 22 June 1961.

149 'The Anti-Poet', in *Oxford Addresses on Poetry* p. 29.

150 DIARIES 6, 8 July 1961; Margot had cabled on 26 June.

151 Ibid. 21–2 July 1961.

152 MAJORCA *unposted* RG to Margot Callas n.d. but from int. ev. June 1962.

153 DIARIES 23 July 1961.

154 MAJORCA *posted but returned* RG to Eleni 27 Aug. 1961.

155 DIARIES 7 (for 'Jess & Ted'), 10 Aug. 1961.

156 'The Personal Muse', in *Oxford Addresses on Poetry* pp. 50, 62, 68.

157 Ibid. p. 81.

158 MAJORCA Tom Matthews to RG 3 Aug. 1961.

159 O'PREY (2) p. 207 RG to Tom Matthews 5 Aug. 1961.

160 As note 148 above.

161 DIARIES 19 Aug. 1961.

162 As note 154 above.

163 Ibid.

164 MS-S p. 513. 'Ouzo Unclouded' was its later title.

165 As note 154 above.

166 Ibid. Partly reproduced in MS-S p. 513.

167 Ibid.

168 MAJORCA Alastair Reid Le Moulin de [?] near Navarra Basses-Pyrénées to RG 1 Sept. 1961.

169 Both the existence of this note and its probable contents have been deduced (perhaps wrongly) from MAJORCA Idries Shah to RG 6 Sept. 1961.

170 MAJORCA Idries Shah to RG 6 Sept. 1961.

171 Ibid. 12 Sept. 1961.

172 Ibid. 21 Sept. 1961.

173 Ibid. 19, 27 Sept. 1961.

174 Ibid. 2/3 Oct. 1961.

CHAPTER 6
THE PERSONAL MUSE

175 MAJORCA press cutting of an interview with Kenneth Allsop which DIARIES show was given by telephone on 7 Jan. 1962 for the *Daily Mail*.

176 *Brothers: No 5 Robert Graves* by Charles Graves in the *Evening Standard*.

177 'Foreword' to *Oxford Addresses on Poetry*.

178 O'PREY (2) p. 208 RG to James Reeves pmk 23 Oct. 1961.

179 AUTHOR Clarissa Graves to RPG and Simon Graves 29 Sept. 1961.

180 As note 178 above. LETTERS covering note to an n.d. shows that RG's brother John was present.

181 As note 177 above.

182 LETTERS 27 Oct. 1961.

183 MAJORCA Lucy Aldridge to BG 14 Nov. 1961 refers to 'a visit from you and Robert . . . last Saturday'.

184 See DIARIES 1961; they also saw Isla Cameron and the Jepsons.

185 MAJORCA James Reeves to

RG 15 Dec. 1961. JR added as an aside that MS-S seemed 'distressed about some book which is about to appear containing libels on you by Herbert Read and another. I hope you annihilate them.' This was a reference to *Truth Is More Sacred*, a book of correspondence between Herbert Read and Edward Dahlberg which contained 'several antagonistic and libellous remarks about Graves'; (O'PREY (2) p. 209) but Watt's solicitors (whom Graves had asked to read the book for libel) advised him not to draw any attention to the attack; and so (having explained to MS-S that Dahlberg had been in Majorca 'five years ago; behaved disgracefully and was mortified that I did not accept him at his own valuation', Graves let the matter drop (MS-S p. 515).

186 MAJORCA Enid Starkie to RG 1 Dec. 1961.

187 TRUST RG to William Graves 3 Jan. 1962.

188 DIARIES 1 Jan. 1962.

189 'The Wreath', in *Collected Poems 1975* p. 238.

190 MAJORCA Tom Matthews London to RG 12 June 1962.

191 MAJORCA Alston Anderson to RG 25 Jan. 1962.

192 Ibid. 4 Feb. 1962.

193 Ibid. 13 March 1962.

194 Catherine Dalton, *Without Walls* 3rd edn 1980.

195 MAJORCA Jenny Nicholson to RG 28 Jan. 1962.

196 As note 192 above.

197 O'PREY (2) p. 212 RG to James Reeves 25 Feb. 1962.

198 Ibid. p. 219 17 Aug. 1962.

199 DIARIES 17 March 1962.

200 'The Unnamed Spell', in *Collected Poems 1975* p. 251.

201 'To Beguile and Betray' in *Man Does, Woman Is* (Cassell 1964) p. 25.

202 DIARIES show that Jenny's letter reached RG on 19 March 1962.

203 MAJORCA Jenny Nicholson to RG 12–16 March 1962.

204 Ibid.

205 Ibid.

206 Catherine Dalton, *Without Walls* p. 197. Extract from CD to RG 6 May 1962 thanks for this sum.

207 AUTHOR Catherine Nicholson to JTRG 24 Sept. 1962.

208 AUTHOR RG to Sally Chilver 5 May 1962.

209 DIARIES 10 May 1962.

210 MAJORCA *unposted* RG to Margot Callas n.d.

211 O'PREY (2) p. 213 RG to Gordon Wasson 30 May 1962.

212 O'PREY (2) p. 215 and MAJORCA Gordon Wasson to RG 5 June 1962.

213 O'PREY (2) pp. 217–18 RG to Gordon Wasson 16 June 1962.

214 O'PREY (2) p. 218.

215 Ibid. RG to Gordon Wasson 25 June 1962.

216 MAJORCA Kingsley Amis,

article on RG for *Show*
magazine, autumn 1962.
217 DIARIES 18 June 1962. RG
describes the theatre as
'suprising and hitherto secret'.
For details of the play, Lucia
Graves in teleph. conv. with
RPG 26 Nov. 1994.
218 MAJORCA W. H. Auden to
RG 6 March 1961.
219 DIARIES 25–7 June 1962.
220 Ibid. 30 June 1962.
221 Ibid. 24 July 1962. The play
(partly written by RG) was called
The Oracle. It had 'above 30
characters in Mallorquin,
Spanish, English, French, Latin';
and leading parts were taken by
Ralph Jacobs, Stella Reeves and
Idries Shah among others.
222 MAJORCA RG to Ralph
Jacobs (who had been in the play
but was then so ill that he was in
hospital for a few days, where he
had a haemorrhage and nearly
died) 26 July 1962.
223 DIARIES 24 July 1962.
224 MAJORCA *unposted* RG to
Margot Callas 30 July (1962);
partly printed in MS-S p. 523.
225 DIARIES 30 June 1962.
226 Ibid. 6 Aug. 1962.
227 Ibid. 9 Aug. 1962.
228 'A Time of Waiting', in *Man
Does, Woman Is* p. 3.
229 See e.g. *The Greek Myths: 1*
(Penguin 1955 Repr. 1962).
230 MAJORCA Jenny Nicholson to
RG 10 Aug. 1962.
231 Kingsley Amis, *Show*
magazine Dec. 1962.

232 BG in conv. with RG Sept.
1994.
233 As note 198 above.
234 Kingsley Amis, *Memoirs*
Hutchinson 1991 p. 212.
235 MS-S p. 519, though he
misdates this letter of 17 Aug. to
27 Aug. 1962.
236 DIARIES 21 Aug. 1962.
237 DIARIES 25 Aug. 1962.
238 DIARIES 10–11 Sept. 1962.
Margot joined RG's sister
Rosaleen, and a woman friend of
Rosaleen's named in AUTHOR
Clarissa Graves to JTRG as Mrs
Aileen Powers.

CHAPTER 7
MARGOT IN ATTENDANCE

239 MAJORCA RG to Margot
Callas n.d.
240 MAJORCA RG to BG 20
Sept. 1962.
241 VICTORIA RG to Selwyn
Jepson 3 or 8 March 1963.
'Who is fairer or wiser than
Beryl? Or who rates Margot
higher than she does? Or who
rates Beryl higher than Margot?
Yet they have so little to say to
one another, except about trifles.'
242 DIARIES Tuesday 18 Sept.
1962.
243 As note 240 above.
244 Ibid. 23 Sept. 1962.
245 Ibid. 25 Sept. 1962.
246 Ibid. 26 Sept. (1962).
247 DIARIES 1–11 Oct. 1962.
248 'Some Instances of Poetic

Vulgarity', in *Mammon and the Black Goddess* (Cassell 1965).

249 DIARIES 24 Oct. 1962. Margot had arrived in London on the 23rd.

250 Ibid. 28 Oct. 1962.

251 Ibid. 1 Nov. 1962.

252 Ibid. 3 Nov. 1962.

253 MAJORCA Selwyn Jepson to RG 28 Feb. 1963.

254 DIARIES 6 Nov. 1962.

255 'Technique in Poetry', in *Mammon and the Black Goddess*.

256 DIARIES 10 Nov. 1962: it was the Threlford Memorial Lecture, and it appears in RG, *Mammon and the Black Goddess*.

257 'The Poet in the Valley of Dry Bones', in *Mammon and the Black Goddess*.

258 MATTHEWS p. 290.

259 MAJORCA James Reeves to RG n.d.

260 DIARIES 4 Dec. 1962.

261 O'PREY (2) pp. 221–2 RG to James Reeves 19 Jan. 1963.

262 VICTORIA RG to Selwyn Jepson 21 Dec. 1962.

263 Ibid. 20 Feb. 1963.

264 MAJORCA *unposted* RG to Margot Callas 28 May 1963.

265 This is speculative.

266 As note 264 above; the money would be repaid by her sale of the mill' in April.

CHAPTER 8
NEUROTIC CASUALTIES

267 DIARIES 1, 2, 3, 9, 16 Jan. 1963.

268 MAJORCA RG to Ralph Jacobs 24 Jan. 1963.

269 VICTORIA RG to Selwyn Jepson 20 Feb. 1963.

270 DIARIES 10–11 Jan. 1963.

271 Ibid. 22 Jan. 1963 The flat was 16 Calatrava.

272 As note 269 above.

273 MAJORCA Ralph Jacobs to RG 18 Jan. 1963.

274 MAJORCA RG to Ralph Jacobs 24 Jan. 1963.

275 As note 269 above.

276 DIARIES 3, 4, 10, 11, 12 Feb. 1963.

277 'A Last Poem', in *Man Does, Woman Is* p. 12.

278 As note 269 above.

279 DIARIES March 1963.

280 'Broken Neck', in *Man Does, Woman Is* p. 57.

281 MAJORCA Margery Terrasa to RG 17 March (1963).

282 DIARIES 4 March 1963. The stories were published the following year in London and New York.

283 Ibid. 12–24 March 1963.

284 Ibid. 31 March–1 April 1963.

285 Ibid. 2 April 1963.

286 Ibid. 3 April 1963 'Esteban came'; 4 April 'Margot in London'; and MAJORCA *unposted* RG to Margot Callas 28 May 1963.

287 As note 264 above.

288 DIARIES 16 April 1963.

289 As note 264 above.

290 O'PREY (2) p. 226 RG to Idries Shah 6 May 1963.

291 DIARIES 23 April 1963 (at

this stage called 'Three Faced Muse').

292 'The Three-Faced', in *Man Does, Woman Is* p. 20.

293 DIARIES 25–6 April 1963.

294 MAJORCA Sam Wanamaker to RG 10 April 1963.

295 DIARIES 27 April 1963.

296 As note 290 above pp. 225–6.

297 MAJORCA R. Gordon Wasson to RG 5 March 1963.

298 DIARIES 28 April 1963. The evidence is enigmatic. Possibly he waited at the airport, and it was there that Margot 'phoned & came'.

299 O'PREY (2) p. 225 RG to Idries Shah 6 May 1963.

300 As note 264 above.

301 DIARIES 28 April 1963.

302 Ibid. 29 April 1963.

303 'Not To Sleep' in *Man Does, Woman Is* p. 47.

304 O'PREY (2) p. 225 RG to James Reeves 2 May 1963.

305 DIARIES 30 April 1963.

306 MAJORCA R. Gordon Wasson to RG 5 April 1963 shows that RG had sent a list of those whom he wanted to be invited.

307 As note 305 above.

308 O'PREY (2) p. 227.

309 DIARIES 1–2 May 1963.

310 As note 304 above.

311 DIARIES 3 May 1963.

CHAPTER 9
THE BLACK GODDESS

312 As note 296 above.

313 MAJORCA *draft/unposted* RG to Margot Callas 22 May 1963.

314 'She Is No Liar', in *Man Does, Woman Is* p. 11.

315 MAJORCA *draft/unposted* RG to Margot Callas 22 May 1963 has RG writing of the necessity for Nichols to reform – a necessity which became 'evident' when RG saw how he had furnished his apartment.

316 As note 296 above.

317 DIARIES 4 May 1963 reads simply: 'N.Y. to New Hope and trouble'. The journey may have had something to do with an interview; as MAJORCA *unposted/draft* RG to Mike Nichols n.d. (on or after 15 May 1963) has RC's complaint that Mike Nichols, on seeing a certain article in print, should have physically assaulted the writer. Why? Because it was Nichols who took RG to New Hope and (meaning well) had passed on some details leading (presumably) to an article which, in Robert's view, had made him a laughing stock to some people. He suggested that an apology would be in order.

318 As note 290 above.

319 Ibid.

320 MAJORCA *draft/unposted* RG to Mike Nichols n.d.

321 MAJORCA *draft* RG to Margot Callas from The Hotel Continental Cambridge Massachusetts.

322 As note 290 above.

323 MS-S p. 525 (the original

document is in the MAJORCA archives).

324 'Seldom Yet Now', in *More Poems 1961* p. 24.

325 See 'In Time', in *Man Does, Woman Is* p. 7.

326 DIARIES 6–11 May 1963.

327 DIARIES 10 May 1963.

328 MAJORCA *unposted/draft* RG to Margot Callas Tuesday evening n.d. (probably 7 May 1963); but other drafts of this letter appear to be as late as 13 or 14 May.

329 '900 Iron Chariots', in *Mammon and the Black Goddess* p.

330 DIARIES 15 May 1963.

331 MAJORCA *unposted/draft* RG to Mike Nichols (on or after 15 May 1963).

332 DIARIES 16 May 1963.

333 O'PREY (2) p. 227.

334 As note 313 above.

335 LETTERS 21 May 1963.

336 DIARIES 21 May 1963.

337 As note 264 above.

338 As note 313 above.

339 'Intimations of the Black Goddess', in *Mammon and the Black Goddess*.

340 Or, as RG expresses it in 'Intimations of the Black Goddess': A poet who elects to worship Ishtar-Anatha-Eurydice, concentrates in himself the emotional struggle which has torn mankind apart: that futile war for dominance waged between men and women on battlefields of the patriarchal

marriage bed. He rejects the crude, self-sufficient male intelligence, yet finds the mild, complacent Vesta insufficient for his spiritual needs. Renascent primitive woman, the White Goddess, to whom he swears allegiance, treats him no less contemptuously than she does anyone else in this man-ruled world . . . There can be no kindness between Ishtar and Enkidu, between Muse and Poet, despite their perverse need for each other. Nor does a return to Vesta's gentle embrace – though he may never have denied her his affection – solve his problem. Marriage does not satisfy the physiological and emotional needs of more than one couple in ten.

341 O'PREY (2) p. 231.

342 O'PREY (2) p. 232 RG to Idries Shah n.d.

343 As note 339.

344 MAJORCA *unposted/draft* RG to Margot Callas n.d.

345 O'PREY (2) p. 233.

346 As note 342.

347 MAJORCA RG to Idries Shah n.d.

348 MAJORCA Margery Terrasa to RG 16 June 1963.

349 MAJORCA Mary Allen to RG 24 March 1963.

350 DIARIES 25, 28 May 1963.

351 MAJORCA Mary Allen to RG 9 June 1963.

352 Ibid. 14 July 1963.

353 MAJORCA *unposted* RG to Margot Callas 4 June 1963.

354 Ibid. 5 June 1963.

355 Ibid.

356 DIARIES 12 June 1963.

357 Ibid. The original has 'bills' not 'debts' and 'simple' not 'city' beauty; and appears in *Poems 1914–1926* pp. 126–7.

358 MAJORCA Jenny Nicholson to RG 6 June 1963.

359 DIARIES 12 June 1963.

360 As note 359 above.

361 'I Will Write', in *Man Does, Woman Is* p. 26.

362 MAJORCA *unposted* RG to Margot Callas 28 June 1963.

363 Ibid. n.d.

364 Ibid. 29 June 1963.

365 Helen Morningstar in conv. with RPG Feb. 1993.

366 Ibid.

367 MAJORCA Mary Allen to RG 6 Aug. 1963.

368 As note 365 above.

Book Seven   Cindy and Poetic Truth   1963–6

CHAPTER I
'GIFT OF SIGHT'

1 Simon Graves in conv. with RPG July 1994. Extracts from the play come from MAJORCA '1963 23 July *Prompt Copy*'.

2 MS-S p. 535.

3 Juan Graves, John de St Jorre and others in conv. with RPG Mar. 1993.

4 O'PREY (2) p. 234 RG to Selwyn Jepson n.d. From int.

evid. about the rewriting of *Much Ado*, this letter must be later than 20 Aug. 1964 when Ken Tynan suggested that he should begin a specimen sample of the work.

5 MAJORCA James Reeves to RG 16 Aug. 1963.

6 VICTORIA RG to Selwyn Jepson 25 Sept. 1963.

7 Anon. in conv. with RPG 4 Feb. 1993.

8 The next few paragraphs are from John de St Jorre in conv. with RPG 6 Mar. 1993, modified by written annotations Dec. 1994. It is George McDowell who recalls RG's finger-wagging.

9 'Gift of Sight', in *Love Respelt* (Cassell 1965) p. 5.

10 RG had the curious idea that his son William would one day be its curator.

11 DIARIES 18 May 1963 '150,000 pesetas to Ramon for Jazz Club'.

12 MAJORCA RG to Ralph Jacobs 10 Oct. 1963. TRUST RG to William Graves 26 Aug. 1963 shows that RG had an unexpected stroke of good fortune, in that 'Ronnie Scott's arrival was a great piece of luck; he consented to prolong his visit a week and play sax every night in return for hotel-fare'.

13 Juan Graves in conv. with RPG 5 Feb. 1993.

14 AUTHOR Clarissa Graves to JTRG 9 Aug. 1963.

15 LETTERS 13 Aug. 1963.

16 Ibid. 15 July 1963.

17 As note 15 above.

18 AUTHOR *copy* RG to Simon Graves 13 Sept. 1963.

19 MAJORCA RG to Ralph Jacobs 10 Oct. 1963.

20 MAJORCA Jenny Nicholson to RG 13 Aug. 1963.

21 MAJORCA Jenny Nicholson to BG 25 Sept. 1963.

22 O'PREY (2) p. 237 RG to Idries Shah 10 Feb. 1964. Has RG writing that Jenny, 'though a *good* woman . . . [had] dissipated all her energies of honour and love to little purpose. I couldn't get through to her about this'.

23 As note 19 above. At some stage there had been a curious sequence of events. After John de St Jorre had left the village, Cindy began using an old Volkswagen, painted in psychedelic colours, that he had left in her care. However, she was a poor driver; and when St Jorre returned to Deyá the following year, the first person he saw as he walked up to the Estanco to do some shopping was Robert, who glared at him and said: 'You'll be very glad to hear that car has been impounded. It was a danger, a menace. It was threatening Aemile's life.' When in the summer of 1965 de St Jorre met Aemile again, and they briefly resumed their affair, she told him that she had driven Robert to Palma, and in trying to park in a narrow space had smashed into two other cars. The police had been called, and when they discovered that the car had no papers, and she had no licence, they would have jailed her but for Robert's intervention.

24 Ibid.

25 MATTHEWS p. 292 In the original, Tom refers to Cindy as 'Emile', a name which she did not adopt until after the meeting he describes.

26 William Graves in conv. with RPG Sept. 1994.

27 O'PREY (2) p. 233 to Selwyn Jepson n.d. (post-20 Aug. 1964) shows that her memory was uncertain: by the following August the 'French' had become 'Basque'.

28 As note 26 above.

29 O'PREY (2) p. 238.

30 VICTORIA RG to Selwyn and Tania Jepson 14 Oct. 1963.

CHAPTER 2
DEATH OF A DAUGHTER

31 LETTERS n.d. (mid-Oct. 1963).

32 AUTHOR pc Clarissa Graves to JTRG pmk 23 Oct. 1963.

33 As note 25 above.

34 As note 18 above.

35 Ibid. 20 Dec. 1963.

36 As note 19 above.

37 LETTERS pmk 15 Oct. 1963. MAJORCA Enid Starkie to RG 19 Oct. 1963 shows that the digs were at 78 Sandfield Road.

38 MAJORCA RG to Ralph Jacobs 18 Nov. 1963.

39 MAJORCA *draft/fragment* RG to Cindy Lee/Emile Laraçuen n.d.

40 AUTHOR *Copy* RG to Simon Graves 20 Dec. 1963.

41 MAJORCA James Reeves to BG 11 Nov. n.d. 'Mary and I can and will definitely come. We will stay with Keith and Valerie Thomas. She is an ex-local girl and Oxford graduate who used to read to me at Chalfont, and she married Keith, who is a History Don at St. John's. Perhaps Robert and or you has met him. Anyway we would like them to meet you, so perhaps we can arrange that.'

42 As note 40 above.

43 TRUST RG to William Graves n.d. (?10 Dec.) 1963.

44 MAJORCA RG to Ralph Jacobs n.d.

45 Ibid. (pre-11 Dec. 1963).

46 DIARIES 4, 6 Jan. 1964.

47 DIARIES 17 Jan. 1964. '2 letters from E: in Hermosilla Mexico on the way back to N.Y.' See also TRUST RG to William Graves 29 Jan. 1964.

48 O'PREY (2) p. 235 RG to Idries Shah 4 Feb. 1964.

49 Ibid.

50 O'PREY (2) p. 236.

51 O'PREY (2) p. 240 RG to Idries Shah 21 May 1964. Has RG describing the craft of writing as 'a means of avoiding confusion and boredom and fading effect and short circuits: by the *order* in which words are placed. Also by the avoidance of unparallel similarities, and changing synonyms for the same subject; mixed metaphors; repetition . . .'

52 See RPG, *Richard Hughes: A Biography* (Deutsch 1994).

53 Ibid. p. 393.

54 AUTHOR Clarissa Graves to JTRG and Mary Graves 7 Feb. 1964.

55 MAJORCA Martha Gellhorn to RG 6 March 1964.

56 As note 54 above.

57 AUTHOR Rosaleen Cooper to JTRG 14 Feb. 1964.

58 AUTHOR *Jenny Nicholson Crosse* an address delivered by Nigel Ryan at the Memorial Service on Mon. 10 Feb. 1964.

59 O'PREY (2) p. 239 RG to Idries Shah n.d. (March 1964).

60 Ibid. p. 237 10 Feb. 1964.

CHAPTER 3
TALK OF LEAVING

61 DIARIES 22 Feb. 1964.

62 MAJORCA *Copy* Mrs John Benson Brooks to MS-S 18 Aug. 1982. She inaccurately recalls the length of the visit as being 'about five weeks'.

63 As note 59 above.

64 DIARIES 22–9 Feb. 1964.

65 As note 59 above.

66 DIARIES 6–8 Jan. 1964.

67 'The Green Castle', in *Man Does, Woman Is* pp. 45–6.

68 As note 59 above.

69 Ibid. RG commented that

Aemilia had been 'thinking hard of late' about 'the ideal relations between real man and real woman'.

70 'Real Woman', in *The Ladies Home Journal* (1964).

71 See for example MAJORCA Alastair Reid to RG n.d. (1961). 'Beryl is a private person: I am a private person. It is not hiding anything: it is simply retaining a part of life to live in one's aloneness, in the silence. One can perceive other people in their silence; but one must not invent explanations of them.'

72 Gamel Woolsey, 'Immutable', in *Middle Earth* (reprinted by Warren House Press, North Walsham, 1979) p. 45.

73 TRUST Aemile Lee to Peggy and John Benson Brooks n.d.

74 MAJORCA Aemile Laraçuen to Ava Gardner 19 March 1964.

76 Ruth Fainlight in conv. with RPG 27 April 1993.

76 'Batxoca', in *Love Respelt* p. 5.

77 As note 59 above.

78 INDIANA (iii) RG to Richard Hughes 30 April 1964. RG also drew Diccon's attention to the correspondence which had followed the publication of a book to which RPG had made a small contribution: *Charterhouse: An Open Examination Written By The Boys*. Reviewing it for the *Sunday Times*, Robert had delivered a blistering and highly controversial attack on his old school. 'Ordinary boys', he declared at one point, 'thrive under their ordeals; others either have nervous breakdowns – a brilliant fifteen-year-old scholar came to me for a long rest cure last year – or survive gloriously' (RG , 'Poet and public school', in the *Sunday Times* 29 March 1964).

79 Alan Sillitoe and Ruth Fainlight in conv. with RPG 27 April 1993.

80 O'PREY (2) p. 241 RG to Idries Shah 21 May 1964.

81 TRUST RG to Ava Gardner 21 June 1964.

82 Ibid. 26 June 1964.

83 O'PREY (2) p. 242 RG to Indries Shah 2 July 1964.

84 Ibid. pp. 242–3.

85 Ibid.

86 TRUST RG to John Benson Brooks 10 July 1964.

87 Ibid. 12 July 1964.

88 O'PREY (2) p. 243.

89 MAJORCA script of *To The Lighthouse*.

90 O'PREY (2) p. 243.

91 TRUST RG to Ava Gardner 22 Aug. 1964.

92 Magnus Magnusson Ed., *Chambers Biographical Dictionary* 5th edn 1990 p. 1484.

93 MAJORCA Ken Tynan of *Iris Productions Ltd* to RG 20 Aug. 1964.

94 Ibid.

95 TRUST RG to Ava Gardner 2 Sept. 1964.

96 MAJORCA RG to Ralph Jacobs 5 Sept. 1964.

97 MAJORCA Ralph Jacobs to RG 10 Sept. 1964.

CHAPTER 4
THE TROUBLE WITH HOWARD

98 Ibid.

99 MAJORCA RG to Ralph Jacobs 13 Sept. 1964.

100 Ibid. 30 Sept. 1964; and for the cyst, see O'PREY (2) p. 244 RG to Tom Matthews 6 Oct. 1964.

101 MAJORCA RG to Ralph Jacobs 30 Sept. 1964.

102 MAJORCA 27 Sept. (1964) Maggie Smith to RG and BG.

103 MAJORCA Ken Tynan to RG 16 Sept. 1964.

104 Ibid. 22 Sept. 1964.

105 MAJORCA 6 Oct. 1964 RG to Ralph Jacobs.

106 TRUST RG to Ava Gardner 8 Oct. 1964.

107 O'PREY (2) p. 224 RG to Tom Matthews 6 Oct. 1964. They set out on Sunday 10 October, caught the ferry to Barcelona, and drove north to Paris.

108 TRUST RG c/o Metcalf Paris to John Benson Brooks n.d.

109 MAJORCA 17 Oct. (1964) RG in Paris (as from St John's College) to Ralph Jacobs.

110 As note 79 above.

111 Their flat was just on the other side of St Giles's Street.

112 DIARIES 27 Oct. 1964.

113 For the 1964 lectures see RG, *Poetic Craft and Principle* (Cassell 1967).

114 MAJORCA RG to Ralph Jacobs 3 Nov. 1964.

115 O'PREY (2) p. 233–4 RG to Selwyn Jepson n.d.

116 TRUST Cindy Lee from Paris to Peggy and John Benson Brooks Nov. 1964.

117 'Son Altesse', in *Collected Poems 1975* p. 307.

118 TRUST RG to John and Peggy Benson Brooks 3 Nov. 1964. Apparently RG had thought of sending Cindy/Aemile to Yugoslavia, but the Consulate wouldn't give her a visa, so it had to be Spain.

119 MAJORCA *unposted/draft* RG to Ralph Jacobs 3 Nov. 1964 and Ibid. RG to (Eleni?) 15 Jan. 1965.

120 DIARIES 9–10 Nov. 1964. Shortly before this, he had given a talk at Eton College. In his Oxford lecture, RG exposed the technical weaknesses in poem after poem taken from Sir Arthur Quiller-Couch's *Oxford Book of English Verse*.

121 'Lecture Three, 1964', in *Poetic Craft and Principle* (Cassell 1967) pp. 80–82.

122 TRUST RG to Ava Gardner 27 Nov. 1964.

123 MAJORCA RG to Ralph Jacobs n.d. (bet. 30 Dec. 1964 and 18 Jan. 1965).

124 TRUST RG to John and Peggy Benson Brooks 10–14 Dec. 1964.

125 TRUST RG to John Benson Brooks 1 Jan. 1965.

126 SPIKE p. 3 RG to Spike Milligan n.d. (soon after 6 Dec. 1964).

127 SPIKE p. 4.

128 Ibid. p. 5.

129 MAJORCA *copy* Mr and Mrs John Benson Brooks to MS-S 18 Aug. 1982.

130 SPIKE p. 20 RG to Spike Milligan post-18 May 1965.

131 Ibid. p. 8 30 Jan. 1965.

132 As note 126 above pp. 3–4.

133 'Between Hyssop And Axe', in *Collected Poems 1975* p. 307.

134 As note 124 above.

135 VICTORIA RG to Selwyn Jepson 14 Dec. 1964.

136 As note 125 above.

137 MAJORCA *unposted/draft* RG to (?Eleni) 15 Jan. 1965.

138 MAJORCA RG to Ralph Jacobs n.d.

139 As note 137 above.

140 MAJORCA RG to Ralph Jacobs 29 Jan. 1965.

141 As note 125 above.

142 As note 137 above.

143 O'PREY (¼(P. ¼½⅝ RG to Alan Sillitoe and Ruth Fainlight 18 Jan. 1965.

144 Ibid.

145 MAJORCA Alan Sillitoe to RG n.d. (post-18 Jan. 1965).

146 MAJORCA Ralph Jacobs to RG 24 Jan. 1965.

CHAPTER 5
TO SEEK FELICITY

147 MAJORCA RG to Ralph Jacobs 29 Jan. 1965.

148 MAJORCA James McKinley to RG 30 Jan. 1965.

149 DIARIES for 1965 gives 'N.Y. State Univ.' (22 Feb); 'Syracuse Univ' (22 Feb.) and 'Yale' (1 March)'.

150 MAJORCA *draft* RG to James McKinley 5 Feb. 1965. In MS-S pp. 542–3 it is erroneously stated that RG was writing to James Metcalf.

151 MAJORCA RG to Ralph Jacobs n.d. (Dec. 64–Jan.65) also has 'Juan emigrates to Australia on Feb 10th with his hands to support him.'

152 DIARIES 10 Feb. 1965.

153 Ibid. 21 Feb. 1965 has 'Cable Beryl'.

154 O'PREY (2) p. 246 RG to Karl Gay n.d.

155 MAJORCA Ralph Jacobs to BG 11 April 1965 has 'Robert is here at last!'; in SPIKE RG to Spike Milligan 22 April 1965, RG says that he was in Mexico 'for a month'; and in O'PREY (2) p. 246 RG to Karl Gay n.d. RG says that he must leave the USA on (?or by) 15 March.

156 VICTORIA RG to Selwyn Jepson 19 June 1965 has a reference to Mexico Gulf; but later references are to Puerto Vallarta –which though not on the Gulf, but on the Pacific, is on the same latitude as the Gulf.

157 TRUST pc RG to Peggy and John Benson Brooks n.d.

158 MAJORCA Ralph Jacobs to BG 11 April 1965.

159 SPIKE p. 12 RG to Spike Milligan 22 April 1965.

160 O'PREY (2) pp. 248–9 RG to Ruth Fainlight 3 May 1965.

161 Ibid.

162 O'PREY (2) pp. 247–8 RG to Karl Gay 14 April 1965. RG headed the letter 'as from 9 Gay St, NY where I'll be soon' and O'PREY (2) p. 247 suggests this letter was written from Mexico; but the evidence of MAJORCA Ralph Jacobs to BG 11 April 1965 is that RG was in NY on that date.

163 DIARIES 16 April 1965 has 'To Deya (?)'.

164 VICTORIA RG to Selwyn Jepson 19 June 1965.

165 William and Elena Graves in conv. with RPG various dates.

166 SPIKE p. 15 RG to Spike Milligan 5 May 1965.

167 O'PREY (2) pp. 248–9 RG to Ruth Fainlight 3 May 1965.

168 As note 166 above.

169 MAJORCA Ruth Fainlight to RG 8 May 1965.

CHAPTER 6

LURE OF MURDER

170 SPIKE p. 20 RG to Spike Milligan post-18 May 1965.

171 SPIKE p. 28 Spike Milligan to RG n.d. (prob. early June, perhaps late May 1965).

172 O'PREY (2) p. 250.

173 As note 79 above.

174 As note 164 above.

175 Ibid.

176 Philip Toynbee, 'Robert Graves at 70', in the *Observer* (magazine supplement) 18 July 1965.

177 RG in Bill Duncalf's 'The Epic That Never Was' (BBC TV 1965).

178 MS-S p. 534.

179 'Lecture Two, 1965', in *Poetic Craft and Principle* p. 134.

180 O'PREY (2) pp. 250–51 RG to James Reeves 21 July 1965.

181 Ibid.

182 VICTORIA RG to Selwyn and Tania Jepson 29 July 1965.

183 John de St Jorre in conv. with RPG 6 March 1993.

184 Ibid.

185 Ibid.

186 'Stolen Jewel', in *Poems 1965–1968* (Cassell 1968) p. 10.

187 'Lure of Murder', in *Poems 1965–1968* p. 7.

188 BG in conv. with RPG 9 and 12 Feb. 1993.

189 As note 7 above.

190 William Graves in conv. with RPG 8 April 1982.

191 Thus VICTORIA RG to Selwyn Jepson 14 May 1966 has 'The Posada which Wm got from me by a trick'.

192 William and Elena Graves in conv. with RPG 8 April 1982.

193 VICTORIA RG to SJ 21 March 1966.

194 Elena Graves in conv. with RPG 1 Feb. 1993.

195 Ibid.

196 As note 192 above.

Notes for pages 414–21 579

197 AUTHOR *Copy* RG to Simon Graves 30 Aug. 1965. MS-S pp. 531–2 shows it was in 1962 that Sam Spiegel introduced RG to Tom Roe, an international lawyer based in Lausanne, whose company 'International Authors' dealt with the finances of authors and others who were domiciled outside their own countries. He bought RG's copyrights, then paid him the money when it was needed. As RG later commented 'My fees came through in perfect order until June [1965]'. But Roe had become involved in the 'Scottish Cadco Pig Project' which (supposedly worth £1,300,000) had collapsed in December 1964 with only £45 in its accounts; and since then, Roe had taken to passing forged dollar bills, while at the same time stealing from his clients' accounts.

198 O'PREY (2) p. 252 RG to Karl Gay 15 Oct. 1965.

199 As note 7 above.

200 TRUST RG to John and Peggy Benson Brooks 27 Sept. 1965.

201 TRUST Cindy Laraçuen Lee to Peggy and John Benson Brooks 27 Sept. 1965.

202 'Lecture Two, 1965', in *Poetic Craft and Principle* p. 149.

203 Versions of this appear in VICTORIA RG to Selwyn Jepson 14 Oct. 1965 and Ibid. n.d. This comes from *Poems 1965–1968* p. 14.

204 VICTORIA RG to Selwyn Jepson 14 Oct. 1965.

205 TRUST BG to Cecily Gittes 16 Oct. (1965).

206 MAJORCA Selwyn Jepson to RG 1 Jan. 1966.

207 DIARIES 26 Oct. 1965 show BG leaving for Russia.

CHAPTER 7
SAGACIOUS FRIEND

208 *Poetic Craft and Principle* p. vii.

209 Ibid. pp. 97–121.

210 Ibid. pp. 125–50. The lecture was given on 9 Nov. 1965.

211 Ibid. pp. 153–79.

212 John Graves and Rosaleen Cooper were also present: Rosaleen much disappointed by the fact that their brother was 'too cluttered by adoring females to give us much time' (see AUTHOR Rosaleen Cooper to JTRG 1 Dec. 1965).

213 MATTHEWS pp. 292–3.

CHAPTER 8
WITHERING HEIGHTS

214 LETTERS n.d. AUTHOR RG to JTRG talks of returning to Majorca on Thursday; from DIARIES 1965 we know that RG was in London up to and including 30 Nov.; and he was back in Majorca for Philip Graves's birth on 6 Dec.

215 AUTHOR RG to Sally Chilver n.d. (post-6 Dec. 1965).

216 Ibid.

217 VICTORIA RG to Selwyn Jepson 26 Dec. 1965.

218 MAJORCA Selwyn Jepson to RG 12 Jan. 1966.

219 VICTORIA RG to Selwyn Jepson 7 Jan. 1966.

220 As note 218 above.

221 Ibid. 16 Jan. 1966. Yet Aemilia had also written to Ruth Fainlight (see MAJORCA RF to RG 20 Jan. 1966) telling her that she felt the first drawing was better.

222 VICTORIA RG to Selwyn Jepson 22 Jan. 1966.

223 Ibid. 1 Feb. 1966.

224 MAJORCA RG to Ralph Jacobs 9 Feb. 1966.

225 MS-S p. 553.

226 Stephen Spender in *The Times* 8 Feb. 1966 p. 11.

227 MS-S p. 553 oddly suggests that RG only wrote this letter 'to annoy, because he hoped it would tease people such as [John] Wain'.

228 RG in *The Times* 16 Feb. 1966 p. 13.

229 MAJORCA Edmund Blunden to RG 20 Feb. 1966.

230 VICTORIA RG to Selwyn Jepson 21 March 1966.

231 AUTHOR RG to Sally Chilver 21 May 1966. 'I have had stomach trouble for nearly three months.'

232 VICTORIA RG to Selwyn Jepson 9 April 1966.

233 MAJORCA Joanna Simon to RG May 1966.

234 VICTORIA RG to Selwyn Jepson 4 May 1966.

235 MAJORCA John Benson Brooks to RG 6 May 1966.

236 TRUST RG to John Benson Brooks 1 June 1966.

237 VICTORIA RG to Selwyn Jepson 20 April 1966.

238 AUTHOR RG to Sally Chilver 21 May 1966 (misdated 1961; pmk Palma 25 May 1966).

239 This may be deduced from MAJORCA RG to Ralph Jacobs 11 May 1966: 'I hope Aemilia will let you have a room in her house! It will be a different sort of summer, that's clear . . .'

240 VICTORIA RG to Selwyn Jepson 14 May 1966.

241 MAJORCA RG to Ralph Jacobs 11 May 1966.

242 As note 240 above.

243 Ibid. RG was disappointed that William and Elena had turned to BG and not to himself for financial support.

244 As note 238 above.

245 MAJORCA Jonathan Boulting to RG 21 May 1966.

246 SPIKE p. 46 Spike Milligan to RG n.d.

247 SPIKE p. 49.

248 Ibid.

249 MAJORCA Michael Horowitz to RG 25 June 1966.

250 MAJORCA Christopher Logue to RG n.d.

251 As note 247 above.

252 RG to the Editor, the *Daily Telegraph*, quoted in Ibid.

253 As note 250 above.

254 As note 249 above.

255 MAJORCA Bernard Miles to RG 17 Nov. 1965.

256 Ibid. 30 Nov. 1965.

257 SPIKE pp. 35, 37, 39 RG to

Spike Milligan 10 April or so, 18 April or so and 18 May 1966.

258 SPIKE pp. 39–40 RG to Spike Milligan 18 May.

259 SPIKE p. 41 Spike Milligan to RG Wed. 25 May 1966.

260 SPIKE pp. 50–51.

261 As note 238 above.

262 AUTHOR 1966 MSS Journal by RPG. Afterwards, walking through the village on the way to supper at C'an Quet, RG said that he had known since RPG was born that they would one day become friends; and he invited him to return for a longer holiday the following year.

263 See MAJORCA RG to Ralph Jacobs 4 April 1967.

264 VICTORIA RG to Selwyn Jepson 20 July 1966.

265 MAJORCA RG to Ralph Jacobs 10 Nov. 1966 has 'the house I had bought for her and me at Puerto Vallarta'.

266 MAJORCA George Simon to RG Sept. 1966.

267 O'PREY (2) p. 258 RG to Ruth Fainlight 17 Dec. 1966.

268 MAJORCA RG to Ralph Jacobs 15 Sept. 1966. It was 'the Dr. Freimann hepatitis cure that Joanne Vance had'.

269 AUTHOR RG to Sally Chilver 18 Sept. 1966.

270 VICTORIA RG to Selwyn Jepson 17 Sept. 1966.

271 As note 269 above.

272 MAJORCA RG to Ralph Jacobs 29 Sept. 1966.

273 SPIKE p. 55 RG to Spike Milligan 17 Sept. 1966.

274 As note 272 above.

275 Ibid.

276 TRUST RG to Ava Gardner 9 Oct. 1966.

277 As note 272 above.

CHAPTER 9
CLOSING ACCOUNTS

278 RG's various contemporary accounts of his correspondence with Aemilia Laraçuen during Sept./Oct. 1966 are not at all consistent, chiefly because the combined shock of her desertion and his operation appear to have left him in a state of considerable mental confusion for some while. So some of what follows is a little speculative.

279 MAJORCA RG to Ralph Jacobs n.d. (24 Oct. 1966); and Ibid. n.d. (?24/25/26 Oct. 1966).

280 MAJORCA RG to Ralph Jacobs n.d. (24/25/26 Oct. 1966).

281 VICTORIA RG to Selwyn Jepson n.d. (but before RG's operation on Mon. 10 Oct. 1966).

282 TRUST RG in St Thomas's to John Benson Brooks (misdated 7 Sept.) 1966.

283 MAJORCA Selwyn Jepson to RG 9 Oct. 1966.

284 MAJORCA RG to Ralph Jacobs 1 Nov. 1966.

285 O'PREY (1) p. 263 RG to Idries Shah 2 Aug. 1967.

286 O'PREY (2) pp. 253–4.

287 RG, 'The Fitz-Omar Cult' in

Tr. RG and Omar Ali-Shah, *The Rubaiyyat of Omar Khayaam* (Penguin Books 1972) p. 7.

288 The previous day (see O'PREY (2) p. 254 23 Oct. 1966) Graves described this as Aemilia's 'first letter since Sept 28th'; but after a) her letter written on 27 Oct., he had received b) a further letter from Aemilia in Mexico, which reached him not long before his operation – and afterwards he was prepared to 'sit it out once more'; and this is now letter c), after which he 'closes accounts'.

289 MAJORCA RG to Ralph Jacobs n.d. (24 Oct. 1966).

290 O'PREY (2) p. 255 RG to Selwyn Jepson 23 Oct. with excisions restored from the original in VICTORIA.

291 As note 289 above.

292 'A Dream Of Hell', in *Poems 1965–1968* pp. 33–4.

293 As note 289 above.

294 Helena Simon in conv. with RPG 25 Aug. 1993.

295 SPIKE p. 56.

Book Eight *Juli 1966–75*

CHAPTER I
TOUSLED PILLOW

1 SPIKE p. 57.

2 'Tousled Pillow', in *Poems 1965–1968* p. 86.

3 O'PREY (2) p. 258 RG to Ruth Fainlight 17 Dec. 1966.

4 MAJORCA RG to Ralph Jacobs 10 Nov. 1966.

5 Ibid. 4 April 1967.

6 Ibid. 6 Jan. 1967.

7 VICTORIA RG to Selwyn Jepson 3 Jan. 1967.

8 Ibid. 31 Dec. 1966.

9 Ibid. n.d.

10 Ibid. 30 Jan. 1967. Some of Aemilia's words have been put back into direct speech.

11 MAJORCA Selwyn Jepson to RG 27 Jan. 1967.

12 VICTORIA RG to Selwyn Jepson 30 Jan. 1967.

13 Ibid. 4 March 1967.

14 As note 5 above.

15 VICTORIA RG to Selwyn Jepson 17 March 1967.

16 A revised version appears as 'With The Gift Of A Lion's Claw', in *Poems 1965–1968* p. 72.

17 As note 5 above.

18 VICTORIA RG to Selwyn Jepson 1 June 1967. The service was on 20 June.

19 TRUST RG to Alan Hodge 26 June 1967.

20 MAJORCA Alan Hodge to RG 20 June 1967.

21 MAJORCA John Betjeman to RG 20 June 1967.

22 MAJORCA Ted Hughes to RG 20 July 1967.

23 MAJORCA draft RG to the Rt Hon. Richard Austin Butler of the Royal Society of Literature 12 April 1962.

24 MAJORCA has considerable correspondence on the subject.

The programme was as follows:
RG read poems such as '1805'
'Vanity' 'The Legs' 'Flying
Crooked' 'An Honest Housewife'
'On Portents' 'The Villagers and
Death' 'The Lost Jewel' 'The
Window Sill' 'Turn of the Moon'
'Lion Lover' 'In Time' and 'Non
Cogunt Astra'. Then Isla read
'Warning to Children' 'The
Castle' 'Pure Death' 'In Broken
Images' 'With the Lips Only'
'Counting the Beats' 'I Will Write'
'Hedges Freaked with Snow' and
'All I Tell You From My Heart'.
Then Robert read 'Grace Notes'
'Not to Sleep' and selections from
privately printed works.

25 MAJORCA air mail George and
Joanna Simon to RG n.d.

26 Joanna Simon in conv. with
RPG 26 April 1993. The verse
was 'Until We Both . . .'

27 MAJORCA Stephanie Sweet to
RG 24 July 1967.

28 Ibid.

CHAPTER 2
SUMMER OF '67

29 TRUST RG to William Graves
14 March 1967.

30 Martin Tallents in conv. on
numerous occasions with RPG.

31 O'PREY (2) p.   RG to Idries
Shah 2 Aug. 1967.

32 AUTHOR RG to Sally Chilver
13 Sept. 1967.

33 Trans. RG and Omar Ali-Shah,
The Rubaiyyat of Omar Khayaam
p. 74.

CHAPTER 3
TO AVOID DROWNING

34 As note 32 above.

35 MAJORCA RG to Ralph Jacobs
25 Sept. 1967.

36 MAJORCA Dept. of Ed. to
Stephanie Sweet 27 Sept. 1967.

37 RG, 'Translating the *Rubaiyyat*'
in *The Crane-Bag and Other
Disputed Subjects* p. 227.

38 AUTHOR RPG to JTRG and
Mary Graves n.d. (but from 35
Bainton Rd, Oxford).

39 As note 32 above.

40 DALTON p. 219 extract of
letter from RG to NN 23 Jan.
1968.

41 AUTHOR RG to Sally Chilver
25 Oct. 1967. And from TRUST
RG to David Sutton 26 Nov.
1967 we learn that it was RG's
grandson James Dalton who
arranged the tour.

42 TRUST RG to David Sutton 26
Nov. 1967.

43 SPIKE p. 73 RG to Spike
Milligan n.d.

44 DALTON p. 138.

45 DALTON p. 165.

46 As note 40 above.

47 DALTON pp. 61–2. AUTHOR
RG to Sally Chilver 25 Oct.
1967 shows that RG flew to
London via San Francisco and
New York, where (SPIKE p. 73
RG to Spike Milligan n.d.) he
'ran into Peter Ustinov hand in
hand with Miss Lilian Gish'.

48 BERG RG to Selwyn Jepson 29
Dec. 1967.

49 SPIKE p. 74 RG to Spike Milligan n.d.

50 What Aemilia wrote has been deduced (somewhat speculatively) from RG's comments in MAJORCA *draft/unposted* RG to Aemilia Laraçuen 22 Dec. 1967.

51 Ibid.

52 As this is a draft, one cannot of course tell to what extent (if any) it was rewritten until the Laraçuen letters become available.

53 MAJORCA RG to Ralph Jacobs 15 Jan. 1968. Some said the necklace was 18th-century costume jewellery.

54 MAJORCA RG to Ralph Jacobs 16 Feb. 1968.

55 BERG RG to Selwyn Jepson 16 Feb. 1968.

56 Ibid. 27 Feb. 1968.

57 MAJORCA *refused as not enough postage on it* RG to Aemilia Laraçuen c/o Solow 69 West 10th St NYC 27 March 1968 (returned 15 May 1968). However, from Ibid. Margery Terrasa to RG and BG 9 Jan. 1968, it is just possible that this 'present' actually came from a small store of jewellery which Aemilia had left with Margery, among which were presents from RG to Aemilia which he was then trying to recover.

58 MAJORCA RG to Aemilia Laraçuen 14 March 1968.

59 As note 57 above.

60 MAJORCA Selwyn Jepson to BG 19 Jan. 1968.

61 MAJORCA Michael Horniman at A. P. Watt to RG 19 April 1968.

62 MAJORCA The BBC producer David Gerard to RG 26 April 1968.

63 MAJORCA Stephanie Sweet from Barcelona to RG 29 Jan. 1969.

64 MS-S p. 550.

65 BG in conv. with RPG Sept. 1994.

66 Ibid. BG went on ahead to Moscow, where all three were befriended by some Sufi friends of Idries Shah.

67 MS-S p. 551 for an extract from RG to MS-S 28 Sept. 1968.

68 BERG RG to Selwyn Jepson 12 July 1968.

CHAPTER 4
DON'T HATE IAGO

69 Ibid.

70 Ibid.

71 These few slightly speculative lines are deduced by working backwards from MAJORCA Joanna Simon to RG 3 July 1968.

72 MAJORCA Joanna Simon to RG 3 July 1968.

73 As note 68 above.

74 DALTON pp. 61–2.

75 Catherine Dalton in conv. with RPG July 1985.

76 MAJORCA Joanna Simon to RG 20 Aug. 1968 has 'No sign

of Aemilia fetching her coat yet. It is hanging in the cupboard in "Robert's room".'

77 As note 75 above.

78 BERG RG to Selwyn Jepson 26 July 1968. William and Elena Graves in conv. with RPG Sept. 1994 report that a turning point came when Peter Ustinov had invited RG and BG to visit him on his yacht, then anchored off Soller. BG had refused to go if 'Cindy' went too, as RG wished. RG then asked WG to drive him and 'Cindy' over. He too refused. So in the end RG gave way, and he and BG and William and Elena went together without Aemilia; and afterwards W & E noticed that 'things began to swing back in the right direction'. However, the date of this event cannot be pinpointed with any degree of accuracy, which is why it has not been included in the main body of the text.

79 MAJORCA Tom Matthews to RG 6 July 1988.

80 BERG RG to Selwyn Jepson 28 Aug. 1968.

81 MAJORCA RG to Enid Starkie 19 July 1968 quoted in Joanna Richardson to RG 16 June 1972.

82 O'PREY (2) p. 270 RG to Karl Gay 27 July 1968.

83 Ibid. For details of the gifts see TRUST RG to David Sutton 31 Aug. 1968.

84 MAJORCA Enid Starkie from Paris to RG 3 Aug. 1968.

85 As note 80 above, 26 Aug. 1968. (Aemilia sent him the cable 'a week ago'.)

86 Ibid.

87 MAJORCA RG to Ralph Jacobs 23 Nov. 1968 has Aemilia and Peter 'still around staying at my cottage'.

88 BERG RG to Selwyn Jepson 28 Aug. 1968.

89 They stayed 5–27 Sept.

90 RG in 'John Aldridge Water-colours 1931–1968' (7–24 May 1969).

91 RG to Enid Starkie 25 Aug. 1968 quoted in MAJORCA Joanna Richardson of Hampstead on 16 June 1972.

92 MAJORCA Enid Starkie to RG 11 and 21 Sept. 1968.

93 RG to Enid Starkie 28 Sept. 1968 quoted in MAJORCA Joanna Richardson of Hampstead on 16 June 1972.

94 MAJORCA *draft/unposted* RG to Leticia de la Valle in Mexico 28 Sept. 1968.

95 MAJORCA RG to Juan Graves 15 Oct. 1968.

96 BERG RG to Selwyn Jepson n.d.

97 O'PREY (2) p. 274.

98 As note 96 above.

99 O'PREY (2) p. 274 RG to Idries Shah 4 Nov. 1968.

100 Ibid.

101 Quoted in BERG RG to Selwyn Jepson 8 Nov. 1968.

102 MAJORCA C. Day-Lewis to RG 28 Oct. 1968 has already received RG's letter.

103 MAJORCA Enid Starkie to

RG 1 Oct. 1968 and Ibid. to BG 20 Oct. 1968.

104 RG in the *Guardian* 28 Oct. 1968.

105 MAJORCA Enid Starkie to RG Dec. 1968.

106 *Life International* 10 June 1968.

107 MAJORCA Amphlett & Co Solctrs of London about Mr L. P. Elwell-Sutton 5 Nov. 1968.

108 MAJORCA RG's lawyers to RG 14 Nov. 1968.

109 MAJORCA has a *copy* of this letter.

110 BERG RG to Selwyn Jepson 8 Nov. 1968.

111 TRUST RG to Colin and Heather Thompson 15 Nov. 1968. The Thompsons were young friends who had spent part of the summer in Deyá, before retreating to the Isle of Lewis.

112 MAJORCA Joanna Simon to RG 24 Nov. 1968.

113 MS-S pp. 552–3.

114 BERG RG to Selwyn Jepson 25 Nov. 1968.

115 MAJORCA Selwyn Jepson to RG 18 Jan. 1959.

116 O'PREY (2) pp. 276–7 RG to Ruth Fainlight 13 Jan. 1969.

117 TRUST RG to Colin and Heather Thompson 28 Jan. 1969.

118 As note 116 above.

119 MAJORCA Peter Weismiller to RG 26 Jan. n.d. (1969).

120 AUTHOR RG to Sally Chilver 4 Feb. 1969.

121 BERG RG to Selwyn Jepson 25 Feb. 1969.

122 MAJORCA Selwyn Jepson to RG 11 Feb. 1969.

123 Ibid.

124 Ibid. 21 Feb. 1969.

125 BERG RG to Selwyn Jepson 25 Feb. 1969.

126 TRUST RG to Colin and Heather Thompson 16 Feb. 1969.

CHAPTER 5
LOSS OF MAGIC

127 MAJORCA RG to Margot Nichols 25 March 1969 (*return to sender* 4 April)

128 O'PREY (2) pp. 277–8 RG to Ruth Fainlight 12 Feb. 1969.

129 TRUST 1990s note by David Sutton accompanying RG's letters to him.

130 TRUST RG to Colin and Heather Thompson 9 May 1969.

131 As note 129 above.

132 MAJORCA Selwyn Jepson to RG 8 June 1969.

133 BERG RG to Selwyn Jepson 10 June 1969.

134 MAJORCA Selwyn Jepson to RG 25 June 1969.

135 TRUST RG to David Sutton 9 October 1971.

136 BERG RG to Selwyn Jepson dated 18 July 1969, but from int. evidence after RG's birthday, and therefore more probably 18 Aug. 1969.

137 MAJORCA This is the interpretation of Selwyn Jepson in SJ to RG 3 Oct. 1969.

138 BERG RG to Selwyn Jepson 7 Oct. 1969.

139 As note 136 above.

140 TRUST RG to David Sutton 1 Oct. 1969.

141 As note 136 above. In another letter TRUST RG to Colin and Heather Thompson 29 July 1969, RG wrote 'Juli came here to the Tower and was the victim of one of the most evil plots that Deyá can show.' She was then 'back in Oslo; but I haven't recovered'. RG harboured a grudge against Sonja until at least September, when Selwyn Jepson, believing quite rightly that there had been nothing inherently disloyal to Robert in her actions, asked him whether it was fair for the sins of the husband to be visited on the wife? This led to a considerable change of heart on RG's part. He could not see Sonja while she remained with Page; but he accepted that she had acted for the best. (MAJORCA Selwyn Jepson to RG 3 Oct. 1969; and BERG RG to Selwyn Jepson 7 Oct. 1969).

142 As note 136 above. Later, in BERG RG to Selwyn Jepson 7 Oct. 1969, RG explains to Jepson that she 'can't account for it [her attraction to Page] now of course, but shudders in horror'.

143 Here, of course, Graves refers to the Chappaquiddick scandal.

144 MAJORCA Selwyn Jepson to RG 15 Aug. 1969.

145 As note 138 above.

146 TRUST RG to Ava Gardner 13 Dec. 1969.

147 TRUST RG to Colin and Heather Thompson 29 July 1969.

148 MAJORCA Frances Power Weismiller to RG and BG 3 Dec. 1969.

149 Ibid. 30 Sept. 1969. RG flew on 21 Oct. to London, where TRUST RG to Colin and Heather Thompson 4, 15 Oct. 1969 shows that he was paid £300 for making a speech during a banquet in the Savoy at the launching of an official history of the First World War.

150 MAJORCA Joanna Simon to RG 25 Nov. 1969.

151 TRUST RG to Colin and Heather Thompson 7 Dec. 1969.

152 As note 146 above.

153 MAJORCA RG to Juan Graves n.d. (?Jan/early Feb. 1970). RG was guaranteed £500 against the proceeds of a limited edition, besides a royalty on the trade edition.

154 BERG RG to Selwyn Jepson 30 Sept. 1969.

155 Ibid. 7 Oct. 1969.

156 Reprinted as RG, 'The Two Births of Dionysus' in *Difficult Questions, Easy Answers* (Cassell 1972) pp. 104–12, where 'scientifically' becomes 'science-wise (as the Americans say)'.

157 See for example MAJORCA R. Gordon Wasson to RG 10 Jan.

1969: 'As for the Bearserks surely Occam's Razor, the law of parsimony, rules here. We need no drug to explain the Bearserks. They were huge, powerful, ordinary brutes, roughnecks the pick of a bad lot . . . would put on an act when the Boss told them to, an act that any moron could perform if he was strong and big enough. You speak of the episode in the Napoleonic Wars as though it had taken place but you cannot prove it. (It was not the Napoleonic Wars but the war between Norway and Sweden.)'

158 MAJORCA R. Gordon Wasson to RG 21 Nov. 1969.

159 See O'PREY (2) pp. 283–5.

160 MS-S p. 558.

161 MAJORCA RG *draft* to Olga 'shortest day of the year' (21 Dec.) 1969.

CHAPTER 6
A MATTER OF HONOUR

162 MS-S pp. 561–2.

163 As note 153 above.

164 This interview appears as RG, 'Speaking Freely' in *Difficult Questions, Easy Answers* pp. 190–213.

165 Ibid. p. 191.

166 Ibid. p. 194.

167 BERG RG to Selwyn Jepson 30 Sept. 1969.

168 Ibid. 6 March 1970 'Just off to Venice . . .'

169 TRUST RG to David Sutton 18 May 1970. In May, RG went with Catherine to Budapest where, as he told Selwyn Jepson, he was 'the senior poet at the Congress of Poets and had a great time'. (BERG RG to Selwyn Jepson 20 May 1970.)

170 BERG RG to Selwyn Jepson 20, 30 May 1970. Juli was dancing for the Royal Festival Ballet. While staying with the Simons, RG wrote these lines, which capture the flavour of the time:

JUNE 18 1970

The United Simons (quote unquote)
Strolled out along the street to vote
Joanna, Heli, George and Juli
The sun was west, the breeze came coolly.
Chris was too young to vote; no doubt
His elders cancelled themselves out
But all kept their selections hid.
It was their duty and they did.

171 Ibid. 4 July 1970.

172 TRUST RG to Colin and Heather Thompson 25 July 1970.

173 Julian Glover and Isla Blair were also visitors; as were RG's nephew RPG, who had recently been married to Anne Fortescue, and was enjoying a second honeymoon at C'an Quet at Robert's expense. Another feature of the summer was that both Elena and Lucia were

heavily pregnant with their second children.

174 MAJORCA Edna O'Brien to RG n.d.

175 BERG RG to Selwyn Jepson 31 July 1970.

176 MAJORCA RG to ?1971.

177 MAJORCA Bernard Miles to RG 14 Jan. 1970.

178 RG earned £182-10-0 (50% of the gross box office), together with the cost of his flights to and from London. 'Herewith your Hawl', wrote Miles, enclosing a cheque for £224-15-0. 'It was a really historic evening and an immense pleasure meeting all your friends as well as listening to you. Come again next year!' MAJORCA Bernard Miles to RG 7 Sept. 1970.

179 MAJORCA Vivien Holzer to RG 30 July 1970. She would soon visit RG in Deyá, where her parents were to celebrate their silver wedding.

180 Ibid. 8 Oct. 1970.

181 Ibid. has 'Remember you mentioned you would go back to London some time in October. Will she [Juli Simon] be there?' RG had been hoping to see Jerome Robbins again, with a view to co-operating with him on a ballet which would probably have involved both Lucia's husband Ramon, and Juli Simon. (O'PREY (2) p. 286 RG to Gordon Wasson n.d.). However, Robbins failed to put in an appearance; and the following

month he wrote from New York pleading ill health, and adding: 'One bright, clear and shining memory of London is being with you and yours, hearing your poems and finding you again. I hope we can see each other soon.' (MAJORCA JR to RG Nov. 1970). But he and RG did not meet again.

182 O'PREY (2) p. 181 says that this was 'not strictly true': shortly before his death, Sirdar Ikbar Ali-Shah *had* written to Graves saying that the manuscript should be produced; but when Graves forwarded the old man's letter to Omar Ali-Shah, Omar claimed not to have received it, and Graves had unfortunately made no copy.

183 O'PREY (2) p. 281 and MAJORCA Idries Shah to RG 30 Oct. 1970.

184 O'PREY (2) pp. 282–3 RG to Idries Shah 11 Nov. 1970.

185 O'PREY (2) p. 283.

CHAPTER 7
THE FIFTH DIMENSION

186 BERG RG to Selwyn Jepson n.d. but from int. evidence post-12 Nov. and pre-28 Nov. 1970. Good news was the safe delivery of Elena's daughter Sofia on 23 October, and of Lucia's daughter Eulalia on 12 November. BG in conv. with RPG Sept. 1994 mentions that it was John Aldridge who put RG in touch

with the London doctor, having benefited from a similar operation himself.

187 MAJORCA RG to Frank Kersnowski Dept. of Eng., Trinity University, San Antonio, Texas, 11 Feb. 1971.

188 MS-S p. 562.

189 LETTERS 27 April 1971.

190 As note 188 above.

191 'Address to the Poets of Hungary' in *Difficult Questions, Easy Answers* pp. 1–4. The date of this address is give as 1970; but MS-S p. 562 declares that it was given on 28 May 1971.

192 It later became sections XXVI and XXVII of RG's *Collected Poems*.

193 *Poems 1970–1972* (Cassell 1972) pp. v–vi.

194 Ibid. p. 15.

195 The original runs: Quinque tibi luces vibrant in nomine: quinque / Isidis in stella cornua sacra deae. / Nonne etiam digitos anuli quinque Isidis ornant? / Ornant te totidem, Julia. . . . Sum, quod amo.

196 TRUST RG to Colin and Heather Thompson pmk 21 July (1971).

197 MAJORCA Marianne Greenwood (a woman friend who was also a respected professional photographer) c/o American Express Salvador, Bahia Brazil to RG 2 April 1971.

198 As note 196 above. Peter Weismiller described him as 'an artist, [and] an extremely hearty

type (he nearly broke my hand several times on the pretext of shaking it, and I was not alone in being so honoured)'. MAJORCA Peter (Weismiller) to RG 25 July n.d. (?1971).

199 MAJORCA Marianne Greenwood Cayenne, French Guiana to RG 6 Sept. 1971. (MG was then the only crew on a small 29-foot yacht one mast no motor on a trip round the world, the captain a young adventurous Frenchman.)

200 MAJORCA *unsent/draft* RG to Josefa 23 March 1972. RG explains that he had been operated upon, leaving his nose clear, but his memory patchy. The result was, he confessed, that sadly he was completely unable to recall anything about his correspondent.

201 LETTERS 7 Oct. 1971.

202 TRUST RG to Ruthven 9 Sept. 1971 'just back from a fortnight in St. Thomas's.

203 TRUST RG to Colin & Heather Thompson 9 Oct. 1971.

204 Ibid.

205 As note 188 above.

206 MAJORCA Tony Richardson to RG 26 Aug. (1971).

207 Ibid. 1 Oct. 1971.

CHAPTER 8
LOSS OF MEMORY

208 LETTERS 30 Jan. 1972.

209 See for example O'PREY (2) pp. 282–3 RG to Idries Shah 11 Nov. 1970.

210 LETTERS 14 Feb, 28 May 1972.

211 Ibid. 22 March 1972.

212 Ibid. 30 Jan. 1972.

213 As note 211 above.

214 As note 65 above. BG adds that Robert Edwards and Pauline Scudamore were both very helpful at this time.

215 MAJORCA Sam Wanamaker to RG Jan 1972; and ibid. A further letter from the Acting Administrator FOM Smith; and AUTHOR RG to Clarissa Graves 29 Ap. 1972. Such limited editions signed by celebrities fetched high prices; and Robert Graves was currently involved in a lucrative arrangement with the artist Paul Hogarth, who had illustrated a number of Graves's poems. As Edward Booth-Clibborn of Motif Editions wrote on 15 May, they would be doing a box of five lithographs to be published in Paris and signed by Graves and Hogarth; then three of those five would be selected for a further 250 sets also signed by poet and artist; and (much later in the year) (the *Daily Telegraph* magazine 8 Dec. 1972) there would also be 'a mass-market version in conjunction with the *Daily Telegraph* which will be sold to their readers at a fairly cheap price'. (MAJORCA Edward Booth-Clibborn to RG 15 May 1972).

216 MAJORCA Tony Richardson to RG 17 March 1972.

217 MAJORCA *copy* RG to Tony Richardson 22 March 1972.

218 MAJORCA Tony Richardson to RG 24 May 1972.

219 MAJORCA Ralph Jacobs to BG and RG Sept. 1972.

220 LETTERS 28 May 1972 and as note 65 above.

221 MAJORCA RG to Ralph Jacobs 1 Oct. 1972. BG in conv. with RPG Sept. 1994 comments that it was 'all right, but a bit too clever – almost a farce: good in its way but not into it'.

222 MAJORCA Hugh Lloyd-Jones of Christ-Church to RG 10 March 1972 has: 'Of course I will write to Julie for March 13th. I am glad you told me. It is good that you had that splendid week's visit. I saw a report of the production of the ballet in the *Daily Express* some weeks ago.'

223 MAJORCA Robert Edwards to RG 4 Aug. 1972.

224 'Love as Lovelessness', in *Collected Poems 1975* p. 513.

225 MAJORCA Juli Simon in a PS of Joanna Simon to RG (?)14th/15th Aug. 1972.

226 LETTERS pmk. Zurich 18 Aug. 1972.

227 MAJORCA RG to Ralph Jacobs 1 Oct. 1972.

228 LETTERS n.d. show that in Nov. RG and BG stayed with the Simons in London for a few days. Sadly, the visit 'was not helped by a burglary' in which Beryl lost £25, and Robert lost his briefcase containing, among

other things, the fifth volume of Lucien's works, 'which had a discourse on dancing from which I wanted to quote'.

229 Ibid. 1 Dec. 1972 and 21 March 1973. See also Edward Booth-Clibborn, in the *Daily Telegraph* magazine, 8 Dec. 1972 p. 47. The presentation was on 1 Dec. 1972.

230 AUTHOR RG to Sally Chilver 9 Nov. 1972.

231 LETTERS n.d. When JTRG 'later mentioned this to Mrs Simon. She thought Robert was mistaken, that he *thought* he had lost the books he had given away to friends'.

232 See for example Ibid. 1, 17 dec. 1972.

233 MAJORCA *unposted* RG to Idries Shah 19 Jan. 1973. Graves wrote that he would with his muse in Glasgow, where Scotland's television service would be broadcasting his talk about Burns. Then he would return briefly to 'Drayton Great Park'.

234 MAJORCA RG to Mary Ellidge 5 Feb. 1973.

235 MAJORCA *unposted* RG to Idries Shah 19 Jan. 1973.

236 'The Scared Child', in *Collected Poems 1975* p. 514.

237 MAJORCA Elizabeth Gould-Davis to RG 1 Dec. 1972.

238 Ibid. 1 Feb. 1973.

239 MS-S p. 561.

240 MAJORCA Colin Wilson to RG 6 May 1970.

241 LETTERS (dict. by BG) 19 Feb. 1973.

242 See AUTHOR Paul Watson to JTRG 29 Nov. 1973, in which Watson says that 'the Americans haven't the money to invest in "one off" films . . . There was a chance of the film being financed totally by the BBC: a co-production with the Drama department and us. All seemed to be going well until the Head of Plays decided he didn't like the script. I'm afraid it was a political judgment rather than artistic.'

243 As note 241 above.

244 SPIKE pp. 121–2.

245 See e.g. Ibid. pp. 106–7.

246 *South Kensington News & Chelsea Post* Fri. 6 April 1973.

247 LETTERS pmk 4 Sept. 1973.

248 MAJORCA John Aldridge to RG 16 Oct. 1973.

249 MATTHEWS p. 328.

250 TRUST BG to CG 24 March 1974.

251 MAJORCA Aldridge to RG 9 May 1974.

252 MAJORCA James Reeves to RG 24 Aug. 1974.

253 BG, 'Notes on Visit to Warsaw Budapest Cracow' Sept.–Oct. 1974.

254 'The Persian Version', in *Collected Poems 1975* p. 146.

255 MAJORCA James Reeves to RG and BG n.d. (1974).

256 MAJORCA John Aldridge to RG 18 Dec. 1974 and Ibid. Tom Matthews to BG 13 Dec.

1974. Tom wrote: 'On December 6 we went to see her for the last time. She was evidently dying then, though of course no-one could tell when it would be.'

257 'P.W.' in *The Times* Thurs. 6 Feb. 1975.

258 SPIKE p. 125 RG to Spike Milligan 9 March 1974.

259 SPIKE p. 128 Spike Milligan to RG 5 April 1974.

260 TRUST BG to CG 13 March 1975.

261 CANELLUÑ Julian Glover to RG 13, 29 May, and programme enc. with 23 July 1975.

262 CANELLUÑ Major E. L. Kirby, Curator of the Royal Welch Fusiliers Regimental Museum at Caernavon Castle, to RG 2 July 1975 recalls the occasion.

263 AUTHOR JTRG Diary 27 June 1975; and Ibid. a typescript account by JTRG of the events of that day.

264 CANELLUÑ John Wain to BG 25 July 1978 recalls the occasion.

CHAPTER 9
IT'S YOUR MOON AND MY
MOON

265 This chapter is entirely taken from i) notes made at the time by the RPG and ii) an unpublished account written a few days later, also by RPG. Most unfashionably, none of the dialogue is invented.

*Book Nine   Death's Narrow
Sea   1975–85*

CHAPTER I
SCREENING *I, CLAUDIUS*

1 MAJORCA Judith Bledsoe to RG and BG 22, 25 July (1975).

2 MAJORCA John Aldridge to RG Dec. 1975.

3 MAJORCA Joanna Simon to RG and BG Nov. 1975.

4 AUTHOR JTRG Diary 14 Jan. 1976.

5 AUTHOR Dora Middleton to JTRG 23 Jan. 1976.

6 AUTHOR NN to Rosaleen Cooper 17 Jan. 1976.

7 MAJORCA Michael Austin to RG c/o A. P. Watt 18 May 1976.

8 MAJORCA Selwyn Jepson to RG 31 Jan. 1976.

9 AUTHOR JTRG Diary 21 July 1976 – a letter from Elizabeth. with news that 'Beryl, & Lucia & family + Tomas' were planning a journey 'to Poland to spend [RG's] royalties, which cannot be taken out of the country'.

10 AUTHOR *copy* (in JTRG's hand) of BG to Rosaleen Cooper 11 July 1976.

11 MS-S pp. 566–7.

12 RG, *I, Claudius* (Arthur Barker 1934) p. 15.

CHAPTER 2

WALKING BACK TO WIMBLEDON

13 AUTHOR JTRG Diary 20 Sept. 1976.
14 Lucia Farran (*née* Graves) in conv. with RPG 16 Aug. 1994.
15 AUTHOR JTRG Diary Tuesday 26 Oct. 1976.
16 Ibid. 2 Nov. 1976.
17 Ibid. 3 Nov. 1976.
18 BG's letter appears in *The Carthusian* Vol 28 No 3 Dec. 1976.
19 MAJORCA James McKinley to BG 28 Oct. 1977: JM has completed five chapters and is going ahead with the remainder.
20 AUTHOR BG to JTRG 11 Jan. 1978 retrospectively explains her position.
21 AUTHOR JTRG Diary 29 Nov. 1976.

CHAPTER 3

UNDER THE INFLUENCE

22 AUTHOR JTRG Diary 2 Dec. 1976.
23 MS-S p. 567.
24 AUTHOR BG to JTRG 11 Feb. 1977.
25 AUTHOR Rosaleen Cooper to JTRG 6 Feb. 1977.
26 MAJORCA Beryl Graves to Tom Matthews n.d. 1977.
27 AUTHOR JTRG Diary 16 Aug. 1977.
28 AUTHOR Sam Graves to JTRG and Mary Graves 19 Aug. 1977.

CHAPTER 4

'MY DEAR OLD FRIEND'

29 As note 14 above.
30 MAJORCA Julian Glover from the Royal Shakespeare Theatre at Stratford upon Avon to BG 11 Oct. 1977.
31 MAJORCA Stella Irwin to RG and BG 2 May 1978.
32 Ralph Jacobs to RG 9 April 1978.
33 MAJORCA Ruth Fainlight to BG 12 July 1978 and AUTHOR Rosaleen Cooper to JTRG 16 July 1978.
34 MAJORCA Tom Matthews to RG 13 July 1978.

CHAPTER 5

HEAVENLY DEYÁ

35 MAJORCA RG to BG 11 Oct. 1977, 8 June and 12 Aug. 1978.
36 MAJORCA Juli Simon to RG and BG 24 Aug. 1978.
37 AUTHOR Lucia Farran to Rosaleen Cooper quoted in Rosaleen Cooper to JTRG 18 Dec. 1978.
38 MAJORCA Joanna Simon to BG n.d. and Ibid. Ruth Fainlight to BG 12 Nov. 1978: 'I hope Robert's arm is on the mend.'
39 MAJORCA Selwyn Jepson to RG 1 Sept. 1978.

CHAPTER 6

DEATH AND DECAY

40 MAJORCA June 1979 obituary

of Alan Hodge in the *Financial Times*.

41 MAJORCA Jane Hodge to BG I guess 30 May (1979).

42 MAJORCA Margery Terrasa to RG and BG 30 Sept. 1978.

43 Ibid. to BG & family 14 Oct. 1979.

44 Ibid. to BG 27 Oct. 1979.

CHAPTER 7
SPELL-BOUND

45 e.g. MAJORCA Paul O'Prey to Tony Baekeland 19 Feb. 1980.

CHAPTER 8
SAD BUT INEVITABLE

46 MS-S p. 567.

47 MAJORCA Jane Hodge to BG 26 April (1983).

48 MAJORCA pc Gretl Aldridge to BG 24 Jan. 1983.

49 As note 47 above.

50 MAJORCA Diana Mancroft to BG 1 March 1983.

51 MAJORCA Biddy from 29 Margaretta Terrace to BG 4 May 1983.

52 MAJORCA Tom Matthews to BG 8 May 1983.

CHAPTER 9
DEATH OF A POET

53 Information in this chapter comes from a record made on the day of RG's death by the present author, based upon telephone conversations with Elizabeth Graves, Paul O'Prey and William Graves's son Philip Graves; and from Tomas Graves in conv. with RPG 10 Feb. 1993; and from BG, William Graves and Elena Graves in conv. with RPG Sept. 1994.

SELECT BIBLIOGRAPHY

For a full bibliography the reader should turn to F. H. Higginson's *Robert Graves: A Bibliography* (St Paul's Bibliographies 1987). What follows is a guide to the more important published sources relevant to the period covered by this volume.

I RELATING TO ROBERT GRAVES'S LIFE BETWEEN 1940 AND 1985

Baker, Deborah, *In Extremis: The Life of Laura Riding* (Hamish Hamilton 1993). Despite what John Carey described as her 'whimsical treatment of chronology', Baker writes with great intelligence, and this, the first fullscale biography of Laura Riding, gives an intriguing account of Riding's post-Graves years.

Dalton, Catherine Dalton [*née* Nicholson], *Without Hardware: Cases of Treason in Australia* (Ochre Press N.S.W. Australia 3rd edn 1980). Quite apart from its central story, this intriguing work quotes extracts from a number of letters written or received by Robert Graves and Nancy Nicholson.

Matthews, T. S. *Under the Influence* (Cassell 1977). This memoir, so valuable when detailing earlier episodes in Robert Graves's life, is inevitably less useful for the 1940–85 period, but still contains a number of unforgettable insights and vignettes.

O'Prey, Paul (ed.) *In Broken Images: Selected Letters of Robert Graves 1914–1946* (Hutchinson 1982); and O'Prey, Paul, *Between Moon and Moon: Selected Letters of Robert Graves 1946–1972* (Hutchinson 1984) O'Prey gives a very thorough account of selected correspondences.

Scudamore, Pauline (ed.), *Dear Robert, Dear Spike: The Graves–Milligan Correspondence* (Alan Sutton 1991) Scudamore's work gives a comprehensive account of Robert Graves's friendship with Spike Milligan, in the course of which some valuable light is shed upon Robert's relationship with his Muses Aemilia Laraçuen and Juli Simon.

Seymour-Smith, Martin, *Robert Graves: His Life and Works* (Hutchinson 1982). The pioneering critical biography: good on criticism, though factually unreliable. A new edition, currently in the press, is said by the author to have a greatly expanded section on Laura Riding.

2 PRINCIPAL PUBLICATIONS BY ROBERT GRAVES BETWEEN 1940 AND 1985

1940 *No More Ghosts: Selected Poems* (London: Faber & Faber) (poems).
Sergeant Lamb of the Ninth (London: Methuen; New York, as *Sergeant Lamb's America*, Random House) (fiction).
The Long Weekend (with Alan Hodge) (London: Faber & Faber; New York: Macmillan 1941) (social history).
1941 *Proceed, Sergeant Lamb* (London: Methuen; New York: Random House) (fiction).
1942 *Work in Hand* (with Alan Hodge and Norman Cameron) (London: The Hogarth Press) (poems).
1943 *The Story of Mary Powell: Wife to Mr. Milton* (London: Methuen; New York, as *Wife to Mr. Milton: The Story of Mary Powell*, Creative Age Press 1944) (fiction).
The Reader Over Your Shoulder (with Alan Hodge) (London: Jonathan Cape; New York: Macmillan 1944) (writer's handbook).
1944 *The Golden Fleece* (London: Cassell; New York, as *Hercules, My Shipmate*, Creative Age Press) (fiction).
1945 *Poems 1938–1945* (London: Cassell; New York: Creative Age Press 1946) (poems).
1946 *King Jesus* (London: Cassell; New York: Creative Age Press) (fiction).
1948 *Collected Poems 1914–1947* (London: Cassell) (poems).
The White Goddess (London: Faber & Faber, rev. 1952, 1966; New York: Creative Age Press, rev. Knopf 1958) (historical grammar of poetic myth).
1949 *Watch the North Wind Rise* (New York: Creative Age Press; London, as *Seven Days in New Crete*, Cassell) (fiction).
The Islands of Unwisdom (New York: Doubleday; London, as *The Isles of Unwisdom*, Cassell 1950) (fiction).
The Common Asphodel: Collected Essays on Poetry 1922–1949 (London: Hamish Hamilton; Pennsylvania: Falcroft Editions 1971) (critical).
1950 *Occupation Writer* (New York: Creative Age Press; London: Cassell 1951) (miscellany).
Apuleius, *The Transformation of Lucius, Otherwise Known as the Golden Ass* (London: Penguin; New York: Farrar Straus 1951) (translation).
1951 *Poems and Satires 1951* (London: Cassell) (poems).
1953 *Poems 1953* (London: Cassell) (poems).
The Nazarene Gospel Restored (with Joshua Podro) (London: Cassell; New York: Doubleday 1954) (religious).
1955 *Collected Poems 1955* (New York: Doubleday) (poems).
Homer's Daughter (London: Cassell; New York: Doubleday) (fiction).

The Crowning Privilege: The Clark Lectures, 1954–5 (London: Cassell; New York: Doubleday 1956) (critical).

Adam's Rib (London: Trianon Press; New York: Yoseloff) (religious).

The Greek Myths (2 vols.) (London and Baltimore: Penguin) (mythology).

Manuel de Jésus Galvan, *The Cross and the Sword* (Bloomington: Indiana University Press; London: Gollancz 1956) (translation).

Pedro Alarcón, *The Infant with the Globe* (London: Trianon Press; New York: Yoseloff 1958) (translation).

1956 *¡Catacrok! Mostly Stories, Mostly Funny* (London: Cassell 1956) (short stories).

George Sand, *Winter in Majorca* (London: Cassell) (translation).

Lucan, *Pharsalia* (London: Penguin) (translation).

1957 *Poems Selected by Himself* (Harmondsworth: Penguin; rev. 1961, 1966, 1972) (poems).

They Hanged My Saintly Billy (London: Cassell; New York: Doubleday) (fiction).

Jesus in Rome (with Joshua Podro) (London: Cassell) (religious).

Suetonius, *The Twelve Caesars* (London: Penguin) (translation).

1958 *The Poems of Robert Graves* (New York: Doubleday) (poems).

Steps (London: Cassell) (miscellany).

5 Pens in Hand (New York: Doubleday) (miscellany).

1959 *Collected Poems 1959* (London: Cassell) (poems).

The Anger of Achilles: Homer's Iliad (New York: Doubleday; London: Cassell 1960) (translation).

1960 *The Penny Fiddle: Poems for Children* (London: Cassell; New York: Doubleday 1961) (poems).

Food for Centaurs (New York: Doubleday) (miscellany).

Greek Gods and Heroes (New York: Doubleday; London, as *Myths of Ancient Greece*, Cassell 1961) (mythology).

1961 *More Poems 1961* (London: Cassell) (poems).

Collected Poems (New York: Doubleday) (poems).

ed. James Reeves, *Selected Poetry and Prose* (London: Hutchinson) (miscellany).

Oxford Addresses on Poetry (London: Cassell; New York: Doubleday 1962) (critical).

1962 *New Poems 1962* (London: Cassell; New York, as *New Poems*, Doubleday 1963) (poems).

The More Deserving Cases: Eighteen Old Poems for Reconsideration (Marlborough: Marlborough College Press; Pennsylvania: Folcroft Editions 1978) (poems).

The Comedies of Terence (New York: Doubleday; London: Cassell 1963) (editor).

The Siege and Fall of Troy (London: Cassell; New York: Doubleday 1963) (historical/mythology).

The Big Green Book (New York: Crowell Collier; London: Penguin 1978) (children's fiction).

1963 *Nine Hundred Iron Chariots* (Cambridge, Massachusetts: M.I.T.) (critical).

1964 *Man Does, Woman Is 1964* (London: Cassell; New York: Doubleday) (poems).

The Hebrew Myths (with Raphael Patai) (New York: Doubleday; London: Cassell) (mythology).

Ann at Highwood Hall: Poems for Children (London: Cassell) (poems).

Collected Short Stories (New York: Doubleday; London: Cassell 1965; London: as *The Shout*, Penguin 1978) (short stories).

1965 *Love Respelt* (London: Cassell) (poems).

Collected Poems 1965 (London: Cassell) (poems).

Majorca Observed (London: Cassell; New York: Doubleday).

Mammon and the Black Goddess (London: Cassell; New York: Doubleday) (critical).

1966 *Seventeen Poems Missing from 'Love Respelt'* (Barnet, Hertfordshire: Stellar Press) (poems).

Collected Poems 1966 (New York: Doubleday) (poems).

Two Wise Children (New York: Harlen Quist: London: W. H. Allen 1967) (children's fiction).

1967 *Rubaiyyat of Omar Khayaam* (with Omar Ali-Shah) (London: Cassell; New York: Doubleday 1968) (translation).

Colophon to 'Love Respelt' (Barnet, Hertfordshire: Stellar Press) (poems).

Poetic Craft and Principle (London: Cassell) (critical).

1968 *Poems 1965–1968* (London: Cassell; New York: Doubleday 1969) (poems)

The Poor Boy Who Followed His Star (London: Cassell; New York: Doubleday 1969) (children's fiction).

1969 *Poems about Love* (London: Cassell; New York: Doubleday) (poems).

Love Respelt Again (New York: Doubleday) (poems).

Beyond Giving (Barnet, Hertfordshire: Stellar Press) (poems).

The Crane Bag (London: Cassell) (miscellany).

On Poetry: Collected Talks and Essays (New York: Doubleday) (critical).

1970 *Poems 1968–1970* (London: Cassell) (poems).

1971 *The Green-Sailed Vessel* (Barnet, Hertfordshire: Stellar Press) (poems).

Poems: Abridged for Dolls and Princes (London: Cassell; New York: Doubleday) (poems).

1972 *Poems 1970–1972* (London: Cassell; New York: Doubleday 1973) (poems).

Difficult Questions, Easy Answers (London: Cassell; New York: Doubleday 1973) (miscellany).

1973 *The Song of Songs* (New York: Clarkson Potter; London: Collins) (translation).

Timeless Meeting: Poems (London: Rota) (poems).

1974 *At the Gate* (London: Rota) (poems).

1975 *Collected Poems 1975* (London: Cassell) (poems).

1977 *New Collected Poems* (New York: Doubleday) (poems).

1980 *An Ancient Castle* (London: Peter Owen) (children's fiction).

INDEX

RG stands for Robert Graves, BG for Beryl Graves.